X-MEN ORIGINS

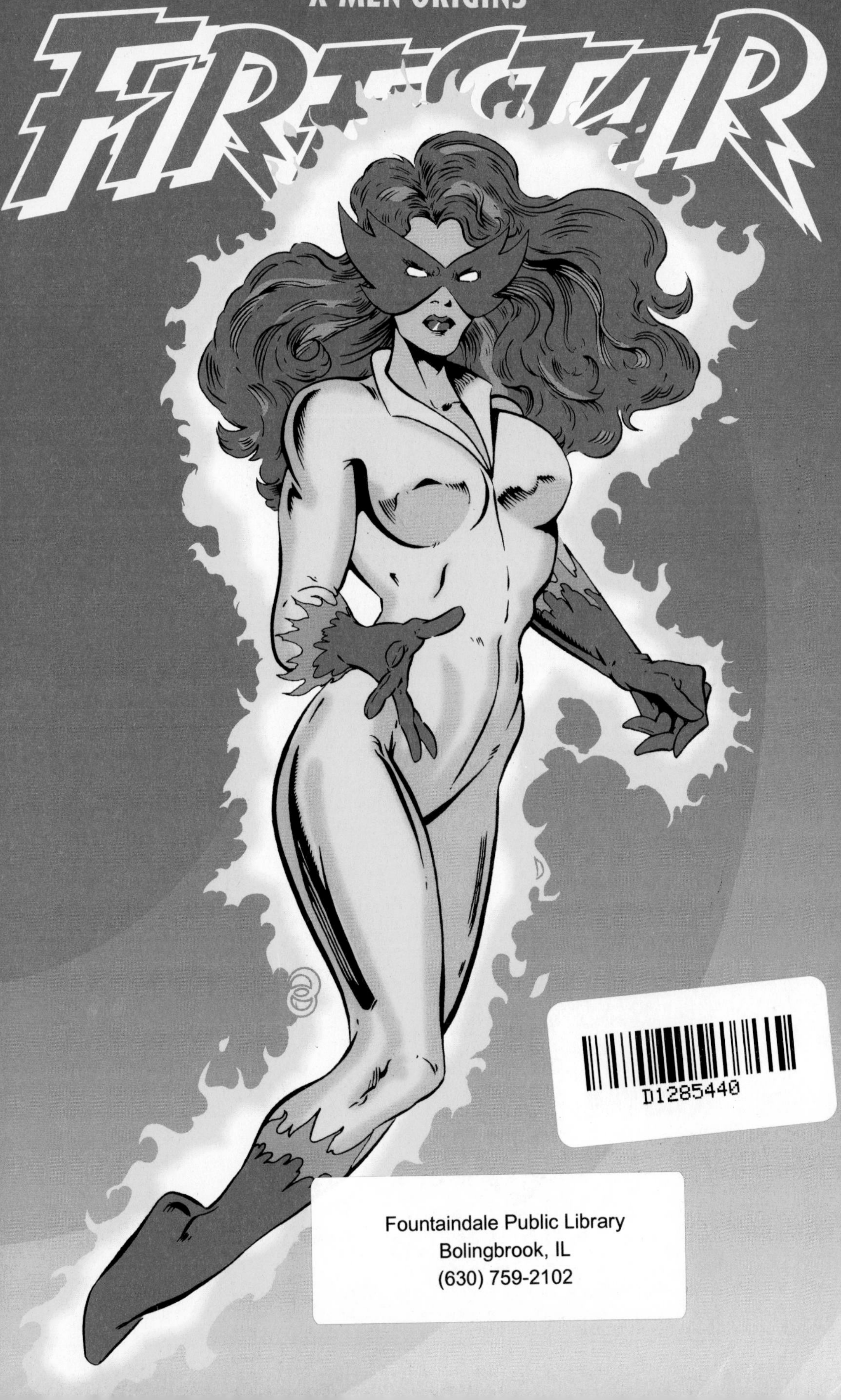
FIRESTAR

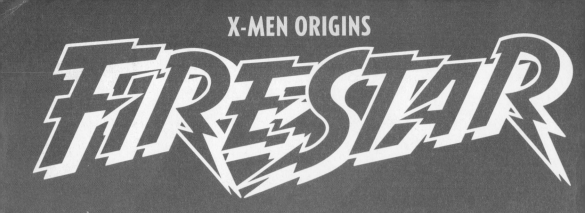

X-MEN ORIGINS

FIRESTAR

Chris Claremont, Tom DeFalco, Marie Javins,
Marcus McLaurin & Sean McKeever with Dennis Marks

writers

Dan Spiegle, John Romita Jr., Mary Wilshire & Dwayne Turner with
Pat Olliffe, Casey Jones, Kano, Nick Dragotta & Chris Giarrusso

pencilers

Vince Colletta, Dan Green, Steve Leialoha, Bob Wiacek,
José Marzan Jr. & Chris Ivy with Livesay, Vince Russell, Kano,
Álvaro López, Nick Dragotta & Chris Giarrusso

inkers

Bob Sharen, Glynis Oliver, Daina Graziunas,
Marcus McLaurin & Lee Loughridge with Chris Giarrusso

colorists

Jim Novak, Tom Orzechowski, Lois Buhalis,
Rick Parker & Artmonkeys' Melanie Olsen with
Dave Sharpe, Diana Albers & Chris Giarrusso

letterers

Peter Sanderson, Terry Kavanagh, Mark Powers & Mark Paniccia

assistant editors

Tom DeFalco, Ann Nocenti, Terry Kavanagh & Nathan Cosby

editors

Barry Windsor-Smith & Veronica Gandini

front cover artists

John Romita Jr. & Al Milgrom

back cover artists

X-Men Created by **Stan Lee & Jack Kirby**

collection editor **Mark D. Beazley**
assistant editor **Caitlin O'Connell**
associate managing editor **Kateri Woody**
associate manager, digital assets **Joe Hochstein**
senior editor, special projects **Jennifer Grünwald**

vp production & special projects **Jeff Youngquist**
research & layout **Jeph York**
production **Jerron Quality Color, ColorTek & Joe Frontirre**
book designer **Adam Del Re**
svp print, sales & marketing **David Gabriel**

editor in chief **Axel Alonso**
chief creative officer **Joe Quesada**
president **Dan Buckley**
executive producer **Alan Fine**

X-MEN ORIGINS: FIRESTAR. Contains material originally published in magazine form as SPIDER-MAN AND HIS AMAZING FRIENDS #1, UNCANNY X-MEN #193, FIRESTAR #1-4, SPIDER-MAN FAMILY: AMAZING FRIENDS and MARVEL COMICS PRESENTS #82-87. First printing 2017. ISBN# 978-1-302-90393-0. Published by MARVEL WORLDWIDE, INC., a subsidiary of MARVEL ENTERTAINMENT, LLC. OFFICE OF PUBLICATION: 135 West 50th Street, New York, NY 10020. **Printed in the U.S.A.** DAN BUCKLEY, President, Marvel Entertainment; JOE QUESADA, Chief Creative Officer; TOM BREVOORT, SVP of Publishing; DAVID BOGART, SVP of Business Affairs & Operations, Publishing & Partnership; C.B. CEBULSKI, VP of Brand Management & Development, Asia; DAVID GABRIEL, SVP of Sales & Marketing, Publishing; JEFF YOUNGQUIST, VP of Production & Special Projects; DAN CARR, Executive Director of Publishing Technology; ALEX MORALES, Director of Publishing Operations; SUSAN CRESPI, Production Manager; STAN LEE, Chairman Emeritus. For information regarding advertising in Marvel Comics or on Marvel.com, please contact Vit DeBellis, Integrated Sales Manager, at vdebellis@marvel.com. For Marvel subscription inquiries, please call 888-511-5480. **Manufactured between 3/3/2017 and 4/4/2017 by LSC COMMUNICATIONS INC., SALEM, VA, USA.**

10 9 8 7 6 5 4 3 2 1

Unlike most Marvel characters, Firestar did not debut in the pages of a comic book — the character was created especially for the 1981 Saturday morning cartoon *Spider-Man and His Amazing Friends*. This one-shot, Firestar's first in-print appearance, adapted the cartoon's pilot episode.

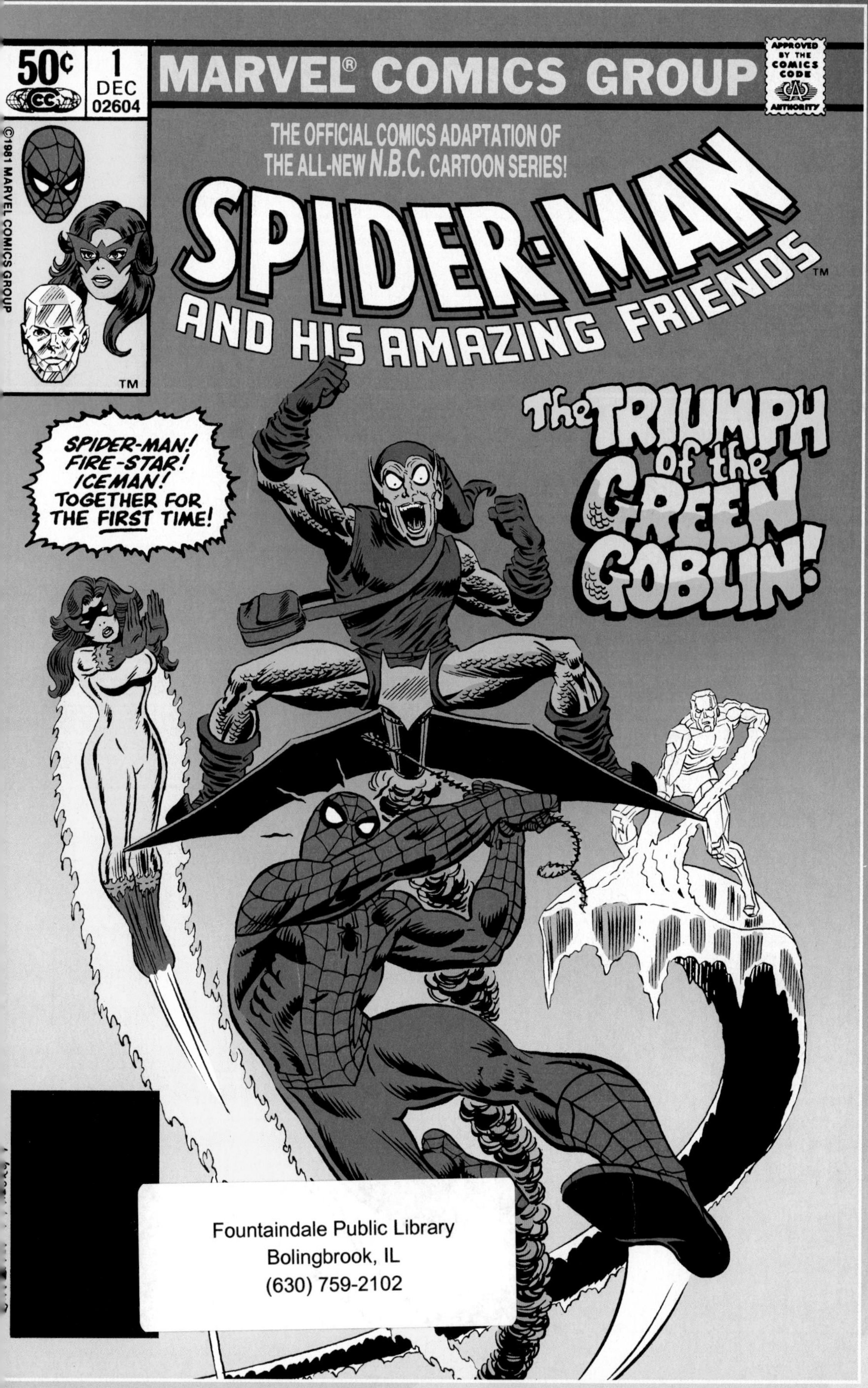

50¢
1
DEC
02604
MARVEL® COMICS GROUP
APPROVED BY THE COMICS CODE AUTHORITY
©1981 MARVEL COMICS GROUP
THE OFFICIAL COMICS ADAPTATION OF THE ALL-NEW N.B.C. CARTOON SERIES!
SPIDER-MAN AND HIS AMAZING FRIENDS™
SPIDER-MAN! FIRE-STAR! ICEMAN! TOGETHER FOR THE FIRST TIME!
The TRIUMPH of the GREEN GOBLIN!

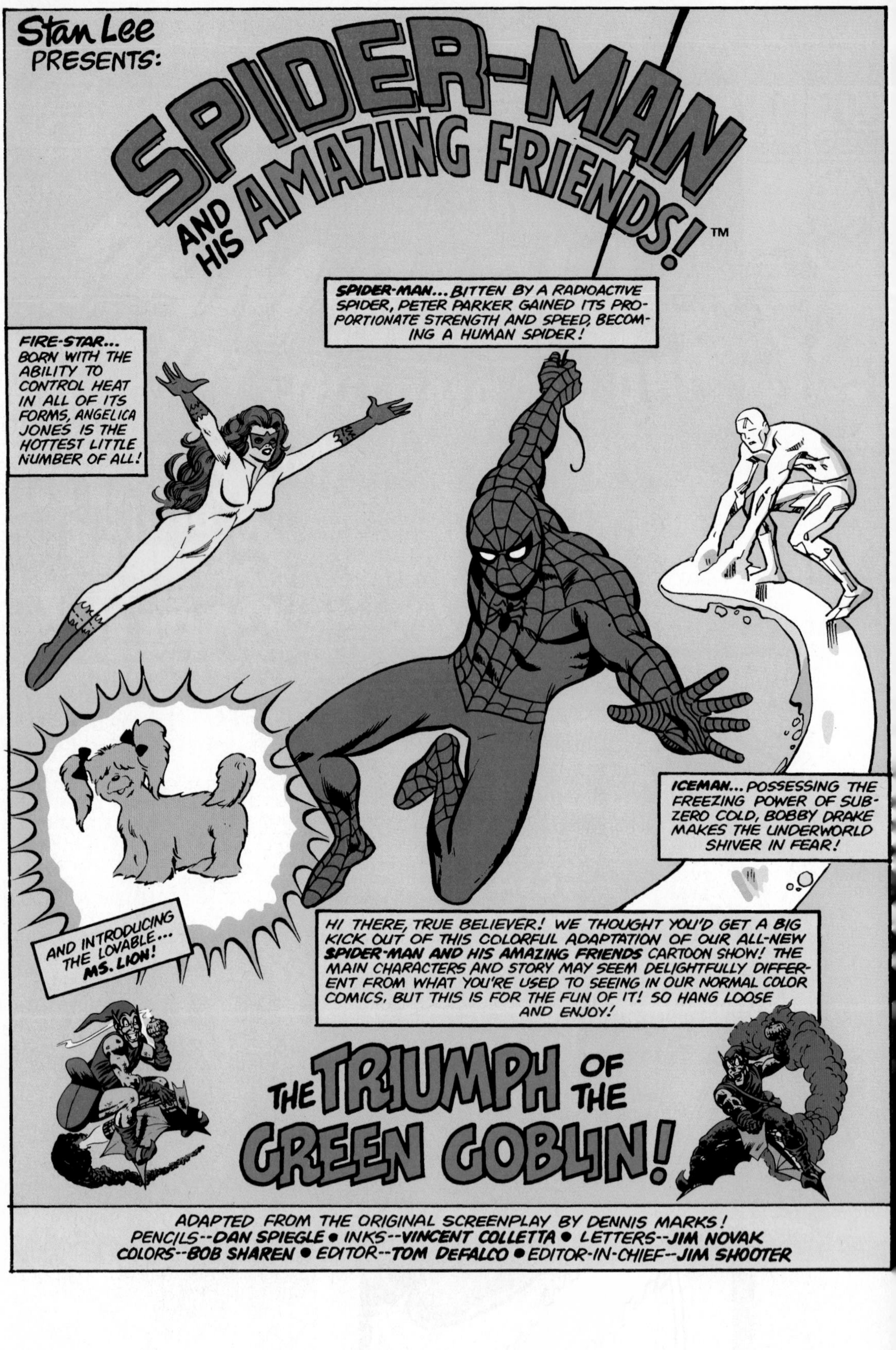

Stan Lee PRESENTS:
SPIDER-MAN AND HIS AMAZING FRIENDS! ™
SPIDER-MAN... BITTEN BY A RADIOACTIVE SPIDER, PETER PARKER GAINED ITS PROPORTIONATE STRENGTH AND SPEED, BECOMING A HUMAN SPIDER!
FIRE-STAR... BORN WITH THE ABILITY TO CONTROL HEAT IN ALL OF ITS FORMS, ANGELICA JONES IS THE HOTTEST LITTLE NUMBER OF ALL!
ICEMAN... POSSESSING THE FREEZING POWER OF SUB-ZERO COLD, BOBBY DRAKE MAKES THE UNDERWORLD SHIVER IN FEAR!
AND INTRODUCING THE LOVABLE... MS. LION!
HI THERE, TRUE BELIEVER! WE THOUGHT YOU'D GET A BIG KICK OUT OF THIS COLORFUL ADAPTATION OF OUR ALL-NEW SPIDER-MAN AND HIS AMAZING FRIENDS CARTOON SHOW! THE MAIN CHARACTERS AND STORY MAY SEEM DELIGHTFULLY DIFFERENT FROM WHAT YOU'RE USED TO SEEING IN OUR NORMAL COLOR COMICS, BUT THIS IS FOR THE FUN OF IT! SO HANG LOOSE AND ENJOY!
THE TRIUMPH OF THE GREEN GOBLIN!
ADAPTED FROM THE ORIGINAL SCREENPLAY BY DENNIS MARKS!
PENCILS--DAN SPIEGLE • INKS--VINCENT COLLETTA • LETTERS--JIM NOVAK
COLORS--BOB SHAREN • EDITOR--TOM DEFALCO • EDITOR-IN-CHIEF--JIM SHOOTER

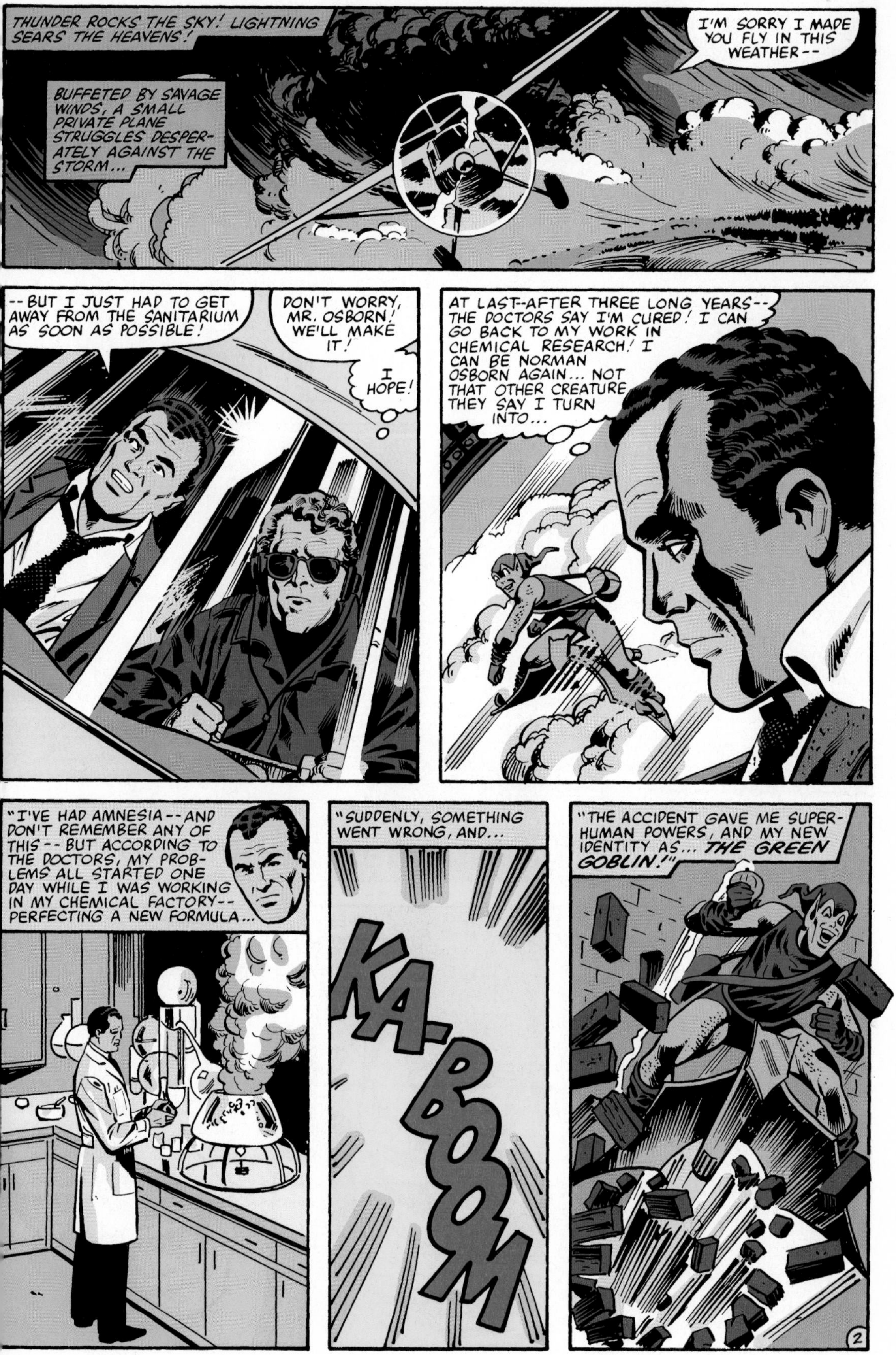
THUNDER ROCKS THE SKY! LIGHTNING SEARS THE HEAVENS!
BUFFETED BY SAVAGE WINDS, A SMALL PRIVATE PLANE STRUGGLES DESPERATELY AGAINST THE STORM...
I'M SORRY I MADE YOU FLY IN THIS WEATHER--
--BUT I JUST HAD TO GET AWAY FROM THE SANITARIUM AS SOON AS POSSIBLE!
DON'T WORRY, MR. OSBORN! WE'LL MAKE IT!
I HOPE!
AT LAST--AFTER THREE LONG YEARS--THE DOCTORS SAY I'M CURED! I CAN GO BACK TO MY WORK IN CHEMICAL RESEARCH! I CAN BE NORMAN OSBORN AGAIN... NOT THAT OTHER CREATURE THEY SAY I TURN INTO...
"I'VE HAD AMNESIA--AND DON'T REMEMBER ANY OF THIS--BUT ACCORDING TO THE DOCTORS, MY PROBLEMS ALL STARTED ONE DAY WHILE I WAS WORKING IN MY CHEMICAL FACTORY--PERFECTING A NEW FORMULA...
"SUDDENLY, SOMETHING WENT WRONG, AND...
KA-BOOM
"THE ACCIDENT GAVE ME SUPER-HUMAN POWERS, AND MY NEW IDENTITY AS... THE GREEN GOBLIN!"
2

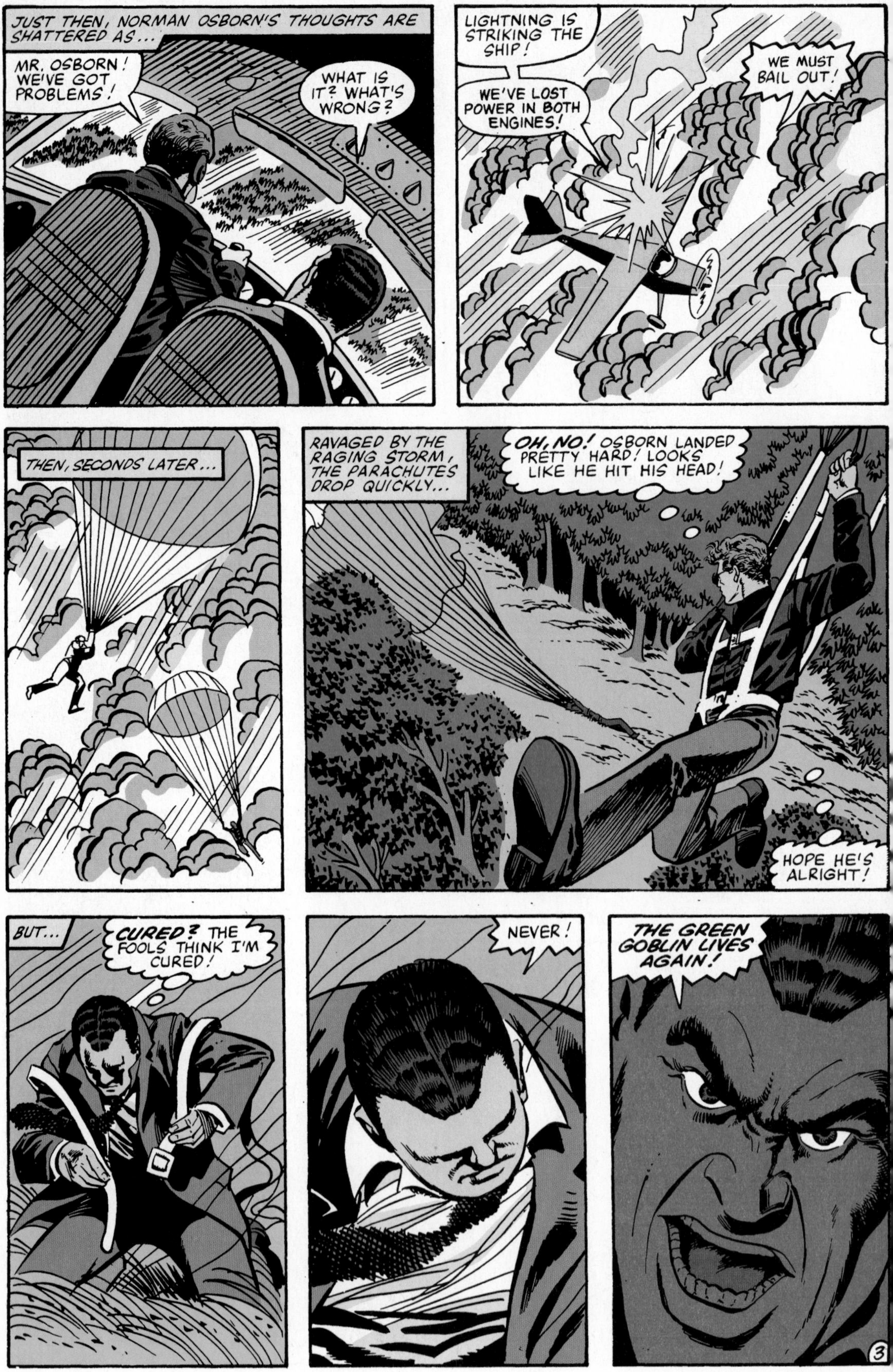
JUST THEN, NORMAN OSBORN'S THOUGHTS ARE SHATTERED AS...
MR. OSBORN! WE'VE GOT PROBLEMS!
WHAT IS IT? WHAT'S WRONG?
LIGHTNING IS STRIKING THE SHIP!
WE'VE LOST POWER IN BOTH ENGINES!
WE MUST BAIL OUT!
THEN, SECONDS LATER...
RAVAGED BY THE RAGING STORM, THE PARACHUTES DROP QUICKLY...
OH, NO! OSBORN LANDED PRETTY HARD! LOOKS LIKE HE HIT HIS HEAD!
HOPE HE'S ALRIGHT!
BUT...
CURED? THE FOOLS THINK I'M CURED!
NEVER!
THE GREEN GOBLIN LIVES AGAIN!
3

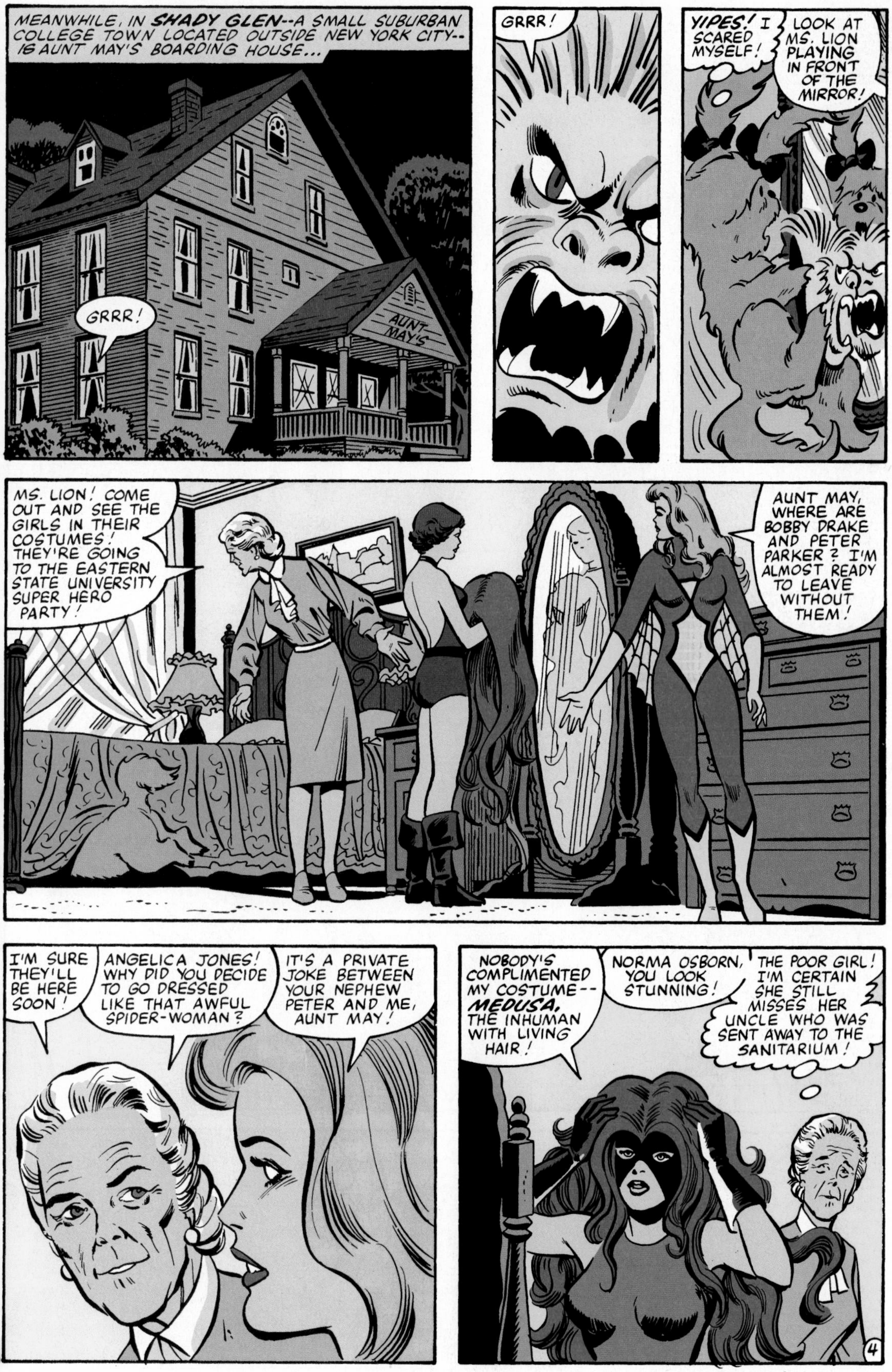
MEANWHILE, IN SHADY GLEN--A SMALL SUBURBAN COLLEGE TOWN LOCATED OUTSIDE NEW YORK CITY--IS AUNT MAY'S BOARDING HOUSE...
GRRR!
AUNT MAY'S
GRRR!
YIPES! I SCARED MYSELF!
LOOK AT MS. LION PLAYING IN FRONT OF THE MIRROR!
MS. LION! COME OUT AND SEE THE GIRLS IN THEIR COSTUMES! THEY'RE GOING TO THE EASTERN STATE UNIVERSITY SUPER HERO PARTY!
AUNT MAY, WHERE ARE BOBBY DRAKE AND PETER PARKER? I'M ALMOST READY TO LEAVE WITHOUT THEM!
I'M SURE THEY'LL BE HERE SOON!
ANGELICA JONES! WHY DID YOU DECIDE TO GO DRESSED LIKE THAT AWFUL SPIDER-WOMAN?
IT'S A PRIVATE JOKE BETWEEN YOUR NEPHEW PETER AND ME, AUNT MAY!
NOBODY'S COMPLIMENTED MY COSTUME--MEDUSA, THE INHUMAN WITH LIVING HAIR!
NORMA OSBORN, YOU LOOK STUNNING!
THE POOR GIRL! I'M CERTAIN SHE STILL MISSES HER UNCLE WHO WAS SENT AWAY TO THE SANITARIUM!
4

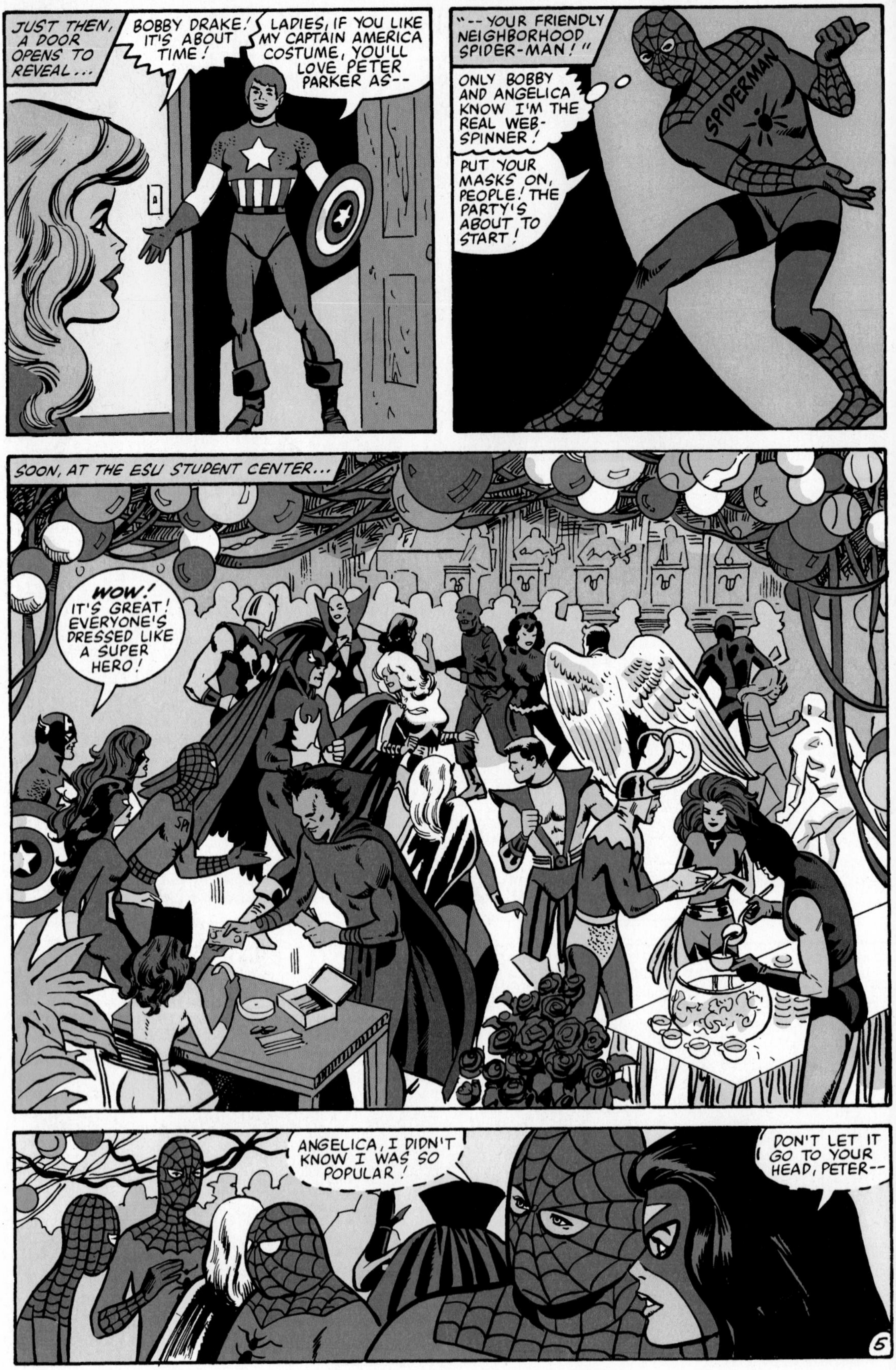
JUST THEN, A DOOR OPENS TO REVEAL...
BOBBY DRAKE! IT'S ABOUT TIME!
LADIES, IF YOU LIKE MY CAPTAIN AMERICA COSTUME, YOU'LL LOVE PETER PARKER AS--
"--YOUR FRIENDLY NEIGHBORHOOD SPIDER-MAN!"
ONLY BOBBY AND ANGELICA KNOW I'M THE REAL WEB-SPINNER!
PUT YOUR MASKS ON, PEOPLE! THE PARTY'S ABOUT TO START!
SPIDERMAN
SOON, AT THE ESU STUDENT CENTER...
WOW! IT'S GREAT! EVERYONE'S DRESSED LIKE A SUPER HERO!
ANGELICA, I DIDN'T KNOW I WAS SO POPULAR!
DON'T LET IT GO TO YOUR HEAD, PETER--
5

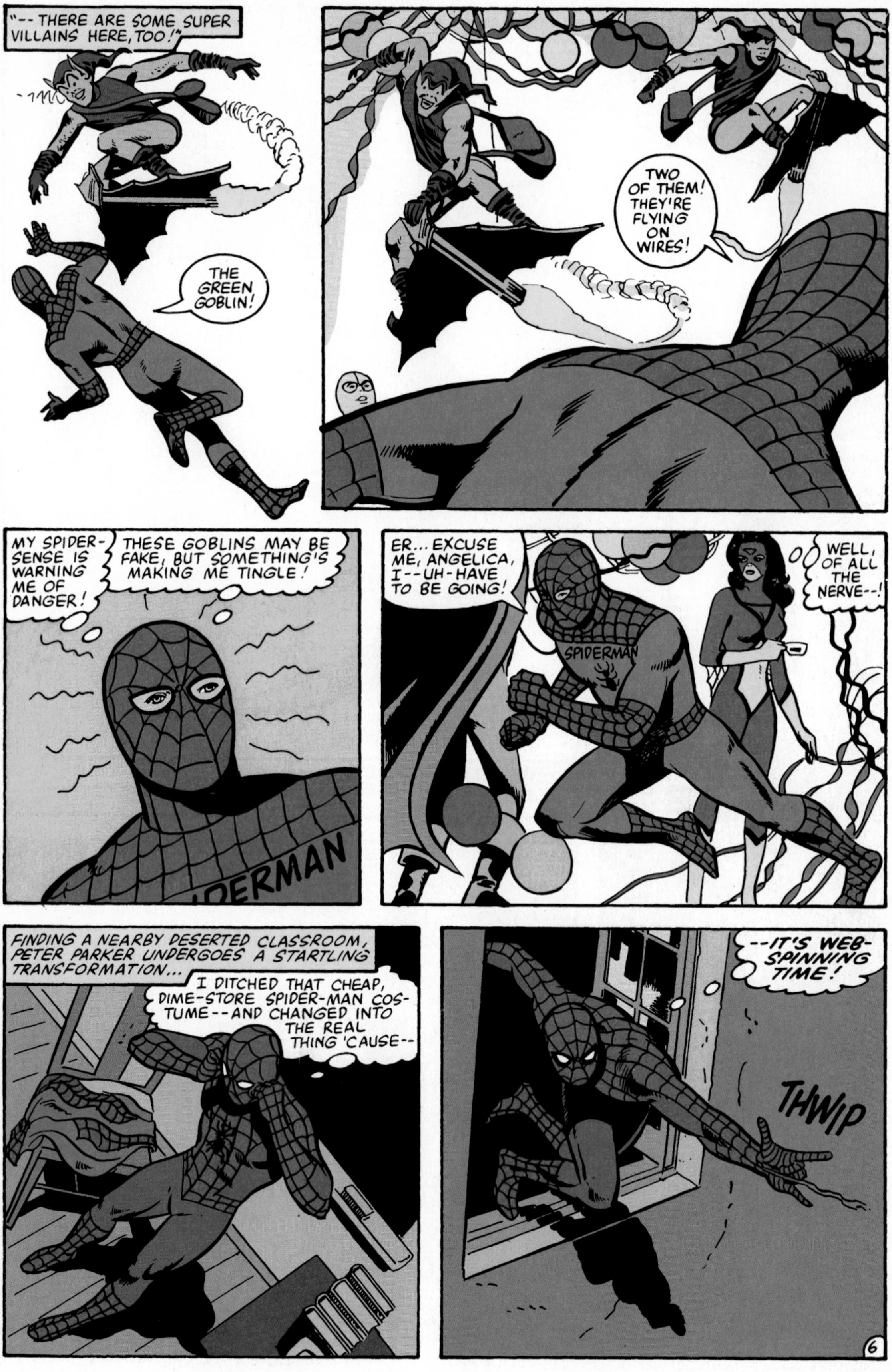
"--THERE ARE SOME SUPER VILLAINS HERE, TOO!"
THE GREEN GOBLIN!
TWO OF THEM! THEY'RE FLYING ON WIRES!
MY SPIDER-SENSE IS WARNING ME OF DANGER!
THESE GOBLINS MAY BE FAKE, BUT SOMETHING'S MAKING ME TINGLE!
SPIDERMAN
ER... EXCUSE ME, ANGELICA, I--UH-HAVE TO BE GOING!
WELL, OF ALL THE NERVE--!
SPIDERMAN
FINDING A NEARBY DESERTED CLASSROOM, PETER PARKER UNDERGOES A STARTLING TRANSFORMATION...
I DITCHED THAT CHEAP, DIME-STORE SPIDER-MAN COSTUME--AND CHANGED INTO THE REAL THING 'CAUSE--
--IT'S WEB-SPINNING TIME!
THWIP
6

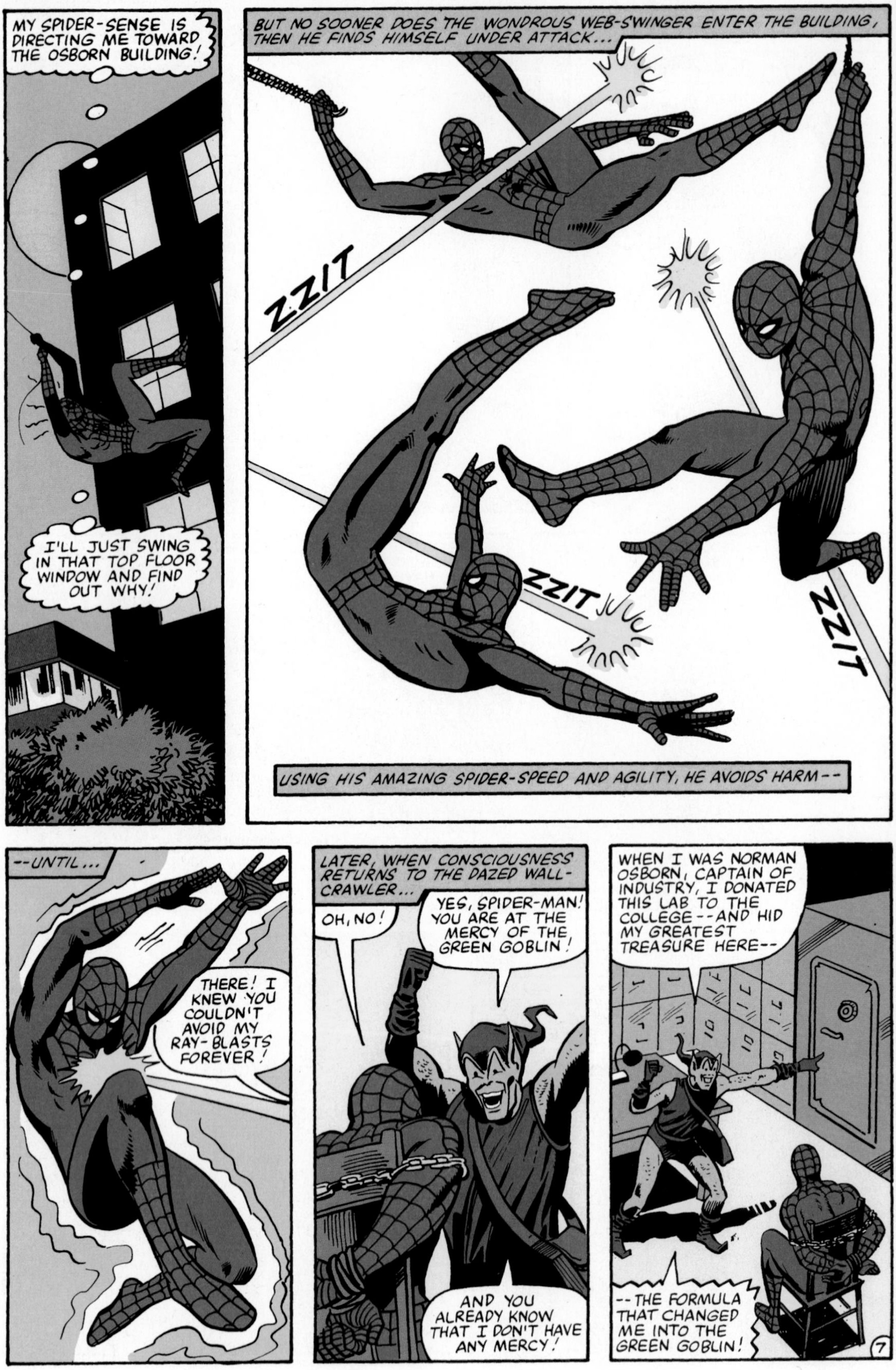
MY SPIDER-SENSE IS DIRECTING ME TOWARD THE OSBORN BUILDING!
I'LL JUST SWING IN THAT TOP FLOOR WINDOW AND FIND OUT WHY!
BUT NO SOONER DOES THE WONDROUS WEB-SWINGER ENTER THE BUILDING, THEN HE FINDS HIMSELF UNDER ATTACK...
ZZIT
ZZIT
ZZIT
USING HIS AMAZING SPIDER-SPEED AND AGILITY, HE AVOIDS HARM--
--UNTIL...
THERE! I KNEW YOU COULDN'T AVOID MY RAY-BLASTS FOREVER!
LATER, WHEN CONSCIOUSNESS RETURNS TO THE DAZED WALL-CRAWLER...
OH, NO!
YES, SPIDER-MAN! YOU ARE AT THE MERCY OF THE GREEN GOBLIN!
AND YOU ALREADY KNOW THAT I DON'T HAVE ANY MERCY!
WHEN I WAS NORMAN OSBORN, CAPTAIN OF INDUSTRY, I DONATED THIS LAB TO THE COLLEGE--AND HID MY GREATEST TREASURE HERE--
--THE FORMULA THAT CHANGED ME INTO THE GREEN GOBLIN!
7

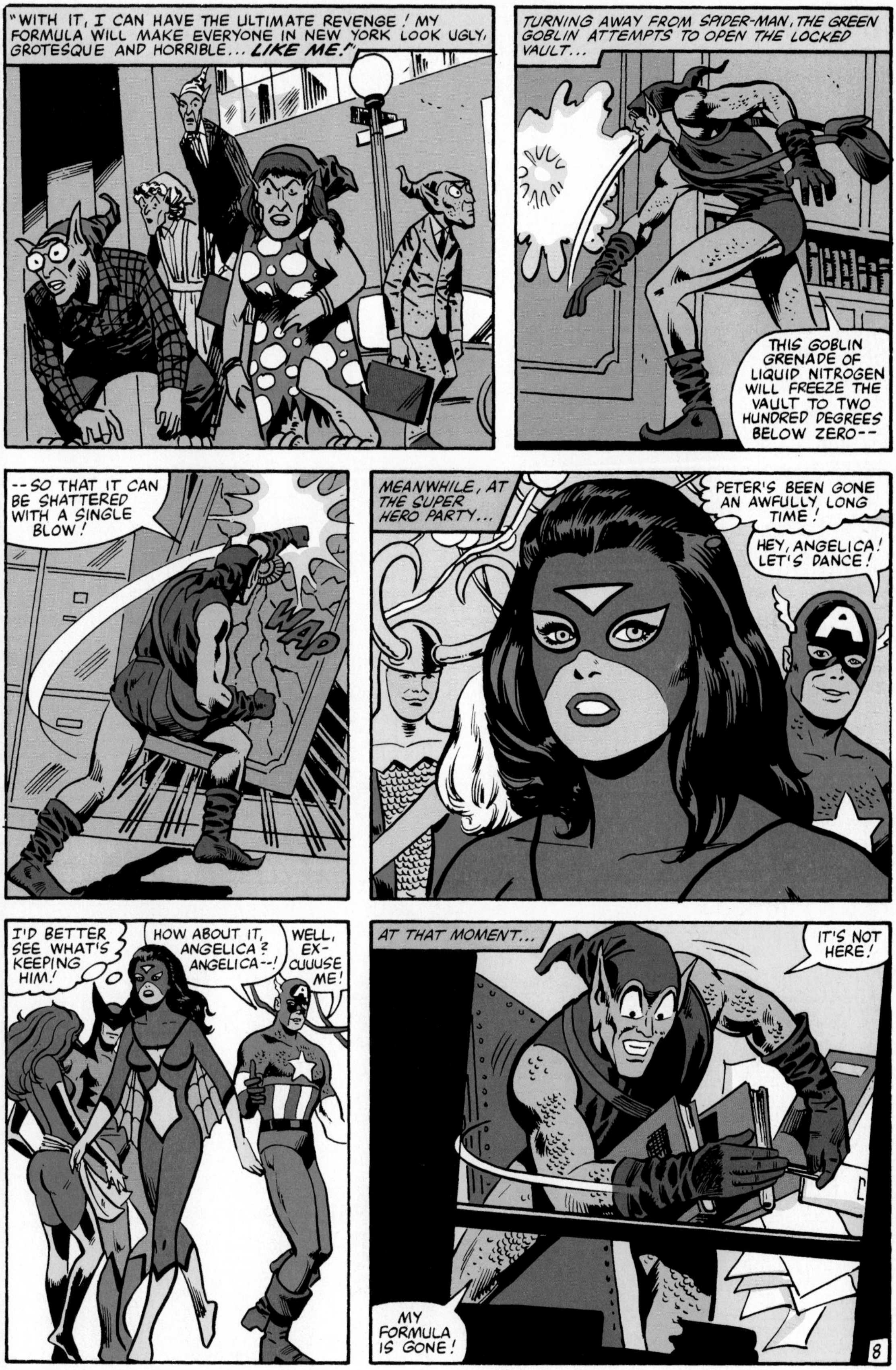
"WITH IT, I CAN HAVE THE ULTIMATE REVENGE! MY FORMULA WILL MAKE EVERYONE IN NEW YORK LOOK UGLY, GROTESQUE AND HORRIBLE... LIKE ME!"
TURNING AWAY FROM SPIDER-MAN, THE GREEN GOBLIN ATTEMPTS TO OPEN THE LOCKED VAULT...
THIS GOBLIN GRENADE OF LIQUID NITROGEN WILL FREEZE THE VAULT TO TWO HUNDRED DEGREES BELOW ZERO--
--SO THAT IT CAN BE SHATTERED WITH A SINGLE BLOW!
WAP
MEANWHILE, AT THE SUPER HERO PARTY...
PETER'S BEEN GONE AN AWFULLY LONG TIME!
HEY, ANGELICA! LET'S DANCE!
I'D BETTER SEE WHAT'S KEEPING HIM!
HOW ABOUT IT, ANGELICA? ANGELICA--!
WELL, EX-CUUUSE ME!
AT THAT MOMENT...
IT'S NOT HERE!
MY FORMULA IS GONE!
8

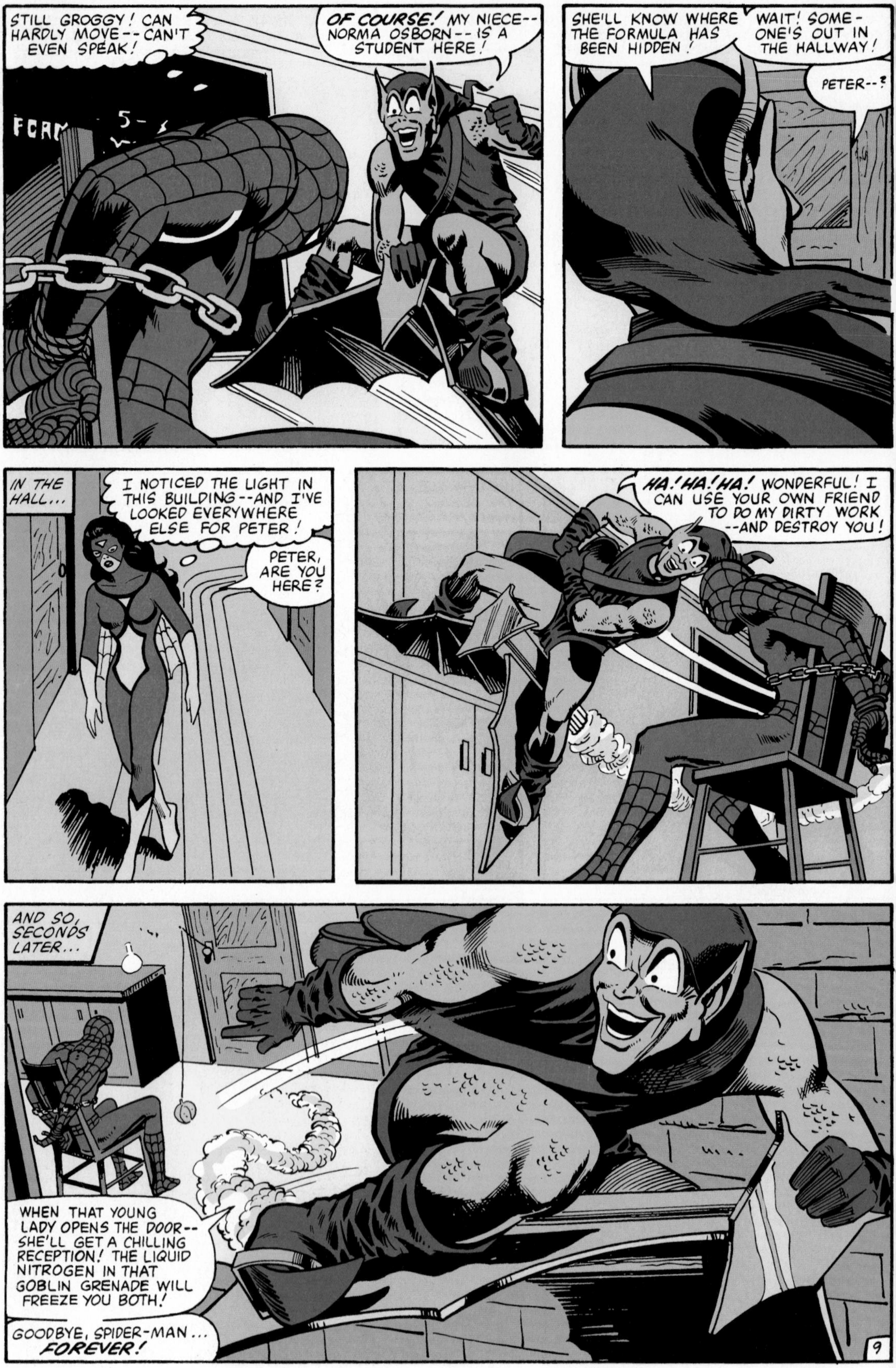
STILL GROGGY! CAN HARDLY MOVE--CAN'T EVEN SPEAK!
OF COURSE! MY NIECE--NORMA OSBORN--IS A STUDENT HERE!
SHE'LL KNOW WHERE THE FORMULA HAS BEEN HIDDEN!
WAIT! SOMEONE'S OUT IN THE HALLWAY!
PETER--?
IN THE HALL...
I NOTICED THE LIGHT IN THIS BUILDING--AND I'VE LOOKED EVERYWHERE ELSE FOR PETER!
PETER, ARE YOU HERE?
HA! HA! HA! WONDERFUL! I CAN USE YOUR OWN FRIEND TO DO MY DIRTY WORK --AND DESTROY YOU!
AND SO, SECONDS LATER...
WHEN THAT YOUNG LADY OPENS THE DOOR--SHE'LL GET A CHILLING RECEPTION! THE LIQUID NITROGEN IN THAT GOBLIN GRENADE WILL FREEZE YOU BOTH!
GOODBYE, SPIDER-MAN... FOREVER!
9

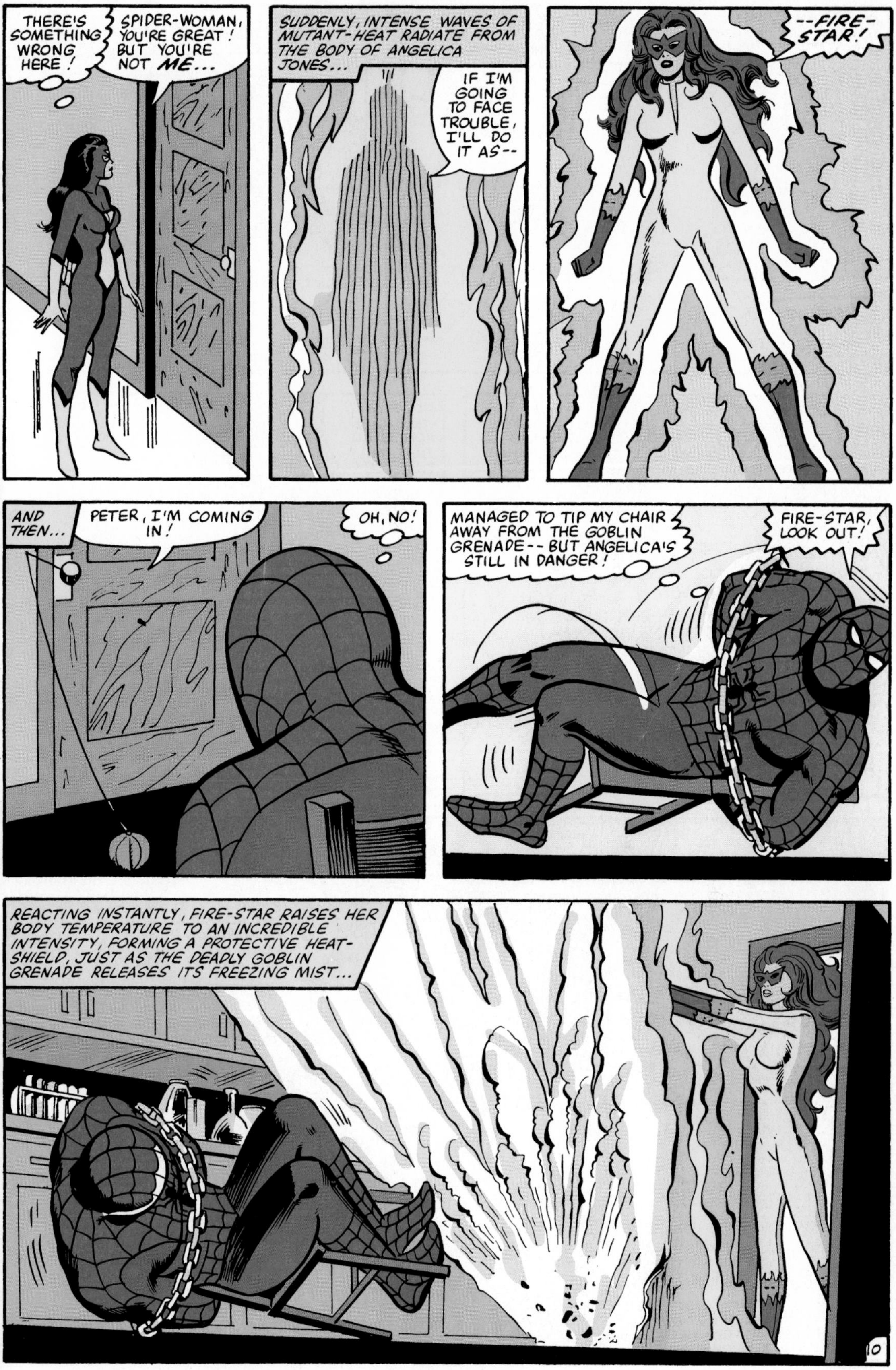

THERE'S SOMETHING WRONG HERE!
SPIDER-WOMAN, YOU'RE GREAT! BUT YOU'RE NOT ME...
SUDDENLY, INTENSE WAVES OF MUTANT-HEAT RADIATE FROM THE BODY OF ANGELICA JONES...
IF I'M GOING TO FACE TROUBLE, I'LL DO IT AS--
--FIRE-STAR!
AND THEN...
PETER, I'M COMING IN!
OH, NO!
MANAGED TO TIP MY CHAIR AWAY FROM THE GOBLIN GRENADE-- BUT ANGELICA'S STILL IN DANGER!
FIRE-STAR, LOOK OUT!
REACTING INSTANTLY, FIRE-STAR RAISES HER BODY TEMPERATURE TO AN INCREDIBLE INTENSITY, FORMING A PROTECTIVE HEAT-SHIELD, JUST AS THE DEADLY GOBLIN GRENADE RELEASES ITS FREEZING MIST...
10

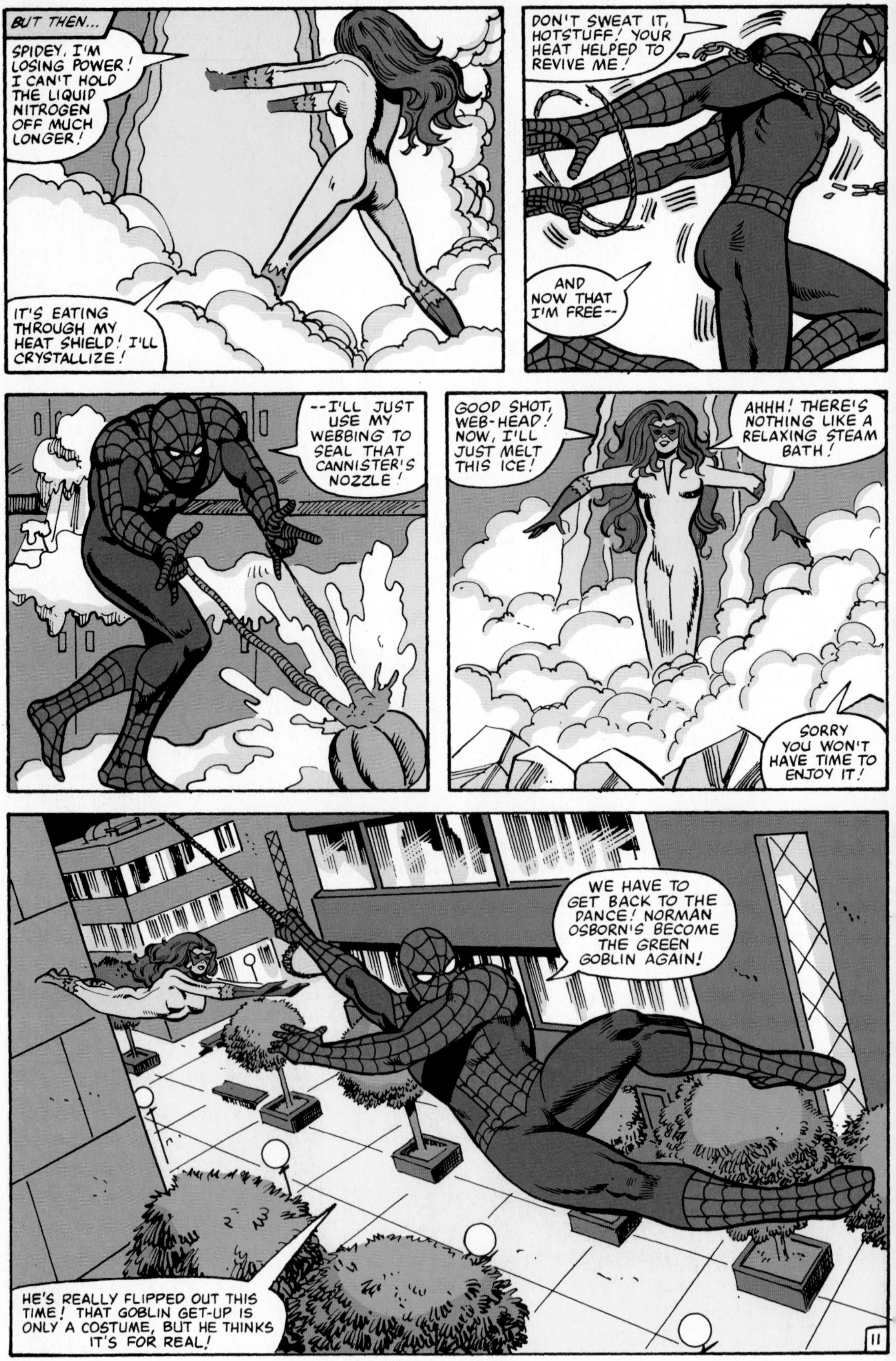
BUT THEN...
SPIDEY, I'M LOSING POWER! I CAN'T HOLD THE LIQUID NITROGEN OFF MUCH LONGER!
IT'S EATING THROUGH MY HEAT SHIELD! I'LL CRYSTALLIZE!
DON'T SWEAT IT, HOTSTUFF! YOUR HEAT HELPED TO REVIVE ME!
AND NOW THAT I'M FREE--
--I'LL JUST USE MY WEBBING TO SEAL THAT CANNISTER'S NOZZLE!
GOOD SHOT, WEB-HEAD! NOW, I'LL JUST MELT THIS ICE!
AHHH! THERE'S NOTHING LIKE A RELAXING STEAM BATH!
SORRY YOU WON'T HAVE TIME TO ENJOY IT!
WE HAVE TO GET BACK TO THE DANCE! NORMAN OSBORN'S BECOME THE GREEN GOBLIN AGAIN!
HE'S REALLY FLIPPED OUT THIS TIME! THAT GOBLIN GET-UP IS ONLY A COSTUME, BUT HE THINKS IT'S FOR REAL!
11

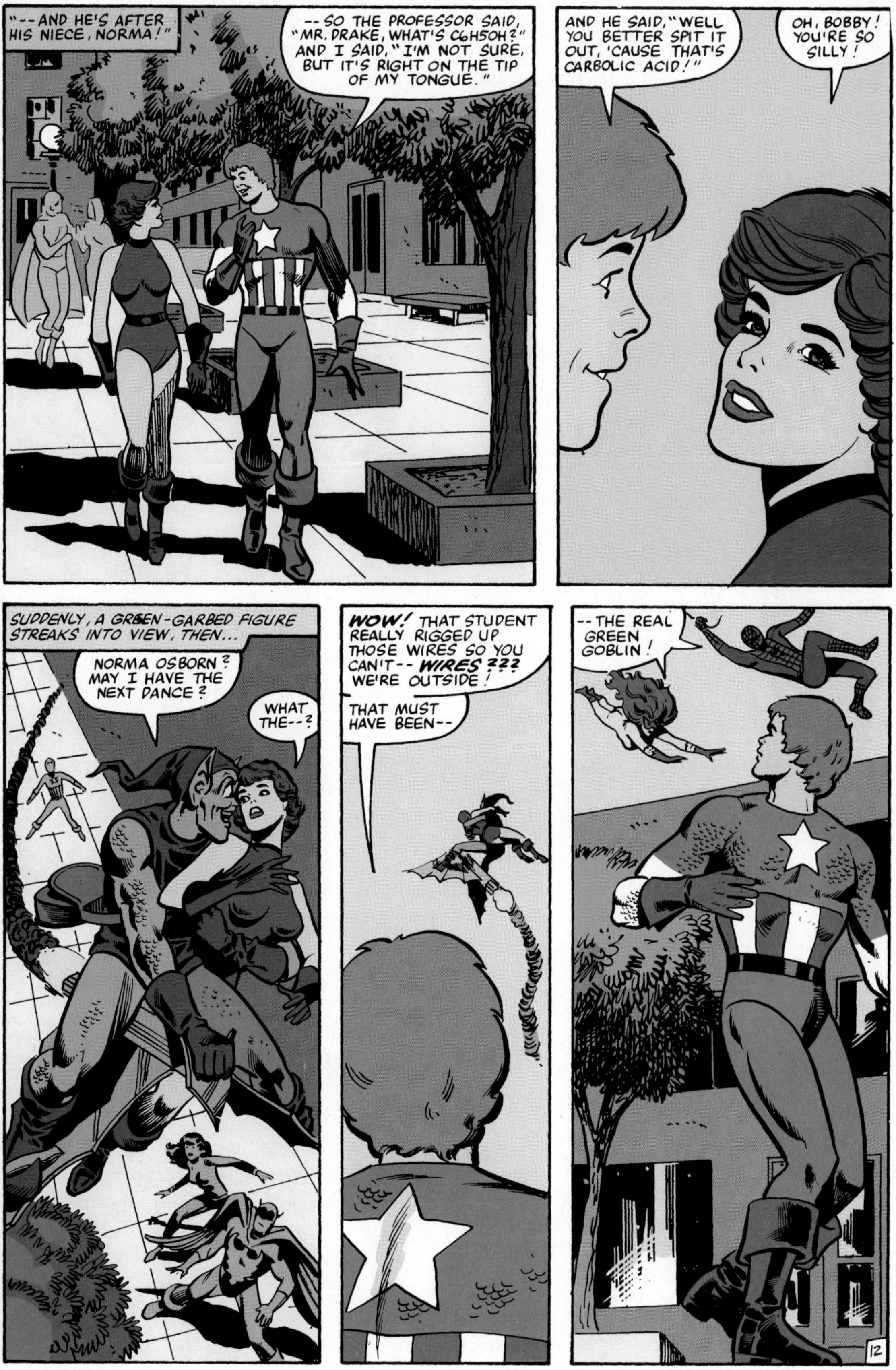
"--AND HE'S AFTER HIS NIECE, NORMA!"
--SO THE PROFESSOR SAID, "MR. DRAKE, WHAT'S C6H5OH?" AND I SAID, "I'M NOT SURE, BUT IT'S RIGHT ON THE TIP OF MY TONGUE."
AND HE SAID, "WELL YOU BETTER SPIT IT OUT, 'CAUSE THAT'S CARBOLIC ACID!"
OH, BOBBY! YOU'RE SO SILLY!
SUDDENLY, A GREEN-GARBED FIGURE STREAKS INTO VIEW, THEN...
NORMA OSBORN? MAY I HAVE THE NEXT DANCE?
WHAT THE--?
WOW! THAT STUDENT REALLY RIGGED UP THOSE WIRES SO YOU CAN'T-- WIRES??? WE'RE OUTSIDE!
THAT MUST HAVE BEEN--
--THE REAL GREEN GOBLIN!
12

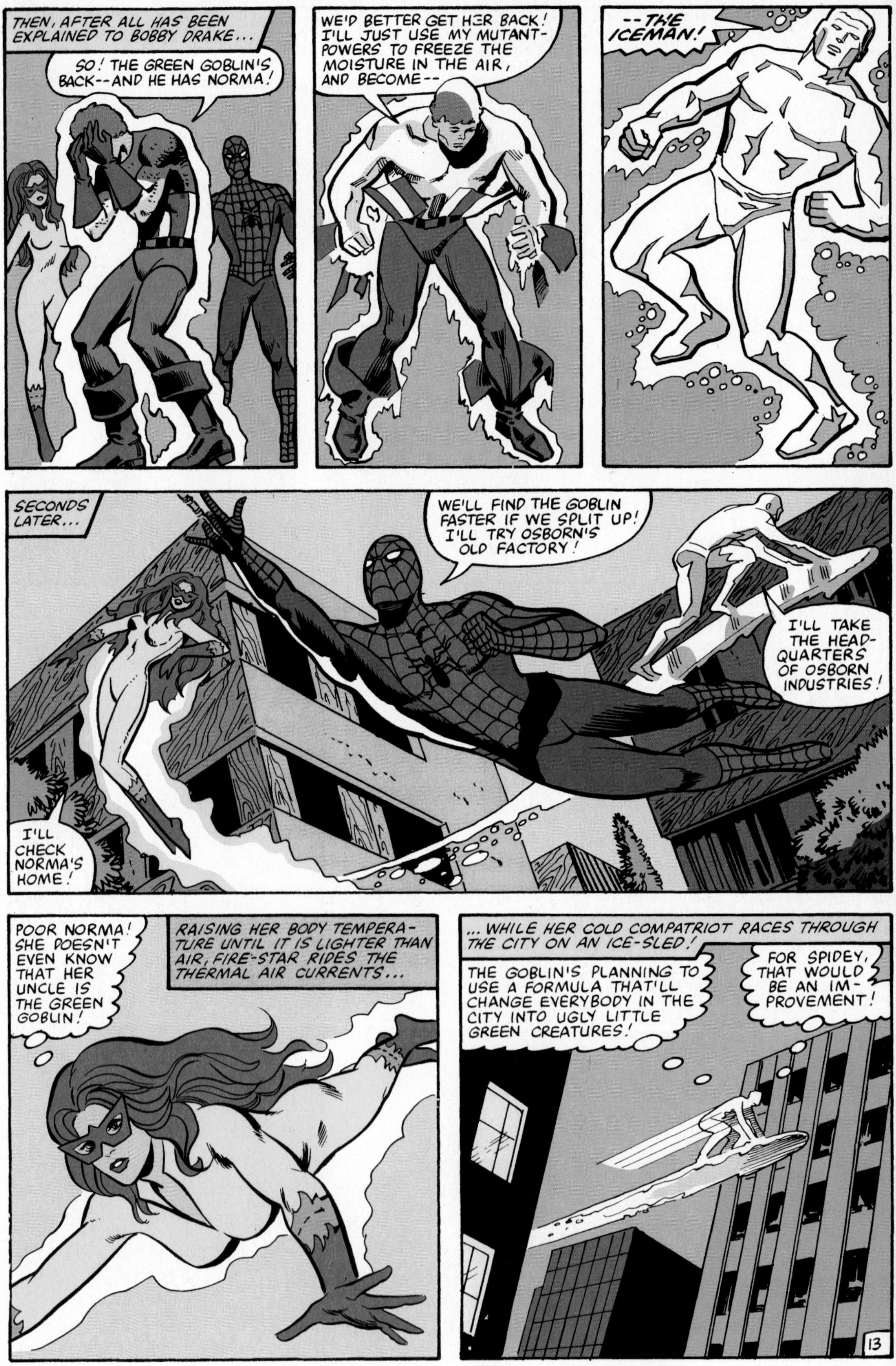
THEN, AFTER ALL HAS BEEN EXPLAINED TO BOBBY DRAKE...
SO! THE GREEN GOBLIN'S BACK--AND HE HAS NORMA!
WE'D BETTER GET HER BACK! I'LL JUST USE MY MUTANT-POWERS TO FREEZE THE MOISTURE IN THE AIR, AND BECOME--
--THE ICEMAN!
SECONDS LATER...
WE'LL FIND THE GOBLIN FASTER IF WE SPLIT UP! I'LL TRY OSBORN'S OLD FACTORY!
I'LL TAKE THE HEAD-QUARTERS OF OSBORN INDUSTRIES!
I'LL CHECK NORMA'S HOME!
POOR NORMA! SHE DOESN'T EVEN KNOW THAT HER UNCLE IS THE GREEN GOBLIN!
RAISING HER BODY TEMPERA-TURE UNTIL IT IS LIGHTER THAN AIR, FIRE-STAR RIDES THE THERMAL AIR CURRENTS...
...WHILE HER COLD COMPATRIOT RACES THROUGH THE CITY ON AN ICE-SLED!
THE GOBLIN'S PLANNING TO USE A FORMULA THAT'LL CHANGE EVERYBODY IN THE CITY INTO UGLY LITTLE GREEN CREATURES!
FOR SPIDEY, THAT WOULD BE AN IM-PROVEMENT!
13

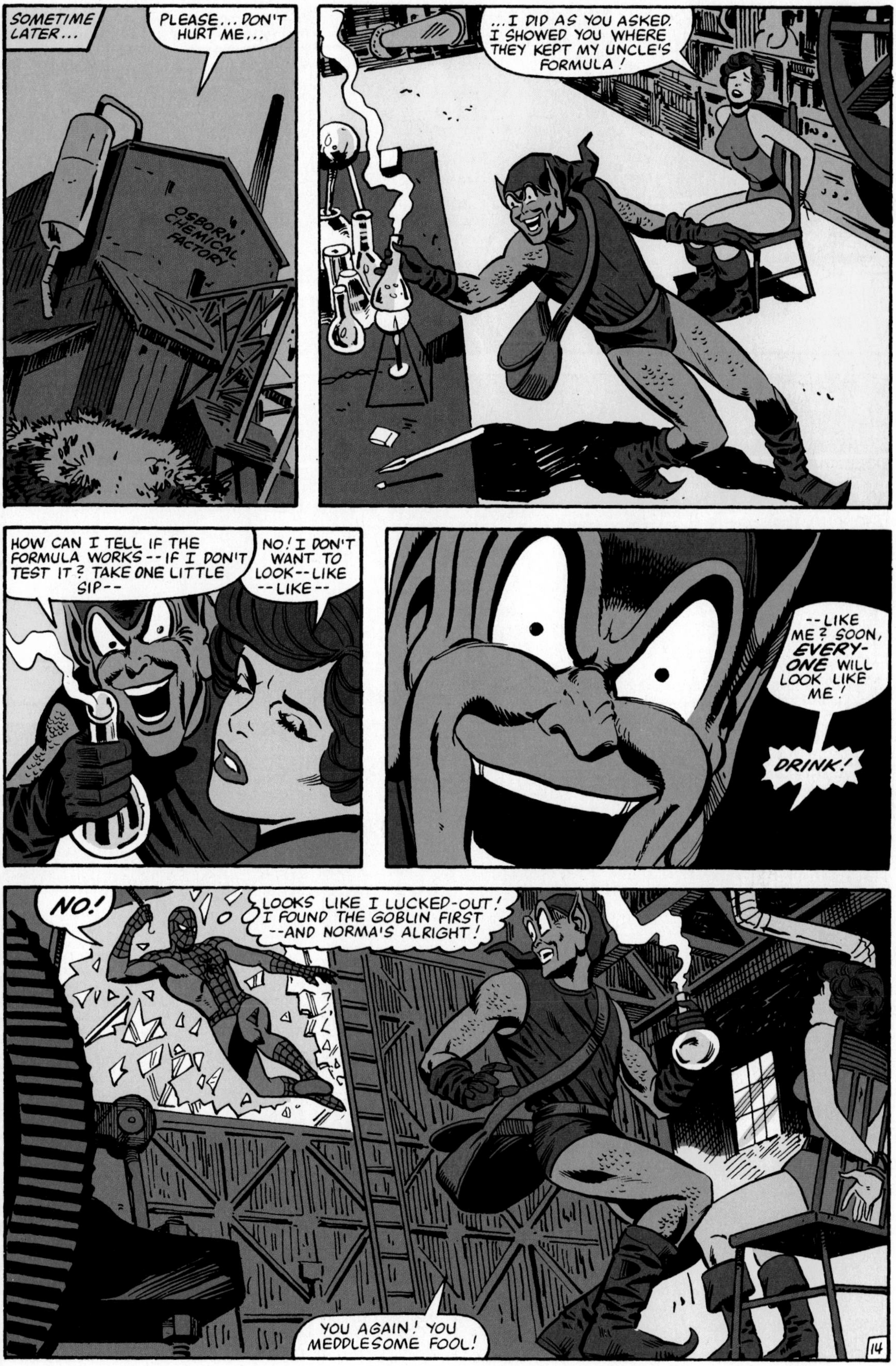

SOMETIME LATER...
PLEASE... DON'T HURT ME...
OSBORN CHEMICAL FACTORY
...I DID AS YOU ASKED. I SHOWED YOU WHERE THEY KEPT MY UNCLE'S FORMULA!
HOW CAN I TELL IF THE FORMULA WORKS--IF I DON'T TEST IT? TAKE ONE LITTLE SIP--
NO! I DON'T WANT TO LOOK--LIKE --LIKE--
--LIKE ME? SOON, EVERYONE WILL LOOK LIKE ME!
DRINK!
NO!
LOOKS LIKE I LUCKED-OUT! I FOUND THE GOBLIN FIRST --AND NORMA'S ALRIGHT!
YOU AGAIN! YOU MEDDLESOME FOOL!
14

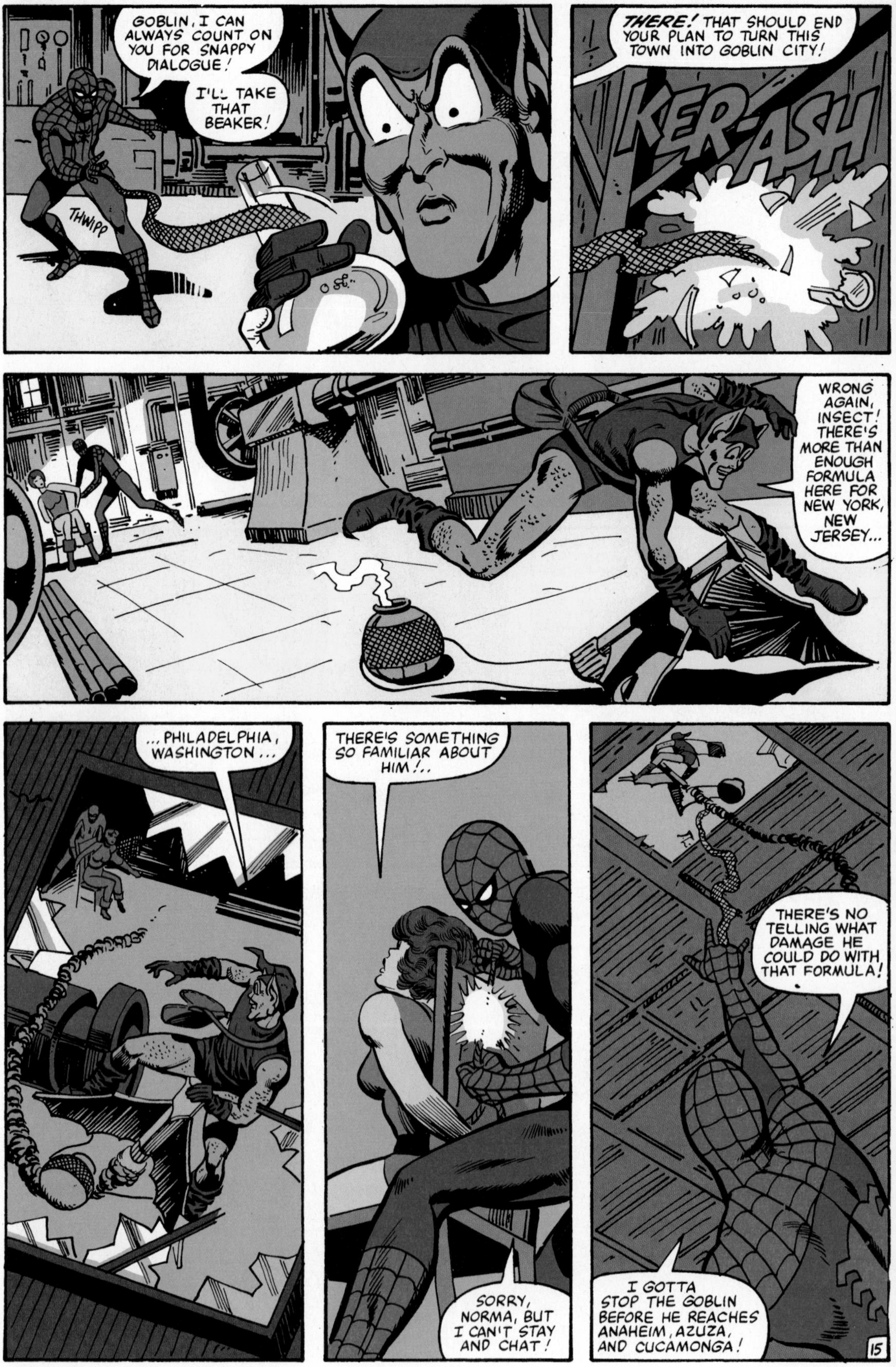

GOBLIN, I CAN ALWAYS COUNT ON YOU FOR SNAPPY DIALOGUE!
I'LL TAKE THAT BEAKER!
THWIPP
THERE! THAT SHOULD END YOUR PLAN TO TURN THIS TOWN INTO GOBLIN CITY!
KER-ASH
WRONG AGAIN, INSECT! THERE'S MORE THAN ENOUGH FORMULA HERE FOR NEW YORK, NEW JERSEY...
...PHILADELPHIA, WASHINGTON...
THERE'S SOMETHING SO FAMILIAR ABOUT HIM!..
SORRY, NORMA, BUT I CAN'T STAY AND CHAT!
THERE'S NO TELLING WHAT DAMAGE HE COULD DO WITH THAT FORMULA!
I GOTTA STOP THE GOBLIN BEFORE HE REACHES ANAHEIM, AZUZA, AND CUCAMONGA!
15

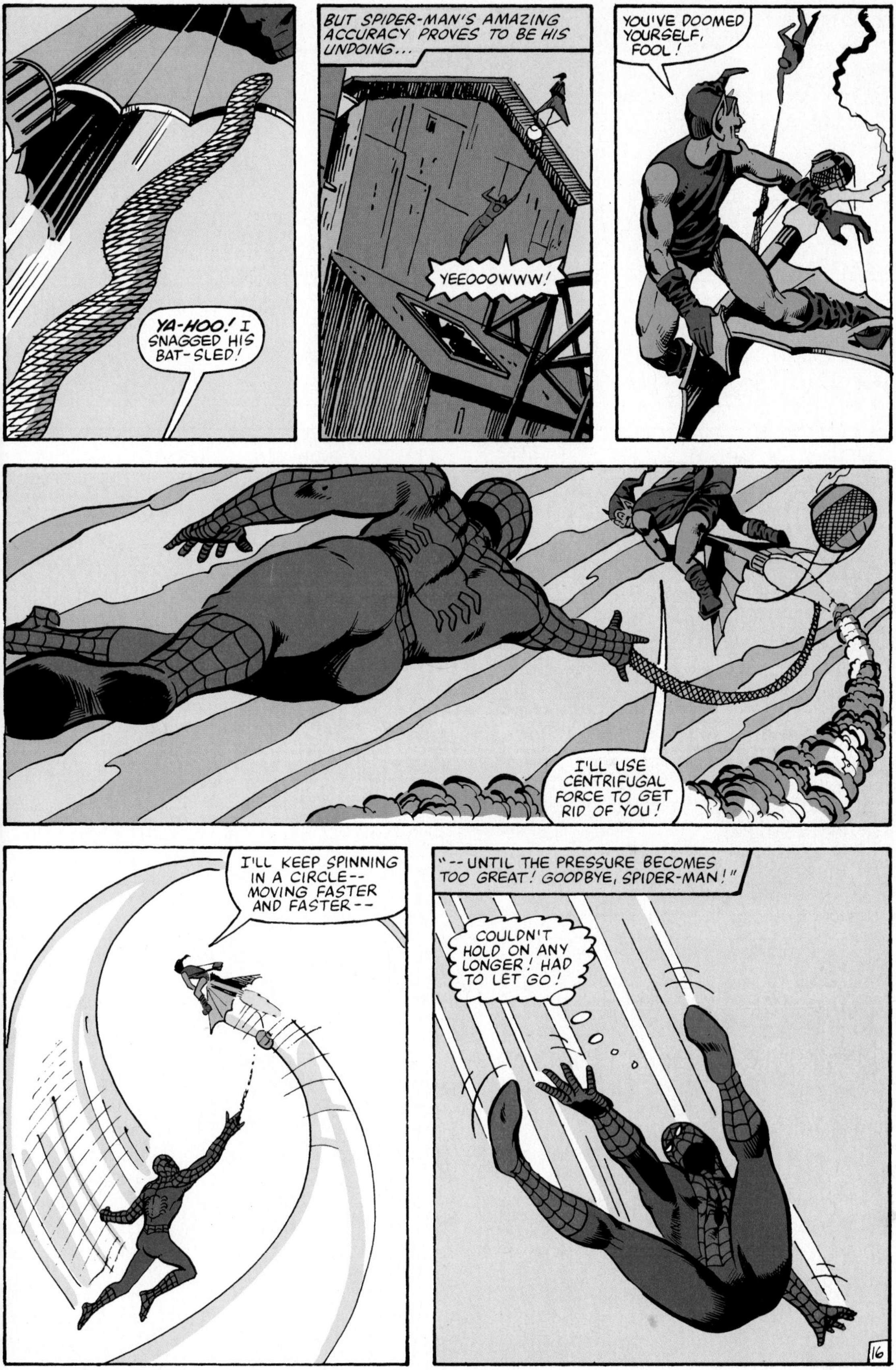

YA-HOO! I SNAGGED HIS BAT-SLED!
BUT SPIDER-MAN'S AMAZING ACCURACY PROVES TO BE HIS UNDOING...
YEEOOOWWW!
YOU'VE DOOMED YOURSELF, FOOL!
I'LL USE CENTRIFUGAL FORCE TO GET RID OF YOU!
I'LL KEEP SPINNING IN A CIRCLE-- MOVING FASTER AND FASTER--
"--UNTIL THE PRESSURE BECOMES TOO GREAT! GOODBYE, SPIDER-MAN!"
COULDN'T HOLD ON ANY LONGER! HAD TO LET GO!
16

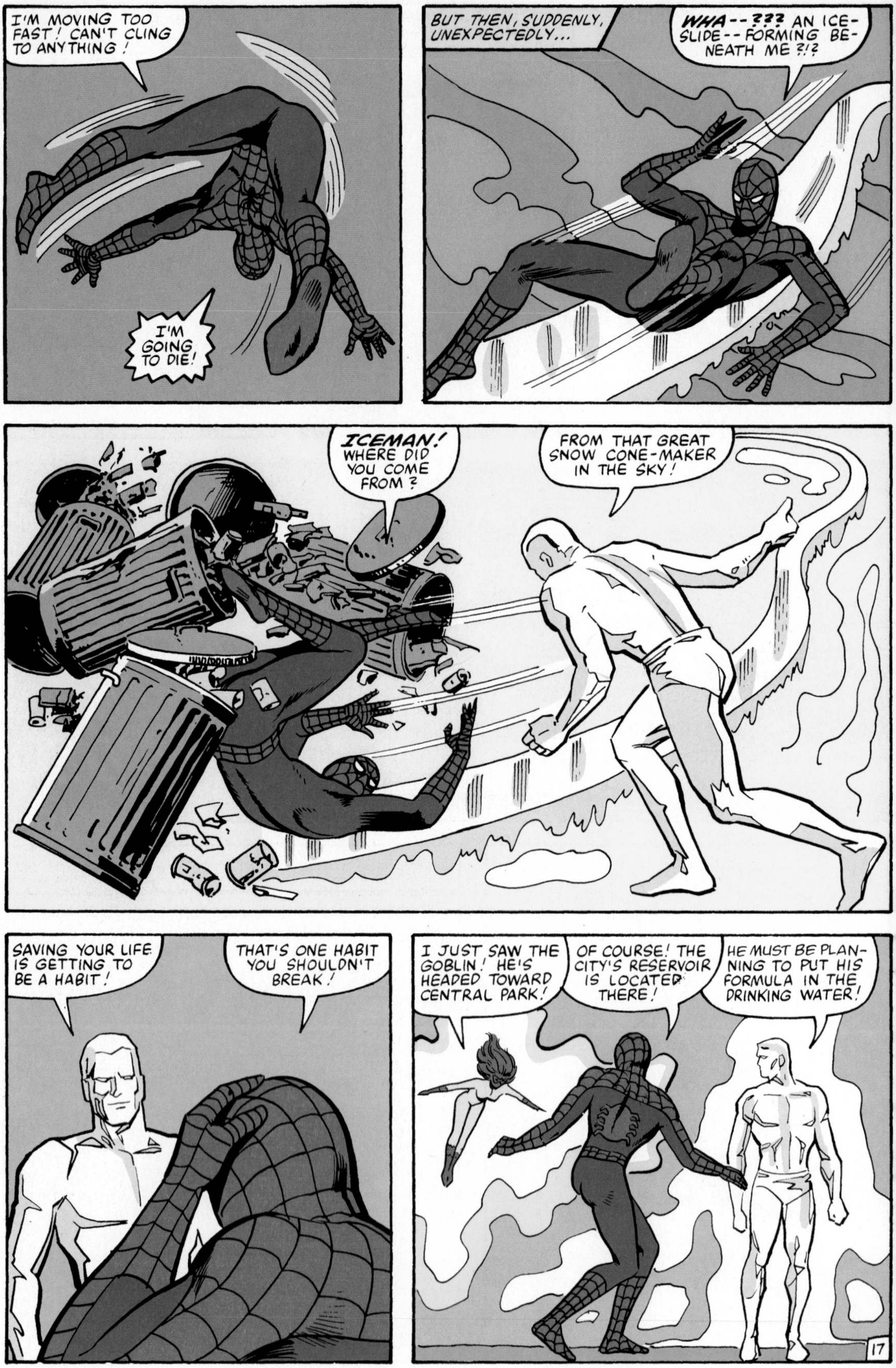
I'M MOVING TOO FAST! CAN'T CLING TO ANYTHING!
I'M GOING TO DIE!
BUT THEN, SUDDENLY, UNEXPECTEDLY...
WHA--??? AN ICE-SLIDE--FORMING BE-NEATH ME ?!?
ICEMAN! WHERE DID YOU COME FROM?
FROM THAT GREAT SNOW CONE-MAKER IN THE SKY!
SAVING YOUR LIFE IS GETTING TO BE A HABIT!
THAT'S ONE HABIT YOU SHOULDN'T BREAK!
I JUST SAW THE GOBLIN! HE'S HEADED TOWARD CENTRAL PARK!
OF COURSE! THE CITY'S RESERVOIR IS LOCATED THERE!
HE MUST BE PLAN-NING TO PUT HIS FORMULA IN THE DRINKING WATER!
17

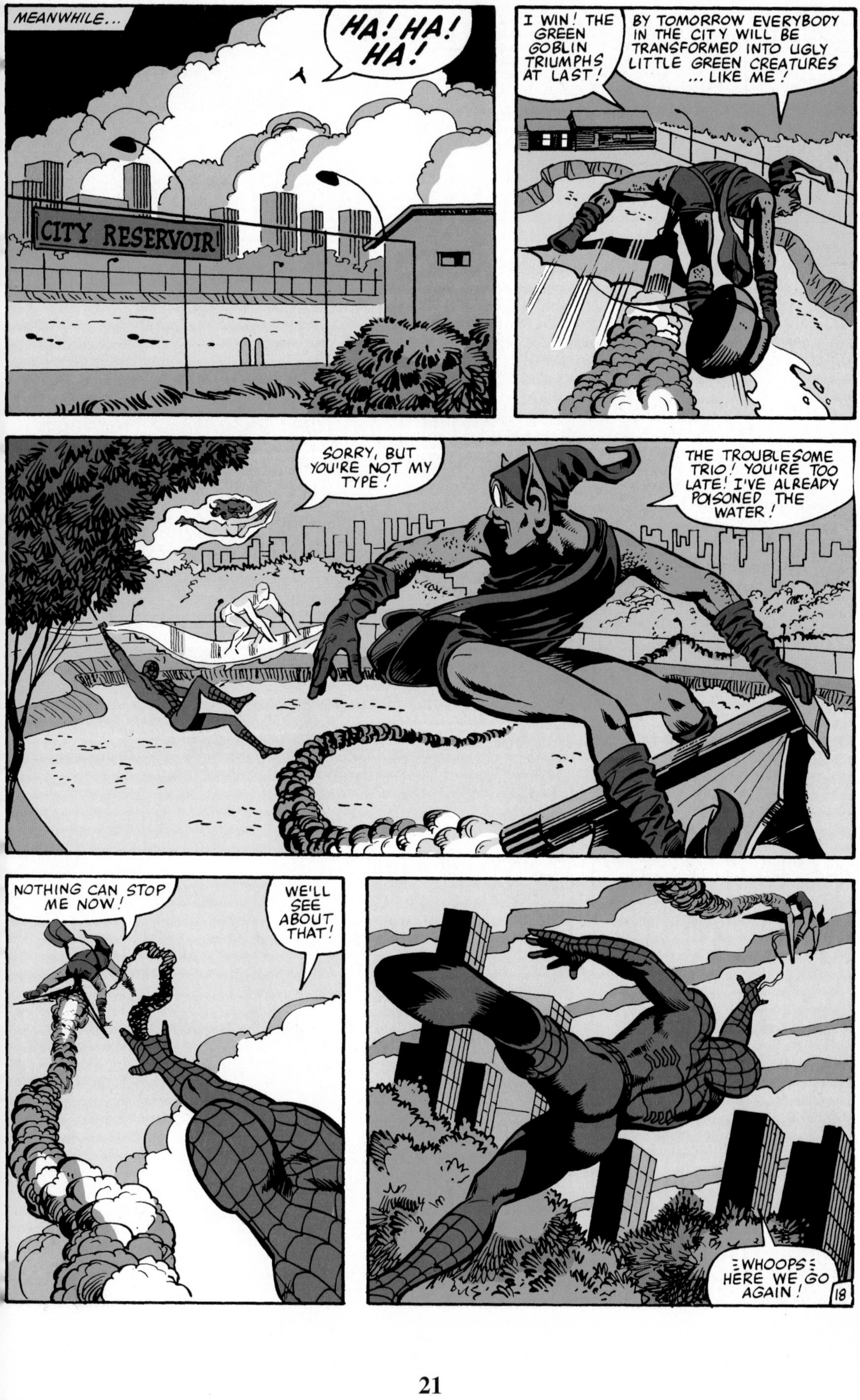
MEANWHILE...
HA! HA! HA!
CITY RESERVOIR
I WIN! THE GREEN GOBLIN TRIUMPHS AT LAST!
BY TOMORROW EVERYBODY IN THE CITY WILL BE TRANSFORMED INTO UGLY LITTLE GREEN CREATURES ... LIKE ME!
SORRY, BUT YOU'RE NOT MY TYPE!
THE TROUBLESOME TRIO! YOU'RE TOO LATE! I'VE ALREADY POISONED THE WATER!
NOTHING CAN STOP ME NOW!
WE'LL SEE ABOUT THAT!
WHOOPS HERE WE GO AGAIN!
18

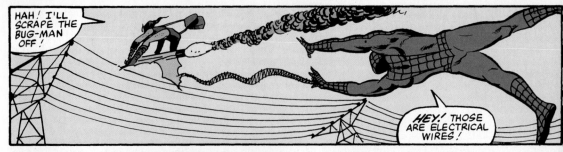

HAH! I'LL SCRAPE THE BUG-MAN OFF!

HEY! THOSE ARE ELECTRICAL WIRES!

THWIP!

FIRING HIS WEBBING AT A NEARBY TREE, SPIDER-MAN SWINGS TO SAFETY, BUT...

IF YOU WANT ME TO LEAVE, WHY NOT SAY SO?

I'M FLYING TOO LOW-- CAN'T PULL UP IN TIME!

AND THEN...

KA-BLOOM

MEANWHILE, BACK AT THE RESERVOIR...

LOOK AT THIS, FIREFLY! I MANAGED TO FREEZE THE ENTIRE RESERVOIR!

GOOD WORK, SNOWFACE! THE GOBLIN'S FORMULA HASN'T HAD A CHANCE TO MIX WITH THE WATER YET!

19

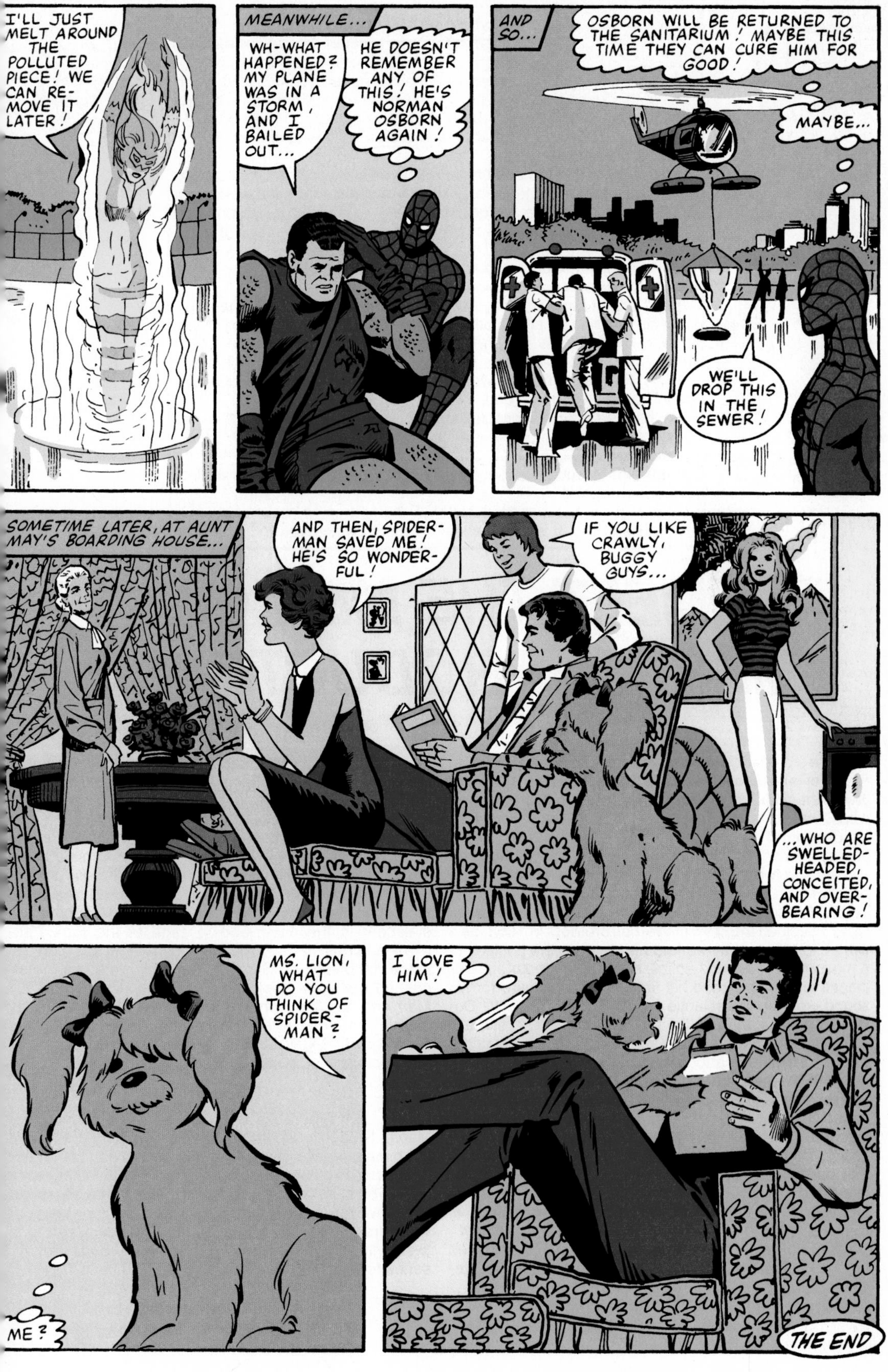
I'LL JUST MELT AROUND THE POLLUTED PIECE! WE CAN REMOVE IT LATER!
MEANWHILE...
WH-WHAT HAPPENED? MY PLANE WAS IN A STORM, AND I BAILED OUT...
HE DOESN'T REMEMBER ANY OF THIS! HE'S NORMAN OSBORN AGAIN!
AND SO...
OSBORN WILL BE RETURNED TO THE SANITARIUM! MAYBE THIS TIME THEY CAN CURE HIM FOR GOOD!
MAYBE...
WE'LL DROP THIS IN THE SEWER!
SOMETIME LATER, AT AUNT MAY'S BOARDING HOUSE...
AND THEN, SPIDER-MAN SAVED ME! HE'S SO WONDERFUL!
IF YOU LIKE CRAWLY, BUGGY GUYS...
...WHO ARE SWELLED-HEADED, CONCEITED, AND OVER-BEARING!
MS. LION, WHAT DO YOU THINK OF SPIDER-MAN?
ME?
I LOVE HIM!
THE END

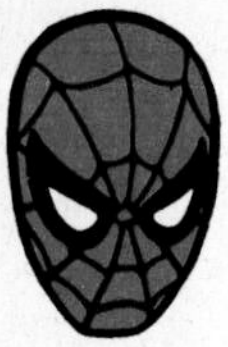

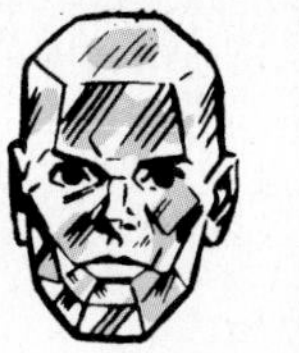

For the past year or so, you may have heard rumors and reports about Marvel getting involved in the wild world of animation. Well, it's true!

And the book you hold in your hands is a result of that involvement!

As of this writing, *"Spider-Man And His Amazing Friends"* is scheduled to make its network debut Saturday, September 12th, on NBC. And this special issue is an adaptation of an upcoming episode of that amazing animated series.

Now, we know that many of you will be a tad bit puzzled by the story. After all, in that far-famed reality known to comics fans the world over as the *Marvel Universe,* Spider-Man rarely—if ever—pals around with the Iceman . . . and there is no young lady called Fire-star. (At least, not yet!) Well, that's because this yarn is adapted from a series which is *itself* an adaptation of the continuing saga of our popular Web-slinger. It's sort of a double adaptation, so to speak.

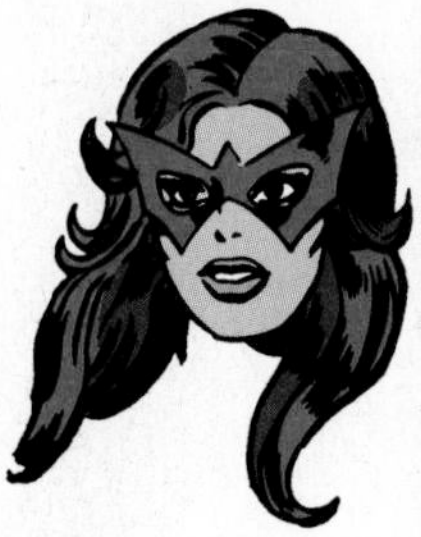

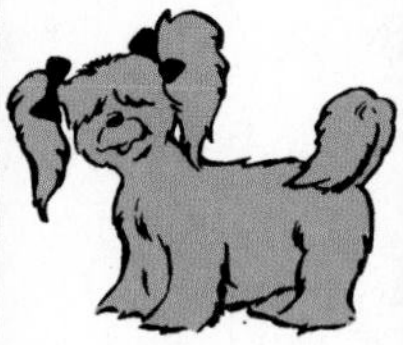

So, if you're a consistency buff and you're worried about where this story fits in amongst all the other Spider-Man tales, then let us put you at ease. This story is not part of the normal fabric of the Marvel Universe. If you wish to consider this a saga of an alternate Marvel reality, then be our guest. But, as we said, it's an adaptation . . . and is only meant to be enjoyed as one.

Be that as it may, this special issue is our way of celebrating Marvel's newest entry into the ever-expanding broadcast medium. And, just as with the comics themselves, animation is not the work of one man! It's a team effort, brought about by the combined talents of several dedicated individuals.

And who are those individuals? We thought you'd never ask!

In other words, this is our sneaky way of inviting you to . . .

MEET THE MEN OF MARVEL PRODUCTIONS!

There's probably no name more familiar to those in the realm of animation than that of DAVID DePATIE, the president of Marvel Productions, Ltd. An industry veteran whose career spans four decades, Dave is responsible for dozens of box office smashes and video success stories. His efforts over the years have earned him two Oscars and two Emmy Awards, as well as a host of other accolades.

David began his career in the field of entertainment when he joined the crew at Warner Brothers in 1952, as a film editor. He shortly worked his way into the position of a motion picture sound editor, rising to immediate prominence when he earned his first Academy Award for his sound work on the science fiction classic, *"THEM!"* DePatie moved up through the ranks at Warners, eventually being named vice-president and general manager of the studio's animated cartoon division.

In 1963, when Warner Brothers decided to do away with its animation department, David DePatie joined with famed animation director Friz Freleng to form the now-legendary partnership known as DePatie-Freleng Enterprises. During the seventeen highly successful years of that partnership, Dave distinguished himself well in the television and motion picture fields, demonstrating equal facility with animation, live-action, and combinations of the two.

Although he's probably best known for his animated productions of the Pink Panther, DePatie has also provided title animation for such feature films as *"A Shot in the Dark," "The Great Race,"* and *"The Hallelujah Trail."* And, though it's a little-known fact, Dave also contributed to the animated special effects of "Star Wars"!

In his current position at the helm of Marvel Productions, Ltd., David DePatie continues to lend his considerable talents to television productions. In less than a year, the Marvel studio has already delivered one prime time special to ABC—"Pink at First Sight," another installment in the never-ending saga of the Pink Panther—and has started production on Dr. Seuss' "The Cat in the Hat Meets the Grinch"—currently slated for broadcast on ABC later this year. And, in addition to *"Spider-Man And His Amazing Friends"* for NBC's fall Saturday morning line-up, DePatie is readying twenty-six new solo episodes of "Spider-Man" for first-run syndication on stations across the country!

****

LEE GUNTHER, the vice-president of production for Marvel Productions, Ltd., is another luminary in the field of animation. Like David DePatie, Lee began his career at Warner Brothers. Signing on in 1957, Gunther spent three years as a film editor and three years as sound effects editor in the animated cartoon division. While at Warners, Lee worked on some fifty commercials, twenty-five theatrical cartoons, and the "Bugs Bunny" series for ABC.

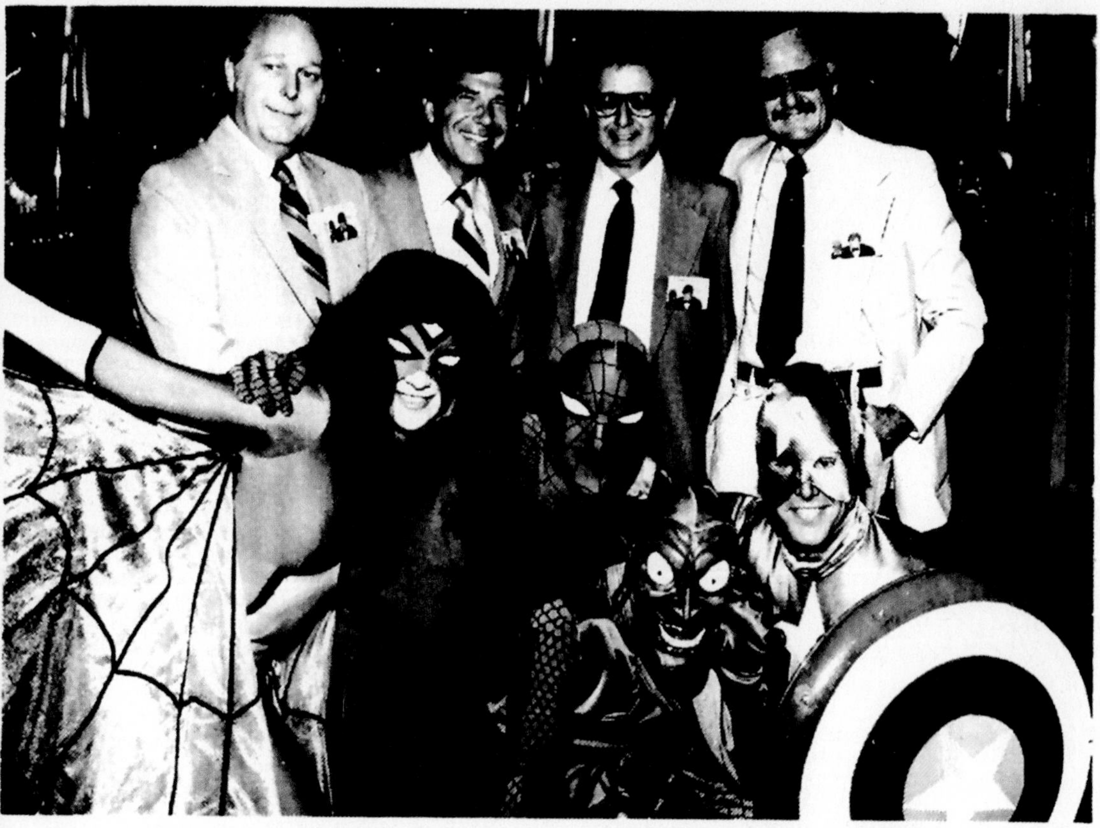

The brain-trust of *Marvel Productions, Ltd.* parties down with four mysterious gate-crashers. (Back row, left to right: Lee Gunther, David DePatie, Jim Galton, and Stan Lee. Front row: Aw, you know!)

Gunther joined DePatie-Freleng Enterprises in 1963, and during his years of work there, he accrued a roster of credits which includes 180 theatrical cartoons, nine television series, eleven television specials, 300 commercials, and was the winner of two Emmys and seven Cleo Awards. Lee is also the recipient of a special Presidential citation for his services in producing "A Force in Readiness," for the United States Marine Corps.

****

DENNIS MARKS, another entertainment industry veteran, is the Marvel Productions creative director. The former producer of Metromedia's *"Wonderama"* series, Dennis has also written and produced hundreds of television and theatrical animation features for numerous companies, including DePatie-Freleng Enterprises, Filmation Studios, and Hanna-Barbera. An instructor of courses on children's programming at the New School for Social Research during the 1970s, Dennis is the producer of *"Spider-Man And His Amazing Friends."*

****

AL BRODAX, best known as the producer and co-writer of the animated Beatles' feature film, *"Yellow Submarine,"* brings three decades of experience to his post as director of program development/special projects for Marvel Productions. Winner of the prestigious George Peabody Award, Al began his career at the William Morris Agency, where he was involved with such classic shows of the golden age of television as *"The Show of*

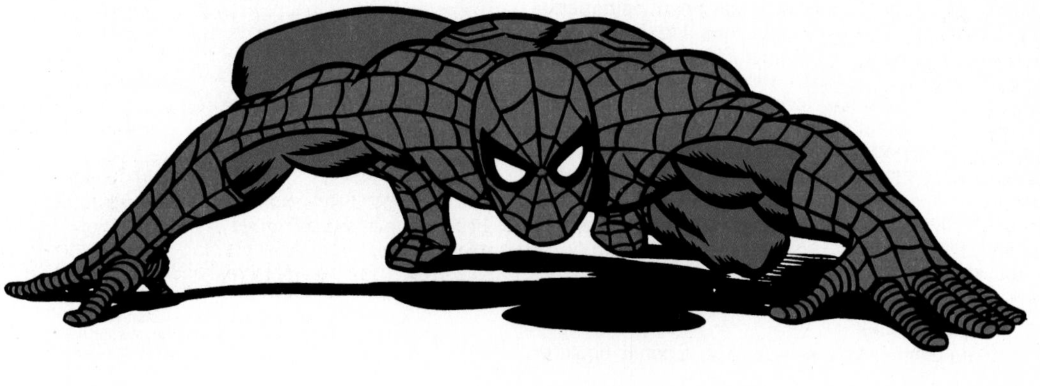

the first time, Stan Lee is the moving force that sparked the birth of Marvel Comics. As editor and head writer, Stan started what became known as the Marvel Age of Comics in 1961, giving the reading public a whole new universe of characters . . . the Fantastic Four, Spider-Man, the Hulk, Dr. Strange, Iron Man, Daredevil, the X-Men, the Inhumans, the Silver Surfer, the Black Panther . . . the list goes on and on and on!

A writer of no small talent, Stan wrote no fewer than two complete comic books a week, for nearly three decades! That may well be the largest amount of published work to ever come out of one man's typewriter. And, in his spare time, Stan wrote newspaper features, radio scripts, special magazines, television scripts, and screenplays. Not one to let little inconveniences stand in his way, Stan persevered in the face of the 1965 East Coast blackout by digging an old manual typewriter out of his closet and typing a complete story by candle light!

But most importantly, Stan revolutionized the comics industry through his popularization of super hero stories which had more relevance to the reader, stories which had a stronger touchstone to reality. And, in so doing, Stan concocted a mythological product of the imagination that's bigger than life, and yet still possesses recognizably human flaws . . . heroes that allow you to both fantasize and empathize, often at the same time.

Stan became publisher of Marvel Comics in 1972, and since then has devoted his time and energy to making Marvel the largest, best-selling comics company in the world.

Currently, Stan is writing the Amazing Spider-Man newspaper strip, working on a new comic book adventure of the Silver Surfer, and supervising the creative development of Marvel Productions, Ltd.
'Nuff said!

Shows," "Pulitzer Prize Playhouse," "Celanese Theatre," and "Omnibus." The writer and producer of over five hundred animated cartoons for television, Al has recently completed a treatment of "The Nutcracker," an 85-minute animated feature film, which will be co-produced by Marvel Productions, Ltd. and Japan's Toei Animation Company, Ltd.

****

JERRY EISENBERG is the senior producer at Marvel Productions. Since joining the animation industry in 1956 at MGM, Jerry has demonstrated his expertise in virtually all aspects of the field, from character design to producing and directing. Jerry's worked for Warner Brothers, Hanna-Barbera, and Sanrio Film. Before joining Marvel, he was the producer of several animated series for Ruby-Spears, including the highly successful "Thundarr!"

****

A soft-spoken gentleman who has been instrumental in the formation of Marvel Productions, Ltd. is JIM GALTON, the president of the Marvel Entertainment Group! An enlightened businessman with three decades of publishing experience to his credit, Jim assumed the presidential chair at Marvel in 1975, and instantly realized the incredible untapped potential which the company possessed. Today, thanks to Galton's careful direction, Marvel has become a worldwide leader in the field of publishing and a major supplier to virtually all forms of entertainment media!

****

STAN LEE really needs no introduction . . . but we'll give him one anyway!

For those of you who are picking up a comic book for

A publisher's work is never done! Stan-the-Man spends a lot of his time on the phone, making sure that Marvel-West keeps in touch with Marvel-East!

Three years later, Firestar debuted in the mainstream Marvel Universe. Though unlike her cartoon counterpart, she was not a friend of the Amazing Spider-Man — but a conflicted member of the Hellions, the mutant students of the villainous Hellfire Club! The following year, Firestar received a miniseries that fleshed out her Marvel Universe backstory.

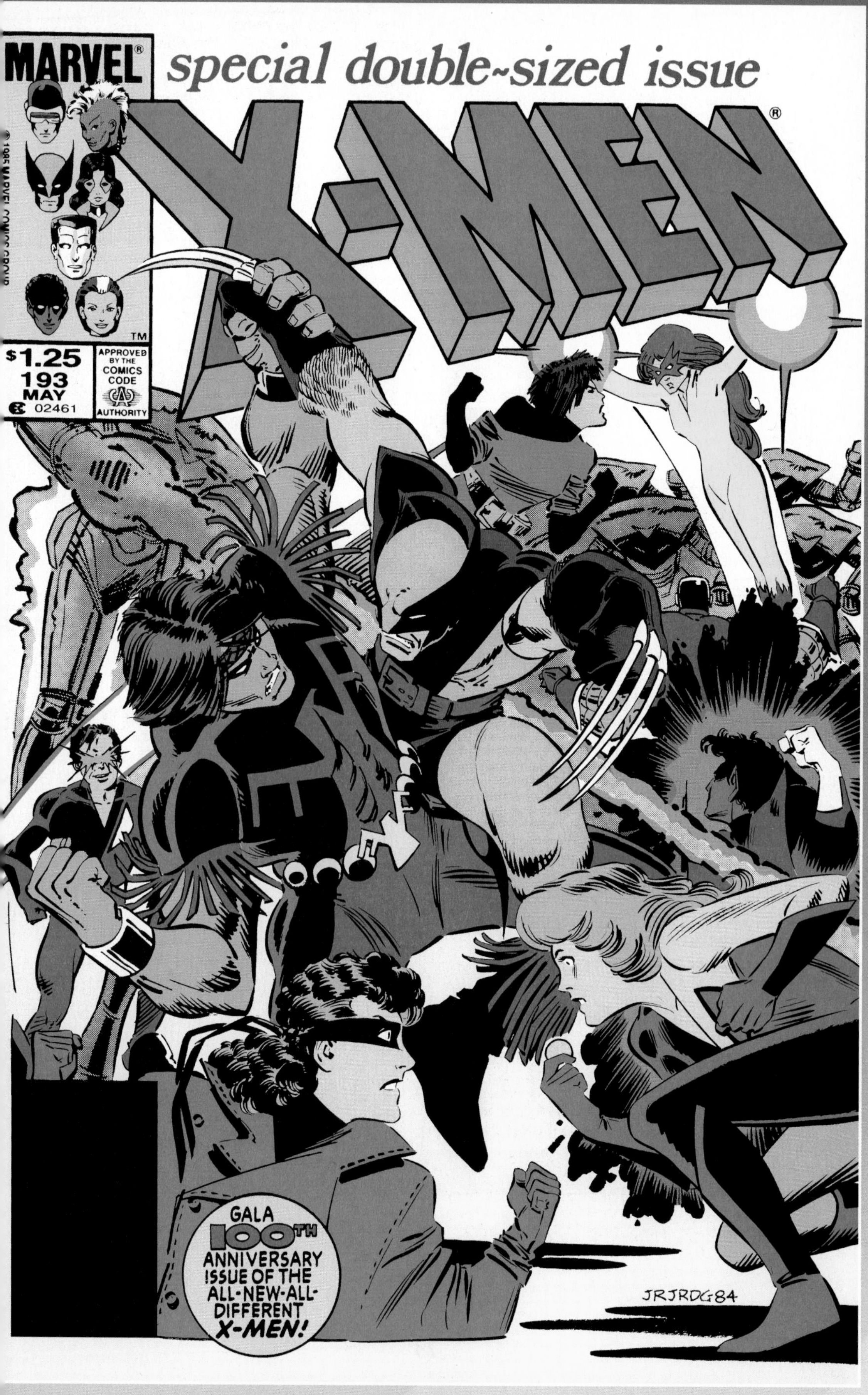

MARVEL
special double-sized issue
X-MEN
TM
$1.25
193
MAY
02461
APPROVED BY THE COMICS CODE AUTHORITY
GALA 100TH ANNIVERSARY ISSUE OF THE ALL-NEW-ALL-DIFFERENT X-MEN!
JRJRDG84

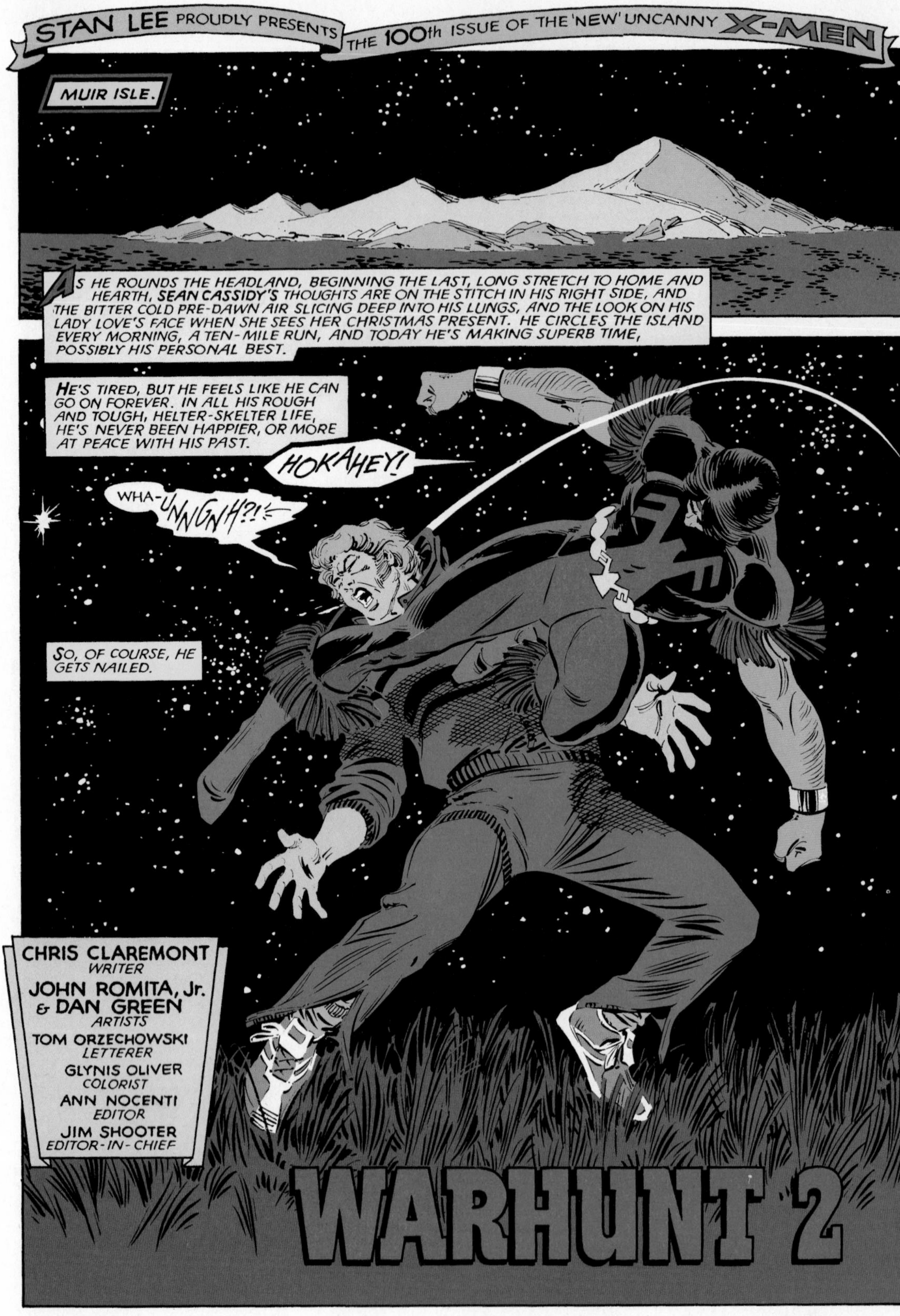
STAN LEE PROUDLY PRESENTS THE 100th ISSUE OF THE 'NEW' UNCANNY X-MEN
MUIR ISLE.
AS HE ROUNDS THE HEADLAND, BEGINNING THE LAST, LONG STRETCH TO HOME AND HEARTH, SEAN CASSIDY'S THOUGHTS ARE ON THE STITCH IN HIS RIGHT SIDE, AND THE BITTER COLD PRE-DAWN AIR SLICING DEEP INTO HIS LUNGS, AND THE LOOK ON HIS LADY LOVE'S FACE WHEN SHE SEES HER CHRISTMAS PRESENT. HE CIRCLES THE ISLAND EVERY MORNING, A TEN-MILE RUN, AND TODAY HE'S MAKING SUPERB TIME, POSSIBLY HIS PERSONAL BEST.
HE'S TIRED, BUT HE FEELS LIKE HE CAN GO ON FOREVER. IN ALL HIS ROUGH AND TOUGH, HELTER-SKELTER LIFE, HE'S NEVER BEEN HAPPIER, OR MORE AT PEACE WITH HIS PAST.
HOKAHEY!
WHA-UNNGNH?!
SO, OF COURSE, HE GETS NAILED.
CHRIS CLAREMONT WRITER
JOHN ROMITA, Jr. & DAN GREEN ARTISTS
TOM ORZECHOWSKI LETTERER
GLYNIS OLIVER COLORIST
ANN NOCENTI EDITOR
JIM SHOOTER EDITOR-IN-CHIEF
WARHUNT 2

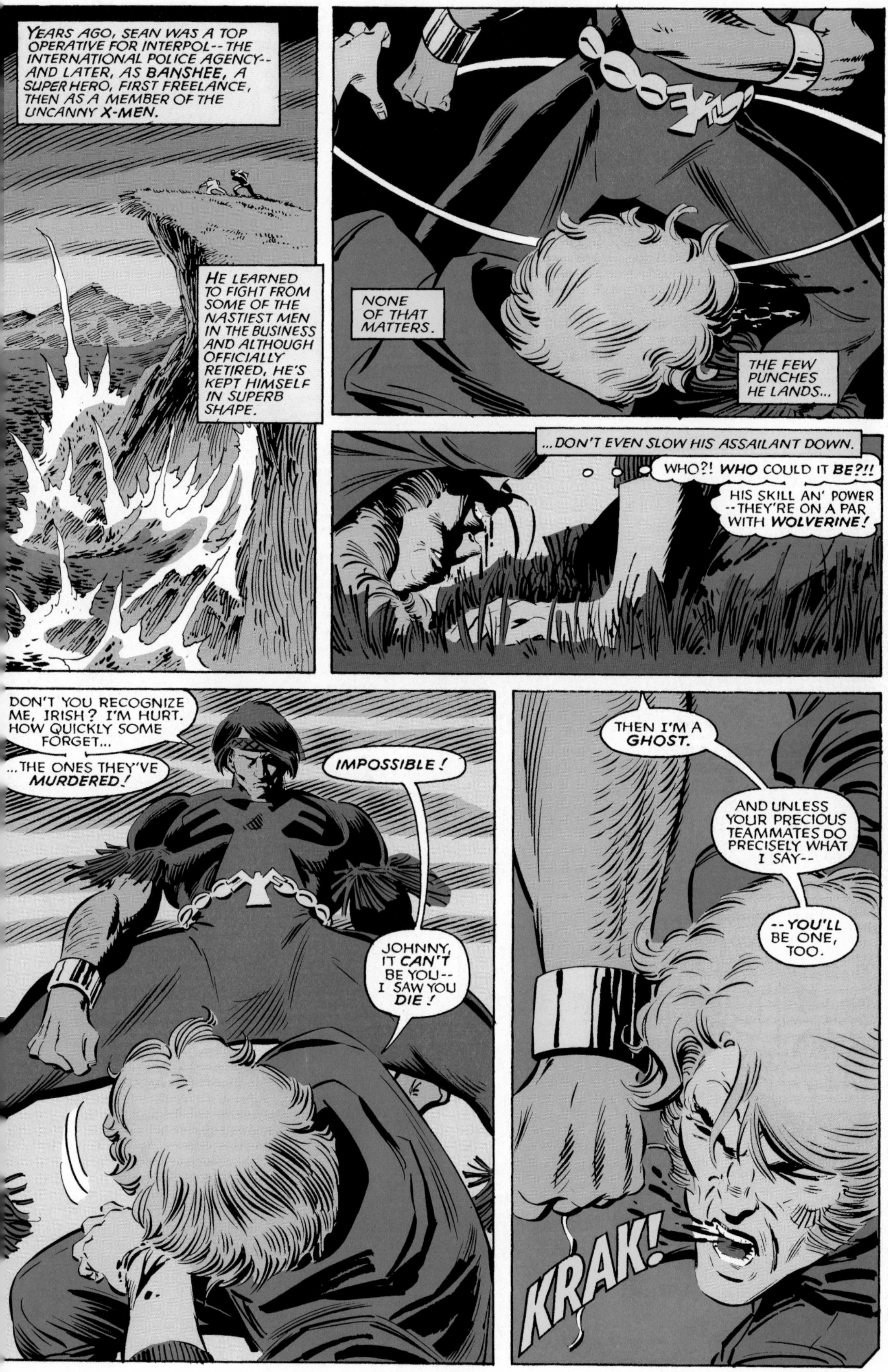

YEARS AGO, SEAN WAS A TOP OPERATIVE FOR INTERPOL--THE INTERNATIONAL POLICE AGENCY--AND LATER, AS BANSHEE, A SUPER HERO, FIRST FREELANCE, THEN AS A MEMBER OF THE UNCANNY X-MEN.
HE LEARNED TO FIGHT FROM SOME OF THE NASTIEST MEN IN THE BUSINESS AND ALTHOUGH OFFICIALLY RETIRED, HE'S KEPT HIMSELF IN SUPERB SHAPE.
NONE OF THAT MATTERS.
THE FEW PUNCHES HE LANDS...
...DON'T EVEN SLOW HIS ASSAILANT DOWN.
WHO?! WHO COULD IT BE?!!
HIS SKILL AN' POWER --THEY'RE ON A PAR WITH WOLVERINE!
DON'T YOU RECOGNIZE ME, IRISH? I'M HURT. HOW QUICKLY SOME FORGET...
...THE ONES THEY'VE MURDERED!
IMPOSSIBLE!
JOHNNY, IT CAN'T BE YOU-- I SAW YOU DIE!
THEN I'M A GHOST.
AND UNLESS YOUR PRECIOUS TEAMMATES DO PRECISELY WHAT I SAY--
--YOU'LL BE ONE, TOO.
KRAK!

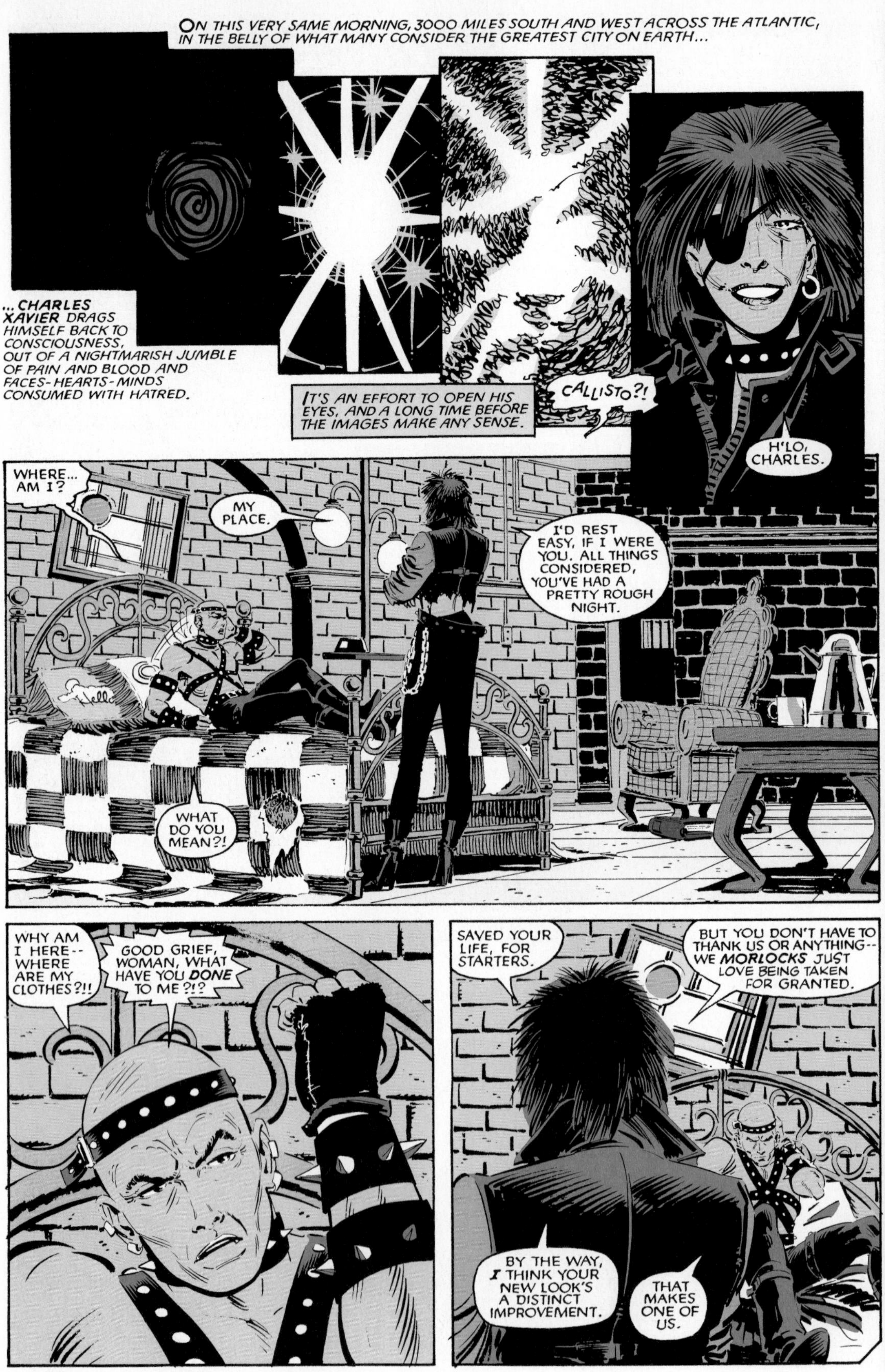
ON THIS VERY SAME MORNING, 3000 MILES SOUTH AND WEST ACROSS THE ATLANTIC, IN THE BELLY OF WHAT MANY CONSIDER THE GREATEST CITY ON EARTH...
...CHARLES XAVIER DRAGS HIMSELF BACK TO CONSCIOUSNESS, OUT OF A NIGHTMARISH JUMBLE OF PAIN AND BLOOD AND FACES-HEARTS-MINDS CONSUMED WITH HATRED.
IT'S AN EFFORT TO OPEN HIS EYES, AND A LONG TIME BEFORE THE IMAGES MAKE ANY SENSE.
CALLISTO?!
H'LO, CHARLES.
WHERE... AM I?
MY PLACE.
I'D REST EASY, IF I WERE YOU. ALL THINGS CONSIDERED, YOU'VE HAD A PRETTY ROUGH NIGHT.
WHAT DO YOU MEAN?!
WHY AM I HERE-- WHERE ARE MY CLOTHES?!!
GOOD GRIEF, WOMAN, WHAT HAVE YOU DONE TO ME?!?
SAVED YOUR LIFE, FOR STARTERS.
BUT YOU DON'T HAVE TO THANK US OR ANYTHING-- WE MORLOCKS JUST LOVE BEING TAKEN FOR GRANTED.
BY THE WAY, I THINK YOUR NEW LOOK'S A DISTINCT IMPROVEMENT.
THAT MAKES ONE OF US.

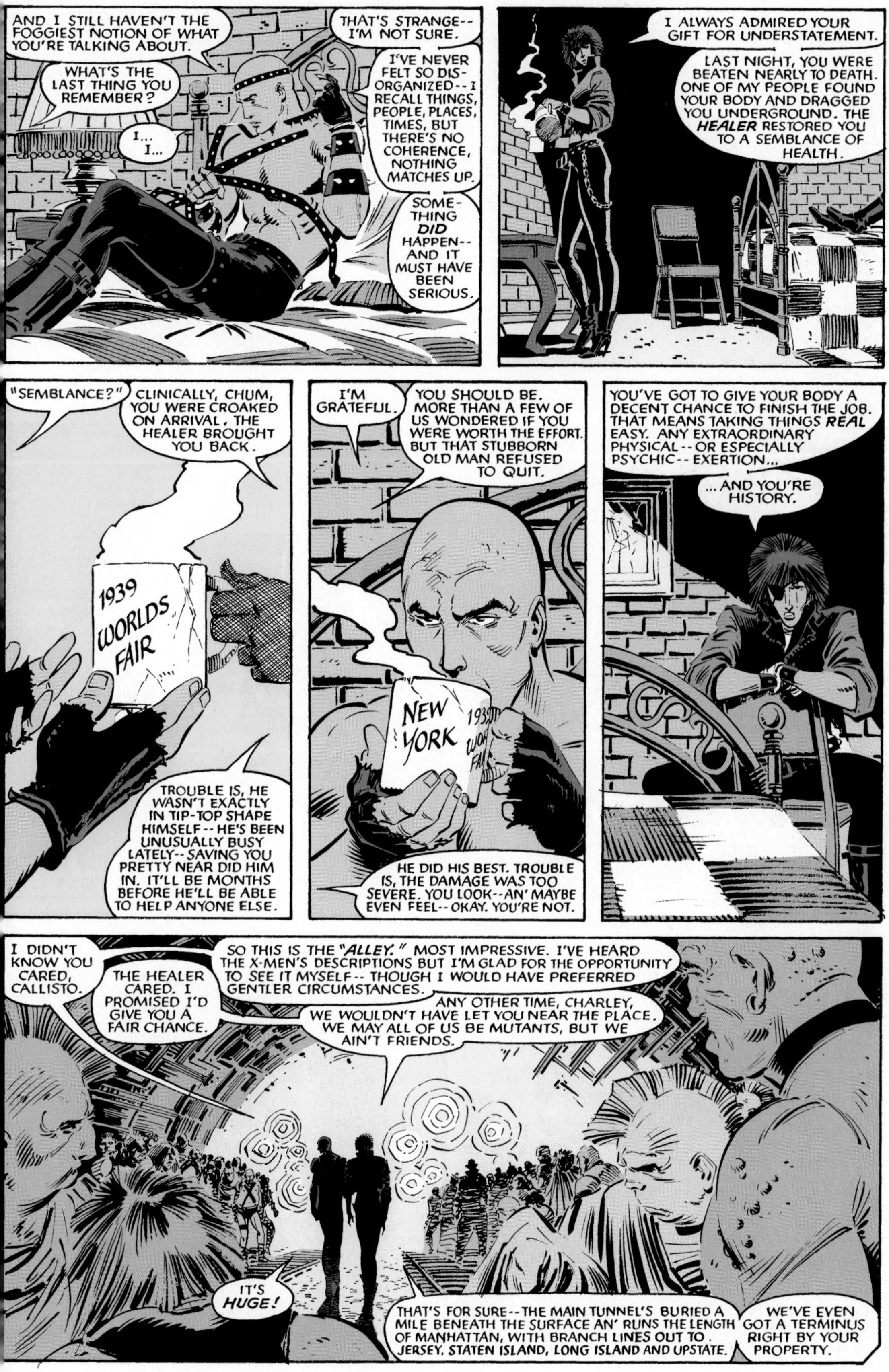

AND I STILL HAVEN'T THE FOGGIEST NOTION OF WHAT YOU'RE TALKING ABOUT.
WHAT'S THE LAST THING YOU REMEMBER?
I... I...
...
THAT'S STRANGE-- I'M NOT SURE.
I'VE NEVER FELT SO DIS-ORGANIZED-- I RECALL THINGS, PEOPLE, PLACES, TIMES, BUT THERE'S NO COHERENCE, NOTHING MATCHES UP.
SOME-THING DID HAPPEN-- AND IT MUST HAVE BEEN SERIOUS.
I ALWAYS ADMIRED YOUR GIFT FOR UNDERSTATEMENT.
LAST NIGHT, YOU WERE BEATEN NEARLY TO DEATH. ONE OF MY PEOPLE FOUND YOUR BODY AND DRAGGED YOU UNDERGROUND. THE HEALER RESTORED YOU TO A SEMBLANCE OF HEALTH.
"SEMBLANCE?"
CLINICALLY, CHUM, YOU WERE CROAKED ON ARRIVAL. THE HEALER BROUGHT YOU BACK.
1939 WORLDS FAIR
TROUBLE IS, HE WASN'T EXACTLY IN TIP-TOP SHAPE HIMSELF-- HE'S BEEN UNUSUALLY BUSY LATELY-- SAVING YOU PRETTY NEAR DID HIM IN. IT'LL BE MONTHS BEFORE HE'LL BE ABLE TO HELP ANYONE ELSE.
I'M GRATEFUL.
YOU SHOULD BE. MORE THAN A FEW OF US WONDERED IF YOU WERE WORTH THE EFFORT. BUT THAT STUBBORN OLD MAN REFUSED TO QUIT.
NEW YORK
HE DID HIS BEST. TROUBLE IS, THE DAMAGE WAS TOO SEVERE. YOU LOOK--AN' MAYBE EVEN FEEL-- OKAY. YOU'RE NOT.
YOU'VE GOT TO GIVE YOUR BODY A DECENT CHANCE TO FINISH THE JOB. THAT MEANS TAKING THINGS REAL EASY. ANY EXTRAORDINARY PHYSICAL -- OR ESPECIALLY PSYCHIC-- EXERTION...
...AND YOU'RE HISTORY.
I DIDN'T KNOW YOU CARED, CALLISTO.
THE HEALER CARED. I PROMISED I'D GIVE YOU A FAIR CHANCE.
SO THIS IS THE "ALLEY." MOST IMPRESSIVE. I'VE HEARD THE X-MEN'S DESCRIPTIONS BUT I'M GLAD FOR THE OPPORTUNITY TO SEE IT MYSELF-- THOUGH I WOULD HAVE PREFERRED GENTLER CIRCUMSTANCES.
ANY OTHER TIME, CHARLEY, WE WOULDN'T HAVE LET YOU NEAR THE PLACE. WE MAY ALL OF US BE MUTANTS, BUT WE AIN'T FRIENDS.
IT'S HUGE!
THAT'S FOR SURE-- THE MAIN TUNNEL'S BURIED A MILE BENEATH THE SURFACE AN' RUNS THE LENGTH OF MANHATTAN, WITH BRANCH LINES OUT TO JERSEY, STATEN ISLAND, LONG ISLAND AND UPSTATE.
WE'VE EVEN GOT A TERMINUS RIGHT BY YOUR PROPERTY.

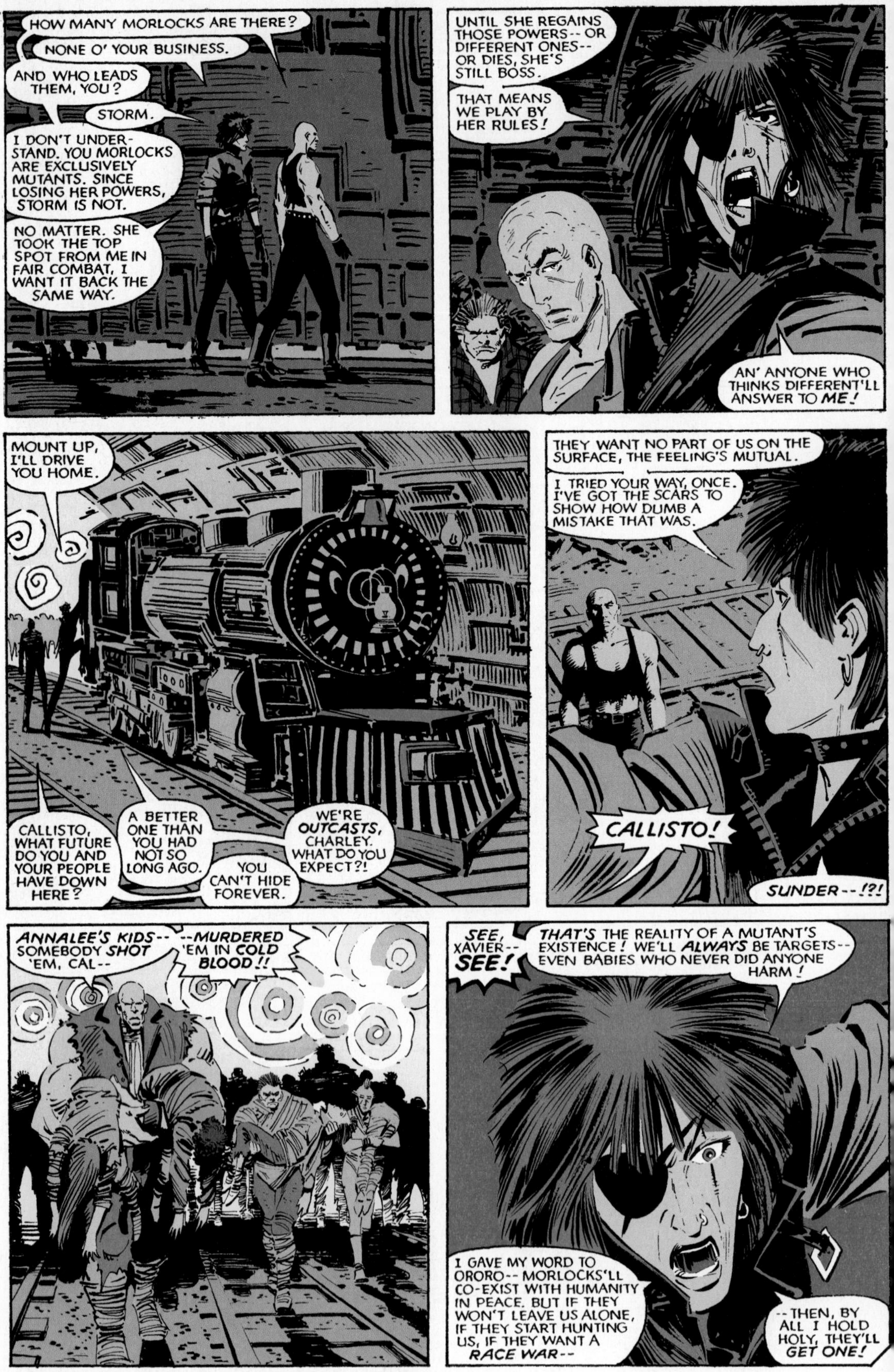
HOW MANY MORLOCKS ARE THERE?
NONE O' YOUR BUSINESS.
AND WHO LEADS THEM, YOU?
STORM.
I DON'T UNDERSTAND. YOU MORLOCKS ARE EXCLUSIVELY MUTANTS. SINCE LOSING HER POWERS, STORM IS NOT.
NO MATTER. SHE TOOK THE TOP SPOT FROM ME IN FAIR COMBAT, I WANT IT BACK THE SAME WAY.
UNTIL SHE REGAINS THOSE POWERS-- OR DIFFERENT ONES-- OR DIES, SHE'S STILL BOSS.
THAT MEANS WE PLAY BY HER RULES!
AN' ANYONE WHO THINKS DIFFERENT'LL ANSWER TO ME!
MOUNT UP, I'LL DRIVE YOU HOME.
CALLISTO, WHAT FUTURE DO YOU AND YOUR PEOPLE HAVE DOWN HERE?
A BETTER ONE THAN YOU HAD NOT SO LONG AGO.
YOU CAN'T HIDE FOREVER.
WE'RE OUTCASTS, CHARLEY. WHAT DO YOU EXPECT?!
THEY WANT NO PART OF US ON THE SURFACE, THE FEELING'S MUTUAL.
I TRIED YOUR WAY, ONCE. I'VE GOT THE SCARS TO SHOW HOW DUMB A MISTAKE THAT WAS.
CALLISTO!
SUNDER--!?!
ANNALEE'S KIDS-- SOMEBODY SHOT 'EM, CAL--
--MURDERED 'EM IN COLD BLOOD!!
SEE, XAVIER-- SEE!
THAT'S THE REALITY OF A MUTANT'S EXISTENCE! WE'LL ALWAYS BE TARGETS-- EVEN BABIES WHO NEVER DID ANYONE HARM!
I GAVE MY WORD TO ORORO-- MORLOCKS'LL CO-EXIST WITH HUMANITY IN PEACE. BUT IF THEY WON'T LEAVE US ALONE, IF THEY START HUNTING US, IF THEY WANT A RACE WAR--
--THEN, BY ALL I HOLD HOLY, THEY'LL GET ONE!

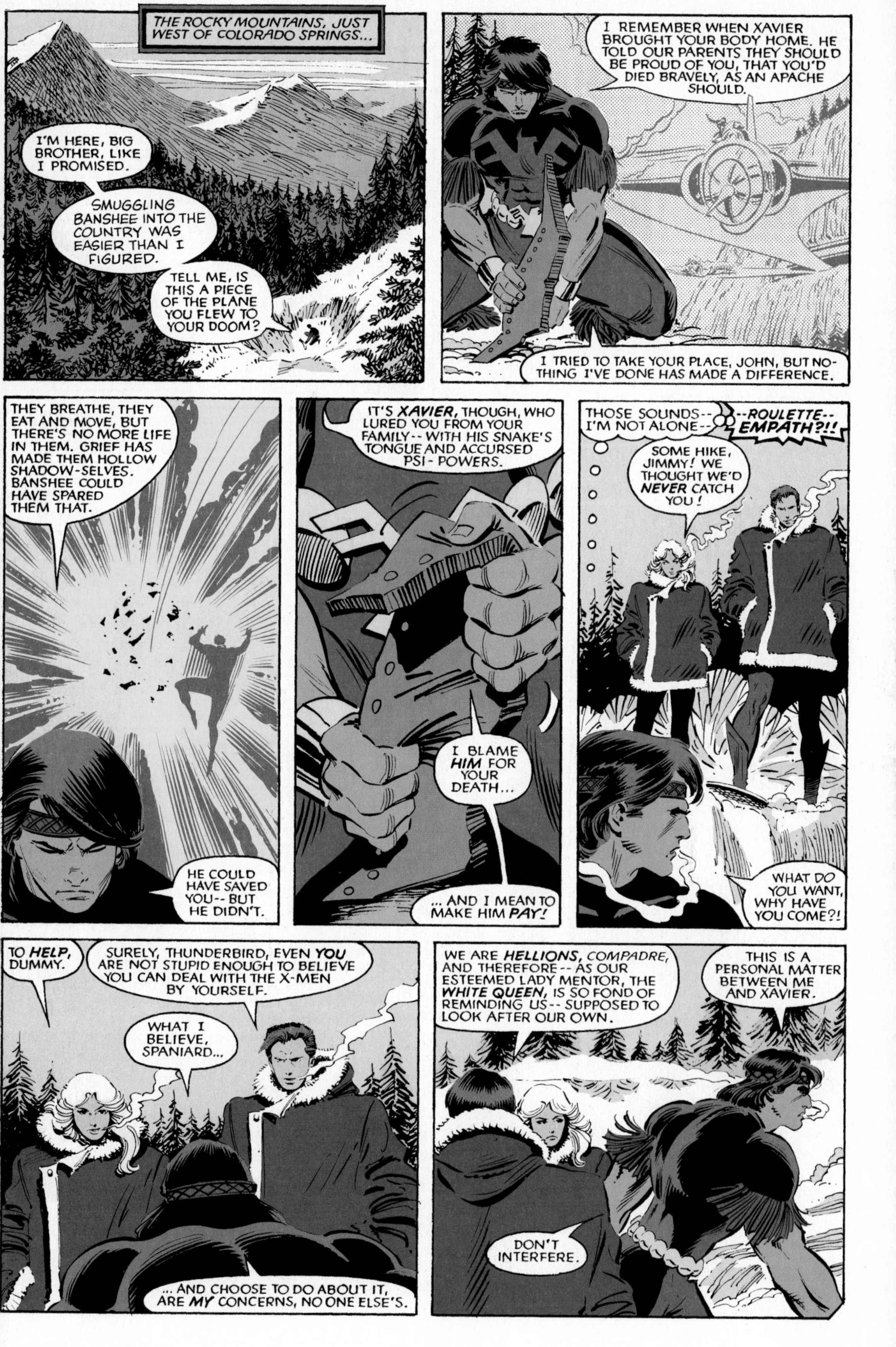
THE ROCKY MOUNTAINS, JUST WEST OF COLORADO SPRINGS...
I'M HERE, BIG BROTHER, LIKE I PROMISED.
SMUGGLING BANSHEE INTO THE COUNTRY WAS EASIER THAN I FIGURED.
TELL ME, IS THIS A PIECE OF THE PLANE YOU FLEW TO YOUR DOOM?
I REMEMBER WHEN XAVIER BROUGHT YOUR BODY HOME. HE TOLD OUR PARENTS THEY SHOULD BE PROUD OF YOU, THAT YOU'D DIED BRAVELY, AS AN APACHE SHOULD.
I TRIED TO TAKE YOUR PLACE, JOHN, BUT NOTHING I'VE DONE HAS MADE A DIFFERENCE.
THEY BREATHE, THEY EAT AND MOVE, BUT THERE'S NO MORE LIFE IN THEM. GRIEF HAS MADE THEM HOLLOW SHADOW-SELVES. BANSHEE COULD HAVE SPARED THEM THAT.
HE COULD HAVE SAVED YOU-- BUT HE DIDN'T.
IT'S XAVIER, THOUGH, WHO LURED YOU FROM YOUR FAMILY-- WITH HIS SNAKE'S TONGUE AND ACCURSED PSI-POWERS.
I BLAME HIM FOR YOUR DEATH...
...AND I MEAN TO MAKE HIM PAY!
THOSE SOUNDS-- I'M NOT ALONE--
--ROULETTE-- EMPATH?!!
SOME HIKE, JIMMY! WE THOUGHT WE'D NEVER CATCH YOU!
WHAT DO YOU WANT, WHY HAVE YOU COME?!
TO HELP, DUMMY.
SURELY, THUNDERBIRD, EVEN YOU ARE NOT STUPID ENOUGH TO BELIEVE YOU CAN DEAL WITH THE X-MEN BY YOURSELF.
WHAT I BELIEVE, SPANIARD...
...AND CHOOSE TO DO ABOUT IT, ARE MY CONCERNS, NO ONE ELSE'S.
WE ARE HELLIONS, COMPADRE, AND THEREFORE-- AS OUR ESTEEMED LADY MENTOR, THE WHITE QUEEN, IS SO FOND OF REMINDING US-- SUPPOSED TO LOOK AFTER OUR OWN.
THIS IS A PERSONAL MATTER BETWEEN ME AND XAVIER.
DON'T INTERFERE.

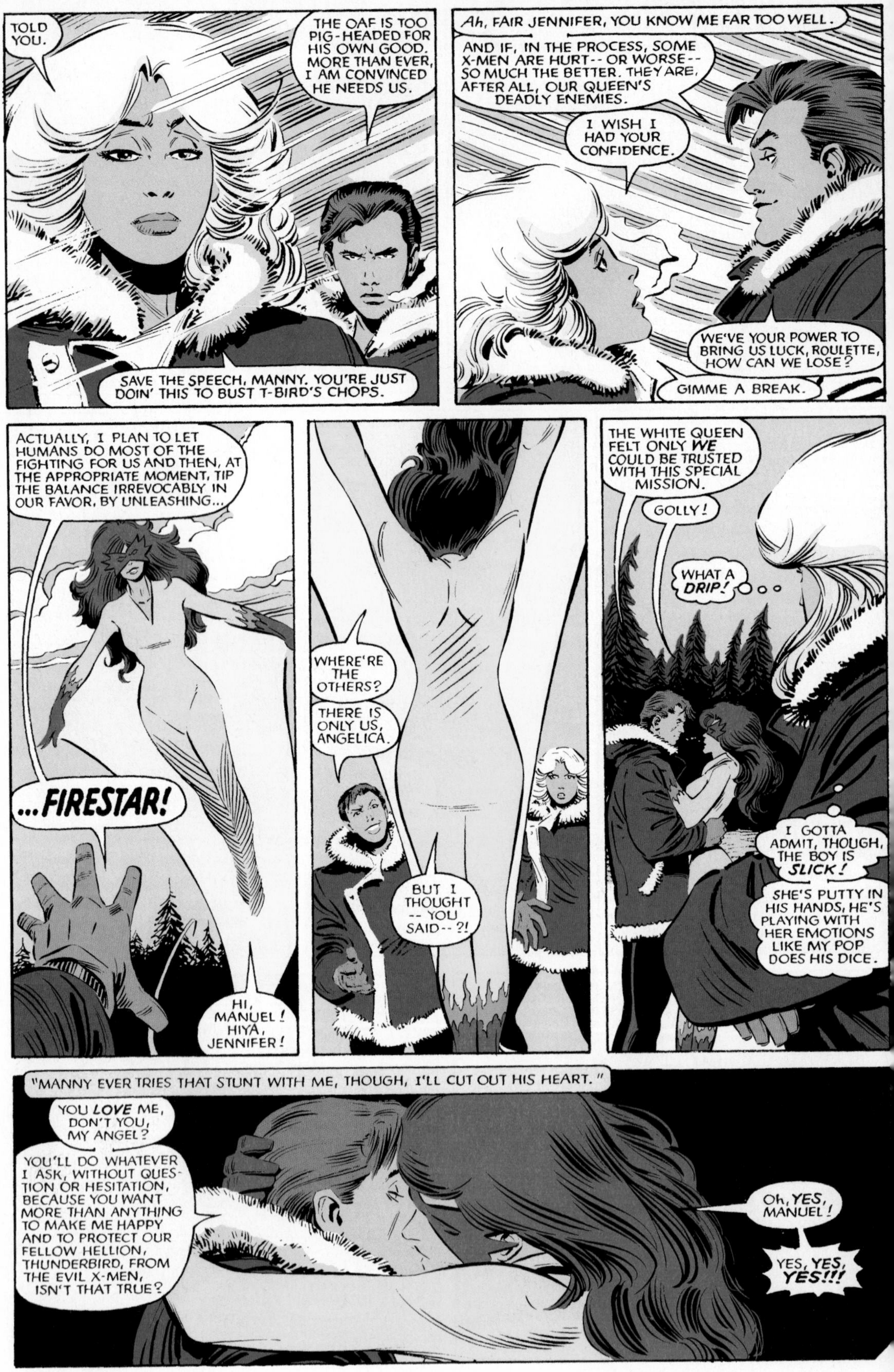

TOLD YOU.
THE OAF IS TOO PIG-HEADED FOR HIS OWN GOOD. MORE THAN EVER, I AM CONVINCED HE NEEDS US.
SAVE THE SPEECH, MANNY. YOU'RE JUST DOIN' THIS TO BUST T-BIRD'S CHOPS.
Ah, FAIR JENNIFER, YOU KNOW ME FAR TOO WELL.
AND IF, IN THE PROCESS, SOME X-MEN ARE HURT-- OR WORSE-- SO MUCH THE BETTER. THEY ARE, AFTER ALL, OUR QUEEN'S DEADLY ENEMIES.
I WISH I HAD YOUR CONFIDENCE.
WE'VE YOUR POWER TO BRING US LUCK, ROULETTE. HOW CAN WE LOSE?
GIMME A BREAK.
ACTUALLY, I PLAN TO LET HUMANS DO MOST OF THE FIGHTING FOR US AND THEN, AT THE APPROPRIATE MOMENT, TIP THE BALANCE IRREVOCABLY IN OUR FAVOR, BY UNLEASHING...
...FIRESTAR!
HI, MANUEL! HIYA, JENNIFER!
WHERE'RE THE OTHERS?
THERE IS ONLY US, ANGELICA.
BUT I THOUGHT -- YOU SAID-- ?!
THE WHITE QUEEN FELT ONLY WE COULD BE TRUSTED WITH THIS SPECIAL MISSION.
GOLLY!
WHAT A DRIP!
I GOTTA ADMIT, THOUGH, THE BOY IS SLICK!
SHE'S PUTTY IN HIS HANDS, HE'S PLAYING WITH HER EMOTIONS LIKE MY POP DOES HIS DICE.
"MANNY EVER TRIES THAT STUNT WITH ME, THOUGH, I'LL CUT OUT HIS HEART."
YOU LOVE ME, DON'T YOU, MY ANGEL?
YOU'LL DO WHATEVER I ASK, WITHOUT QUESTION OR HESITATION, BECAUSE YOU WANT MORE THAN ANYTHING TO MAKE ME HAPPY AND TO PROTECT OUR FELLOW HELLION, THUNDERBIRD, FROM THE EVIL X-MEN, ISN'T THAT TRUE?
Oh, YES, MANUEL!
YES, YES, YES!!!

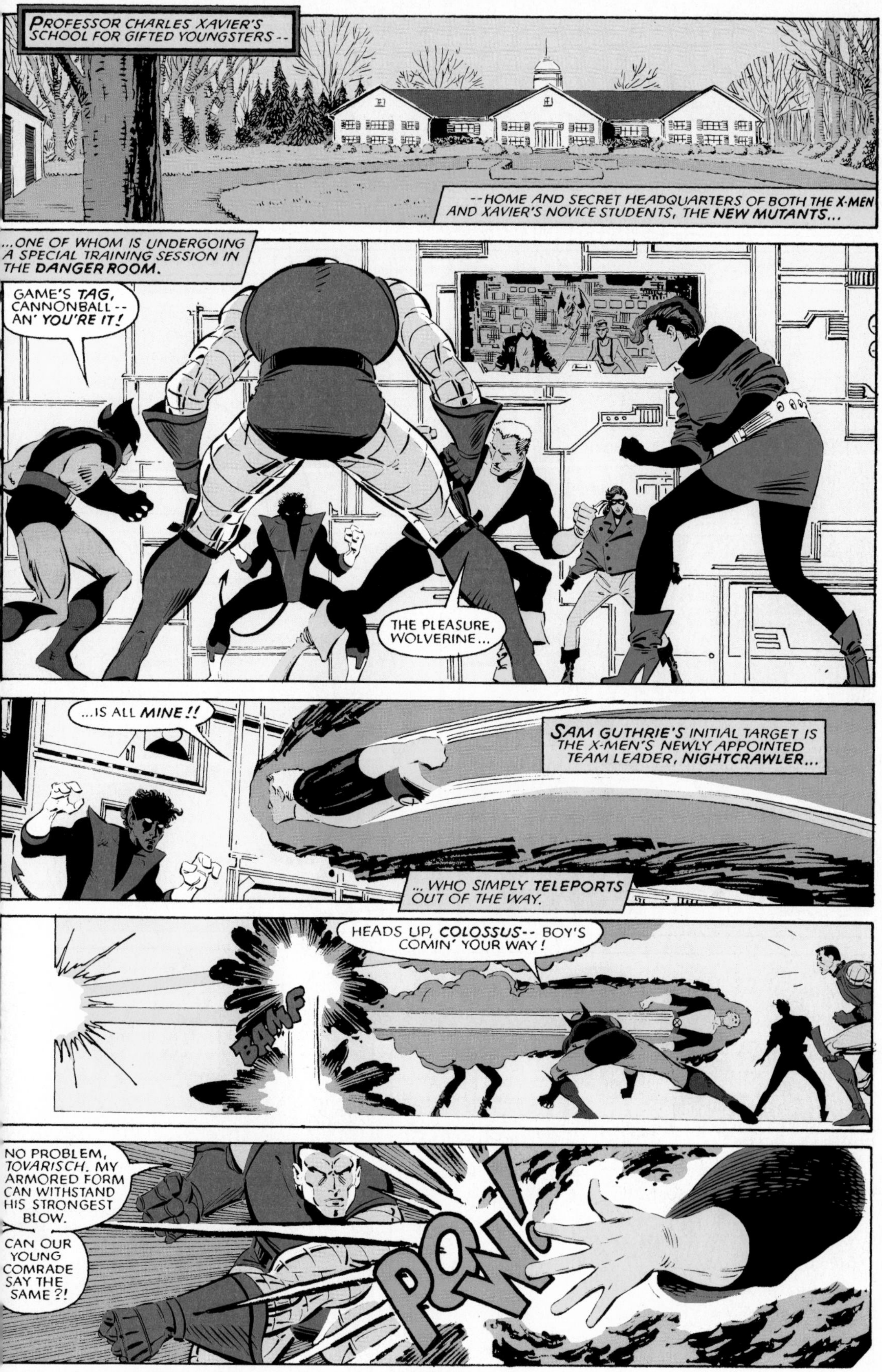

PROFESSOR CHARLES XAVIER'S SCHOOL FOR GIFTED YOUNGSTERS --
--HOME AND SECRET HEADQUARTERS OF BOTH THE X-MEN AND XAVIER'S NOVICE STUDENTS, THE NEW MUTANTS...
...ONE OF WHOM IS UNDERGOING A SPECIAL TRAINING SESSION IN THE DANGER ROOM.
GAME'S TAG, CANNONBALL -- AN' YOU'RE IT!
THE PLEASURE, WOLVERINE...
...IS ALL MINE!!
SAM GUTHRIE'S INITIAL TARGET IS THE X-MEN'S NEWLY APPOINTED TEAM LEADER, NIGHTCRAWLER...
...WHO SIMPLY TELEPORTS OUT OF THE WAY.
HEADS UP, COLOSSUS-- BOY'S COMIN' YOUR WAY!
BAMF
NO PROBLEM, TOVARISCH. MY ARMORED FORM CAN WITHSTAND HIS STRONGEST BLOW.
CAN OUR YOUNG COMRADE SAY THE SAME?!
POW!

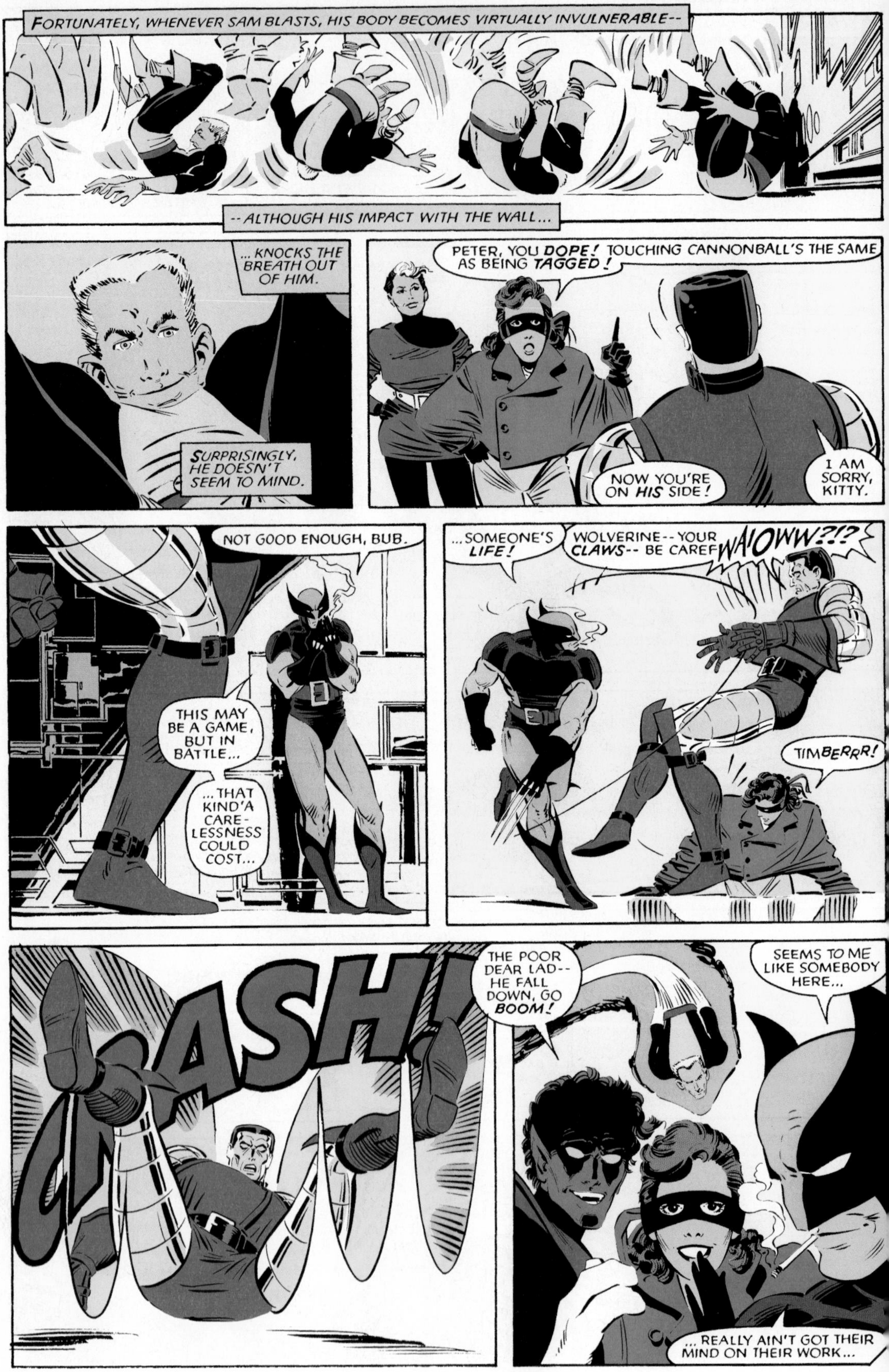
FORTUNATELY, WHENEVER SAM BLASTS, HIS BODY BECOMES VIRTUALLY INVULNERABLE--
--ALTHOUGH HIS IMPACT WITH THE WALL...
...KNOCKS THE BREATH OUT OF HIM.
SURPRISINGLY, HE DOESN'T SEEM TO MIND.
PETER, YOU DOPE! TOUCHING CANNONBALL'S THE SAME AS BEING TAGGED!
NOW YOU'RE ON HIS SIDE!
I AM SORRY, KITTY.
NOT GOOD ENOUGH, BUB.
THIS MAY BE A GAME, BUT IN BATTLE...
...THAT KIND'A CARE-LESSNESS COULD COST...
...SOMEONE'S LIFE!
WOLVERINE--YOUR CLAWS-- BE CAREF
WAIOWW?!?
TIMBERRR!
CRASH!
THE POOR DEAR LAD-- HE FALL DOWN, GO BOOM!
SEEMS TO ME LIKE SOMEBODY HERE...
...REALLY AIN'T GOT THEIR MIND ON THEIR WORK...

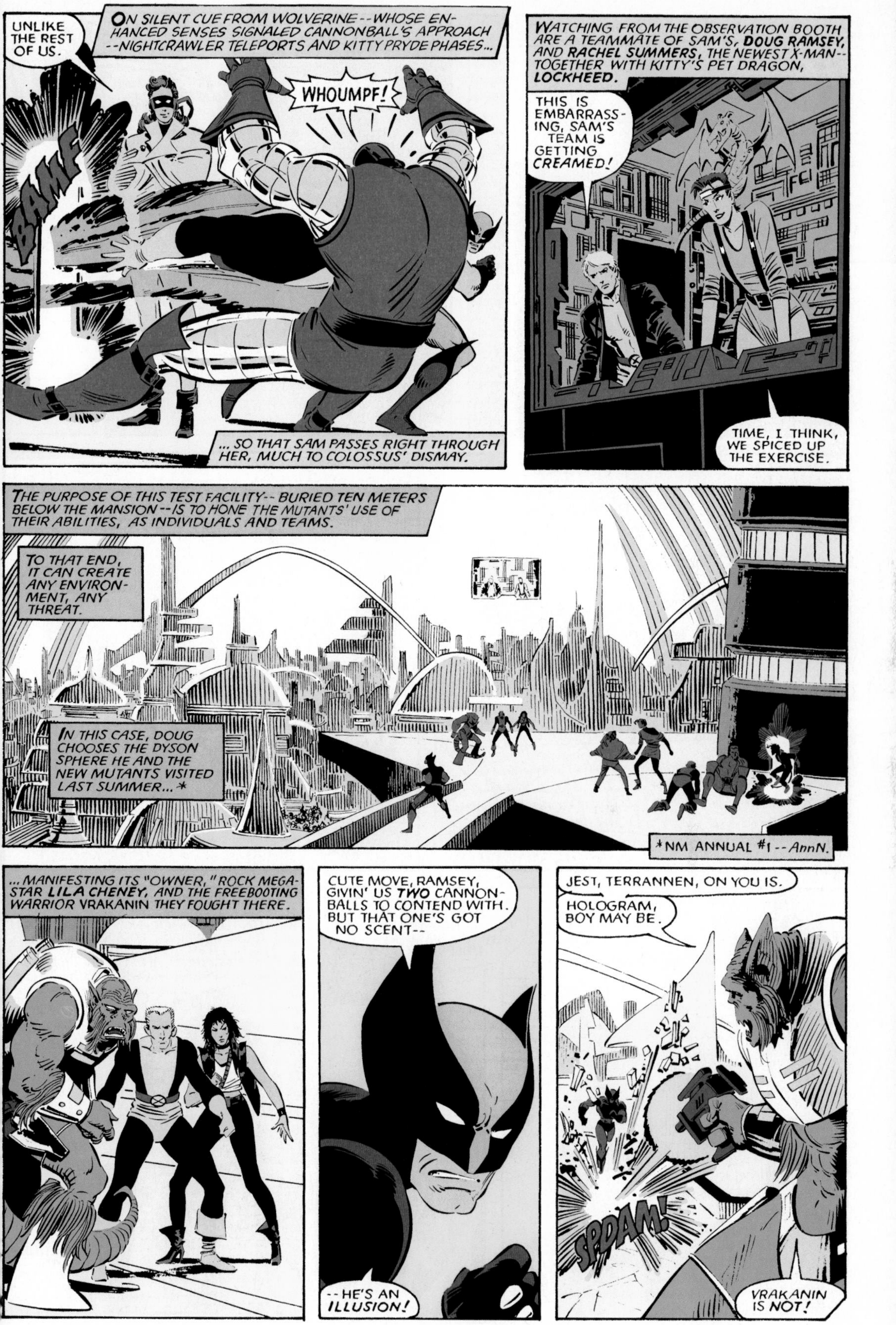
UNLIKE THE REST OF US.
ON SILENT CUE FROM WOLVERINE--WHOSE ENHANCED SENSES SIGNALED CANNONBALL'S APPROACH --NIGHTCRAWLER TELEPORTS AND KITTY PRYDE PHASES...
WHOUMPF!
BAMF
...SO THAT SAM PASSES RIGHT THROUGH HER, MUCH TO COLOSSUS' DISMAY.
WATCHING FROM THE OBSERVATION BOOTH ARE A TEAMMATE OF SAM'S, DOUG RAMSEY, AND RACHEL SUMMERS, THE NEWEST X-MAN--TOGETHER WITH KITTY'S PET DRAGON, LOCKHEED.
THIS IS EMBARRASSING, SAM'S TEAM IS GETTING CREAMED!
TIME, I THINK, WE SPICED UP THE EXERCISE.
THE PURPOSE OF THIS TEST FACILITY-- BURIED TEN METERS BELOW THE MANSION --IS TO HONE THE MUTANTS' USE OF THEIR ABILITIES, AS INDIVIDUALS AND TEAMS.
TO THAT END, IT CAN CREATE ANY ENVIRONMENT, ANY THREAT.
IN THIS CASE, DOUG CHOOSES THE DYSON SPHERE HE AND THE NEW MUTANTS VISITED LAST SUMMER...*
*NM ANNUAL #1 --AnnN.
...MANIFESTING ITS "OWNER," ROCK MEGA-STAR LILA CHENEY, AND THE FREEBOOTING WARRIOR VRAKANIN THEY FOUGHT THERE.
CUTE MOVE, RAMSEY, GIVIN' US TWO CANNONBALLS TO CONTEND WITH. BUT THAT ONE'S GOT NO SCENT--
--HE'S AN ILLUSION!
JEST, TERRANNEN, ON YOU IS.
HOLOGRAM, BOY MAY BE.
SPDAM!
VRAKANIN IS NOT!

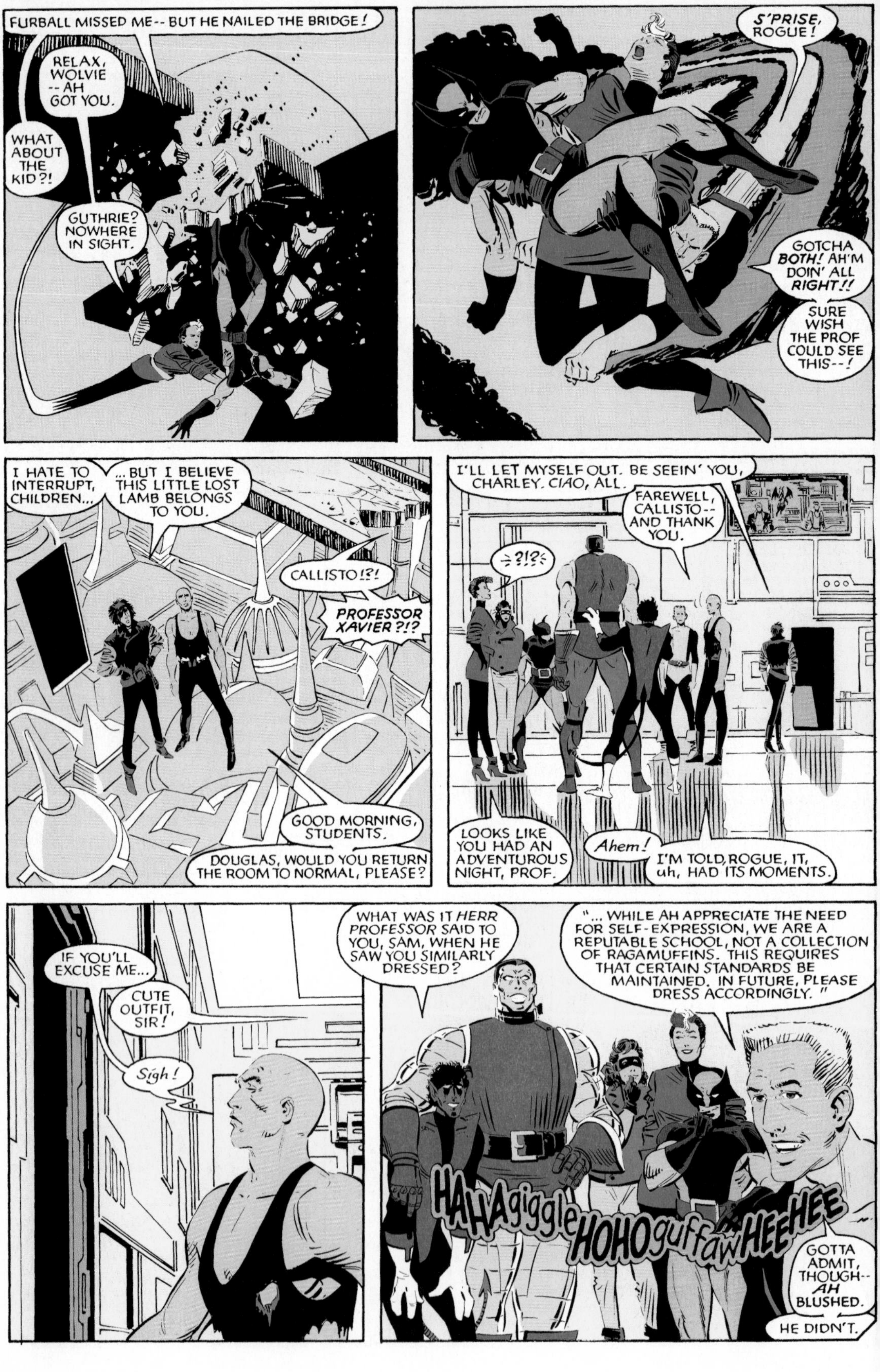
FURBALL MISSED ME-- BUT HE NAILED THE BRIDGE!
RELAX, WOLVIE --AH GOT YOU.
WHAT ABOUT THE KID?!
GUTHRIE? NOWHERE IN SIGHT.
S'PRISE, ROGUE!
GOTCHA BOTH! AH'M DOIN' ALL RIGHT!!
SURE WISH THE PROF COULD SEE THIS--!
I HATE TO INTERRUPT, CHILDREN...
...BUT I BELIEVE THIS LITTLE LOST LAMB BELONGS TO YOU.
CALLISTO!?!
PROFESSOR XAVIER?!?
GOOD MORNING, STUDENTS.
DOUGLAS, WOULD YOU RETURN THE ROOM TO NORMAL, PLEASE?
I'LL LET MYSELF OUT. BE SEEIN' YOU, CHARLEY. CIAO, ALL.
FAREWELL, CALLISTO-- AND THANK YOU.
?!?
LOOKS LIKE YOU HAD AN ADVENTUROUS NIGHT, PROF.
Ahem!
I'M TOLD, ROGUE, IT, uh, HAD ITS MOMENTS.
IF YOU'LL EXCUSE ME...
CUTE OUTFIT, SIR!
Sigh!
WHAT WAS IT HERR PROFESSOR SAID TO YOU, SAM, WHEN HE SAW YOU SIMILARLY DRESSED?
"...WHILE AH APPRECIATE THE NEED FOR SELF-EXPRESSION, WE ARE A REPUTABLE SCHOOL, NOT A COLLECTION OF RAGAMUFFINS. THIS REQUIRES THAT CERTAIN STANDARDS BE MAINTAINED. IN FUTURE, PLEASE DRESS ACCORDINGLY."
HAHAgiggleHOHOguffawHEEHEE
GOTTA ADMIT, THOUGH-- AH BLUSHED.
HE DIDN'T.

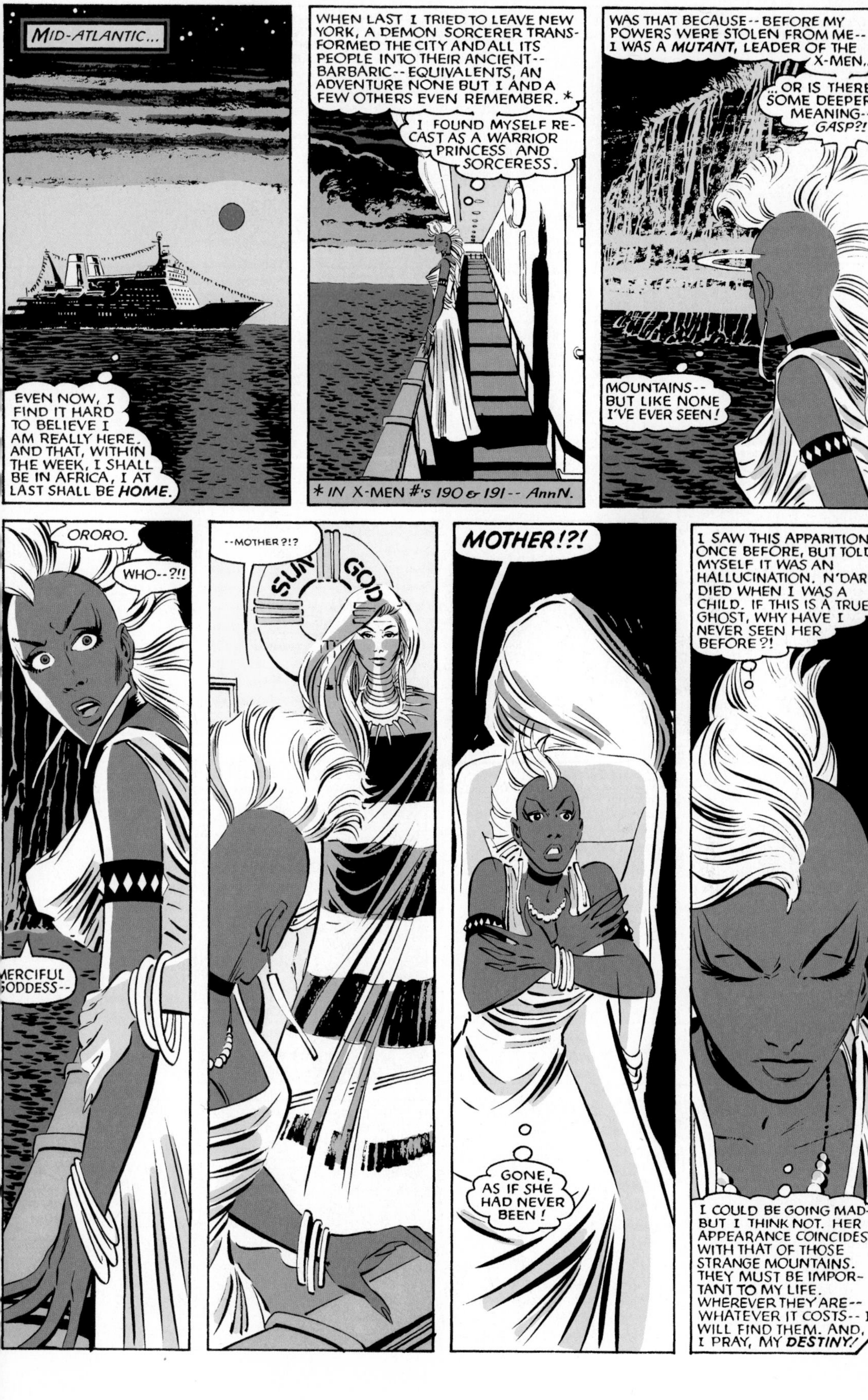

MID-ATLANTIC...
EVEN NOW, I FIND IT HARD TO BELIEVE I AM REALLY HERE. AND THAT, WITHIN THE WEEK, I SHALL BE IN AFRICA, I AT LAST SHALL BE HOME.
WHEN LAST I TRIED TO LEAVE NEW YORK, A DEMON SORCERER TRANSFORMED THE CITY AND ALL ITS PEOPLE INTO THEIR ANCIENT-- BARBARIC-- EQUIVALENTS, AN ADVENTURE NONE BUT I AND A FEW OTHERS EVEN REMEMBER. *
I FOUND MYSELF RECAST AS A WARRIOR PRINCESS AND SORCERESS.
* IN X-MEN #'s 190 & 191 -- AnnN.
WAS THAT BECAUSE-- BEFORE MY POWERS WERE STOLEN FROM ME-- I WAS A MUTANT, LEADER OF THE X-MEN...
...OR IS THERE SOME DEEPER MEANING-- GASP?!?
MOUNTAINS-- BUT LIKE NONE I'VE EVER SEEN!
ORORO.
WHO--?!!
MERCIFUL GODDESS--
--MOTHER?!?
SUN GOD
MOTHER!?!
GONE, AS IF SHE HAD NEVER BEEN!
I SAW THIS APPARITION ONCE BEFORE, BUT TOLD MYSELF IT WAS AN HALLUCINATION. N'DARE DIED WHEN I WAS A CHILD. IF THIS IS A TRUE GHOST, WHY HAVE I NEVER SEEN HER BEFORE?!
I COULD BE GOING MAD-- BUT I THINK NOT. HER APPEARANCE COINCIDES WITH THAT OF THOSE STRANGE MOUNTAINS. THEY MUST BE IMPORTANT TO MY LIFE. WHEREVER THEY ARE-- WHATEVER IT COSTS-- I WILL FIND THEM. AND, I PRAY, MY DESTINY!

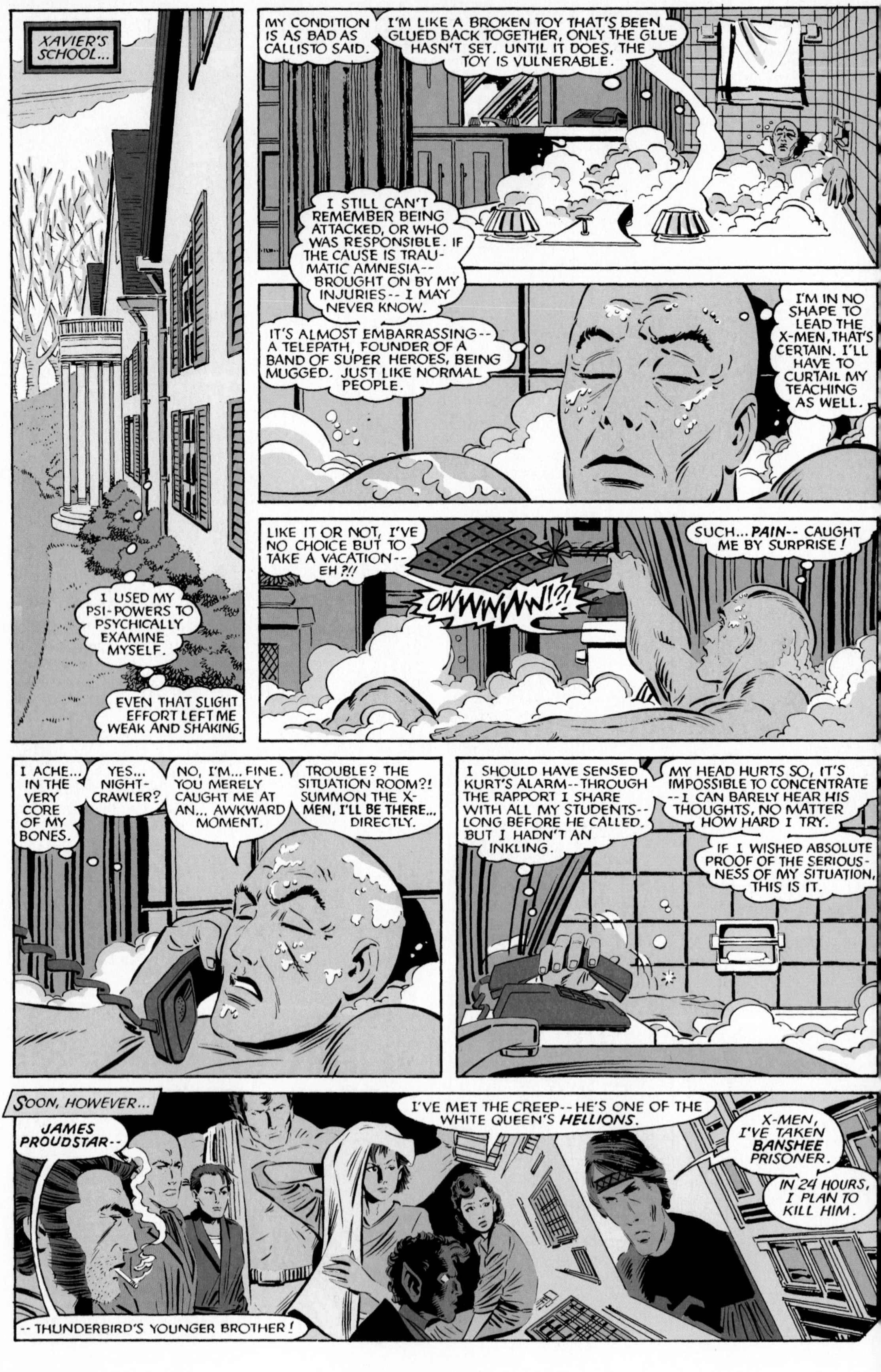
XAVIER'S SCHOOL...
MY CONDITION IS AS BAD AS CALLISTO SAID.
I'M LIKE A BROKEN TOY THAT'S BEEN GLUED BACK TOGETHER, ONLY THE GLUE HASN'T SET. UNTIL IT DOES, THE TOY IS VULNERABLE.
I STILL CAN'T REMEMBER BEING ATTACKED, OR WHO WAS RESPONSIBLE. IF THE CAUSE IS TRAUMATIC AMNESIA-- BROUGHT ON BY MY INJURIES-- I MAY NEVER KNOW.
IT'S ALMOST EMBARRASSING-- A TELEPATH, FOUNDER OF A BAND OF SUPER HEROES, BEING MUGGED. JUST LIKE NORMAL PEOPLE.
I'M IN NO SHAPE TO LEAD THE X-MEN, THAT'S CERTAIN. I'LL HAVE TO CURTAIL MY TEACHING AS WELL.
LIKE IT OR NOT, I'VE NO CHOICE BUT TO TAKE A VACATION-- EH ?!!
BREEP BREEP BREEP
OWWWWW!?!
SUCH... PAIN-- CAUGHT ME BY SURPRISE!
I USED MY PSI-POWERS TO PSYCHICALLY EXAMINE MYSELF.
EVEN THAT SLIGHT EFFORT LEFT ME WEAK AND SHAKING.
I ACHE... IN THE VERY CORE OF MY BONES.
YES... NIGHTCRAWLER?
NO, I'M... FINE. YOU MERELY CAUGHT ME AT AN... AWKWARD MOMENT.
TROUBLE? THE SITUATION ROOM?! SUMMON THE X-MEN, I'LL BE THERE... DIRECTLY.
I SHOULD HAVE SENSED KURT'S ALARM--THROUGH THE RAPPORT I SHARE WITH ALL MY STUDENTS-- LONG BEFORE HE CALLED. BUT I HADN'T AN INKLING.
MY HEAD HURTS SO, IT'S IMPOSSIBLE TO CONCENTRATE --I CAN BARELY HEAR HIS THOUGHTS, NO MATTER HOW HARD I TRY.
IF I WISHED ABSOLUTE PROOF OF THE SERIOUSNESS OF MY SITUATION, THIS IS IT.
SOON, HOWEVER...
JAMES PROUDSTAR--
I'VE MET THE CREEP-- HE'S ONE OF THE WHITE QUEEN'S HELLIONS.
X-MEN, I'VE TAKEN BANSHEE PRISONER.
IN 24 HOURS, I PLAN TO KILL HIM.
-- THUNDERBIRD'S YOUNGER BROTHER!

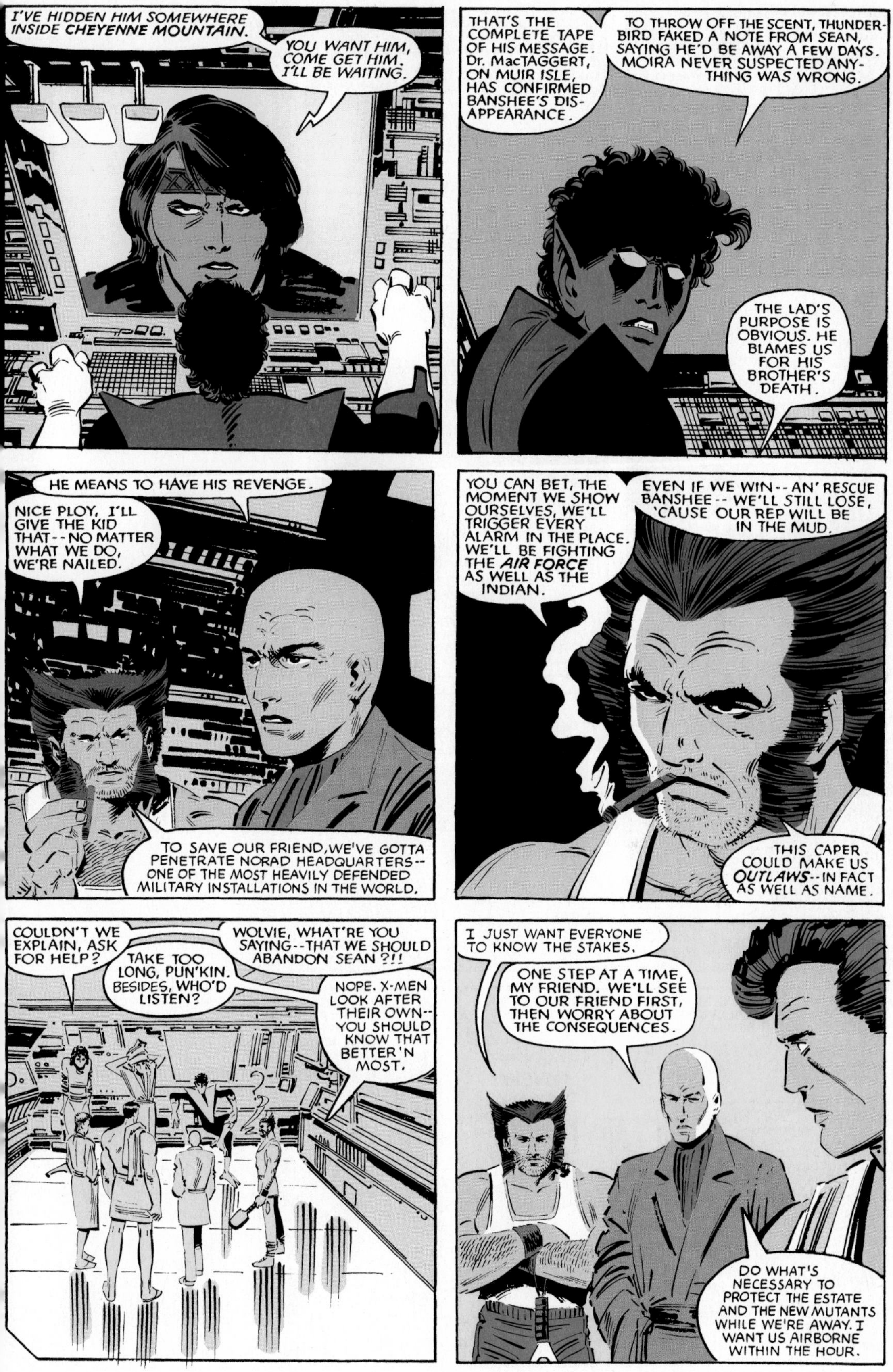
I'VE HIDDEN HIM SOMEWHERE INSIDE CHEYENNE MOUNTAIN.
YOU WANT HIM, COME GET HIM. I'LL BE WAITING.
THAT'S THE COMPLETE TAPE OF HIS MESSAGE. Dr. MacTAGGERT, ON MUIR ISLE, HAS CONFIRMED BANSHEE'S DISAPPEARANCE.
TO THROW OFF THE SCENT, THUNDERBIRD FAKED A NOTE FROM SEAN, SAYING HE'D BE AWAY A FEW DAYS. MOIRA NEVER SUSPECTED ANYTHING WAS WRONG.
THE LAD'S PURPOSE IS OBVIOUS. HE BLAMES US FOR HIS BROTHER'S DEATH.
HE MEANS TO HAVE HIS REVENGE.
NICE PLOY, I'LL GIVE THE KID THAT--NO MATTER WHAT WE DO, WE'RE NAILED.
TO SAVE OUR FRIEND, WE'VE GOTTA PENETRATE NORAD HEADQUARTERS--ONE OF THE MOST HEAVILY DEFENDED MILITARY INSTALLATIONS IN THE WORLD.
YOU CAN BET, THE MOMENT WE SHOW OURSELVES, WE'LL TRIGGER EVERY ALARM IN THE PLACE. WE'LL BE FIGHTING THE AIR FORCE AS WELL AS THE INDIAN.
EVEN IF WE WIN--AN' RESCUE BANSHEE--WE'LL STILL LOSE, 'CAUSE OUR REP WILL BE IN THE MUD.
THIS CAPER COULD MAKE US OUTLAWS--IN FACT AS WELL AS NAME.
COULDN'T WE EXPLAIN, ASK FOR HELP?
TAKE TOO LONG, PUN'KIN. BESIDES, WHO'D LISTEN?
WOLVIE, WHAT'RE YOU SAYING--THAT WE SHOULD ABANDON SEAN ?!!
NOPE. X-MEN LOOK AFTER THEIR OWN--YOU SHOULD KNOW THAT BETTER'N MOST.
I JUST WANT EVERYONE TO KNOW THE STAKES.
ONE STEP AT A TIME, MY FRIEND. WE'LL SEE TO OUR FRIEND FIRST, THEN WORRY ABOUT THE CONSEQUENCES.
DO WHAT'S NECESSARY TO PROTECT THE ESTATE AND THE NEW MUTANTS WHILE WE'RE AWAY. I WANT US AIRBORNE WITHIN THE HOUR.

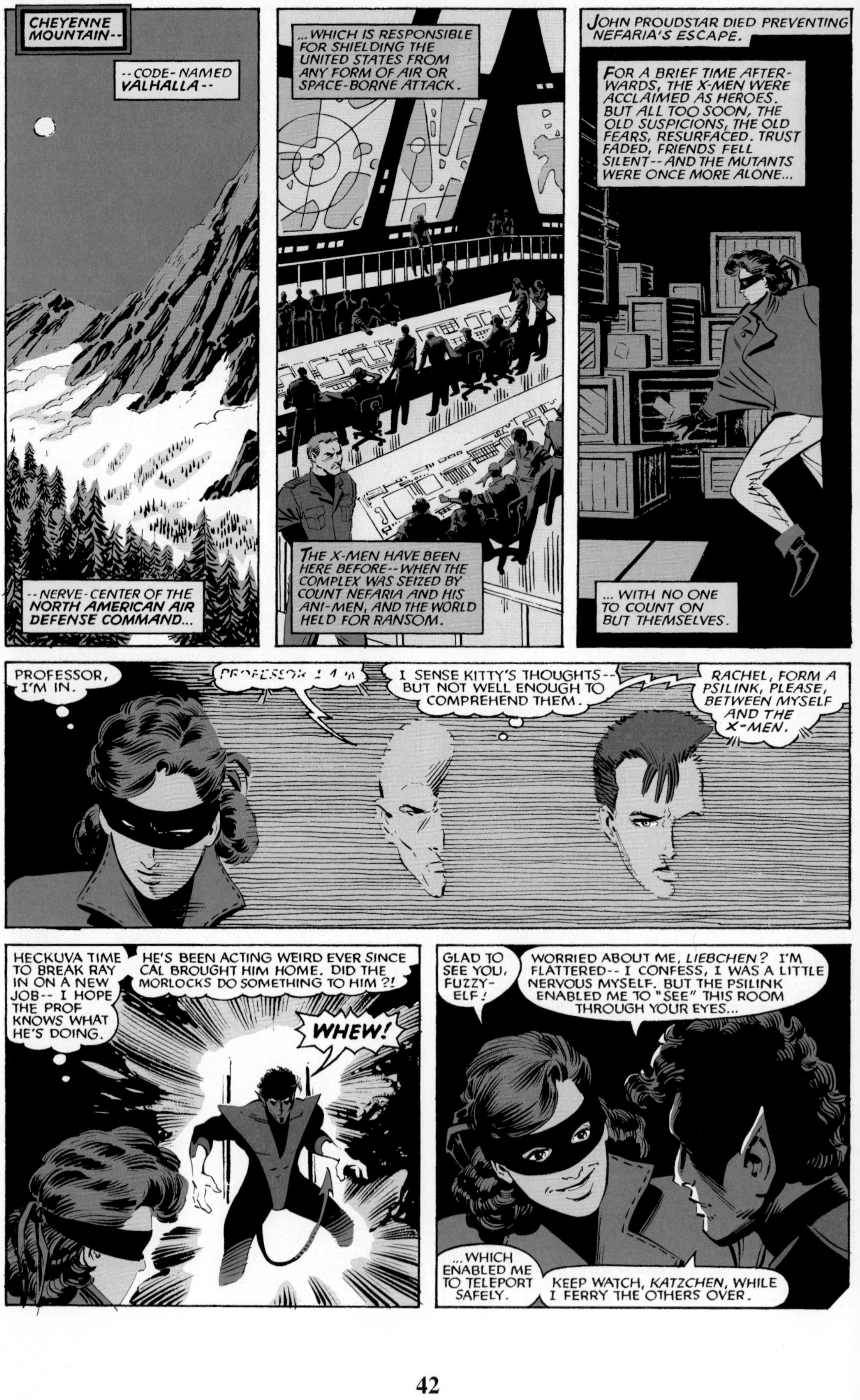
CHEYENNE MOUNTAIN--
--CODE-NAMED VALHALLA--
--NERVE-CENTER OF THE NORTH AMERICAN AIR DEFENSE COMMAND...
...WHICH IS RESPONSIBLE FOR SHIELDING THE UNITED STATES FROM ANY FORM OF AIR OR SPACE-BORNE ATTACK.
THE X-MEN HAVE BEEN HERE BEFORE--WHEN THE COMPLEX WAS SEIZED BY COUNT NEFARIA AND HIS ANI-MEN, AND THE WORLD HELD FOR RANSOM.
JOHN PROUDSTAR DIED PREVENTING NEFARIA'S ESCAPE.
FOR A BRIEF TIME AFTERWARDS, THE X-MEN WERE ACCLAIMED AS HEROES. BUT ALL TOO SOON, THE OLD SUSPICIONS, THE OLD FEARS, RESURFACED. TRUST FADED, FRIENDS FELL SILENT--AND THE MUTANTS WERE ONCE MORE ALONE...
...WITH NO ONE TO COUNT ON BUT THEMSELVES.
PROFESSOR, I'M IN.
I SENSE KITTY'S THOUGHTS--BUT NOT WELL ENOUGH TO COMPREHEND THEM.
RACHEL, FORM A PSILINK, PLEASE, BETWEEN MYSELF AND THE X-MEN.
HECKUVA TIME TO BREAK RAY IN ON A NEW JOB-- I HOPE THE PROF KNOWS WHAT HE'S DOING.
HE'S BEEN ACTING WEIRD EVER SINCE CAL BROUGHT HIM HOME. DID THE MORLOCKS DO SOMETHING TO HIM ?!
WHEW!
GLAD TO SEE YOU, FUZZY-ELF!
WORRIED ABOUT ME, LIEBCHEN? I'M FLATTERED-- I CONFESS, I WAS A LITTLE NERVOUS MYSELF. BUT THE PSILINK ENABLED ME TO "SEE" THIS ROOM THROUGH YOUR EYES...
...WHICH ENABLED ME TO TELEPORT SAFELY.
KEEP WATCH, KATZCHEN, WHILE I FERRY THE OTHERS OVER.

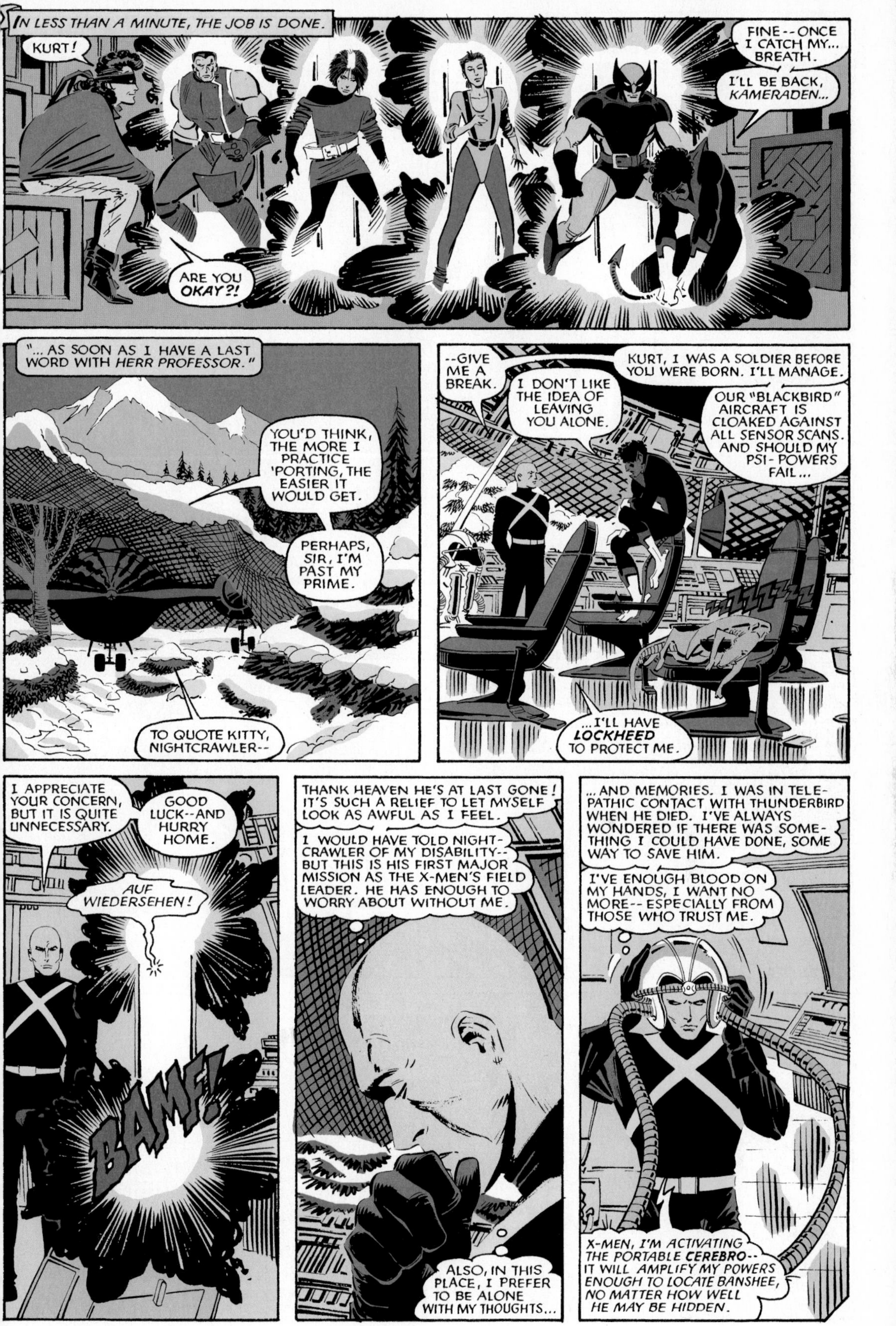
IN LESS THAN A MINUTE, THE JOB IS DONE.
KURT!
ARE YOU OKAY?!
FINE--ONCE I CATCH MY... BREATH.
I'LL BE BACK, KAMERADEN...
"... AS SOON AS I HAVE A LAST WORD WITH HERR PROFESSOR."
YOU'D THINK, THE MORE I PRACTICE 'PORTING, THE EASIER IT WOULD GET.
PERHAPS, SIR, I'M PAST MY PRIME.
TO QUOTE KITTY, NIGHTCRAWLER--
--GIVE ME A BREAK.
I DON'T LIKE THE IDEA OF LEAVING YOU ALONE.
KURT, I WAS A SOLDIER BEFORE YOU WERE BORN. I'LL MANAGE.
OUR "BLACKBIRD" AIRCRAFT IS CLOAKED AGAINST ALL SENSOR SCANS. AND SHOULD MY PSI-POWERS FAIL...
...I'LL HAVE LOCKHEED TO PROTECT ME.
I APPRECIATE YOUR CONCERN, BUT IT IS QUITE UNNECESSARY.
GOOD LUCK--AND HURRY HOME.
AUF WIEDERSEHEN!
BAMF!
THANK HEAVEN HE'S AT LAST GONE! IT'S SUCH A RELIEF TO LET MYSELF LOOK AS AWFUL AS I FEEL.
I WOULD HAVE TOLD NIGHTCRAWLER OF MY DISABILITY--BUT THIS IS HIS FIRST MAJOR MISSION AS THE X-MEN'S FIELD LEADER. HE HAS ENOUGH TO WORRY ABOUT WITHOUT ME.
ALSO, IN THIS PLACE, I PREFER TO BE ALONE WITH MY THOUGHTS...
...AND MEMORIES. I WAS IN TELEPATHIC CONTACT WITH THUNDERBIRD WHEN HE DIED. I'VE ALWAYS WONDERED IF THERE WAS SOMETHING I COULD HAVE DONE, SOME WAY TO SAVE HIM.
I'VE ENOUGH BLOOD ON MY HANDS, I WANT NO MORE--ESPECIALLY FROM THOSE WHO TRUST ME.
X-MEN, I'M ACTIVATING THE PORTABLE CEREBRO--IT WILL AMPLIFY MY POWERS ENOUGH TO LOCATE BANSHEE, NO MATTER HOW WELL HE MAY BE HIDDEN.

HOWEVER, RIGHT OUTSIDE, HER PRESENCE MASKED BY A PSISCREEN BUILT INTO HER HELLIONS UNIFORM...

BLACK DISK, CHROME-DOME--

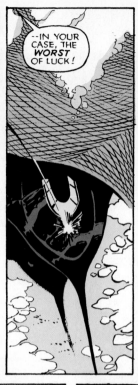

--IN YOUR CASE, THE *WORST* OF LUCK!

AND, ABOARD THE "BLACKBIRD"...

SHORT-CIRCUIT-- SYSTEMS FEEDBACK--!?!

AHRRGH!

XAVIER'S BELLOW OF AGONY...

...WAKES KITTY'S DRAGON, IN TIME TO SEE EMPATH'S HURRIED ENTRANCE--

--BUT BEFORE LOCKHEED CAN ACT, HE'S HIT WITH SUCH A CONCENTRATED BURST OF PURE, PRIMAL TERROR...

...THAT BY THE TIME THE SMALL BEAST REALIZES WHAT HE'S DOING, HE'S MILES AWAY, FLEEING FOR HIS LIFE.

FLUSH WITH THAT INITIAL VICTORY, MANUEL TURNS ON XAVIER...

FROM KITTY'S DESCRIPTION, THIS MUST BE *EMPATH!*

HIS STRENGTH IS FORMIDABLE, AND MINE AT LOW EBB-- MY HEAD IS REELING FROM THAT POWER SURGE. I...DON'T WANT TO RESIST!

HE'S MAKING ME *LIKE* HIM--! BUT... WHERE MY EMOTIONS YIELD -- MY INTELLECT WILL *NOT!*

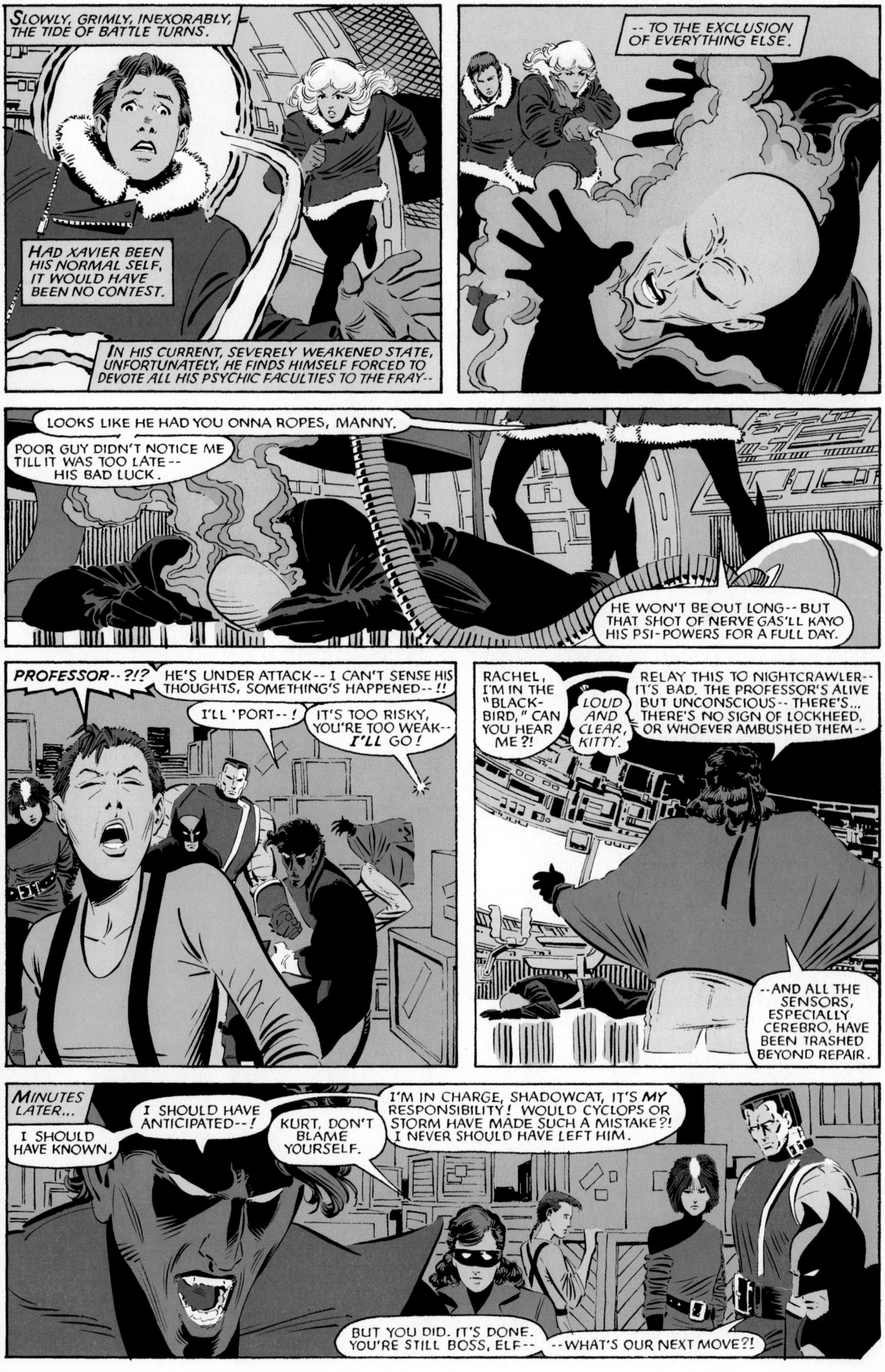

SLOWLY, GRIMLY, INEXORABLY, THE TIDE OF BATTLE TURNS.
HAD XAVIER BEEN HIS NORMAL SELF, IT WOULD HAVE BEEN NO CONTEST.
IN HIS CURRENT, SEVERELY WEAKENED STATE, UNFORTUNATELY, HE FINDS HIMSELF FORCED TO DEVOTE ALL HIS PSYCHIC FACULTIES TO THE FRAY--
-- TO THE EXCLUSION OF EVERYTHING ELSE.
LOOKS LIKE HE HAD YOU ONNA ROPES, MANNY.
POOR GUY DIDN'T NOTICE ME TILL IT WAS TOO LATE -- HIS BAD LUCK.
HE WON'T BE OUT LONG-- BUT THAT SHOT OF NERVE GAS'LL KAYO HIS PSI-POWERS FOR A FULL DAY.
PROFESSOR--?!?
HE'S UNDER ATTACK-- I CAN'T SENSE HIS THOUGHTS, SOMETHING'S HAPPENED--!!
I'LL 'PORT--!
IT'S TOO RISKY, YOU'RE TOO WEAK-- I'LL GO!
RACHEL, I'M IN THE "BLACK-BIRD," CAN YOU HEAR ME?!
LOUD AND CLEAR, KITTY.
RELAY THIS TO NIGHTCRAWLER-- IT'S BAD. THE PROFESSOR'S ALIVE BUT UNCONSCIOUS-- THERE'S... THERE'S NO SIGN OF LOCKHEED, OR WHOEVER AMBUSHED THEM--
--AND ALL THE SENSORS, ESPECIALLY CEREBRO, HAVE BEEN TRASHED BEYOND REPAIR.
MINUTES LATER...
I SHOULD HAVE KNOWN.
I SHOULD HAVE ANTICIPATED--!
KURT, DON'T BLAME YOURSELF.
I'M IN CHARGE, SHADOWCAT, IT'S MY RESPONSIBILITY! WOULD CYCLOPS OR STORM HAVE MADE SUCH A MISTAKE?! I NEVER SHOULD HAVE LEFT HIM.
BUT YOU DID. IT'S DONE. YOU'RE STILL BOSS, ELF--
--WHAT'S OUR NEXT MOVE?!

RACHEL, YOU'RE OUR BACK-UP TELEPATH. SCAN FOR BANSHEE-- YOU SHOULD BE ABLE TO DETECT HIM, EVEN WITHOUT CEREBRO'S AID.

NO.

WHAT--?!?

NO!

THAT'S WHAT I DID--IN *MY* ERA--BUT HOW CAN I TELL THEM, TELL *ANYONE*?! I WAS A *HOUND!* THE GOVERNMENT FORCED ME TO USE MY PSI-SKILLS TO HUNT DOWN MUTANTS.

A FEW THEY CAPTURED--

--BUT MOST WERE *KILLED!*

STRANGERS--FRIENDS-- *FAMILY*--SLAUGHTERED LIKE ANIMALS--

--BECAUSE OF *ME!*

BY THE WHITE WOLF!

RACHEL ...???

I HOPE SHE'LL BE OKAY, LOGAN.

DEFINE THE TERM, PUN'KIN.

RAY'S GOT SECRETS--MEMORIES--PROB'LY GUILTS-- THAT'RE TEARING HER APART. LIKE SOME WHO SURVIVED THE HOLOCAUST, SHE MAYBE FEELS ASHAMED FOR HAVING LIVED, AN' FOR THE PRICE SHE PAID TO DO IT. THAT'S A HURT THE LIKE OF WHICH WE CAN'T IMAGINE.

SHE'LL EITHER COME TO TERMS WITH IT, OR BE DESTROYED.

CAN'T WORRY ABOUT HER NOW, THOUGH, KIT. BANSHEE'S GOT PRIORITY. I'VE SPOTTED HIS SCENT.

THE TRAIL IS IMPOSSIBLY FAINT, BUT WOLVERINE FOLLOWS IT WITH EASE...

...KITTY PHASING THE TWO OF THEM DEEP INTO THE MOUNTAIN COMPLEX...

...TAKING OCCASIONAL, HURRIED DETOURS ALONG THE WAY AROUND ANYONE THEY FIND IN THEIR PATH.

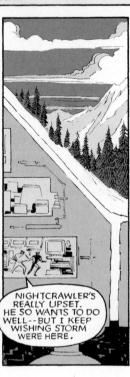

NIGHTCRAWLER'S REALLY UPSET. HE SO WANTS TO DO WELL--BUT I KEEP WISHING STORM WERE HERE.

WE MAKE DO WITH WHAT'S AT HAND, DARLIN'-- WE GOT NOBODY BETTER.

THAT'S COMFORTING.

QUIT WORRYIN'!

IT'S A WASTE OF EFFORT, AN' WE GOT NONE TO SPARE.

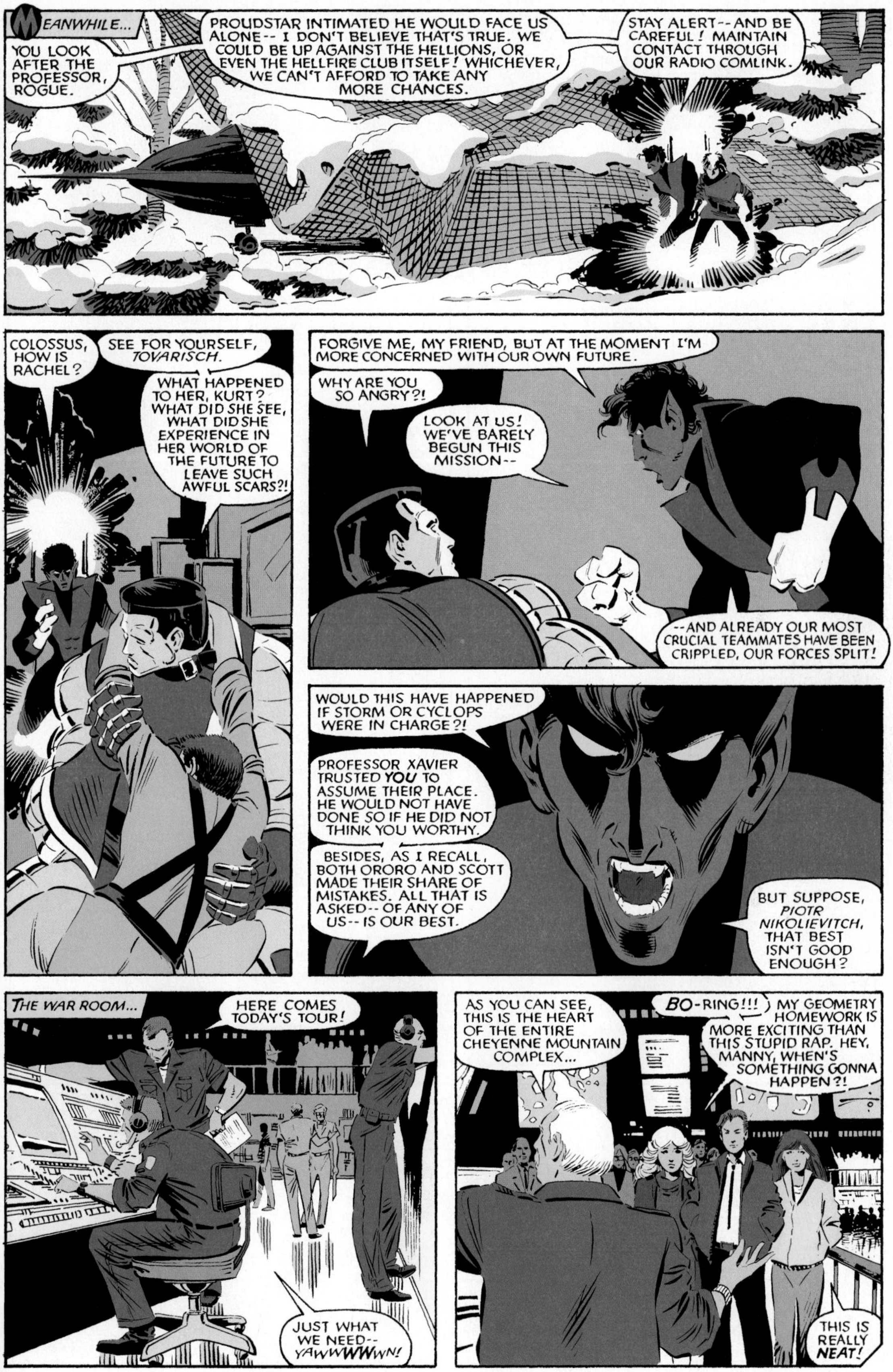
MEANWHILE...
YOU LOOK AFTER THE PROFESSOR, ROGUE.
PROUDSTAR INTIMATED HE WOULD FACE US ALONE-- I DON'T BELIEVE THAT'S TRUE. WE COULD BE UP AGAINST THE HELLIONS, OR EVEN THE HELLFIRE CLUB ITSELF! WHICHEVER, WE CAN'T AFFORD TO TAKE ANY MORE CHANCES.
STAY ALERT--AND BE CAREFUL! MAINTAIN CONTACT THROUGH OUR RADIO COMLINK.
COLOSSUS, HOW IS RACHEL?
SEE FOR YOURSELF, TOVARISCH.
WHAT HAPPENED TO HER, KURT? WHAT DID SHE SEE, WHAT DID SHE EXPERIENCE IN HER WORLD OF THE FUTURE TO LEAVE SUCH AWFUL SCARS?!
FORGIVE ME, MY FRIEND, BUT AT THE MOMENT I'M MORE CONCERNED WITH OUR OWN FUTURE.
WHY ARE YOU SO ANGRY?!
LOOK AT US! WE'VE BARELY BEGUN THIS MISSION--
--AND ALREADY OUR MOST CRUCIAL TEAMMATES HAVE BEEN CRIPPLED, OUR FORCES SPLIT!
WOULD THIS HAVE HAPPENED IF STORM OR CYCLOPS WERE IN CHARGE?!
PROFESSOR XAVIER TRUSTED YOU TO ASSUME THEIR PLACE. HE WOULD NOT HAVE DONE SO IF HE DID NOT THINK YOU WORTHY.
BESIDES, AS I RECALL, BOTH ORORO AND SCOTT MADE THEIR SHARE OF MISTAKES. ALL THAT IS ASKED-- OF ANY OF US-- IS OUR BEST.
BUT SUPPOSE, PIOTR NIKOLIEVITCH, THAT BEST ISN'T GOOD ENOUGH?
THE WAR ROOM...
HERE COMES TODAY'S TOUR!
JUST WHAT WE NEED-- YAWWWWWN!
AS YOU CAN SEE, THIS IS THE HEART OF THE ENTIRE CHEYENNE MOUNTAIN COMPLEX...
BO-RING!!! MY GEOMETRY HOMEWORK IS MORE EXCITING THAN THIS STUPID RAP. HEY, MANNY, WHEN'S SOMETHING GONNA HAPPEN?!
THIS IS REALLY NEAT!

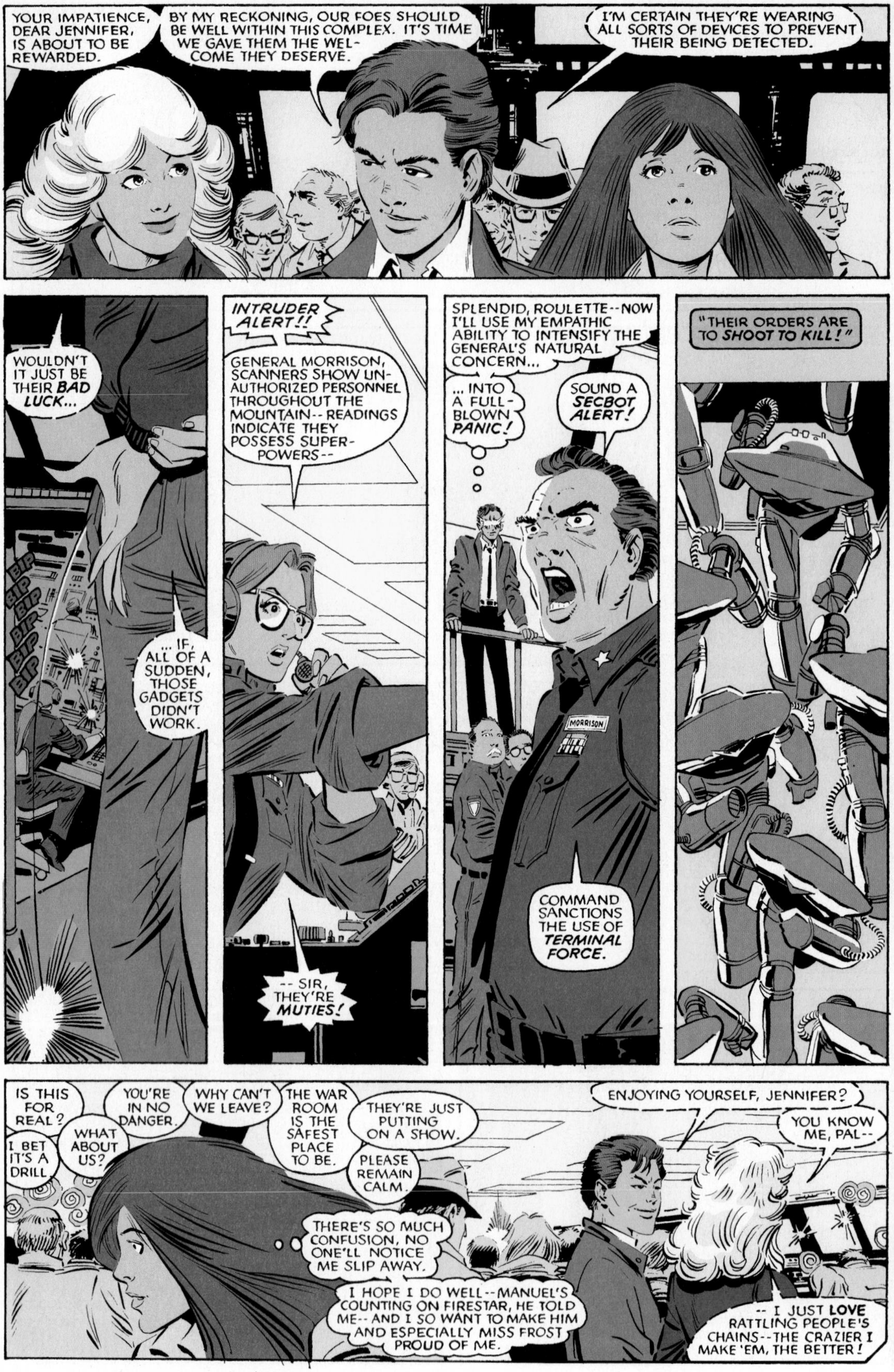
YOUR IMPATIENCE, DEAR JENNIFER, IS ABOUT TO BE REWARDED.
BY MY RECKONING, OUR FOES SHOULD BE WELL WITHIN THIS COMPLEX. IT'S TIME WE GAVE THEM THE WELCOME THEY DESERVE.
I'M CERTAIN THEY'RE WEARING ALL SORTS OF DEVICES TO PREVENT THEIR BEING DETECTED.
WOULDN'T IT JUST BE THEIR BAD LUCK...
BIP BIP BIP BIP BIP BIP BIP BIP
... IF, ALL OF A SUDDEN, THOSE GADGETS DIDN'T WORK.
INTRUDER ALERT!!
GENERAL MORRISON, SCANNERS SHOW UNAUTHORIZED PERSONNEL THROUGHOUT THE MOUNTAIN-- READINGS INDICATE THEY POSSESS SUPER-POWERS--
-- SIR, THEY'RE MUTIES!
SPLENDID, ROULETTE-- NOW I'LL USE MY EMPATHIC ABILITY TO INTENSIFY THE GENERAL'S NATURAL CONCERN...
... INTO A FULL-BLOWN PANIC!
SOUND A SECBOT ALERT!
MORRISON
COMMAND SANCTIONS THE USE OF TERMINAL FORCE.
"THEIR ORDERS ARE TO SHOOT TO KILL!"
IS THIS FOR REAL?
I BET IT'S A DRILL
YOU'RE IN NO DANGER.
WHAT ABOUT US?
WHY CAN'T WE LEAVE?
THE WAR ROOM IS THE SAFEST PLACE TO BE.
THEY'RE JUST PUTTING ON A SHOW.
PLEASE REMAIN CALM.
THERE'S SO MUCH CONFUSION, NO ONE'LL NOTICE ME SLIP AWAY.
I HOPE I DO WELL-- MANUEL'S COUNTING ON FIRESTAR, HE TOLD ME-- AND I SO WANT TO MAKE HIM AND ESPECIALLY MISS FROST PROUD OF ME.
ENJOYING YOURSELF, JENNIFER?
YOU KNOW ME, PAL--
-- I JUST LOVE RATTLING PEOPLE'S CHAINS-- THE CRAZIER I MAKE 'EM, THE BETTER!

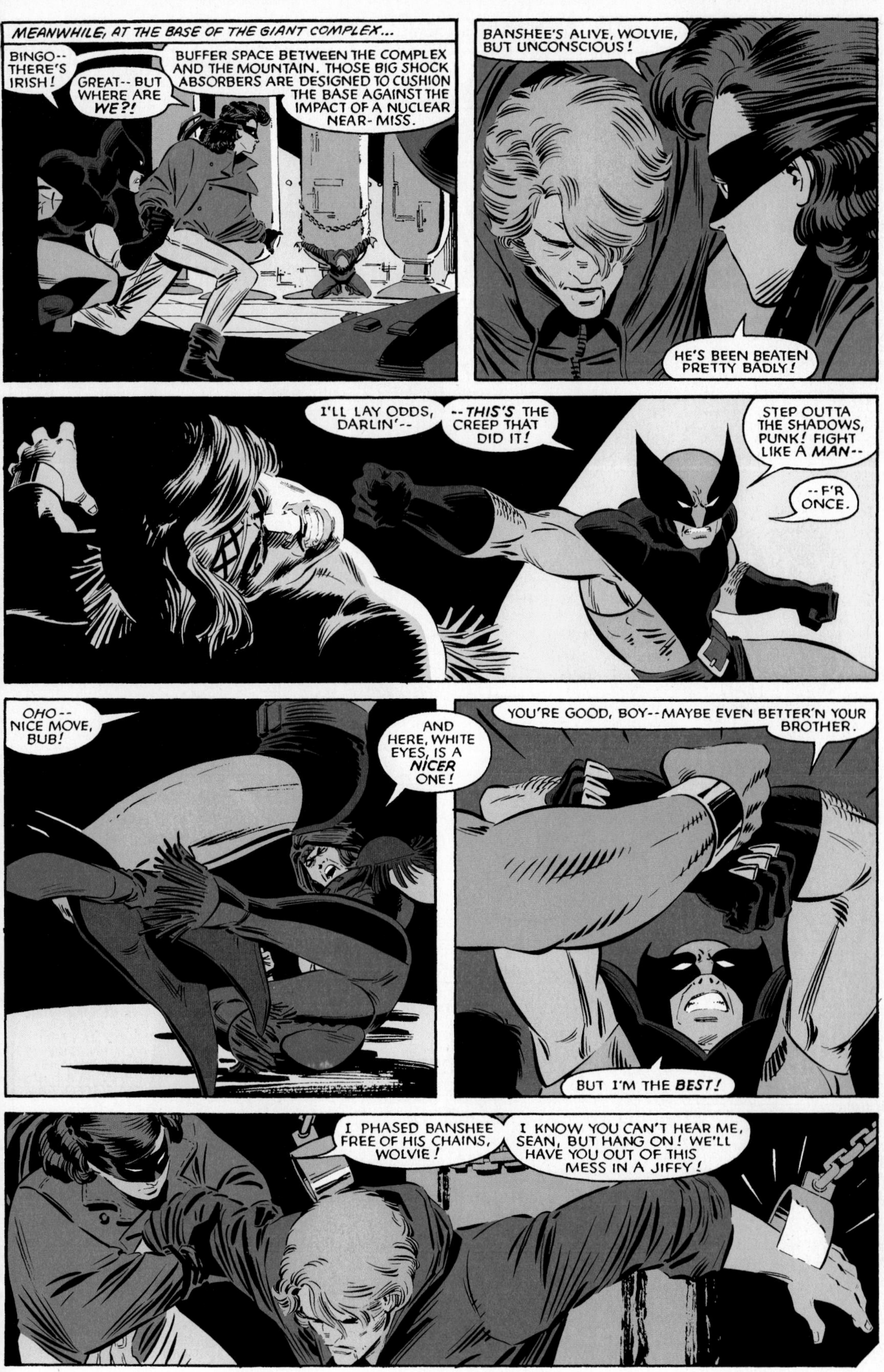

MEANWHILE, AT THE BASE OF THE GIANT COMPLEX...
BINGO-- THERE'S IRISH!
GREAT-- BUT WHERE ARE WE?!
BUFFER SPACE BETWEEN THE COMPLEX AND THE MOUNTAIN. THOSE BIG SHOCK ABSORBERS ARE DESIGNED TO CUSHION THE BASE AGAINST THE IMPACT OF A NUCLEAR NEAR-MISS.
BANSHEE'S ALIVE, WOLVIE, BUT UNCONSCIOUS!
HE'S BEEN BEATEN PRETTY BADLY!
I'LL LAY ODDS, DARLIN'--
--THIS'S THE CREEP THAT DID IT!
STEP OUTTA THE SHADOWS, PUNK! FIGHT LIKE A MAN--
--F'R ONCE.
OHO-- NICE MOVE, BUB!
AND HERE, WHITE EYES, IS A NICER ONE!
YOU'RE GOOD, BOY--MAYBE EVEN BETTER'N YOUR BROTHER.
BUT I'M THE BEST!
I PHASED BANSHEE FREE OF HIS CHAINS, WOLVIE!
I KNOW YOU CAN'T HEAR ME, SEAN, BUT HANG ON! WE'LL HAVE YOU OUT OF THIS MESS IN A JIFFY!

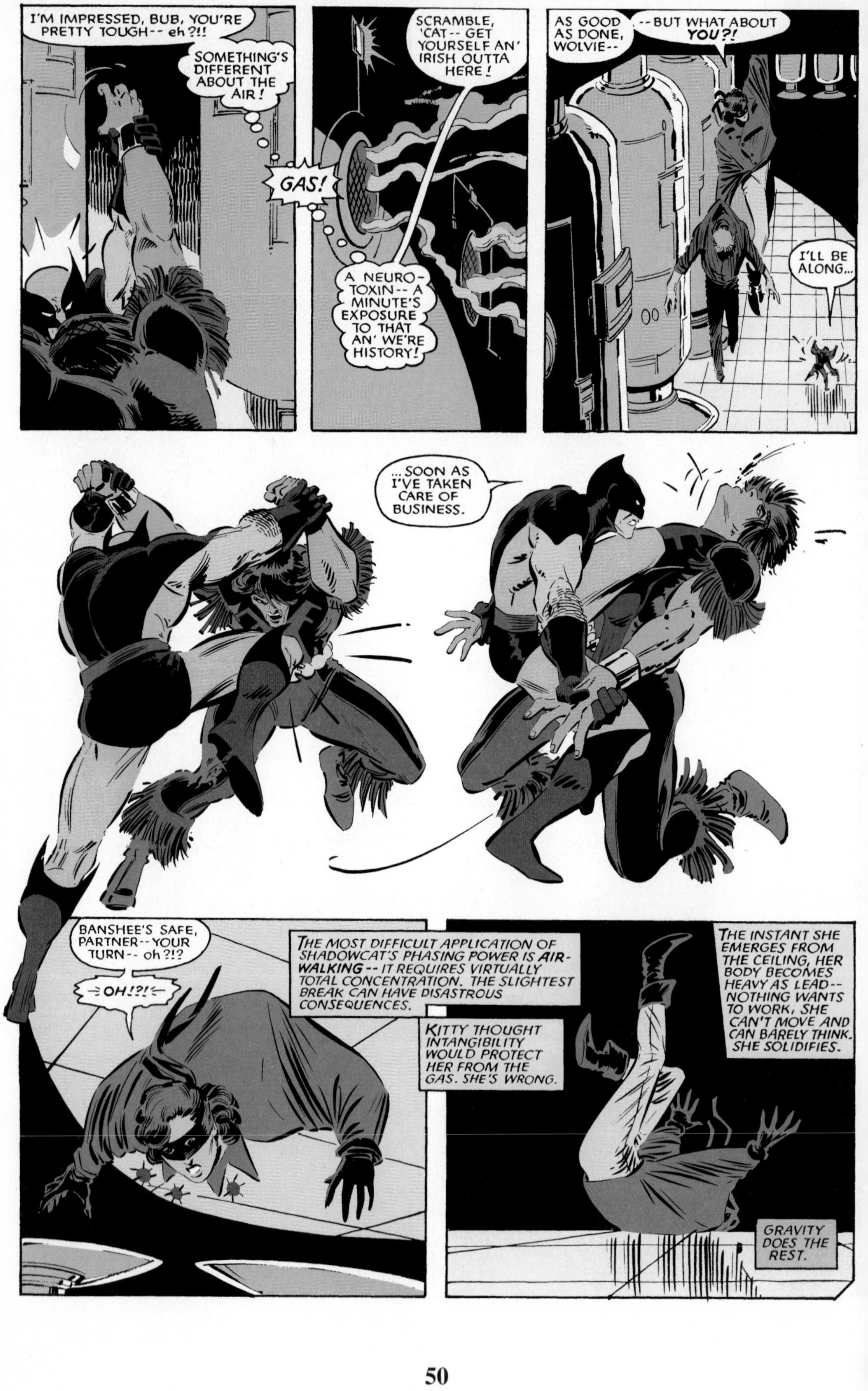

I'M IMPRESSED, BUB, YOU'RE PRETTY TOUGH-- eh?!!
SOMETHING'S DIFFERENT ABOUT THE AIR!
GAS!
A NEURO-TOXIN-- A MINUTE'S EXPOSURE TO THAT AN' WE'RE HISTORY!
SCRAMBLE, 'CAT-- GET YOURSELF AN' IRISH OUTTA HERE!
AS GOOD AS DONE, WOLVIE--
--BUT WHAT ABOUT YOU?!
I'LL BE ALONG...
...SOON AS I'VE TAKEN CARE OF BUSINESS.
BANSHEE'S SAFE, PARTNER-- YOUR TURN-- oh?!?
OH!?!
THE MOST DIFFICULT APPLICATION OF SHADOWCAT'S PHASING POWER IS AIR-WALKING-- IT REQUIRES VIRTUALLY TOTAL CONCENTRATION. THE SLIGHTEST BREAK CAN HAVE DISASTROUS CONSEQUENCES.
KITTY THOUGHT INTANGIBILITY WOULD PROTECT HER FROM THE GAS. SHE'S WRONG.
THE INSTANT SHE EMERGES FROM THE CEILING, HER BODY BECOMES HEAVY AS LEAD-- NOTHING WANTS TO WORK, SHE CAN'T MOVE AND CAN BARELY THINK. SHE SOLIDIFIES.
GRAVITY DOES THE REST.

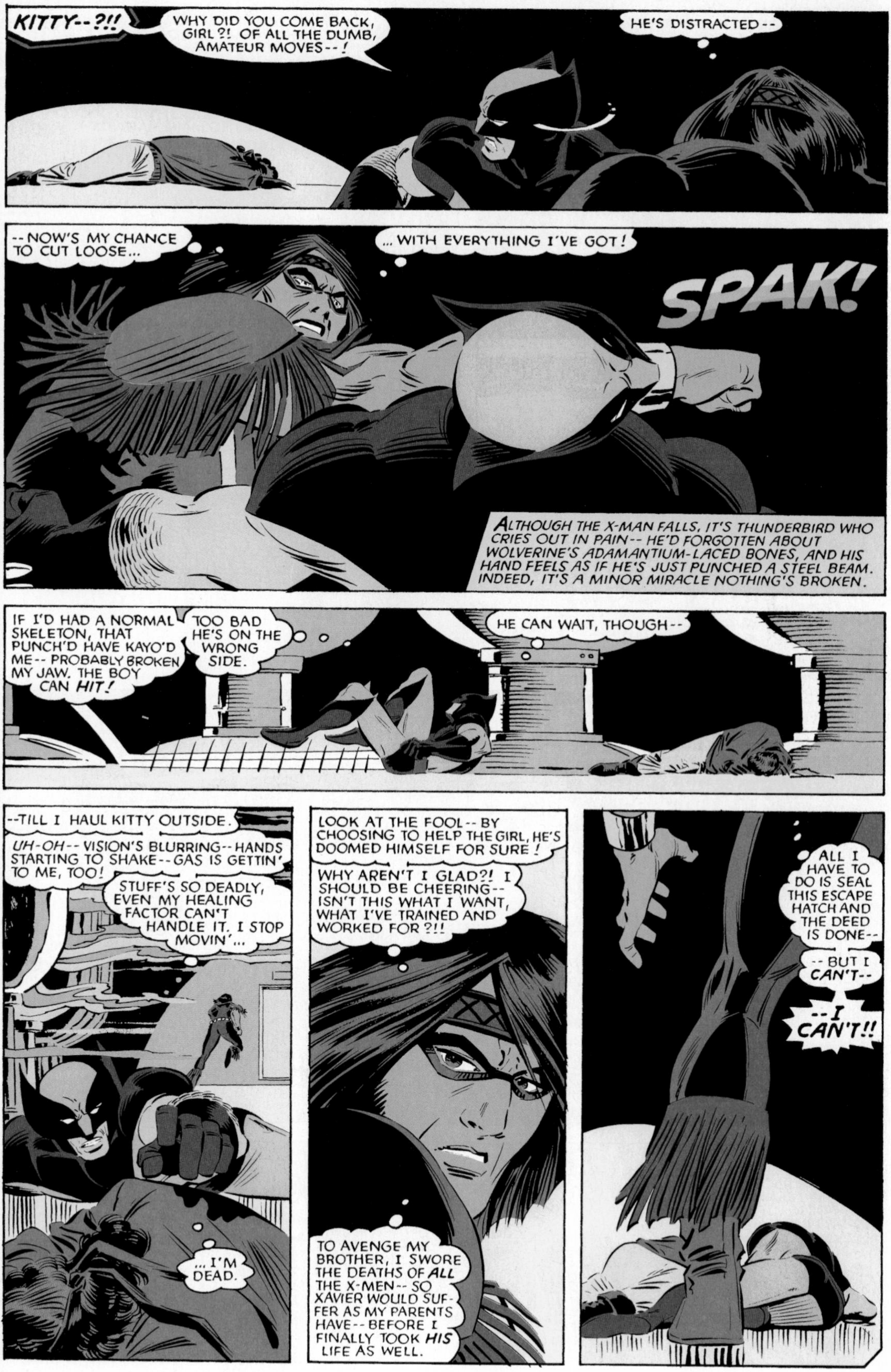

KITTY--?!!
WHY DID YOU COME BACK, GIRL?! OF ALL THE DUMB, AMATEUR MOVES--!
HE'S DISTRACTED--
--NOW'S MY CHANCE TO CUT LOOSE...
...WITH EVERYTHING I'VE GOT!
SPAK!
ALTHOUGH THE X-MAN FALLS, IT'S THUNDERBIRD WHO CRIES OUT IN PAIN-- HE'D FORGOTTEN ABOUT WOLVERINE'S ADAMANTIUM-LACED BONES, AND HIS HAND FEELS AS IF HE'S JUST PUNCHED A STEEL BEAM. INDEED, IT'S A MINOR MIRACLE NOTHING'S BROKEN.
IF I'D HAD A NORMAL SKELETON, THAT PUNCH'D HAVE KAYO'D ME-- PROBABLY BROKEN MY JAW. THE BOY CAN HIT!
TOO BAD HE'S ON THE WRONG SIDE.
HE CAN WAIT, THOUGH--
--TILL I HAUL KITTY OUTSIDE.
UH-OH-- VISION'S BLURRING-- HANDS STARTING TO SHAKE-- GAS IS GETTIN' TO ME, TOO!
STUFF'S SO DEADLY, EVEN MY HEALING FACTOR CAN'T HANDLE IT. I STOP MOVIN'...
...I'M DEAD.
LOOK AT THE FOOL-- BY CHOOSING TO HELP THE GIRL, HE'S DOOMED HIMSELF FOR SURE!
WHY AREN'T I GLAD?! I SHOULD BE CHEERING-- ISN'T THIS WHAT I WANT, WHAT I'VE TRAINED AND WORKED FOR?!!
TO AVENGE MY BROTHER, I SWORE THE DEATHS OF ALL THE X-MEN-- SO XAVIER WOULD SUFFER AS MY PARENTS HAVE-- BEFORE I FINALLY TOOK HIS LIFE AS WELL.
ALL I HAVE TO DO IS SEAL THIS ESCAPE HATCH AND THE DEED IS DONE--
--BUT I CAN'T--
--I CAN'T!!

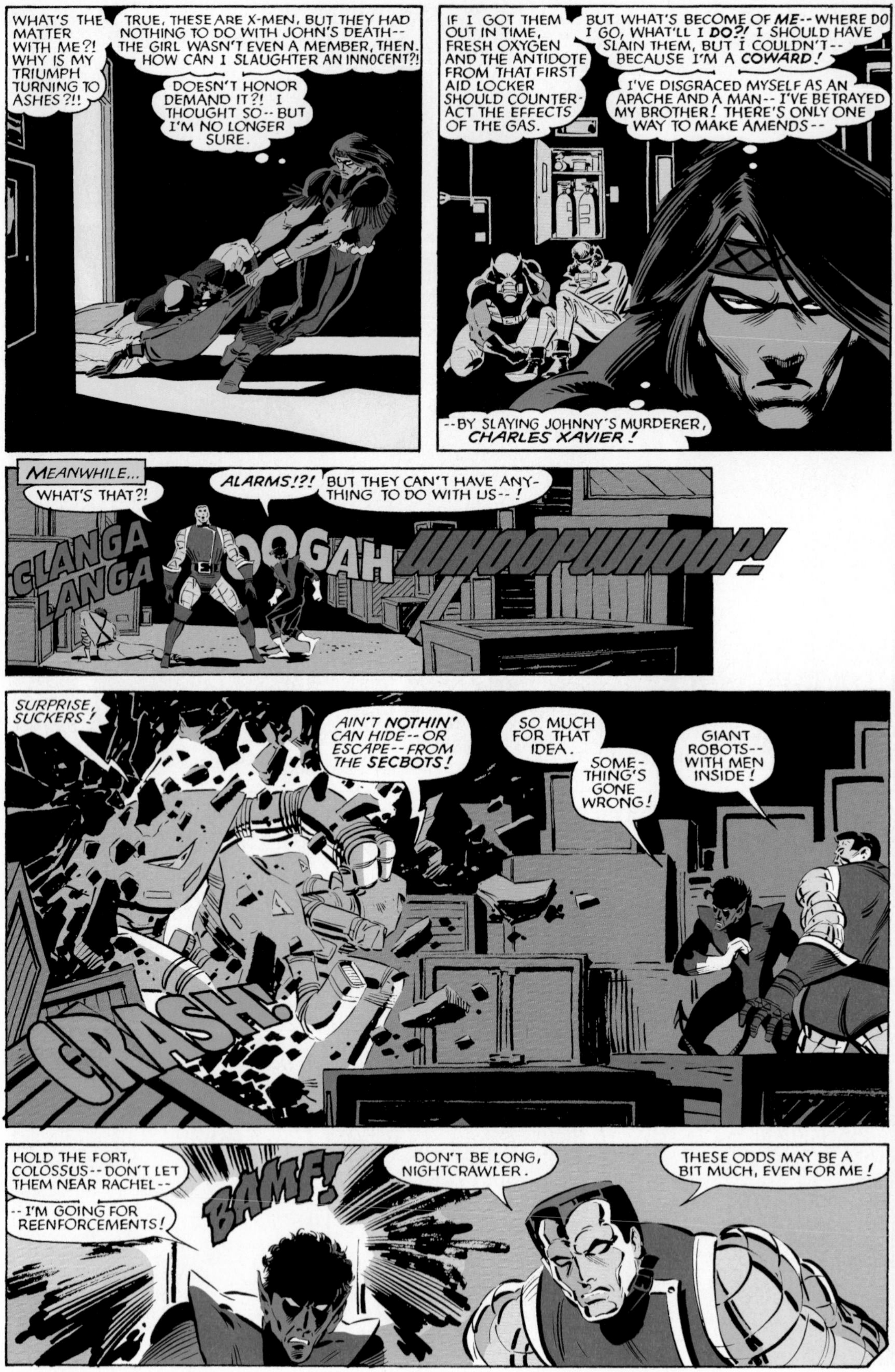
WHAT'S THE MATTER WITH ME?! WHY IS MY TRIUMPH TURNING TO ASHES?!!
TRUE, THESE ARE X-MEN, BUT THEY HAD NOTHING TO DO WITH JOHN'S DEATH-- THE GIRL WASN'T EVEN A MEMBER, THEN. HOW CAN I SLAUGHTER AN INNOCENT?!
DOESN'T HONOR DEMAND IT?! I THOUGHT SO-- BUT I'M NO LONGER SURE.
IF I GOT THEM OUT IN TIME, FRESH OXYGEN AND THE ANTIDOTE FROM THAT FIRST AID LOCKER SHOULD COUNTERACT THE EFFECTS OF THE GAS.
BUT WHAT'S BECOME OF ME-- WHERE DO I GO, WHAT'LL I DO?! I SHOULD HAVE SLAIN THEM, BUT I COULDN'T-- BECAUSE I'M A COWARD!
I'VE DISGRACED MYSELF AS AN APACHE AND A MAN-- I'VE BETRAYED MY BROTHER! THERE'S ONLY ONE WAY TO MAKE AMENDS--
--BY SLAYING JOHNNY'S MURDERER, CHARLES XAVIER!
MEANWHILE...
WHAT'S THAT?!
ALARMS!?!
BUT THEY CAN'T HAVE ANYTHING TO DO WITH US--!
CLANGA LANGA
OOGAH
WHOOPWHOOP!
SURPRISE, SUCKERS!
AIN'T NOTHIN' CAN HIDE-- OR ESCAPE-- FROM THE SECBOTS!
SO MUCH FOR THAT IDEA.
SOMETHING'S GONE WRONG!
GIANT ROBOTS-- WITH MEN INSIDE!
CRASH!
HOLD THE FORT, COLOSSUS-- DON'T LET THEM NEAR RACHEL--
--I'M GOING FOR REENFORCEMENTS!
BAMF!
DON'T BE LONG, NIGHTCRAWLER.
THESE ODDS MAY BE A BIT MUCH, EVEN FOR ME!

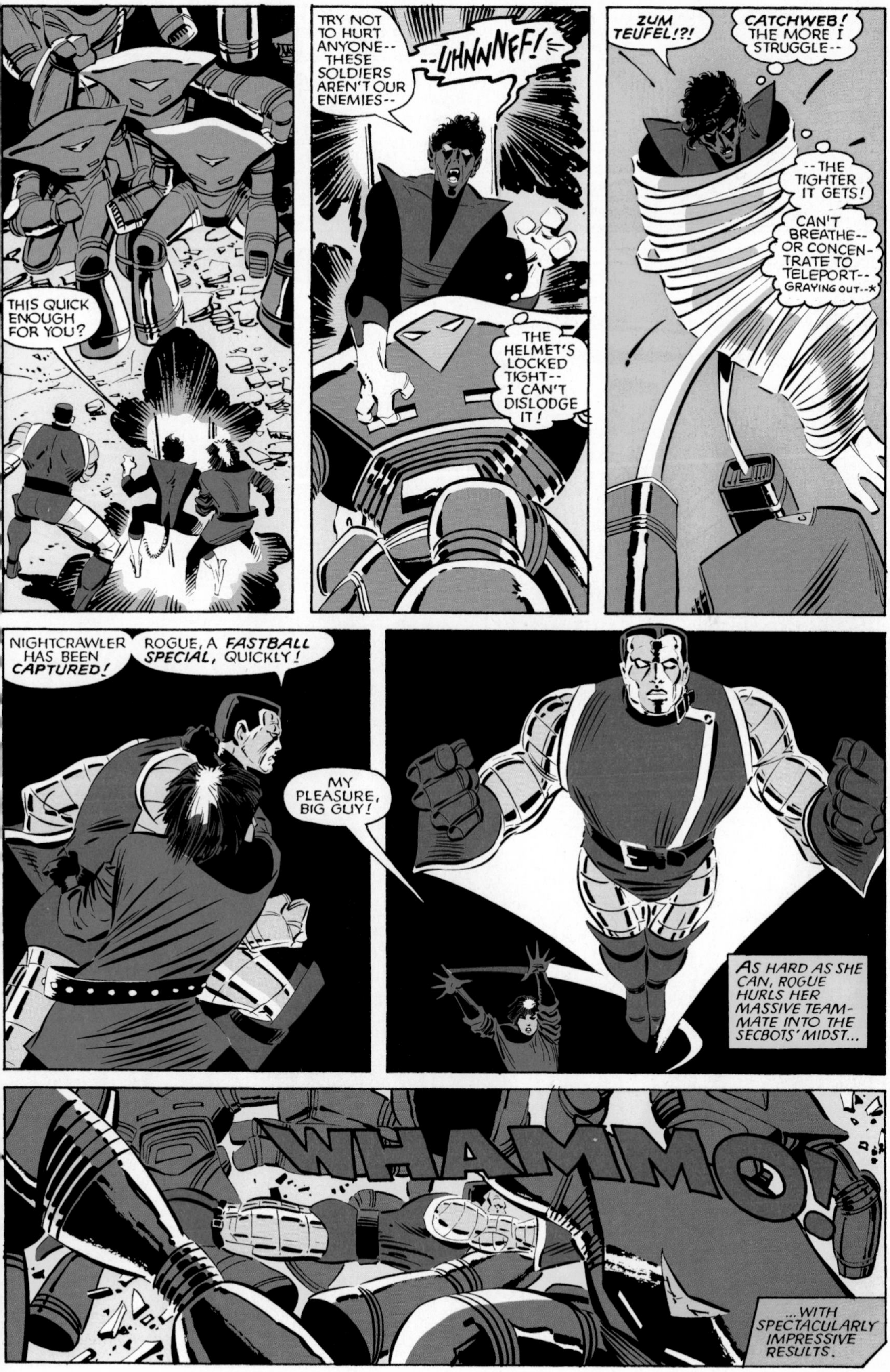
THIS QUICK ENOUGH FOR YOU?
TRY NOT TO HURT ANYONE-- THESE SOLDIERS AREN'T OUR ENEMIES--
--UHNNNFF!
THE HELMET'S LOCKED TIGHT-- I CAN'T DISLODGE IT!
ZUM TEUFEL!?!
CATCHWEB! THE MORE I STRUGGLE--
--THE TIGHTER IT GETS!
CAN'T BREATHE-- OR CONCEN-TRATE TO TELEPORT-- GRAYING OUT--*
NIGHTCRAWLER HAS BEEN CAPTURED!
ROGUE, A FASTBALL SPECIAL, QUICKLY!
MY PLEASURE, BIG GUY!
AS HARD AS SHE CAN, ROGUE HURLS HER MASSIVE TEAM-MATE INTO THE SECBOTS' MIDST...
WHAMMO!
...WITH SPECTACULARLY IMPRESSIVE RESULTS.

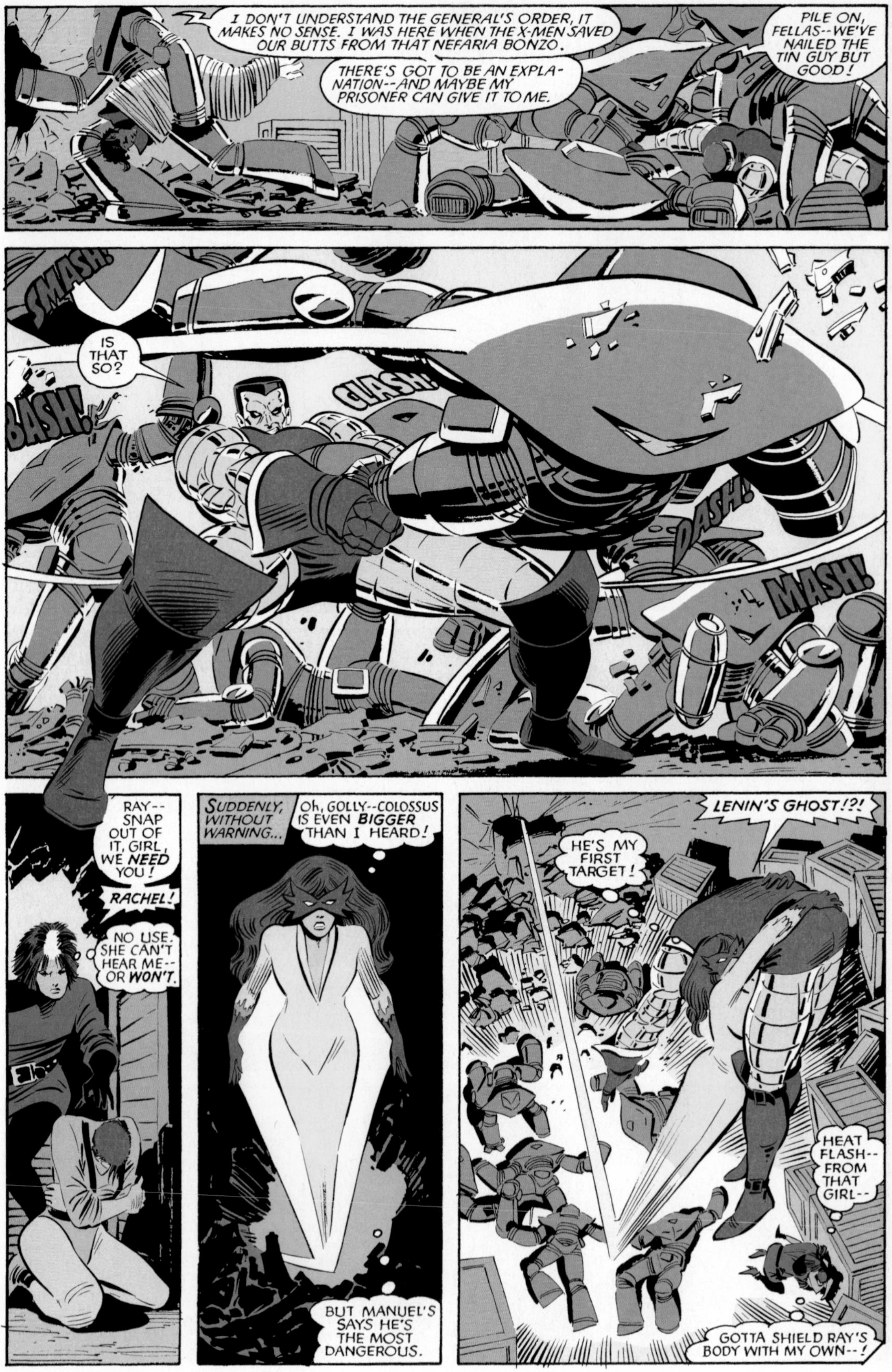
I DON'T UNDERSTAND THE GENERAL'S ORDER, IT MAKES NO SENSE. I WAS HERE WHEN THE X-MEN SAVED OUR BUTTS FROM THAT NEFARIA BONZO.
THERE'S GOT TO BE AN EXPLANATION--AND MAYBE MY PRISONER CAN GIVE IT TO ME.
PILE ON, FELLAS--WE'VE NAILED THE TIN GUY BUT GOOD!
SMASH!
IS THAT SO?
BASH!
CLASH!
DASH!
MASH!
RAY--SNAP OUT OF IT, GIRL, WE NEED YOU!
RACHEL!
NO USE. SHE CAN'T HEAR ME--OR WON'T.
SUDDENLY, WITHOUT WARNING...
Oh, GOLLY--COLOSSUS IS EVEN BIGGER THAN I HEARD!
BUT MANUEL'S SAYS HE'S THE MOST DANGEROUS.
LENIN'S GHOST!?!
HE'S MY FIRST TARGET!
HEAT FLASH--FROM THAT GIRL--
GOTTA SHIELD RAY'S BODY WITH MY OWN--!

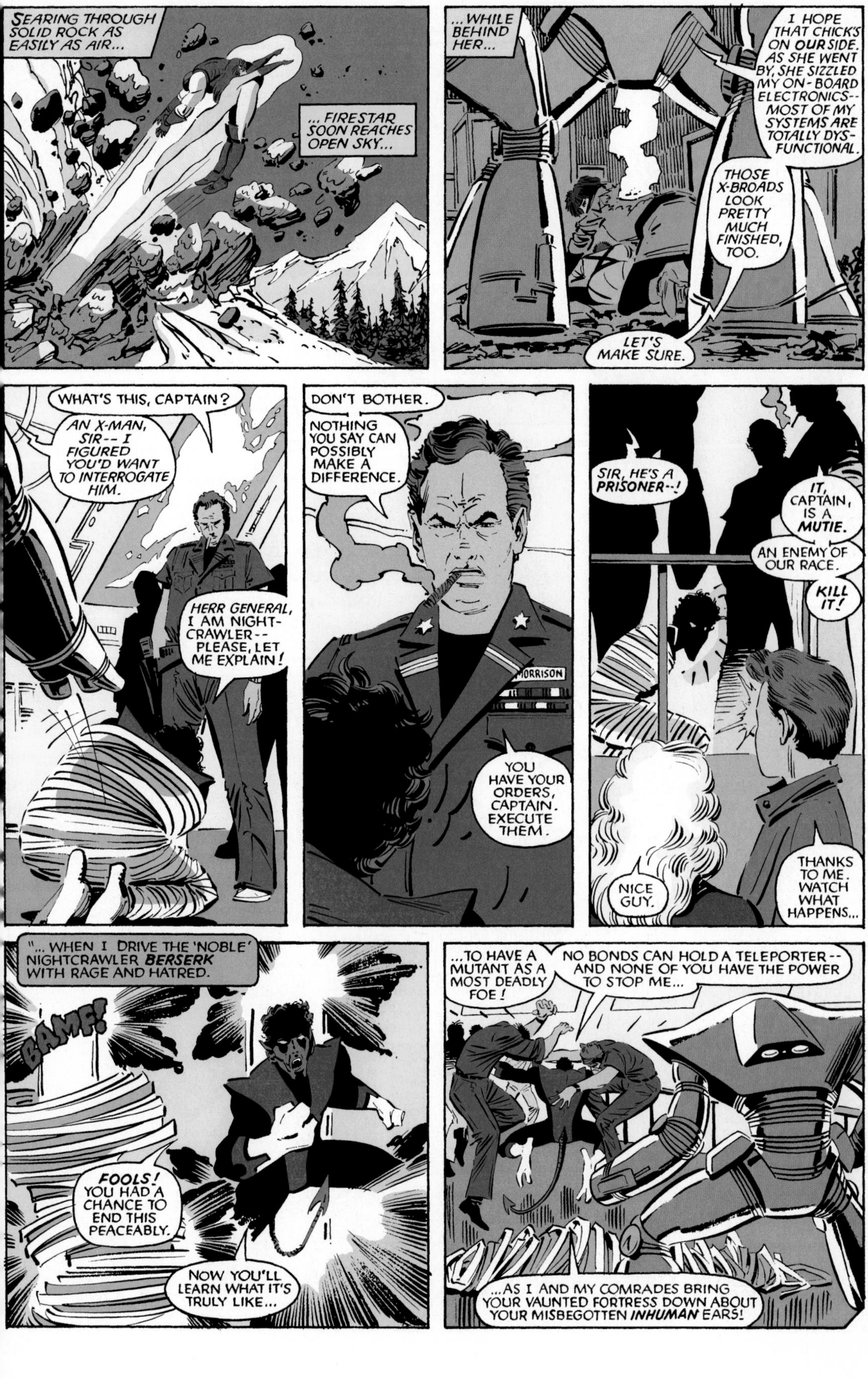
SEARING THROUGH SOLID ROCK AS EASILY AS AIR...
...FIRESTAR SOON REACHES OPEN SKY...
...WHILE BEHIND HER...
I HOPE THAT CHICK'S ON OUR SIDE. AS SHE WENT BY, SHE SIZZLED MY ON-BOARD ELECTRONICS--MOST OF MY SYSTEMS ARE TOTALLY DYS-FUNCTIONAL.
THOSE X-BROADS LOOK PRETTY MUCH FINISHED, TOO.
LET'S MAKE SURE.
WHAT'S THIS, CAPTAIN?
AN X-MAN, SIR-- I FIGURED YOU'D WANT TO INTERROGATE HIM.
HERR GENERAL, I AM NIGHT-CRAWLER--PLEASE, LET ME EXPLAIN!
DON'T BOTHER.
NOTHING YOU SAY CAN POSSIBLY MAKE A DIFFERENCE.
MORRISON
YOU HAVE YOUR ORDERS, CAPTAIN. EXECUTE THEM.
SIR, HE'S A PRISONER--!
IT, CAPTAIN, IS A MUTIE.
AN ENEMY OF OUR RACE.
KILL IT!
NICE GUY.
THANKS TO ME. WATCH WHAT HAPPENS...
"...WHEN I DRIVE THE 'NOBLE' NIGHTCRAWLER BERSERK WITH RAGE AND HATRED.
BAMF!
FOOLS! YOU HAD A CHANCE TO END THIS PEACEABLY.
NOW YOU'LL LEARN WHAT IT'S TRULY LIKE...
...TO HAVE A MUTANT AS A MOST DEADLY FOE!
NO BONDS CAN HOLD A TELEPORTER--AND NONE OF YOU HAVE THE POWER TO STOP ME...
...AS I AND MY COMRADES BRING YOUR VAUNTED FORTRESS DOWN ABOUT YOUR MISBEGOTTEN INHUMAN EARS!

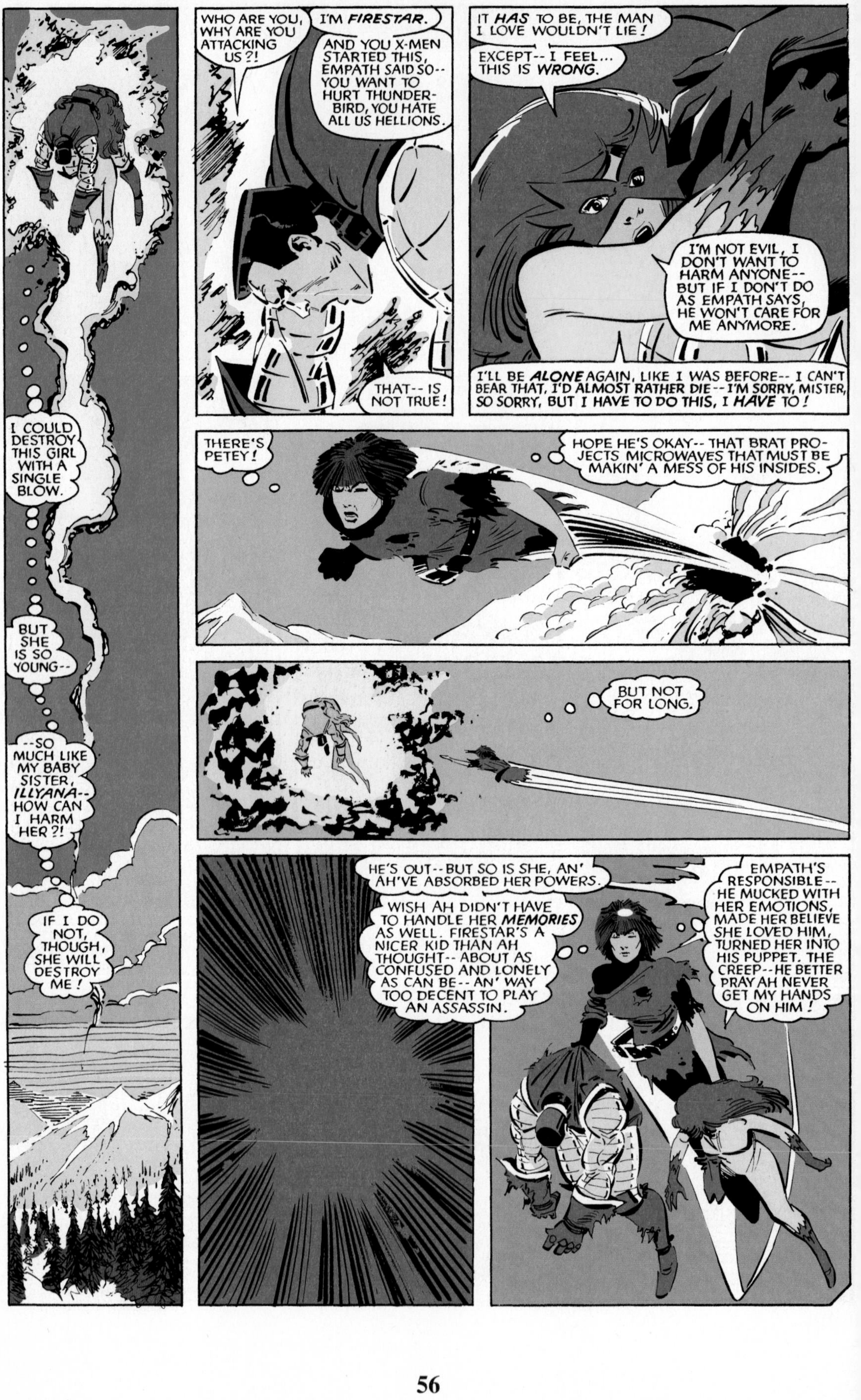

WHO ARE YOU, WHY ARE YOU ATTACKING US?!
I'M FIRESTAR.
AND YOU X-MEN STARTED THIS, EMPATH SAID SO-- YOU WANT TO HURT THUNDERBIRD, YOU HATE ALL US HELLIONS.
THAT-- IS NOT TRUE!
IT HAS TO BE, THE MAN I LOVE WOULDN'T LIE!
EXCEPT-- I FEEL... THIS IS WRONG.
I'M NOT EVIL, I DON'T WANT TO HARM ANYONE-- BUT IF I DON'T DO AS EMPATH SAYS, HE WON'T CARE FOR ME ANYMORE.
I'LL BE ALONE AGAIN, LIKE I WAS BEFORE-- I CAN'T BEAR THAT, I'D ALMOST RATHER DIE-- I'M SORRY, MISTER, SO SORRY, BUT I HAVE TO DO THIS, I HAVE TO!
I COULD DESTROY THIS GIRL WITH A SINGLE BLOW.
BUT SHE IS SO YOUNG--
--SO MUCH LIKE MY BABY SISTER, ILLYANA-- HOW CAN I HARM HER?!
IF I DO NOT, THOUGH, SHE WILL DESTROY ME!
THERE'S PETEY!
HOPE HE'S OKAY-- THAT BRAT PROJECTS MICROWAVES THAT MUST BE MAKIN' A MESS OF HIS INSIDES.
BUT NOT FOR LONG.
HE'S OUT-- BUT SO IS SHE, AN' AH'VE ABSORBED HER POWERS.
WISH AH DIDN'T HAVE TO HANDLE HER MEMORIES AS WELL. FIRESTAR'S A NICER KID THAN AH THOUGHT-- ABOUT AS CONFUSED AND LONELY AS CAN BE-- AN' WAY TOO DECENT TO PLAY AN ASSASSIN.
EMPATH'S RESPONSIBLE-- HE MUCKED WITH HER EMOTIONS, MADE HER BELIEVE SHE LOVED HIM, TURNED HER INTO HIS PUPPET. THE CREEP-- HE BETTER PRAY AH NEVER GET MY HANDS ON HIM!

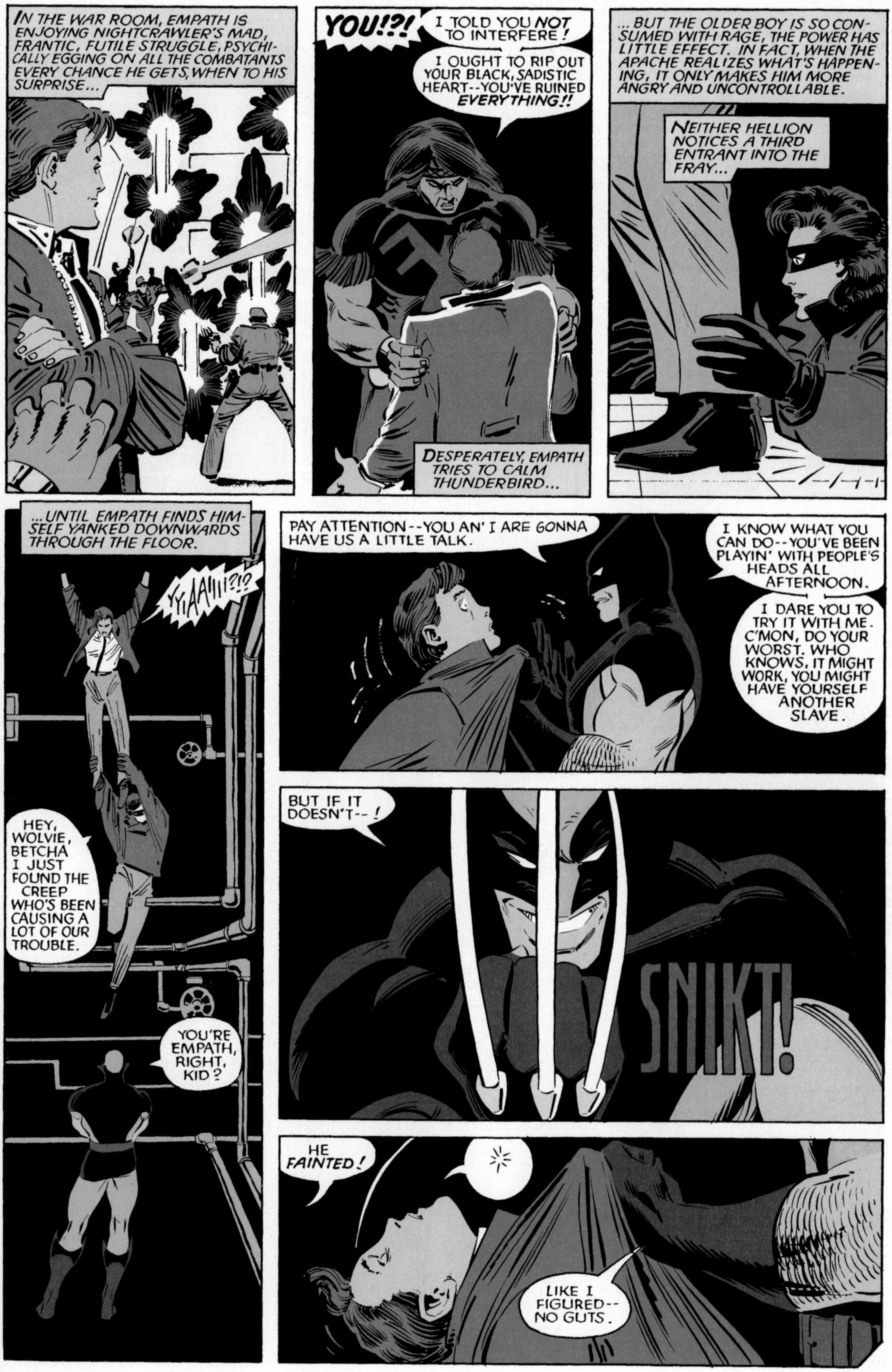
IN THE WAR ROOM, EMPATH IS ENJOYING NIGHTCRAWLER'S MAD, FRANTIC, FUTILE STRUGGLE, PSYCHICALLY EGGING ON ALL THE COMBATANTS EVERY CHANCE HE GETS, WHEN TO HIS SURPRISE...
YOU!?!
I TOLD YOU NOT TO INTERFERE!
I OUGHT TO RIP OUT YOUR BLACK, SADISTIC HEART--YOU'VE RUINED EVERYTHING!!
DESPERATELY, EMPATH TRIES TO CALM THUNDERBIRD...
...BUT THE OLDER BOY IS SO CONSUMED WITH RAGE, THE POWER HAS LITTLE EFFECT. IN FACT, WHEN THE APACHE REALIZES WHAT'S HAPPENING, IT ONLY MAKES HIM MORE ANGRY AND UNCONTROLLABLE.
NEITHER HELLION NOTICES A THIRD ENTRANT INTO THE FRAY...
...UNTIL EMPATH FINDS HIMSELF YANKED DOWNWARDS THROUGH THE FLOOR.
YYIAA!!!?!?
HEY, WOLVIE, BETCHA I JUST FOUND THE CREEP WHO'S BEEN CAUSING A LOT OF OUR TROUBLE.
YOU'RE EMPATH, RIGHT, KID?
PAY ATTENTION--YOU AN' I ARE GONNA HAVE US A LITTLE TALK.
I KNOW WHAT YOU CAN DO--YOU'VE BEEN PLAYIN' WITH PEOPLE'S HEADS ALL AFTERNOON.
I DARE YOU TO TRY IT WITH ME. C'MON, DO YOUR WORST. WHO KNOWS, IT MIGHT WORK, YOU MIGHT HAVE YOURSELF ANOTHER SLAVE.
BUT IF IT DOESN'T--!
SNIKT!
HE FAINTED!
LIKE I FIGURED--NO GUTS.

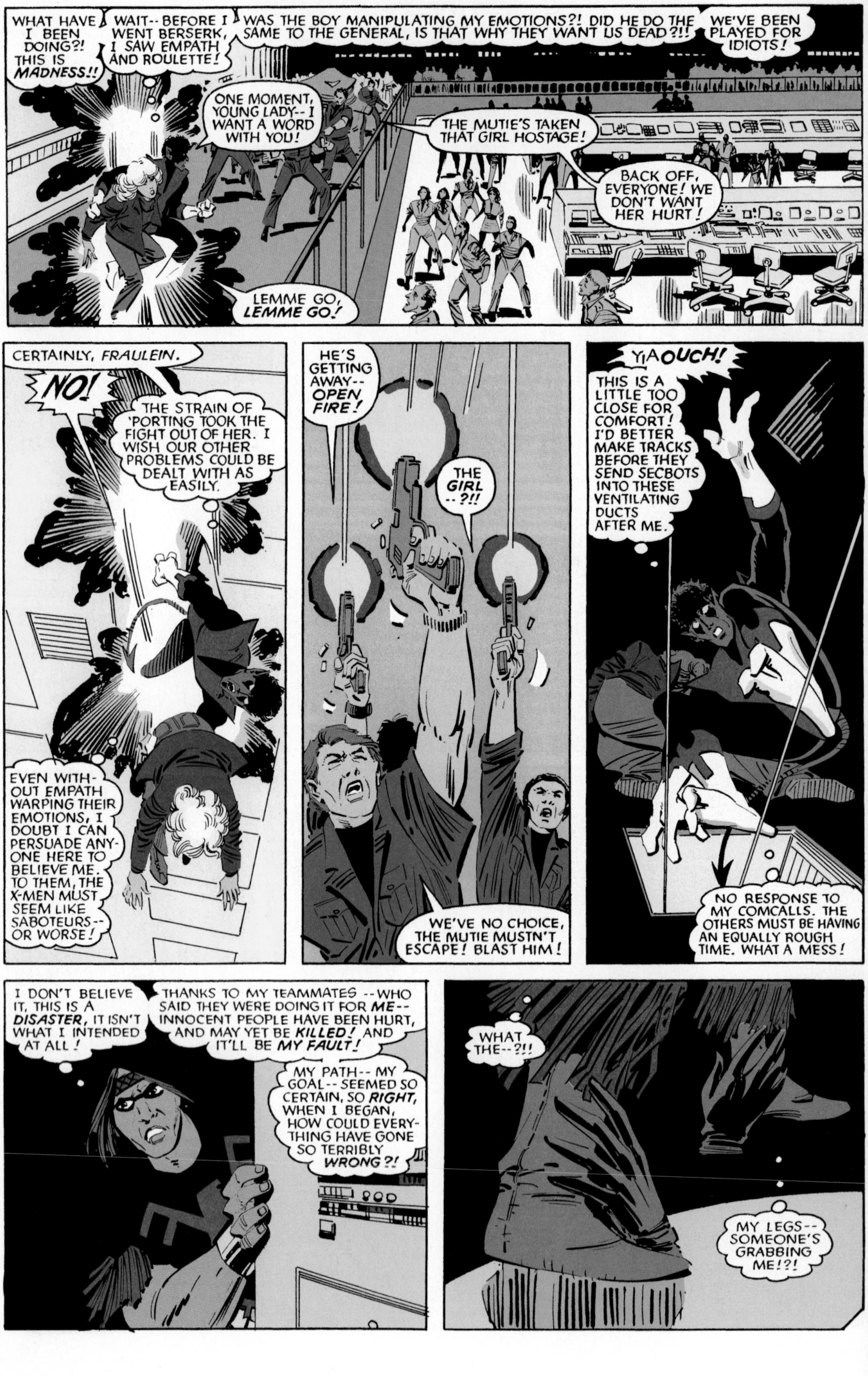
WHAT HAVE I BEEN DOING?! THIS IS MADNESS!!
WAIT-- BEFORE I WENT BERSERK, I SAW EMPATH AND ROULETTE!
WAS THE BOY MANIPULATING MY EMOTIONS?! DID HE DO THE SAME TO THE GENERAL, IS THAT WHY THEY WANT US DEAD?!!
WE'VE BEEN PLAYED FOR IDIOTS!
ONE MOMENT, YOUNG LADY-- I WANT A WORD WITH YOU!
THE MUTIE'S TAKEN THAT GIRL HOSTAGE!
BACK OFF, EVERYONE! WE DON'T WANT HER HURT!
LEMME GO, LEMME GO!
CERTAINLY, FRAULEIN.
NO!
THE STRAIN OF 'PORTING TOOK THE FIGHT OUT OF HER. I WISH OUR OTHER PROBLEMS COULD BE DEALT WITH AS EASILY.
EVEN WITHOUT EMPATH WARPING THEIR EMOTIONS, I DOUBT I CAN PERSUADE ANYONE HERE TO BELIEVE ME. TO THEM, THE X-MEN MUST SEEM LIKE SABOTEURS-- OR WORSE!
HE'S GETTING AWAY-- OPEN FIRE!
THE GIRL--?!!
WE'VE NO CHOICE, THE MUTIE MUSTN'T ESCAPE! BLAST HIM!
YIAOUCH!
THIS IS A LITTLE TOO CLOSE FOR COMFORT! I'D BETTER MAKE TRACKS BEFORE THEY SEND SECBOTS INTO THESE VENTILATING DUCTS AFTER ME.
NO RESPONSE TO MY COMCALLS. THE OTHERS MUST BE HAVING AN EQUALLY ROUGH TIME. WHAT A MESS!
I DON'T BELIEVE IT, THIS IS A DISASTER, IT ISN'T WHAT I INTENDED AT ALL!
THANKS TO MY TEAMMATES --WHO SAID THEY WERE DOING IT FOR ME-- INNOCENT PEOPLE HAVE BEEN HURT, AND MAY YET BE KILLED! AND IT'LL BE MY FAULT!
MY PATH-- MY GOAL-- SEEMED SO CERTAIN, SO RIGHT, WHEN I BEGAN, HOW COULD EVERYTHING HAVE GONE SO TERRIBLY WRONG?!
WHAT THE--?!!
MY LEGS-- SOMEONE'S GRABBING ME!?!

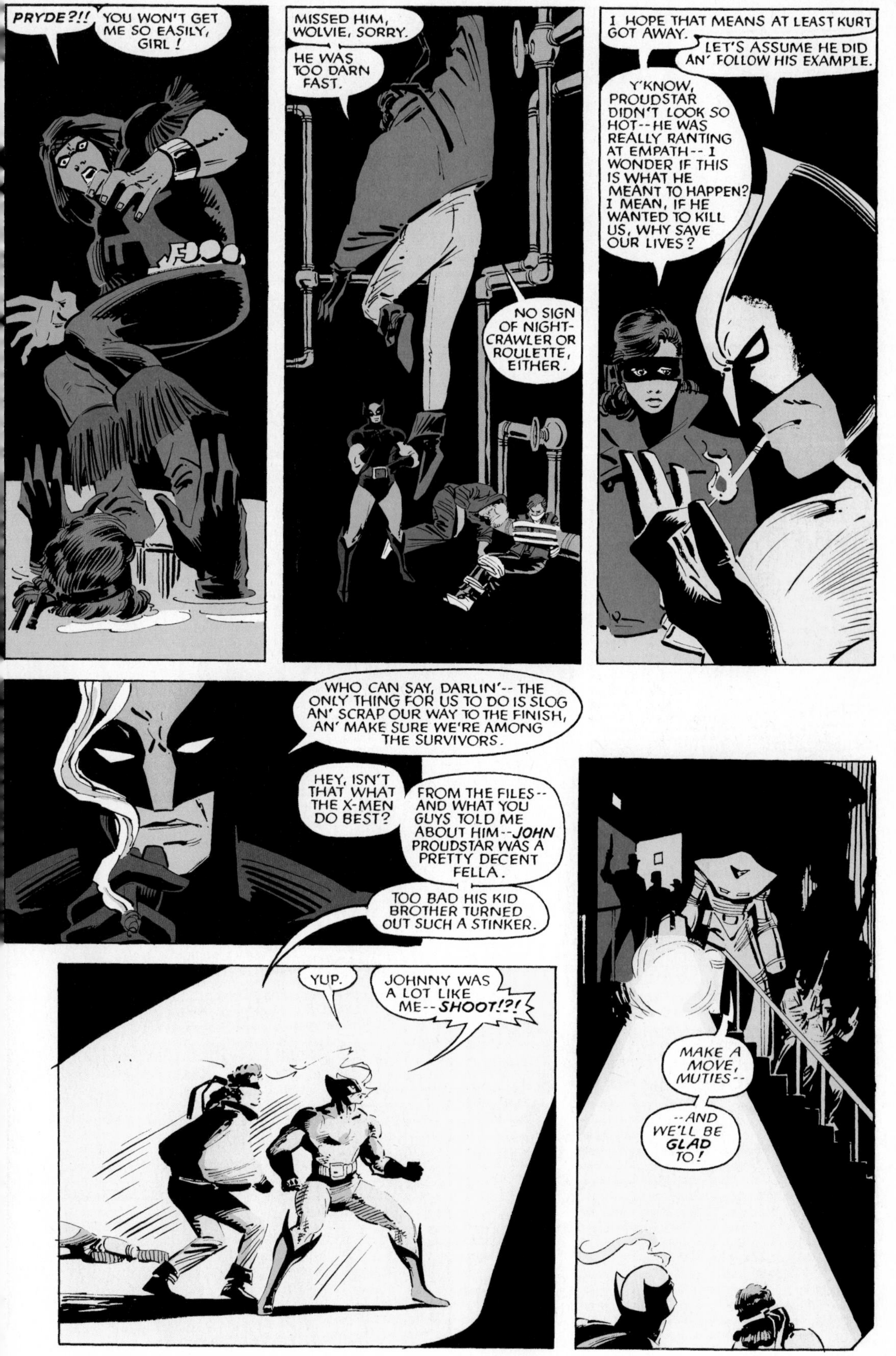
PRYDE?!!
YOU WON'T GET ME SO EASILY, GIRL!
MISSED HIM, WOLVIE, SORRY.
HE WAS TOO DARN FAST.
NO SIGN OF NIGHT-CRAWLER OR ROULETTE, EITHER.
I HOPE THAT MEANS AT LEAST KURT GOT AWAY.
LET'S ASSUME HE DID AN' FOLLOW HIS EXAMPLE.
Y'KNOW, PROUDSTAR DIDN'T LOOK SO HOT--HE WAS REALLY RANTING AT EMPATH-- I WONDER IF THIS IS WHAT HE MEANT TO HAPPEN? I MEAN, IF HE WANTED TO KILL US, WHY SAVE OUR LIVES?
WHO CAN SAY, DARLIN'-- THE ONLY THING FOR US TO DO IS SLOG AN' SCRAP OUR WAY TO THE FINISH, AN' MAKE SURE WE'RE AMONG THE SURVIVORS.
HEY, ISN'T THAT WHAT THE X-MEN DO BEST?
FROM THE FILES-- AND WHAT YOU GUYS TOLD ME ABOUT HIM--JOHN PROUDSTAR WAS A PRETTY DECENT FELLA.
TOO BAD HIS KID BROTHER TURNED OUT SUCH A STINKER.
YUP.
JOHNNY WAS A LOT LIKE ME--SHOOT!?!
MAKE A MOVE, MUTIES--
--AND WE'LL BE GLAD TO!

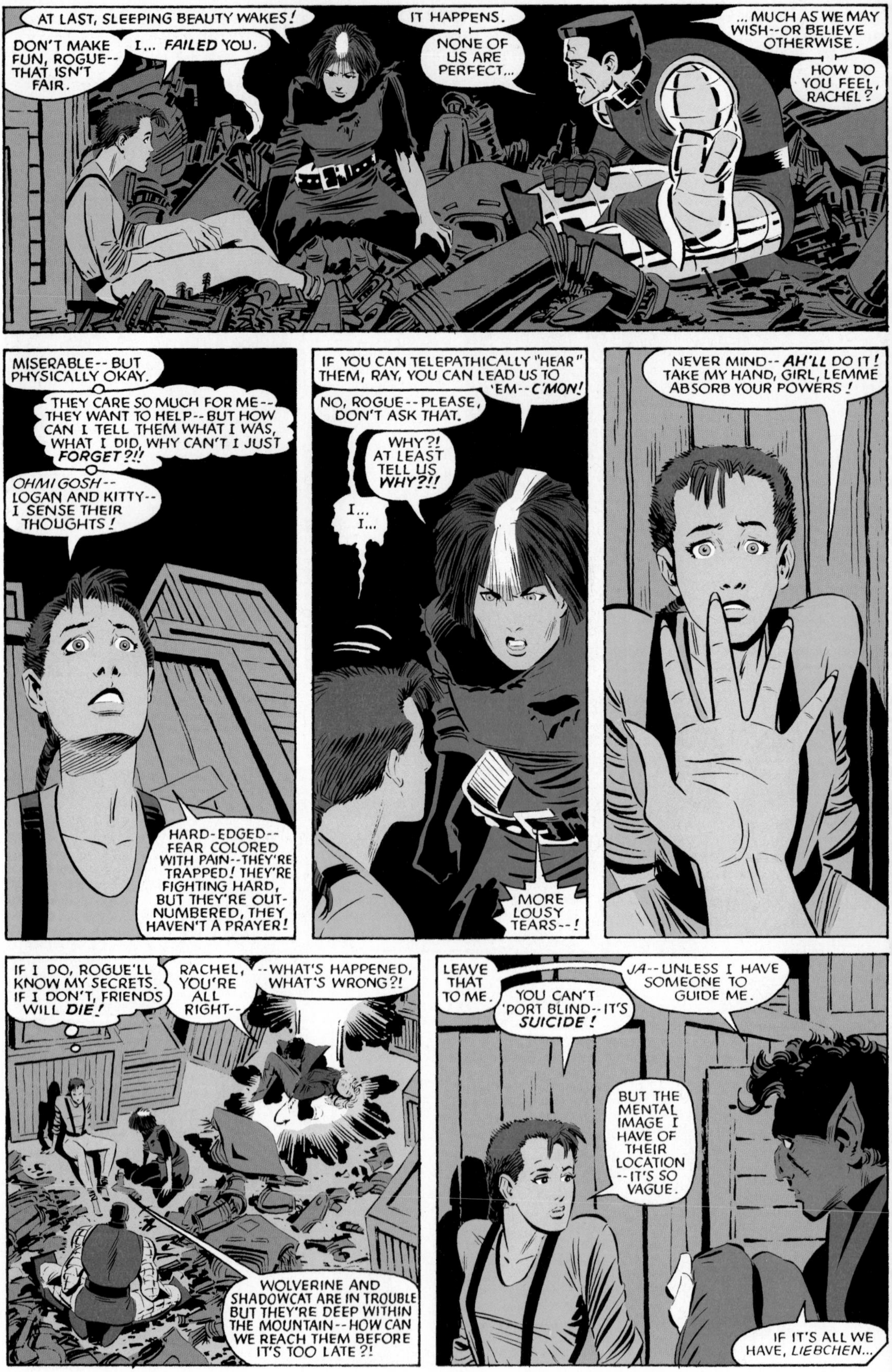
AT LAST, SLEEPING BEAUTY WAKES!
DON'T MAKE FUN, ROGUE-- THAT ISN'T FAIR.
I... FAILED YOU.
IT HAPPENS.
NONE OF US ARE PERFECT...
...MUCH AS WE MAY WISH--OR BELIEVE OTHERWISE.
HOW DO YOU FEEL, RACHEL?
MISERABLE-- BUT PHYSICALLY OKAY.
THEY CARE SO MUCH FOR ME-- THEY WANT TO HELP-- BUT HOW CAN I TELL THEM WHAT I WAS, WHAT I DID, WHY CAN'T I JUST FORGET?!!
OHMIGOSH-- LOGAN AND KITTY-- I SENSE THEIR THOUGHTS!
HARD-EDGED-- FEAR COLORED WITH PAIN--THEY'RE TRAPPED! THEY'RE FIGHTING HARD, BUT THEY'RE OUT-NUMBERED, THEY HAVEN'T A PRAYER!
IF YOU CAN TELEPATHICALLY "HEAR" THEM, RAY, YOU CAN LEAD US TO 'EM--C'MON!
NO, ROGUE-- PLEASE, DON'T ASK THAT.
WHY?! AT LEAST TELL US WHY?!!
I... I...
MORE LOUSY TEARS--!
NEVER MIND-- AH'LL DO IT! TAKE MY HAND, GIRL, LEMME ABSORB YOUR POWERS!
IF I DO, ROGUE'LL KNOW MY SECRETS. IF I DON'T, FRIENDS WILL DIE!
RACHEL, YOU'RE ALL RIGHT--
--WHAT'S HAPPENED, WHAT'S WRONG?!
WOLVERINE AND SHADOWCAT ARE IN TROUBLE BUT THEY'RE DEEP WITHIN THE MOUNTAIN--HOW CAN WE REACH THEM BEFORE IT'S TOO LATE?!
LEAVE THAT TO ME.
YOU CAN'T 'PORT BLIND--IT'S SUICIDE!
JA--UNLESS I HAVE SOMEONE TO GUIDE ME.
BUT THE MENTAL IMAGE I HAVE OF THEIR LOCATION --IT'S SO VAGUE.
IF IT'S ALL WE HAVE, LIEBCHEN...

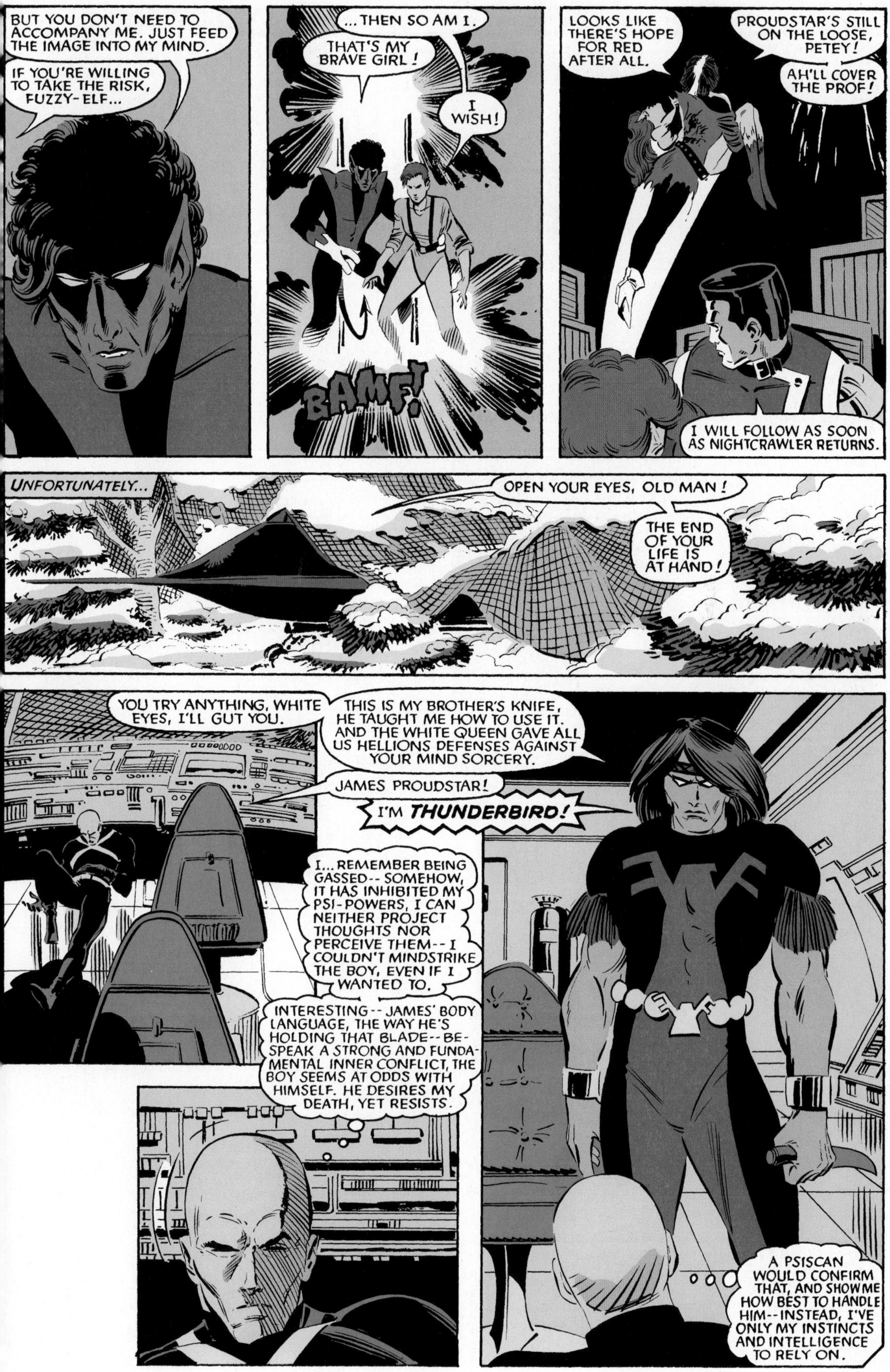
BUT YOU DON'T NEED TO ACCOMPANY ME. JUST FEED THE IMAGE INTO MY MIND.
IF YOU'RE WILLING TO TAKE THE RISK, FUZZY-ELF...
...THEN SO AM I.
THAT'S MY BRAVE GIRL!
I WISH!
BAMF!
LOOKS LIKE THERE'S HOPE FOR RED AFTER ALL.
PROUDSTAR'S STILL ON THE LOOSE, PETEY!
AH'LL COVER THE PROF!
I WILL FOLLOW AS SOON AS NIGHTCRAWLER RETURNS.
UNFORTUNATELY...
OPEN YOUR EYES, OLD MAN!
THE END OF YOUR LIFE IS AT HAND!
YOU TRY ANYTHING, WHITE EYES, I'LL GUT YOU.
THIS IS MY BROTHER'S KNIFE, HE TAUGHT ME HOW TO USE IT. AND THE WHITE QUEEN GAVE ALL US HELLIONS DEFENSES AGAINST YOUR MIND SORCERY.
JAMES PROUDSTAR!
I'M THUNDERBIRD!
I... REMEMBER BEING GASSED-- SOMEHOW, IT HAS INHIBITED MY PSI-POWERS, I CAN NEITHER PROJECT THOUGHTS NOR PERCEIVE THEM-- I COULDN'T MINDSTRIKE THE BOY, EVEN IF I WANTED TO.
INTERESTING-- JAMES' BODY LANGUAGE, THE WAY HE'S HOLDING THAT BLADE-- BE-SPEAK A STRONG AND FUNDA-MENTAL INNER CONFLICT, THE BOY SEEMS AT ODDS WITH HIMSELF. HE DESIRES MY DEATH, YET RESISTS.
A PSISCAN WOULD CONFIRM THAT, AND SHOW ME HOW BEST TO HANDLE HIM--INSTEAD, I'VE ONLY MY INSTINCTS AND INTELLIGENCE TO RELY ON.

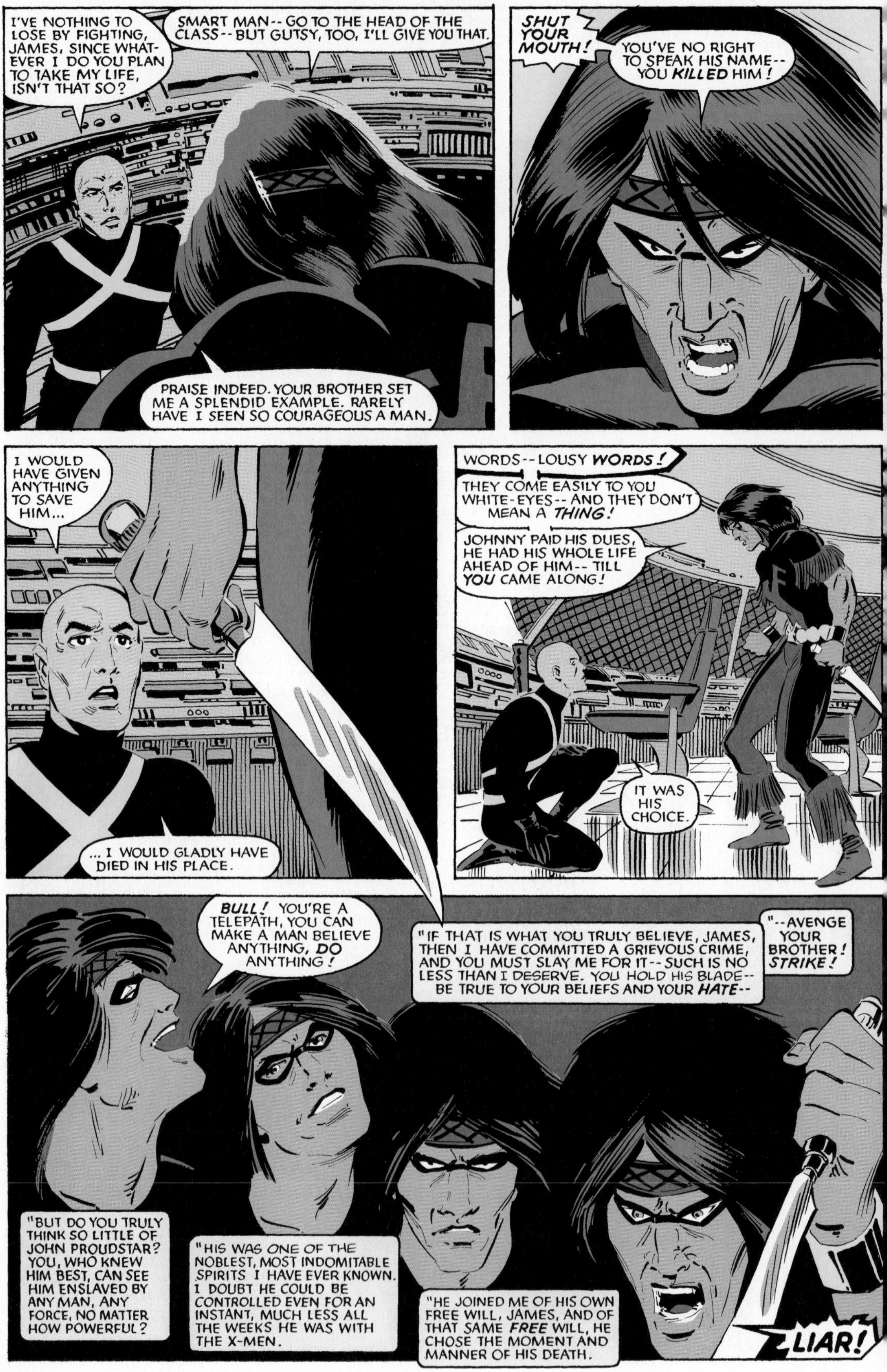

I'VE NOTHING TO LOSE BY FIGHTING, JAMES, SINCE WHATEVER I DO YOU PLAN TO TAKE MY LIFE, ISN'T THAT SO?
SMART MAN-- GO TO THE HEAD OF THE CLASS-- BUT GUTSY, TOO, I'LL GIVE YOU THAT.
PRAISE INDEED. YOUR BROTHER SET ME A SPLENDID EXAMPLE. RARELY HAVE I SEEN SO COURAGEOUS A MAN.
SHUT YOUR MOUTH!
YOU'VE NO RIGHT TO SPEAK HIS NAME-- YOU KILLED HIM!
I WOULD HAVE GIVEN ANYTHING TO SAVE HIM...
...I WOULD GLADLY HAVE DIED IN HIS PLACE.
WORDS--LOUSY WORDS!
THEY COME EASILY TO YOU WHITE-EYES-- AND THEY DON'T MEAN A THING!
JOHNNY PAID HIS DUES, HE HAD HIS WHOLE LIFE AHEAD OF HIM-- TILL YOU CAME ALONG!
IT WAS HIS CHOICE.
BULL! YOU'RE A TELEPATH, YOU CAN MAKE A MAN BELIEVE ANYTHING, DO ANYTHING!
"IF THAT IS WHAT YOU TRULY BELIEVE, JAMES, THEN I HAVE COMMITTED A GRIEVOUS CRIME, AND YOU MUST SLAY ME FOR IT--SUCH IS NO LESS THAN I DESERVE. YOU HOLD HIS BLADE-- BE TRUE TO YOUR BELIEFS AND YOUR HATE--
"--AVENGE YOUR BROTHER! STRIKE!
"BUT DO YOU TRULY THINK SO LITTLE OF JOHN PROUDSTAR? YOU, WHO KNEW HIM BEST, CAN SEE HIM ENSLAVED BY ANY MAN, ANY FORCE, NO MATTER HOW POWERFUL?
"HIS WAS ONE OF THE NOBLEST, MOST INDOMITABLE SPIRITS I HAVE EVER KNOWN. I DOUBT HE COULD BE CONTROLLED EVEN FOR AN INSTANT, MUCH LESS ALL THE WEEKS HE WAS WITH THE X-MEN.
"HE JOINED ME OF HIS OWN FREE WILL, JAMES, AND OF THAT SAME FREE WILL, HE CHOSE THE MOMENT AND MANNER OF HIS DEATH.
LIAR!

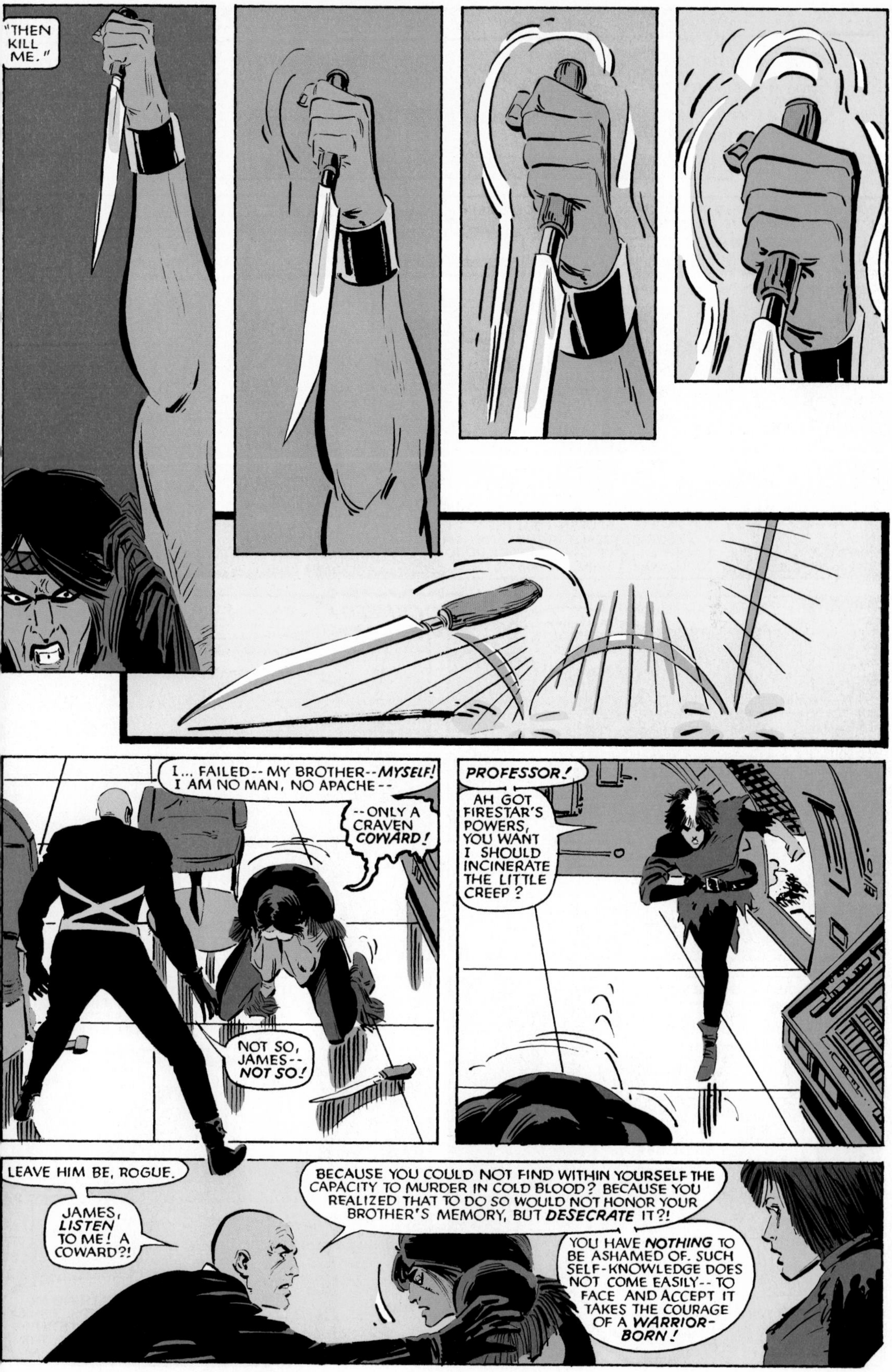

"THEN KILL ME."
I... FAILED-- MY BROTHER-- MYSELF! I AM NO MAN, NO APACHE--
--ONLY A CRAVEN COWARD!
NOT SO, JAMES-- NOT SO!
PROFESSOR!
AH GOT FIRESTAR'S POWERS, YOU WANT I SHOULD INCINERATE THE LITTLE CREEP?
LEAVE HIM BE, ROGUE.
JAMES, LISTEN TO ME! A COWARD?!
BECAUSE YOU COULD NOT FIND WITHIN YOURSELF THE CAPACITY TO MURDER IN COLD BLOOD? BECAUSE YOU REALIZED THAT TO DO SO WOULD NOT HONOR YOUR BROTHER'S MEMORY, BUT DESECRATE IT?!
YOU HAVE NOTHING TO BE ASHAMED OF. SUCH SELF-KNOWLEDGE DOES NOT COME EASILY-- TO FACE AND ACCEPT IT TAKES THE COURAGE OF A WARRIOR-BORN!

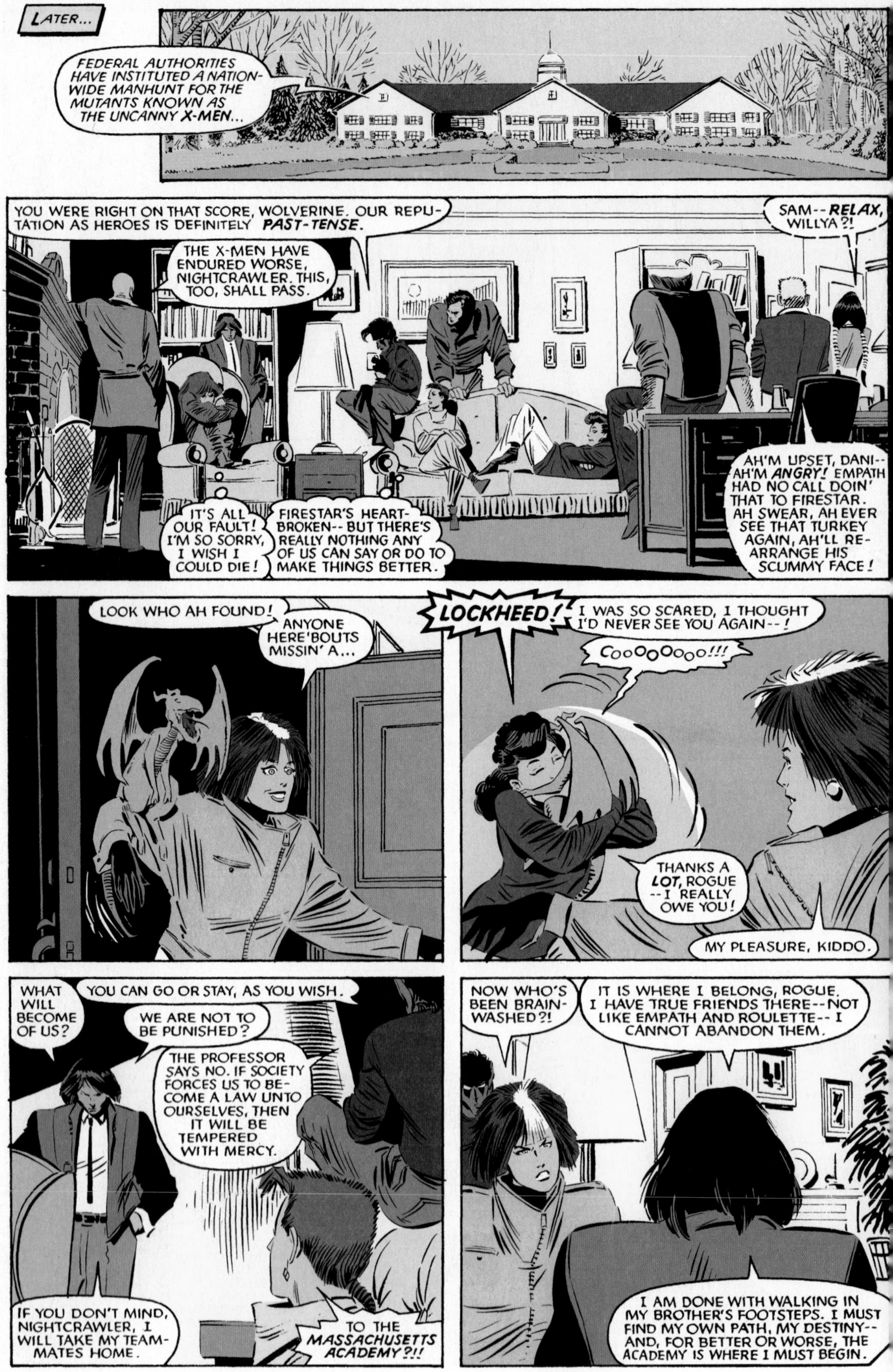
LATER...
FEDERAL AUTHORITIES HAVE INSTITUTED A NATION-WIDE MANHUNT FOR THE MUTANTS KNOWN AS THE UNCANNY X-MEN...
YOU WERE RIGHT ON THAT SCORE, WOLVERINE. OUR REPUTATION AS HEROES IS DEFINITELY PAST-TENSE.
SAM--RELAX, WILLYA?!
THE X-MEN HAVE ENDURED WORSE, NIGHTCRAWLER. THIS, TOO, SHALL PASS.
IT'S ALL OUR FAULT! I'M SO SORRY, I WISH I COULD DIE!
FIRESTAR'S HEART-BROKEN--BUT THERE'S REALLY NOTHING ANY OF US CAN SAY OR DO TO MAKE THINGS BETTER.
AH'M UPSET, DANI--AH'M ANGRY! EMPATH HAD NO CALL DOIN' THAT TO FIRESTAR. AH SWEAR, AH EVER SEE THAT TURKEY AGAIN, AH'LL RE-ARRANGE HIS SCUMMY FACE!
LOOK WHO AH FOUND!
ANYONE HERE'BOUTS MISSIN' A...
LOCKHEED!
I WAS SO SCARED, I THOUGHT I'D NEVER SEE YOU AGAIN--!
COOOOOOOO!!!
THANKS A LOT, ROGUE--I REALLY OWE YOU!
MY PLEASURE, KIDDO.
WHAT WILL BECOME OF US?
YOU CAN GO OR STAY, AS YOU WISH.
WE ARE NOT TO BE PUNISHED?
THE PROFESSOR SAYS NO. IF SOCIETY FORCES US TO BECOME A LAW UNTO OURSELVES, THEN IT WILL BE TEMPERED WITH MERCY.
IF YOU DON'T MIND, NIGHTCRAWLER, I WILL TAKE MY TEAMMATES HOME.
TO THE MASSACHUSETTS ACADEMY?!!
NOW WHO'S BEEN BRAINWASHED?!
IT IS WHERE I BELONG, ROGUE. I HAVE TRUE FRIENDS THERE--NOT LIKE EMPATH AND ROULETTE--I CANNOT ABANDON THEM.
I AM DONE WITH WALKING IN MY BROTHER'S FOOTSTEPS. I MUST FIND MY OWN PATH, MY DESTINY--AND, FOR BETTER OR WORSE, THE ACADEMY IS WHERE I MUST BEGIN.

AND YOU, CHILD? YOU ARE *WELCOME* TO STAY WITH US.

THEY WEREN'T YOUR FAULT, ANGELICA.

EVEN AFTER ALL THE AWFUL THINGS I DID?

AND THEY CANNOT MASK YOUR GOOD HEART AND SOUL.

I'D *LOVE* TO, PROFESSOR--

--BUT... I CAN'T.

I'VE HAD ROTTEN CLASSMATES LIKE EMPATH BEFORE, KIDS WHO LOVED TO PICK ON ME-- BUT I'VE NEVER KNOWN ANYONE, 'CEPT MY DAD...

...AS KIND AS *MISS FROST.*

I CAN'T RUN OUT ON HER. IT'S SOMETHING ROULETTE OR EMPATH WOULD DO-- I DON'T WANT TO BE LIKE THEM.

I UNDERSTAND.

I PRAY THE WHITE QUEEN PROVES DESERVING OF SUCH TRUST.

SHOULD CIRCUMSTAN- CES CHANGE, HOWEVER, ANGELICA...

...YOU WILL *ALWAYS* HAVE A PLACE HERE.

WOULD IT HELP, SIR, IF I TURNED MYSELF IN, TOLD THE FEDS WHAT REALLY HAPPENED? MAYBE THAT'D GET YOU OFF THE HOOK?!

NOTHING IN CHEYENNE MOUNTAIN WAS DAMAGED THAT WAS NOT EASILY-- AND IMMEDIATELY-- REPAIRED.

THE NATION WAS NEVER IN DANGER, JAMES-- AND YOU HAVE ENOUGH TO COPE WITH WITHOUT ADDING A POSSIBLE LIFETIME IN PRISON TO YOUR BURDENS.

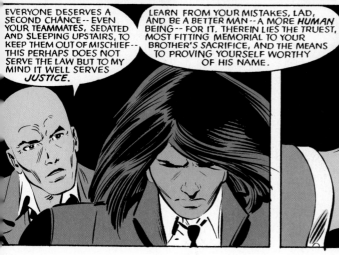

EVERYONE DESERVES A SECOND CHANCE-- EVEN YOUR TEAMMATES, SEDATED AND SLEEPING UPSTAIRS, TO KEEP THEM OUT OF MISCHIEF-- THIS PERHAPS DOES NOT SERVE THE LAW BUT TO MY MIND IT WELL SERVES *JUSTICE.*

LEARN FROM YOUR MISTAKES, LAD, AND BE A BETTER MAN-- A MORE *HUMAN* BEING-- FOR IT. THEREIN LIES THE TRUEST, MOST FITTING MEMORIAL TO YOUR BROTHER'S SACRIFICE, AND THE MEANS TO PROVING YOURSELF WORTHY OF HIS NAME.

I'LL... TRY, PROFESSOR--

--MY VERY BEST!

EPILOGUE

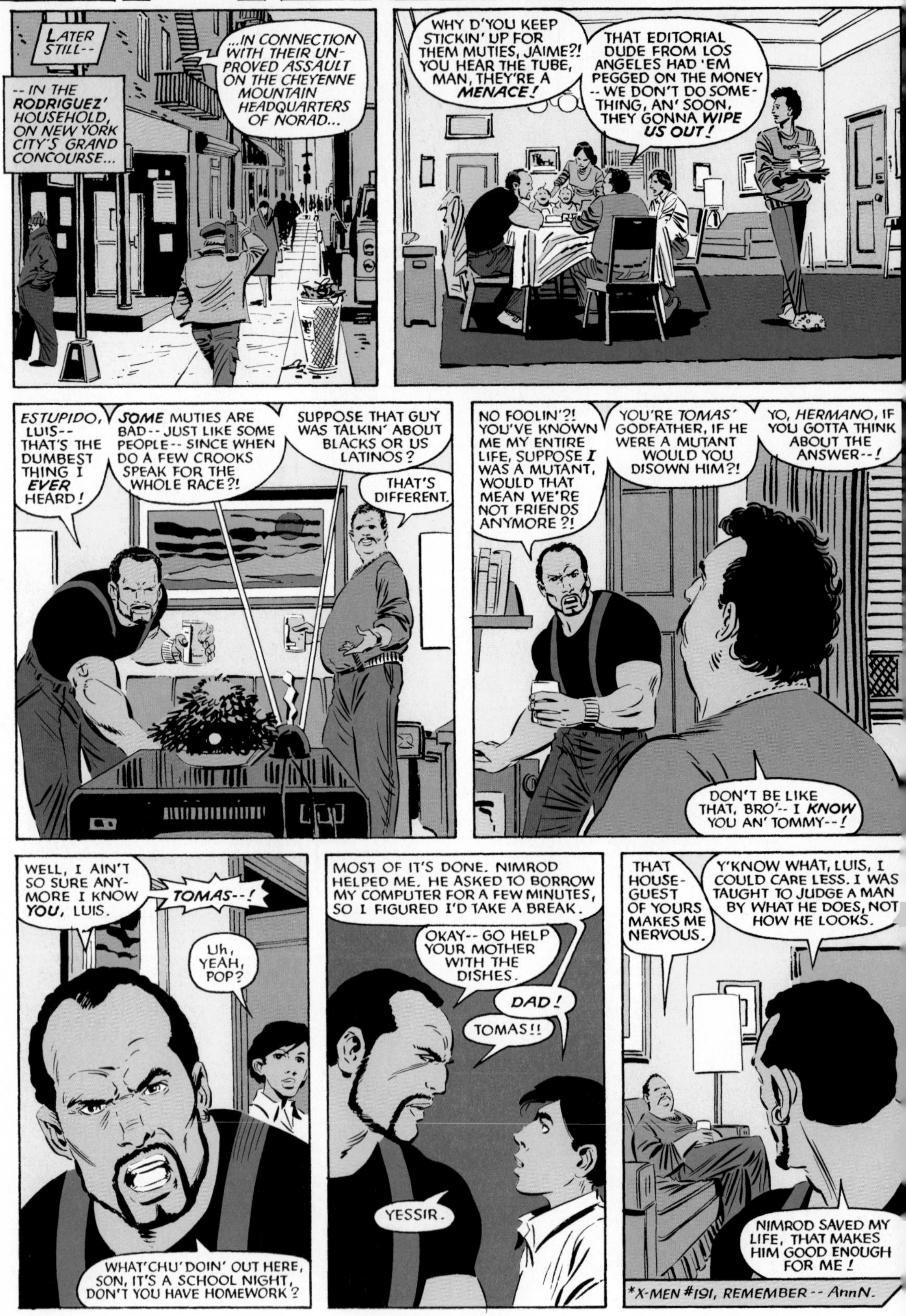
LATER STILL--
-- IN THE RODRIGUEZ' HOUSEHOLD, ON NEW YORK CITY'S GRAND CONCOURSE...
...IN CONNECTION WITH THEIR UNPROVED ASSAULT ON THE CHEYENNE MOUNTAIN HEADQUARTERS OF NORAD...
WHY D'YOU KEEP STICKIN' UP FOR THEM MUTIES, JAIME?! YOU HEAR THE TUBE, MAN, THEY'RE A MENACE!
THAT EDITORIAL DUDE FROM LOS ANGELES HAD 'EM PEGGED ON THE MONEY -- WE DON'T DO SOMETHING, AN' SOON, THEY GONNA WIPE US OUT!
ESTUPIDO, LUIS-- THAT'S THE DUMBEST THING I EVER HEARD!
SOME MUTIES ARE BAD-- JUST LIKE SOME PEOPLE-- SINCE WHEN DO A FEW CROOKS SPEAK FOR THE WHOLE RACE?!
SUPPOSE THAT GUY WAS TALKIN' ABOUT BLACKS OR US LATINOS?
THAT'S DIFFERENT.
NO FOOLIN'?! YOU'VE KNOWN ME MY ENTIRE LIFE, SUPPOSE I WAS A MUTANT, WOULD THAT MEAN WE'RE NOT FRIENDS ANYMORE?!
YOU'RE TOMAS' GODFATHER, IF HE WERE A MUTANT WOULD YOU DISOWN HIM?!
YO, HERMANO, IF YOU GOTTA THINK ABOUT THE ANSWER--!
DON'T BE LIKE THAT, BRO'-- I KNOW YOU AN' TOMMY--!
WELL, I AIN'T SO SURE ANYMORE I KNOW YOU, LUIS.
TOMAS--!
Uh, YEAH, POP?
WHAT'CHU'DOIN' OUT HERE, SON, IT'S A SCHOOL NIGHT, DON'T YOU HAVE HOMEWORK?
MOST OF IT'S DONE. NIMROD HELPED ME. HE ASKED TO BORROW MY COMPUTER FOR A FEW MINUTES, SO I FIGURED I'D TAKE A BREAK.
OKAY-- GO HELP YOUR MOTHER WITH THE DISHES.
DAD!
TOMAS!!
YESSIR.
THAT HOUSE-GUEST OF YOURS MAKES ME NERVOUS.
Y'KNOW WHAT, LUIS, I COULD CARE LESS. I WAS TAUGHT TO JUDGE A MAN BY WHAT HE DOES, NOT HOW HE LOOKS.
NIMROD SAVED MY LIFE, THAT MAKES HIM GOOD ENOUGH FOR ME!
*X-MEN #191, REMEMBER -- AnnN.

OBSERVATION: PHYSICAL APPEARANCE DRAWS UNWANTED ATTENTION TO THIS UNIT, MAY JEOPARDIZE BOTH UNIT AND MISSION.

CONCLUSION: FEATURES AND BEHAVIOR MUST BE FURTHER MODIFIED TO BLEND MORE WITH INDIGENOUS POPULACE.

THOMAS RODRIGUEZ' COMPUTER SYSTEM IS PRIMITIVE-- VIRTUALLY NO MEMORY, WOEFULLY SLOW-WITTED, ARCHAIC IN DESIGN AND CONSTRUCTION--

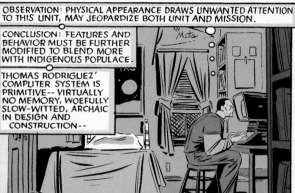

-- HOWEVER, MODEM ALLOWS THIS UNIT TO LINK WITH HIGHER-ORDER MAINFRAMES.

MUTANT ENTITY CODEX *RACHEL SUMMERS* ESCAPED TERMINATION BY SHIFTING HER PHYSICAL BEING THROUGH TIME. HUNTER ENTITY CODEX *NIMROD*-- THIS UNIT-- ATTEMPTED TO MECHANICALLY REPLICATE PROCEDURE.

UNIT FOUND HIMSELF CAUGHT IN AN UNUSUAL ENERGY FLUX FOR WHICH MEMORY CELLS HAD NO ANALOGUE OR EXPLANATION, AND SWEPT TO THIS SPACE/TIME CONTINUUM.

INTERROGATION OF OTHER SYSTEMS REVEALS SIGNIFICANT ANOMALIES BETWEEN HISTORICAL DATA IN THIS UNIT'S FILES AND THEIRS, THE WORLD AS THIS UNIT REMEMBERS IT AND AS IT CURRENTLY EXISTS.

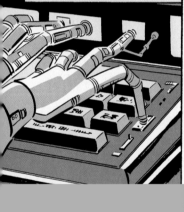

CONCLUSION: THIS UNIT MOVED *CROSSTIME* AS WELL AS DOWN.

AND RESIDES ON AN EARTH THAT IS SIMILAR TO, BUT NOT HIS OWN.

QUERY: WHAT NEXT?

NIMROD'S PRIMARY PROGRAMMING IS TO DEFEND HUMANITY.

IN THIS UNIT'S ORIGIN TIME, FULFILLMENT REQUIRED THE EXTERMINATION OF MUTANTKIND. BUT DOES THE SAME HOLD TRUE HERE? IF THE OPERATIONAL PARAMETERS CHANGE, DOES THAT NOT ALSO CHANGE THE CONCLUSION?

INSUFFICIENT DATA FOR PROPER ANALYSIS-- MORE IS REQUIRED BEFORE FINAL DECISION.

...INTERRUPT THIS PROGRAM FOR A SPECIAL NEWS BULLETIN--

--THE SUPER-VILLAIN, *JUGGERNAUT*, HAS BEEN SIGHTED IN LOWER MANHATTAN. POLICE SWAT UNITS ARE ON THE ALERT AND THE AVENGERS HAVE BEEN NOTIFIED...

...STAY TUNED FOR FURTHER DETAILS.

THIS UNIT'S DUTY IS CLEAR-- NIMROD WILL LOCATE AND *NEUTRALIZE* THOSE ANOMALIES LABELLED AS *OUTLAWS*: THE *JUGGERNAUT*...

...AND THE *UNCANNY X-MEN*. THEY WILL BE *TERMINATED*.

TO *LEN WEIN* AND *DAVE COCKRUM*, WHO HAD THE DREAM... AND *TOM ORZECHOWSKI* AND *GLYNIS WEIN*, WHO'VE BEEN WITH US FROM THE VERY BEGINNING.

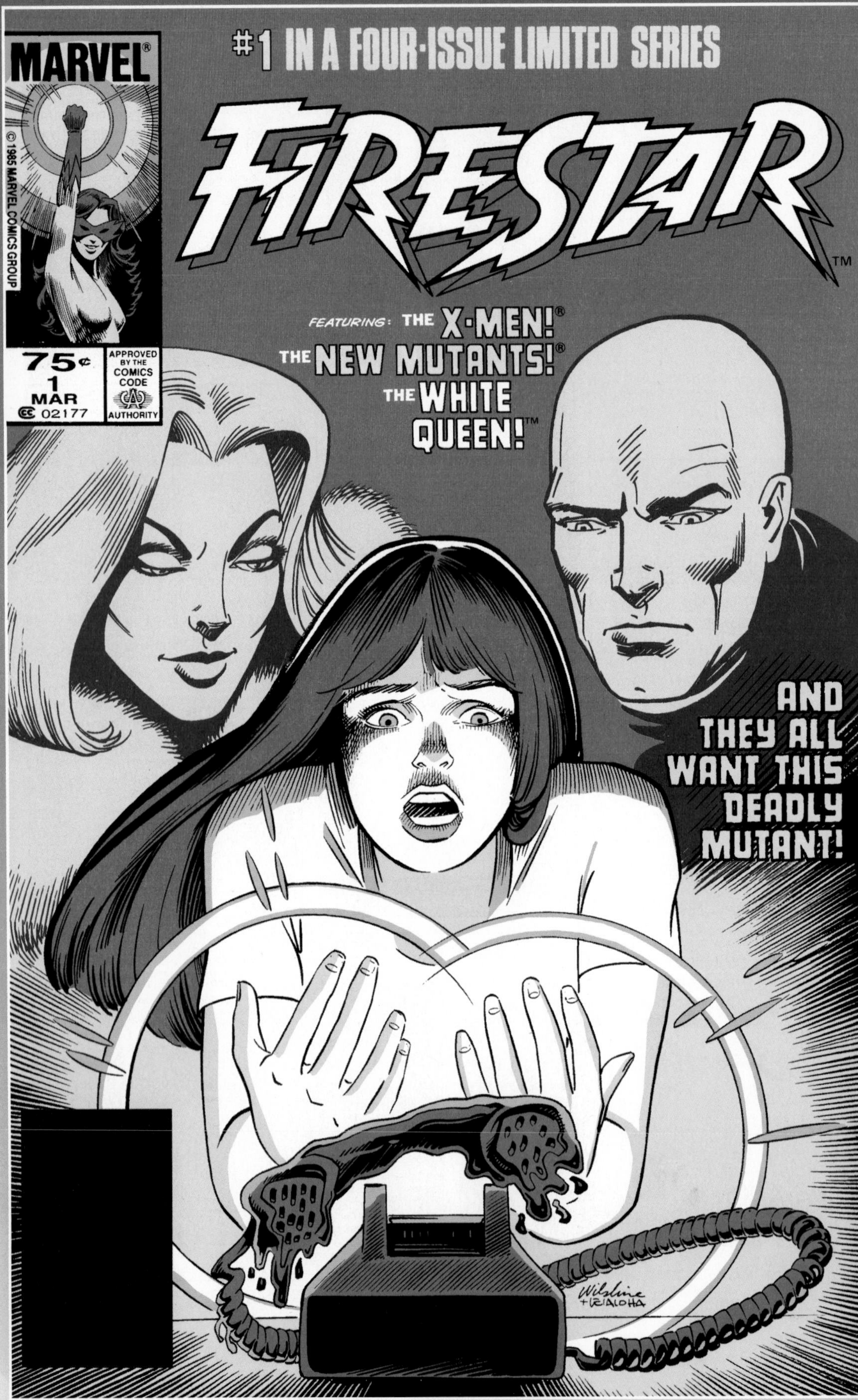

#1 IN A FOUR-ISSUE LIMITED SERIES
MARVEL®
© 1985 MARVEL COMICS GROUP
75¢
1
MAR
02177
APPROVED BY THE COMICS CODE AUTHORITY
FIRESTAR™
FEATURING: THE X-MEN!®
THE NEW MUTANTS!®
THE WHITE QUEEN!™
AND THEY ALL WANT THIS DEADLY MUTANT!

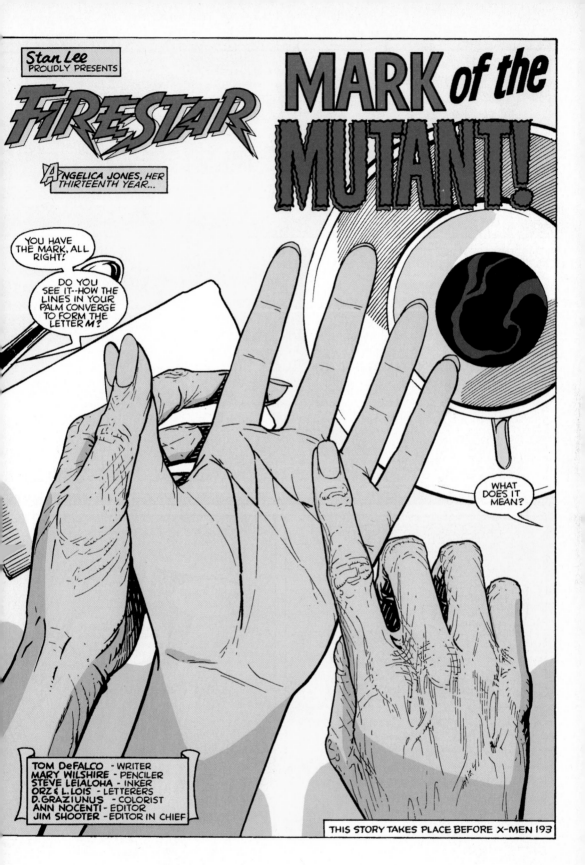

Stan Lee PROUDLY PRESENTS

FiReStAr

MARK of the MUTANT!

ANGELICA JONES, HER THIRTEENTH YEAR...

YOU HAVE THE MARK, ALL RIGHT!

DO YOU SEE IT--HOW THE LINES IN YOUR PALM CONVERGE TO FORM THE LETTER M?

WHAT DOES IT MEAN?

TOM DeFALCO - WRITER
MARY WILSHIRE - PENCILER
STEVE LEIALOHA - INKER
ORZ & L. LOIS - LETTERERS
D. GRAZIUNUS - COLORIST
ANN NOCENTI - EDITOR
JIM SHOOTER - EDITOR IN CHIEF

THIS STORY TAKES PLACE BEFORE X-MEN 193.

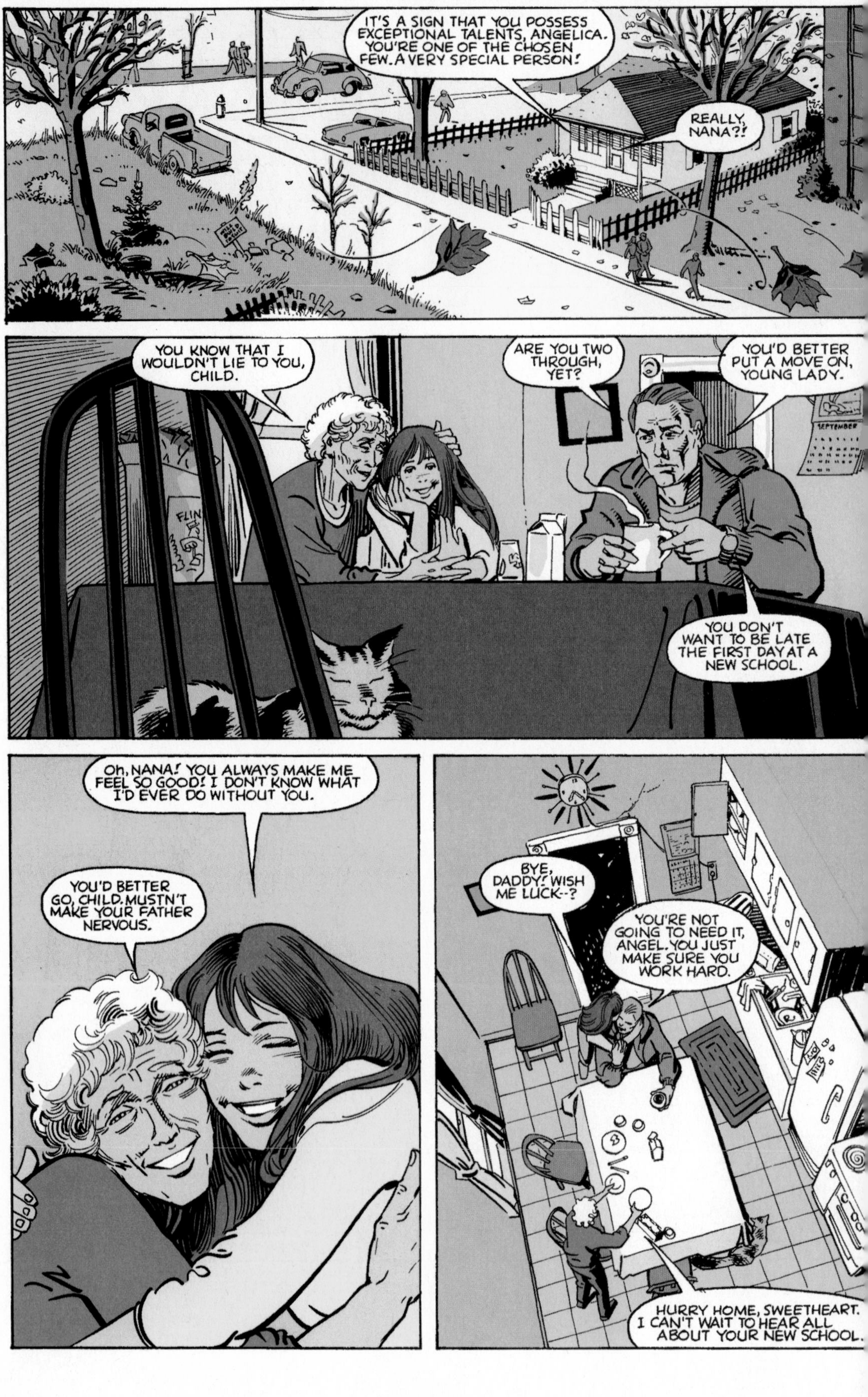

IT'S A SIGN THAT YOU POSSESS EXCEPTIONAL TALENTS, ANGELICA. YOU'RE ONE OF THE CHOSEN FEW. A VERY SPECIAL PERSON!
REALLY, NANA?!
YOU KNOW THAT I WOULDN'T LIE TO YOU, CHILD.
ARE YOU TWO THROUGH, YET?
YOU'D BETTER PUT A MOVE ON, YOUNG LADY.
YOU DON'T WANT TO BE LATE THE FIRST DAY AT A NEW SCHOOL.
Oh, NANA! YOU ALWAYS MAKE ME FEEL SO GOOD! I DON'T KNOW WHAT I'D EVER DO WITHOUT YOU.
YOU'D BETTER GO, CHILD. MUSTN'T MAKE YOUR FATHER NERVOUS.
BYE, DADDY! WISH ME LUCK--?
YOU'RE NOT GOING TO NEED IT, ANGEL. YOU JUST MAKE SURE YOU WORK HARD.
HURRY HOME, SWEETHEART. I CAN'T WAIT TO HEAR ALL ABOUT YOUR NEW SCHOOL.

SLAM

Y'KNOW, MA, I REALLY WISH YOU WOULDN'T MAKE SUCH A FUSS OVER ANGELICA. IT ISN'T RIGHT TO TELL HER SHE'S SO SPECIAL--WHEN SHE'S ONLY AN AVERAGE STUDENT.

WHY NOT? WHAT'S THE HARM IN IT?

THE CHILD COULD USE SOME ENCOURAGEMENT. SHE'S VERY INTELLIGENT-- AND IT ISN'T HER FAULT THAT SHE LOST HER MOTHER--OR THAT SHE'S CONSTANTLY MOVING FROM SCHOOL TO SCHOOL BECAUSE OF YOUR JOB!

GET OFF MY BACK, MA! YOU KNOW HOW MUCH I HATE TO KEEP UPROOTING THE FAMILY, BUT I'VE GOT TO GO WHERE THERE'S WORK...

I KNOW, SON, AND I DON'T MEAN TO CRITICIZE. IT'S JUST THAT A SENSITIVE GIRL LIKE ANGELICA NEEDS...

UNN

MA--!

I--I'M ALL RIGHT, BARTHOLOMEW! JUST GIVE ME A SECOND TO CATCH MY BREATH...

THE SPELLS SEEM TO BE GETTING WORSE, MA. THERE'S GOTTA BE SOMETHING WE CAN DO! MAYBE ANOTHER DOCTOR--!

NO, SON! WE'VE ALREADY WASTED ENOUGH MONEY ON DOCTORS.

THERE ISN'T ANYTHING THEY CAN DO FOR ME. I'M JUST AN OLD WOMAN WHO'S STARTING TO WEAR OUT.

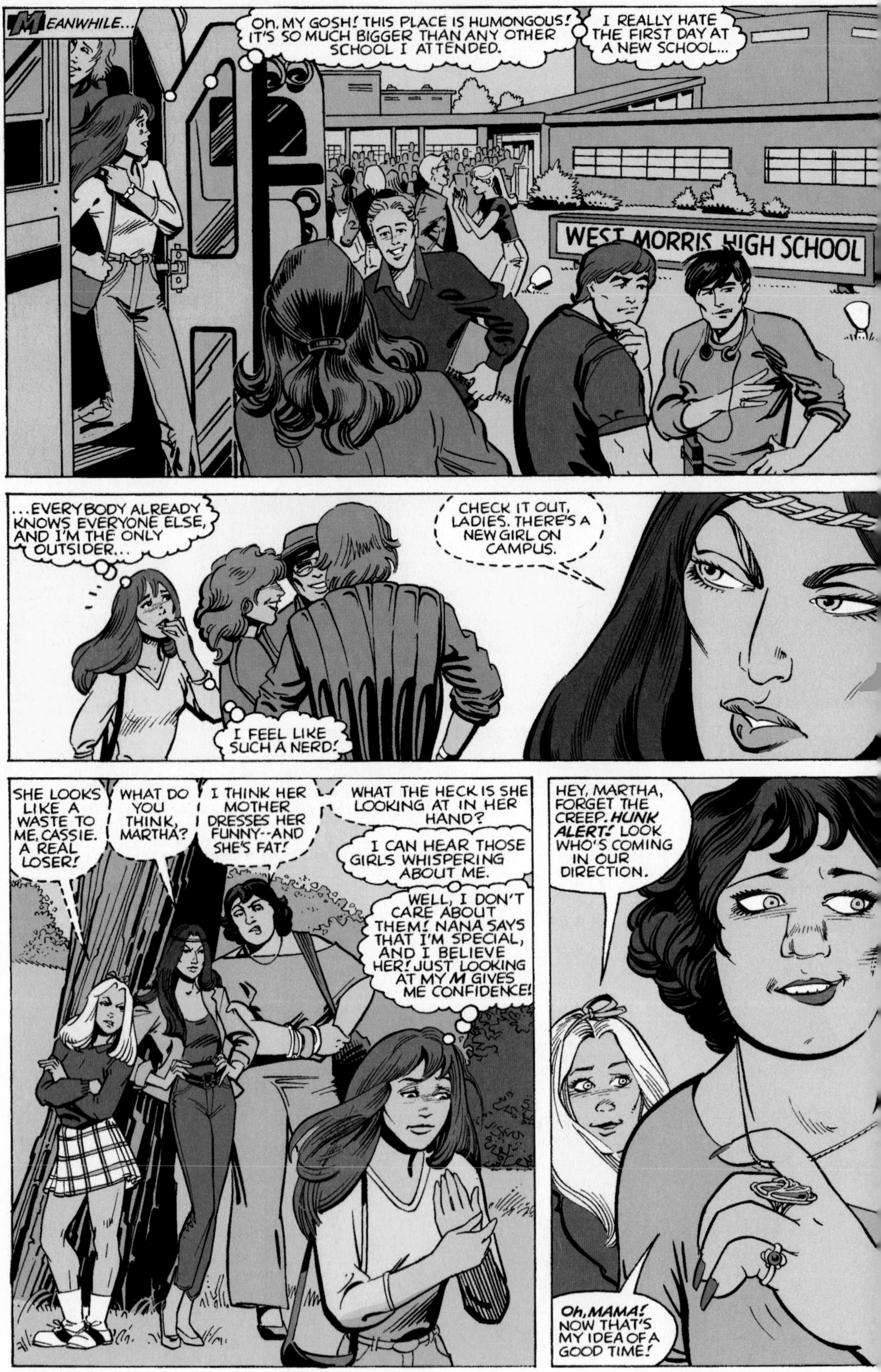
MEANWHILE...
Oh, MY GOSH! THIS PLACE IS HUMONGOUS! IT'S SO MUCH BIGGER THAN ANY OTHER SCHOOL I ATTENDED.
I REALLY HATE THE FIRST DAY AT A NEW SCHOOL...
WEST MORRIS HIGH SCHOOL
...EVERYBODY ALREADY KNOWS EVERYONE ELSE, AND I'M THE ONLY OUTSIDER...
CHECK IT OUT, LADIES. THERE'S A NEW GIRL ON CAMPUS.
I FEEL LIKE SUCH A NERD!
SHE LOOKS LIKE A WASTE TO ME, CASSIE. A REAL LOSER!
WHAT DO YOU THINK, MARTHA?
I THINK HER MOTHER DRESSES HER FUNNY--AND SHE'S FAT!
WHAT THE HECK IS SHE LOOKING AT IN HER HAND?
I CAN HEAR THOSE GIRLS WHISPERING ABOUT ME.
WELL, I DON'T CARE ABOUT THEM! NANA SAYS THAT I'M SPECIAL, AND I BELIEVE HER! JUST LOOKING AT MY M GIVES ME CONFIDENCE!
HEY, MARTHA, FORGET THE CREEP. HUNK ALERT! LOOK WHO'S COMING IN OUR DIRECTION.
Oh, MAMA! NOW THAT'S MY IDEA OF A GOOD TIME!

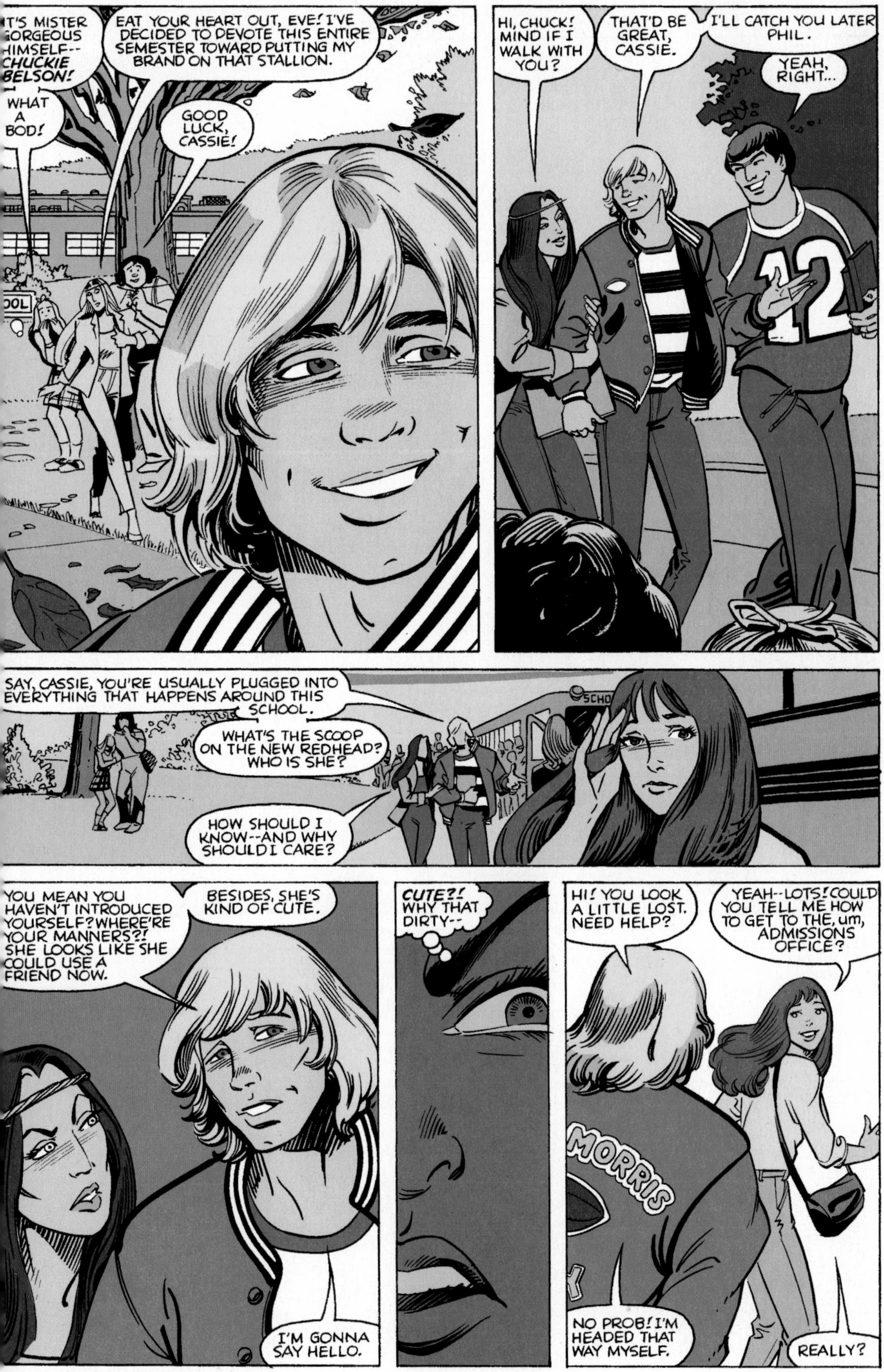

IT'S MISTER GORGEOUS HIMSELF-- CHUCKIE BELSON!
EAT YOUR HEART OUT, EVE! I'VE DECIDED TO DEVOTE THIS ENTIRE SEMESTER TOWARD PUTTING MY BRAND ON THAT STALLION.
WHAT A BOD!
GOOD LUCK, CASSIE!
HI, CHUCK! MIND IF I WALK WITH YOU?
THAT'D BE GREAT, CASSIE.
I'LL CATCH YOU LATER PHIL.
YEAH, RIGHT...
12
SAY, CASSIE, YOU'RE USUALLY PLUGGED INTO EVERYTHING THAT HAPPENS AROUND THIS SCHOOL.
WHAT'S THE SCOOP ON THE NEW REDHEAD? WHO IS SHE?
HOW SHOULD I KNOW--AND WHY SHOULD I CARE?
YOU MEAN YOU HAVEN'T INTRODUCED YOURSELF? WHERE'RE YOUR MANNERS?! SHE LOOKS LIKE SHE COULD USE A FRIEND NOW.
BESIDES, SHE'S KIND OF CUTE.
I'M GONNA SAY HELLO.
CUTE?! WHY THAT DIRTY--
HI! YOU LOOK A LITTLE LOST. NEED HELP?
YEAH--LOTS! COULD YOU TELL ME HOW TO GET TO THE, um, ADMISSIONS OFFICE?
MORRIS
NO PROB! I'M HEADED THAT WAY MYSELF.
REALLY?

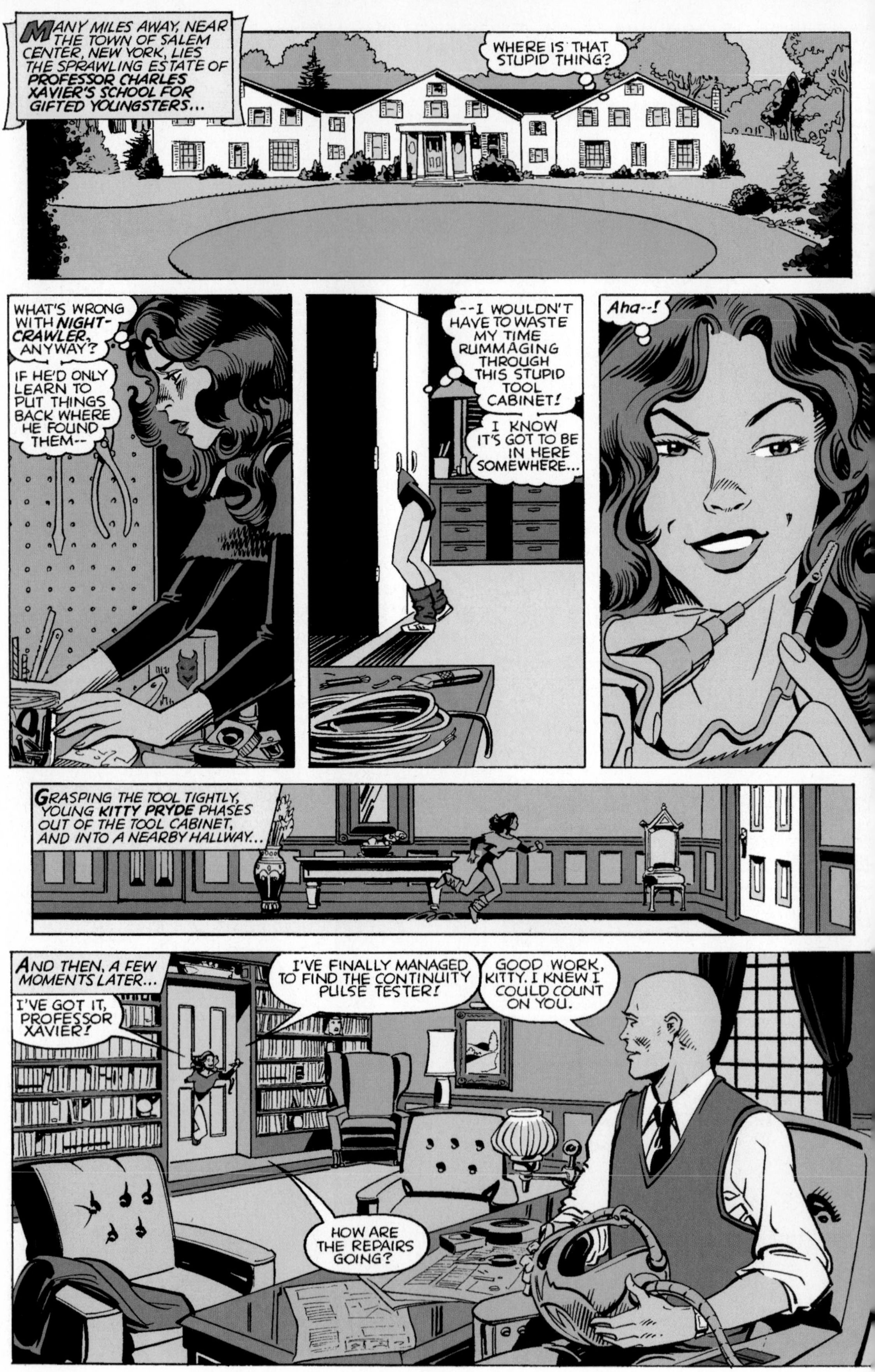

MANY MILES AWAY, NEAR THE TOWN OF SALEM CENTER, NEW YORK, LIES THE SPRAWLING ESTATE OF PROFESSOR CHARLES XAVIER'S SCHOOL FOR GIFTED YOUNGSTERS...
WHERE IS THAT STUPID THING?
WHAT'S WRONG WITH NIGHTCRAWLER, ANYWAY?
IF HE'D ONLY LEARN TO PUT THINGS BACK WHERE HE FOUND THEM--
--I WOULDN'T HAVE TO WASTE MY TIME RUMMAGING THROUGH THIS STUPID TOOL CABINET!
I KNOW IT'S GOT TO BE IN HERE SOMEWHERE...
Aha--!
GRASPING THE TOOL TIGHTLY, YOUNG KITTY PRYDE PHASES OUT OF THE TOOL CABINET, AND INTO A NEARBY HALLWAY...
AND THEN, A FEW MOMENTS LATER...
I'VE GOT IT, PROFESSOR XAVIER!
I'VE FINALLY MANAGED TO FIND THE CONTINUITY PULSE TESTER!
GOOD WORK, KITTY. I KNEW I COULD COUNT ON YOU.
HOW ARE THE REPAIRS GOING?

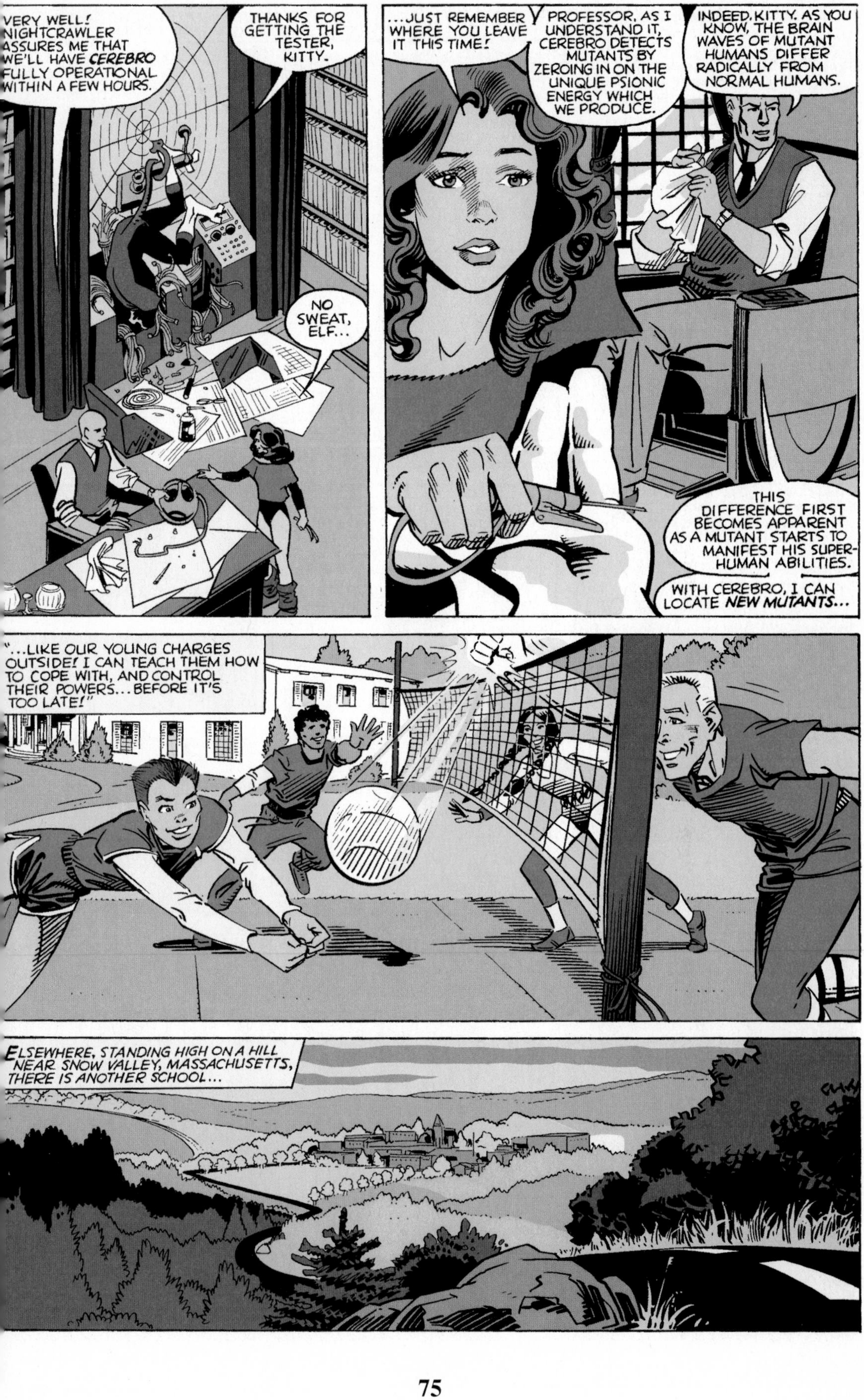
VERY WELL! NIGHTCRAWLER ASSURES ME THAT WE'LL HAVE *CEREBRO* FULLY OPERATIONAL WITHIN A FEW HOURS.
THANKS FOR GETTING THE TESTER, KITTY.
NO SWEAT, ELF...
...JUST REMEMBER WHERE YOU LEAVE IT THIS TIME!
PROFESSOR, AS I UNDERSTAND IT, CEREBRO DETECTS MUTANTS BY ZEROING IN ON THE UNIQUE PSIONIC ENERGY WHICH WE PRODUCE.
INDEED, KITTY. AS YOU KNOW, THE BRAIN WAVES OF MUTANT HUMANS DIFFER RADICALLY FROM NORMAL HUMANS.
THIS DIFFERENCE FIRST BECOMES APPARENT AS A MUTANT STARTS TO MANIFEST HIS SUPER-HUMAN ABILITIES.
WITH CEREBRO, I CAN LOCATE ***NEW MUTANTS***...
"...LIKE OUR YOUNG CHARGES OUTSIDE! I CAN TEACH THEM HOW TO COPE WITH, AND CONTROL THEIR POWERS... BEFORE IT'S TOO LATE!"
ELSEWHERE, STANDING HIGH ON A HILL NEAR SNOW VALLEY, MASSACHUSETTS, THERE IS ANOTHER SCHOOL...

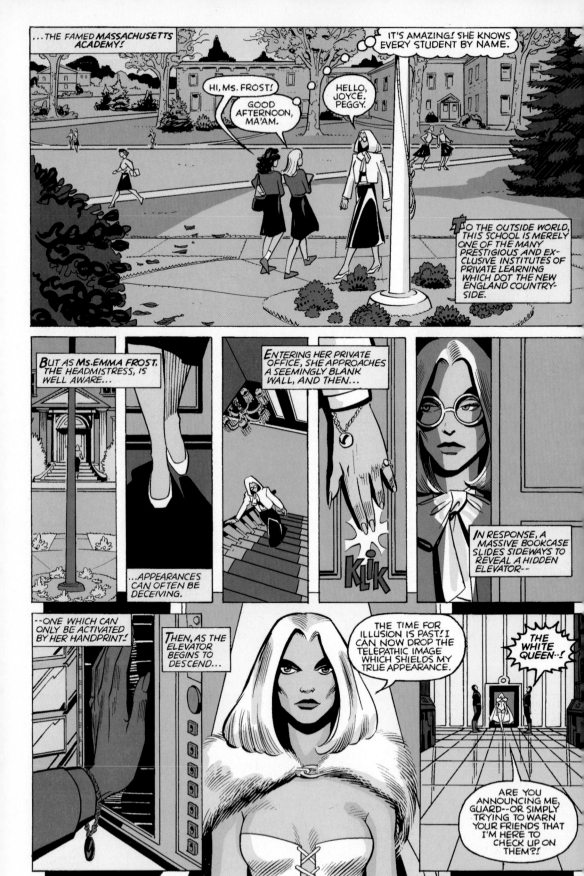

...THE FAMED *MASSACHUSETTS ACADEMY!*

IT'S AMAZING! SHE KNOWS EVERY STUDENT BY NAME.

HI, MS. FROST!

GOOD AFTERNOON, MA'AM.

HELLO, JOYCE, PEGGY.

To THE OUTSIDE WORLD, THIS SCHOOL IS MERELY ONE OF THE MANY PRESTIGIOUS AND EXCLUSIVE INSTITUTES OF PRIVATE LEARNING WHICH DOT THE NEW ENGLAND COUNTRYSIDE.

BUT AS *MS. EMMA FROST,* THE HEADMISTRESS, IS WELL AWARE...

ENTERING HER PRIVATE OFFICE, SHE APPROACHES A SEEMINGLY BLANK WALL, AND THEN...

...APPEARANCES CAN OFTEN BE DECEIVING.

KLIK

IN RESPONSE, A MASSIVE BOOKCASE SLIDES SIDEWAYS TO REVEAL A HIDDEN ELEVATOR--

--ONE WHICH CAN ONLY BE ACTIVATED BY HER HANDPRINT!

THEN, AS THE ELEVATOR BEGINS TO DESCEND...

THE TIME FOR ILLUSION IS PAST! I CAN NOW DROP THE TELEPATHIC IMAGE WHICH SHIELDS MY TRUE APPEARANCE.

THE WHITE QUEEN--!

ARE YOU ANNOUNCING ME, GUARD--OR SIMPLY TRYING TO WARN YOUR FRIENDS THAT I'M HERE TO CHECK UP ON THEM?!

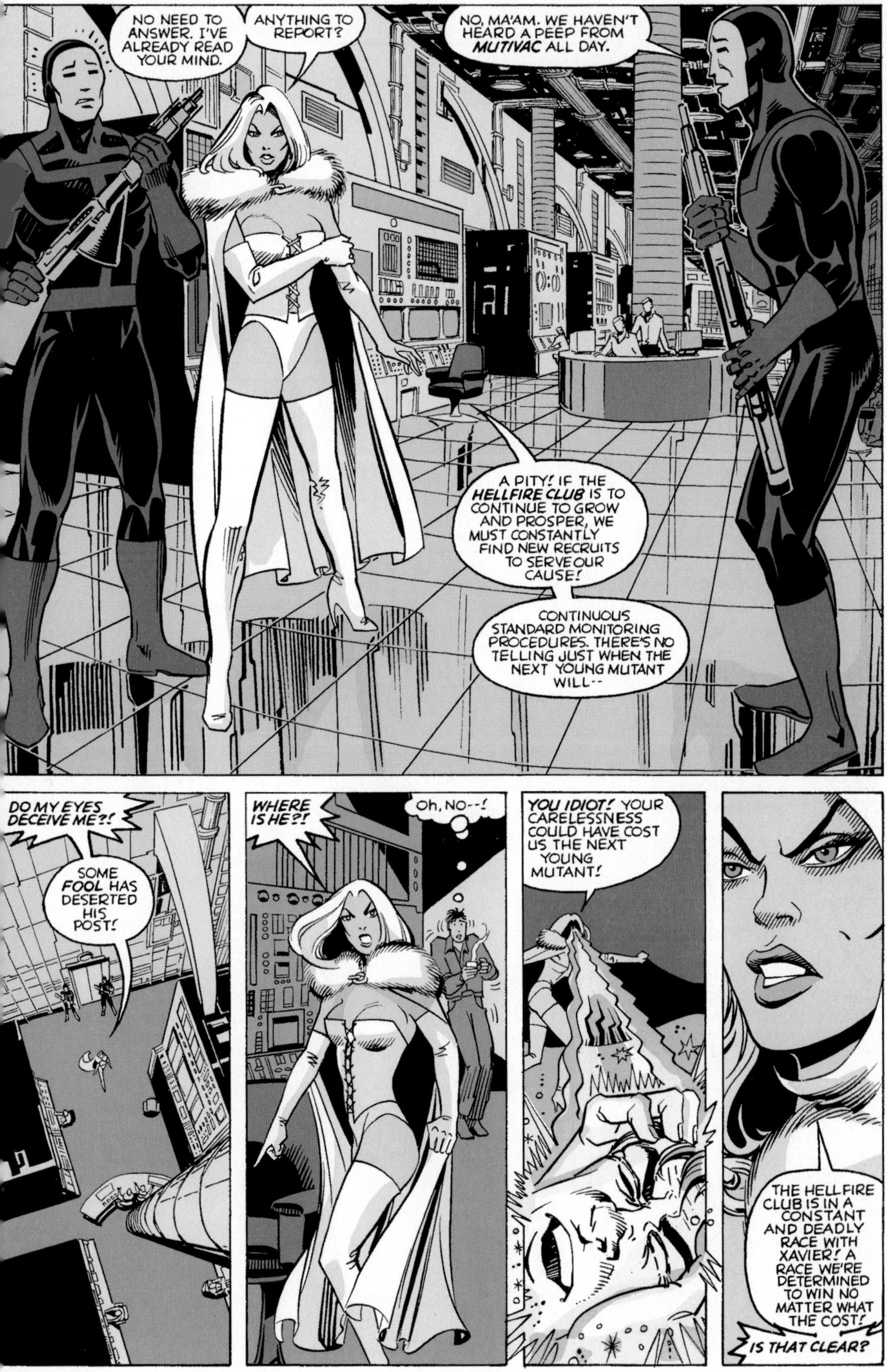
NO NEED TO ANSWER. I'VE ALREADY READ YOUR MIND.
ANYTHING TO REPORT?
NO, MA'AM. WE HAVEN'T HEARD A PEEP FROM MUTIVAC ALL DAY.
A PITY! IF THE HELLFIRE CLUB IS TO CONTINUE TO GROW AND PROSPER, WE MUST CONSTANTLY FIND NEW RECRUITS TO SERVE OUR CAUSE!
CONTINUOUS STANDARD MONITORING PROCEDURES. THERE'S NO TELLING JUST WHEN THE NEXT YOUNG MUTANT WILL--
DO MY EYES DECEIVE ME?!
SOME FOOL HAS DESERTED HIS POST!
WHERE IS HE?!
Oh, NO--!
YOU IDIOT! YOUR CARELESSNESS COULD HAVE COST US THE NEXT YOUNG MUTANT!
THE HELLFIRE CLUB IS IN A CONSTANT AND DEADLY RACE WITH XAVIER! A RACE WE'RE DETERMINED TO WIN NO MATTER WHAT THE COST!
IS THAT CLEAR?

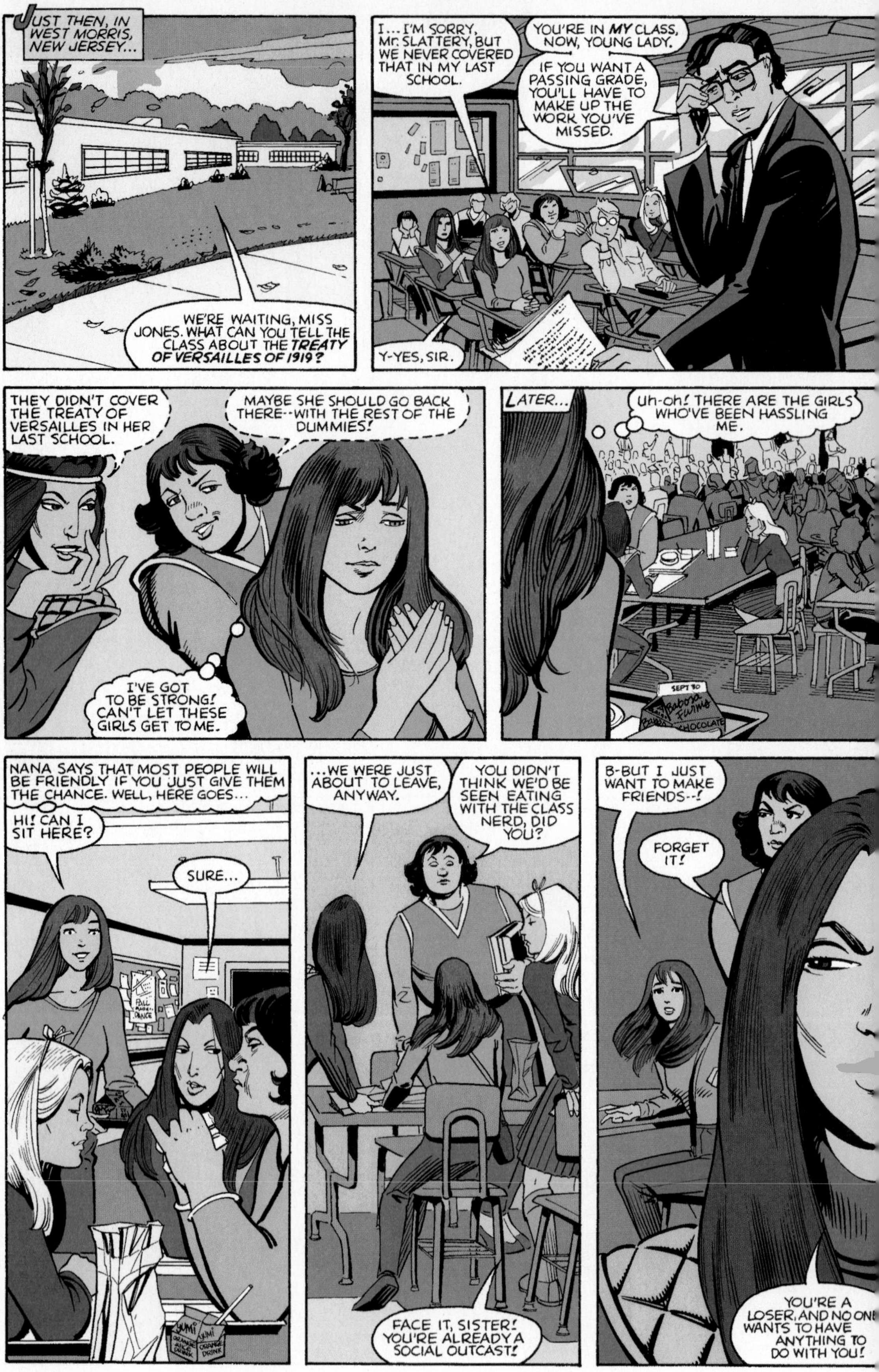

JUST THEN, IN WEST MORRIS, NEW JERSEY...
WE'RE WAITING, MISS JONES. WHAT CAN YOU TELL THE CLASS ABOUT THE TREATY OF VERSAILLES OF 1919?
I... I'M SORRY, Mr. SLATTERY, BUT WE NEVER COVERED THAT IN MY LAST SCHOOL.
YOU'RE IN MY CLASS, NOW, YOUNG LADY.
IF YOU WANT A PASSING GRADE, YOU'LL HAVE TO MAKE UP THE WORK YOU'VE MISSED.
Y-YES, SIR.
THEY DIDN'T COVER THE TREATY OF VERSAILLES IN HER LAST SCHOOL.
MAYBE SHE SHOULD GO BACK THERE--WITH THE REST OF THE DUMMIES!
I'VE GOT TO BE STRONG! CAN'T LET THESE GIRLS GET TO ME.
LATER...
Uh-oh! THERE ARE THE GIRLS WHO'VE BEEN HASSLING ME.
SEPT 30
Babosa Farms
CHOCOLATE
NANA SAYS THAT MOST PEOPLE WILL BE FRIENDLY IF YOU JUST GIVE THEM THE CHANCE. WELL, HERE GOES...
HI! CAN I SIT HERE?
SURE...
FALL DANCE
...WE WERE JUST ABOUT TO LEAVE, ANYWAY.
YOU DIDN'T THINK WE'D BE SEEN EATING WITH THE CLASS NERD, DID YOU?
FACE IT, SISTER! YOU'RE ALREADY A SOCIAL OUTCAST!
B-BUT I JUST WANT TO MAKE FRIENDS--!
FORGET IT!
YOU'RE A LOSER, AND NO ONE WANTS TO HAVE ANYTHING TO DO WITH YOU!

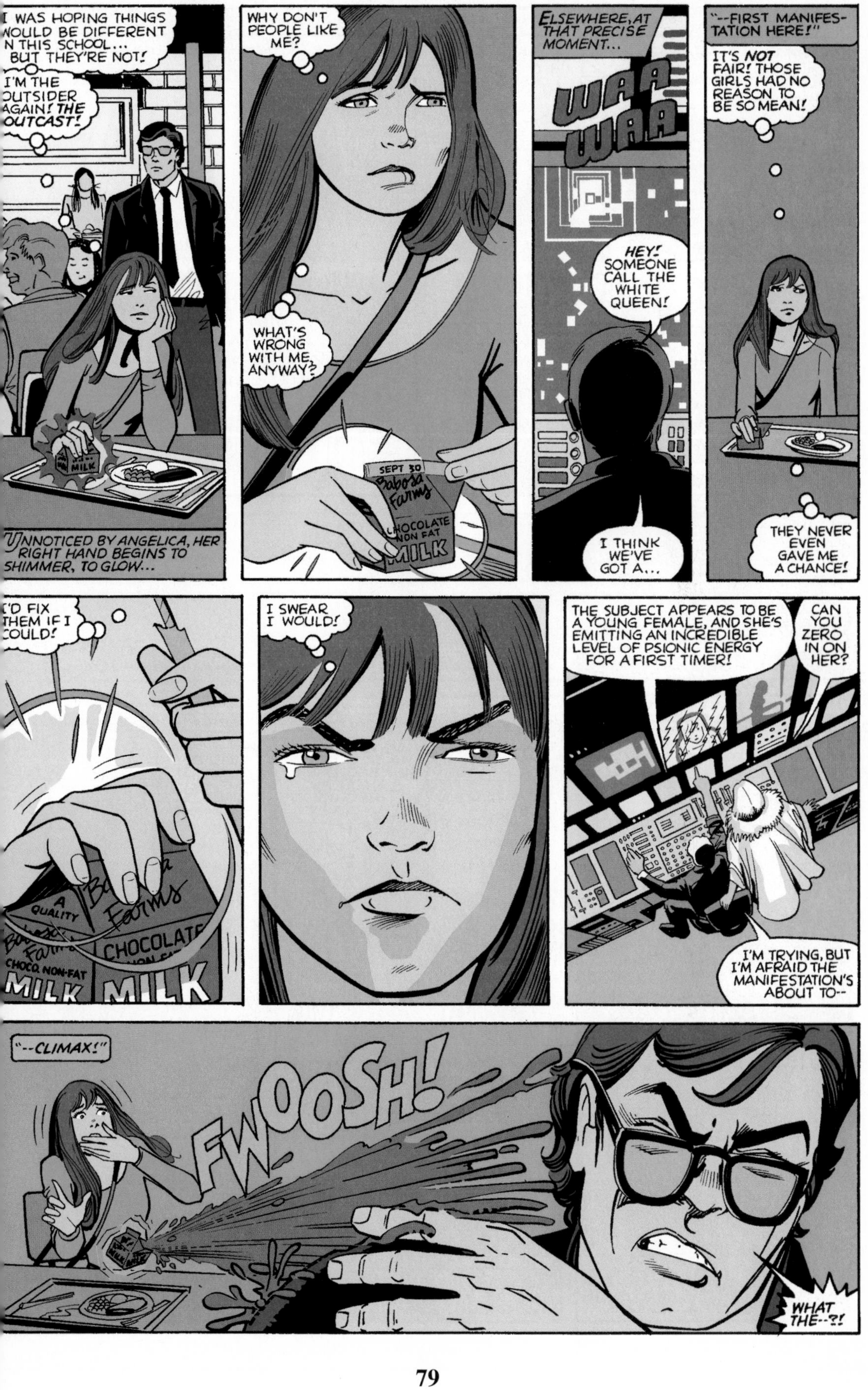
I WAS HOPING THINGS WOULD BE DIFFERENT IN THIS SCHOOL... BUT THEY'RE NOT!
I'M THE OUTSIDER AGAIN! THE OUTCAST!
MILK
UNNOTICED BY ANGELICA, HER RIGHT HAND BEGINS TO SHIMMER, TO GLOW...
WHY DON'T PEOPLE LIKE ME?
WHAT'S WRONG WITH ME, ANYWAY?
SEPT 30
Babosa Farms
CHOCOLATE NON FAT MILK
ELSEWHERE, AT THAT PRECISE MOMENT...
WAA WAA
HEY! SOMEONE CALL THE WHITE QUEEN!
I THINK WE'VE GOT A...
"--FIRST MANIFESTATION HERE!"
IT'S NOT FAIR! THOSE GIRLS HAD NO REASON TO BE SO MEAN!
THEY NEVER EVEN GAVE ME A CHANCE!
I'D FIX THEM IF I COULD!
A QUALITY
CHOCOLATE
CHOCO. NON-FAT
MILK MILK
I SWEAR I WOULD!
THE SUBJECT APPEARS TO BE A YOUNG FEMALE, AND SHE'S EMITTING AN INCREDIBLE LEVEL OF PSIONIC ENERGY FOR A FIRST TIMER!
CAN YOU ZERO IN ON HER?
I'M TRYING, BUT I'M AFRAID THE MANIFESTATION'S ABOUT TO--
"--CLIMAX!"
FWOOSH!
WHAT THE--?!

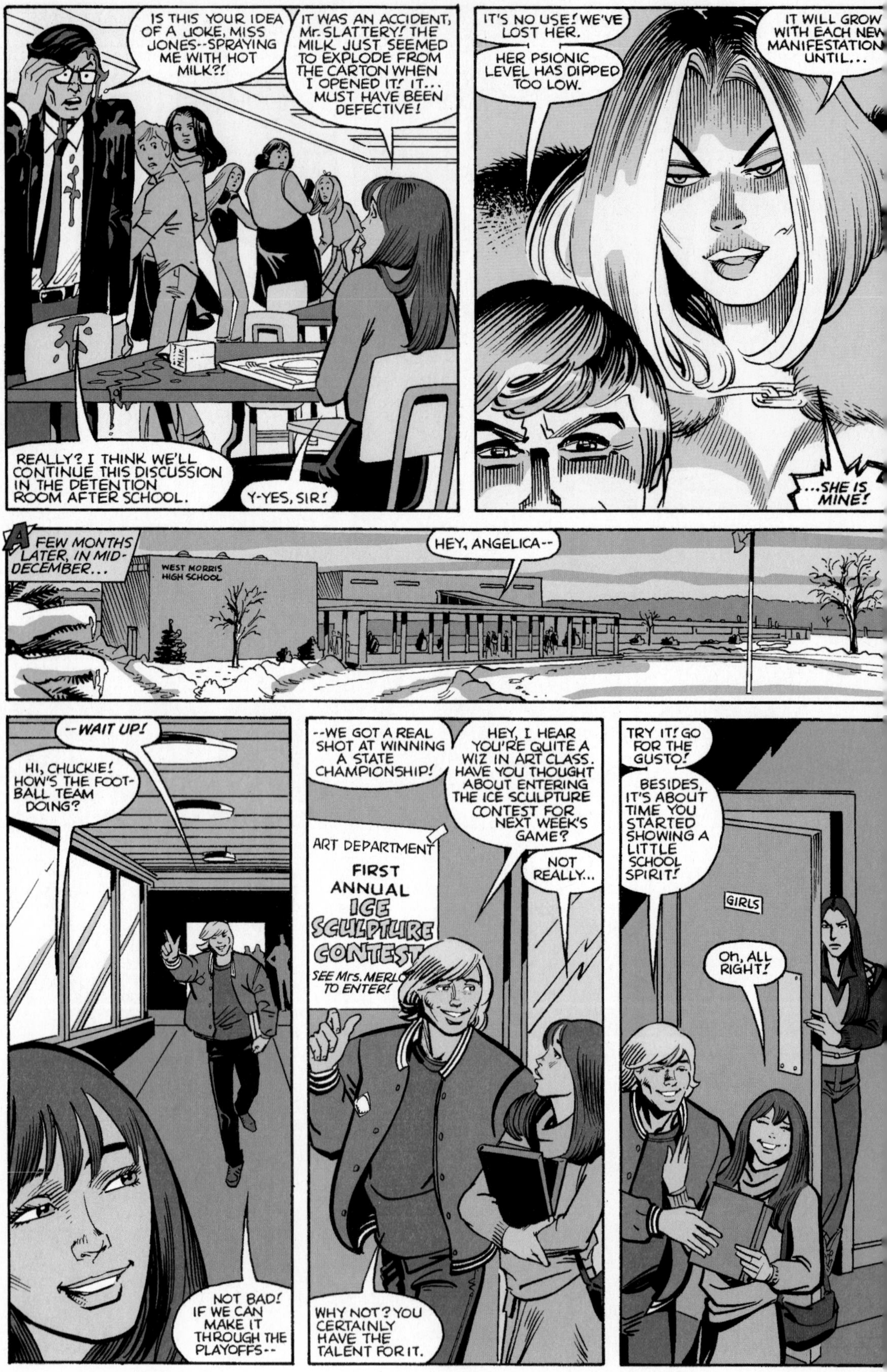

IS THIS YOUR IDEA OF A JOKE, MISS JONES--SPRAYING ME WITH HOT MILK?!
IT WAS AN ACCIDENT, Mr. SLATTERY! THE MILK JUST SEEMED TO EXPLODE FROM THE CARTON WHEN I OPENED IT! IT... MUST HAVE BEEN DEFECTIVE!
MILK
REALLY? I THINK WE'LL CONTINUE THIS DISCUSSION IN THE DETENTION ROOM AFTER SCHOOL.
Y-YES, SIR!
IT'S NO USE! WE'VE LOST HER.
HER PSIONIC LEVEL HAS DIPPED TOO LOW.
IT WILL GROW WITH EACH NEW MANIFESTATION UNTIL...
...SHE IS MINE!
A FEW MONTHS LATER, IN MID-DECEMBER...
WEST MORRIS HIGH SCHOOL
HEY, ANGELICA--
--WAIT UP!
HI, CHUCKIE! HOW'S THE FOOTBALL TEAM DOING?
NOT BAD! IF WE CAN MAKE IT THROUGH THE PLAYOFFS--
--WE GOT A REAL SHOT AT WINNING A STATE CHAMPIONSHIP!
HEY, I HEAR YOU'RE QUITE A WIZ IN ART CLASS. HAVE YOU THOUGHT ABOUT ENTERING THE ICE SCULPTURE CONTEST FOR NEXT WEEK'S GAME?
ART DEPARTMENT
FIRST ANNUAL ICE SCULPTURE CONTEST
SEE Mrs. MERLO TO ENTER!
NOT REALLY...
WHY NOT? YOU CERTAINLY HAVE THE TALENT FOR IT.
TRY IT! GO FOR THE GUSTO!
BESIDES, IT'S ABOUT TIME YOU STARTED SHOWING A LITTLE SCHOOL SPIRIT!
GIRLS
Oh, ALL RIGHT!

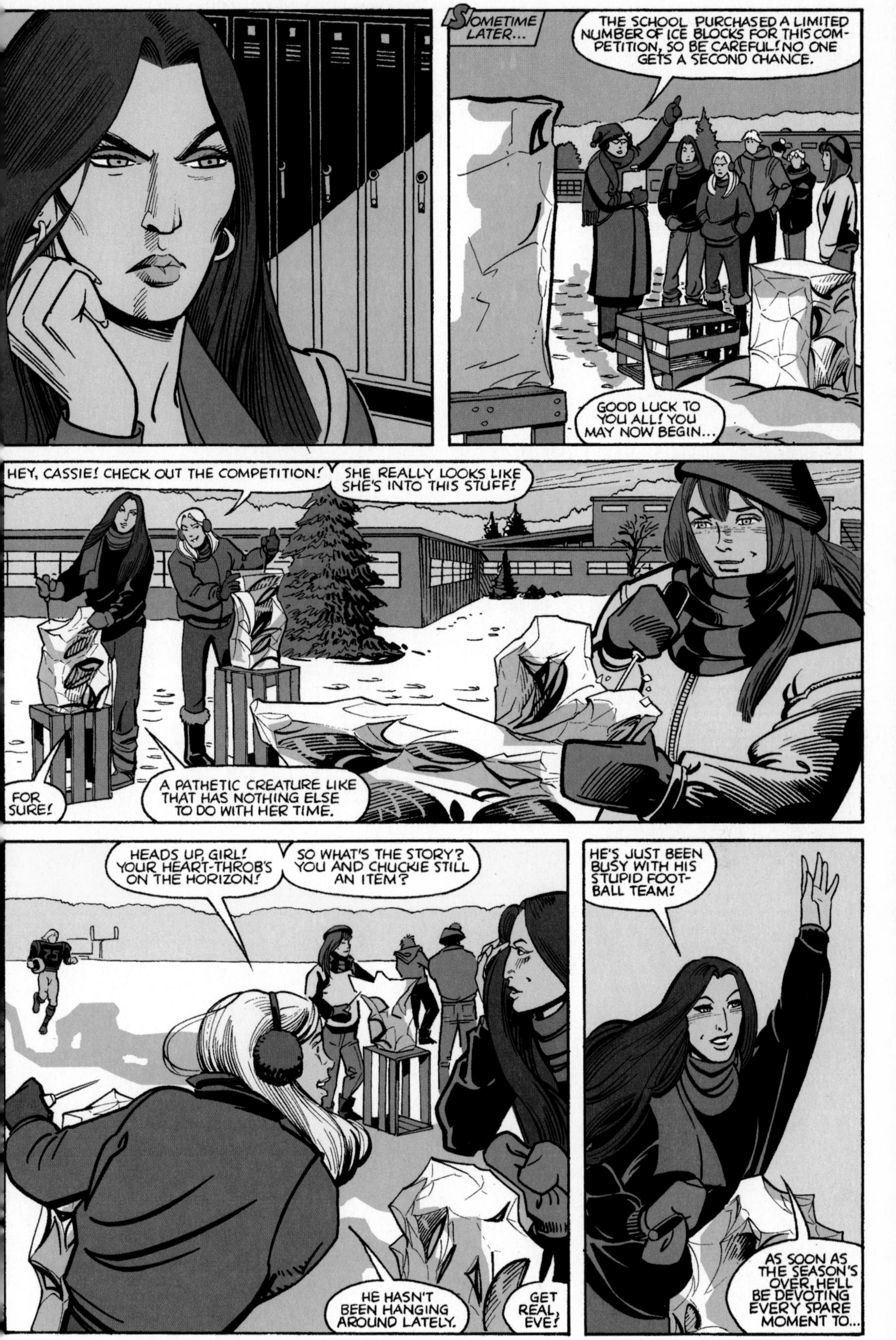
SOMETIME LATER...
THE SCHOOL PURCHASED A LIMITED NUMBER OF ICE BLOCKS FOR THIS COMPETITION, SO BE CAREFUL! NO ONE GETS A SECOND CHANCE.
GOOD LUCK TO YOU ALL! YOU MAY NOW BEGIN...
HEY, CASSIE! CHECK OUT THE COMPETITION!
SHE REALLY LOOKS LIKE SHE'S INTO THIS STUFF!
FOR SURE!
A PATHETIC CREATURE LIKE THAT HAS NOTHING ELSE TO DO WITH HER TIME.
HEADS UP, GIRL! YOUR HEART-THROB'S ON THE HORIZON!
SO WHAT'S THE STORY? YOU AND CHUCKIE STILL AN ITEM?
HE HASN'T BEEN HANGING AROUND LATELY.
GET REAL, EVE!
HE'S JUST BEEN BUSY WITH HIS STUPID FOOTBALL TEAM!
AS SOON AS THE SEASON'S OVER, HE'LL BE DEVOTING EVERY SPARE MOMENT TO...

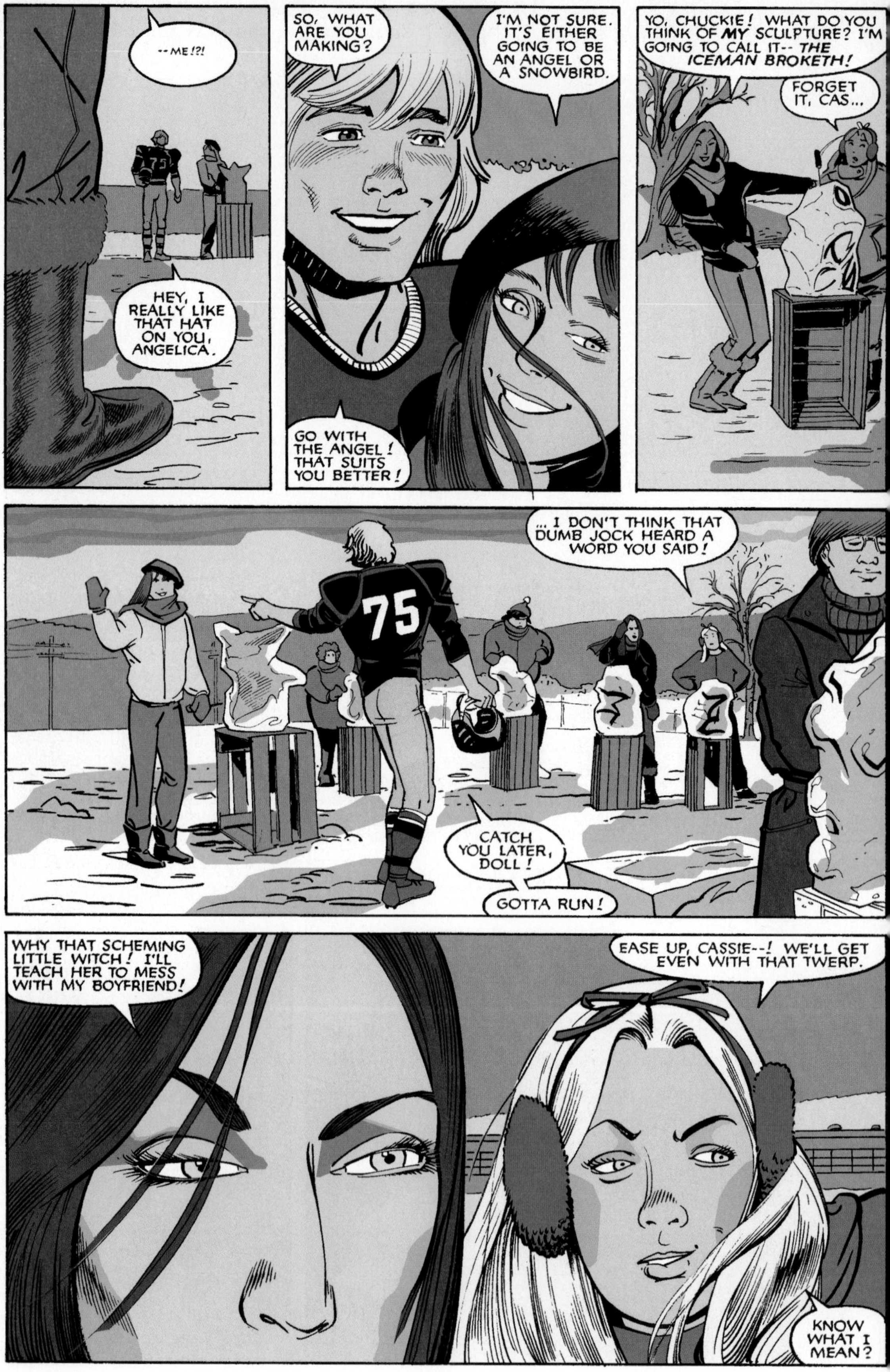
--ME!?!
HEY, I REALLY LIKE THAT HAT ON YOU, ANGELICA.
SO, WHAT ARE YOU MAKING?
I'M NOT SURE. IT'S EITHER GOING TO BE AN ANGEL OR A SNOWBIRD.
GO WITH THE ANGEL! THAT SUITS YOU BETTER!
YO, CHUCKIE! WHAT DO YOU THINK OF MY SCULPTURE? I'M GOING TO CALL IT-- THE ICEMAN BROKETH!
FORGET IT, CAS...
75
...I DON'T THINK THAT DUMB JOCK HEARD A WORD YOU SAID!
CATCH YOU LATER, DOLL!
GOTTA RUN!
WHY THAT SCHEMING LITTLE WITCH! I'LL TEACH HER TO MESS WITH MY BOYFRIEND!
EASE UP, CASSIE--! WE'LL GET EVEN WITH THAT TWERP.
KNOW WHAT I MEAN?

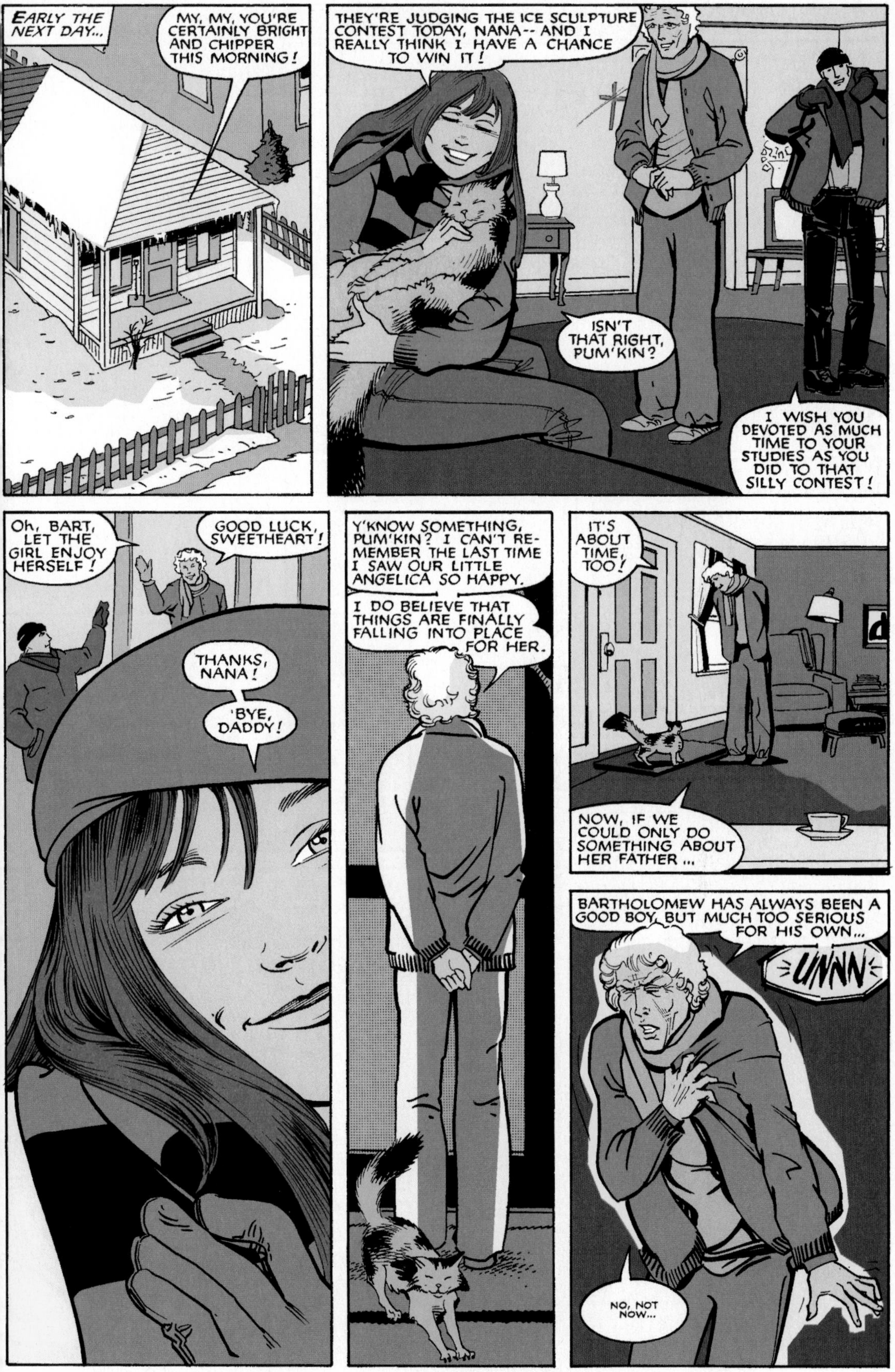
EARLY THE NEXT DAY...
MY, MY, YOU'RE CERTAINLY BRIGHT AND CHIPPER THIS MORNING!
THEY'RE JUDGING THE ICE SCULPTURE CONTEST TODAY, NANA-- AND I REALLY THINK I HAVE A CHANCE TO WIN IT!
ISN'T THAT RIGHT, PUM'KIN?
I WISH YOU DEVOTED AS MUCH TIME TO YOUR STUDIES AS YOU DID TO THAT SILLY CONTEST!
Oh, BART, LET THE GIRL ENJOY HERSELF!
GOOD LUCK, SWEETHEART!
THANKS, NANA!
'BYE, DADDY!
Y'KNOW SOMETHING, PUM'KIN? I CAN'T REMEMBER THE LAST TIME I SAW OUR LITTLE ANGELICA SO HAPPY.
I DO BELIEVE THAT THINGS ARE FINALLY FALLING INTO PLACE FOR HER.
IT'S ABOUT TIME, TOO!
NOW, IF WE COULD ONLY DO SOMETHING ABOUT HER FATHER ...
BARTHOLOMEW HAS ALWAYS BEEN A GOOD BOY, BUT MUCH TOO SERIOUS FOR HIS OWN...
UNNN
NO, NOT NOW...

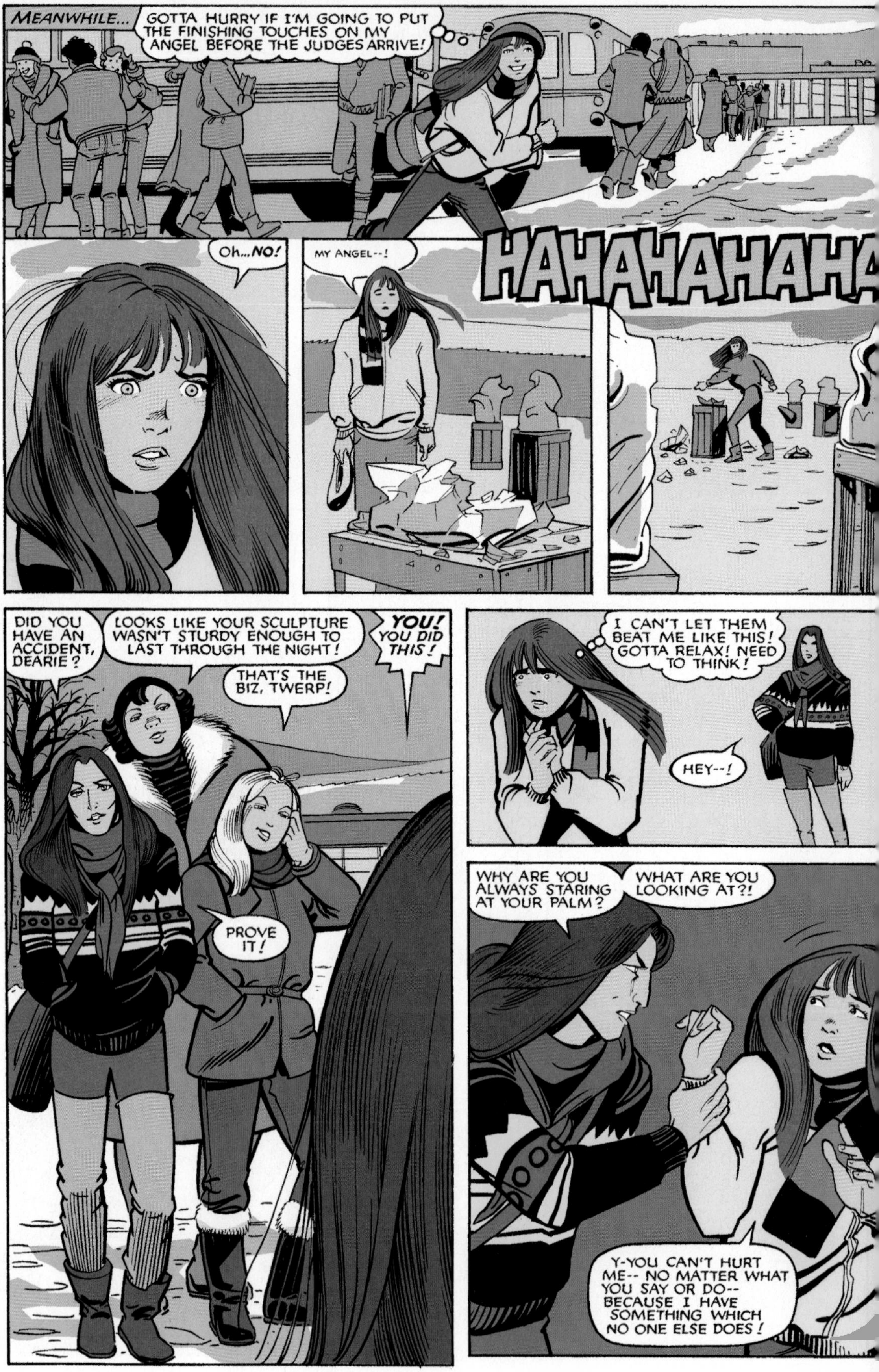
MEANWHILE...
GOTTA HURRY IF I'M GOING TO PUT THE FINISHING TOUCHES ON MY ANGEL BEFORE THE JUDGES ARRIVE!
Oh...NO!
MY ANGEL--!
HAHAHAHAHAHA
DID YOU HAVE AN ACCIDENT, DEARIE?
LOOKS LIKE YOUR SCULPTURE WASN'T STURDY ENOUGH TO LAST THROUGH THE NIGHT!
THAT'S THE BIZ, TWERP!
YOU! YOU DID THIS!
PROVE IT!
I CAN'T LET THEM BEAT ME LIKE THIS! GOTTA RELAX! NEED TO THINK!
HEY--!
WHY ARE YOU ALWAYS STARING AT YOUR PALM?
WHAT ARE YOU LOOKING AT?!
Y-YOU CAN'T HURT ME-- NO MATTER WHAT YOU SAY OR DO-- BECAUSE I HAVE SOMETHING WHICH NO ONE ELSE DOES!

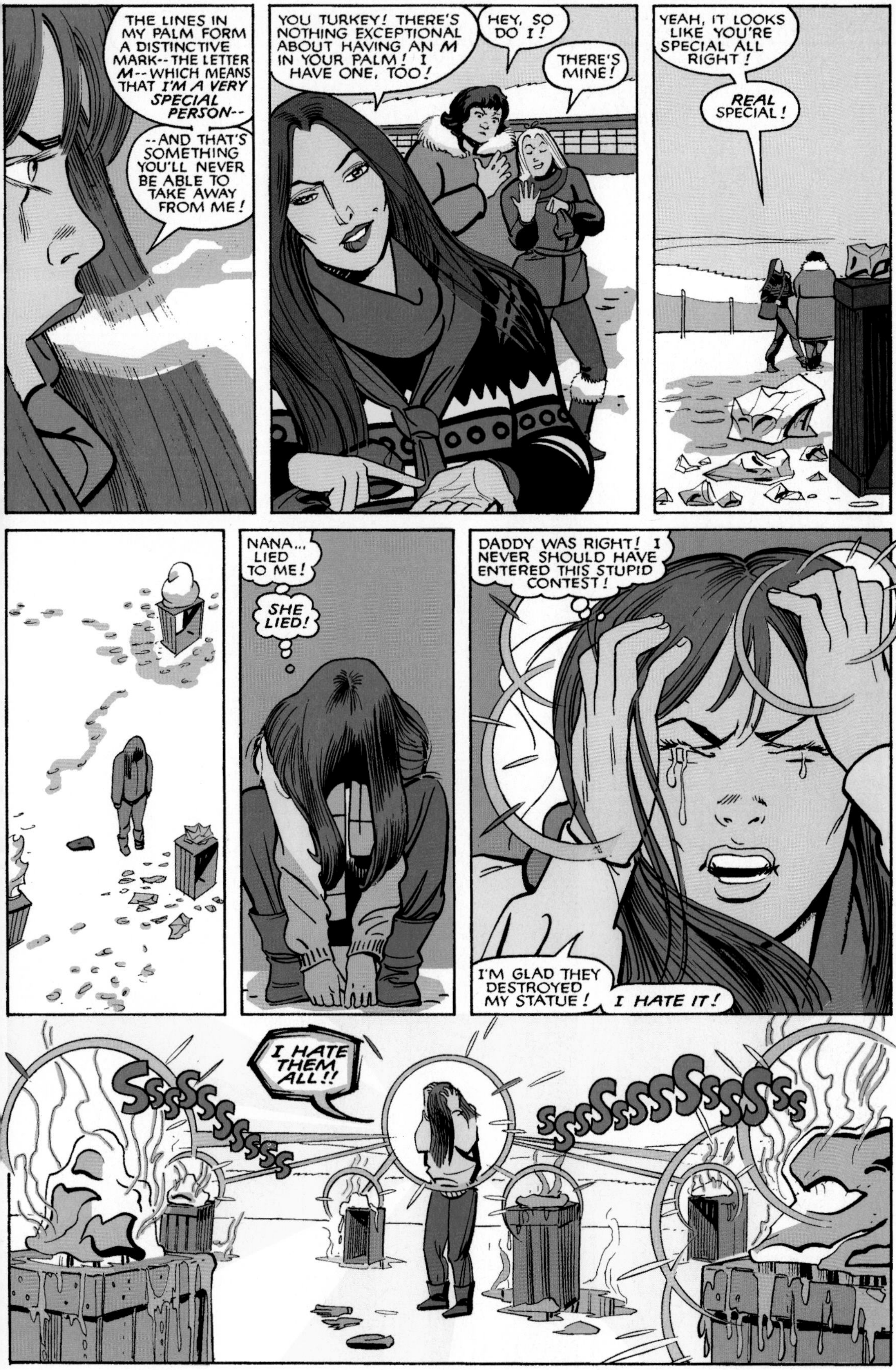
THE LINES IN MY PALM FORM A DISTINCTIVE MARK-- THE LETTER M-- WHICH MEANS THAT I'M A VERY SPECIAL PERSON--
--AND THAT'S SOMETHING YOU'LL NEVER BE ABLE TO TAKE AWAY FROM ME!
YOU TURKEY! THERE'S NOTHING EXCEPTIONAL ABOUT HAVING AN M IN YOUR PALM! I HAVE ONE, TOO!
HEY, SO DO I!
THERE'S MINE!
YEAH, IT LOOKS LIKE YOU'RE SPECIAL ALL RIGHT!
REAL SPECIAL!
NANA... LIED TO ME!
SHE LIED!
DADDY WAS RIGHT! I NEVER SHOULD HAVE ENTERED THIS STUPID CONTEST!
I'M GLAD THEY DESTROYED MY STATUE!
I HATE IT!
SSSSSSSSSSS
I HATE THEM ALL!!
SSSSSSSSSSSSSS

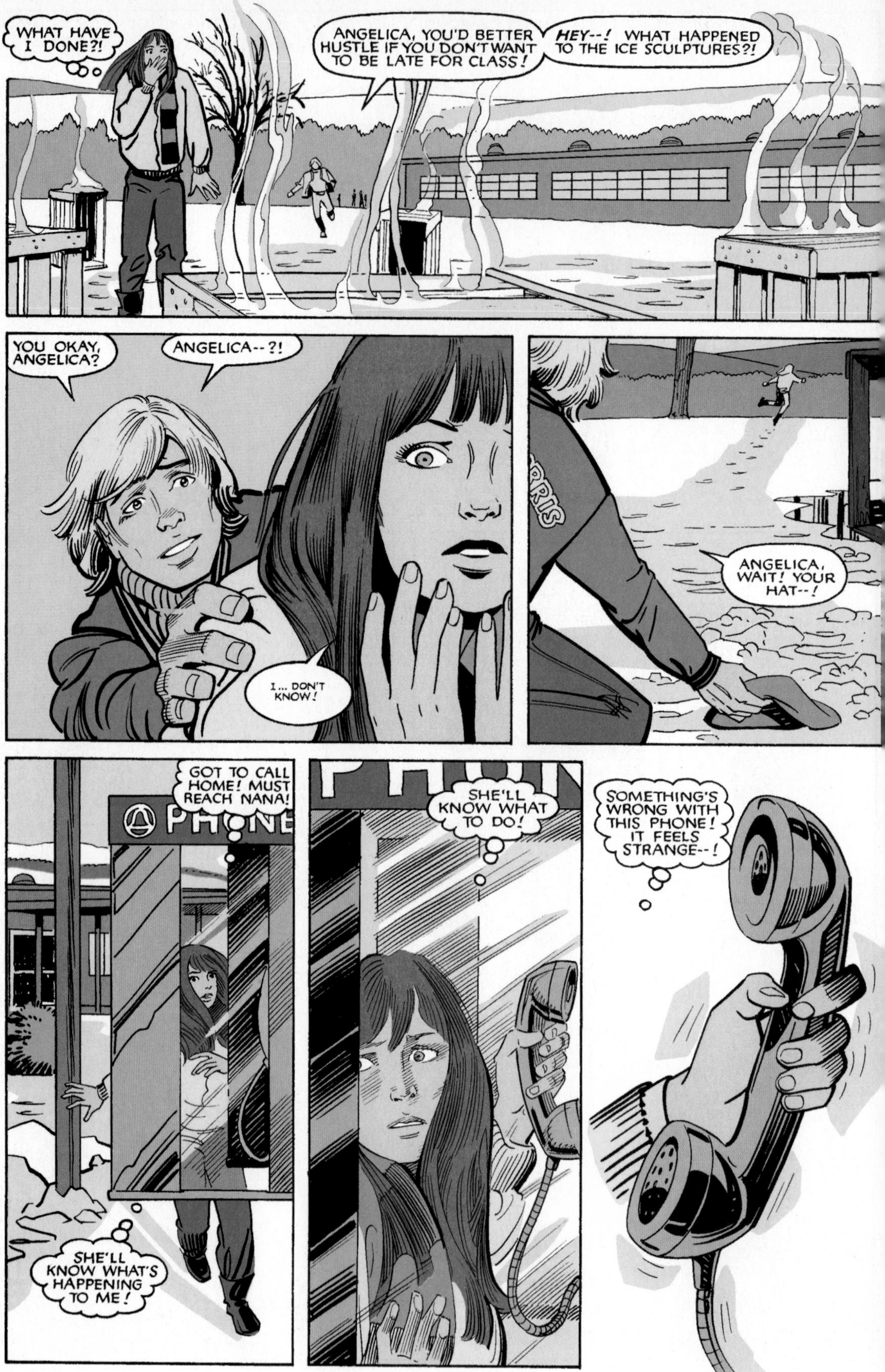
WHAT HAVE I DONE?!
ANGELICA, YOU'D BETTER HUSTLE IF YOU DON'T WANT TO BE LATE FOR CLASS!
HEY--! WHAT HAPPENED TO THE ICE SCULPTURES?!
YOU OKAY, ANGELICA?
ANGELICA--?!
I... DON'T KNOW!
ANGELICA, WAIT! YOUR HAT--!
GOT TO CALL HOME! MUST REACH NANA!
PHONE
SHE'LL KNOW WHAT'S HAPPENING TO ME!
SHE'LL KNOW WHAT TO DO!
SOMETHING'S WRONG WITH THIS PHONE! IT FEELS STRANGE--!

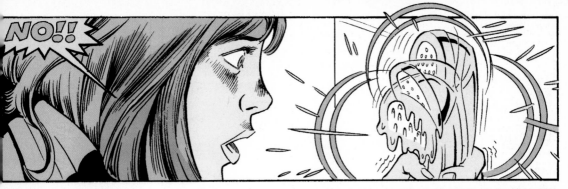

NO!!

AT THAT VERY MOMENT...

CEREBRO HAS DETECTED THE PRESENCE OF A YOUNG MUTANT!

BE SILENT! CLEAR YOUR MINDS OF ALL THOUGHTS!

THERE MUST BE NO INTERFERENCE AS I USE MY OWN TELEPATHIC POWERS TO INCREASE CEREBRO'S ABILITY TO PINPOINT THE LOCATION!

GOT HER! THE COMPUTER HAS LOCKED ONTO HER COORDINATES!

SHE'S IN NEW JERSEY!

EXCELLENT! HAVE MY PRIVATE JET PREPARED FOR AN IMMEDIATE TAKE-OFF, AND ARRANGE FOR A LIMOSINE TO MEET ME WHEN I LAND.

I SHALL PERSONALLY COLLECT THIS ONE. THE POOR THING...

"...SHE MUST BE TERRIFIED!"

"WELL, SHE'LL GET USED TO IT..."

"...IF I HAVE MY WAY, *TERROR* WILL SOON BECOME A WAY OF LIFE TO HER!"

NEVER THOUGHT I'D MAKE IT ALL THE WAY HOME!

HEY! WHY IS THAT AMBULANCE-- AND THOSE COP CARS--IN FRONT OF MY HOUSE?!

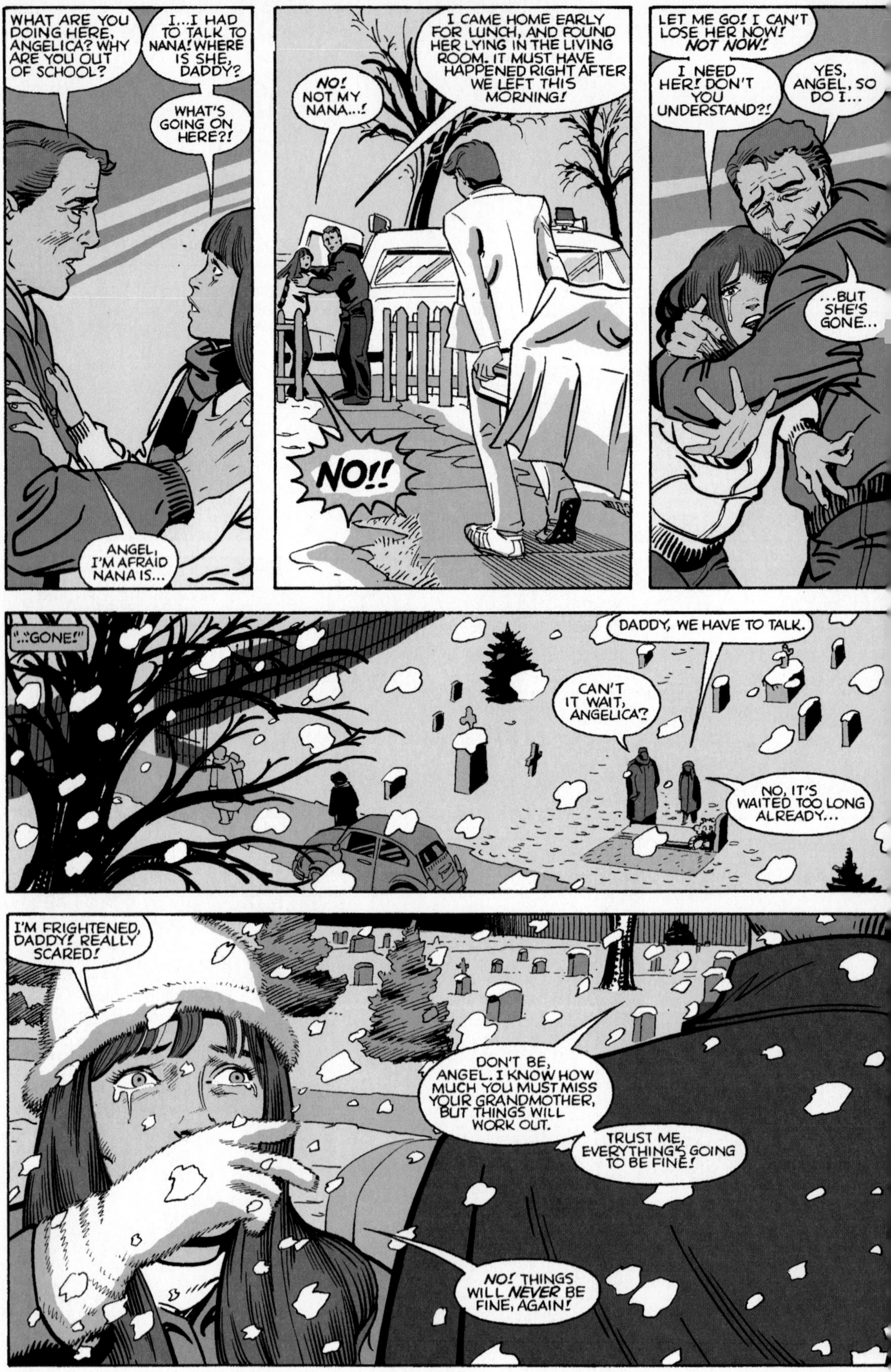
WHAT ARE YOU DOING HERE, ANGELICA? WHY ARE YOU OUT OF SCHOOL?
I...I HAD TO TALK TO NANA! WHERE IS SHE, DADDY?
WHAT'S GOING ON HERE?!
ANGEL, I'M AFRAID NANA IS...
I CAME HOME EARLY FOR LUNCH, AND FOUND HER LYING IN THE LIVING ROOM. IT MUST HAVE HAPPENED RIGHT AFTER WE LEFT THIS MORNING!
NO! NOT MY NANA...!
NO!!
LET ME GO! I CAN'T LOSE HER NOW! NOT NOW!
I NEED HER! DON'T YOU UNDERSTAND?!
YES, ANGEL, SO DO I...
...BUT SHE'S GONE...
"...GONE!"
DADDY, WE HAVE TO TALK.
CAN'T IT WAIT, ANGELICA?
NO, IT'S WAITED TOO LONG ALREADY...
I'M FRIGHTENED, DADDY! REALLY SCARED!
DON'T BE, ANGEL. I KNOW HOW MUCH YOU MUST MISS YOUR GRANDMOTHER, BUT THINGS WILL WORK OUT.
TRUST ME, EVERYTHING'S GOING TO BE FINE!
NO! THINGS WILL NEVER BE FINE, AGAIN!

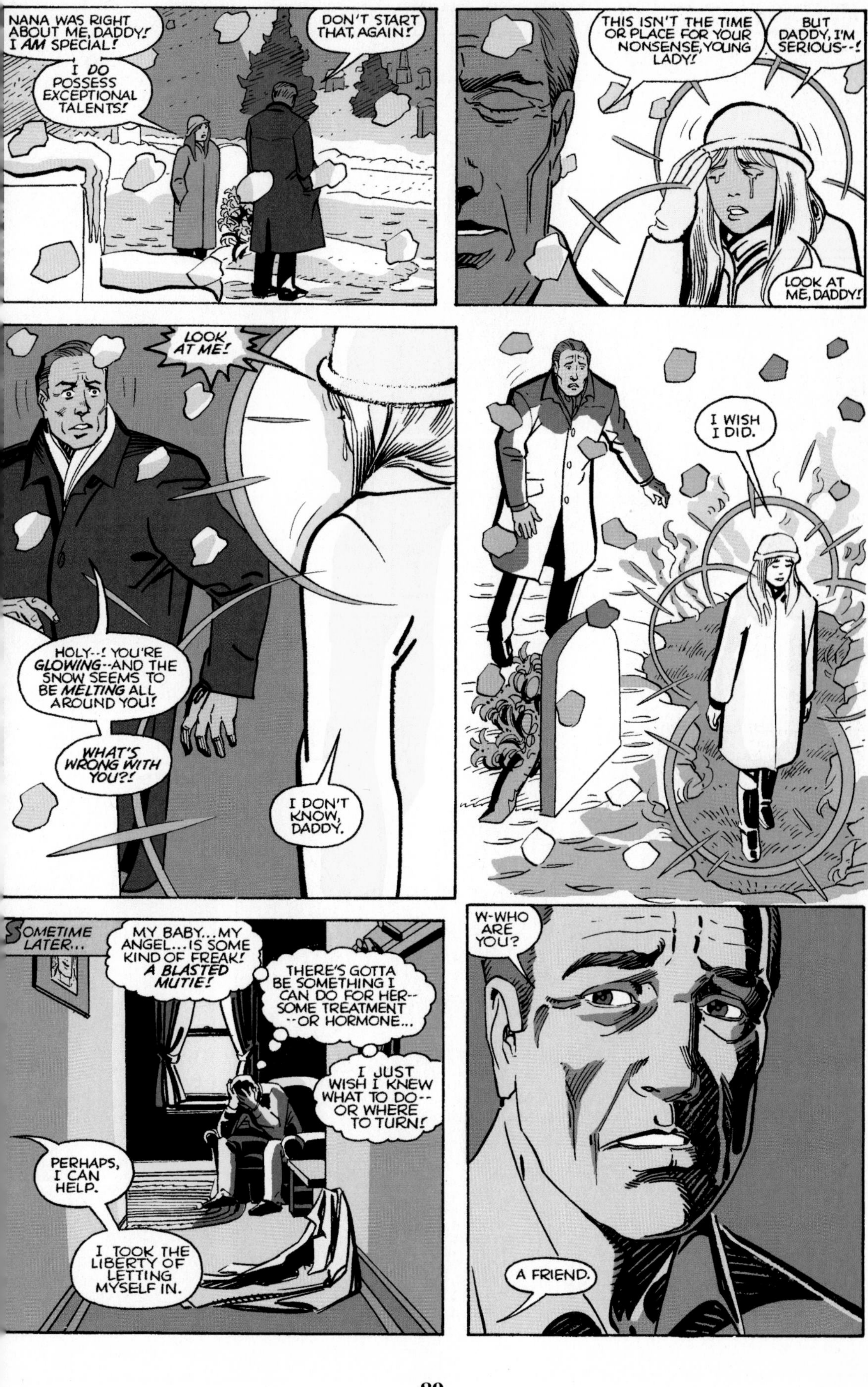
NANA WAS RIGHT ABOUT ME, DADDY! I AM SPECIAL!
I DO POSSESS EXCEPTIONAL TALENTS!
DON'T START THAT, AGAIN!
THIS ISN'T THE TIME OR PLACE FOR YOUR NONSENSE, YOUNG LADY!
BUT DADDY, I'M SERIOUS--!
LOOK AT ME, DADDY!
LOOK AT ME!
HOLY--! YOU'RE GLOWING--AND THE SNOW SEEMS TO BE MELTING ALL AROUND YOU!
WHAT'S WRONG WITH YOU?!
I DON'T KNOW, DADDY.
I WISH I DID.
SOMETIME LATER...
MY BABY...MY ANGEL...IS SOME KIND OF FREAK! A BLASTED MUTIE!
THERE'S GOTTA BE SOMETHING I CAN DO FOR HER-- SOME TREATMENT --OR HORMONE...
I JUST WISH I KNEW WHAT TO DO-- OR WHERE TO TURN!
PERHAPS, I CAN HELP.
I TOOK THE LIBERTY OF LETTING MYSELF IN.
W-WHO ARE YOU?
A FRIEND.

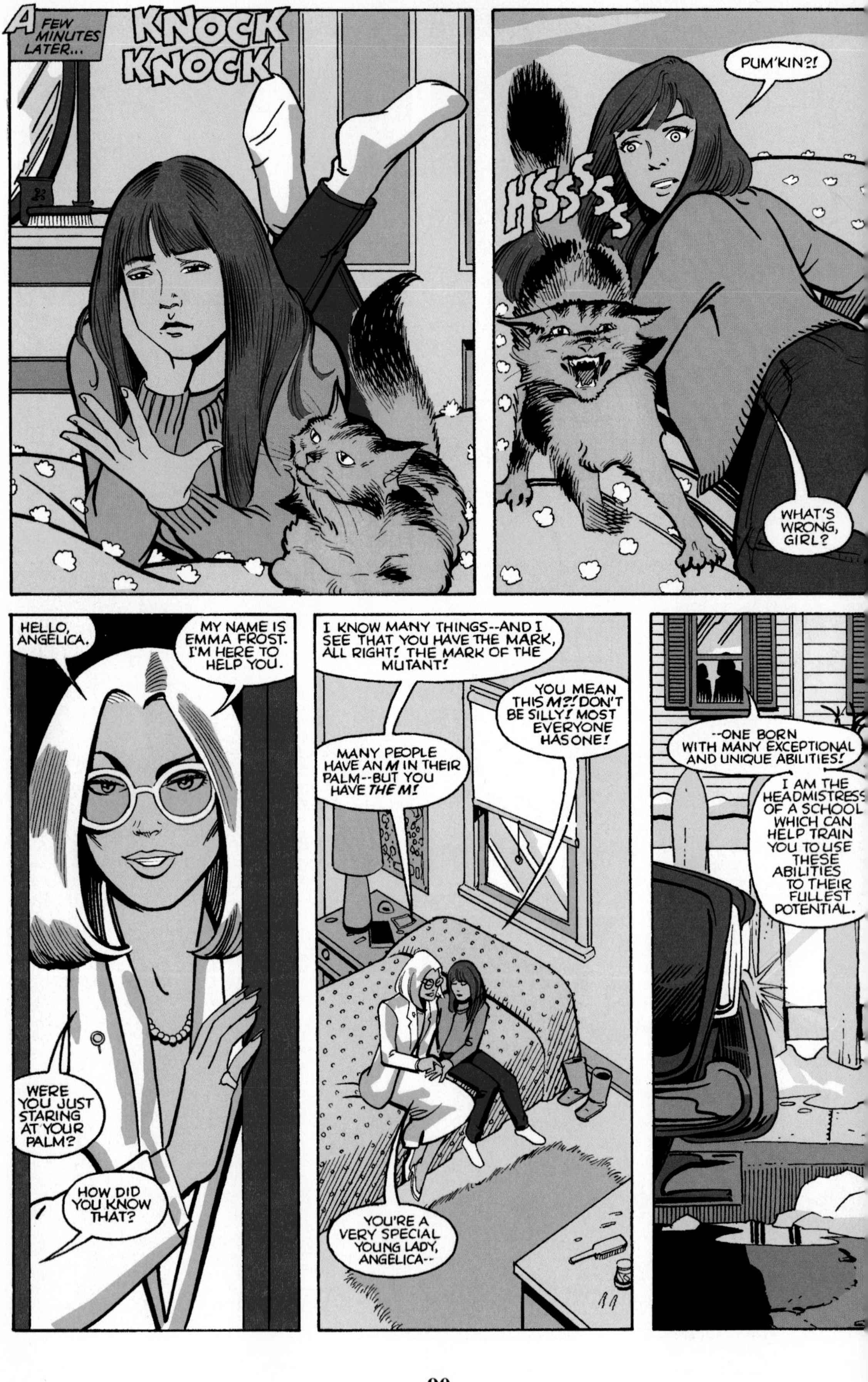
A FEW MINUTES LATER...
KNOCK KNOCK
PUM'KIN?!
HSSSSS
WHAT'S WRONG, GIRL?
HELLO, ANGELICA.
MY NAME IS EMMA FROST. I'M HERE TO HELP YOU.
WERE YOU JUST STARING AT YOUR PALM?
HOW DID YOU KNOW THAT?
I KNOW MANY THINGS--AND I SEE THAT YOU HAVE THE MARK, ALL RIGHT! THE MARK OF THE MUTANT!
YOU MEAN THIS M?! DON'T BE SILLY! MOST EVERYONE HAS ONE!
MANY PEOPLE HAVE AN M IN THEIR PALM--BUT YOU HAVE THE M!
YOU'RE A VERY SPECIAL YOUNG LADY, ANGELICA--
--ONE BORN WITH MANY EXCEPTIONAL AND UNIQUE ABILITIES!
I AM THE HEADMISTRESS OF A SCHOOL WHICH CAN HELP TRAIN YOU TO USE THESE ABILITIES TO THEIR FULLEST POTENTIAL.

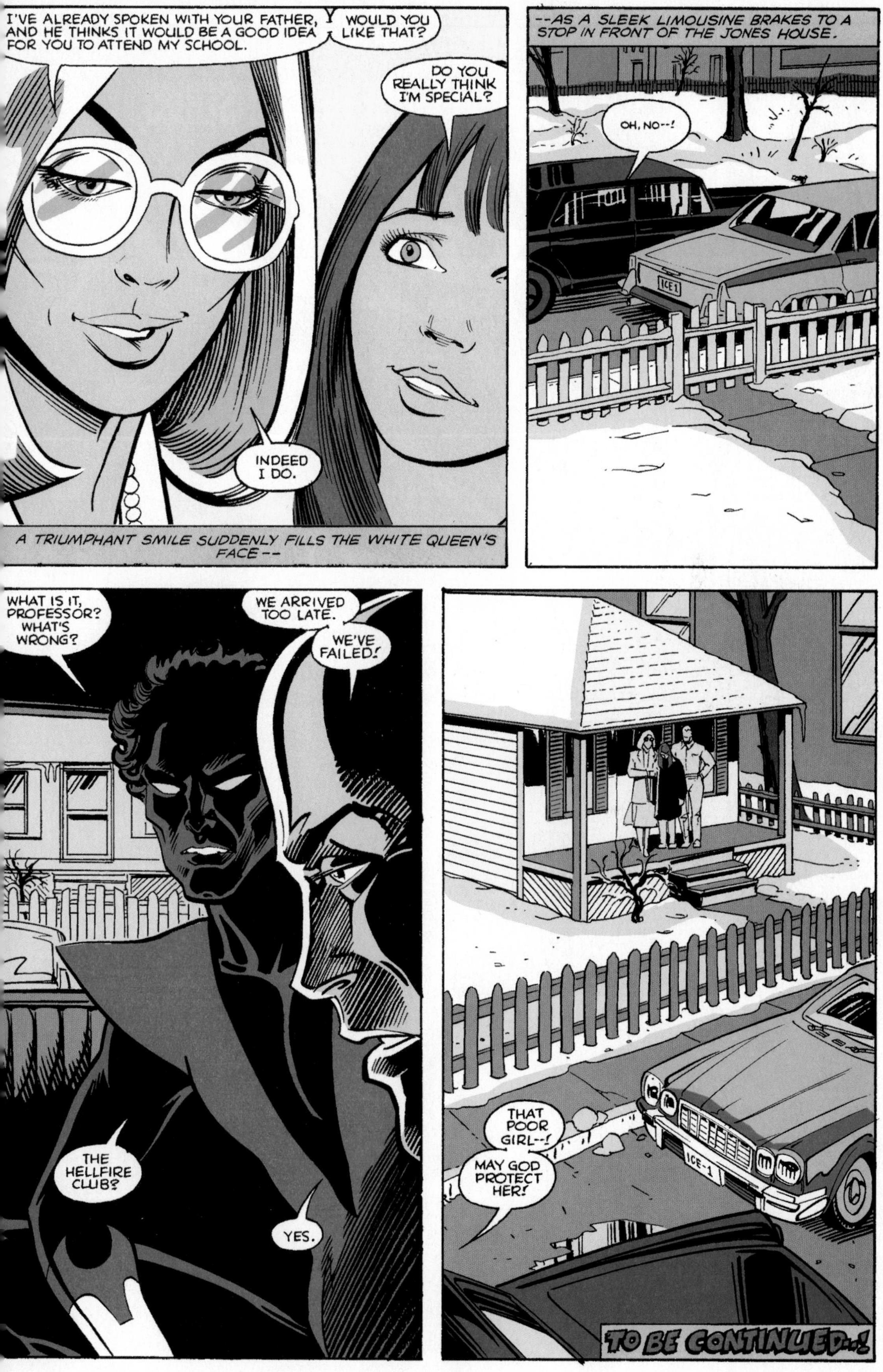
I'VE ALREADY SPOKEN WITH YOUR FATHER, AND HE THINKS IT WOULD BE A GOOD IDEA FOR YOU TO ATTEND MY SCHOOL.
WOULD YOU LIKE THAT?
DO YOU REALLY THINK I'M SPECIAL?
INDEED I DO.
A TRIUMPHANT SMILE SUDDENLY FILLS THE WHITE QUEEN'S FACE--
--AS A SLEEK LIMOUSINE BRAKES TO A STOP IN FRONT OF THE JONES HOUSE.
OH, NO--!
ICE 1
WHAT IS IT, PROFESSOR? WHAT'S WRONG?
WE ARRIVED TOO LATE.
WE'VE FAILED!
THE HELLFIRE CLUB?
YES.
THAT POOR GIRL--!
MAY GOD PROTECT HER!
ICE-1
TO BE CONTINUED..!

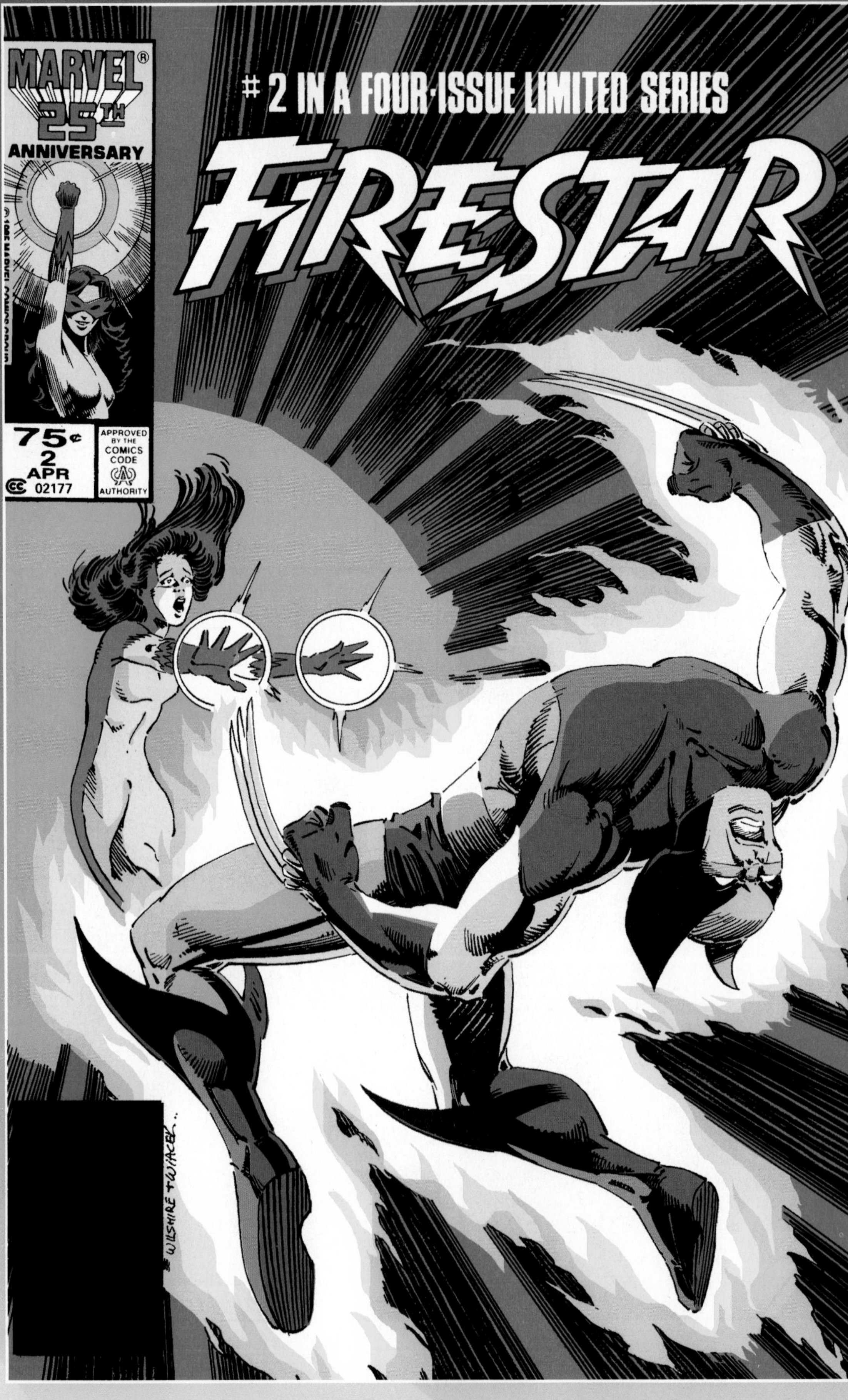
MARVEL®
25TH
ANNIVERSARY
2 IN A FOUR-ISSUE LIMITED SERIES
FIRESTAR
75¢
2
APR
CC 02177
APPROVED BY THE COMICS CODE AUTHORITY
WILSHIRE + WIACEK

STAN LEE PRESENTS: FIRESTAR

Unable to cope with the fact that his only daughter is a mutant possessing strange and uncanny powers, *Bartholemew Jones* quickly entrusts her education and training to *Ms. Emma Frost*, headmistress of the prestigious *Massachusetts Academy*. Unknown to Jones, Frost is secretly a member of the *Inner Council of the Hellfire Club*, an organization determined to dominate the world!

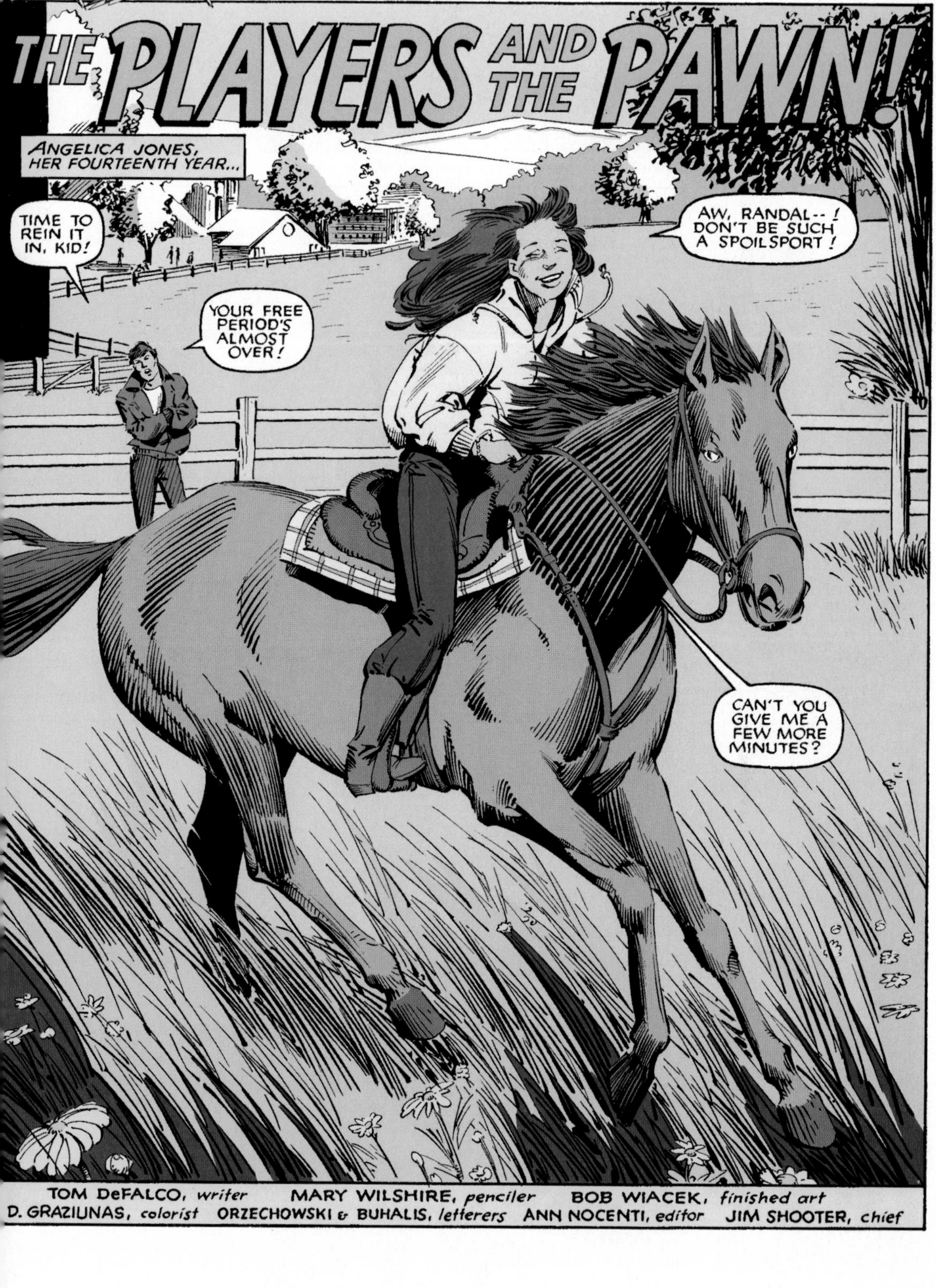

THE PLAYERS AND THE PAWN!
ANGELICA JONES, HER FOURTEENTH YEAR...
TIME TO REIN IT IN, KID!
YOUR FREE PERIOD'S ALMOST OVER!
AW, RANDAL-- ! DON'T BE SUCH A SPOILSPORT!
CAN'T YOU GIVE ME A FEW MORE MINUTES?
TOM DeFALCO, writer MARY WILSHIRE, penciler BOB WIACEK, finished art
D. GRAZIUNAS, colorist ORZECHOWSKI & BUHALIS, letterers ANN NOCENTI, editor JIM SHOOTER, chief

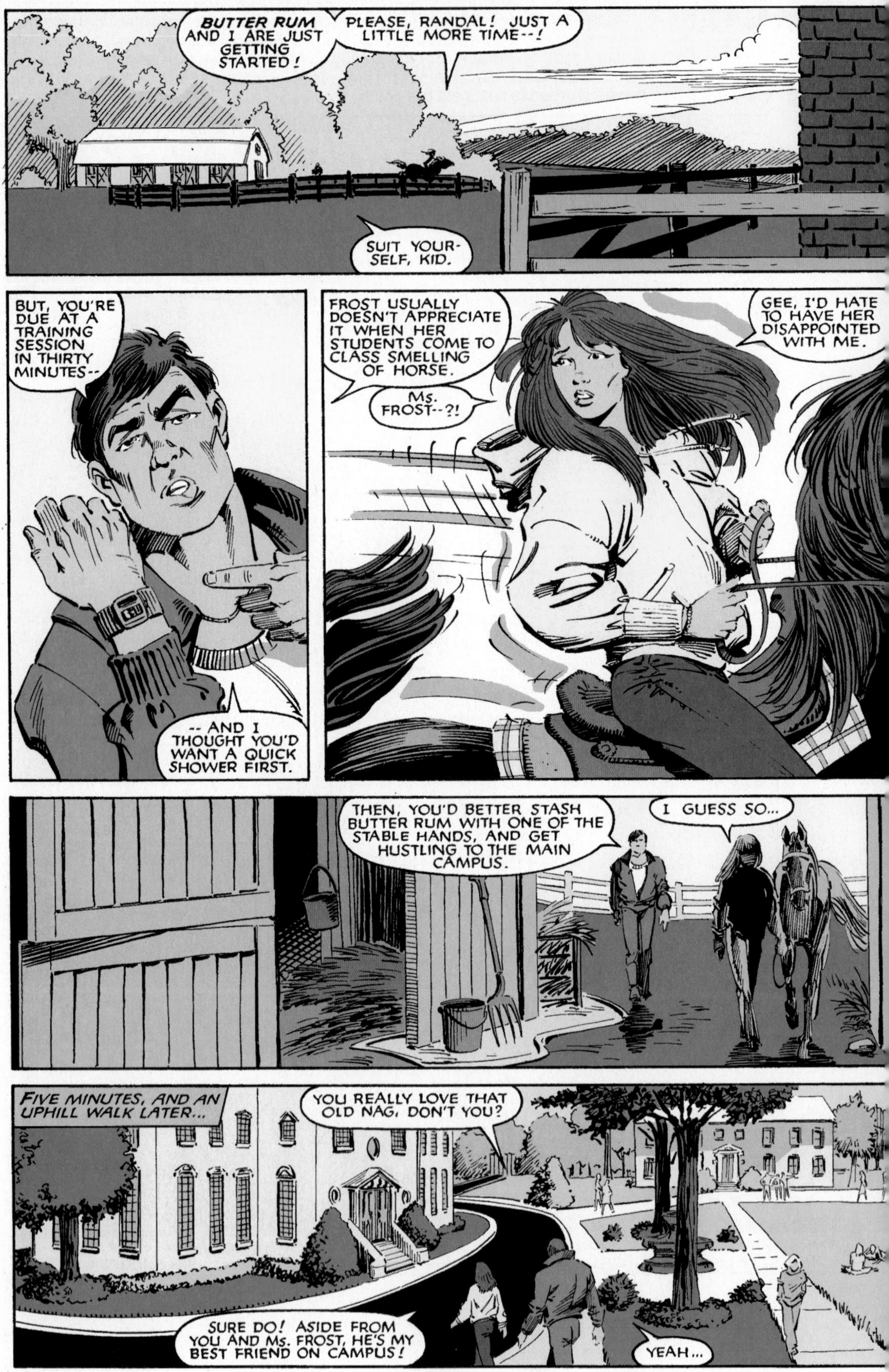
BUTTER RUM AND I ARE JUST GETTING STARTED!
PLEASE, RANDAL! JUST A LITTLE MORE TIME--!
SUIT YOURSELF, KID.
BUT, YOU'RE DUE AT A TRAINING SESSION IN THIRTY MINUTES--
-- AND I THOUGHT YOU'D WANT A QUICK SHOWER FIRST.
FROST USUALLY DOESN'T APPRECIATE IT WHEN HER STUDENTS COME TO CLASS SMELLING OF HORSE.
Ms. FROST--?!
GEE, I'D HATE TO HAVE HER DISAPPOINTED WITH ME.
THEN, YOU'D BETTER STASH BUTTER RUM WITH ONE OF THE STABLE HANDS, AND GET HUSTLING TO THE MAIN CAMPUS.
I GUESS SO...
FIVE MINUTES, AND AN UPHILL WALK LATER...
YOU REALLY LOVE THAT OLD NAG, DON'T YOU?
SURE DO! ASIDE FROM YOU AND Ms. FROST, HE'S MY BEST FRIEND ON CAMPUS!
YEAH...

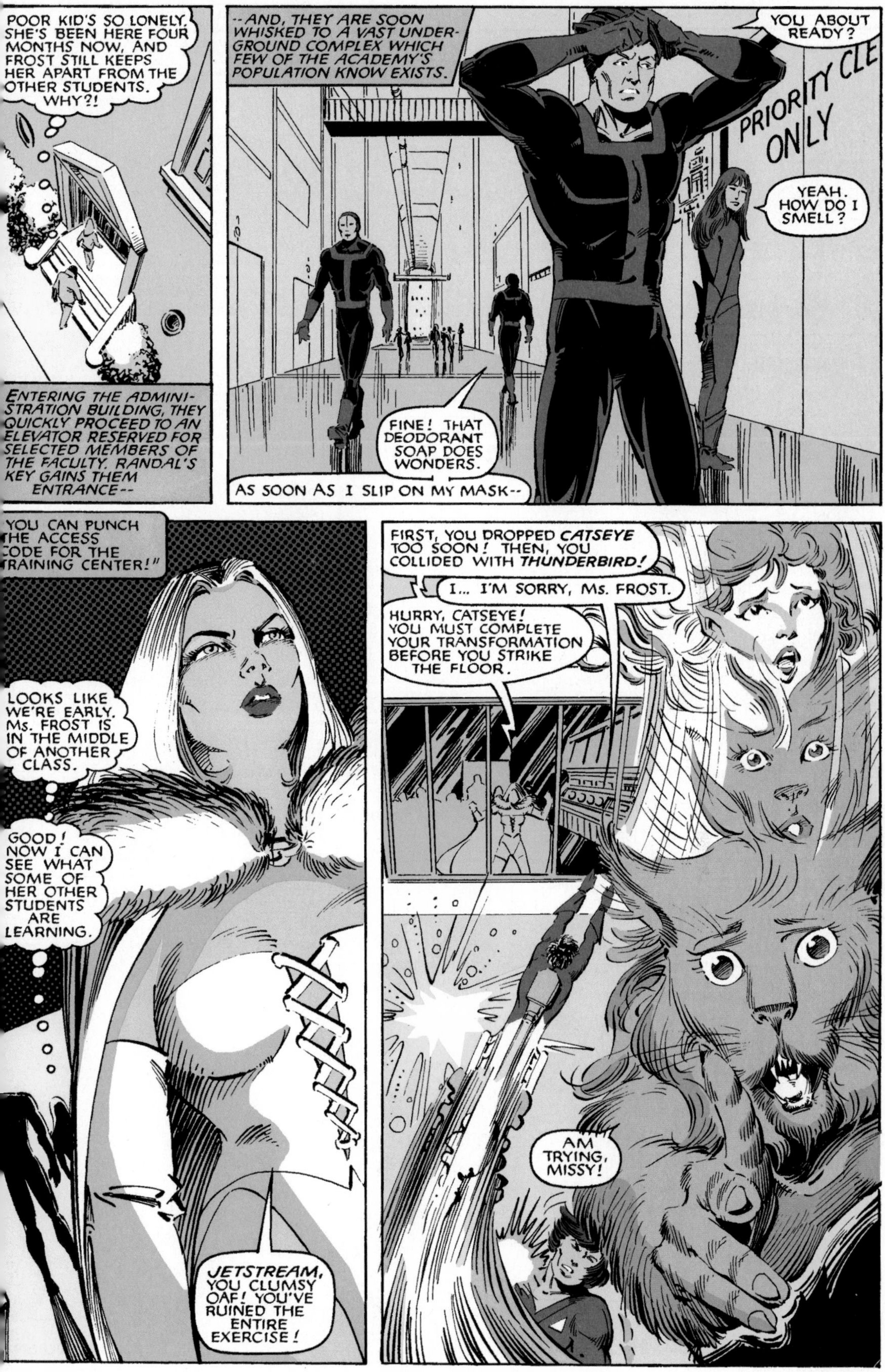
POOR KID'S SO LONELY. SHE'S BEEN HERE FOUR MONTHS NOW, AND FROST STILL KEEPS HER APART FROM THE OTHER STUDENTS. WHY?!
ENTERING THE ADMINISTRATION BUILDING, THEY QUICKLY PROCEED TO AN ELEVATOR RESERVED FOR SELECTED MEMBERS OF THE FACULTY. RANDAL'S KEY GAINS THEM ENTRANCE--
--AND, THEY ARE SOON WHISKED TO A VAST UNDERGROUND COMPLEX WHICH FEW OF THE ACADEMY'S POPULATION KNOW EXISTS.
FINE! THAT DEODORANT SOAP DOES WONDERS.
AS SOON AS I SLIP ON MY MASK--
YOU ABOUT READY?
PRIORITY CLE
ONLY
YEAH. HOW DO I SMELL?
YOU CAN PUNCH THE ACCESS CODE FOR THE TRAINING CENTER!"
LOOKS LIKE WE'RE EARLY. Ms. FROST IS IN THE MIDDLE OF ANOTHER CLASS.
GOOD! NOW I CAN SEE WHAT SOME OF HER OTHER STUDENTS ARE LEARNING.
JETSTREAM, YOU CLUMSY OAF! YOU'VE RUINED THE ENTIRE EXERCISE!
FIRST, YOU DROPPED CATSEYE TOO SOON! THEN, YOU COLLIDED WITH THUNDERBIRD!
I... I'M SORRY, Ms. FROST.
HURRY, CATSEYE! YOU MUST COMPLETE YOUR TRANSFORMATION BEFORE YOU STRIKE THE FLOOR.
AM TRYING, MISSY!

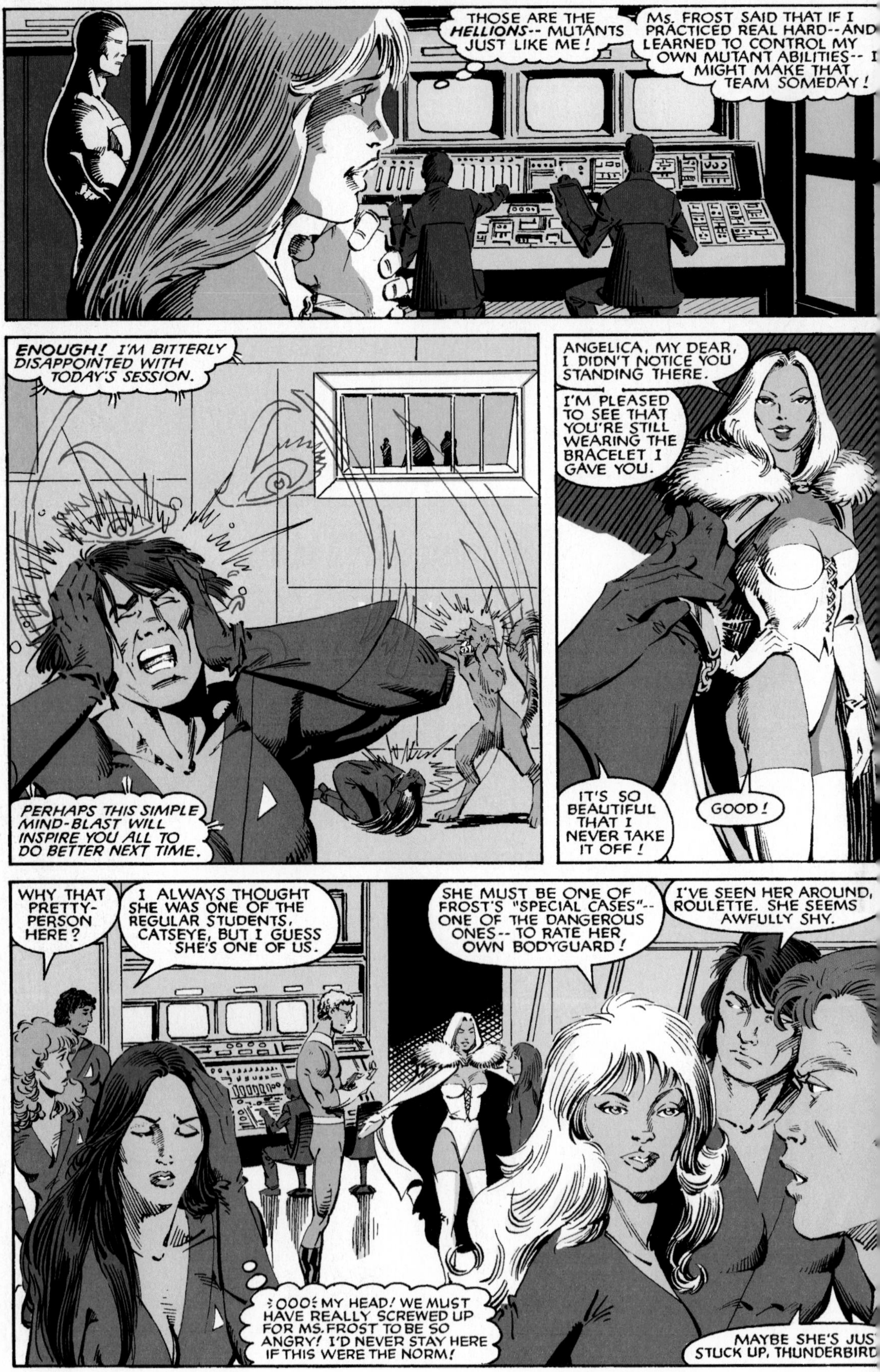
THOSE ARE THE HELLIONS-- MUTANTS JUST LIKE ME!
Ms. FROST SAID THAT IF I PRACTICED REAL HARD--AND LEARNED TO CONTROL MY OWN MUTANT ABILITIES-- I MIGHT MAKE THAT TEAM SOMEDAY!
ENOUGH! I'M BITTERLY DISAPPOINTED WITH TODAY'S SESSION.
PERHAPS THIS SIMPLE MIND-BLAST WILL INSPIRE YOU ALL TO DO BETTER NEXT TIME.
ANGELICA, MY DEAR, I DIDN'T NOTICE YOU STANDING THERE.
I'M PLEASED TO SEE THAT YOU'RE STILL WEARING THE BRACELET I GAVE YOU.
IT'S SO BEAUTIFUL THAT I NEVER TAKE IT OFF!
GOOD!
WHY THAT PRETTY-PERSON HERE?
I ALWAYS THOUGHT SHE WAS ONE OF THE REGULAR STUDENTS, CATSEYE, BUT I GUESS SHE'S ONE OF US.
SHE MUST BE ONE OF FROST'S "SPECIAL CASES"-- ONE OF THE DANGEROUS ONES-- TO RATE HER OWN BODYGUARD!
I'VE SEEN HER AROUND, ROULETTE. SHE SEEMS AWFULLY SHY.
OOO! MY HEAD! WE MUST HAVE REALLY SCREWED UP FOR MS. FROST TO BE SO ANGRY! I'D NEVER STAY HERE IF THIS WERE THE NORM!
MAYBE SHE'S JUS STUCK UP, THUNDERBIRD

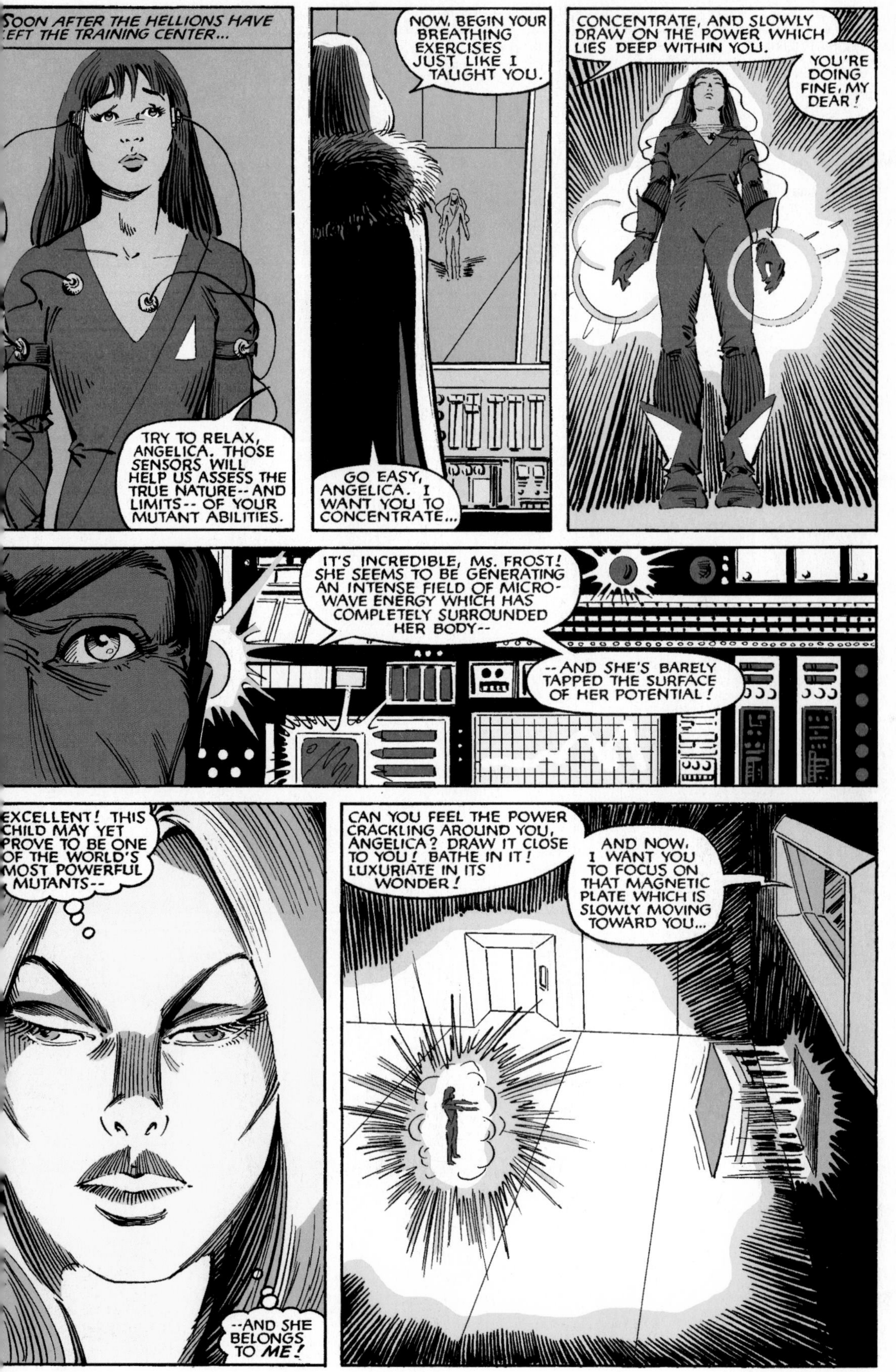
SOON AFTER THE HELLIONS HAVE LEFT THE TRAINING CENTER...
TRY TO RELAX, ANGELICA. THOSE SENSORS WILL HELP US ASSESS THE TRUE NATURE-- AND LIMITS-- OF YOUR MUTANT ABILITIES.
NOW, BEGIN YOUR BREATHING EXERCISES JUST LIKE I TAUGHT YOU.
GO EASY, ANGELICA. I WANT YOU TO CONCENTRATE...
CONCENTRATE, AND SLOWLY DRAW ON THE POWER WHICH LIES DEEP WITHIN YOU.
YOU'RE DOING FINE, MY DEAR!
IT'S INCREDIBLE, Ms. FROST! SHE SEEMS TO BE GENERATING AN INTENSE FIELD OF MICRO-WAVE ENERGY WHICH HAS COMPLETELY SURROUNDED HER BODY--
--AND SHE'S BARELY TAPPED THE SURFACE OF HER POTENTIAL!
EXCELLENT! THIS CHILD MAY YET PROVE TO BE ONE OF THE WORLD'S MOST POWERFUL MUTANTS--
--AND SHE BELONGS TO ME!
CAN YOU FEEL THE POWER CRACKLING AROUND YOU, ANGELICA? DRAW IT CLOSE TO YOU! BATHE IN IT! LUXURIATE IN ITS WONDER!
AND NOW, I WANT YOU TO FOCUS ON THAT MAGNETIC PLATE WHICH IS SLOWLY MOVING TOWARD YOU...

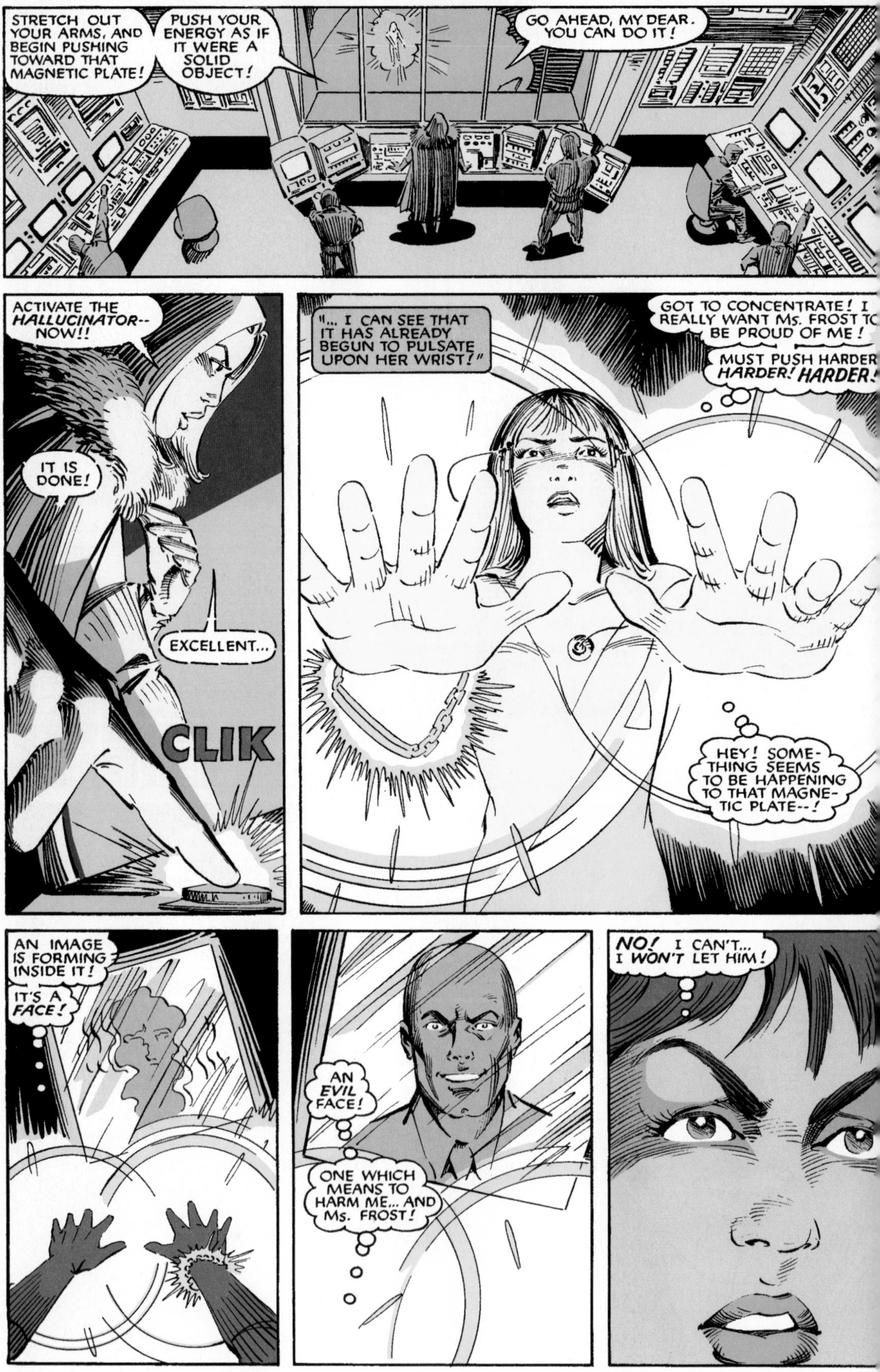
STRETCH OUT YOUR ARMS, AND BEGIN PUSHING TOWARD THAT MAGNETIC PLATE!
PUSH YOUR ENERGY AS IF IT WERE A SOLID OBJECT!
GO AHEAD, MY DEAR. YOU CAN DO IT!
ACTIVATE THE *HALLUCINATOR*-- NOW!!
IT IS DONE!
EXCELLENT...
CLIK
"... I CAN SEE THAT IT HAS ALREADY BEGUN TO PULSATE UPON HER WRIST!"
GOT TO CONCENTRATE! I REALLY WANT Ms. FROST TO BE PROUD OF ME!
MUST PUSH HARDER *HARDER! HARDER!*
HEY! SOMETHING SEEMS TO BE HAPPENING TO THAT MAGNETIC PLATE--!
AN IMAGE IS FORMING INSIDE IT!
IT'S A *FACE!*
AN *EVIL* FACE!
ONE WHICH MEANS TO HARM ME... AND Ms. FROST!
NO! I CAN'T... I *WON'T* LET HIM!

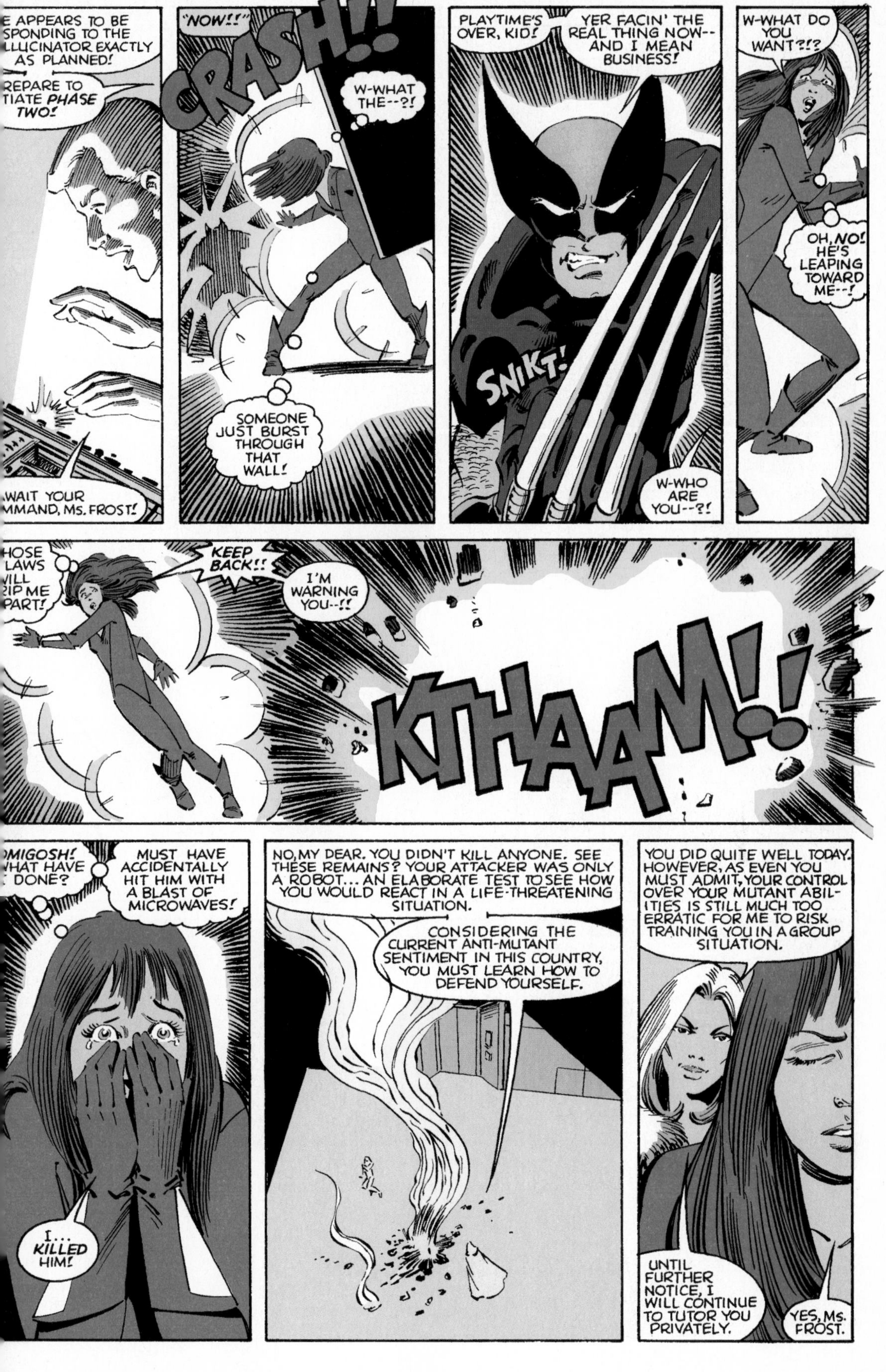
E APPEARS TO BE
SPONDING TO THE
LLUCINATOR EXACTLY
AS PLANNED!
REPARE TO
TIATE PHASE
TWO!
WAIT YOUR
MMAND, MS. FROST!
"NOW!!"
CRASH!!
W-WHAT
THE--?!
SOMEONE
JUST BURST
THROUGH
THAT
WALL!
PLAYTIME'S
OVER, KID!
YER FACIN' THE
REAL THING NOW--
AND I MEAN
BUSINESS!
SNIKT!
W-WHO
ARE
YOU--?!
W-WHAT DO
YOU
WANT?!?
OH, NO!
HE'S
LEAPING
TOWARD
ME--!
HOSE
LAWS
VILL
RIP ME
PART!
KEEP
BACK!!
I'M
WARNING
YOU--!!
KTHAAM!!
OMIGOSH!
WHAT HAVE
DONE?
MUST HAVE
ACCIDENTALLY
HIT HIM WITH
A BLAST OF
MICROWAVES!
I...
KILLED
HIM!
NO, MY DEAR. YOU DIDN'T KILL ANYONE. SEE THESE REMAINS? YOUR ATTACKER WAS ONLY A ROBOT... AN ELABORATE TEST TO SEE HOW YOU WOULD REACT IN A LIFE-THREATENING SITUATION.
CONSIDERING THE CURRENT ANTI-MUTANT SENTIMENT IN THIS COUNTRY, YOU MUST LEARN HOW TO DEFEND YOURSELF.
YOU DID QUITE WELL TODAY. HOWEVER, AS EVEN YOU MUST ADMIT, YOUR CONTROL OVER YOUR MUTANT ABILITIES IS STILL MUCH TOO ERRATIC FOR ME TO RISK TRAINING YOU IN A GROUP SITUATION.
UNTIL FURTHER NOTICE, I WILL CONTINUE TO TUTOR YOU PRIVATELY.
YES, MS. FROST.

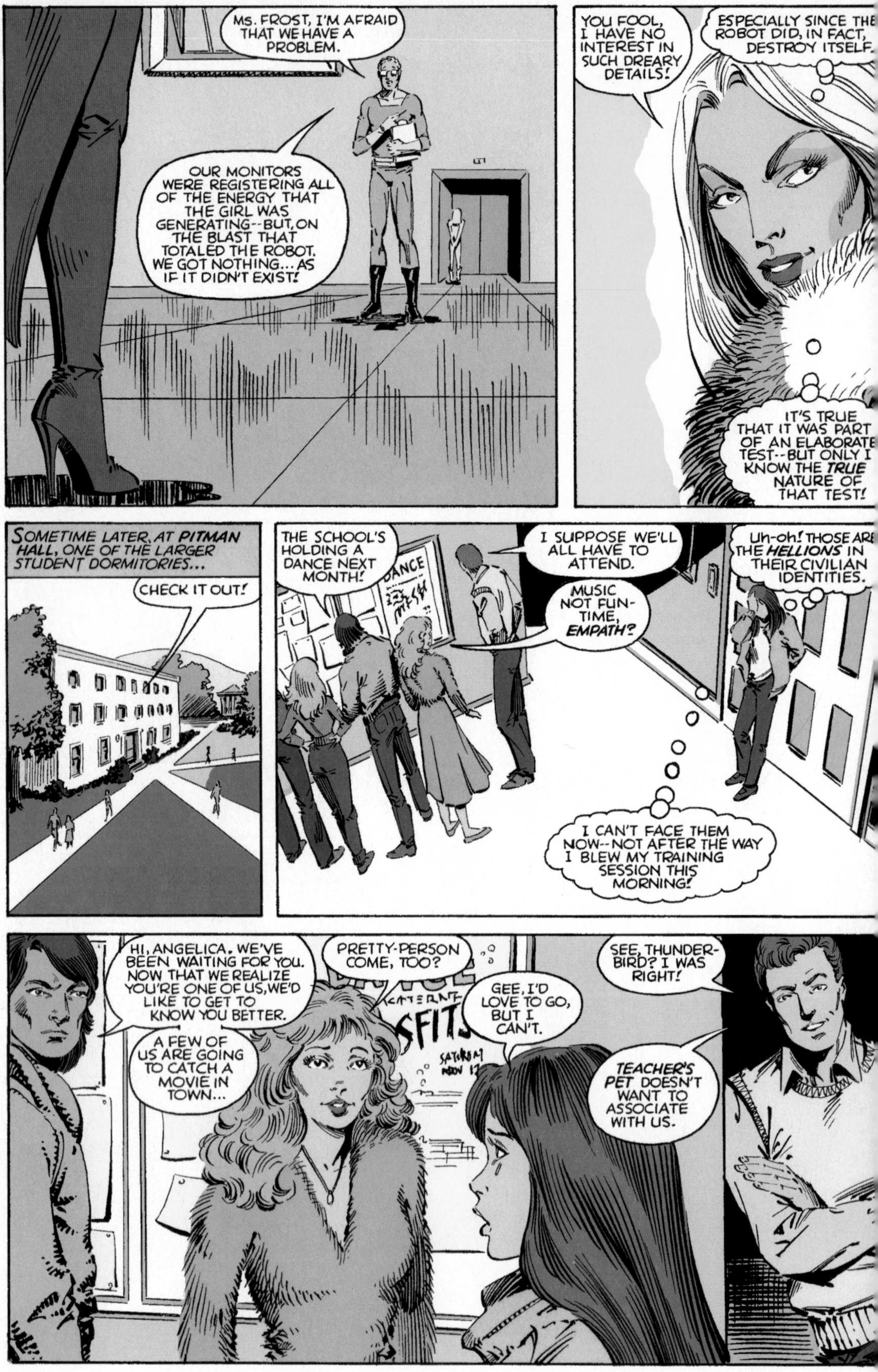

Ms. FROST, I'M AFRAID THAT WE HAVE A PROBLEM.
OUR MONITORS WERE REGISTERING ALL OF THE ENERGY THAT THE GIRL WAS GENERATING--BUT, ON THE BLAST THAT TOTALED THE ROBOT. WE GOT NOTHING... AS IF IT DIDN'T EXIST!
YOU FOOL, I HAVE NO INTEREST IN SUCH DREARY DETAILS!
ESPECIALLY SINCE THE ROBOT DID, IN FACT, DESTROY ITSELF.
IT'S TRUE THAT IT WAS PART OF AN ELABORATE TEST--BUT ONLY I KNOW THE TRUE NATURE OF THAT TEST!
SOMETIME LATER, AT PITMAN HALL, ONE OF THE LARGER STUDENT DORMITORIES...
CHECK IT OUT!
THE SCHOOL'S HOLDING A DANCE NEXT MONTH!
I SUPPOSE WE'LL ALL HAVE TO ATTEND.
MUSIC NOT FUN-TIME, EMPATH?
Uh-oh! THOSE ARE THE HELLIONS IN THEIR CIVILIAN IDENTITIES.
I CAN'T FACE THEM NOW--NOT AFTER THE WAY I BLEW MY TRAINING SESSION THIS MORNING!
HI, ANGELICA. WE'VE BEEN WAITING FOR YOU. NOW THAT WE REALIZE YOU'RE ONE OF US, WE'D LIKE TO GET TO KNOW YOU BETTER.
A FEW OF US ARE GOING TO CATCH A MOVIE IN TOWN...
PRETTY-PERSON COME, TOO?
GEE, I'D LOVE TO GO, BUT I CAN'T.
SEE, THUNDER-BIRD? I WAS RIGHT!
TEACHER'S PET DOESN'T WANT TO ASSOCIATE WITH US.

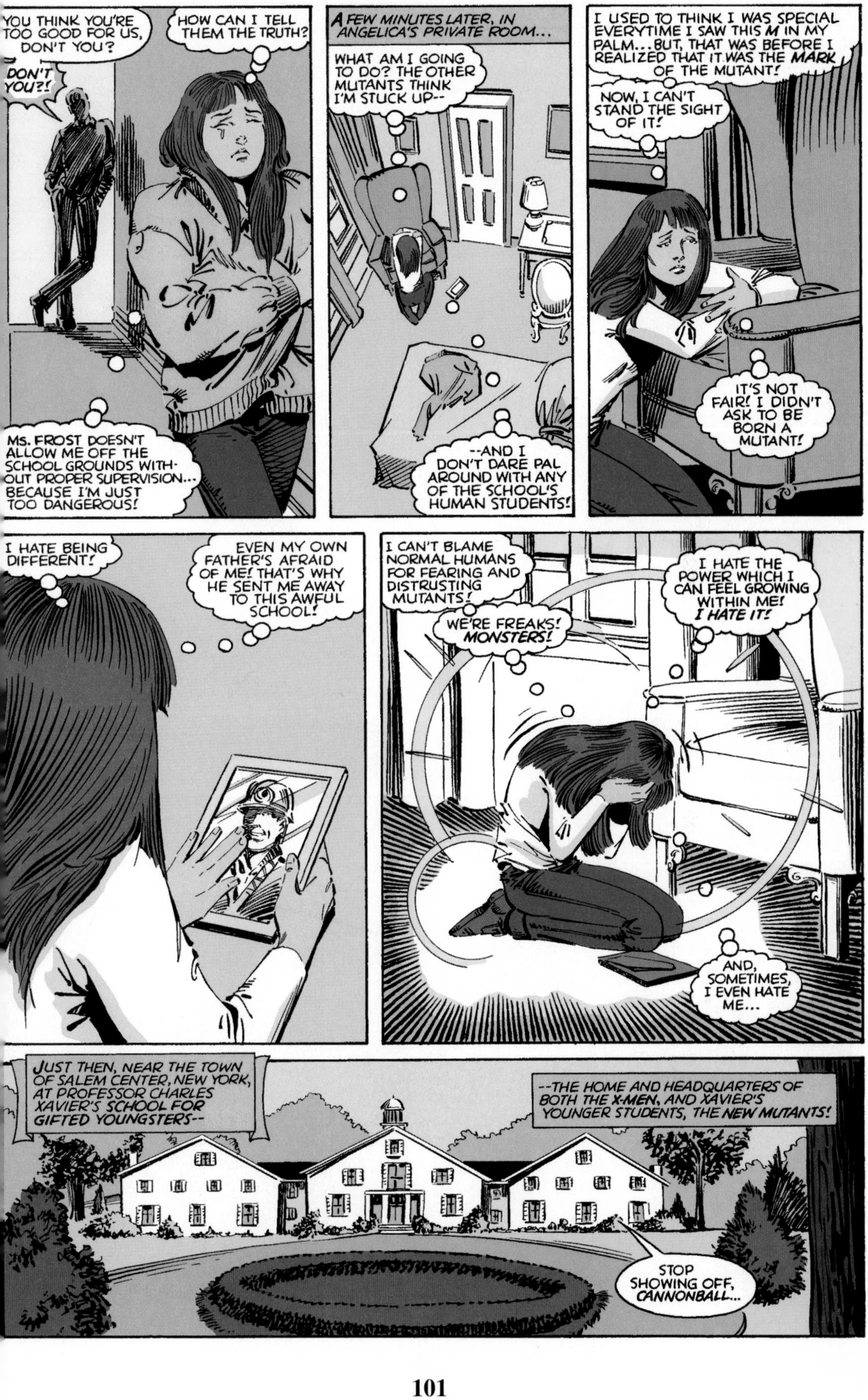
YOU THINK YOU'RE TOO GOOD FOR US, DON'T YOU?
DON'T YOU?!
HOW CAN I TELL THEM THE TRUTH?
MS. FROST DOESN'T ALLOW ME OFF THE SCHOOL GROUNDS WITHOUT PROPER SUPERVISION... BECAUSE I'M JUST TOO DANGEROUS!
A FEW MINUTES LATER, IN ANGELICA'S PRIVATE ROOM...
WHAT AM I GOING TO DO? THE OTHER MUTANTS THINK I'M STUCK UP--
--AND I DON'T DARE PAL AROUND WITH ANY OF THE SCHOOL'S HUMAN STUDENTS!
I USED TO THINK I WAS SPECIAL EVERYTIME I SAW THIS M IN MY PALM...BUT, THAT WAS BEFORE I REALIZED THAT IT WAS THE MARK OF THE MUTANT!
NOW, I CAN'T STAND THE SIGHT OF IT!
IT'S NOT FAIR! I DIDN'T ASK TO BE BORN A MUTANT!
I HATE BEING DIFFERENT!
EVEN MY OWN FATHER'S AFRAID OF ME! THAT'S WHY HE SENT ME AWAY TO THIS AWFUL SCHOOL!
I CAN'T BLAME NORMAL HUMANS FOR FEARING AND DISTRUSTING MUTANTS!
WE'RE FREAKS! MONSTERS!
I HATE THE POWER WHICH I CAN FEEL GROWING WITHIN ME! I HATE IT!
AND, SOMETIMES, I EVEN HATE ME...
JUST THEN, NEAR THE TOWN OF SALEM CENTER, NEW YORK, AT PROFESSOR CHARLES XAVIER'S SCHOOL FOR GIFTED YOUNGSTERS--
--THE HOME AND HEADQUARTERS OF BOTH THE X-MEN, AND XAVIER'S YOUNGER STUDENTS, THE NEW MUTANTS!
STOP SHOWING OFF, CANNONBALL...

...THIS TRAINING SESSION IS ALREADY OVER!

I KNOW, SUNSPOT, BUT I'M JUST TOO KEYED UP TO RELAX!

MIRAGE, HAVE YOU NOTICED THE STRANGE WAY SAM HAS BEEN ACTING LATELY?

WHO HASN'T, WOLFS-BANE?

I THINK HE'S STILL SMITTEN WITH MAGMA!

ME? WHY ME?

IF YOU WANT MY OPINION, YOU SHOULD BE FLATTERE GIRL. SAM GUTHRIE'S CUTE.

THANK YOU, MAGIK, BUT I REALLY DON'T NEED YOUR OPINIONS!

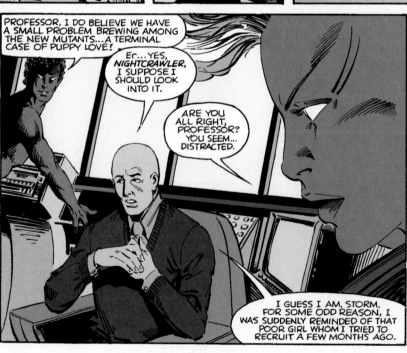

PROFESSOR, I DO BELIEVE WE HAVE A SMALL PROBLEM BREWING AMONG THE NEW MUTANTS...A TERMINAL CASE OF PUPPY LOVE!

Er...YES, NIGHTCRAWLER, I SUPPOSE I SHOULD LOOK INTO IT.

ARE YOU ALL RIGHT, PROFESSOR? YOU SEEM... DISTRACTED.

I GUESS I AM, STORM. FOR SOME ODD REASON, I WAS SUDDENLY REMINDED OF THAT POOR GIRL WHOM I TRIED TO RECRUIT A FEW MONTHS AGO.

I BELIEVE HER NAME WAS JONES...

ISN'T SHE THE ONE THAT FROST BEAT US TO?

YES, I'M STILL HAUNTED BY THE FACT THAT I COULDN'T PREVENT HER FROM FALLING INTO THE HANDS OF A MONSTER LIKE THE WHITE QUEEN!

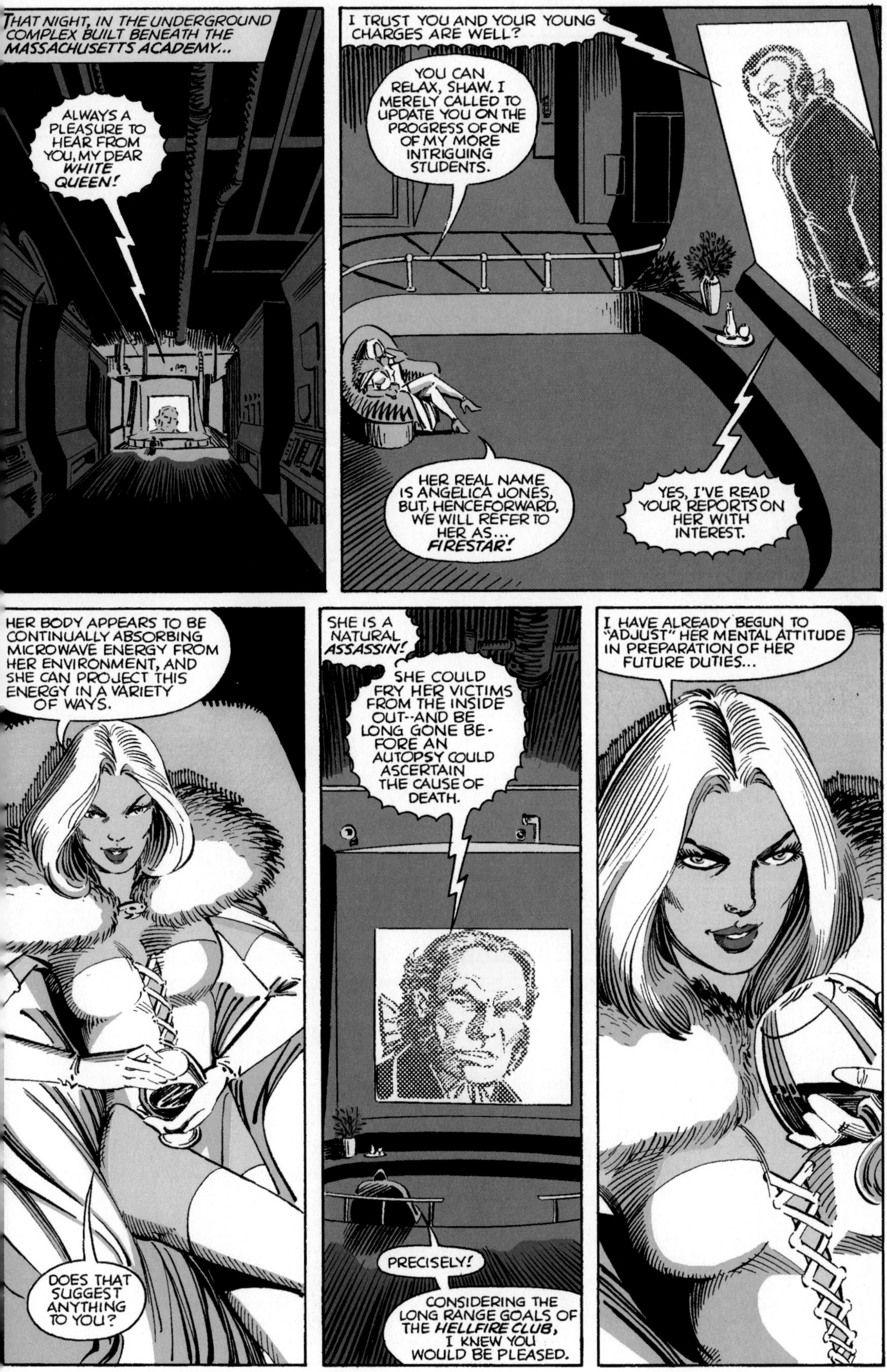
THAT NIGHT, IN THE UNDERGROUND COMPLEX BUILT BENEATH THE MASSACHUSETTS ACADEMY...
ALWAYS A PLEASURE TO HEAR FROM YOU, MY DEAR WHITE QUEEN!
I TRUST YOU AND YOUR YOUNG CHARGES ARE WELL?
YOU CAN RELAX, SHAW. I MERELY CALLED TO UPDATE YOU ON THE PROGRESS OF ONE OF MY MORE INTRIGUING STUDENTS.
HER REAL NAME IS ANGELICA JONES, BUT, HENCEFORWARD, WE WILL REFER TO HER AS... FIRESTAR!
YES, I'VE READ YOUR REPORTS ON HER WITH INTEREST.
HER BODY APPEARS TO BE CONTINUALLY ABSORBING MICROWAVE ENERGY FROM HER ENVIRONMENT, AND SHE CAN PROJECT THIS ENERGY IN A VARIETY OF WAYS.
DOES THAT SUGGEST ANYTHING TO YOU?
SHE IS A NATURAL ASSASSIN!
SHE COULD FRY HER VICTIMS FROM THE INSIDE OUT--AND BE LONG GONE BEFORE AN AUTOPSY COULD ASCERTAIN THE CAUSE OF DEATH.
PRECISELY!
CONSIDERING THE LONG RANGE GOALS OF THE HELLFIRE CLUB, I KNEW YOU WOULD BE PLEASED.
I HAVE ALREADY BEGUN TO "ADJUST" HER MENTAL ATTITUDE IN PREPARATION OF HER FUTURE DUTIES...

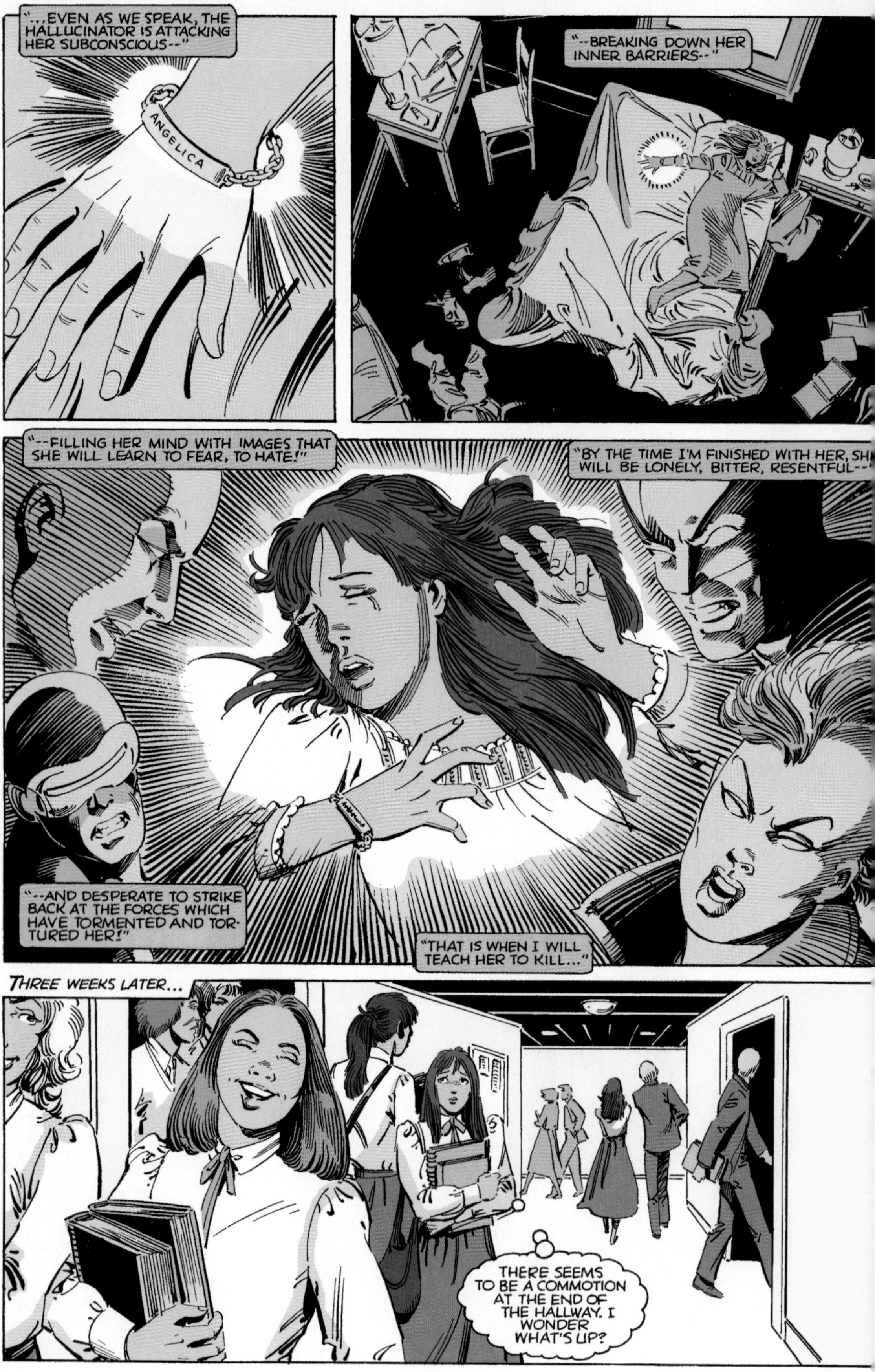
"...EVEN AS WE SPEAK, THE HALLUCINATOR IS ATTACKING HER SUBCONSCIOUS--"
ANGELICA
"--BREAKING DOWN HER INNER BARRIERS--"
"--FILLING HER MIND WITH IMAGES THAT SHE WILL LEARN TO FEAR, TO HATE!"
"BY THE TIME I'M FINISHED WITH HER, SHE WILL BE LONELY, BITTER, RESENTFUL--"
"--AND DESPERATE TO STRIKE BACK AT THE FORCES WHICH HAVE TORMENTED AND TORTURED HER!"
"THAT IS WHEN I WILL TEACH HER TO KILL..."
THREE WEEKS LATER...
THERE SEEMS TO BE A COMMOTION AT THE END OF THE HALLWAY. I WONDER WHAT'S UP?

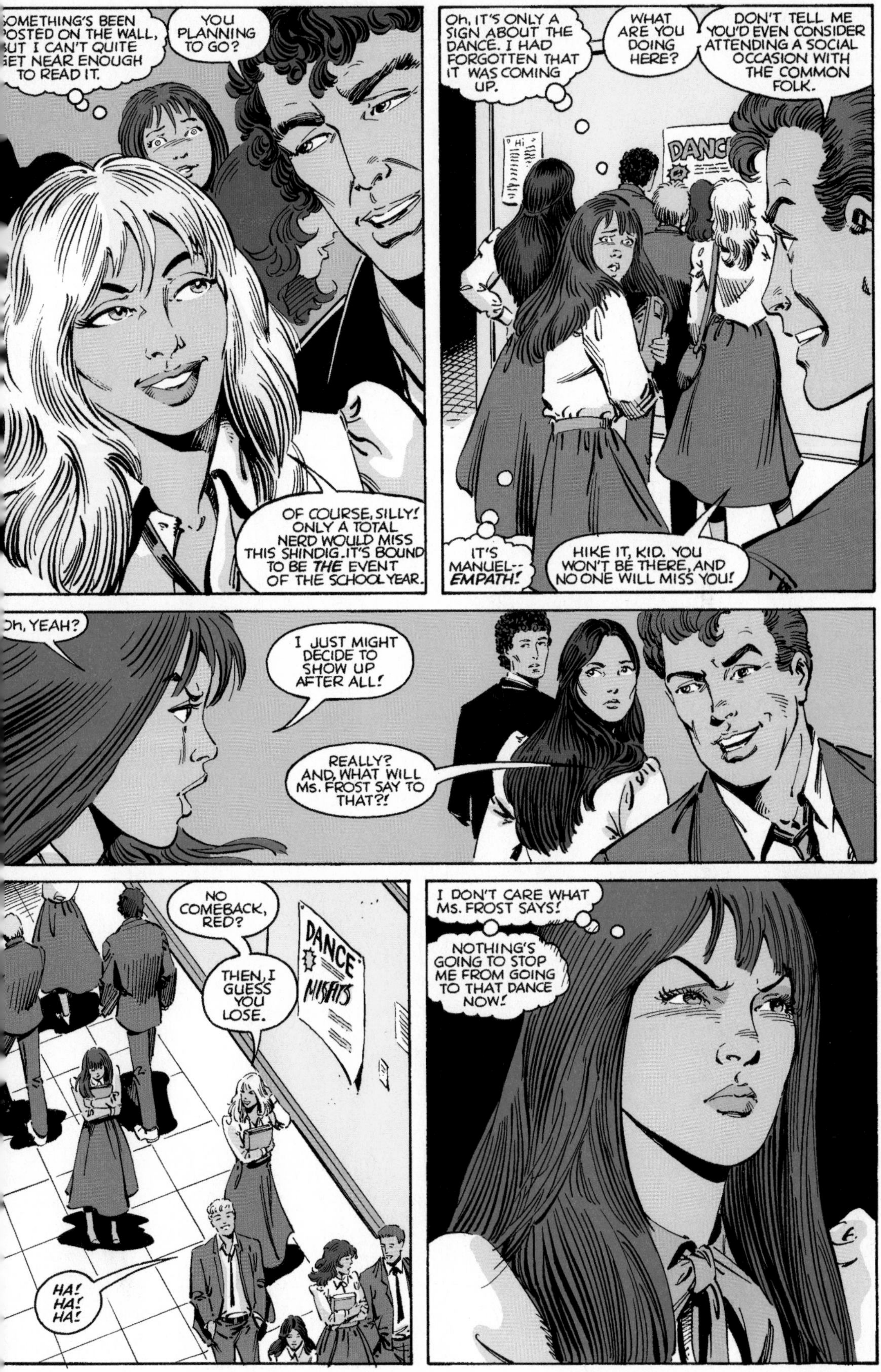
OMETHING'S BEEN POSTED ON THE WALL, BUT I CAN'T QUITE GET NEAR ENOUGH TO READ IT.
YOU PLANNING TO GO?
OF COURSE, SILLY! ONLY A TOTAL NERD WOULD MISS THIS SHINDIG. IT'S BOUND TO BE *THE* EVENT OF THE SCHOOL YEAR.
Oh, IT'S ONLY A SIGN ABOUT THE DANCE. I HAD FORGOTTEN THAT IT WAS COMING UP.
WHAT ARE YOU DOING HERE?
DON'T TELL ME YOU'D EVEN CONSIDER ATTENDING A SOCIAL OCCASION WITH THE COMMON FOLK.
DANCE
IT'S MANUEL-- *EMPATH!*
HIKE IT, KID. YOU WON'T BE THERE, AND NO ONE WILL MISS YOU!
Oh, YEAH?
I JUST MIGHT DECIDE TO SHOW UP AFTER ALL!
REALLY? AND, WHAT WILL Ms. FROST SAY TO THAT?!
NO COMEBACK, RED?
THEN, I GUESS YOU LOSE.
DANCE
HA! HA! HA!
I DON'T CARE WHAT Ms. FROST SAYS!
NOTHING'S GOING TO STOP ME FROM GOING TO THAT DANCE NOW!

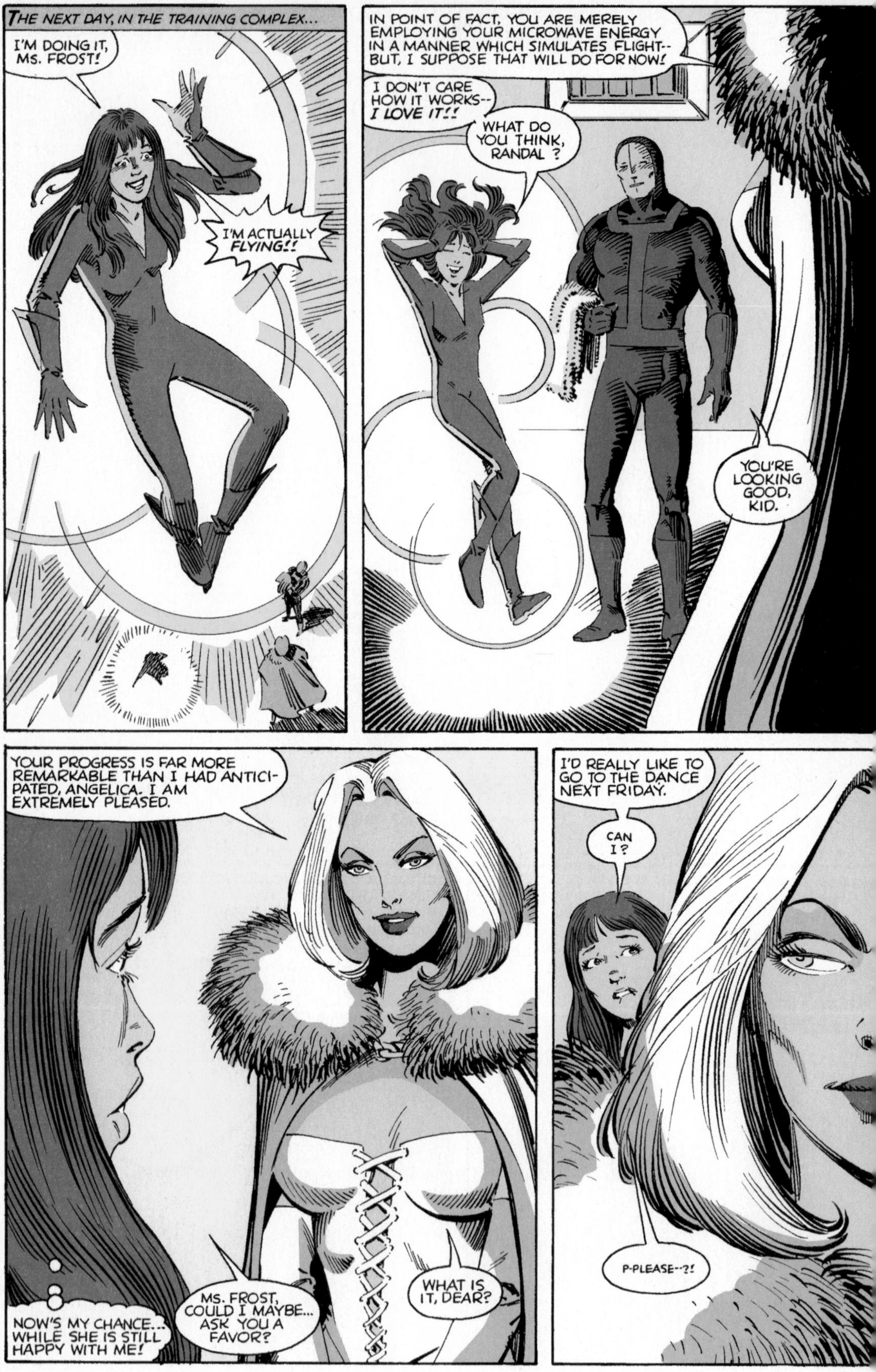
THE NEXT DAY, IN THE TRAINING COMPLEX...
I'M DOING IT, MS. FROST!
I'M ACTUALLY FLYING!!
IN POINT OF FACT, YOU ARE MERELY EMPLOYING YOUR MICROWAVE ENERGY IN A MANNER WHICH SIMULATES FLIGHT-- BUT, I SUPPOSE THAT WILL DO FOR NOW!
I DON'T CARE HOW IT WORKS-- I LOVE IT!!
WHAT DO YOU THINK, RANDAL ?
YOU'RE LOOKING GOOD, KID.
YOUR PROGRESS IS FAR MORE REMARKABLE THAN I HAD ANTICI-PATED, ANGELICA. I AM EXTREMELY PLEASED.
NOW'S MY CHANCE... WHILE SHE IS STILL HAPPY WITH ME!
MS. FROST, COULD I MAYBE... ASK YOU A FAVOR?
WHAT IS IT, DEAR?
I'D REALLY LIKE TO GO TO THE DANCE NEXT FRIDAY.
CAN I?
P-PLEASE--?!

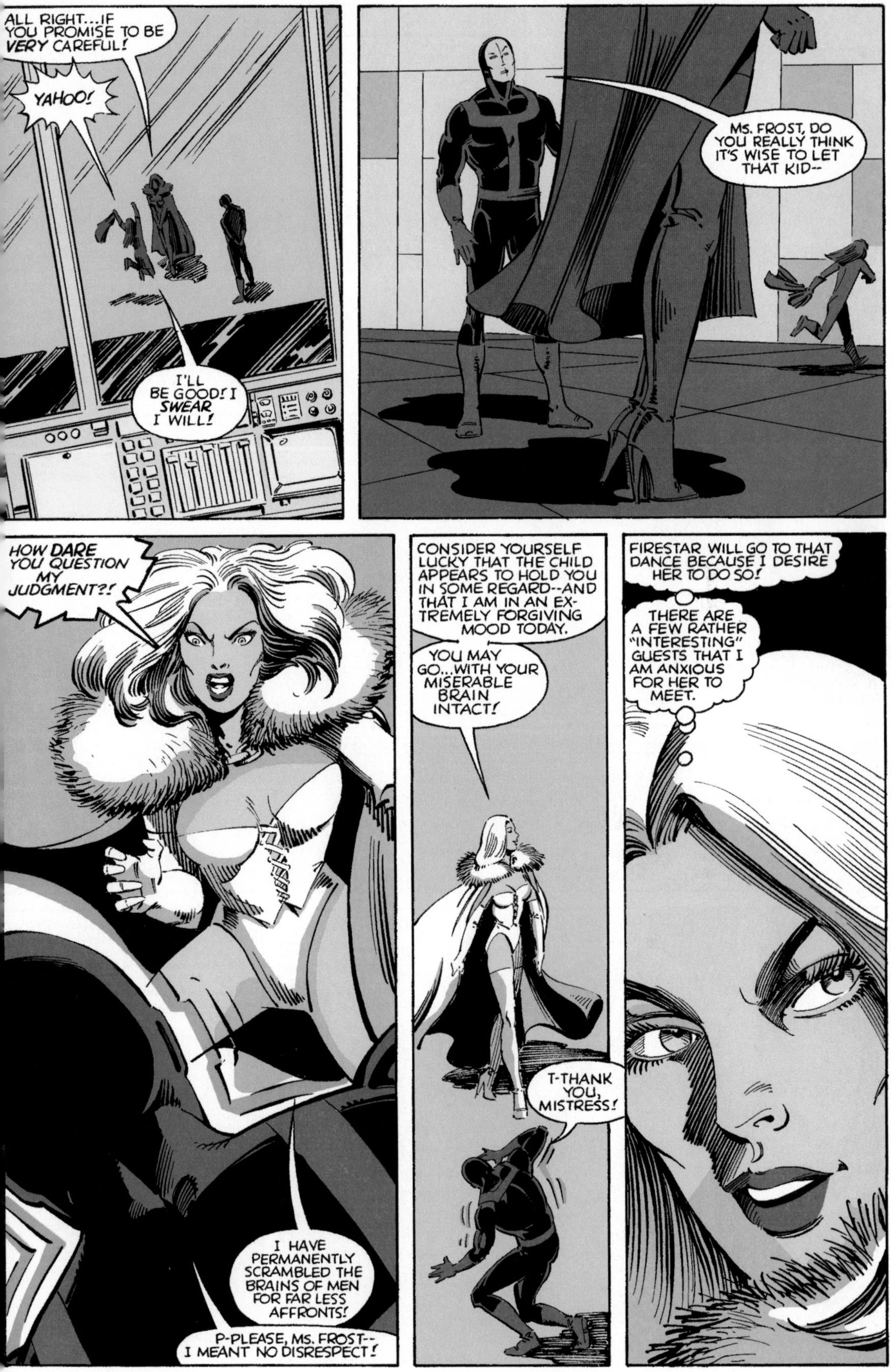
ALL RIGHT...IF YOU PROMISE TO BE VERY CAREFUL!
YAHOO!
I'LL BE GOOD! I SWEAR I WILL!
MS. FROST, DO YOU REALLY THINK IT'S WISE TO LET THAT KID--
HOW DARE YOU QUESTION MY JUDGMENT?!
I HAVE PERMANENTLY SCRAMBLED THE BRAINS OF MEN FOR FAR LESS AFFRONTS!
P-PLEASE, MS. FROST--I MEANT NO DISRESPECT!
CONSIDER YOURSELF LUCKY THAT THE CHILD APPEARS TO HOLD YOU IN SOME REGARD--AND THAT I AM IN AN EXTREMELY FORGIVING MOOD TODAY.
YOU MAY GO...WITH YOUR MISERABLE BRAIN INTACT!
T-THANK YOU, MISTRESS!
FIRESTAR WILL GO TO THAT DANCE BECAUSE I DESIRE HER TO DO SO!
THERE ARE A FEW RATHER "INTERESTING" GUESTS THAT I AM ANXIOUS FOR HER TO MEET.

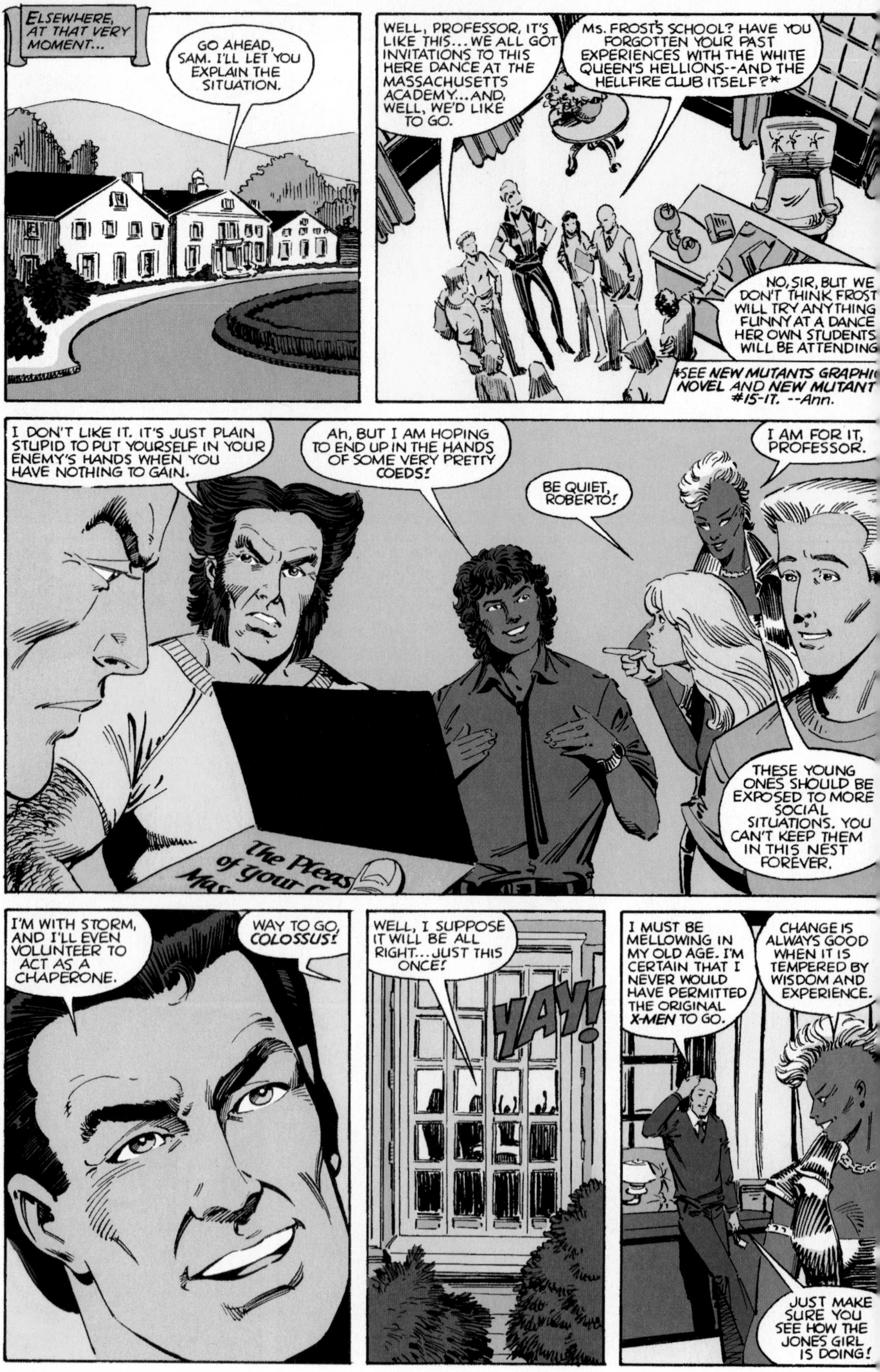
ELSEWHERE, AT THAT VERY MOMENT...
GO AHEAD, SAM. I'LL LET YOU EXPLAIN THE SITUATION.
WELL, PROFESSOR, IT'S LIKE THIS... WE ALL GOT INVITATIONS TO THIS HERE DANCE AT THE MASSACHUSETTS ACADEMY... AND, WELL, WE'D LIKE TO GO.
Ms. FROST'S SCHOOL? HAVE YOU FORGOTTEN YOUR PAST EXPERIENCES WITH THE WHITE QUEEN'S HELLIONS--AND THE HELLFIRE CLUB ITSELF?*
NO, SIR, BUT WE DON'T THINK FROST WILL TRY ANYTHING FUNNY AT A DANCE HER OWN STUDENTS WILL BE ATTENDING
*SEE NEW MUTANTS GRAPHIC NOVEL AND NEW MUTANTS #15-17. --Ann.
I DON'T LIKE IT. IT'S JUST PLAIN STUPID TO PUT YOURSELF IN YOUR ENEMY'S HANDS WHEN YOU HAVE NOTHING TO GAIN.
Ah, BUT I AM HOPING TO END UP IN THE HANDS OF SOME VERY PRETTY COEDS!
BE QUIET, ROBERTO!
I AM FOR IT, PROFESSOR.
THESE YOUNG ONES SHOULD BE EXPOSED TO MORE SOCIAL SITUATIONS. YOU CAN'T KEEP THEM IN THIS NEST FOREVER.
I'M WITH STORM, AND I'LL EVEN VOLUNTEER TO ACT AS A CHAPERONE.
WAY TO GO, COLOSSUS!
WELL, I SUPPOSE IT WILL BE ALL RIGHT... JUST THIS ONCE!
YAY!
I MUST BE MELLOWING IN MY OLD AGE. I'M CERTAIN THAT I NEVER WOULD HAVE PERMITTED THE ORIGINAL X-MEN TO GO.
CHANGE IS ALWAYS GOOD WHEN IT IS TEMPERED BY WISDOM AND EXPERIENCE.
JUST MAKE SURE YOU SEE HOW THE JONES GIRL IS DOING!

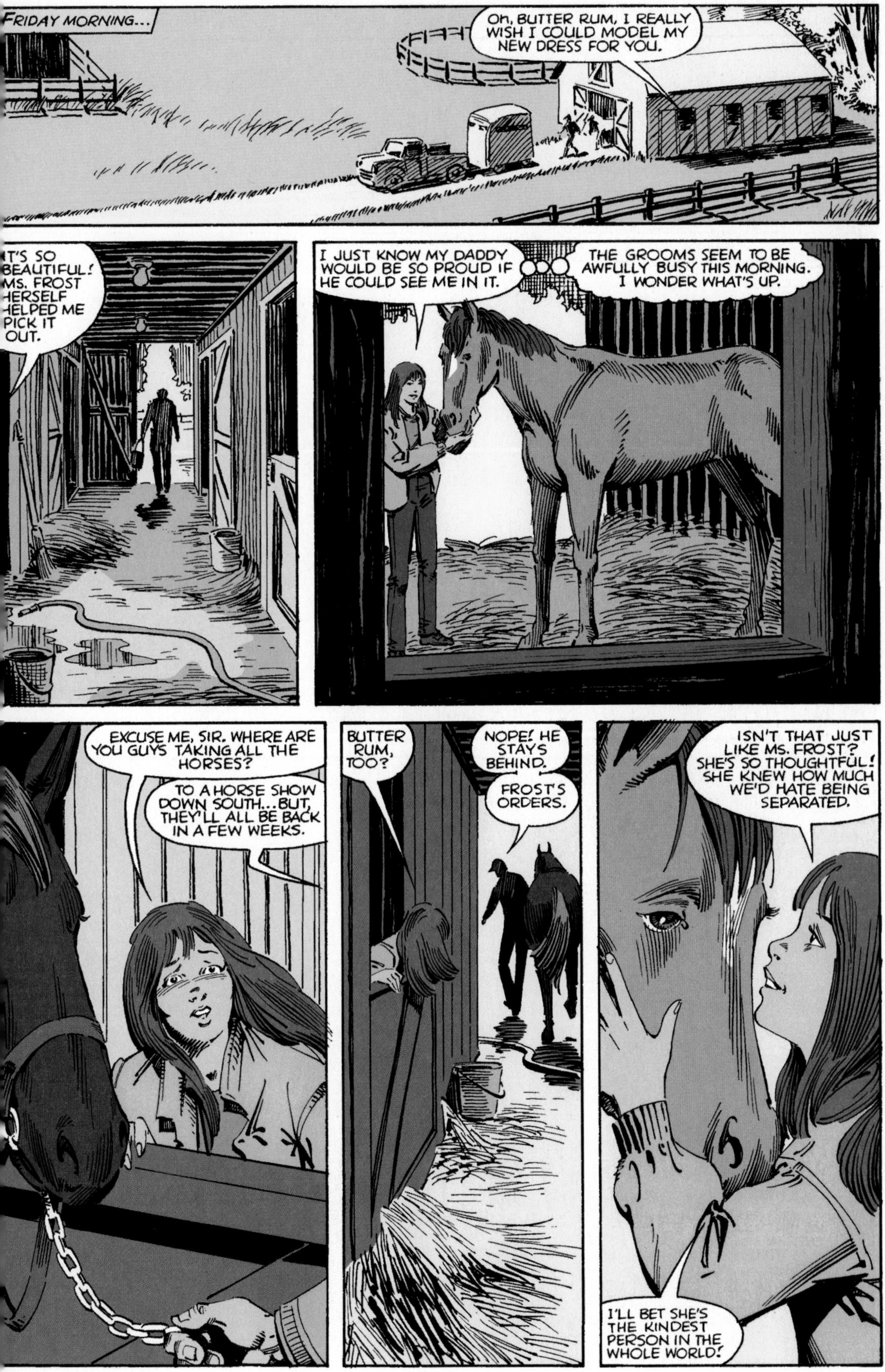
FRIDAY MORNING...
OH, BUTTER RUM, I REALLY WISH I COULD MODEL MY NEW DRESS FOR YOU.
IT'S SO BEAUTIFUL! MS. FROST HERSELF HELPED ME PICK IT OUT.
I JUST KNOW MY DADDY WOULD BE SO PROUD IF HE COULD SEE ME IN IT.
THE GROOMS SEEM TO BE AWFULLY BUSY THIS MORNING. I WONDER WHAT'S UP.
EXCUSE ME, SIR. WHERE ARE YOU GUYS TAKING ALL THE HORSES?
TO A HORSE SHOW DOWN SOUTH...BUT, THEY'LL ALL BE BACK IN A FEW WEEKS.
BUTTER RUM, TOO?
NOPE! HE STAYS BEHIND.
FROST'S ORDERS.
ISN'T THAT JUST LIKE MS. FROST? SHE'S SO THOUGHTFUL! SHE KNEW HOW MUCH WE'D HATE BEING SEPARATED.
I'LL BET SHE'S THE KINDEST PERSON IN THE WHOLE WORLD!

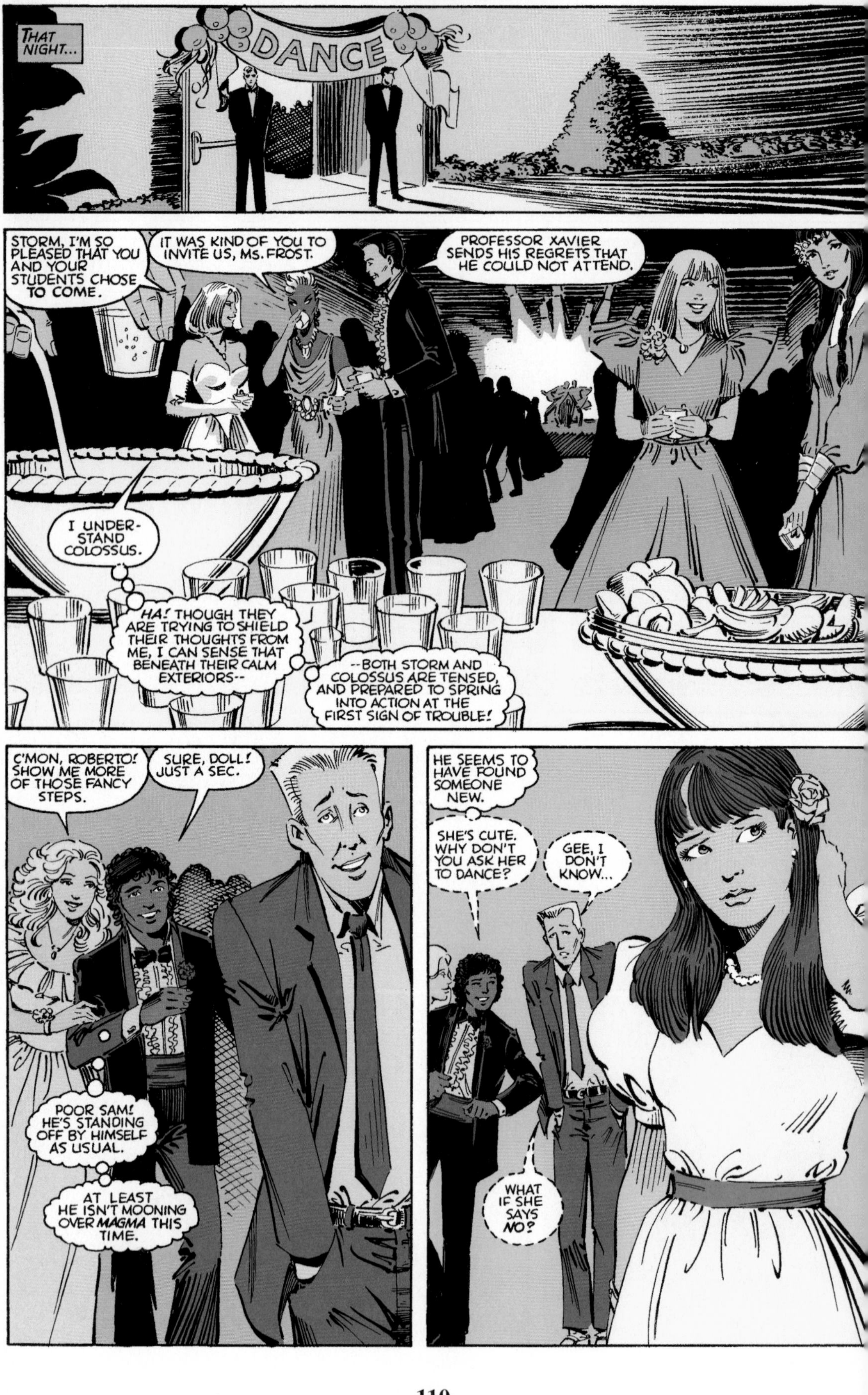
THAT NIGHT...
DANCE
STORM, I'M SO PLEASED THAT YOU AND YOUR STUDENTS CHOSE TO COME.
IT WAS KIND OF YOU TO INVITE US, MS. FROST.
PROFESSOR XAVIER SENDS HIS REGRETS THAT HE COULD NOT ATTEND.
I UNDER-STAND COLOSSUS.
HA! THOUGH THEY ARE TRYING TO SHIELD THEIR THOUGHTS FROM ME, I CAN SENSE THAT BENEATH THEIR CALM EXTERIORS--
--BOTH STORM AND COLOSSUS ARE TENSED, AND PREPARED TO SPRING INTO ACTION AT THE FIRST SIGN OF TROUBLE!
C'MON, ROBERTO! SHOW ME MORE OF THOSE FANCY STEPS.
SURE, DOLL! JUST A SEC.
POOR SAM! HE'S STANDING OFF BY HIMSELF AS USUAL.
AT LEAST HE ISN'T MOONING OVER MAGMA THIS TIME.
HE SEEMS TO HAVE FOUND SOMEONE NEW.
SHE'S CUTE. WHY DON'T YOU ASK HER TO DANCE?
GEE, I DON'T KNOW...
WHAT IF SHE SAYS NO?

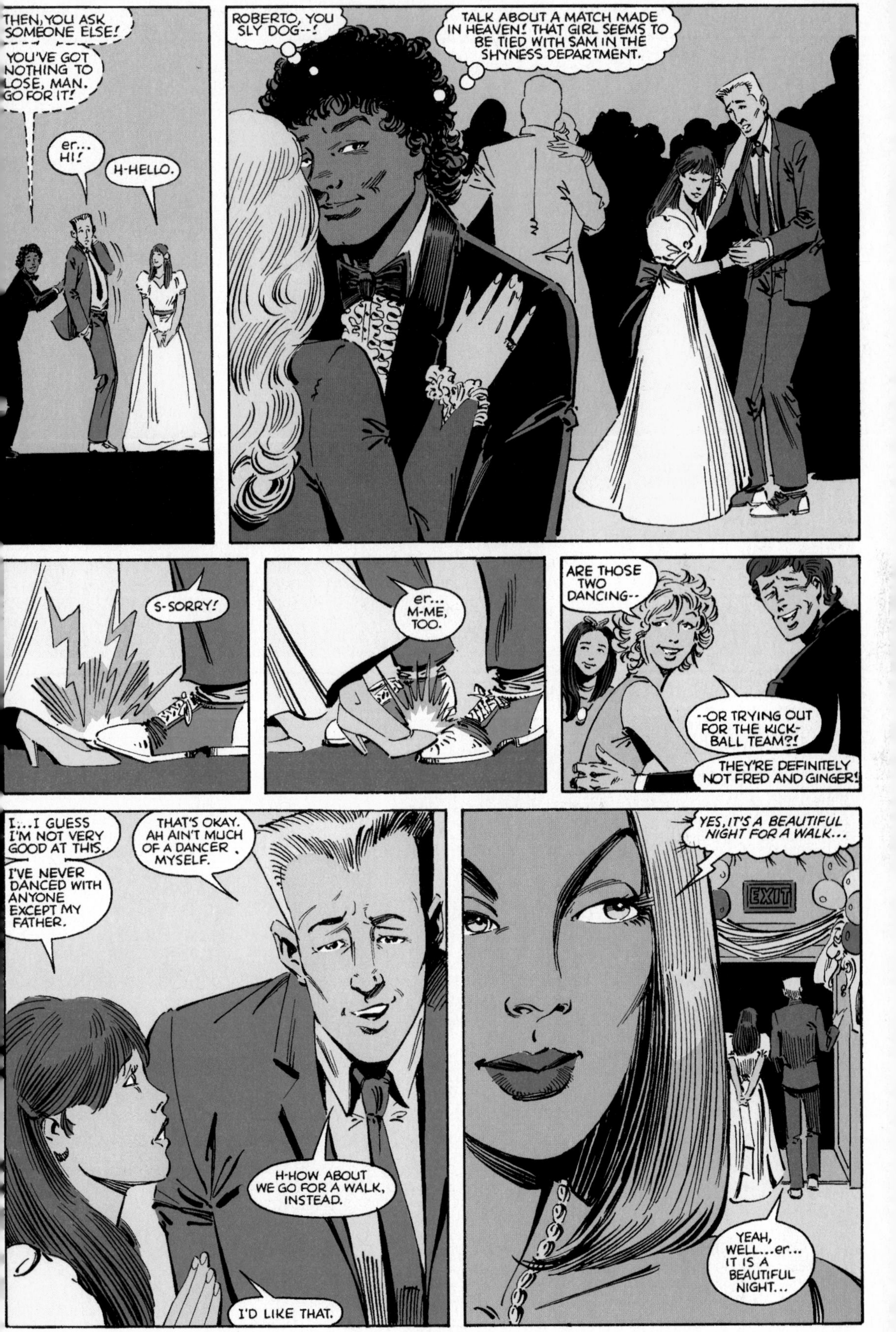
THEN, YOU ASK SOMEONE ELSE!
YOU'VE GOT NOTHING TO LOSE, MAN. GO FOR IT!
er... HI!
H-HELLO.
ROBERTO, YOU SLY DOG--!
TALK ABOUT A MATCH MADE IN HEAVEN! THAT GIRL SEEMS TO BE TIED WITH SAM IN THE SHYNESS DEPARTMENT.
S-SORRY!
er... M-ME, TOO.
ARE THOSE TWO DANCING--
--OR TRYING OUT FOR THE KICK-BALL TEAM?!
THEY'RE DEFINITELY NOT FRED AND GINGER!
I...I GUESS I'M NOT VERY GOOD AT THIS.
I'VE NEVER DANCED WITH ANYONE EXCEPT MY FATHER.
THAT'S OKAY. AH AIN'T MUCH OF A DANCER MYSELF.
H-HOW ABOUT WE GO FOR A WALK, INSTEAD.
I'D LIKE THAT.
YES, IT'S A BEAUTIFUL NIGHT FOR A WALK...
EXIT
YEAH, WELL...er... IT IS A BEAUTIFUL NIGHT...

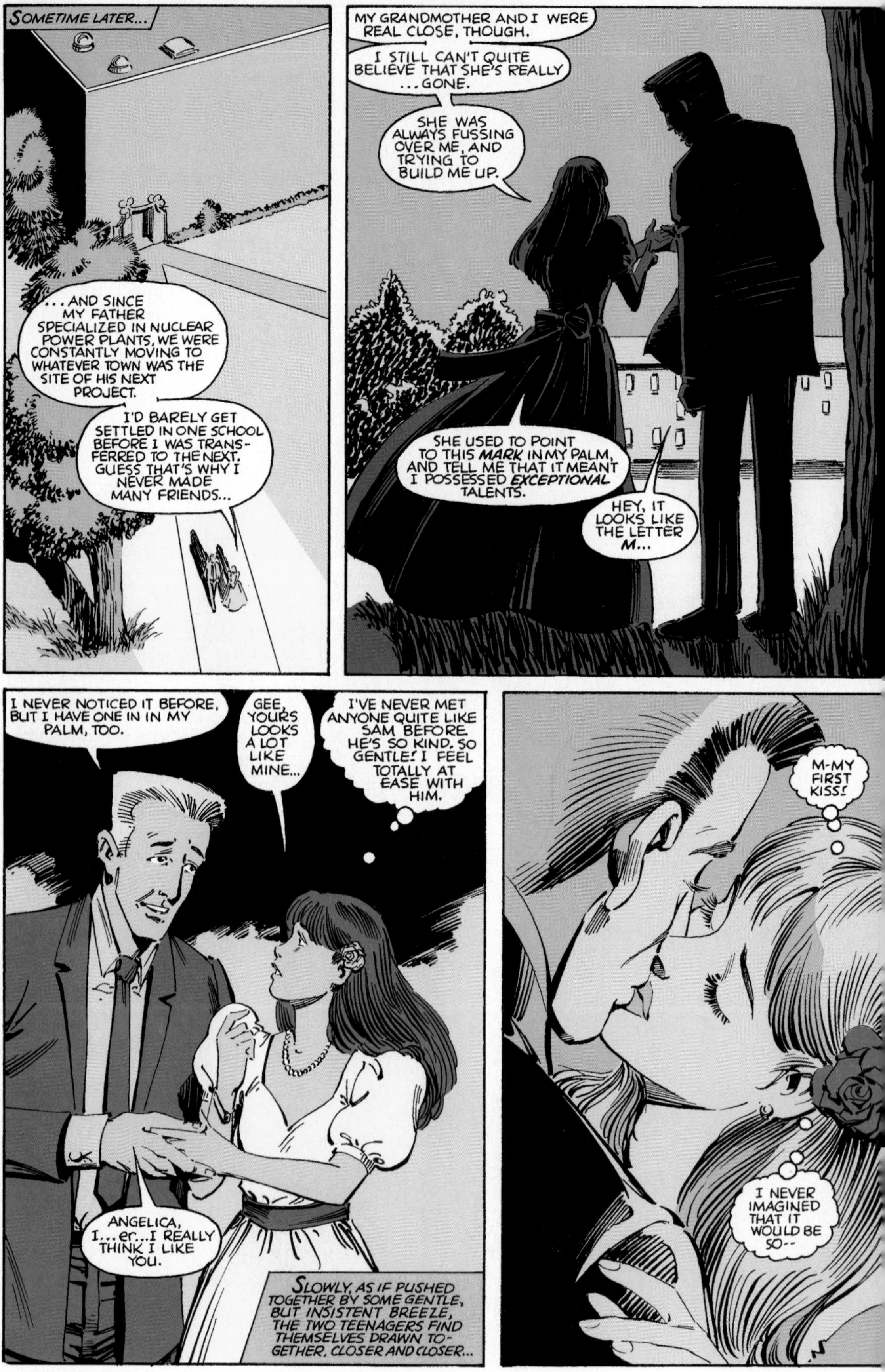
SOMETIME LATER...
...AND SINCE MY FATHER SPECIALIZED IN NUCLEAR POWER PLANTS, WE WERE CONSTANTLY MOVING TO WHATEVER TOWN WAS THE SITE OF HIS NEXT PROJECT.
I'D BARELY GET SETTLED IN ONE SCHOOL BEFORE I WAS TRANS-FERRED TO THE NEXT. GUESS THAT'S WHY I NEVER MADE MANY FRIENDS...
MY GRANDMOTHER AND I WERE REAL CLOSE, THOUGH.
I STILL CAN'T QUITE BELIEVE THAT SHE'S REALLY ...GONE.
SHE WAS ALWAYS FUSSING OVER ME, AND TRYING TO BUILD ME UP.
SHE USED TO POINT TO THIS MARK IN MY PALM, AND TELL ME THAT IT MEANT I POSSESSED EXCEPTIONAL TALENTS.
HEY, IT LOOKS LIKE THE LETTER M...
I NEVER NOTICED IT BEFORE, BUT I HAVE ONE IN IN MY PALM, TOO.
GEE, YOURS LOOKS A LOT LIKE MINE...
I'VE NEVER MET ANYONE QUITE LIKE SAM BEFORE. HE'S SO KIND. SO GENTLE! I FEEL TOTALLY AT EASE WITH HIM.
ANGELICA, I...er...I REALLY THINK I LIKE YOU.
SLOWLY, AS IF PUSHED TOGETHER BY SOME GENTLE, BUT INSISTENT BREEZE, THE TWO TEENAGERS FIND THEMSELVES DRAWN TO-GETHER, CLOSER AND CLOSER...
M-MY FIRST KISS!
I NEVER IMAGINED THAT IT WOULD BE SO--

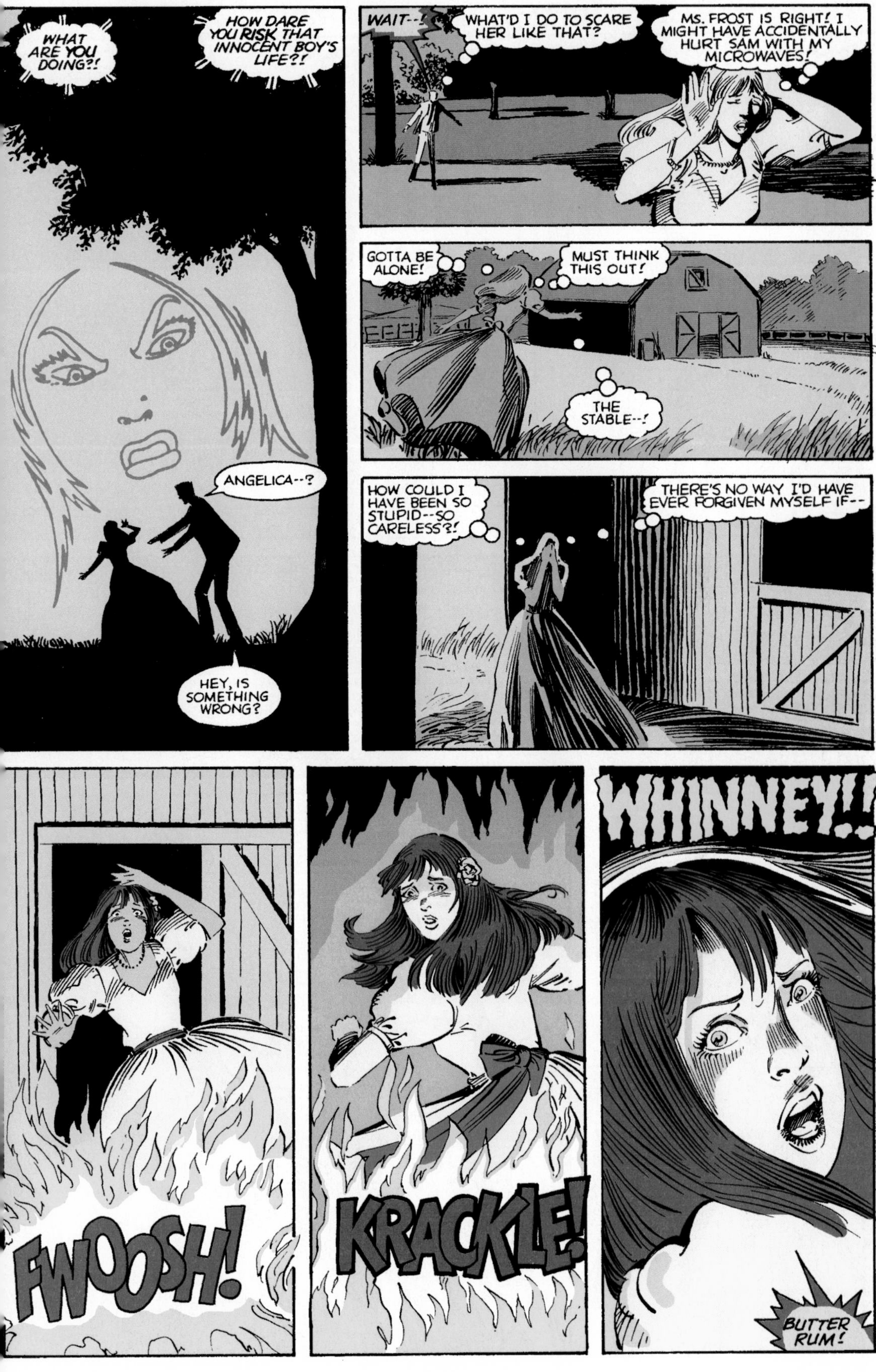

WHAT ARE YOU DOING?!
HOW DARE YOU RISK THAT INNOCENT BOY'S LIFE?!
ANGELICA--?
HEY, IS SOMETHING WRONG?
WAIT--!
WHAT'D I DO TO SCARE HER LIKE THAT?
MS. FROST IS RIGHT! I MIGHT HAVE ACCIDENTALLY HURT SAM WITH MY MICROWAVES!
GOTTA BE ALONE!
MUST THINK THIS OUT!
THE STABLE--!
HOW COULD I HAVE BEEN SO STUPID--SO CARELESS?!
THERE'S NO WAY I'D HAVE EVER FORGIVEN MYSELF IF--
FWOOSH!
KRACKLE!
WHINNEY!!
BUTTER RUM!

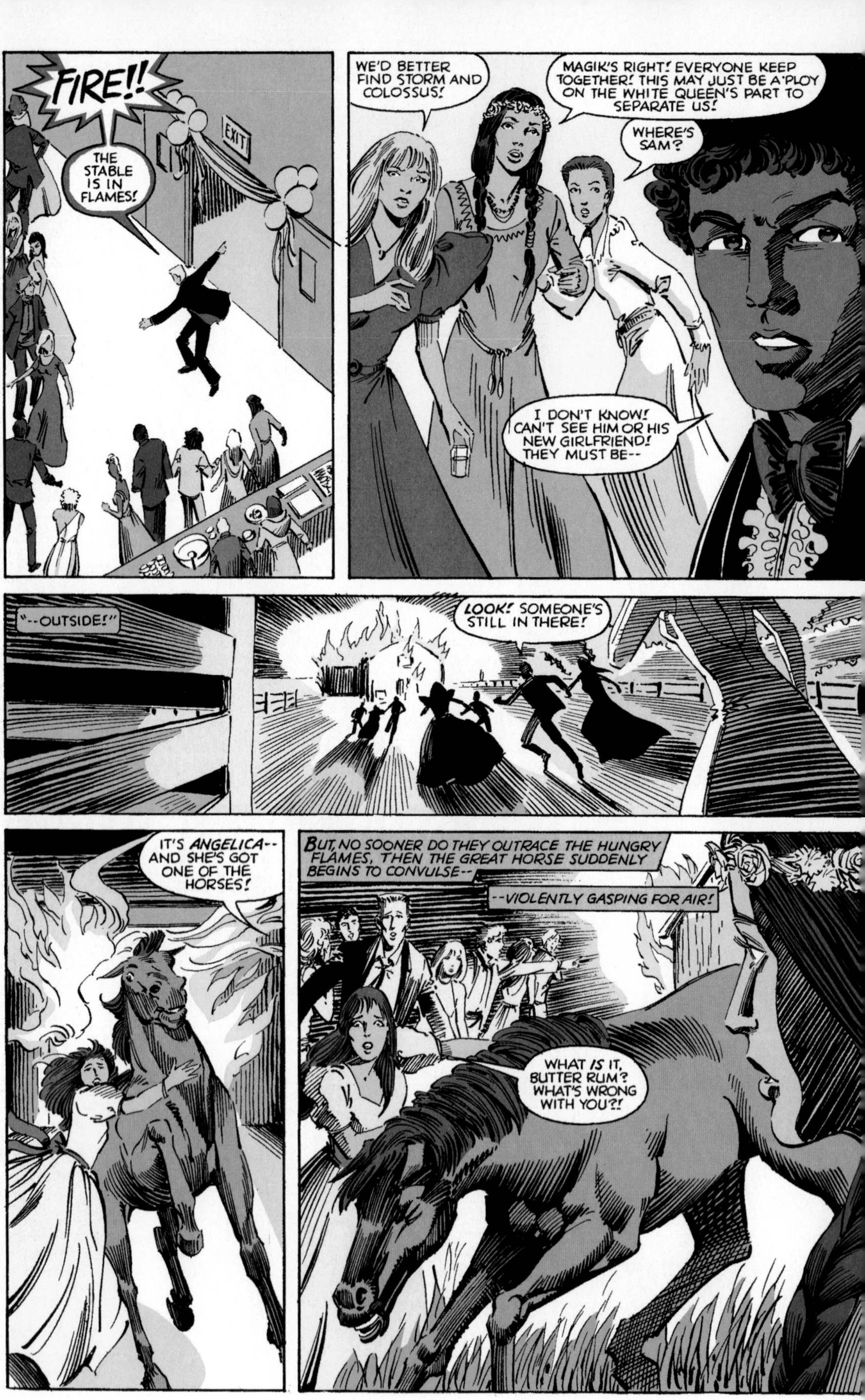
FIRE!!
THE STABLE IS IN FLAMES!
WE'D BETTER FIND STORM AND COLOSSUS!
MAGIK'S RIGHT! EVERYONE KEEP TOGETHER! THIS MAY JUST BE A 'PLOY ON THE WHITE QUEEN'S PART TO SEPARATE US!
WHERE'S SAM?
I DON'T KNOW! CAN'T SEE HIM OR HIS NEW GIRLFRIEND! THEY MUST BE--
"--OUTSIDE!"
LOOK! SOMEONE'S STILL IN THERE!
IT'S ANGELICA-- AND SHE'S GOT ONE OF THE HORSES!
BUT, NO SOONER DO THEY OUTRACE THE HUNGRY FLAMES, THEN THE GREAT HORSE SUDDENLY BEGINS TO CONVULSE--
--VIOLENTLY GASPING FOR AIR!
WHAT IS IT, BUTTER RUM? WHAT'S WRONG WITH YOU?!

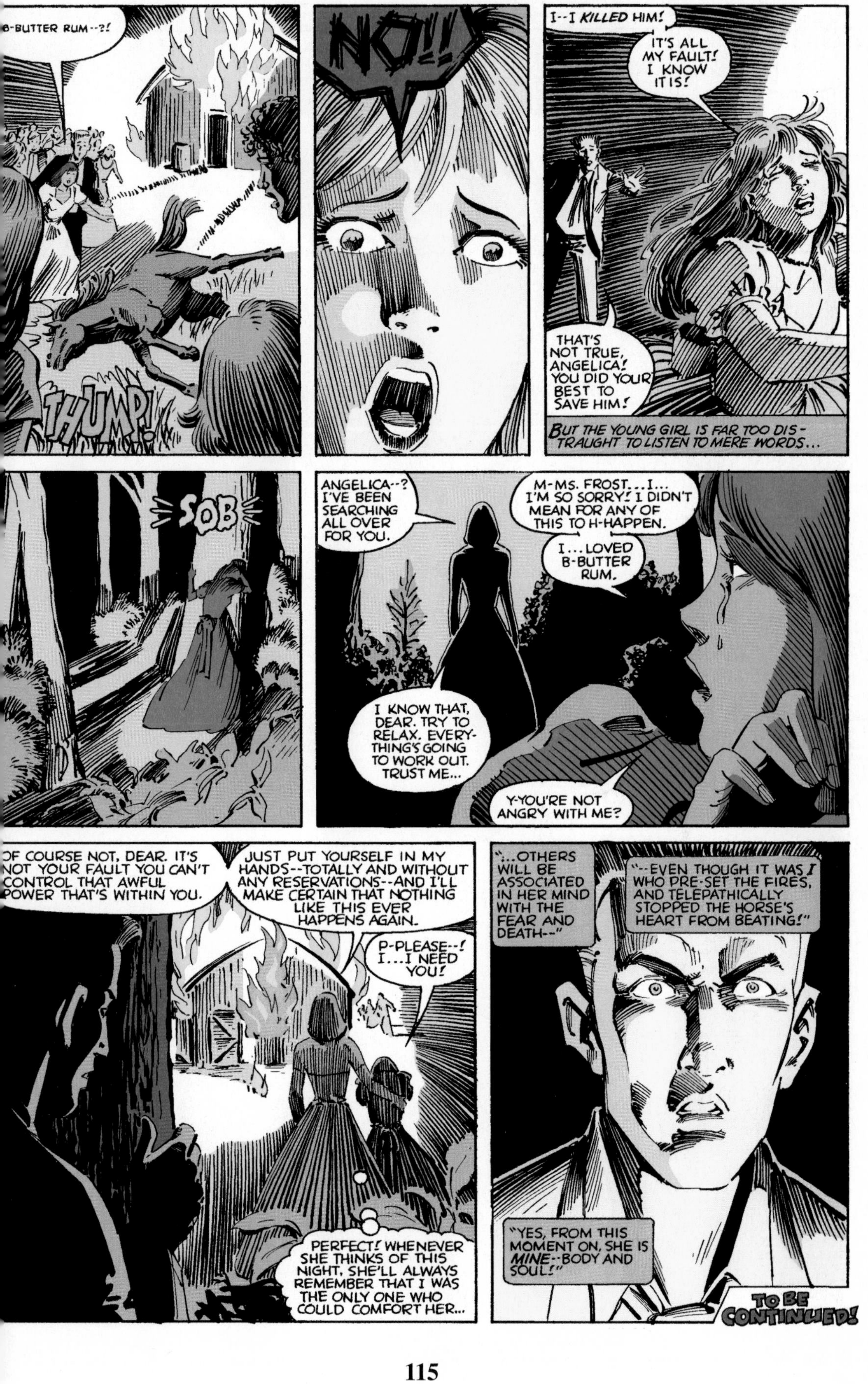
B-BUTTER RUM--?!
THUMP!
NO!!
I--I KILLED HIM!
IT'S ALL MY FAULT! I KNOW IT IS!
THAT'S NOT TRUE, ANGELICA! YOU DID YOUR BEST TO SAVE HIM!
BUT THE YOUNG GIRL IS FAR TOO DISTRAUGHT TO LISTEN TO MERE WORDS...
SOB
ANGELICA--? I'VE BEEN SEARCHING ALL OVER FOR YOU.
M-MS. FROST...I... I'M SO SORRY! I DIDN'T MEAN FOR ANY OF THIS TO H-HAPPEN.
I...LOVED B-BUTTER RUM.
I KNOW THAT, DEAR. TRY TO RELAX. EVERYTHING'S GOING TO WORK OUT. TRUST ME...
Y-YOU'RE NOT ANGRY WITH ME?
OF COURSE NOT, DEAR. IT'S NOT YOUR FAULT YOU CAN'T CONTROL THAT AWFUL POWER THAT'S WITHIN YOU.
JUST PUT YOURSELF IN MY HANDS--TOTALLY AND WITHOUT ANY RESERVATIONS--AND I'LL MAKE CERTAIN THAT NOTHING LIKE THIS EVER HAPPENS AGAIN.
P-PLEASE--! I...I NEED YOU!
PERFECT! WHENEVER SHE THINKS OF THIS NIGHT, SHE'LL ALWAYS REMEMBER THAT I WAS THE ONLY ONE WHO COULD COMFORT HER...
"...OTHERS WILL BE ASSOCIATED IN HER MIND WITH THE FEAR AND DEATH--"
"--EVEN THOUGH IT WAS I WHO PRE-SET THE FIRES, AND TELEPATHICALLY STOPPED THE HORSE'S HEART FROM BEATING!"
"YES, FROM THIS MOMENT ON, SHE IS MINE--BODY AND SOUL!"
TO BE CONTINUED!

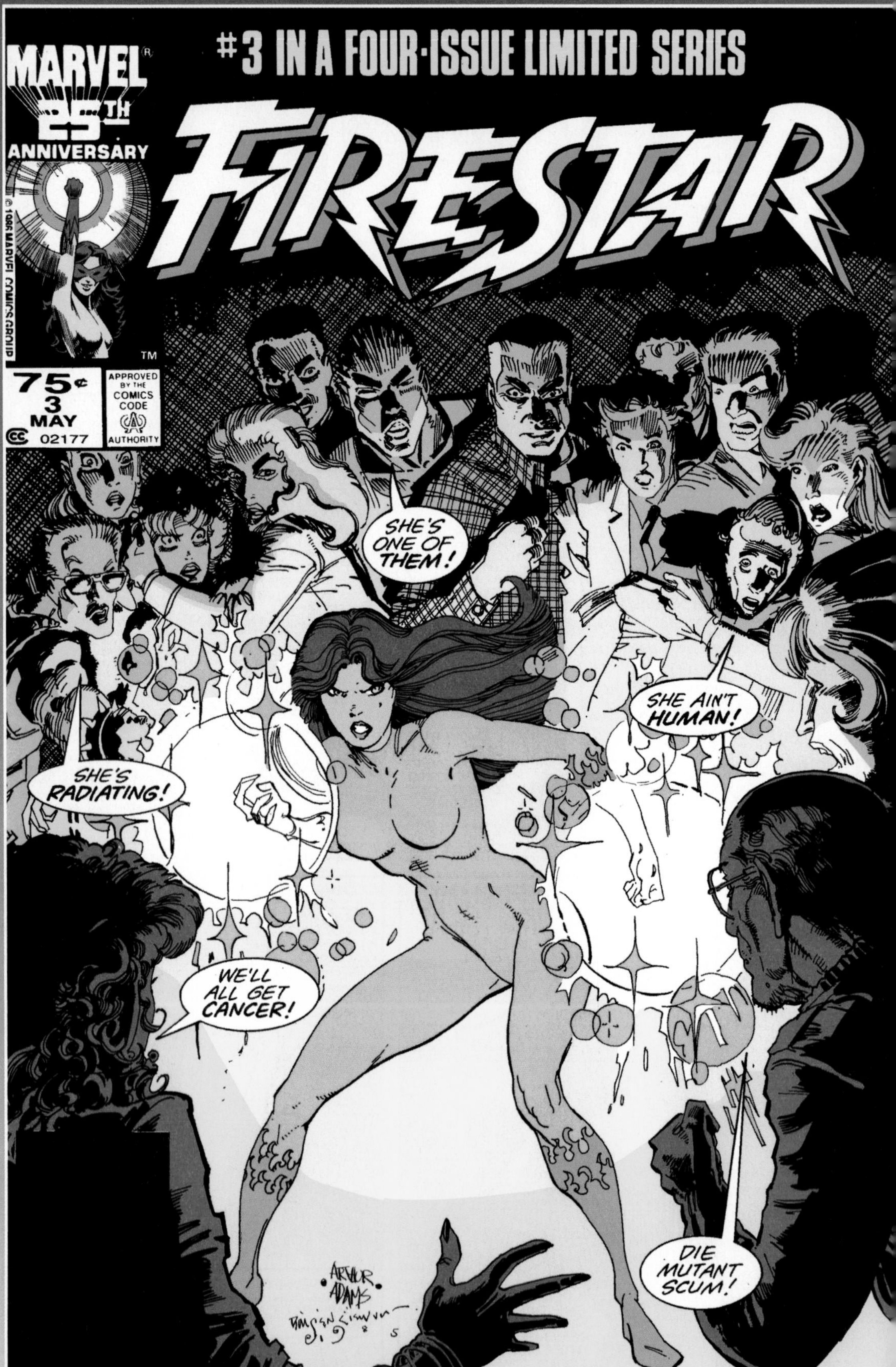

#3 IN A FOUR-ISSUE LIMITED SERIES
MARVEL®
25TH ANNIVERSARY
© 1986 MARVEL COMICS GROUP
FIRESTAR
TM
75¢
3
MAY
02177
APPROVED BY THE COMICS CODE AUTHORITY
SHE'S ONE OF THEM!
SHE AIN'T HUMAN!
SHE'S RADIATING!
WE'LL ALL GET CANCER!
DIE MUTANT SCUM!

Unable to cope with the fact that his only daughter is a mutant possessing strange and ncanny powers, *Bartholomew Jones* quickly entrusts her education and training to *Ms. mma Frost*, headmistress of the prestigious *Massachusetts Academy*. Secretly a member f the *Inner Council of the Hellfire Club*, an organization determined to dominate the world, rost plans to mold young *Angelica* into the ultimate weapon—a human killing machine!!

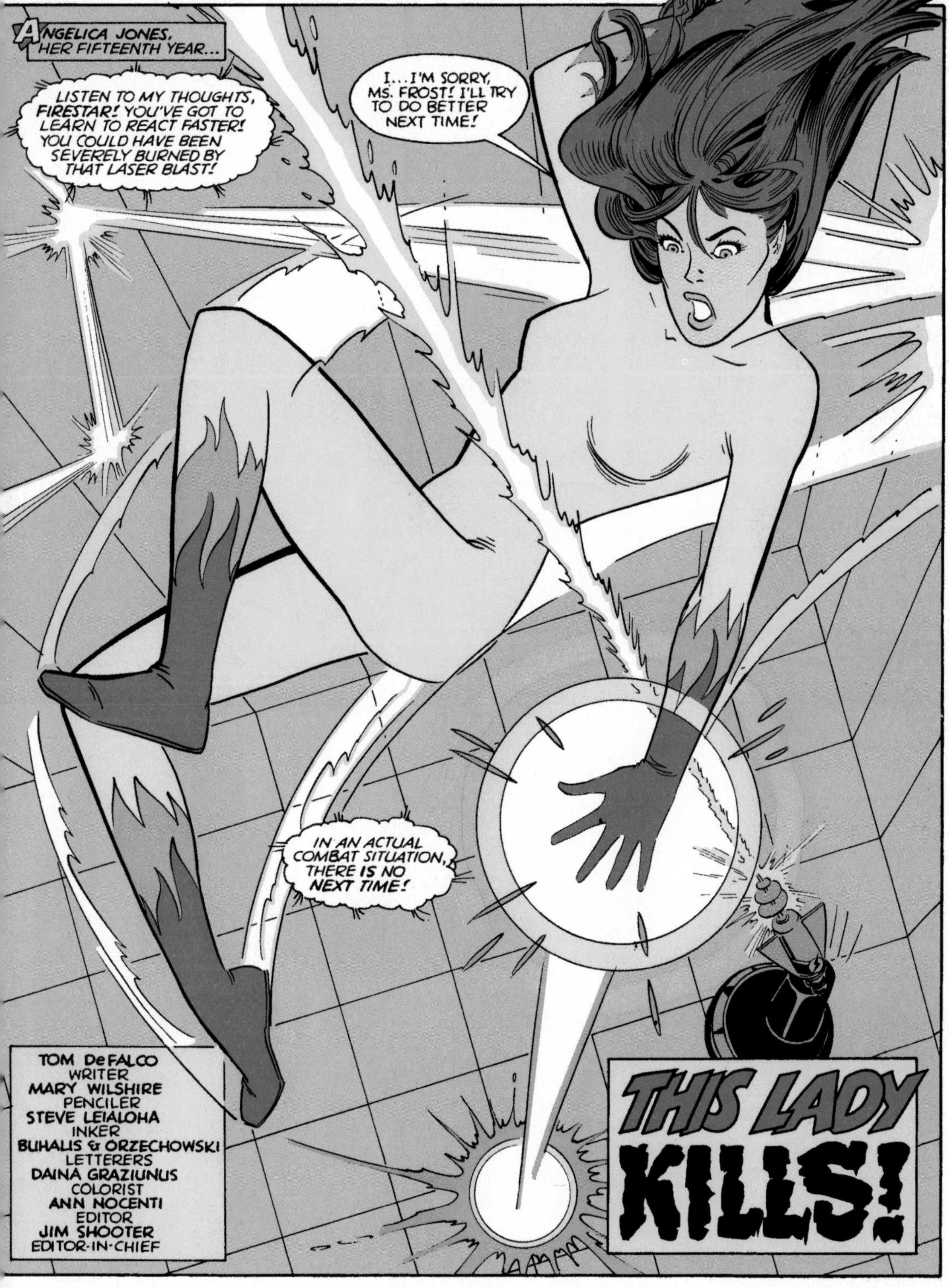
ANGELICA JONES, HER FIFTEENTH YEAR...
LISTEN TO MY THOUGHTS, FIRESTAR! YOU'VE GOT TO LEARN TO REACT FASTER! YOU COULD HAVE BEEN SEVERELY BURNED BY THAT LASER BLAST!
I...I'M SORRY, MS. FROST! I'LL TRY TO DO BETTER NEXT TIME!
IN AN ACTUAL COMBAT SITUATION, THERE IS NO NEXT TIME!
TOM DeFALCO WRITER
MARY WILSHIRE PENCILER
STEVE LEIALOHA INKER
BUHALIS & ORZECHOWSKI LETTERERS
DAINA GRAZIUNUS COLORIST
ANN NOCENTI EDITOR
JIM SHOOTER EDITOR-IN-CHIEF
THIS LADY KILLS!

YOU CAN'T ALLOW YOURSELF THE LUXURY OF THINKING THROUGH EVERY ONE OF YOUR ACTIONS! YOUR REFLEXES MUST BE HONED TO RESPOND TO DANGER AUTOMATICALLY!

LET YOUR MICROWAVE ENERGY FLOW OUT OF YOUR BODY NATURALLY! INSTINCTIVELY!

I...I'M TRYING!

BE CAREFUL! YOU'RE MUCH TOO OFF-BALANCE TO ASSAULT THAT LASER CANNON EFFECTIVELY!

STRAIGHTEN YOURSELF OUT, BEFORE IT CAN DRAW A BEAD ON YOU! THEN SWOOP DOWN AND...

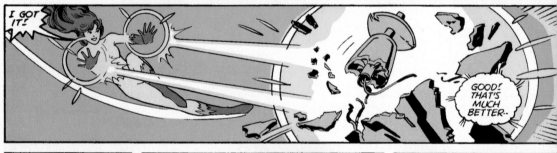

I GOT IT!

GOOD! THAT'S MUCH BETTER--

--BUT THIS TRAINING SESSION IS FAR FROM OVER!

ROBOTS!!

BWAMM!

GOT TO PULL BACK UNTIL I CAN GET MYSELF INTO THE PROPER POSITION TO--

---ATTACK!

YAHOO!

DON'T GET OVER-CONFIDENT, YOUNG LADY! THE SECOND ROBOT ALREADY HAS YOU IN ITS SIGHTS!

I SEE IT!

HOW'S *THAT* FOR A QUICK COMEBACK?

VERY IMPRESSIVE!

HOWEVER, WHEN YOU'RE IN THE FIELD, YOU DARE NOT RELAX YOUR GUARD FOR AN INSTANT!

SOUNDS LIKE SOME TYPE OF MACHINE-GUN!

BRAT-TA-TA

WHAT THE--?!

IT'S PROFESSOR XAVIER--?!

DIE, YOU LITTLE MUTANT *WITCH!!*

≥Ugnn≤

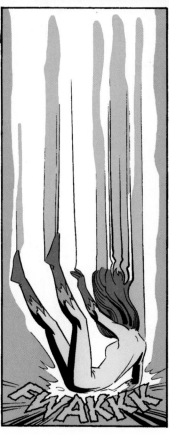

FWAKKK

FOR LONG MOMENTS, THE YOUNG GIRL LIES STILL. SILENT. AND, THEN...

I...GUESS I DIDN'T DO VERY WELL TODAY.

DID I?

119

IF THAT GUN HAD BEEN FIRING REAL BULLETS, INSTEAD OF GELATIN DUMMIES, I'D BE WASHING YOU OFF THE WALLS RIGHT NOW.

ARE YOU ALL RIGHT?

I'M REAL SORE--BUT NOTHING SEEMS TO BE DAMAGED EXCEPT MY PRIDE.

I FEEL LIKE A TOTAL JERK FOR BLOWING MY CONCENTRATION ENOUGH FOR ME TO FALL OUT OF THE AIR LIKE THAT!

A FEW BRUISES WILL HELP YOU TO REMEMBER TODAY'S LESSON--YOU CAN *NEVER* HESITATE WHEN YOUR LIFE IS IN DANGER!

YOU MUST STRIKE QUICKLY AND EFFICIENTLY!

IT'S EASY TO BLOW AWAY ROBOTS AND CANNONS, AND JUNK LIKE THAT. BUT, PEOPLE... THAT'S HARDER.

I COULD NEVER USE MY MICROWAVES TO ACTUALLY HURT SOMEONE.

YOU WEAK, SIMPERING FOOL! WITH TIME, I'LL CHANGE THAT ATTITUDE.

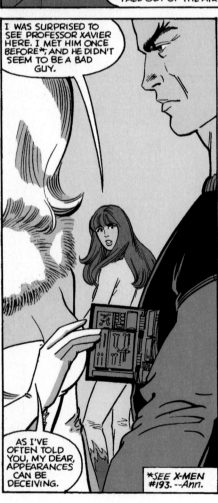

I WAS SURPRISED TO SEE PROFESSOR XAVIER HERE. I MET HIM ONCE BEFORE*, AND HE DIDN'T SEEM TO BE A BAD GUY.

AS I'VE OFTEN TOLD YOU, MY DEAR, APPEARANCES CAN BE DECEIVING.

*SEE X-MEN #193. --Ann.

ANGELICA, I REALIZE THAT THESE TRAINING SESSIONS ARE VERY HARD ON YOU, BUT-- TRUST ME--THEY ARE VERY NECESSARY!

THE ANTI-MUTANT SENTIMENTS ARE GROWING IN THIS COUNTRY. NORMAL HUMANS HATE US! FEAR US!

SOMEDAY, AND I PRAY THAT DAY NEVER COMES, YOU MAY HAVE TO USE YOUR POWERS TO PROTECT YOURSELF, OR SOMEONE YOU LOVE. I JUST WANT YOU TO BE READY!

I UNDERSTAND, MS. FROST. I'LL TRY TO DO BETTER!

SHE'S SO NAIVE! SHE BELIEVES EVERYTHING I SAY!

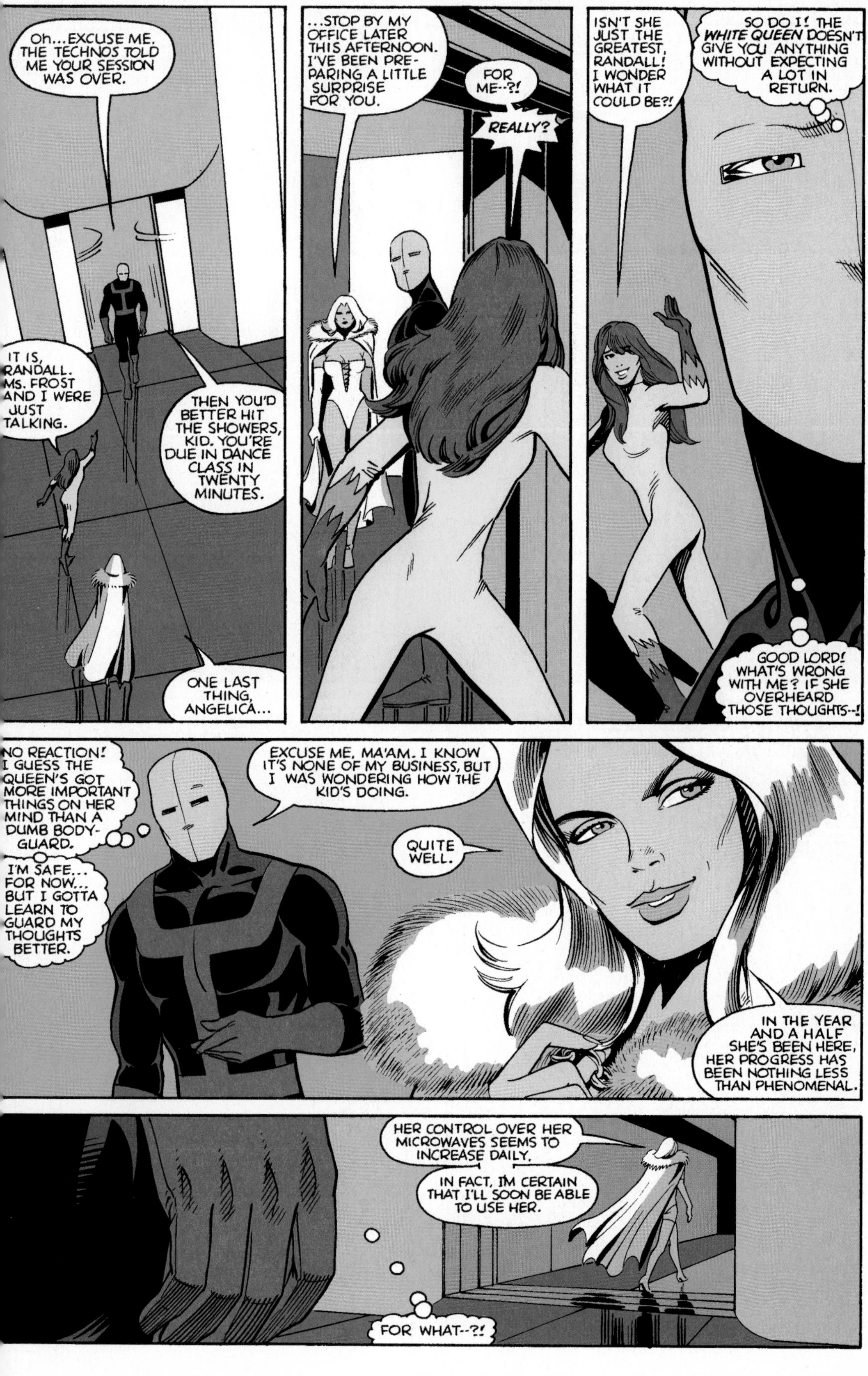
Oh...EXCUSE ME. THE TECHNOS TOLD ME YOUR SESSION WAS OVER.
IT IS, RANDALL. MS. FROST AND I WERE JUST TALKING.
THEN YOU'D BETTER HIT THE SHOWERS, KID. YOU'RE DUE IN DANCE CLASS IN TWENTY MINUTES.
ONE LAST THING, ANGELICA...
...STOP BY MY OFFICE LATER THIS AFTERNOON. I'VE BEEN PRE-PARING A LITTLE SURPRISE FOR YOU.
FOR ME--?!
REALLY?
ISN'T SHE JUST THE GREATEST, RANDALL! I WONDER WHAT IT COULD BE?!
SO DO I! THE WHITE QUEEN DOESN'T GIVE YOU ANYTHING WITHOUT EXPECTING A LOT IN RETURN.
GOOD LORD! WHAT'S WRONG WITH ME? IF SHE OVERHEARD THOSE THOUGHTS--!
NO REACTION! I GUESS THE QUEEN'S GOT MORE IMPORTANT THINGS ON HER MIND THAN A DUMB BODY-GUARD.
I'M SAFE... FOR NOW... BUT I GOTTA LEARN TO GUARD MY THOUGHTS BETTER.
EXCUSE ME, MA'AM. I KNOW IT'S NONE OF MY BUSINESS, BUT I WAS WONDERING HOW THE KID'S DOING.
QUITE WELL.
IN THE YEAR AND A HALF SHE'S BEEN HERE, HER PROGRESS HAS BEEN NOTHING LESS THAN PHENOMENAL.
HER CONTROL OVER HER MICROWAVES SEEMS TO INCREASE DAILY.
IN FACT, I'M CERTAIN THAT I'LL SOON BE ABLE TO USE HER.
FOR WHAT--?!

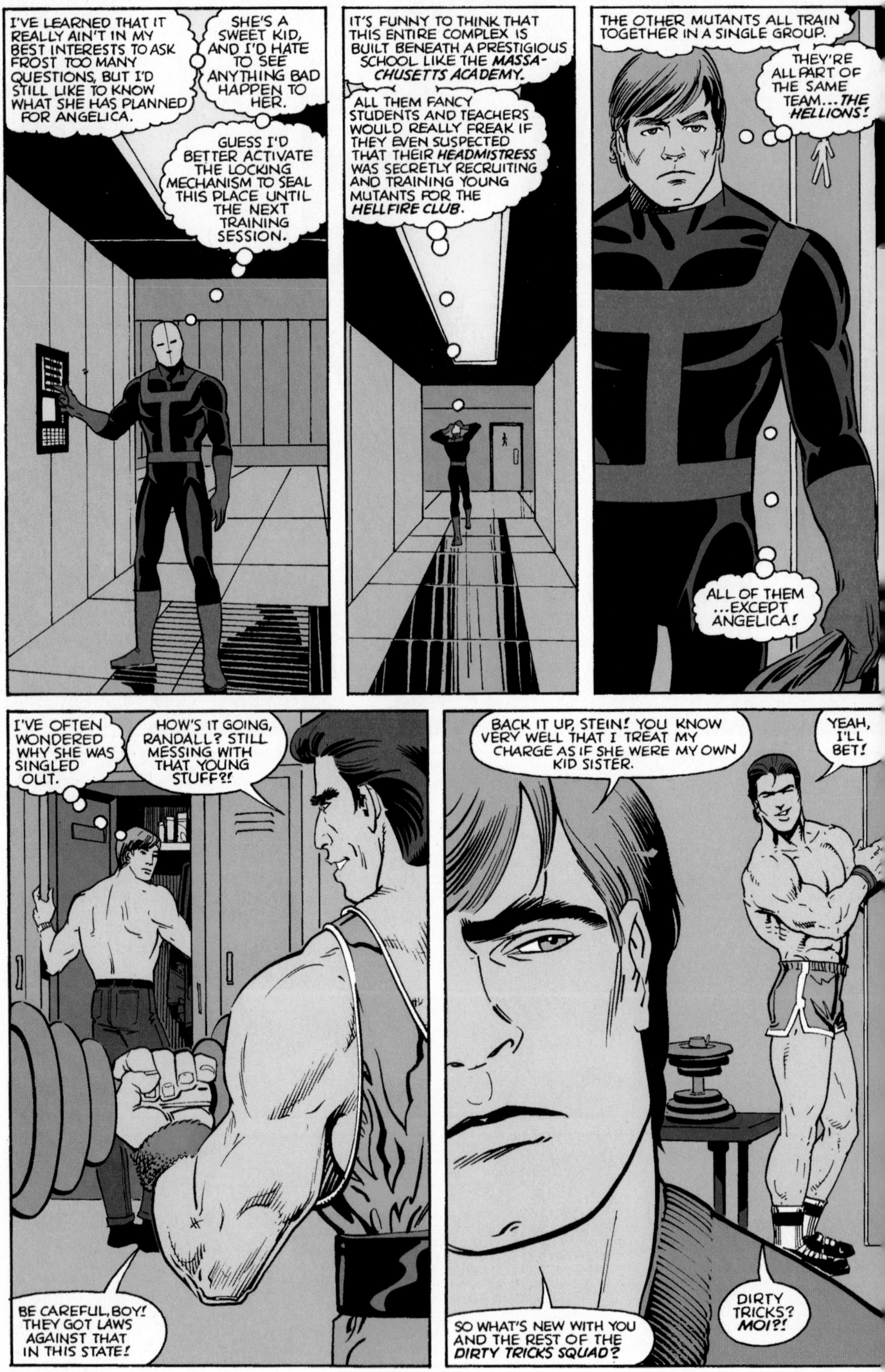

I'VE LEARNED THAT IT REALLY AIN'T IN MY BEST INTERESTS TO ASK FROST TOO MANY QUESTIONS, BUT I'D STILL LIKE TO KNOW WHAT SHE HAS PLANNED FOR ANGELICA.
SHE'S A SWEET KID, AND I'D HATE TO SEE ANYTHING BAD HAPPEN TO HER.
GUESS I'D BETTER ACTIVATE THE LOCKING MECHANISM TO SEAL THIS PLACE UNTIL THE NEXT TRAINING SESSION.
IT'S FUNNY TO THINK THAT THIS ENTIRE COMPLEX IS BUILT BENEATH A PRESTIGIOUS SCHOOL LIKE THE MASSACHUSETTS ACADEMY.
ALL THEM FANCY STUDENTS AND TEACHERS WOULD REALLY FREAK IF THEY EVEN SUSPECTED THAT THEIR HEADMISTRESS WAS SECRETLY RECRUITING AND TRAINING YOUNG MUTANTS FOR THE HELLFIRE CLUB.
THE OTHER MUTANTS ALL TRAIN TOGETHER IN A SINGLE GROUP.
THEY'RE ALL PART OF THE SAME TEAM...THE HELLIONS!
ALL OF THEM ...EXCEPT ANGELICA!
I'VE OFTEN WONDERED WHY SHE WAS SINGLED OUT.
HOW'S IT GOING, RANDALL? STILL MESSING WITH THAT YOUNG STUFF?!
BE CAREFUL, BOY! THEY GOT LAWS AGAINST THAT IN THIS STATE!
BACK IT UP, STEIN! YOU KNOW VERY WELL THAT I TREAT MY CHARGE AS IF SHE WERE MY OWN KID SISTER.
YEAH, I'LL BET!
SO WHAT'S NEW WITH YOU AND THE REST OF THE DIRTY TRICKS SQUAD?
DIRTY TRICKS? MOI?!

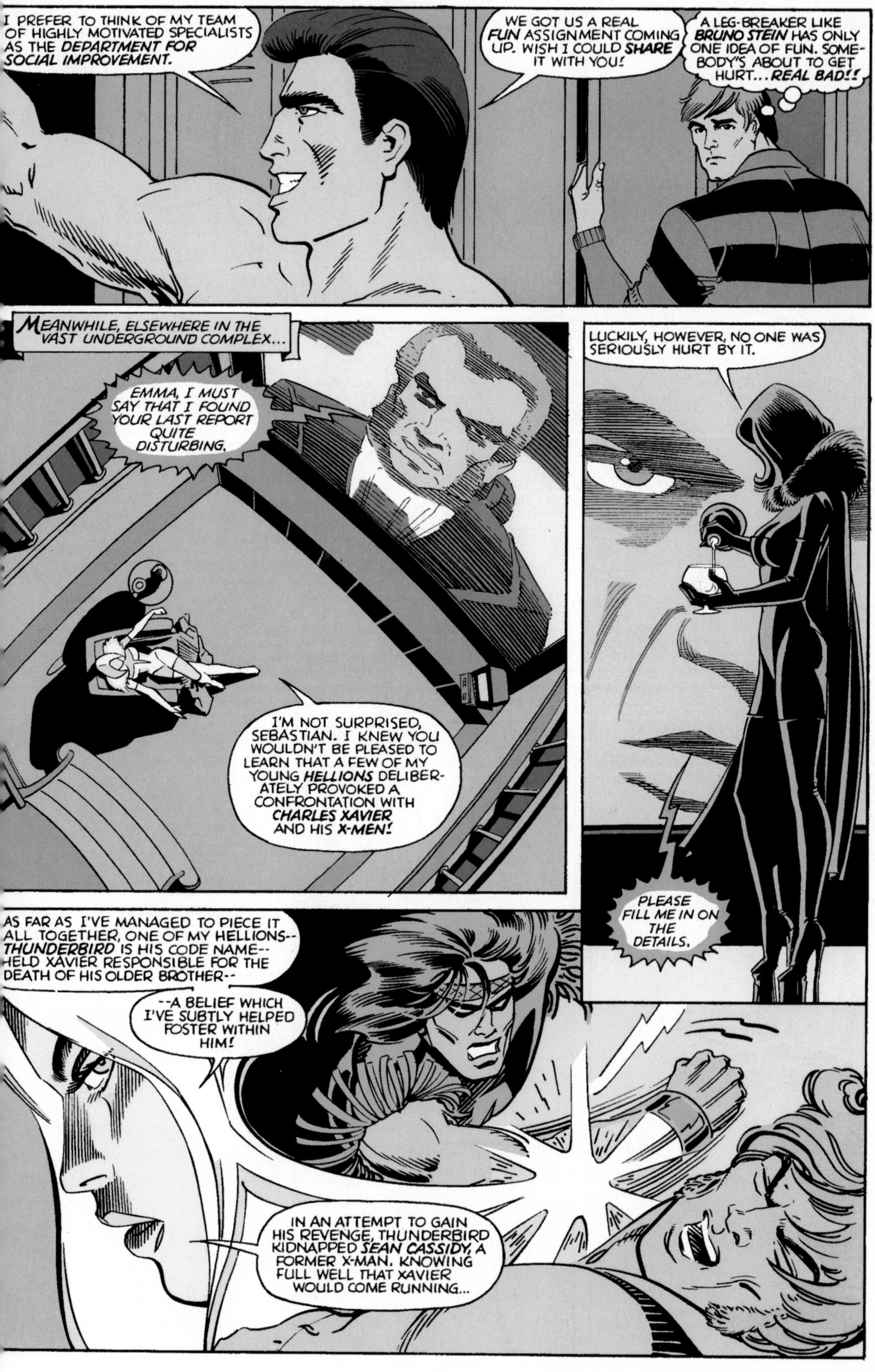
I PREFER TO THINK OF MY TEAM OF HIGHLY MOTIVATED SPECIALISTS AS THE DEPARTMENT FOR SOCIAL IMPROVEMENT.
WE GOT US A REAL FUN ASSIGNMENT COMING UP. WISH I COULD SHARE IT WITH YOU!
A LEG-BREAKER LIKE BRUNO STEIN HAS ONLY ONE IDEA OF FUN. SOMEBODY'S ABOUT TO GET HURT... REAL BAD!!
MEANWHILE, ELSEWHERE IN THE VAST UNDERGROUND COMPLEX...
EMMA, I MUST SAY THAT I FOUND YOUR LAST REPORT QUITE DISTURBING.
I'M NOT SURPRISED, SEBASTIAN. I KNEW YOU WOULDN'T BE PLEASED TO LEARN THAT A FEW OF MY YOUNG HELLIONS DELIBERATELY PROVOKED A CONFRONTATION WITH CHARLES XAVIER AND HIS X-MEN!
LUCKILY, HOWEVER, NO ONE WAS SERIOUSLY HURT BY IT.
PLEASE FILL ME IN ON THE DETAILS.
AS FAR AS I'VE MANAGED TO PIECE IT ALL TOGETHER, ONE OF MY HELLIONS--THUNDERBIRD IS HIS CODE NAME--HELD XAVIER RESPONSIBLE FOR THE DEATH OF HIS OLDER BROTHER--
--A BELIEF WHICH I'VE SUBTLY HELPED FOSTER WITHIN HIM!
IN AN ATTEMPT TO GAIN HIS REVENGE, THUNDERBIRD KIDNAPPED SEAN CASSIDY, A FORMER X-MAN. KNOWING FULL WELL THAT XAVIER WOULD COME RUNNING...

TWO OF THUNDERBIRD'S TEAMMATES-- *EMPATH* AND *ROULETTE*-- DECIDED TO JOIN IN THE FUN.

EMPATH EVEN USED HIS MUTANT ABILITY TO INFLUENCE EMOTIONS TO CON *FIRESTAR* INTO COMING ALONG!

IN EFFECT, HE USED HER AS HIS FIGHTING PAWN. PEOPLE ARE MERELY OBJECTS TO EMPATH, AND HE WOULD HAVE WILLINGLY SACRIFICED HER IF IT HAD SUITED HIS PURPOSE.

IN THIS INSTANCE, THAT DID NOT PROVE TO BE NECESSARY. NO SOONER DID THUNDER- BIRD CAPTURE XAVIER, THAN THE WILY CHARLES SOMEHOW MANAGED TO CONVINCE THE BOY THAT HE WASN'T GUILTY OF CAUSING THE BROTHER'S DEATH!*

*AS RELATED IN X-MEN #193.--Ann.

IT APPEARS THAT YOUR *MONTHS* OF TELEPATHICALLY WORKING ON THUNDERBIRD'S SUBCONSCIOUS WERE IN VAIN.

PERHAPS, I WAS JUST A BIT TOO SUBTLE.

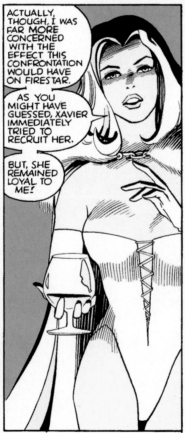

ACTUALLY, THOUGH, I WAS FAR MORE CONCERNED WITH THE EFFECT THIS CONFRONTATION WOULD HAVE ON FIRESTAR.

AS YOU MIGHT HAVE GUESSED, XAVIER IMMEDIATELY TRIED TO RECRUIT HER.

BUT, SHE REMAINED LOYAL TO ME!

THE LITTLE FOOL! SHE ACTUALLY WORSHIPS ME-- LITTLE DREAMING THAT I AM SECRETLY TRAINING HER TO BECOME THE HELLFIRE CLUB'S MOST DEADLY ASSASSIN!

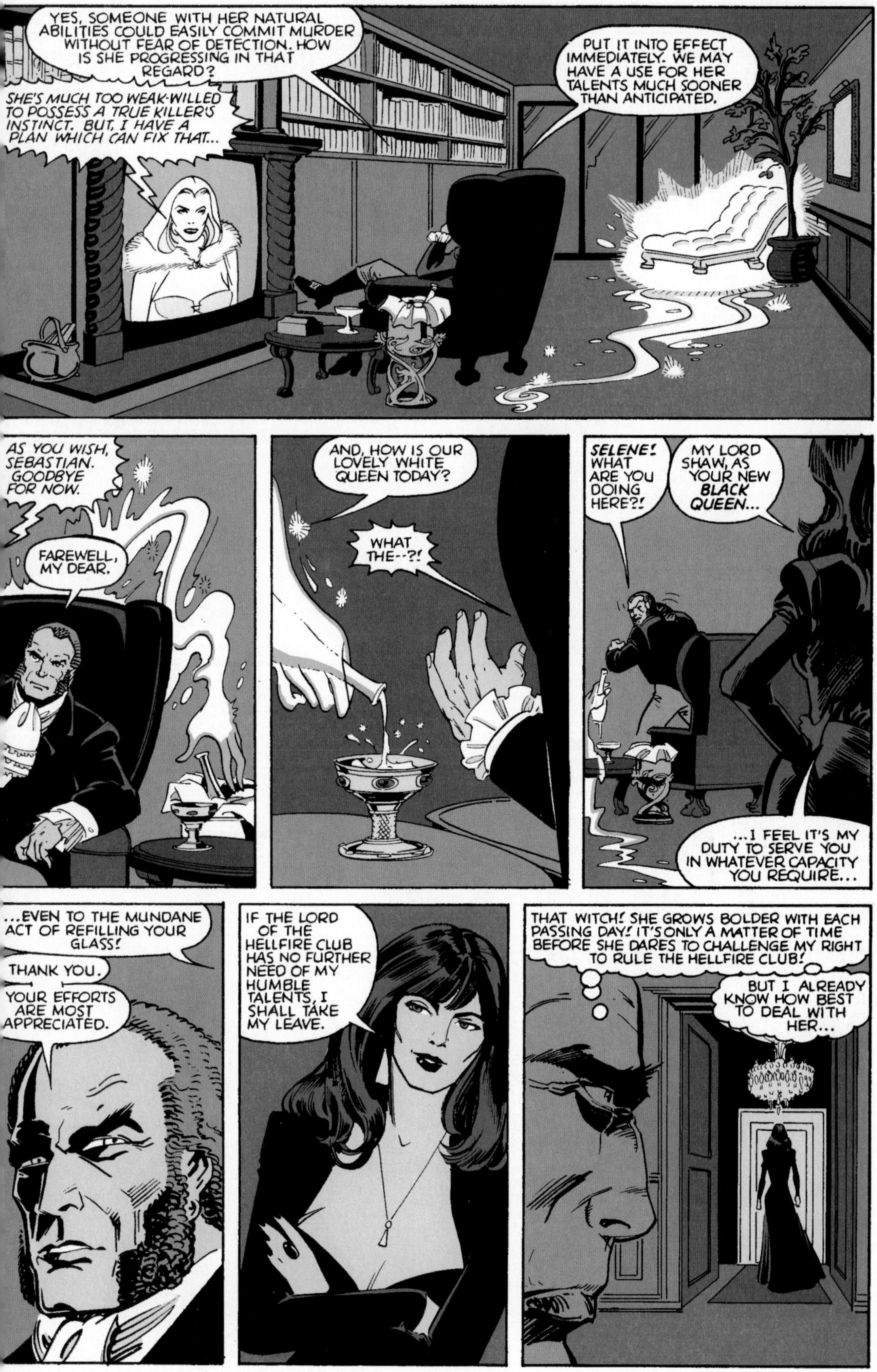
YES, SOMEONE WITH HER NATURAL ABILITIES COULD EASILY COMMIT MURDER WITHOUT FEAR OF DETECTION. HOW IS SHE PROGRESSING IN THAT REGARD?
SHE'S MUCH TOO WEAK-WILLED TO POSSESS A TRUE KILLER'S INSTINCT. BUT, I HAVE A PLAN WHICH CAN FIX THAT...
PUT IT INTO EFFECT IMMEDIATELY. WE MAY HAVE A USE FOR HER TALENTS MUCH SOONER THAN ANTICIPATED.
AS YOU WISH, SEBASTIAN. GOODBYE FOR NOW.
FAREWELL, MY DEAR.
AND, HOW IS OUR LOVELY WHITE QUEEN TODAY?
WHAT THE--?!
SELENE! WHAT ARE YOU DOING HERE?!
MY LORD SHAW, AS YOUR NEW BLACK QUEEN...
...I FEEL IT'S MY DUTY TO SERVE YOU IN WHATEVER CAPACITY YOU REQUIRE...
...EVEN TO THE MUNDANE ACT OF REFILLING YOUR GLASS!
THANK YOU.
YOUR EFFORTS ARE MOST APPRECIATED.
IF THE LORD OF THE HELLFIRE CLUB HAS NO FURTHER NEED OF MY HUMBLE TALENTS, I SHALL TAKE MY LEAVE.
THAT WITCH! SHE GROWS BOLDER WITH EACH PASSING DAY! IT'S ONLY A MATTER OF TIME BEFORE SHE DARES TO CHALLENGE MY RIGHT TO RULE THE HELLFIRE CLUB!
BUT I ALREADY KNOW HOW BEST TO DEAL WITH HER...

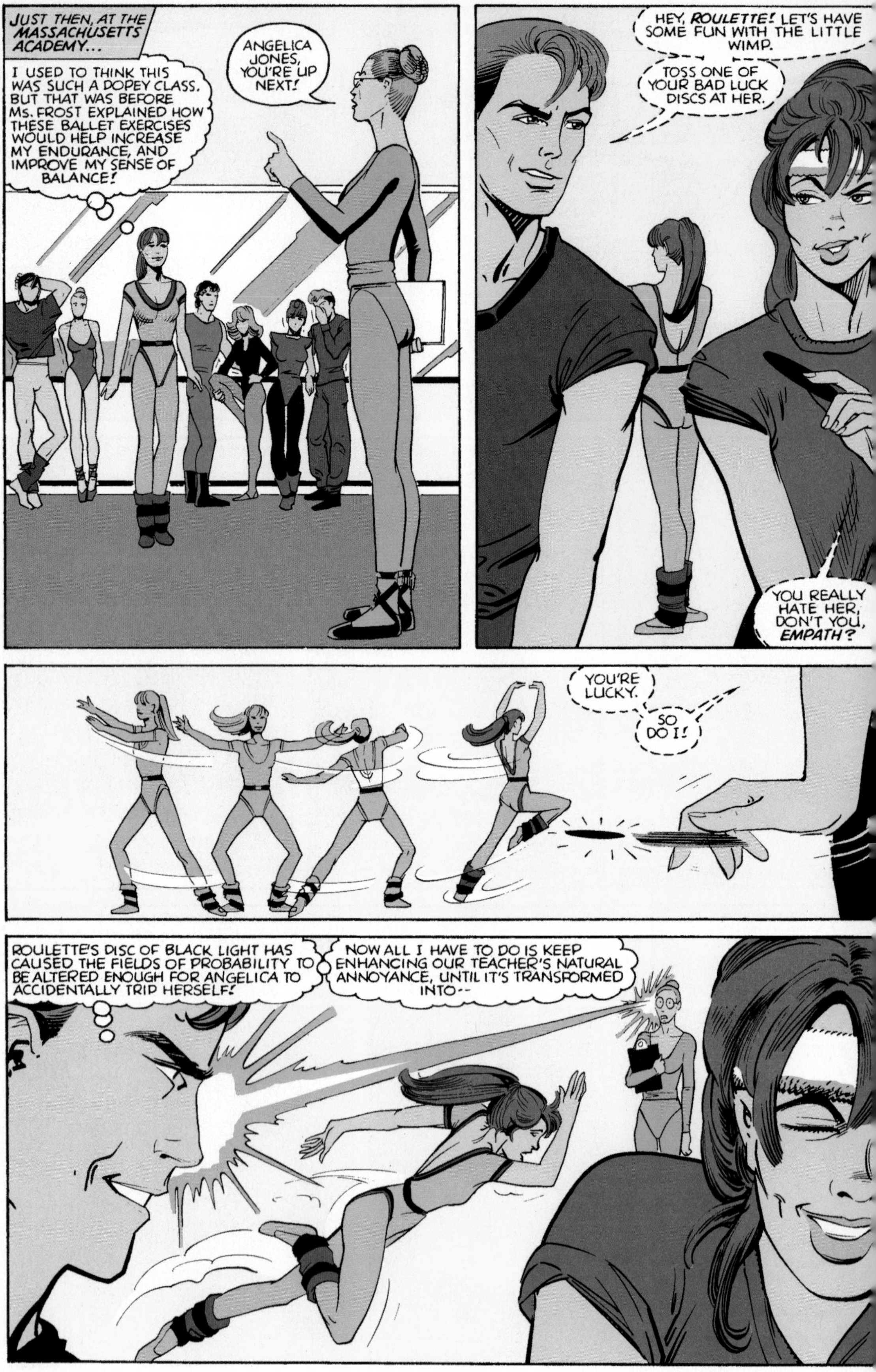

JUST THEN, AT THE MASSACHUSETTS ACADEMY...
I USED TO THINK THIS WAS SUCH A DOPEY CLASS. BUT THAT WAS BEFORE Ms. FROST EXPLAINED HOW THESE BALLET EXERCISES WOULD HELP INCREASE MY ENDURANCE, AND IMPROVE MY SENSE OF BALANCE!
ANGELICA JONES, YOU'RE UP NEXT!
HEY, ROULETTE! LET'S HAVE SOME FUN WITH THE LITTLE WIMP.
TOSS ONE OF YOUR BAD LUCK DISCS AT HER.
YOU REALLY HATE HER, DON'T YOU, EMPATH?
YOU'RE LUCKY.
SO DO I!
ROULETTE'S DISC OF BLACK LIGHT HAS CAUSED THE FIELDS OF PROBABILITY TO BE ALTERED ENOUGH FOR ANGELICA TO ACCIDENTALLY TRIP HERSELF!
NOW ALL I HAVE TO DO IS KEEP ENHANCING OUR TEACHER'S NATURAL ANNOYANCE, UNTIL IT'S TRANSFORMED INTO--

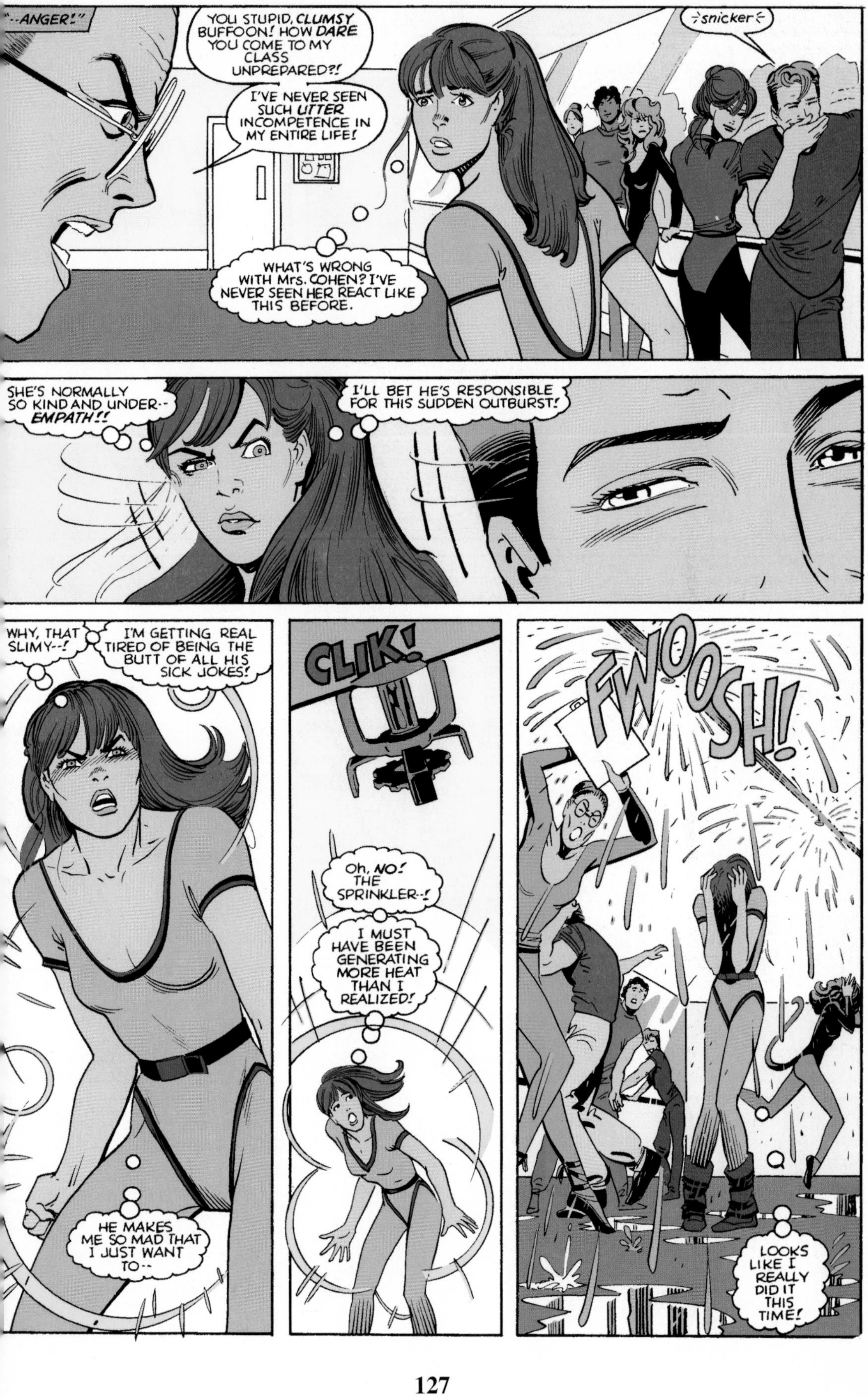
"--ANGER!"
YOU STUPID, CLUMSY BUFFOON! HOW DARE YOU COME TO MY CLASS UNPREPARED?!
I'VE NEVER SEEN SUCH UTTER INCOMPETENCE IN MY ENTIRE LIFE!
WHAT'S WRONG WITH Mrs. COHEN? I'VE NEVER SEEN HER REACT LIKE THIS BEFORE.
snicker
SHE'S NORMALLY SO KIND AND UNDER-- EMPATH!!
I'LL BET HE'S RESPONSIBLE FOR THIS SUDDEN OUTBURST!
WHY, THAT SLIMY--!
I'M GETTING REAL TIRED OF BEING THE BUTT OF ALL HIS SICK JOKES!
HE MAKES ME SO MAD THAT I JUST WANT TO--
CLIK!
Oh, NO! THE SPRINKLER--!
I MUST HAVE BEEN GENERATING MORE HEAT THAN I REALIZED!
FWOOSH!
LOOKS LIKE I REALLY DID IT THIS TIME!

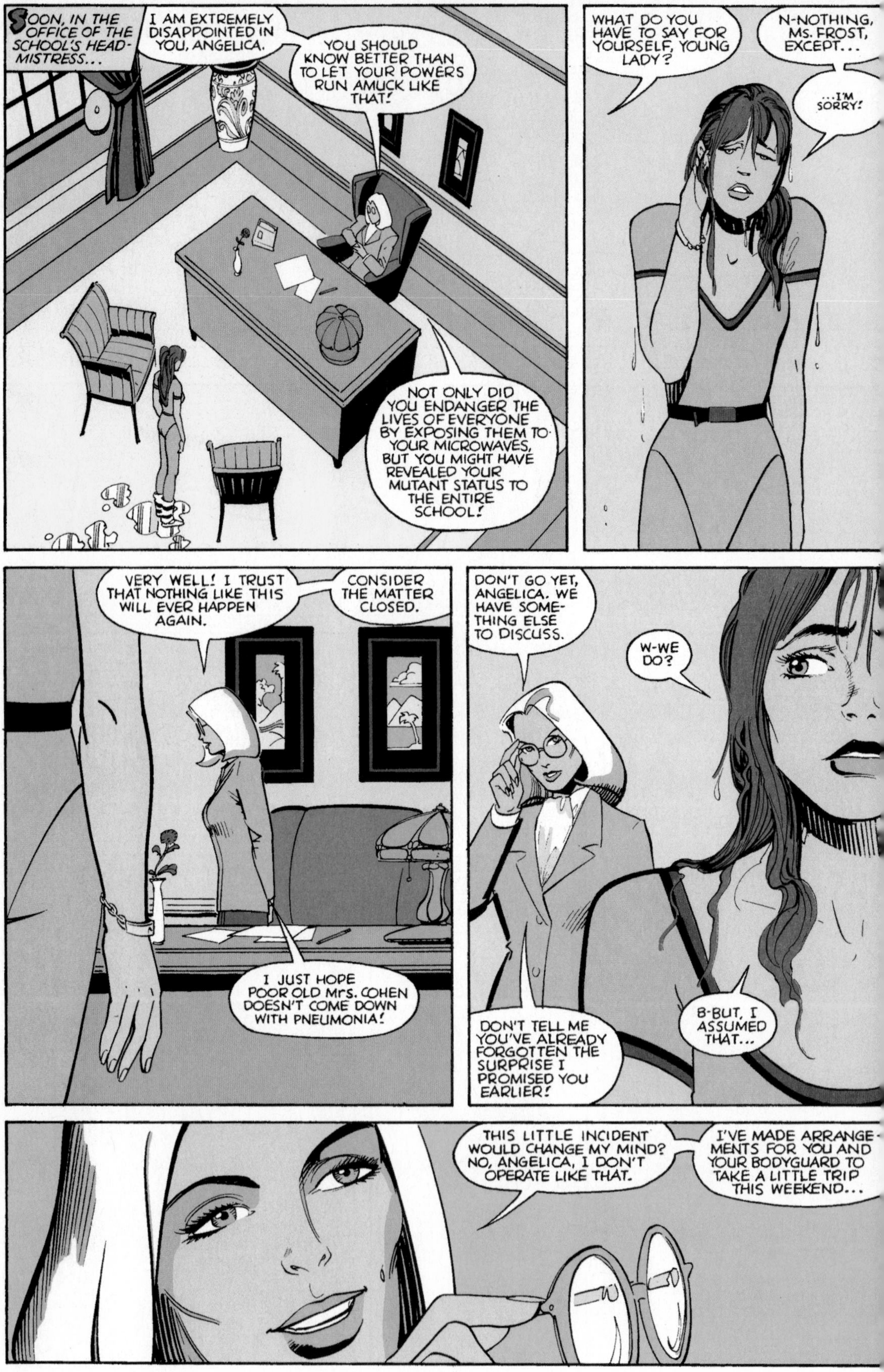
SOON, IN THE OFFICE OF THE SCHOOL'S HEAD-MISTRESS...
I AM EXTREMELY DISAPPOINTED IN YOU, ANGELICA.
YOU SHOULD KNOW BETTER THAN TO LET YOUR POWERS RUN AMUCK LIKE THAT!
NOT ONLY DID YOU ENDANGER THE LIVES OF EVERYONE BY EXPOSING THEM TO YOUR MICROWAVES, BUT YOU MIGHT HAVE REVEALED YOUR MUTANT STATUS TO THE ENTIRE SCHOOL!
WHAT DO YOU HAVE TO SAY FOR YOURSELF, YOUNG LADY?
N-NOTHING, Ms. FROST, EXCEPT...
...I'M SORRY!
VERY WELL! I TRUST THAT NOTHING LIKE THIS WILL EVER HAPPEN AGAIN.
CONSIDER THE MATTER CLOSED.
I JUST HOPE POOR OLD Mrs. COHEN DOESN'T COME DOWN WITH PNEUMONIA!
DON'T GO YET, ANGELICA. WE HAVE SOME-THING ELSE TO DISCUSS.
W-WE DO?
DON'T TELL ME YOU'VE ALREADY FORGOTTEN THE SURPRISE I PROMISED YOU EARLIER!
B-BUT, I ASSUMED THAT...
THIS LITTLE INCIDENT WOULD CHANGE MY MIND? NO, ANGELICA, I DON'T OPERATE LIKE THAT.
I'VE MADE ARRANGE-MENTS FOR YOU AND YOUR BODYGUARD TO TAKE A LITTLE TRIP THIS WEEKEND...

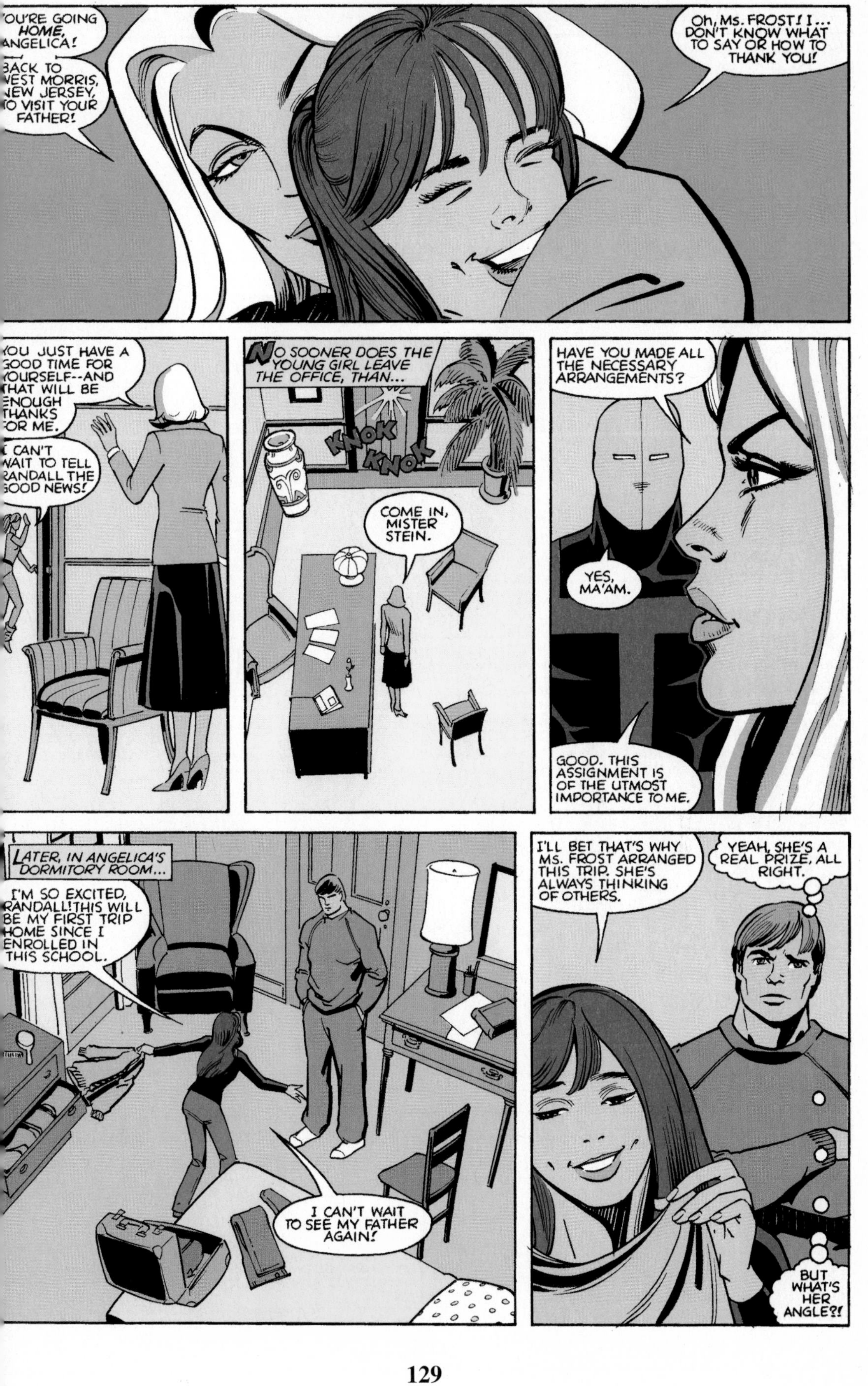
OU'RE GOING HOME, ANGELICA!
BACK TO VEST MORRIS, NEW JERSEY, TO VISIT YOUR FATHER!
Oh, Ms. FROST! I... DON'T KNOW WHAT TO SAY OR HOW TO THANK YOU!
YOU JUST HAVE A GOOD TIME FOR YOURSELF--AND THAT WILL BE ENOUGH THANKS FOR ME.
I CAN'T WAIT TO TELL RANDALL THE GOOD NEWS!
NO SOONER DOES THE YOUNG GIRL LEAVE THE OFFICE, THAN...
KNOK KNOK
COME IN, MISTER STEIN.
HAVE YOU MADE ALL THE NECESSARY ARRANGEMENTS?
YES, MA'AM.
GOOD. THIS ASSIGNMENT IS OF THE UTMOST IMPORTANCE TO ME.
LATER, IN ANGELICA'S DORMITORY ROOM...
I'M SO EXCITED, RANDALL! THIS WILL BE MY FIRST TRIP HOME SINCE I ENROLLED IN THIS SCHOOL.
I CAN'T WAIT TO SEE MY FATHER AGAIN!
I'LL BET THAT'S WHY MS. FROST ARRANGED THIS TRIP. SHE'S ALWAYS THINKING OF OTHERS.
YEAH, SHE'S A REAL PRIZE, ALL RIGHT.
BUT WHAT'S HER ANGLE?!

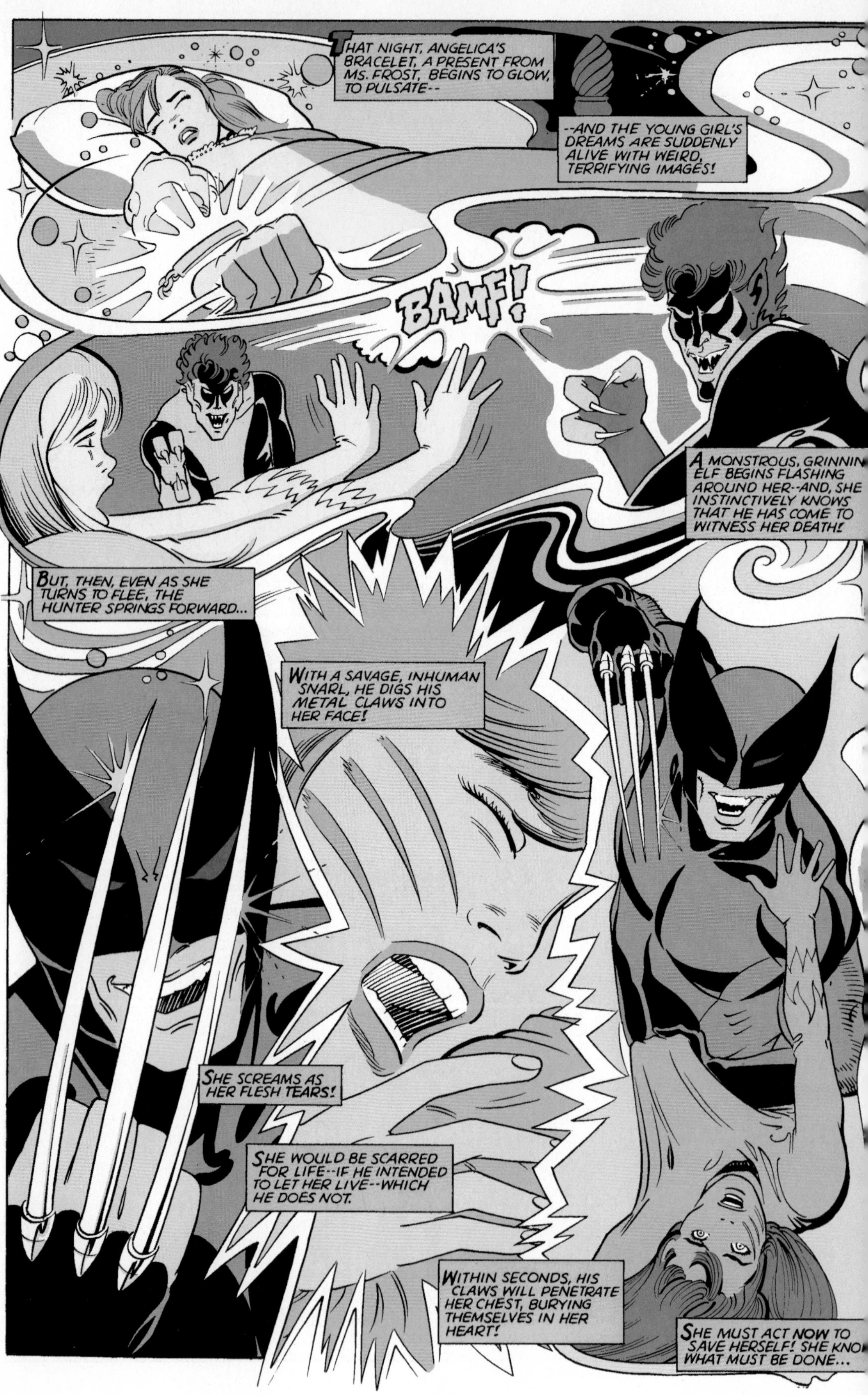
THAT NIGHT, ANGELICA'S BRACELET, A PRESENT FROM MS. FROST, BEGINS TO GLOW, TO PULSATE--
--AND THE YOUNG GIRL'S DREAMS ARE SUDDENLY ALIVE WITH WEIRD, TERRIFYING IMAGES!
BAMF!
A MONSTROUS, GRINNIN ELF BEGINS FLASHING AROUND HER--AND, SHE INSTINCTIVELY KNOWS THAT HE HAS COME TO WITNESS HER DEATH!
BUT, THEN, EVEN AS SHE TURNS TO FLEE, THE HUNTER SPRINGS FORWARD...
WITH A SAVAGE, INHUMAN SNARL, HE DIGS HIS METAL CLAWS INTO HER FACE!
SHE SCREAMS AS HER FLESH TEARS!
SHE WOULD BE SCARRED FOR LIFE--IF HE INTENDED TO LET HER LIVE--WHICH HE DOES NOT.
WITHIN SECONDS, HIS CLAWS WILL PENETRATE HER CHEST, BURYING THEMSELVES IN HER HEART!
SHE MUST ACT NOW TO SAVE HERSELF! SHE KNO WHAT MUST BE DONE...

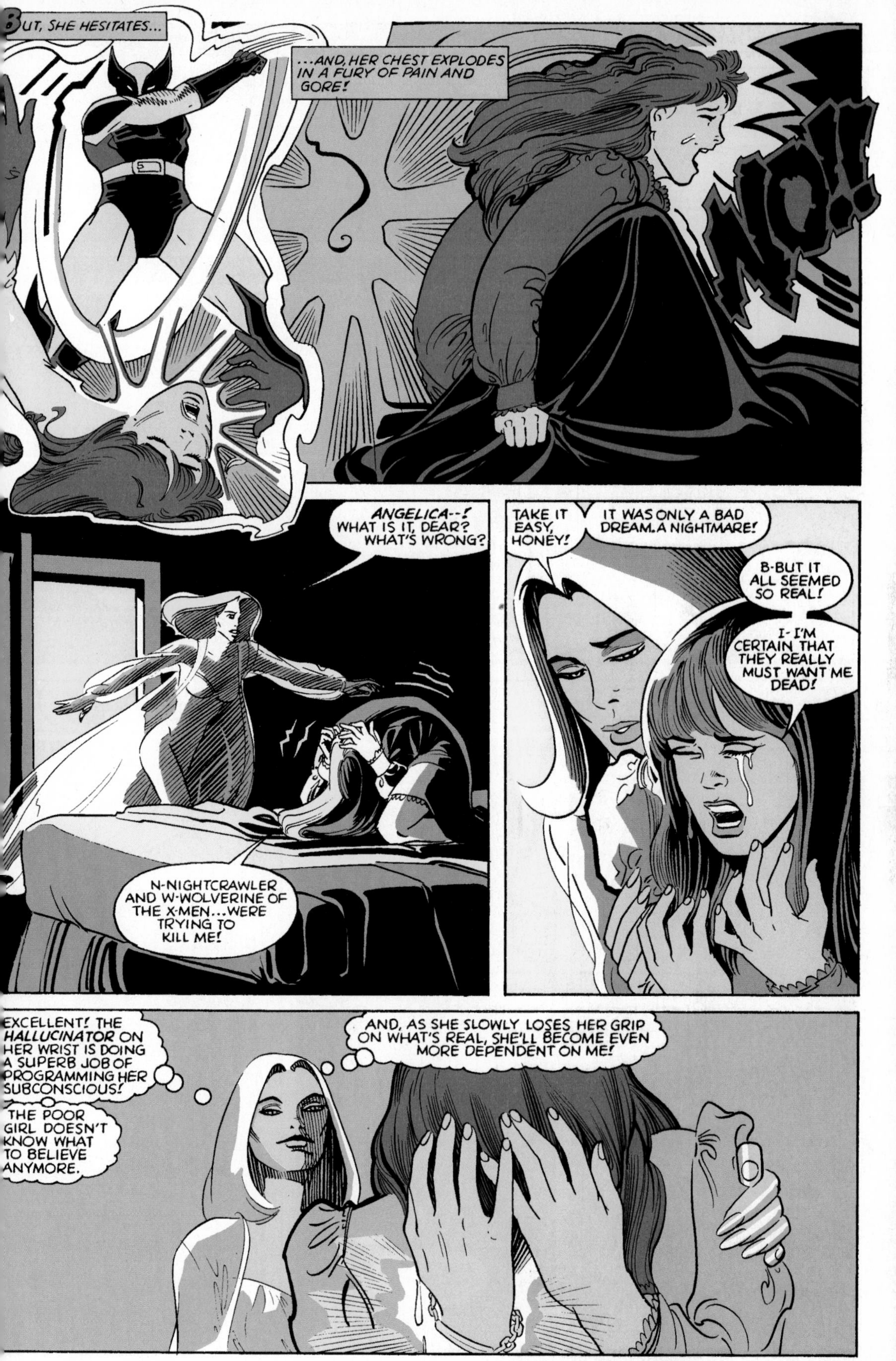
BUT, SHE HESITATES...
...AND, HER CHEST EXPLODES IN A FURY OF PAIN AND GORE!
NO!!
ANGELICA--! WHAT IS IT, DEAR? WHAT'S WRONG?
N-NIGHTCRAWLER AND W-WOLVERINE OF THE X-MEN...WERE TRYING TO KILL ME!
TAKE IT EASY, HONEY!
IT WAS ONLY A BAD DREAM. A NIGHTMARE!
B-BUT IT ALL SEEMED SO REAL!
I- I'M CERTAIN THAT THEY REALLY MUST WANT ME DEAD!
EXCELLENT! THE HALLUCINATOR ON HER WRIST IS DOING A SUPERB JOB OF PROGRAMMING HER SUBCONSCIOUS!
THE POOR GIRL DOESN'T KNOW WHAT TO BELIEVE ANYMORE.
AND, AS SHE SLOWLY LOSES HER GRIP ON WHAT'S REAL, SHE'LL BECOME EVEN MORE DEPENDENT ON ME!

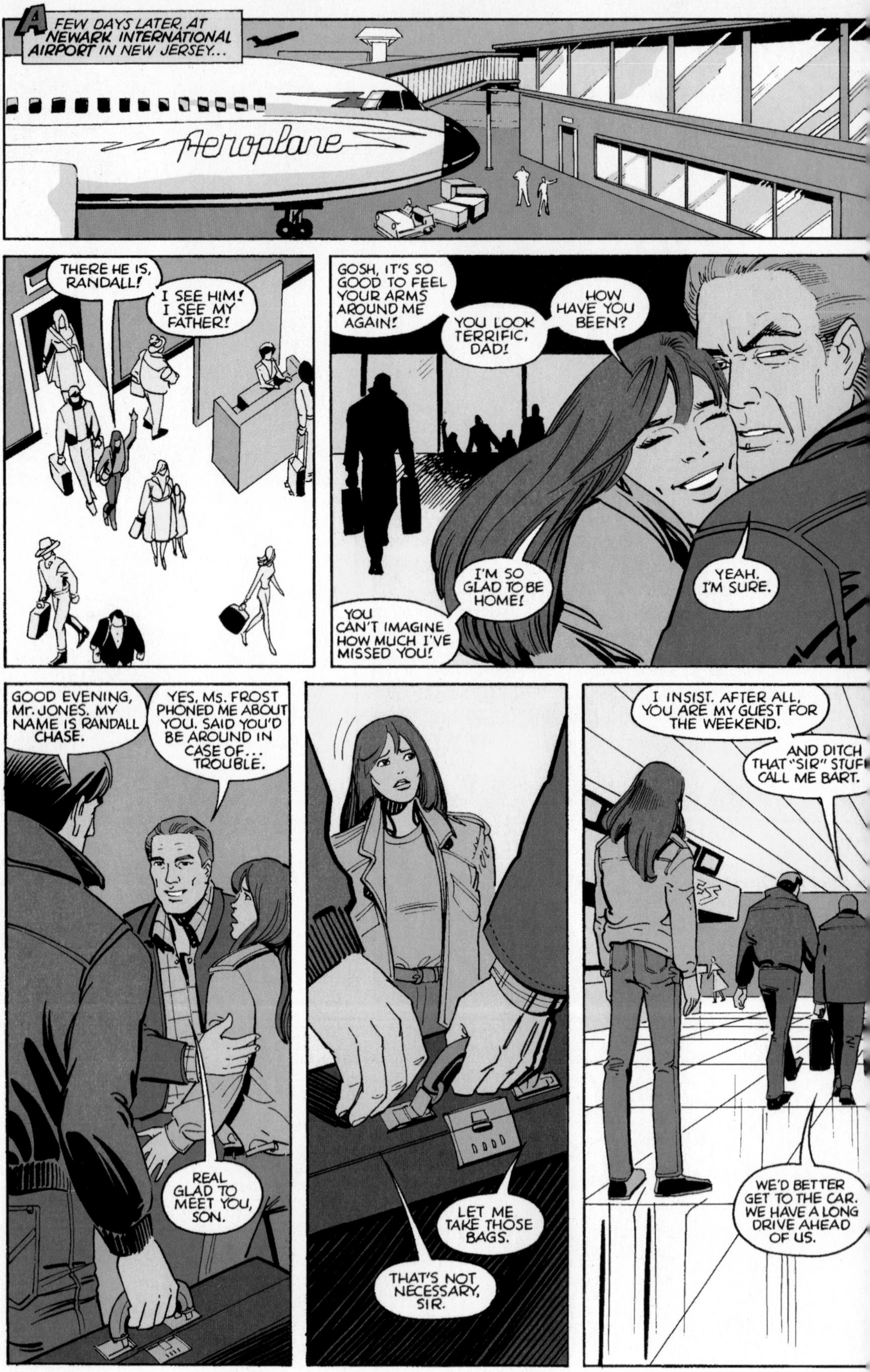
A FEW DAYS LATER, AT NEWARK INTERNATIONAL AIRPORT IN NEW JERSEY...
Aeroplane
THERE HE IS, RANDALL!
I SEE HIM! I SEE MY FATHER!
GOSH, IT'S SO GOOD TO FEEL YOUR ARMS AROUND ME AGAIN!
YOU LOOK TERRIFIC, DAD!
HOW HAVE YOU BEEN?
I'M SO GLAD TO BE HOME!
YOU CAN'T IMAGINE HOW MUCH I'VE MISSED YOU!
YEAH. I'M SURE.
GOOD EVENING, Mr. JONES. MY NAME IS RANDALL CHASE.
YES, Ms. FROST PHONED ME ABOUT YOU. SAID YOU'D BE AROUND IN CASE OF... TROUBLE.
REAL GLAD TO MEET YOU, SON.
LET ME TAKE THOSE BAGS.
THAT'S NOT NECESSARY, SIR.
I INSIST. AFTER ALL, YOU ARE MY GUEST FOR THE WEEKEND.
AND DITCH THAT "SIR" STUF CALL ME BART.
WE'D BETTER GET TO THE CAR. WE HAVE A LONG DRIVE AHEAD OF US.

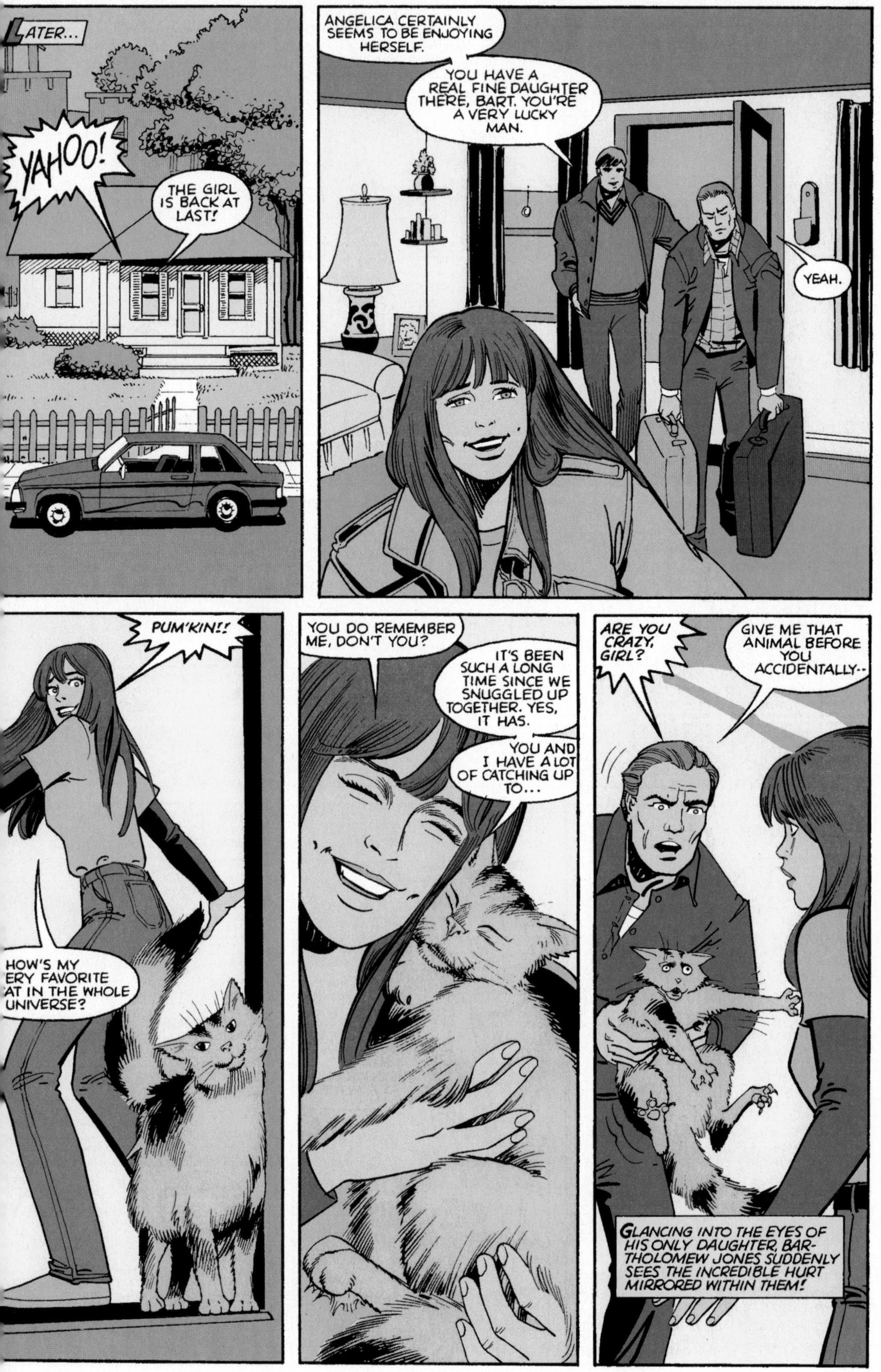
LATER...
YAHOO!
THE GIRL IS BACK AT LAST!
ANGELICA CERTAINLY SEEMS TO BE ENJOYING HERSELF.
YOU HAVE A REAL FINE DAUGHTER THERE, BART. YOU'RE A VERY LUCKY MAN.
YEAH.
PUM'KIN!!
HOW'S MY ERY FAVORITE AT IN THE WHOLE UNIVERSE?
YOU DO REMEMBER ME, DON'T YOU?
IT'S BEEN SUCH A LONG TIME SINCE WE SNUGGLED UP TOGETHER. YES, IT HAS.
YOU AND I HAVE A LOT OF CATCHING UP TO...
ARE YOU CRAZY, GIRL?
GIVE ME THAT ANIMAL BEFORE YOU ACCIDENTALLY--
GLANCING INTO THE EYES OF HIS ONLY DAUGHTER, BARTHOLOMEW JONES SUDDENLY SEES THE INCREDIBLE HURT MIRRORED WITHIN THEM!

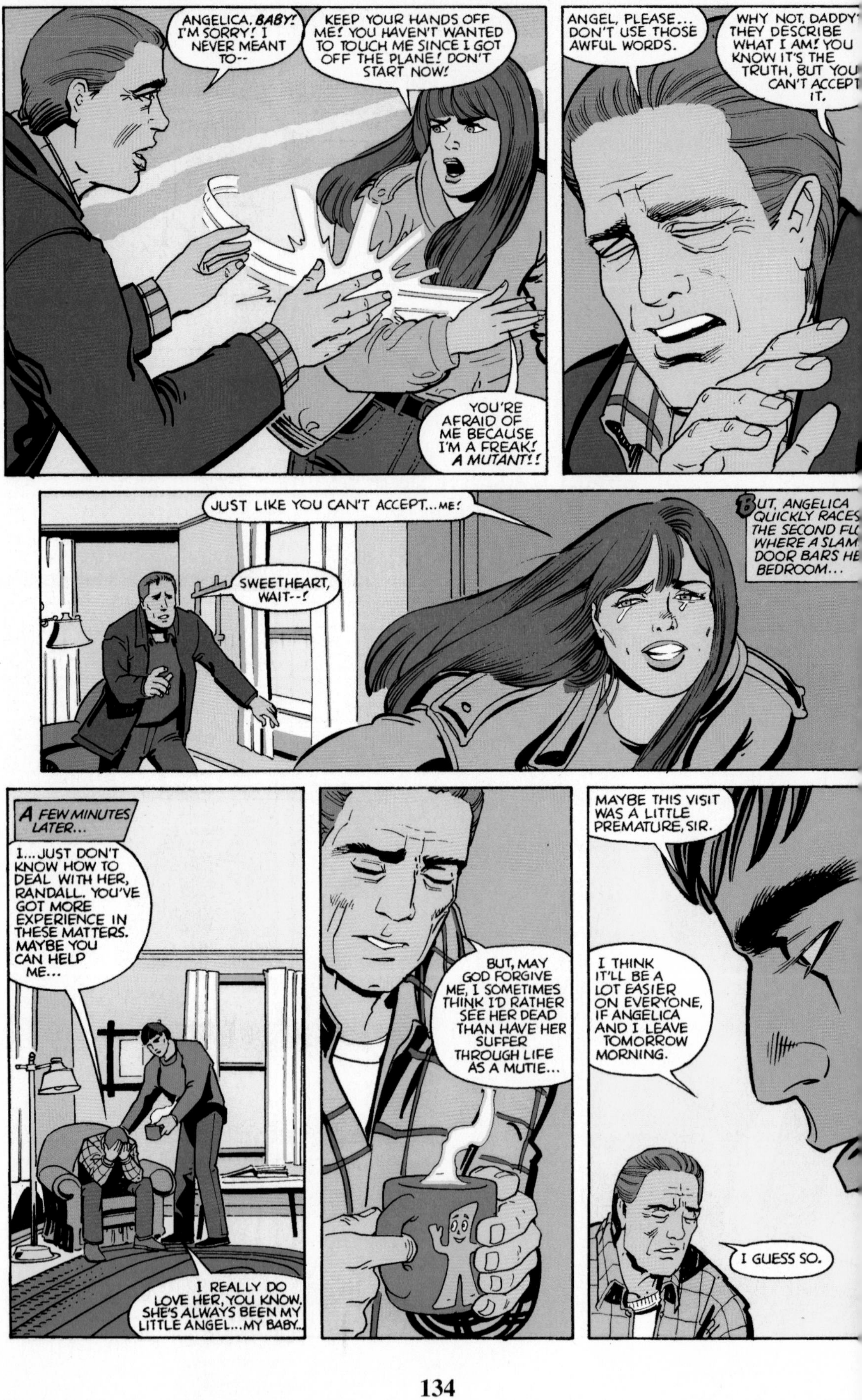
ANGELICA, BABY! I'M SORRY! I NEVER MEANT TO--
KEEP YOUR HANDS OFF ME! YOU HAVEN'T WANTED TO TOUCH ME SINCE I GOT OFF THE PLANE! DON'T START NOW!
YOU'RE AFRAID OF ME BECAUSE I'M A FREAK! A MUTANT!!
ANGEL, PLEASE... DON'T USE THOSE AWFUL WORDS.
WHY NOT, DADDY? THEY DESCRIBE WHAT I AM! YOU KNOW IT'S THE TRUTH, BUT YOU CAN'T ACCEPT IT.
JUST LIKE YOU CAN'T ACCEPT...ME!
SWEETHEART, WAIT--!
BUT, ANGELICA QUICKLY RACES THE SECOND FL WHERE A SLAM DOOR BARS HE BEDROOM...
A FEW MINUTES LATER...
I...JUST DON'T KNOW HOW TO DEAL WITH HER, RANDALL. YOU'VE GOT MORE EXPERIENCE IN THESE MATTERS. MAYBE YOU CAN HELP ME...
I REALLY DO LOVE HER, YOU KNOW. SHE'S ALWAYS BEEN MY LITTLE ANGEL...MY BABY...
BUT, MAY GOD FORGIVE ME, I SOMETIMES THINK I'D RATHER SEE HER DEAD THAN HAVE HER SUFFER THROUGH LIFE AS A MUTIE...
MAYBE THIS VISIT WAS A LITTLE PREMATURE, SIR.
I THINK IT'LL BE A LOT EASIER ON EVERYONE, IF ANGELICA AND I LEAVE TOMORROW MORNING.
I GUESS SO.

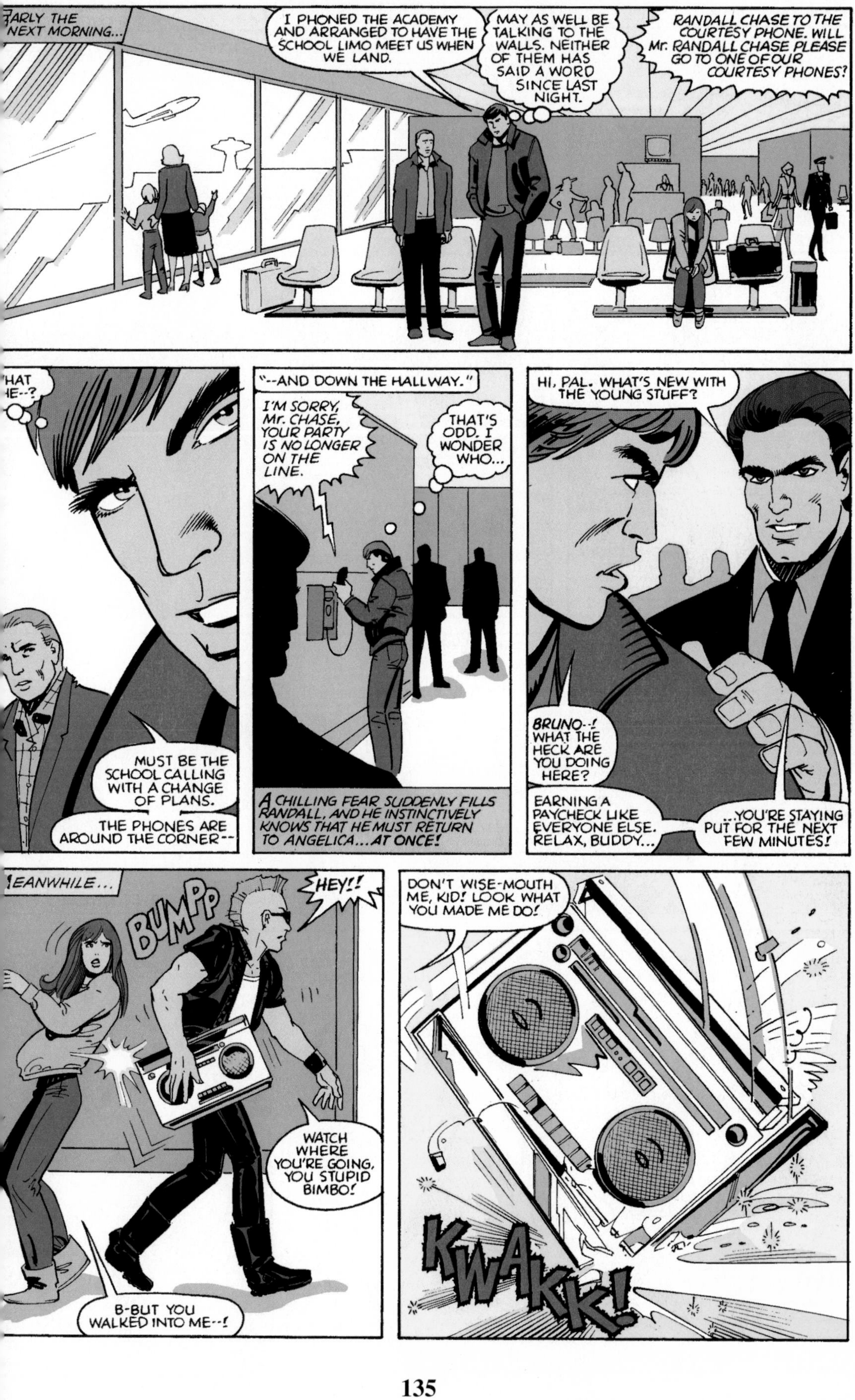

EARLY THE NEXT MORNING...
I PHONED THE ACADEMY AND ARRANGED TO HAVE THE SCHOOL LIMO MEET US WHEN WE LAND.
MAY AS WELL BE TALKING TO THE WALLS. NEITHER OF THEM HAS SAID A WORD SINCE LAST NIGHT.
RANDALL CHASE TO THE COURTESY PHONE. WILL Mr. RANDALL CHASE PLEASE GO TO ONE OF OUR COURTESY PHONES?
WHAT THE--?
MUST BE THE SCHOOL CALLING WITH A CHANGE OF PLANS.
THE PHONES ARE AROUND THE CORNER--
"--AND DOWN THE HALLWAY."
I'M SORRY, Mr. CHASE, YOUR PARTY IS NO LONGER ON THE LINE.
THAT'S ODD. I WONDER WHO...
A CHILLING FEAR SUDDENLY FILLS RANDALL, AND HE INSTINCTIVELY KNOWS THAT HE MUST RETURN TO ANGELICA... AT ONCE!
HI, PAL. WHAT'S NEW WITH THE YOUNG STUFF?
BRUNO--! WHAT THE HECK ARE YOU DOING HERE?
EARNING A PAYCHECK LIKE EVERYONE ELSE. RELAX, BUDDY...
...YOU'RE STAYING PUT FOR THE NEXT FEW MINUTES!
MEANWHILE...
BUMPP
HEY!!
WATCH WHERE YOU'RE GOING, YOU STUPID BIMBO!
B-BUT YOU WALKED INTO ME--!
DON'T WISE-MOUTH ME, KID! LOOK WHAT YOU MADE ME DO!
KWAKK!

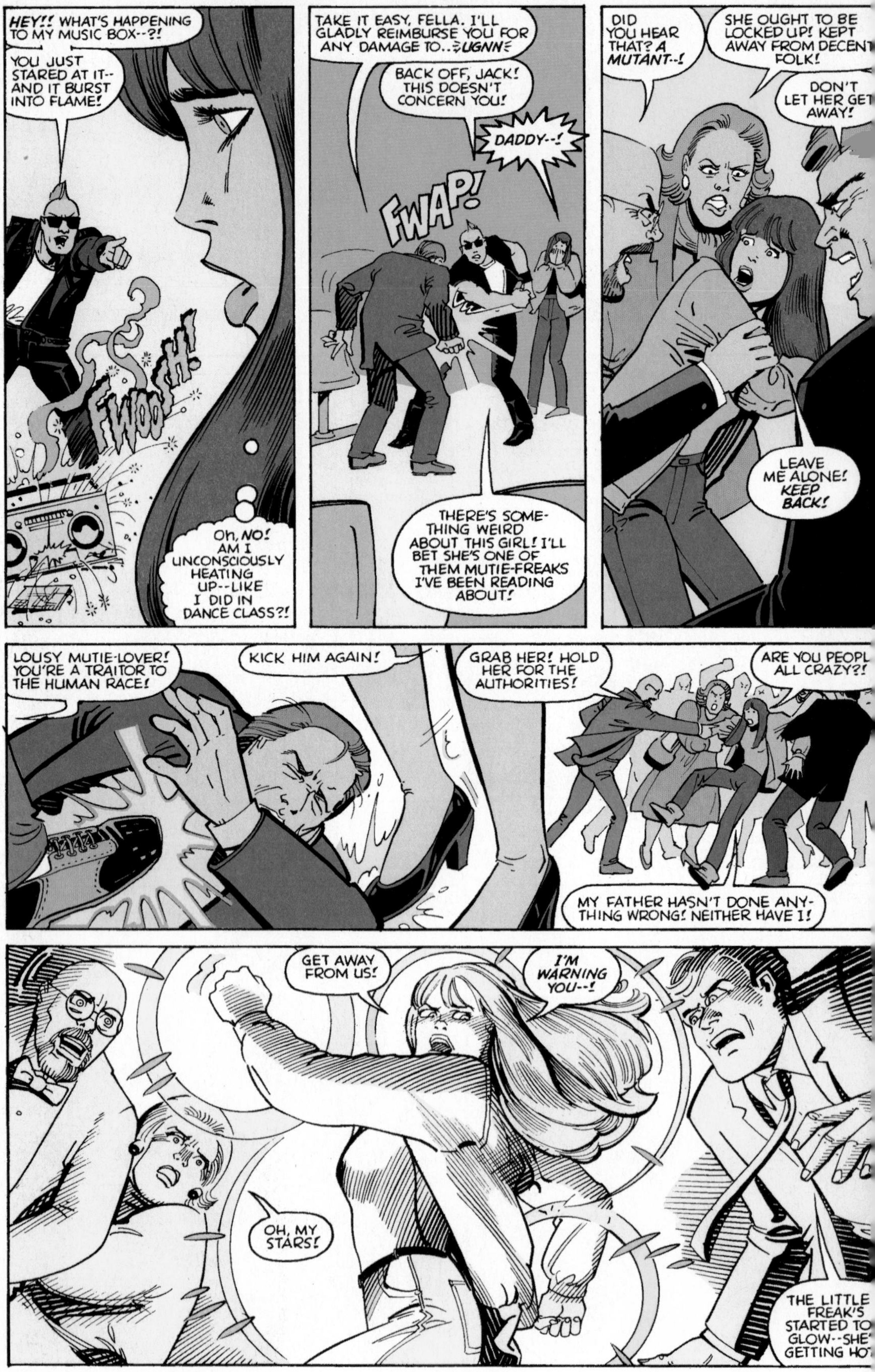

HEY!! WHAT'S HAPPENING TO MY MUSIC BOX--?!
YOU JUST STARED AT IT-- AND IT BURST INTO FLAME!
FWOOSH!
Oh, NO! AM I UNCONSCIOUSLY HEATING UP--LIKE I DID IN DANCE CLASS?!
TAKE IT EASY, FELLA. I'LL GLADLY REIMBURSE YOU FOR ANY DAMAGE TO..UGNN
BACK OFF, JACK! THIS DOESN'T CONCERN YOU!
DADDY--!
FWAP!
THERE'S SOMETHING WEIRD ABOUT THIS GIRL! I'LL BET SHE'S ONE OF THEM MUTIE-FREAKS I'VE BEEN READING ABOUT!
DID YOU HEAR THAT? A MUTANT--!
SHE OUGHT TO BE LOCKED UP! KEPT AWAY FROM DECENT FOLK!
DON'T LET HER GET AWAY!
LEAVE ME ALONE! KEEP BACK!
LOUSY MUTIE-LOVER! YOU'RE A TRAITOR TO THE HUMAN RACE!
KICK HIM AGAIN!
GRAB HER! HOLD HER FOR THE AUTHORITIES!
ARE YOU PEOPL ALL CRAZY?!
MY FATHER HASN'T DONE ANYTHING WRONG! NEITHER HAVE I!
GET AWAY FROM US!
I'M WARNING YOU--!
OH, MY STARS!
THE LITTLE FREAK'S STARTED TO GLOW--SHE GETTING HO

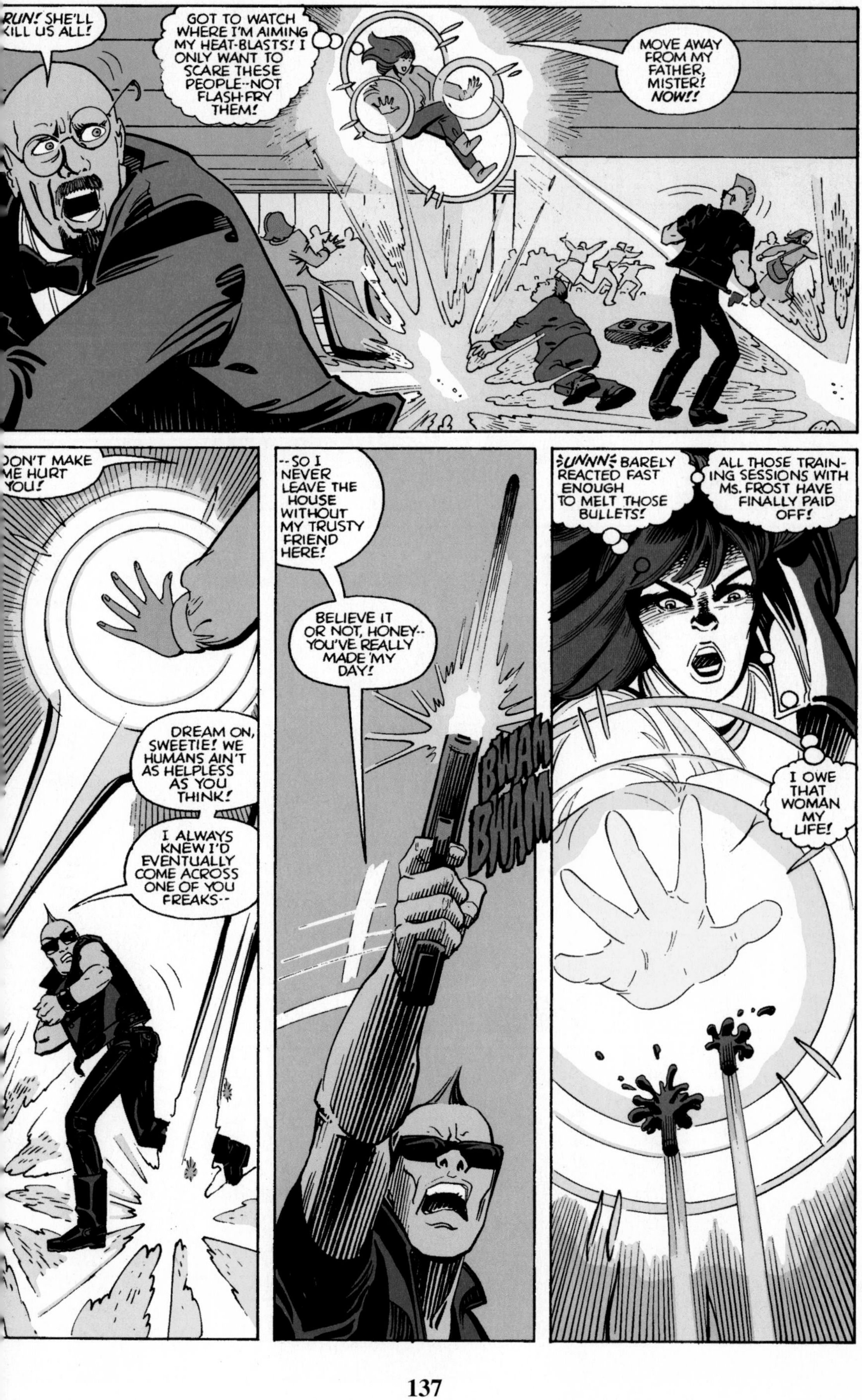

RUN! SHE'LL KILL US ALL!
GOT TO WATCH WHERE I'M AIMING MY HEAT-BLASTS! I ONLY WANT TO SCARE THESE PEOPLE--NOT FLASH-FRY THEM!
MOVE AWAY FROM MY FATHER, MISTER! NOW!!
DON'T MAKE ME HURT YOU!
DREAM ON, SWEETIE! WE HUMANS AIN'T AS HELPLESS AS YOU THINK!
I ALWAYS KNEW I'D EVENTUALLY COME ACROSS ONE OF YOU FREAKS--
--SO I NEVER LEAVE THE HOUSE WITHOUT MY TRUSTY FRIEND HERE!
BELIEVE IT OR NOT, HONEY--YOU'VE REALLY MADE MY DAY!
BWAM
BWAM
UNNN! BARELY REACTED FAST ENOUGH TO MELT THOSE BULLETS!
ALL THOSE TRAINING SESSIONS WITH MS. FROST HAVE FINALLY PAID OFF!
I OWE THAT WOMAN MY LIFE!

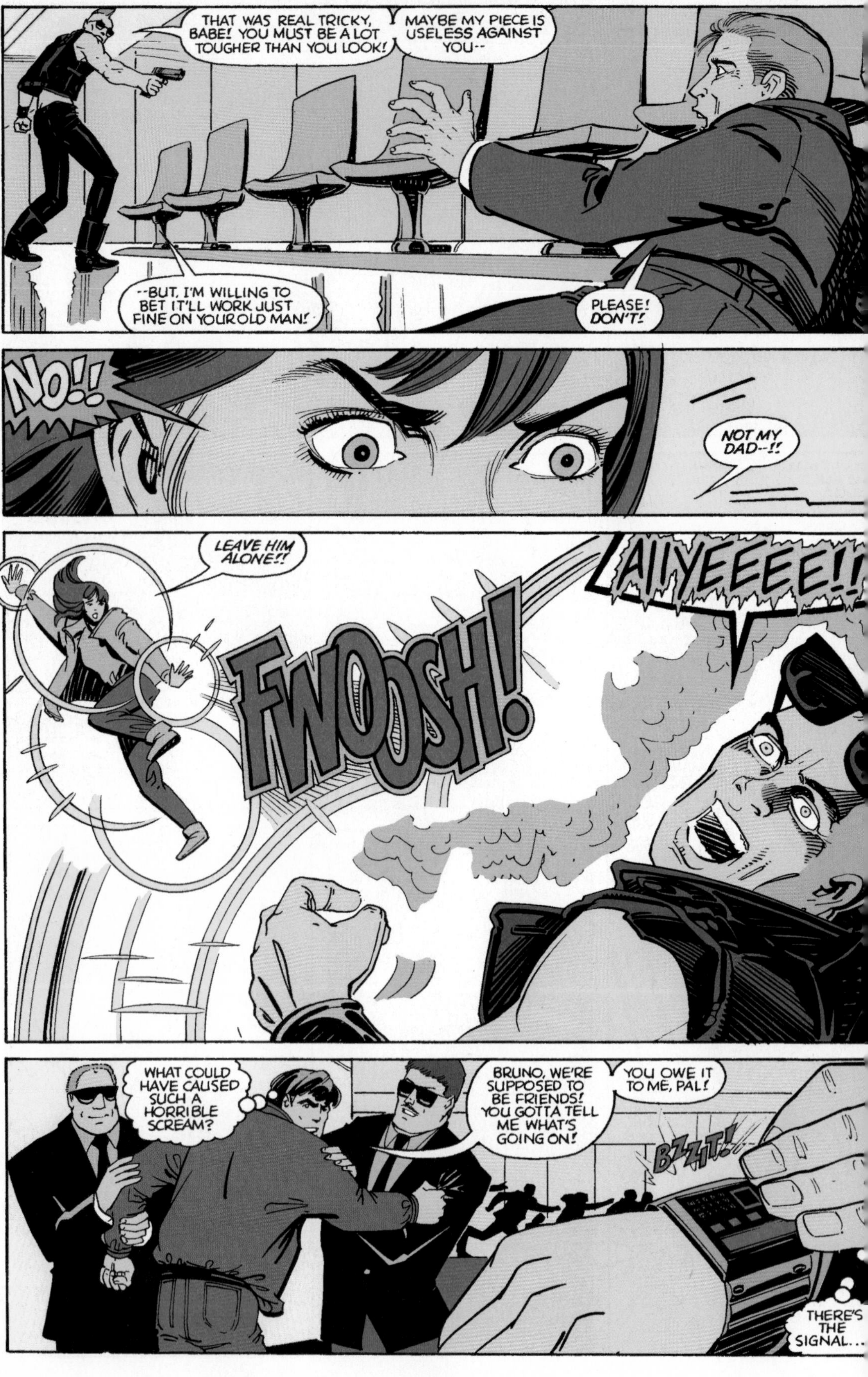
THAT WAS REAL TRICKY, BABE! YOU MUST BE A LOT TOUGHER THAN YOU LOOK!
MAYBE MY PIECE IS USELESS AGAINST YOU--
--BUT, I'M WILLING TO BET IT'LL WORK JUST FINE ON YOUR OLD MAN!
PLEASE! DON'T!
NO!!
NOT MY DAD--!!
LEAVE HIM ALONE!!
AIIYEEEE!!
FWOOSH!
WHAT COULD HAVE CAUSED SUCH A HORRIBLE SCREAM?
BRUNO, WE'RE SUPPOSED TO BE FRIENDS! YOU GOTTA TELL ME WHAT'S GOING ON!
YOU OWE IT TO ME, PAL!
BZZIT!
THERE'S THE SIGNAL...

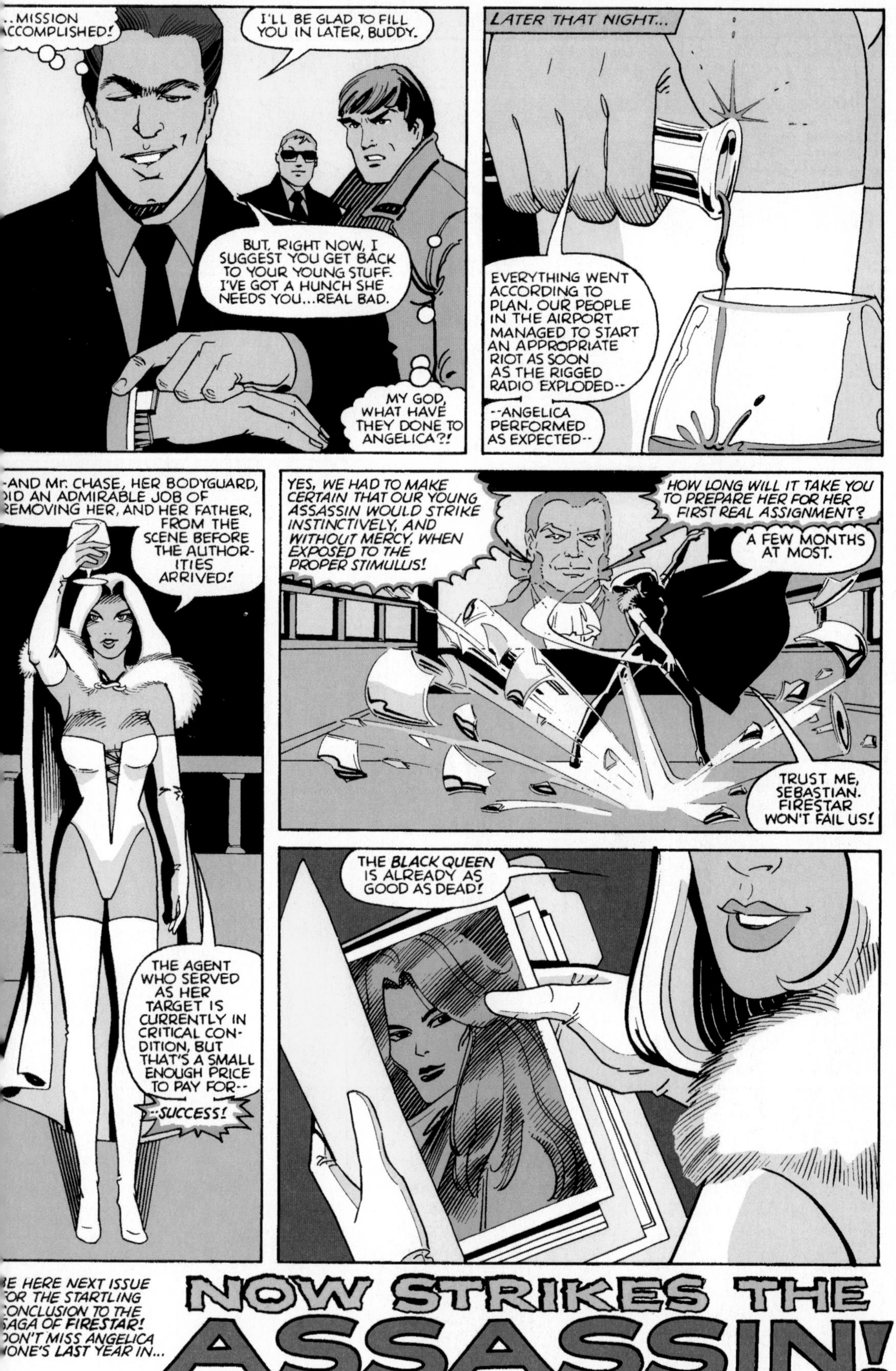
..MISSION ACCOMPLISHED!
I'LL BE GLAD TO FILL YOU IN LATER, BUDDY.
BUT, RIGHT NOW, I SUGGEST YOU GET BACK TO YOUR YOUNG STUFF. I'VE GOT A HUNCH SHE NEEDS YOU...REAL BAD.
MY GOD, WHAT HAVE THEY DONE TO ANGELICA?!
LATER THAT NIGHT...
EVERYTHING WENT ACCORDING TO PLAN. OUR PEOPLE IN THE AIRPORT MANAGED TO START AN APPROPRIATE RIOT AS SOON AS THE RIGGED RADIO EXPLODED--
--ANGELICA PERFORMED AS EXPECTED--
-AND Mr. CHASE, HER BODYGUARD, DID AN ADMIRABLE JOB OF REMOVING HER, AND HER FATHER, FROM THE SCENE BEFORE THE AUTHORITIES ARRIVED!
THE AGENT WHO SERVED AS HER TARGET IS CURRENTLY IN CRITICAL CONDITION, BUT THAT'S A SMALL ENOUGH PRICE TO PAY FOR--
--SUCCESS!
YES, WE HAD TO MAKE CERTAIN THAT OUR YOUNG ASSASSIN WOULD STRIKE INSTINCTIVELY, AND WITHOUT MERCY, WHEN EXPOSED TO THE PROPER STIMULUS!
HOW LONG WILL IT TAKE YOU TO PREPARE HER FOR HER FIRST REAL ASSIGNMENT?
A FEW MONTHS AT MOST.
TRUST ME, SEBASTIAN. FIRESTAR WON'T FAIL US!
THE BLACK QUEEN IS ALREADY AS GOOD AS DEAD!
BE HERE NEXT ISSUE FOR THE STARTLING CONCLUSION TO THE SAGA OF FIRESTAR! DON'T MISS ANGELICA JONE'S LAST YEAR IN...
NOW STRIKES THE ASSASSIN!

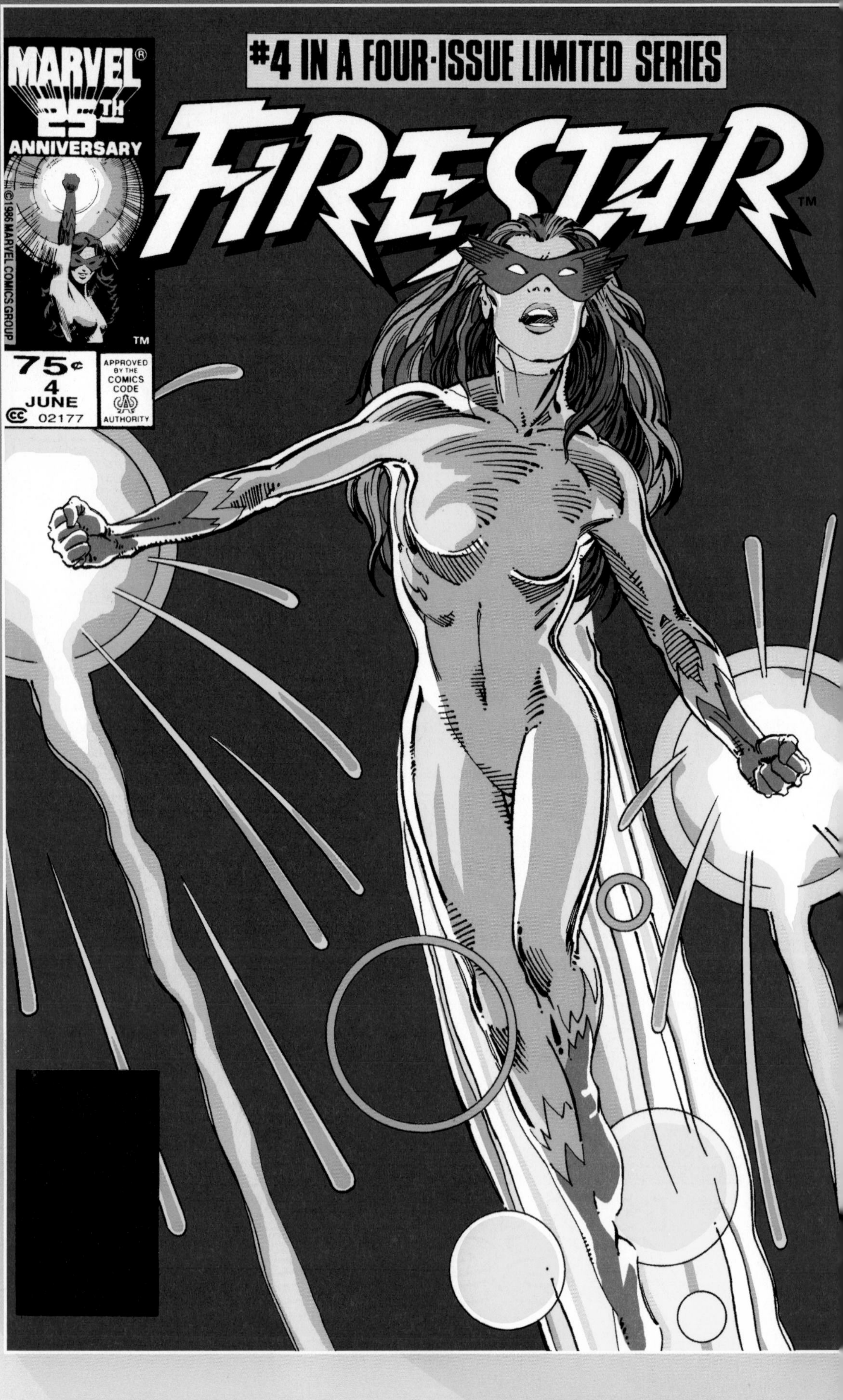

MARVEL®
25TH
ANNIVERSARY
©1986 MARVEL COMICS GROUP
TM
#4 IN A FOUR-ISSUE LIMITED SERIES
FIRESTAR™
75¢
4
JUNE
02177
APPROVED BY THE COMICS CODE AUTHORITY

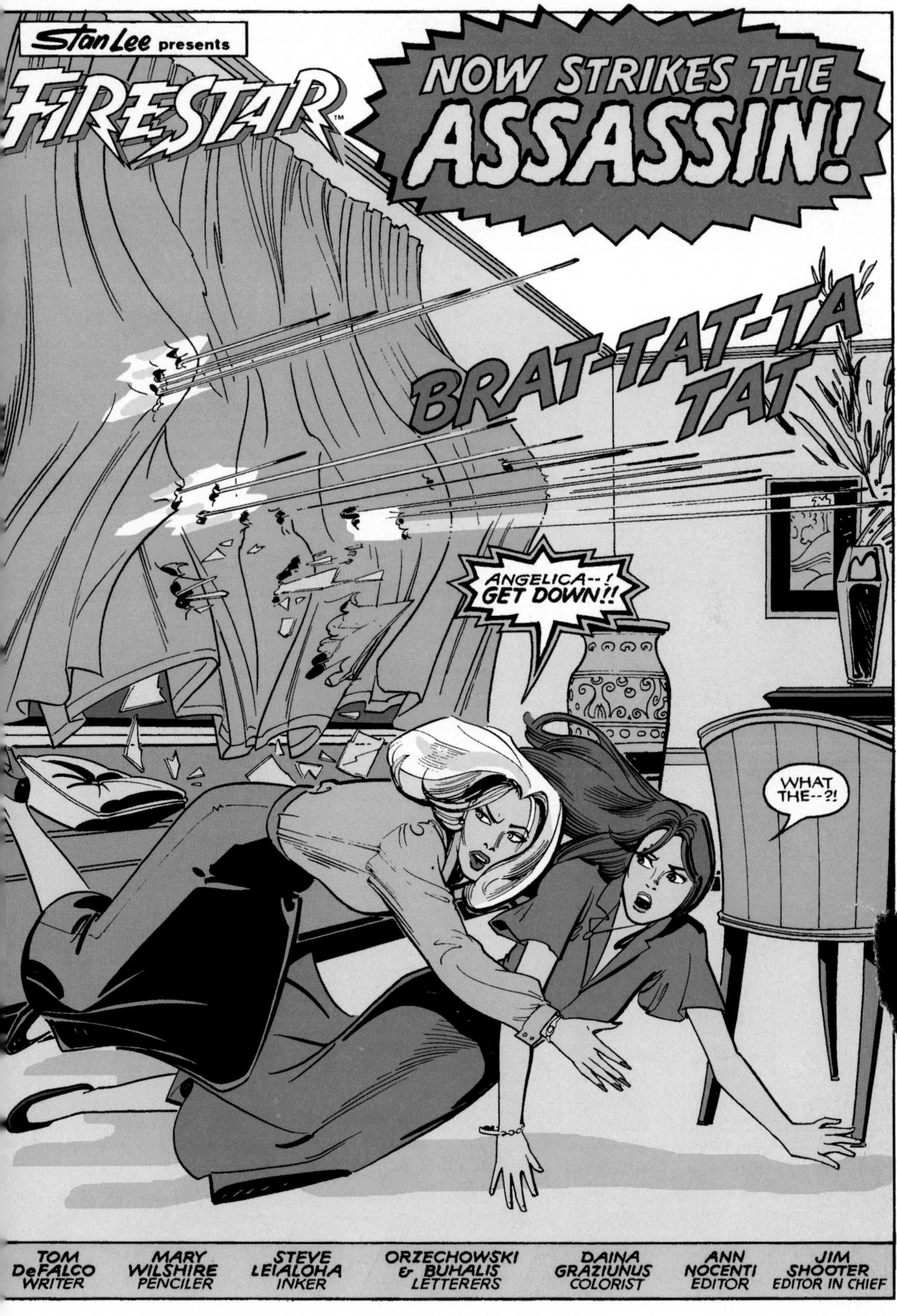
Stan Lee presents
FIRESTAR™
NOW STRIKES THE ASSASSIN!
BRAT-TAT-TA TAT
ANGELICA--! GET DOWN!!
WHAT THE--?!
TOM DeFALCO WRITER
MARY WILSHIRE PENCILER
STEVE LEIALOHA INKER
ORZECHOWSKI & BUHALIS LETTERERS
DAINA GRAZIUNUS COLORIST
ANN NOCENTI EDITOR
JIM SHOOTER EDITOR IN CHIEF

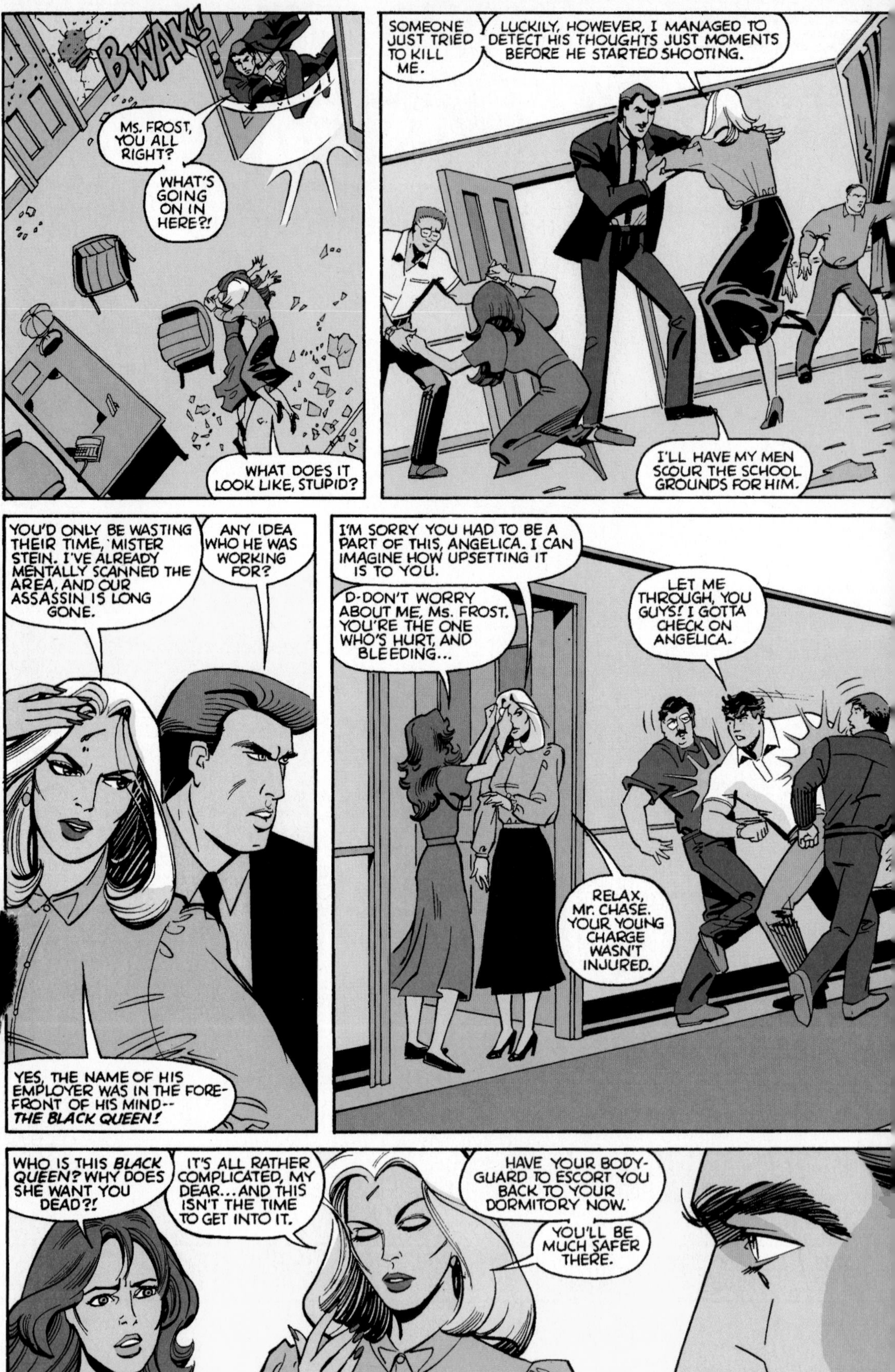
BWAK!
MS. FROST, YOU ALL RIGHT?
WHAT'S GOING ON IN HERE?!
WHAT DOES IT LOOK LIKE, STUPID?
SOMEONE JUST TRIED TO KILL ME.
LUCKILY, HOWEVER, I MANAGED TO DETECT HIS THOUGHTS JUST MOMENTS BEFORE HE STARTED SHOOTING.
I'LL HAVE MY MEN SCOUR THE SCHOOL GROUNDS FOR HIM.
YOU'D ONLY BE WASTING THEIR TIME, MISTER STEIN. I'VE ALREADY MENTALLY SCANNED THE AREA, AND OUR ASSASSIN IS LONG GONE.
ANY IDEA WHO HE WAS WORKING FOR?
YES, THE NAME OF HIS EMPLOYER WAS IN THE FORE-FRONT OF HIS MIND-- THE BLACK QUEEN!
I'M SORRY YOU HAD TO BE A PART OF THIS, ANGELICA. I CAN IMAGINE HOW UPSETTING IT IS TO YOU.
D-DON'T WORRY ABOUT ME, Ms. FROST. YOU'RE THE ONE WHO'S HURT, AND BLEEDING...
LET ME THROUGH, YOU GUYS! I GOTTA CHECK ON ANGELICA.
RELAX, Mr. CHASE. YOUR YOUNG CHARGE WASN'T INJURED.
WHO IS THIS BLACK QUEEN? WHY DOES SHE WANT YOU DEAD?!
IT'S ALL RATHER COMPLICATED, MY DEAR... AND THIS ISN'T THE TIME TO GET INTO IT.
HAVE YOUR BODY-GUARD TO ESCORT YOU BACK TO YOUR DORMITORY NOW.
YOU'LL BE MUCH SAFER THERE.

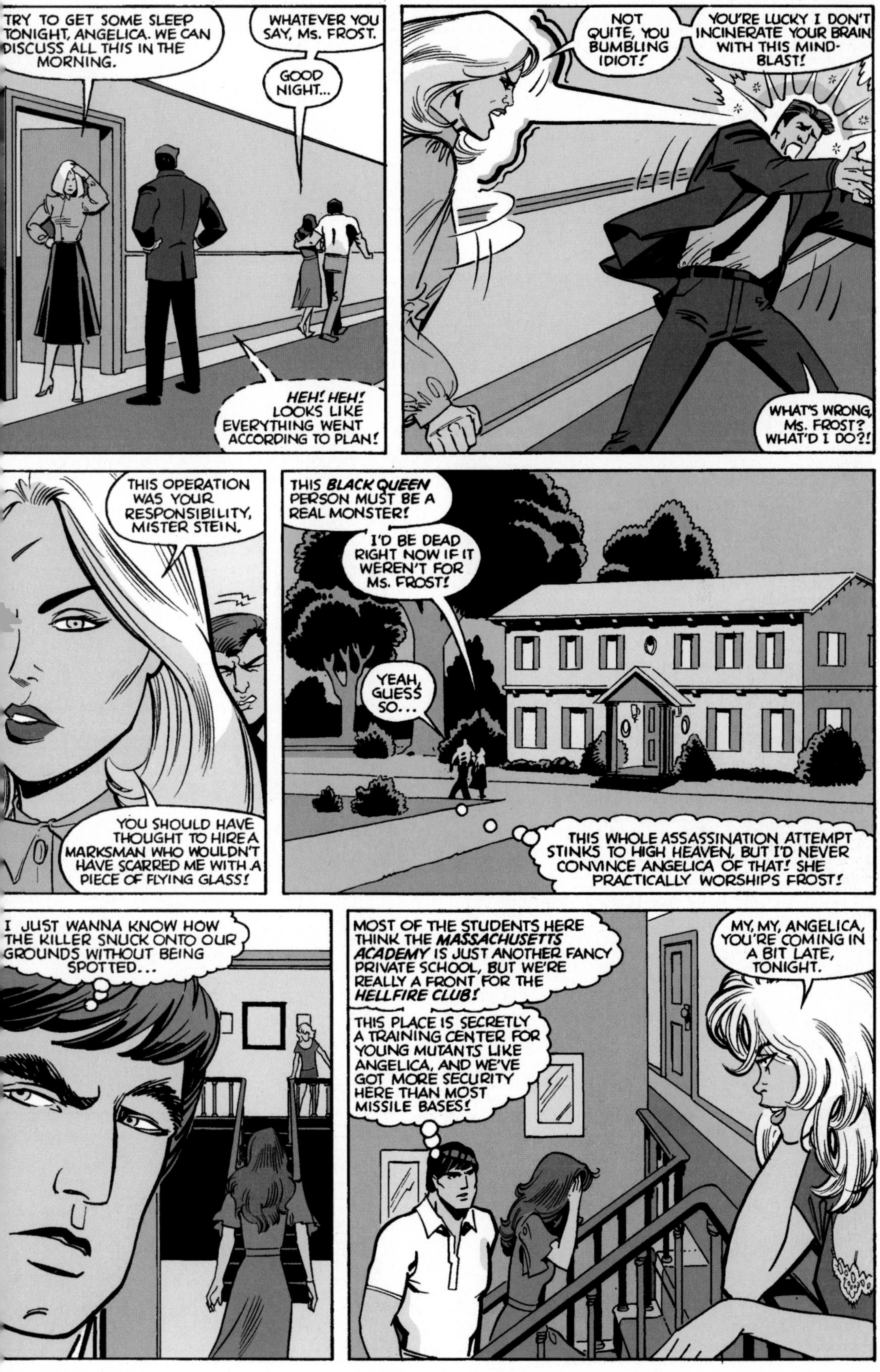
TRY TO GET SOME SLEEP TONIGHT, ANGELICA. WE CAN DISCUSS ALL THIS IN THE MORNING.
WHATEVER YOU SAY, Ms. FROST.
GOOD NIGHT...
HEH! HEH! LOOKS LIKE EVERYTHING WENT ACCORDING TO PLAN!
NOT QUITE, YOU BUMBLING IDIOT!
YOU'RE LUCKY I DON'T INCINERATE YOUR BRAIN WITH THIS MIND-BLAST!
WHAT'S WRONG, Ms. FROST? WHAT'D I DO?!
THIS OPERATION WAS YOUR RESPONSIBILITY, MISTER STEIN.
YOU SHOULD HAVE THOUGHT TO HIRE A MARKSMAN WHO WOULDN'T HAVE SCARRED ME WITH A PIECE OF FLYING GLASS!
THIS BLACK QUEEN PERSON MUST BE A REAL MONSTER!
I'D BE DEAD RIGHT NOW IF IT WEREN'T FOR Ms. FROST!
YEAH, GUESS SO...
THIS WHOLE ASSASSINATION ATTEMPT STINKS TO HIGH HEAVEN, BUT I'D NEVER CONVINCE ANGELICA OF THAT! SHE PRACTICALLY WORSHIPS FROST!
I JUST WANNA KNOW HOW THE KILLER SNUCK ONTO OUR GROUNDS WITHOUT BEING SPOTTED...
MOST OF THE STUDENTS HERE THINK THE MASSACHUSETTS ACADEMY IS JUST ANOTHER FANCY PRIVATE SCHOOL, BUT WE'RE REALLY A FRONT FOR THE HELLFIRE CLUB!
THIS PLACE IS SECRETLY A TRAINING CENTER FOR YOUNG MUTANTS LIKE ANGELICA, AND WE'VE GOT MORE SECURITY HERE THAN MOST MISSILE BASES!
MY, MY, ANGELICA, YOU'RE COMING IN A BIT LATE, TONIGHT.

YOU PEOPLE HAVE ANY IDEA WHAT ALL THE RUCKUS WAS ABOUT OUTSIDE?

NOTHING TO WORRY ABOUT.

JUST A COUPLE OF WISE GUYS SHOOTING OFF SOME FIRECRACKERS.

GO BACK TO BED!

FIRE-CRACKERS?!

SOUNDS LIKE SOMEONE JUST TOLD YOU TO MIND YOUR OWN BUSINESS, LOVE.

YOU GOT A REAL BAD SCARE TO-NIGHT, KID.

YOU SURE YOU'RE OKAY?

I GUESS SO...

ACTUALLY, I'M A LOT MORE WORRIED ABOUT MS. FROST.

EVEN YOU DON'T REALIZE HOW MUCH SHE MEANS TO ME.

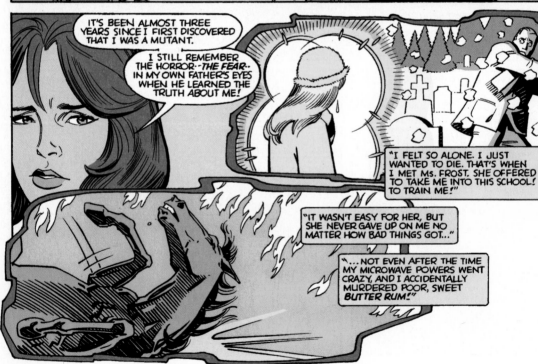

IT'S BEEN ALMOST THREE YEARS SINCE I FIRST DISCOVERED THAT I WAS A MUTANT.

I STILL REMEMBER THE HORROR--*THE FEAR*--IN MY OWN FATHER'S EYES WHEN HE LEARNED THE TRUTH ABOUT ME!

"I FELT SO ALONE. I JUST WANTED TO DIE. THAT'S WHEN I MET MS. FROST. SHE OFFERED TO TAKE ME INTO THIS SCHOOL! TO TRAIN ME!"

"IT WASN'T EASY FOR HER, BUT SHE NEVER GAVE UP ON ME NO MATTER HOW BAD THINGS GOT..."

"...NOT EVEN AFTER THE TIME MY MICROWAVE POWERS WENT CRAZY, AND I ACCIDENTALLY MURDERED POOR, SWEET *BUTTER RUM!*"

144

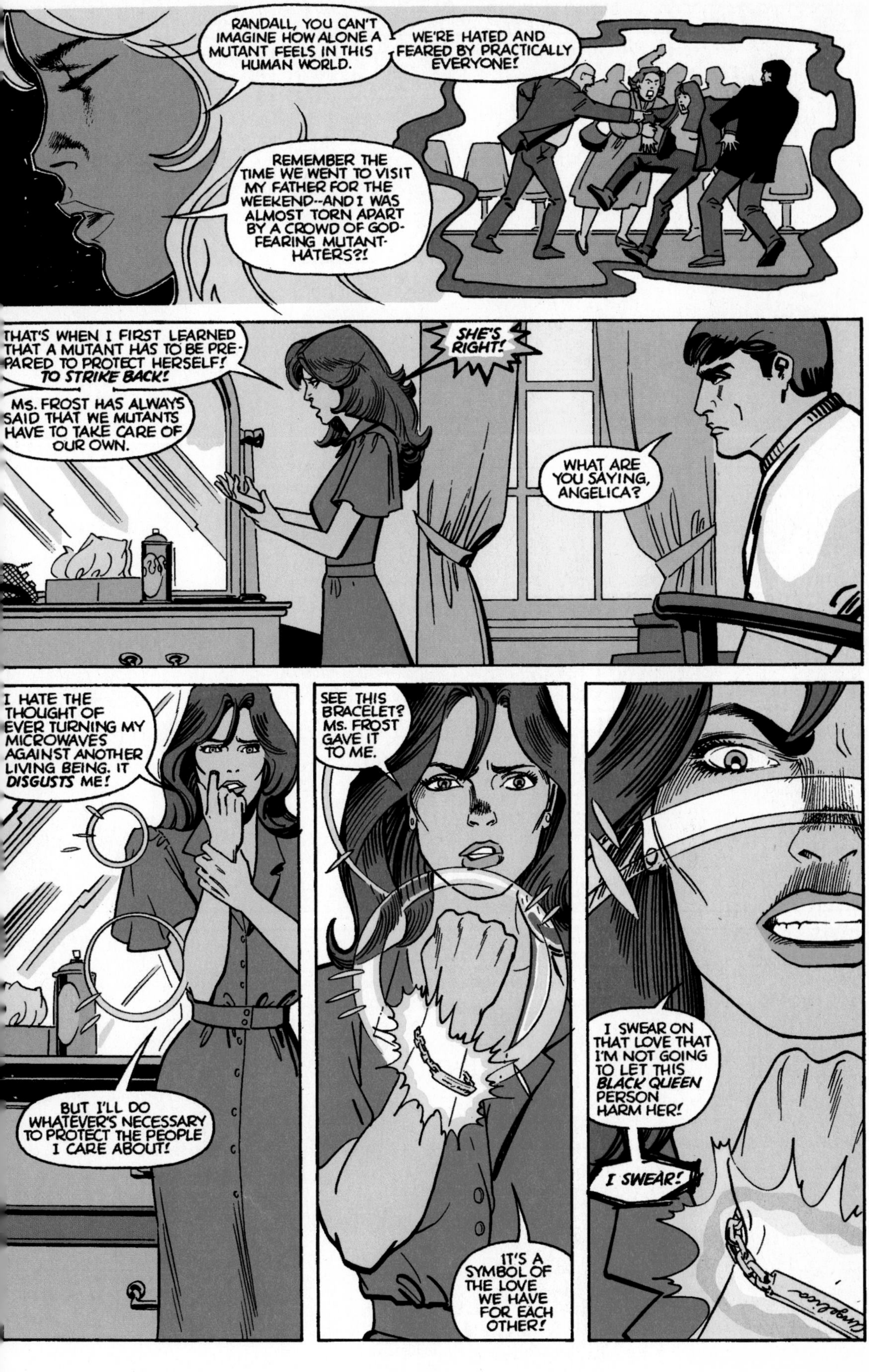
RANDALL, YOU CAN'T IMAGINE HOW ALONE A MUTANT FEELS IN THIS HUMAN WORLD.
WE'RE HATED AND FEARED BY PRACTICALLY EVERYONE!
REMEMBER THE TIME WE WENT TO VISIT MY FATHER FOR THE WEEKEND--AND I WAS ALMOST TORN APART BY A CROWD OF GOD-FEARING MUTANT-HATERS?!
THAT'S WHEN I FIRST LEARNED THAT A MUTANT HAS TO BE PREPARED TO PROTECT HERSELF! TO STRIKE BACK!
MS. FROST HAS ALWAYS SAID THAT WE MUTANTS HAVE TO TAKE CARE OF OUR OWN.
SHE'S RIGHT!
WHAT ARE YOU SAYING, ANGELICA?
I HATE THE THOUGHT OF EVER TURNING MY MICROWAVES AGAINST ANOTHER LIVING BEING. IT DISGUSTS ME!
BUT I'LL DO WHATEVER'S NECESSARY TO PROTECT THE PEOPLE I CARE ABOUT!
SEE THIS BRACELET? MS. FROST GAVE IT TO ME.
IT'S A SYMBOL OF THE LOVE WE HAVE FOR EACH OTHER!
I SWEAR ON THAT LOVE THAT I'M NOT GOING TO LET THIS BLACK QUEEN PERSON HARM HER!
I SWEAR!
Angelica

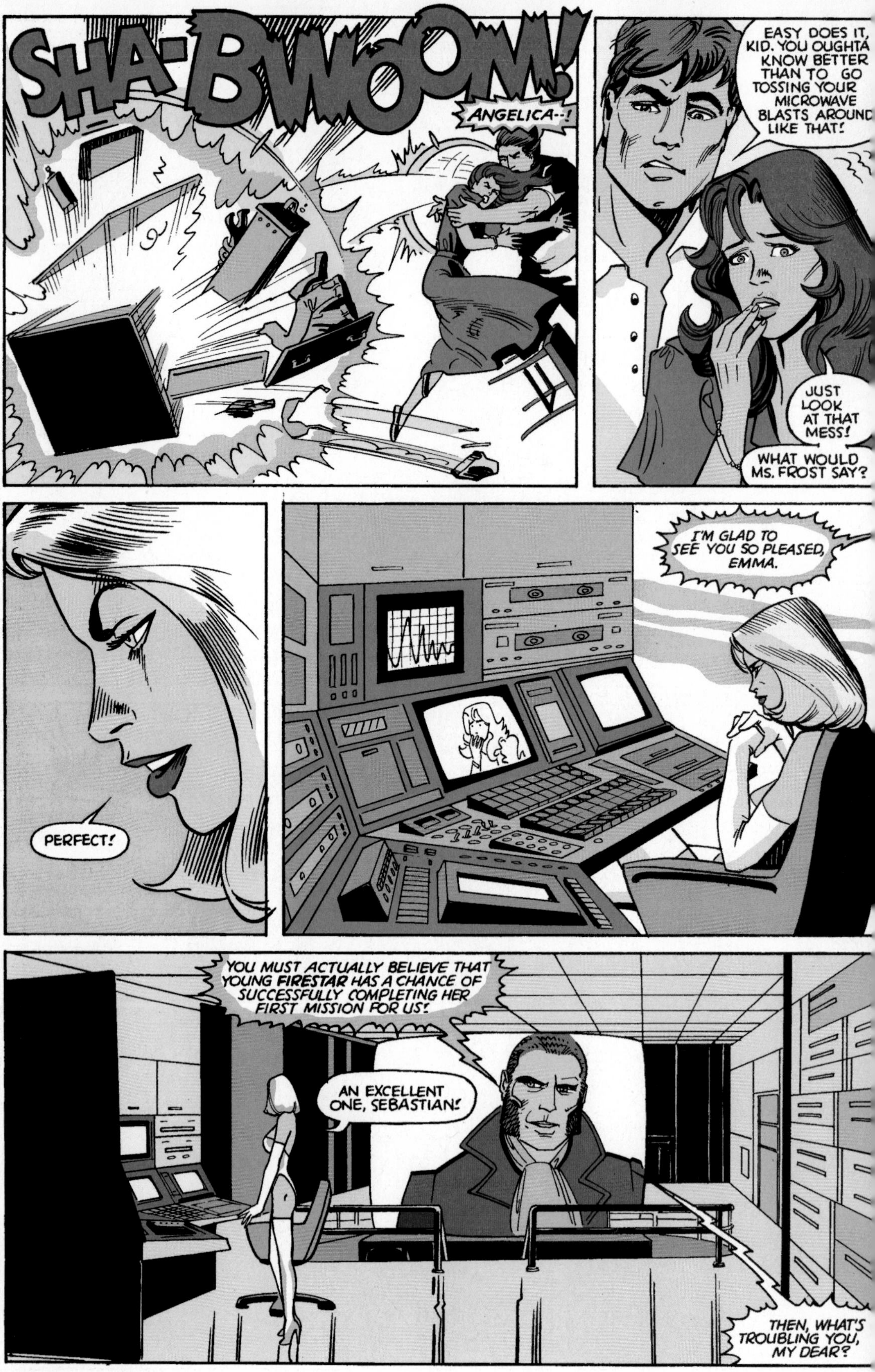
SHA-BWOOM!
ANGELICA--!
EASY DOES IT, KID. YOU OUGHTA KNOW BETTER THAN TO GO TOSSING YOUR MICROWAVE BLASTS AROUND LIKE THAT!
JUST LOOK AT THAT MESS!
WHAT WOULD MS. FROST SAY?
PERFECT!
I'M GLAD TO SEE YOU SO PLEASED, EMMA.
YOU MUST ACTUALLY BELIEVE THAT YOUNG FIRESTAR HAS A CHANCE OF SUCCESSFULLY COMPLETING HER FIRST MISSION FOR US!
AN EXCELLENT ONE, SEBASTIAN!
THEN, WHAT'S TROUBLING YOU, MY DEAR?

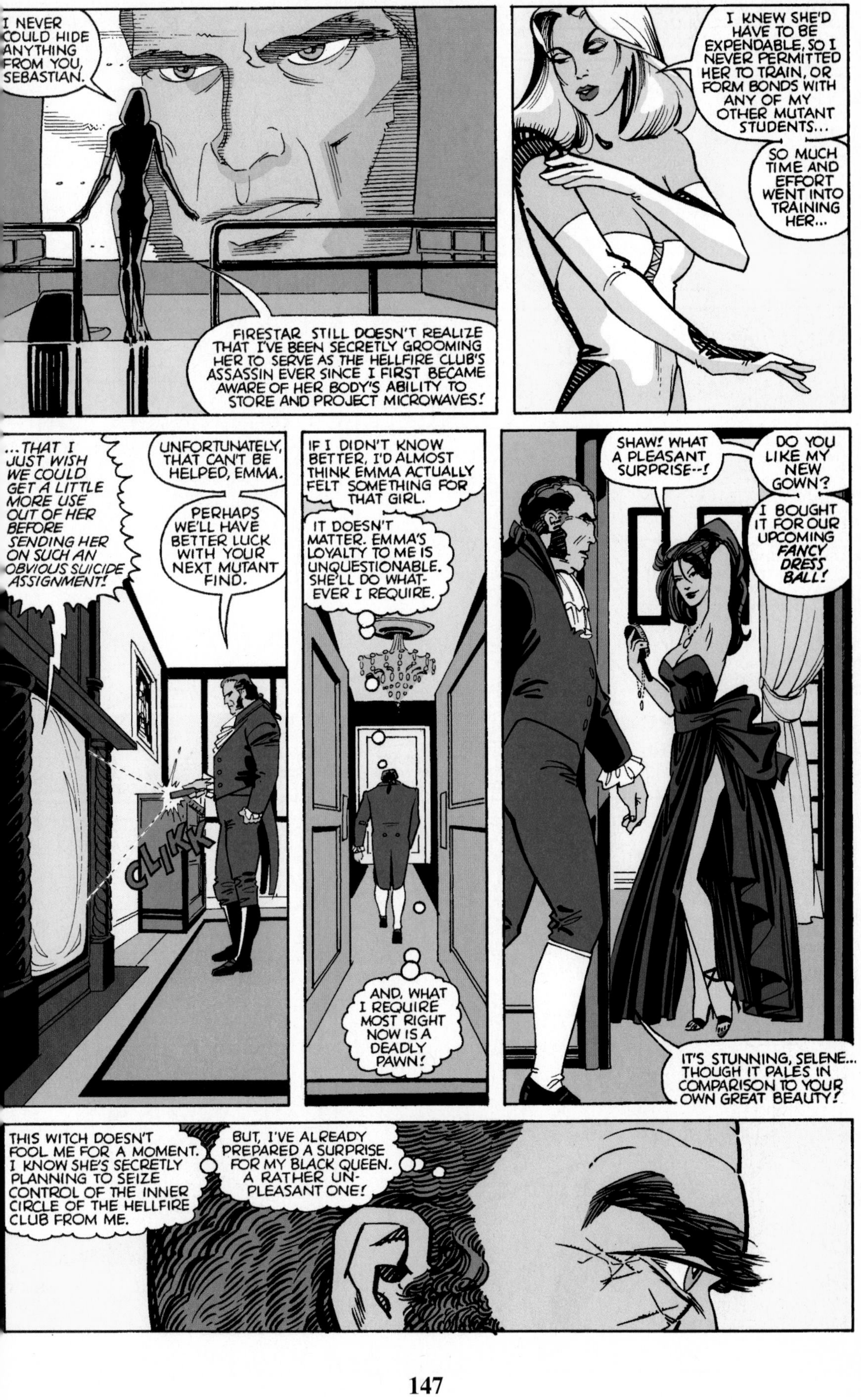
I NEVER COULD HIDE ANYTHING FROM YOU, SEBASTIAN.
FIRESTAR STILL DOESN'T REALIZE THAT I'VE BEEN SECRETLY GROOMING HER TO SERVE AS THE HELLFIRE CLUB'S ASSASSIN EVER SINCE I FIRST BECAME AWARE OF HER BODY'S ABILITY TO STORE AND PROJECT MICROWAVES!
I KNEW SHE'D HAVE TO BE EXPENDABLE, SO I NEVER PERMITTED HER TO TRAIN, OR FORM BONDS WITH ANY OF MY OTHER MUTANT STUDENTS...
SO MUCH TIME AND EFFORT WENT INTO TRAINING HER...
...THAT I JUST WISH WE COULD GET A LITTLE MORE USE OUT OF HER BEFORE SENDING HER ON SUCH AN OBVIOUS SUICIDE ASSIGNMENT!
UNFORTUNATELY, THAT CAN'T BE HELPED, EMMA.
PERHAPS WE'LL HAVE BETTER LUCK WITH YOUR NEXT MUTANT FIND.
CLIKK
IF I DIDN'T KNOW BETTER, I'D ALMOST THINK EMMA ACTUALLY FELT SOMETHING FOR THAT GIRL.
IT DOESN'T MATTER. EMMA'S LOYALTY TO ME IS UNQUESTIONABLE. SHE'LL DO WHATEVER I REQUIRE.
AND, WHAT I REQUIRE MOST RIGHT NOW IS A DEADLY PAWN!
SHAW! WHAT A PLEASANT SURPRISE--!
DO YOU LIKE MY NEW GOWN?
I BOUGHT IT FOR OUR UPCOMING FANCY DRESS BALL!
IT'S STUNNING, SELENE... THOUGH IT PALES IN COMPARISON TO YOUR OWN GREAT BEAUTY!
THIS WITCH DOESN'T FOOL ME FOR A MOMENT. I KNOW SHE'S SECRETLY PLANNING TO SEIZE CONTROL OF THE INNER CIRCLE OF THE HELLFIRE CLUB FROM ME.
BUT, I'VE ALREADY PREPARED A SURPRISE FOR MY BLACK QUEEN. A RATHER UNPLEASANT ONE!

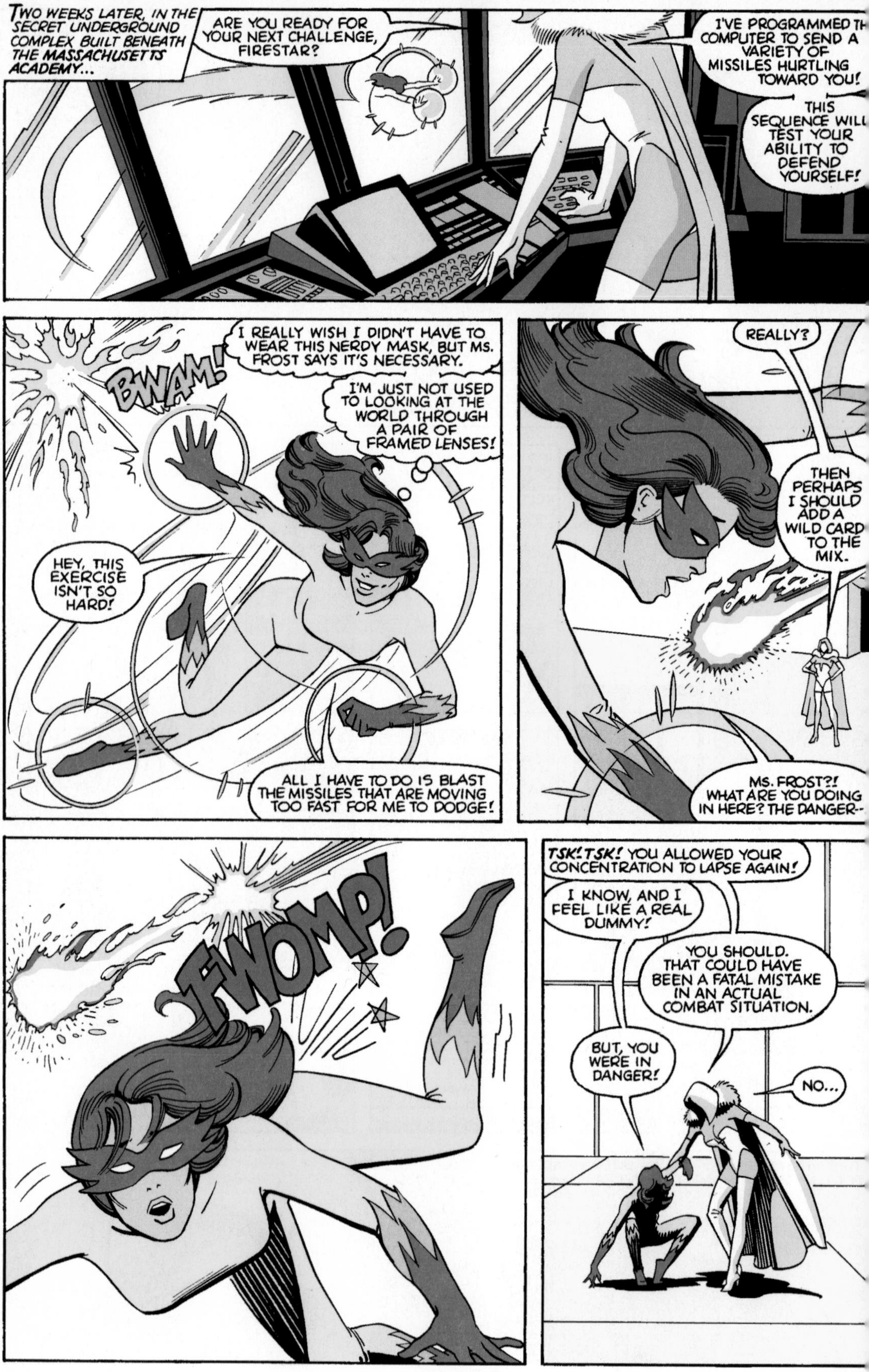
TWO WEEKS LATER, IN THE SECRET UNDERGROUND COMPLEX BUILT BENEATH THE MASSACHUSETTS ACADEMY...
ARE YOU READY FOR YOUR NEXT CHALLENGE, FIRESTAR?
I'VE PROGRAMMED TH COMPUTER TO SEND A VARIETY OF MISSILES HURTLING TOWARD YOU!
THIS SEQUENCE WILL TEST YOUR ABILITY TO DEFEND YOURSELF!
I REALLY WISH I DIDN'T HAVE TO WEAR THIS NERDY MASK, BUT MS. FROST SAYS IT'S NECESSARY.
BWAM!
I'M JUST NOT USED TO LOOKING AT THE WORLD THROUGH A PAIR OF FRAMED LENSES!
HEY, THIS EXERCISE ISN'T SO HARD!
ALL I HAVE TO DO IS BLAST THE MISSILES THAT ARE MOVING TOO FAST FOR ME TO DODGE!
REALLY?
THEN PERHAPS I SHOULD ADD A WILD CARD TO THE MIX.
MS. FROST?! WHAT ARE YOU DOING IN HERE? THE DANGER--
FWOMP!
TSK! TSK! YOU ALLOWED YOUR CONCENTRATION TO LAPSE AGAIN!
I KNOW, AND I FEEL LIKE A REAL DUMMY!
YOU SHOULD. THAT COULD HAVE BEEN A FATAL MISTAKE IN AN ACTUAL COMBAT SITUATION.
BUT, YOU WERE IN DANGER!
NO...

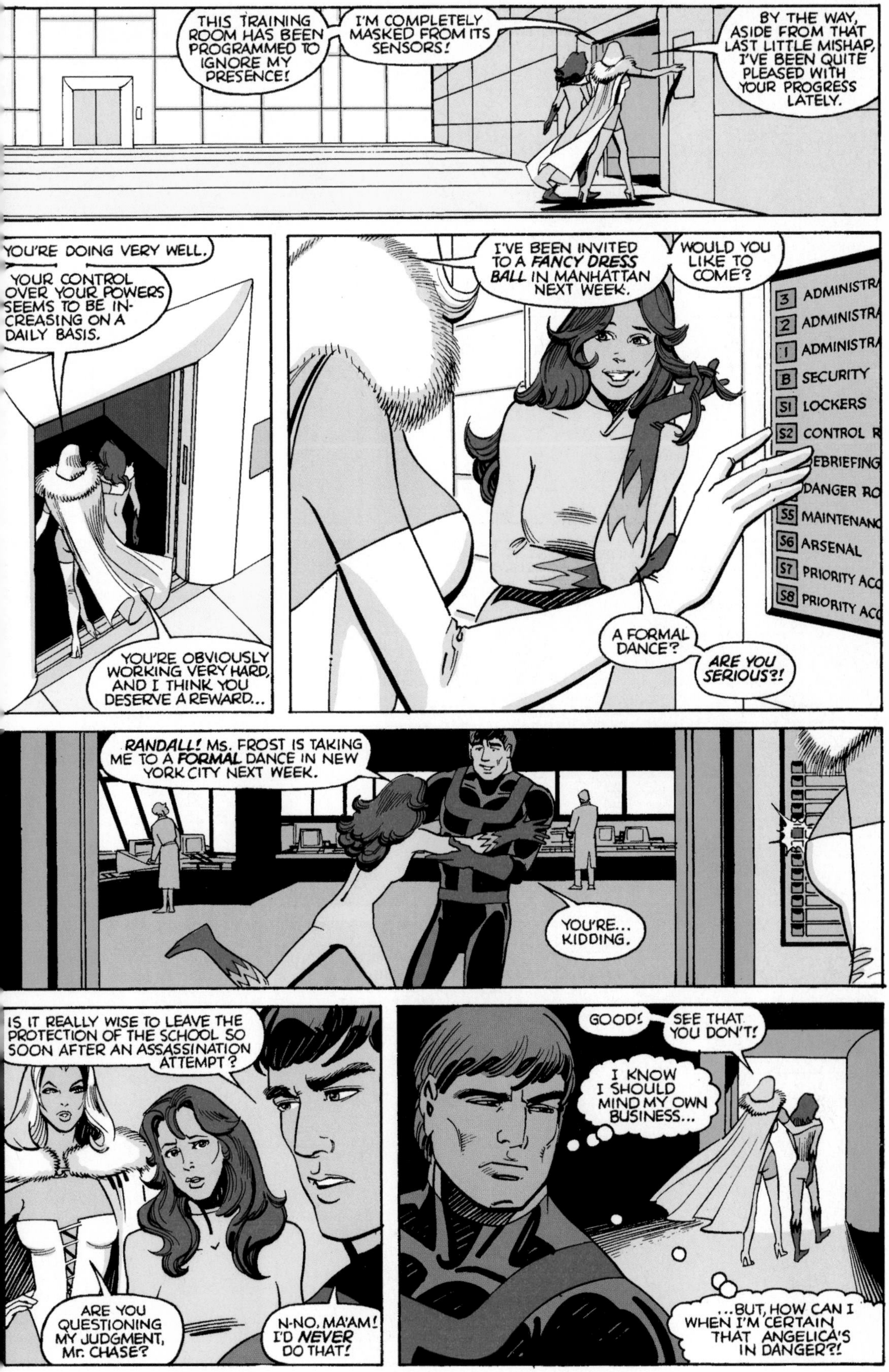
THIS TRAINING ROOM HAS BEEN PROGRAMMED TO IGNORE MY PRESENCE!
I'M COMPLETELY MASKED FROM ITS SENSORS!
BY THE WAY, ASIDE FROM THAT LAST LITTLE MISHAP, I'VE BEEN QUITE PLEASED WITH YOUR PROGRESS LATELY.
YOU'RE DOING VERY WELL.
YOUR CONTROL OVER YOUR POWERS SEEMS TO BE IN-CREASING ON A DAILY BASIS.
YOU'RE OBVIOUSLY WORKING VERY HARD, AND I THINK YOU DESERVE A REWARD...
I'VE BEEN INVITED TO A FANCY DRESS BALL IN MANHATTAN NEXT WEEK.
WOULD YOU LIKE TO COME?
A FORMAL DANCE?
ARE YOU SERIOUS?!
3 ADMINISTRA
2 ADMINISTRA
1 ADMINISTRA
B SECURITY
S1 LOCKERS
S2 CONTROL R
EBRIEFING
DANGER RO
S5 MAINTENANC
S6 ARSENAL
S7 PRIORITY ACC
S8 PRIORITY ACC
RANDALL! Ms. FROST IS TAKING ME TO A FORMAL DANCE IN NEW YORK CITY NEXT WEEK.
YOU'RE... KIDDING.
IS IT REALLY WISE TO LEAVE THE PROTECTION OF THE SCHOOL SO SOON AFTER AN ASSASSINATION ATTEMPT?
ARE YOU QUESTIONING MY JUDGMENT, Mr. CHASE?
N-NO, MA'AM! I'D NEVER DO THAT!
GOOD!
SEE THAT YOU DON'T!
I KNOW I SHOULD MIND MY OWN BUSINESS...
...BUT, HOW CAN I WHEN I'M CERTAIN THAT ANGELICA'S IN DANGER?!

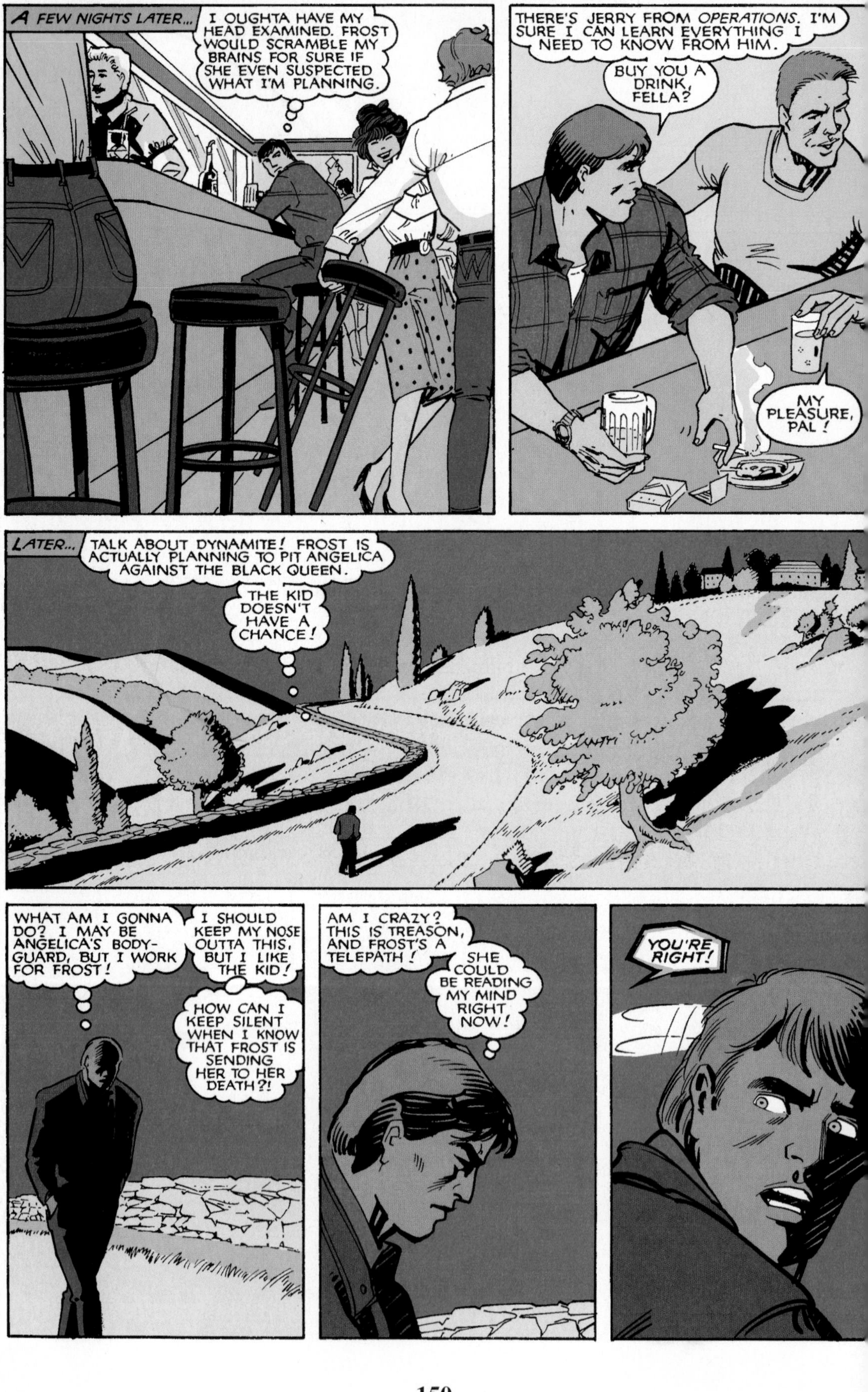
A FEW NIGHTS LATER...
I OUGHTA HAVE MY HEAD EXAMINED. FROST WOULD SCRAMBLE MY BRAINS FOR SURE IF SHE EVEN SUSPECTED WHAT I'M PLANNING.
THERE'S JERRY FROM OPERATIONS. I'M SURE I CAN LEARN EVERYTHING I NEED TO KNOW FROM HIM.
BUY YOU A DRINK, FELLA?
MY PLEASURE, PAL!
LATER...
TALK ABOUT DYNAMITE! FROST IS ACTUALLY PLANNING TO PIT ANGELICA AGAINST THE BLACK QUEEN.
THE KID DOESN'T HAVE A CHANCE!
WHAT AM I GONNA DO? I MAY BE ANGELICA'S BODY-GUARD, BUT I WORK FOR FROST!
I SHOULD KEEP MY NOSE OUTTA THIS, BUT I LIKE THE KID!
HOW CAN I KEEP SILENT WHEN I KNOW THAT FROST IS SENDING HER TO HER DEATH?!
AM I CRAZY? THIS IS TREASON, AND FROST'S A TELEPATH!
SHE COULD BE READING MY MIND RIGHT NOW!
YOU'RE RIGHT!

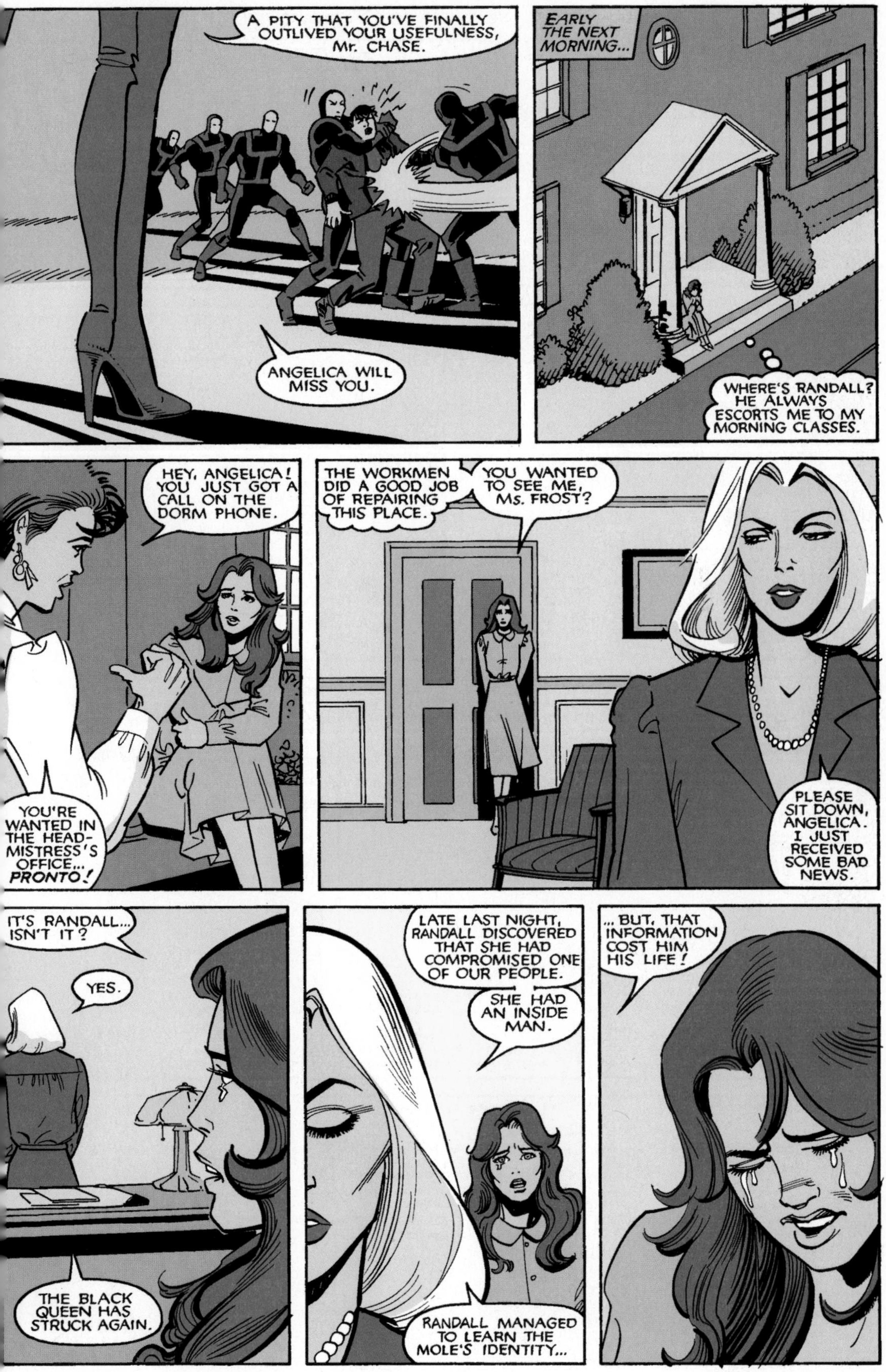
A PITY THAT YOU'VE FINALLY OUTLIVED YOUR USEFULNESS, Mr. CHASE.
ANGELICA WILL MISS YOU.
EARLY THE NEXT MORNING...
WHERE'S RANDALL? HE ALWAYS ESCORTS ME TO MY MORNING CLASSES.
HEY, ANGELICA! YOU JUST GOT A CALL ON THE DORM PHONE.
YOU'RE WANTED IN THE HEAD-MISTRESS'S OFFICE... PRONTO!
THE WORKMEN DID A GOOD JOB OF REPAIRING THIS PLACE.
YOU WANTED TO SEE ME, Ms. FROST?
PLEASE SIT DOWN, ANGELICA. I JUST RECEIVED SOME BAD NEWS.
IT'S RANDALL... ISN'T IT?
YES.
THE BLACK QUEEN HAS STRUCK AGAIN.
LATE LAST NIGHT, RANDALL DISCOVERED THAT SHE HAD COMPROMISED ONE OF OUR PEOPLE.
SHE HAD AN INSIDE MAN.
RANDALL MANAGED TO LEARN THE MOLE'S IDENTITY...
...BUT, THAT INFORMATION COST HIM HIS LIFE!

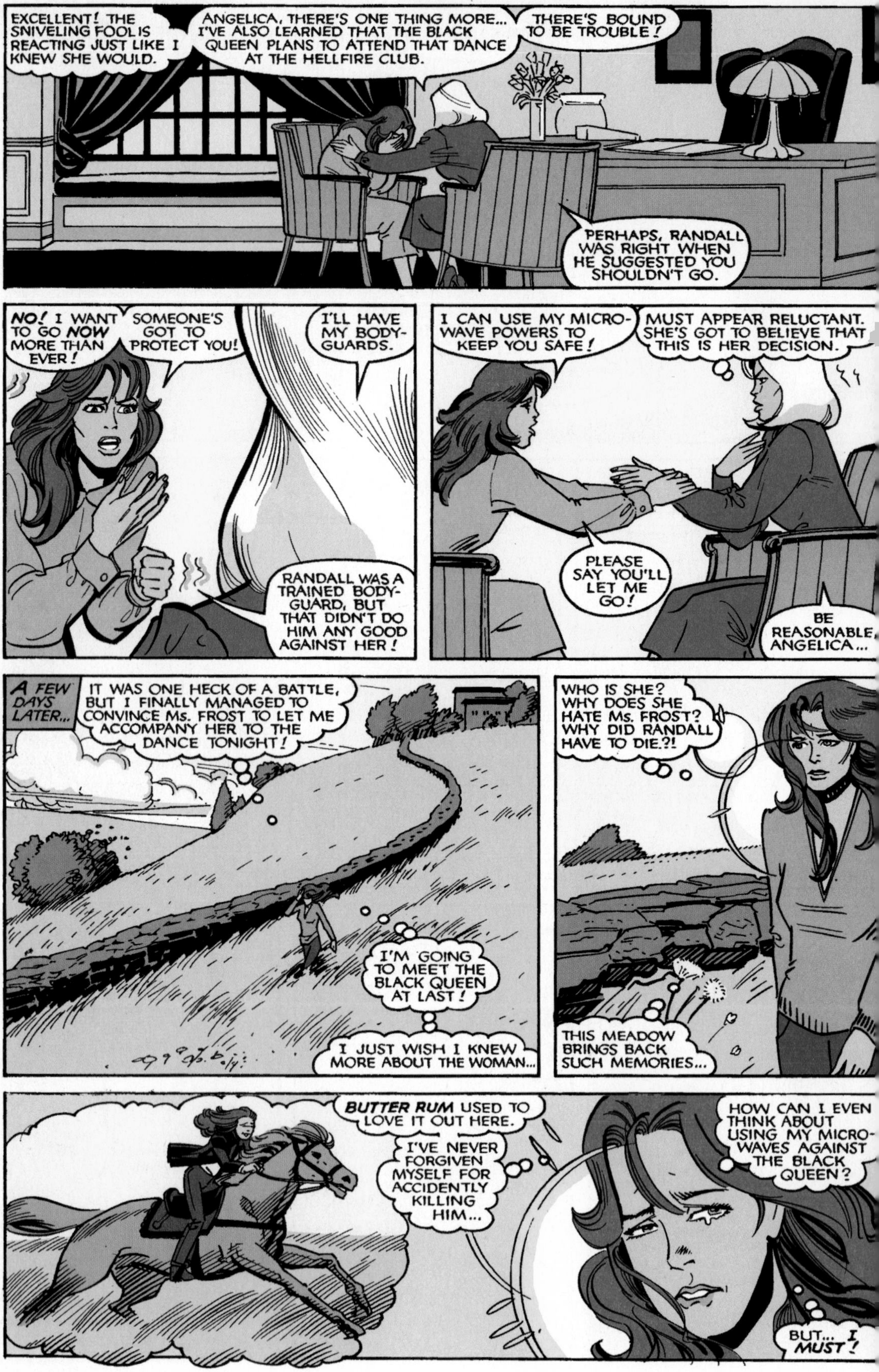
EXCELLENT! THE SNIVELING FOOL IS REACTING JUST LIKE I KNEW SHE WOULD.
ANGELICA, THERE'S ONE THING MORE... I'VE ALSO LEARNED THAT THE BLACK QUEEN PLANS TO ATTEND THAT DANCE AT THE HELLFIRE CLUB.
THERE'S BOUND TO BE TROUBLE!
PERHAPS, RANDALL WAS RIGHT WHEN HE SUGGESTED YOU SHOULDN'T GO.
NO! I WANT TO GO NOW MORE THAN EVER!
SOMEONE'S GOT TO PROTECT YOU!
I'LL HAVE MY BODY-GUARDS.
RANDALL WAS A TRAINED BODY-GUARD, BUT THAT DIDN'T DO HIM ANY GOOD AGAINST HER!
I CAN USE MY MICRO-WAVE POWERS TO KEEP YOU SAFE!
MUST APPEAR RELUCTANT. SHE'S GOT TO BELIEVE THAT THIS IS HER DECISION.
PLEASE SAY YOU'LL LET ME GO!
BE REASONABLE, ANGELICA...
A FEW DAYS LATER...
IT WAS ONE HECK OF A BATTLE, BUT I FINALLY MANAGED TO CONVINCE Ms. FROST TO LET ME ACCOMPANY HER TO THE DANCE TONIGHT!
I'M GOING TO MEET THE BLACK QUEEN AT LAST!
I JUST WISH I KNEW MORE ABOUT THE WOMAN...
WHO IS SHE? WHY DOES SHE HATE Ms. FROST? WHY DID RANDALL HAVE TO DIE.?!
THIS MEADOW BRINGS BACK SUCH MEMORIES...
BUTTER RUM USED TO LOVE IT OUT HERE.
I'VE NEVER FORGIVEN MYSELF FOR ACCIDENTLY KILLING HIM...
HOW CAN I EVEN THINK ABOUT USING MY MICRO-WAVES AGAINST THE BLACK QUEEN?
BUT... I MUST!

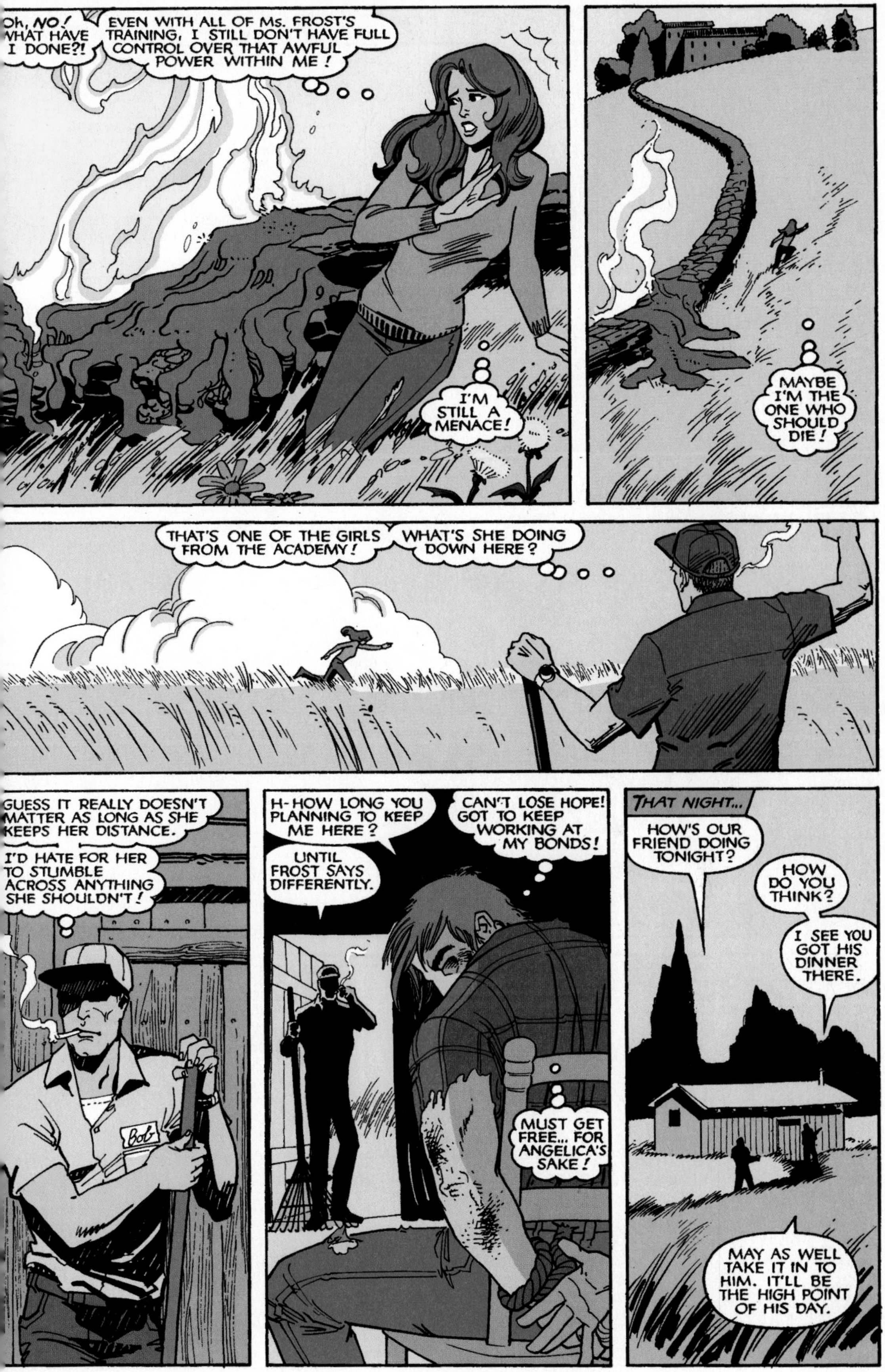
Oh, NO! WHAT HAVE I DONE?!
EVEN WITH ALL OF Ms. FROST'S TRAINING, I STILL DON'T HAVE FULL CONTROL OVER THAT AWFUL POWER WITHIN ME!
I'M STILL A MENACE!
MAYBE I'M THE ONE WHO SHOULD DIE!
THAT'S ONE OF THE GIRLS FROM THE ACADEMY!
WHAT'S SHE DOING DOWN HERE?
GUESS IT REALLY DOESN'T MATTER AS LONG AS SHE KEEPS HER DISTANCE.
I'D HATE FOR HER TO STUMBLE ACROSS ANYTHING SHE SHOULDN'T!
Bob
H-HOW LONG YOU PLANNING TO KEEP ME HERE?
UNTIL FROST SAYS DIFFERENTLY.
CAN'T LOSE HOPE! GOT TO KEEP WORKING AT MY BONDS!
MUST GET FREE... FOR ANGELICA'S SAKE!
THAT NIGHT...
HOW'S OUR FRIEND DOING TONIGHT?
HOW DO YOU THINK?
I SEE YOU GOT HIS DINNER THERE.
MAY AS WELL TAKE IT IN TO HIM. IT'LL BE THE HIGH POINT OF HIS DAY.

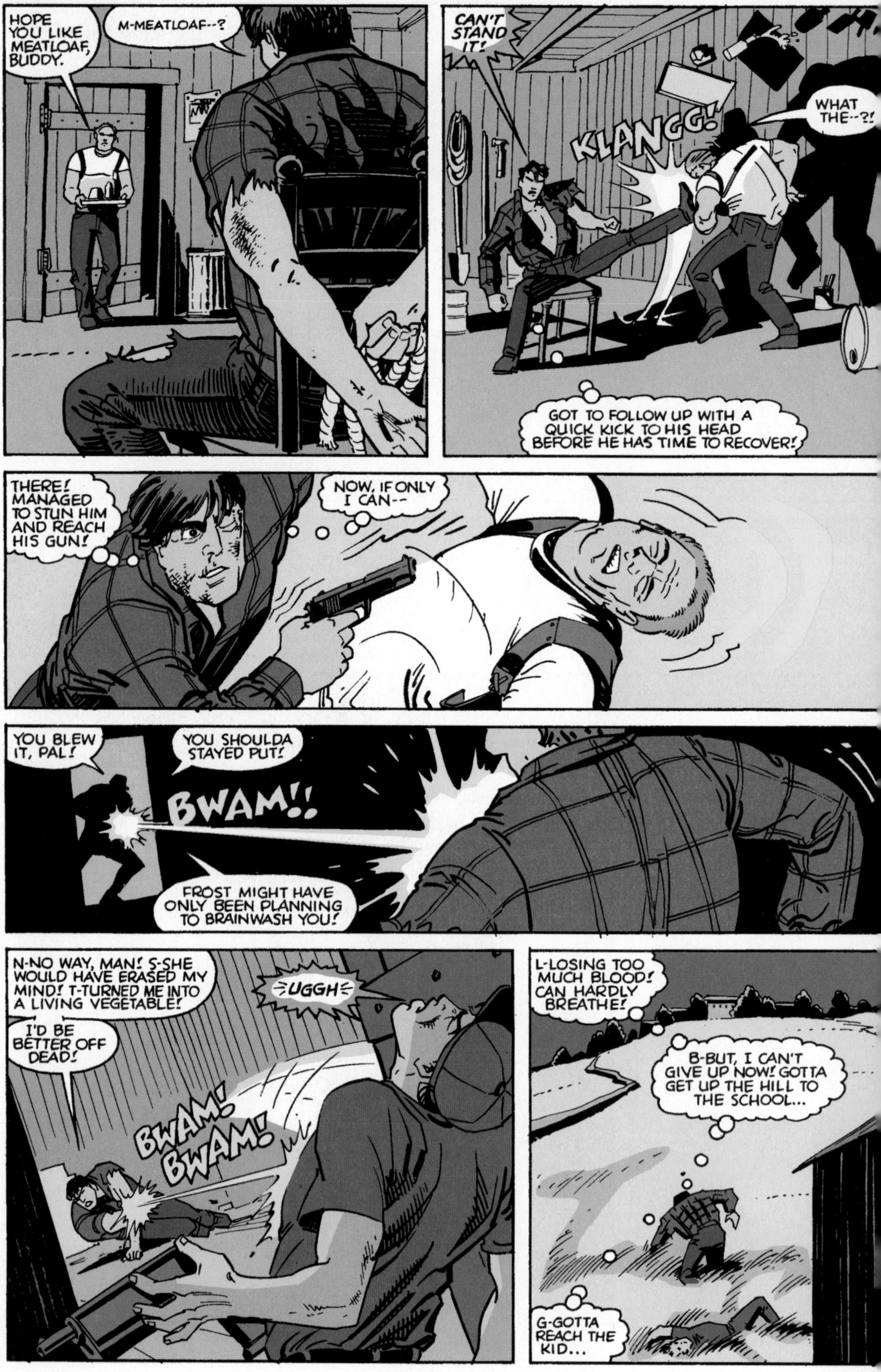

HOPE YOU LIKE MEATLOAF, BUDDY.
M-MEATLOAF--?
CAN'T STAND IT!
KLANGG!
WHAT THE--?!
GOT TO FOLLOW UP WITH A QUICK KICK TO HIS HEAD BEFORE HE HAS TIME TO RECOVER!
THERE! MANAGED TO STUN HIM AND REACH HIS GUN!
NOW, IF ONLY I CAN--
YOU BLEW IT, PAL!
YOU SHOULDA STAYED PUT!
BWAM!!
FROST MIGHT HAVE ONLY BEEN PLANNING TO BRAINWASH YOU!
N-NO WAY, MAN! S-SHE WOULD HAVE ERASED MY MIND! T-TURNED ME INTO A LIVING VEGETABLE!
I'D BE BETTER OFF DEAD!
UGGH
BWAM! BWAM!
L-LOSING TOO MUCH BLOOD! CAN HARDLY BREATHE!
B-BUT, I CAN'T GIVE UP NOW! GOTTA GET UP THE HILL TO THE SCHOOL...
G-GOTTA REACH THE KID...

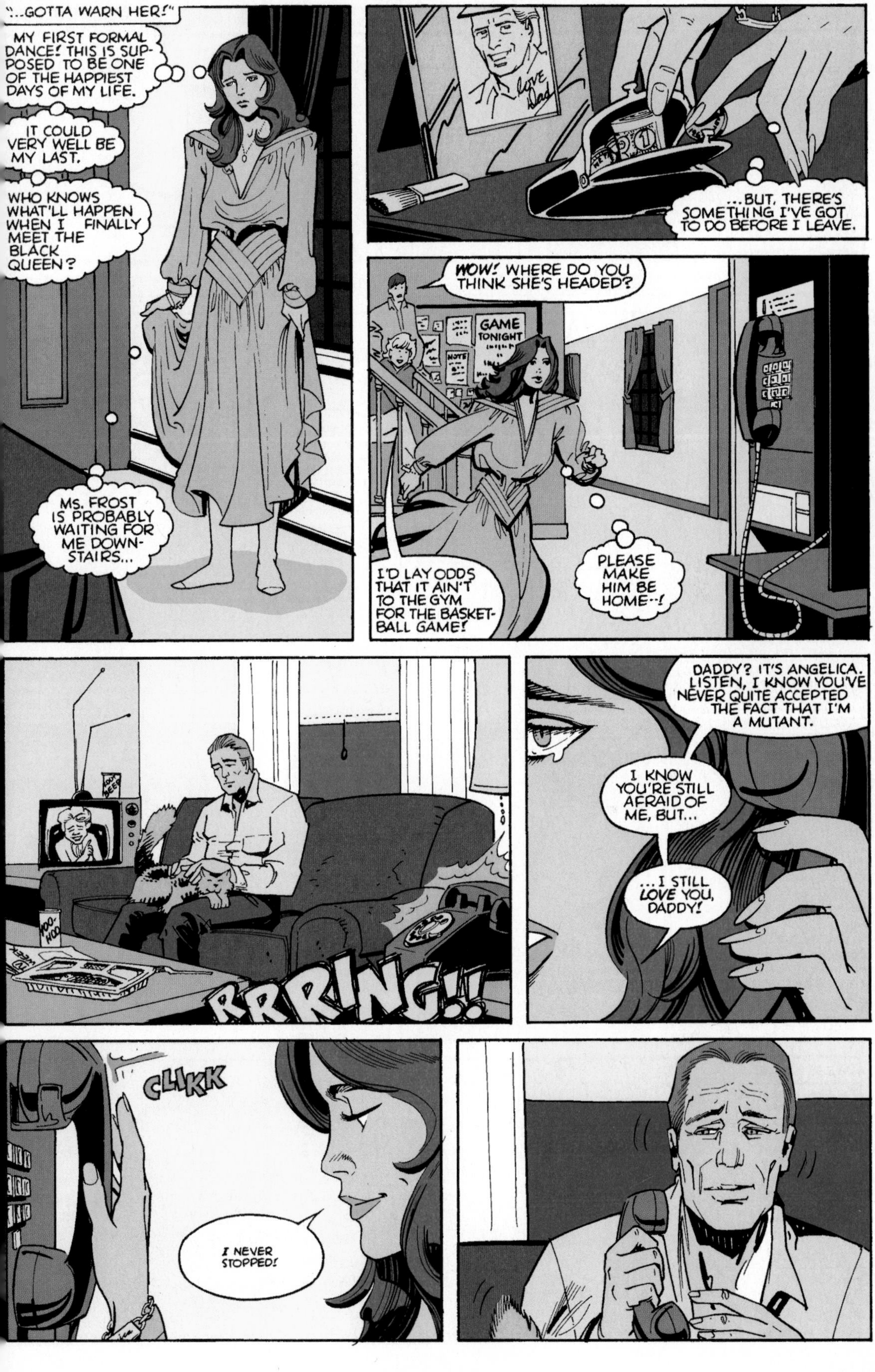
"...GOTTA WARN HER!"
MY FIRST FORMAL DANCE! THIS IS SUPPOSED TO BE ONE OF THE HAPPIEST DAYS OF MY LIFE.
IT COULD VERY WELL BE MY LAST.
WHO KNOWS WHAT'LL HAPPEN WHEN I FINALLY MEET THE BLACK QUEEN?
MS. FROST IS PROBABLY WAITING FOR ME DOWNSTAIRS...
Love Dad
...BUT, THERE'S SOMETHING I'VE GOT TO DO BEFORE I LEAVE.
WOW! WHERE DO YOU THINK SHE'S HEADED?
GAME TONIGHT
I'D LAY ODDS THAT IT AIN'T TO THE GYM FOR THE BASKETBALL GAME!
PLEASE MAKE HIM BE HOME--!
RRRING!!
DADDY? IT'S ANGELICA. LISTEN, I KNOW YOU'VE NEVER QUITE ACCEPTED THE FACT THAT I'M A MUTANT.
I KNOW YOU'RE STILL AFRAID OF ME, BUT...
...I STILL LOVE YOU, DADDY!
CLIKK
I NEVER STOPPED!

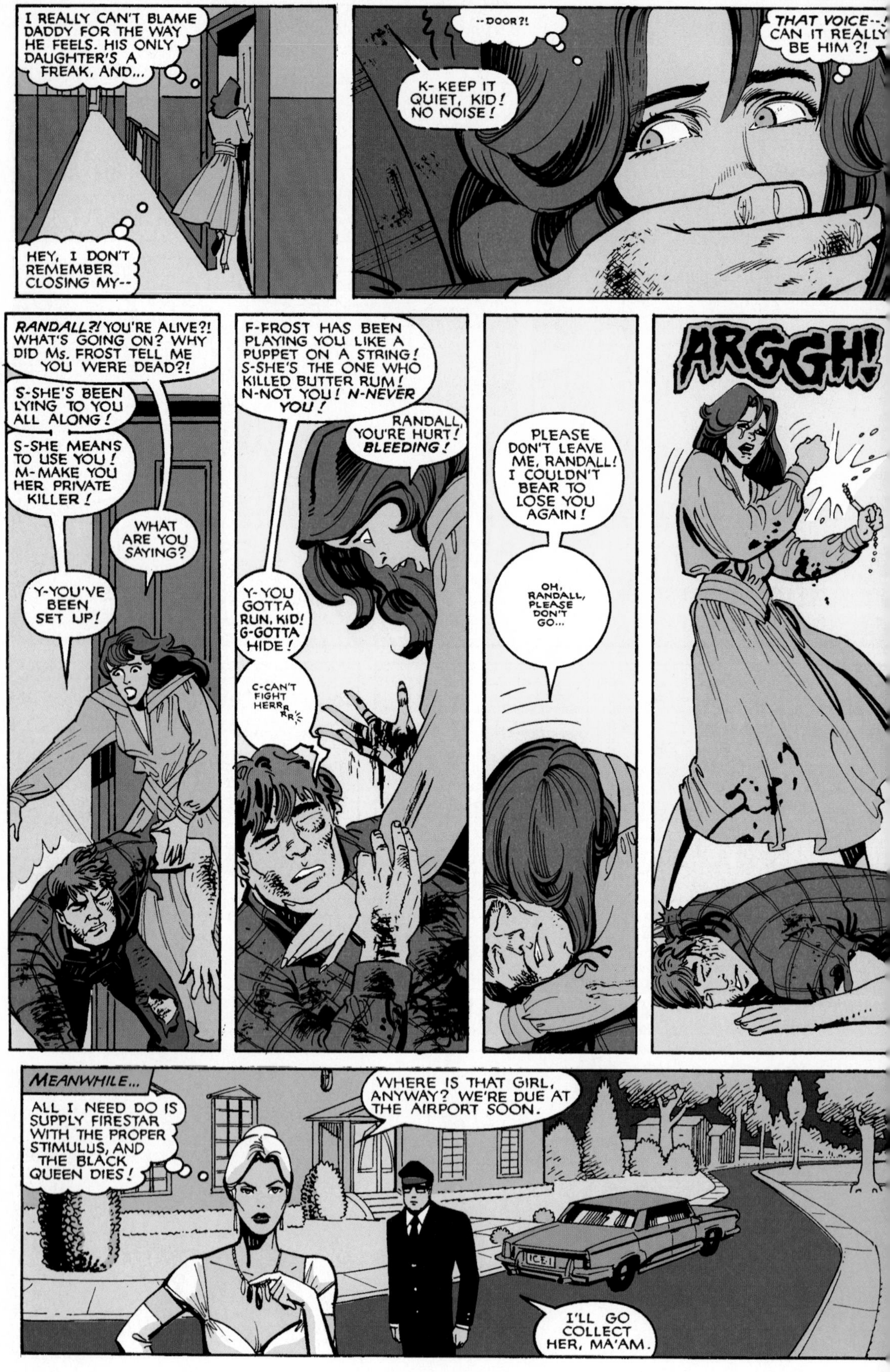

I REALLY CAN'T BLAME DADDY FOR THE WAY HE FEELS. HIS ONLY DAUGHTER'S A FREAK, AND...
HEY, I DON'T REMEMBER CLOSING MY--
--DOOR?!
K-KEEP IT QUIET, KID! NO NOISE!
THAT VOICE--! CAN IT REALLY BE HIM?!
RANDALL?! YOU'RE ALIVE?! WHAT'S GOING ON? WHY DID Ms. FROST TELL ME YOU WERE DEAD?!
S-SHE'S BEEN LYING TO YOU ALL ALONG!
S-SHE MEANS TO USE YOU! M-MAKE YOU HER PRIVATE KILLER!
WHAT ARE YOU SAYING?
Y-YOU'VE BEEN SET UP!
F-FROST HAS BEEN PLAYING YOU LIKE A PUPPET ON A STRING! S-SHE'S THE ONE WHO KILLED BUTTER RUM! N-NOT YOU! N-NEVER YOU!
RANDALL, YOU'RE HURT! BLEEDING!
Y-YOU GOTTA RUN, KID! G-GOTTA HIDE!
C-CAN'T FIGHT HERRRR
PLEASE DON'T LEAVE ME, RANDALL! I COULDN'T BEAR TO LOSE YOU AGAIN!
OH, RANDALL, PLEASE DON'T GO...
ARGGH!
MEANWHILE...
ALL I NEED DO IS SUPPLY FIRESTAR WITH THE PROPER STIMULUS, AND THE BLACK QUEEN DIES!
WHERE IS THAT GIRL, ANYWAY? WE'RE DUE AT THE AIRPORT SOON.
ICE 1
I'LL GO COLLECT HER, MA'AM.

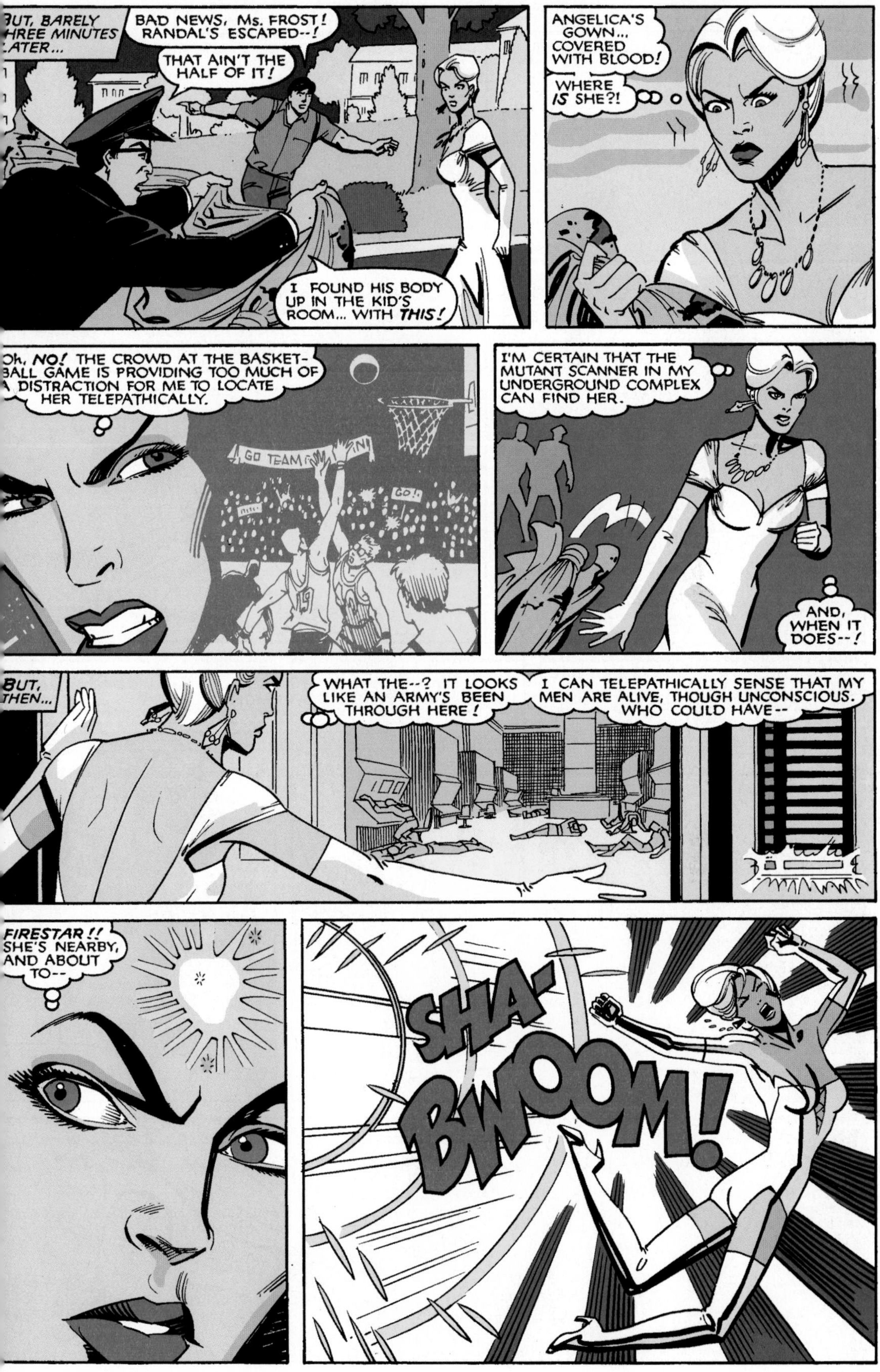
BUT, BARELY THREE MINUTES LATER...
BAD NEWS, Ms. FROST! RANDAL'S ESCAPED--!
THAT AIN'T THE HALF OF IT!
I FOUND HIS BODY UP IN THE KID'S ROOM... WITH THIS!
ANGELICA'S GOWN... COVERED WITH BLOOD!
WHERE IS SHE?!
Oh, NO! THE CROWD AT THE BASKETBALL GAME IS PROVIDING TOO MUCH OF A DISTRACTION FOR ME TO LOCATE HER TELEPATHICALLY.
GO TEAM
GO!
I'M CERTAIN THAT THE MUTANT SCANNER IN MY UNDERGROUND COMPLEX CAN FIND HER.
AND, WHEN IT DOES--!
BUT, THEN...
WHAT THE--? IT LOOKS LIKE AN ARMY'S BEEN THROUGH HERE!
I CAN TELEPATHICALLY SENSE THAT MY MEN ARE ALIVE, THOUGH UNCONSCIOUS. WHO COULD HAVE--
FIRESTAR!! SHE'S NEARBY, AND ABOUT TO--
SHA-BWOOM!

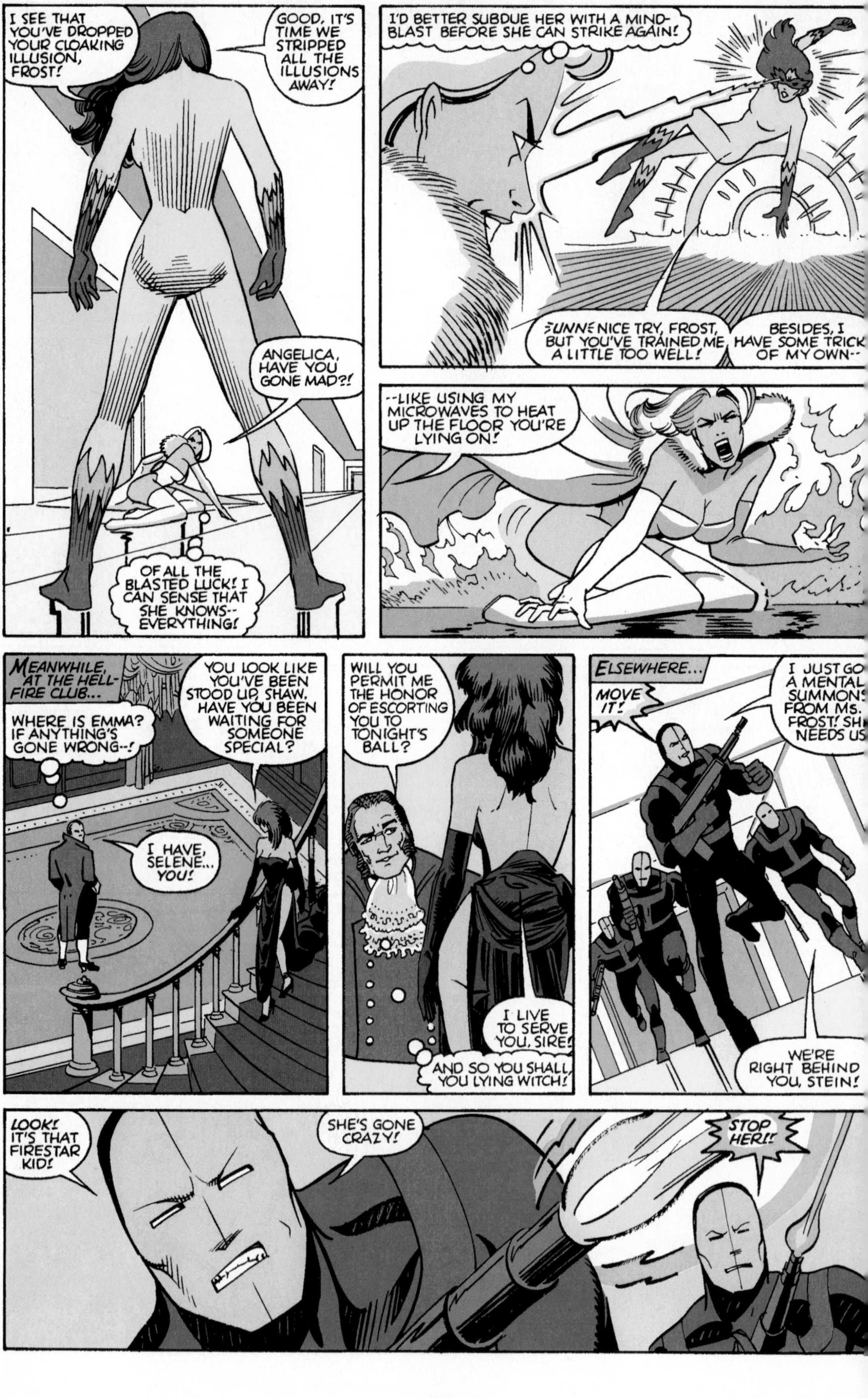

I SEE THAT YOU'VE DROPPED YOUR CLOAKING ILLUSION, FROST!
GOOD. IT'S TIME WE STRIPPED ALL THE ILLUSIONS AWAY!
ANGELICA, HAVE YOU GONE MAD?!
OF ALL THE BLASTED LUCK! I CAN SENSE THAT SHE KNOWS--EVERYTHING!
I'D BETTER SUBDUE HER WITH A MIND-BLAST BEFORE SHE CAN STRIKE AGAIN!
UNN NICE TRY, FROST, BUT YOU'VE TRAINED ME A LITTLE TOO WELL!
BESIDES, I HAVE SOME TRICK OF MY OWN--
--LIKE USING MY MICROWAVES TO HEAT UP THE FLOOR YOU'RE LYING ON!
MEANWHILE, AT THE HELL-FIRE CLUB...
WHERE IS EMMA? IF ANYTHING'S GONE WRONG--!
YOU LOOK LIKE YOU'VE BEEN STOOD UP, SHAW. HAVE YOU BEEN WAITING FOR SOMEONE SPECIAL?
I HAVE, SELENE... YOU!
WILL YOU PERMIT ME THE HONOR OF ESCORTING YOU TO TONIGHT'S BALL?
I LIVE TO SERVE YOU, SIRE!
AND SO YOU SHALL, YOU LYING WITCH!
ELSEWHERE...
MOVE IT!
I JUST GO A MENTAL SUMMON FROM MS. FROST! SH NEEDS US
WE'RE RIGHT BEHIND YOU, STEIN!
LOOK! IT'S THAT FIRESTAR KID!
SHE'S GONE CRAZY!
STOP HER!!

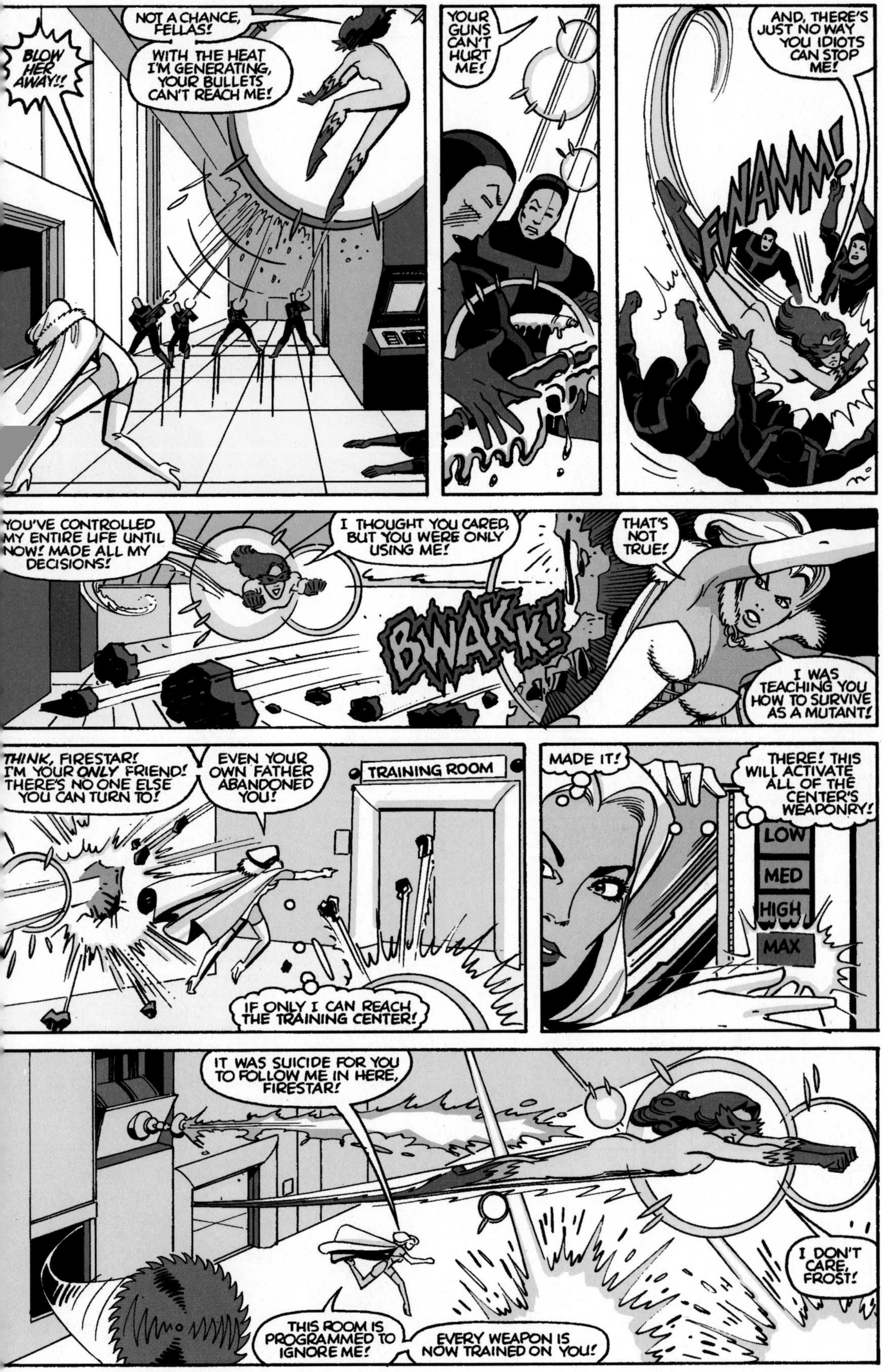

BLOW HER AWAY!!
NOT A CHANCE, FELLAS!
WITH THE HEAT I'M GENERATING, YOUR BULLETS CAN'T REACH ME!
YOUR GUNS CAN'T HURT ME!
AND, THERE'S JUST NO WAY YOU IDIOTS CAN STOP ME!
FWANM!
YOU'VE CONTROLLED MY ENTIRE LIFE UNTIL NOW! MADE ALL MY DECISIONS!
I THOUGHT YOU CARED, BUT YOU WERE ONLY USING ME!
BWAKK!
THAT'S NOT TRUE!
I WAS TEACHING YOU HOW TO SURVIVE AS A MUTANT!
THINK, FIRESTAR! I'M YOUR ONLY FRIEND! THERE'S NO ONE ELSE YOU CAN TURN TO!
EVEN YOUR OWN FATHER ABANDONED YOU!
TRAINING ROOM
IF ONLY I CAN REACH THE TRAINING CENTER!
MADE IT!
THERE! THIS WILL ACTIVATE ALL OF THE CENTER'S WEAPONRY!
LOW
MED
HIGH
MAX
IT WAS SUICIDE FOR YOU TO FOLLOW ME IN HERE, FIRESTAR!
THIS ROOM IS PROGRAMMED TO IGNORE ME!
EVERY WEAPON IS NOW TRAINED ON YOU!
I DON'T CARE, FROST!

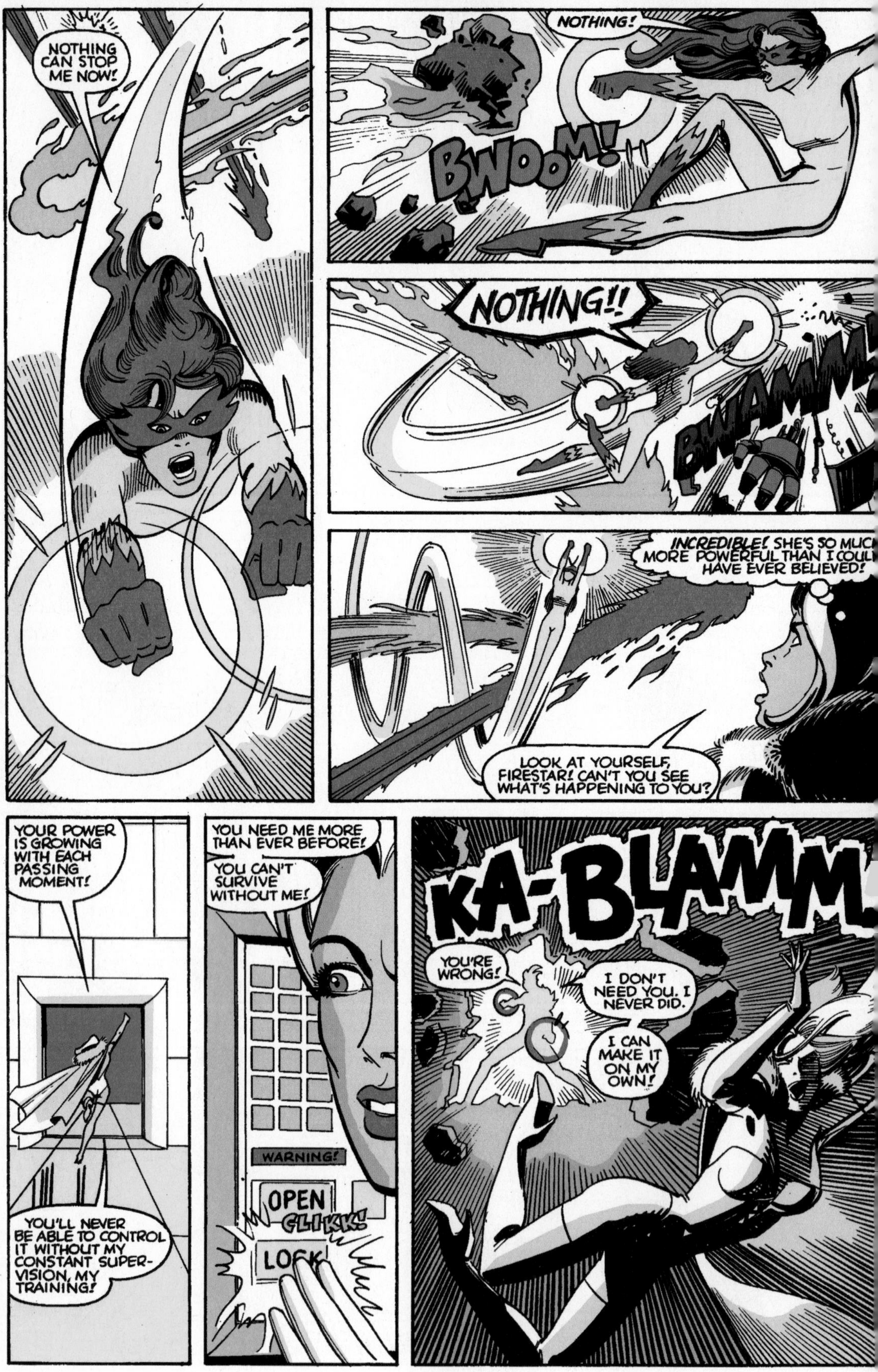
NOTHING CAN STOP ME NOW!
NOTHING!
BWOOM!
NOTHING!!
BWAMM
INCREDIBLE! SHE'S SO MUCH MORE POWERFUL THAN I COULD HAVE EVER BELIEVED!
LOOK AT YOURSELF, FIRESTAR! CAN'T YOU SEE WHAT'S HAPPENING TO YOU?
YOUR POWER IS GROWING WITH EACH PASSING MOMENT!
YOU'LL NEVER BE ABLE TO CONTROL IT WITHOUT MY CONSTANT SUPER-VISION, MY TRAINING!
YOU NEED ME MORE THAN EVER BEFORE!
YOU CAN'T SURVIVE WITHOUT ME!
WARNING!
OPEN
CLIKK!
LOCK
KA-BLAMM
YOU'RE WRONG!
I DON'T NEED YOU. I NEVER DID.
I CAN MAKE IT ON MY OWN!

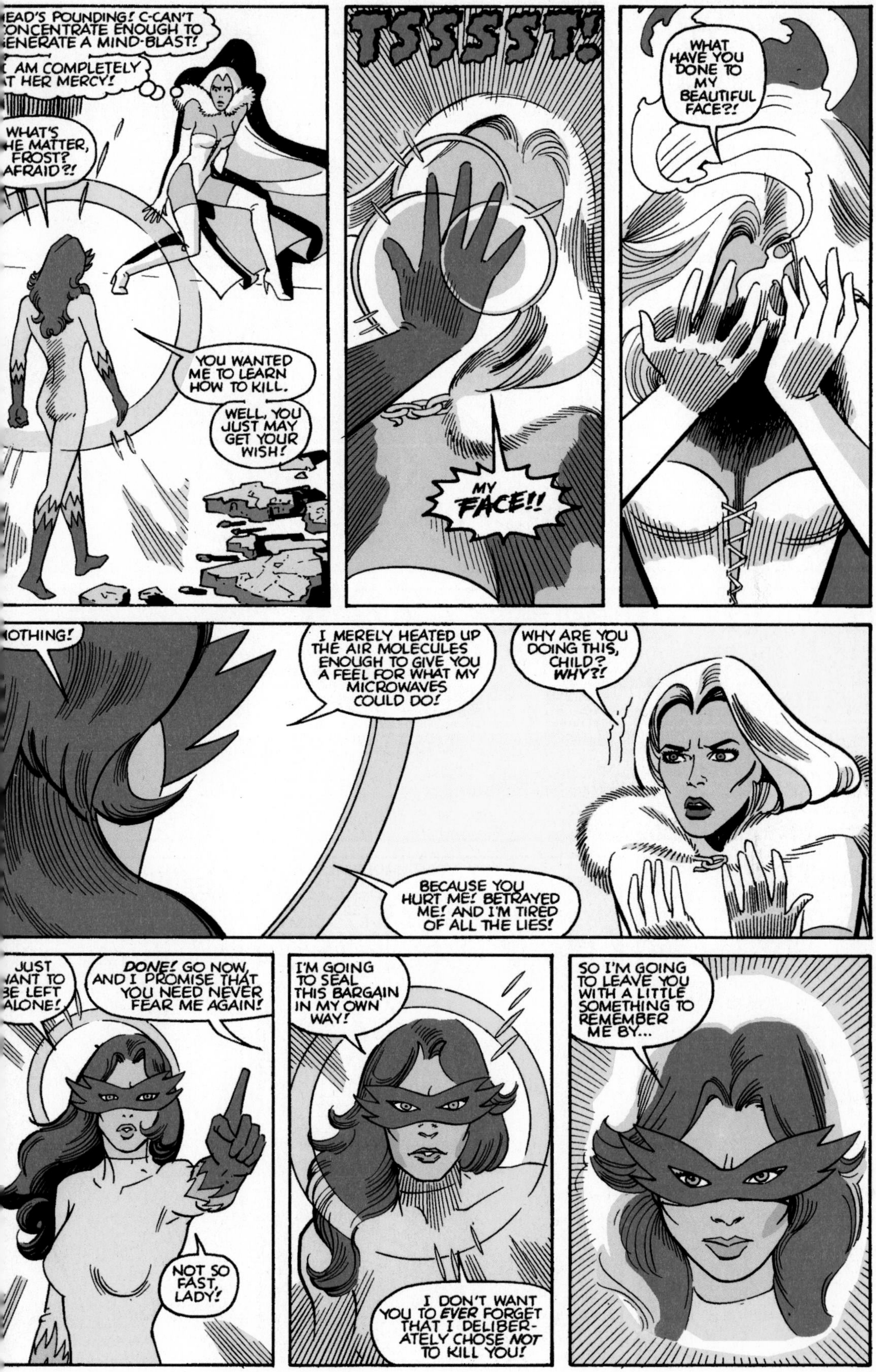
EAD'S POUNDING! C-CAN'T ONCENTRATE ENOUGH TO ENERATE A MIND-BLAST!
AM COMPLETELY T HER MERCY!
WHAT'S HE MATTER, FROST? AFRAID?!
YOU WANTED ME TO LEARN HOW TO KILL.
WELL, YOU JUST MAY GET YOUR WISH!
TSSSSST!
MY FACE!!
WHAT HAVE YOU DONE TO MY BEAUTIFUL FACE?!
OTHING!
I MERELY HEATED UP THE AIR MOLECULES ENOUGH TO GIVE YOU A FEEL FOR WHAT MY MICROWAVES COULD DO!
WHY ARE YOU DOING THIS, CHILD? WHY?!
BECAUSE YOU HURT ME! BETRAYED ME! AND I'M TIRED OF ALL THE LIES!
JUST ANT TO E LEFT ALONE!
DONE! GO NOW, AND I PROMISE THAT YOU NEED NEVER FEAR ME AGAIN!
NOT SO FAST, LADY!
I'M GOING TO SEAL THIS BARGAIN IN MY OWN WAY!
I DON'T WANT YOU TO EVER FORGET THAT I DELIBER-ATELY CHOSE NOT TO KILL YOU!
SO I'M GOING TO LEAVE YOU WITH A LITTLE SOMETHING TO REMEMBER ME BY...

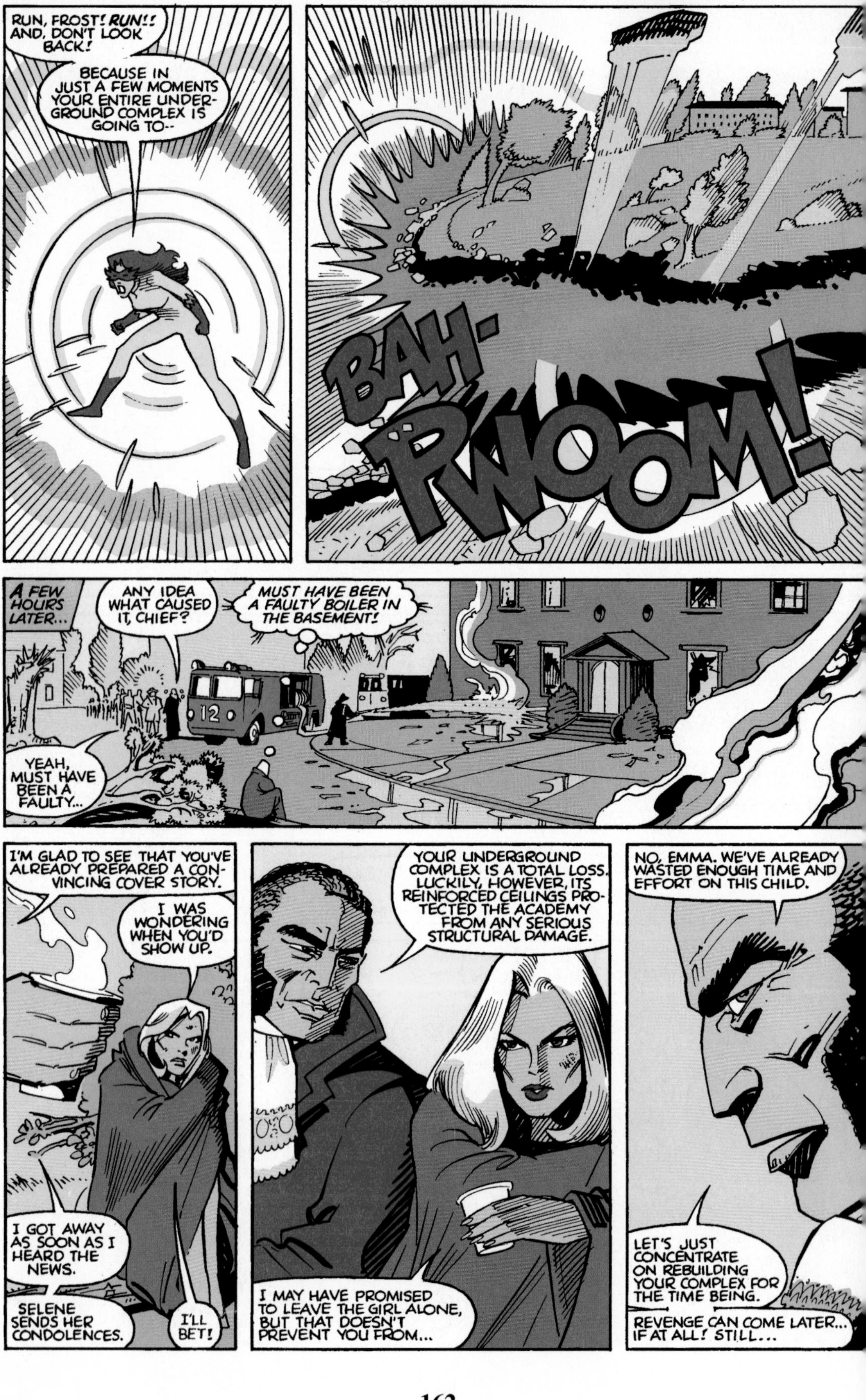

RUN, FROST! RUN!! AND, DON'T LOOK BACK!
BECAUSE IN JUST A FEW MOMENTS YOUR ENTIRE UNDERGROUND COMPLEX IS GOING TO--
BAH-RWOOM!
A FEW HOURS LATER...
ANY IDEA WHAT CAUSED IT, CHIEF?
MUST HAVE BEEN A FAULTY BOILER IN THE BASEMENT!
YEAH, MUST HAVE BEEN A FAULTY...
I'M GLAD TO SEE THAT YOU'VE ALREADY PREPARED A CONVINCING COVER STORY.
I WAS WONDERING WHEN YOU'D SHOW UP.
I GOT AWAY AS SOON AS I HEARD THE NEWS.
SELENE SENDS HER CONDOLENCES.
I'LL BET!
YOUR UNDERGROUND COMPLEX IS A TOTAL LOSS. LUCKILY, HOWEVER, ITS REINFORCED CEILINGS PROTECTED THE ACADEMY FROM ANY SERIOUS STRUCTURAL DAMAGE.
I MAY HAVE PROMISED TO LEAVE THE GIRL ALONE, BUT THAT DOESN'T PREVENT YOU FROM...
NO, EMMA. WE'VE ALREADY WASTED ENOUGH TIME AND EFFORT ON THIS CHILD.
LET'S JUST CONCENTRATE ON REBUILDING YOUR COMPLEX FOR THE TIME BEING.
REVENGE CAN COME LATER... IF AT ALL! STILL...

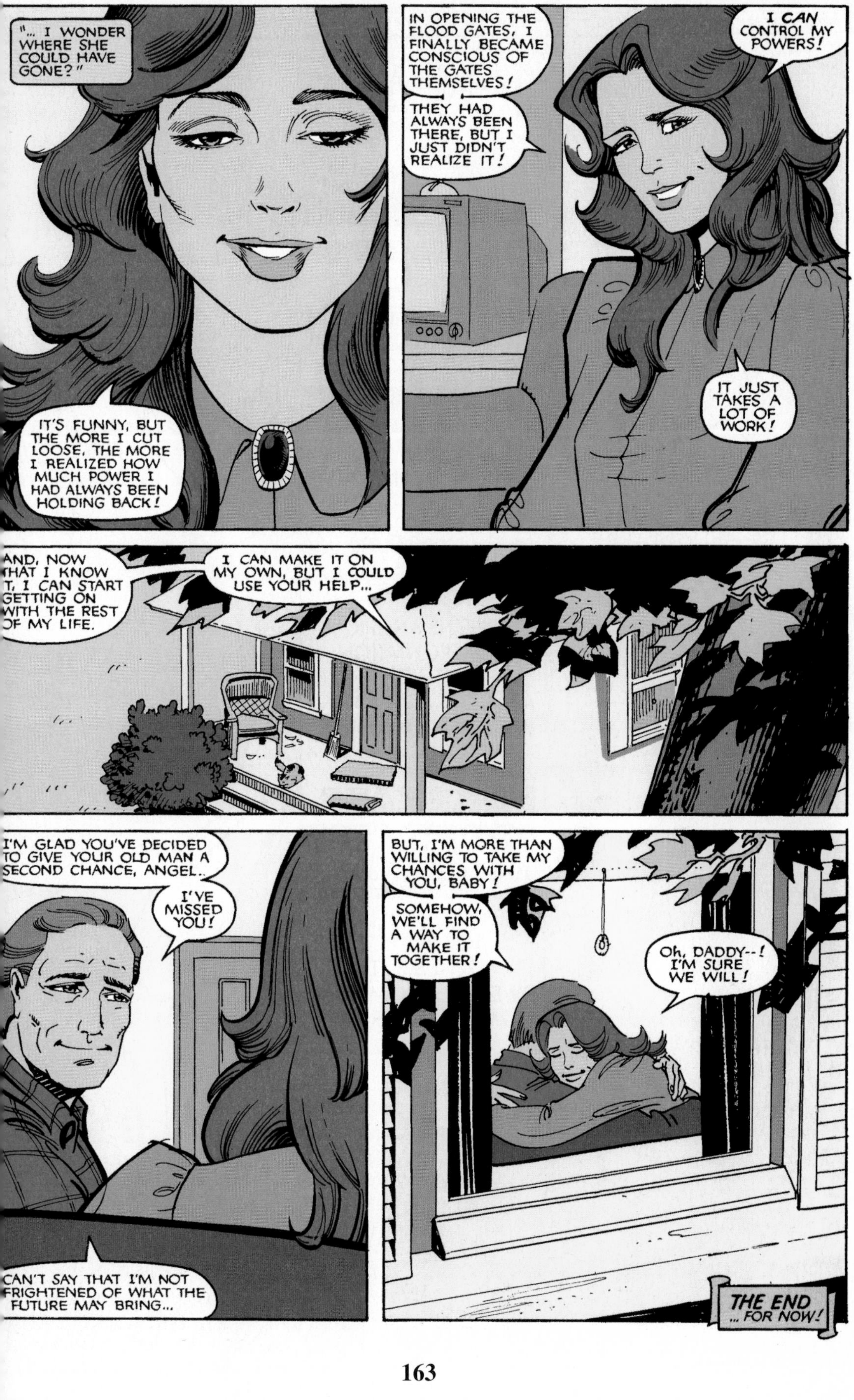

"... I WONDER WHERE SHE COULD HAVE GONE?"
IT'S FUNNY, BUT THE MORE I CUT LOOSE, THE MORE I REALIZED HOW MUCH POWER I HAD ALWAYS BEEN HOLDING BACK!
IN OPENING THE FLOOD GATES, I FINALLY BECAME CONSCIOUS OF THE GATES THEMSELVES!
THEY HAD ALWAYS BEEN THERE, BUT I JUST DIDN'T REALIZE IT!
I CAN CONTROL MY POWERS!
IT JUST TAKES A LOT OF WORK!
AND, NOW THAT I KNOW IT, I CAN START GETTING ON WITH THE REST OF MY LIFE.
I CAN MAKE IT ON MY OWN, BUT I COULD USE YOUR HELP...
I'M GLAD YOU'VE DECIDED TO GIVE YOUR OLD MAN A SECOND CHANCE, ANGEL..
I'VE MISSED YOU!
CAN'T SAY THAT I'M NOT FRIGHTENED OF WHAT THE FUTURE MAY BRING...
BUT, I'M MORE THAN WILLING TO TAKE MY CHANCES WITH YOU, BABY!
SOMEHOW, WE'LL FIND A WAY TO MAKE IT TOGETHER!
Oh, DADDY--! I'M SURE WE WILL!
THE END ... FOR NOW!

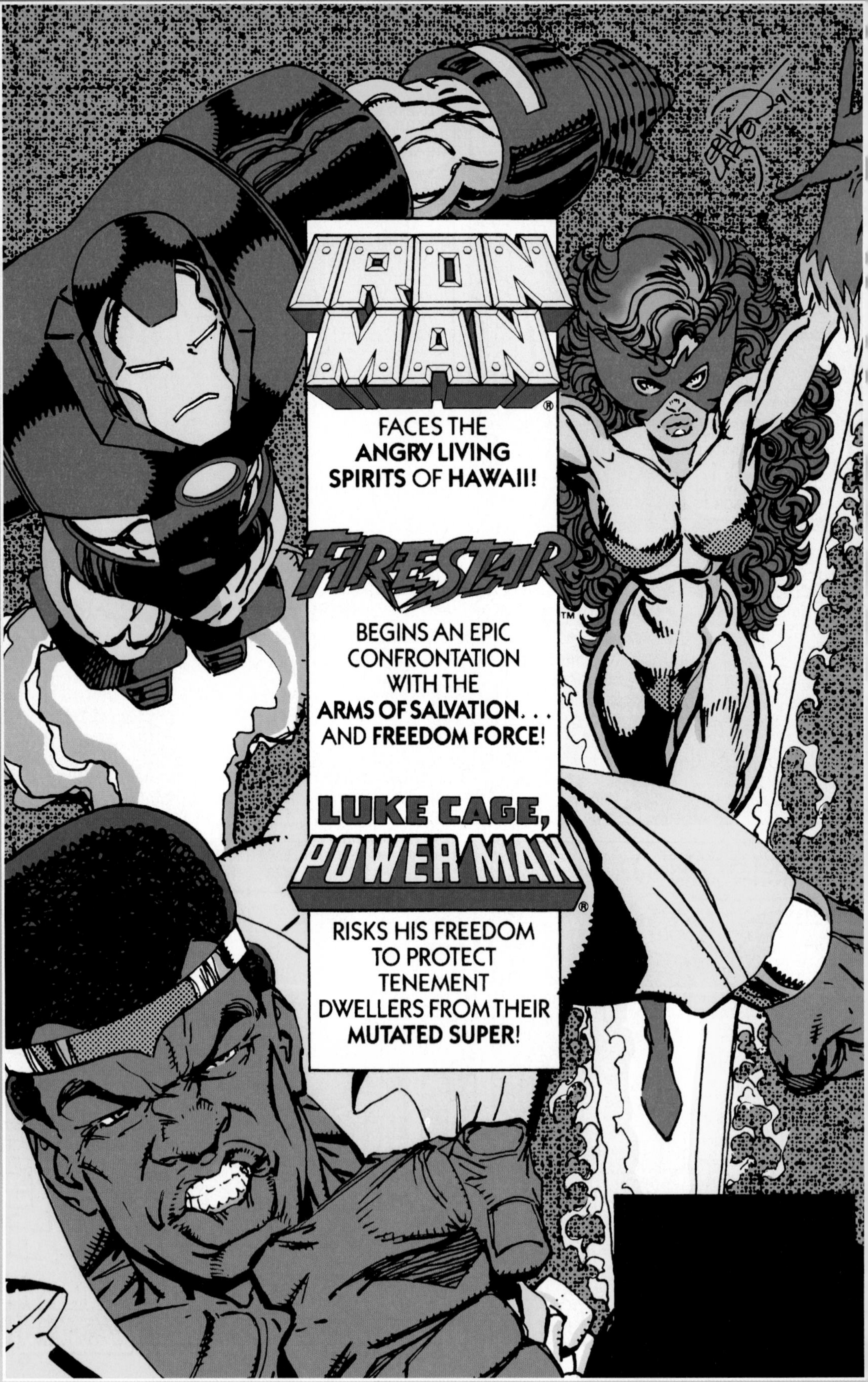
IRON MAN®
FACES THE ANGRY LIVING SPIRITS OF HAWAII!
FIRESTAR™
BEGINS AN EPIC CONFRONTATION WITH THE ARMS OF SALVATION. . . AND FREEDOM FORCE!
LUKE CAGE, POWER MAN®
RISKS HIS FREEDOM TO PROTECT TENEMENT DWELLERS FROM THEIR MUTATED SUPER!

Writers: Marie Javins & Marcus McLaurin • Penciler: Dwayne Turner • Inker: Jose Marzan Jr. • Colorist: Marcus McLaurin
Letterer: Rick Parker • Assistant Editor: Mark Powers • Editor: Terry Kavanagh

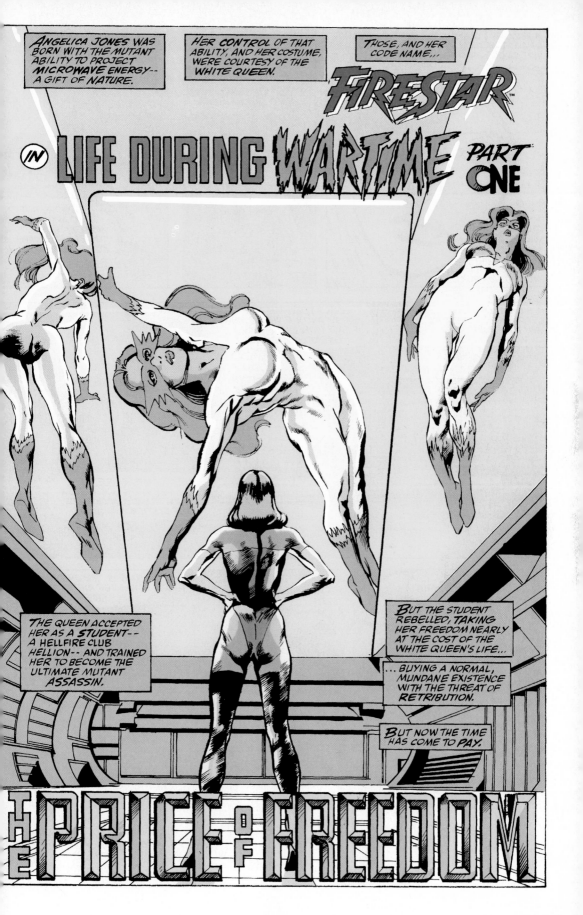

ANGELICA JONES WAS BORN WITH THE MUTANT ABILITY TO PROJECT MICROWAVE ENERGY-- A GIFT OF NATURE.

HER CONTROL OF THAT ABILITY, AND HER COSTUME, WERE COURTESY OF THE WHITE QUEEN.

THOSE, AND HER CODE NAME...

FIRESTAR

IN LIFE DURING WARTIME PART ONE

THE QUEEN ACCEPTED HER AS A STUDENT-- A HELLFIRE CLUB HELLION-- AND TRAINED HER TO BECOME THE ULTIMATE MUTANT ASSASSIN.

BUT THE STUDENT REBELLED, TAKING HER FREEDOM NEARLY AT THE COST OF THE WHITE QUEEN'S LIFE...

...BUYING A NORMAL, MUNDANE EXISTENCE WITH THE THREAT OF RETRIBUTION.

BUT NOW THE TIME HAS COME TO PAY.

THE PRICE OF FREEDOM

A *TOUCH* IS ALL IT WILL TAKE. ONE TOUCH AND THIS INFORMA-TION WILL BE FED--UNTRACEABLY--INTO *FREEDOM FORCE'S* COMPUTERS.

FIRESTAR WILL BE THE NEXT *TARGET* OF THE GOVERN-MENT'S PRIVATE *MUTANT HUNTERS.*

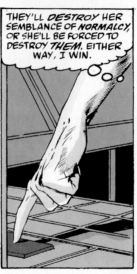

THEY'LL *DESTROY* HER SEMBLANCE OF *NORMALCY,* OR SHE'LL BE FORCED TO DESTROY *THEM.* EITHER WAY, I WIN.

I SWORE NOT TO GO AFTER HER *MYSELF,* BUT NOT TO LET HER ESCAPE *COMPLETELY.*

" THE LITTLE *COW* HAS TO LEARN, NO ONE BETRAYS *EMMA FROST,* THE *WHITE QUEEN.*

" NO ONE..."

...COULD *TOUCH* US OUT THERE, *MEG!* AND WE WOULD'VE WON IF THEY DIDN'T HAVE SUCH A GREAT GOALIE!

SHE WAS UNSTOPPABLE! MAYBE SHE'S A *MUTIE!*

NEXT TIME, *ANGE,* WE'LL TELL HER SHE'S GOT TO SLOW DOWN OR WE'LL MAKE HER *REGISTER!* HA-HA-HA--

NOT SO *FUNNY.* THE *REGISTRATION* HYSTERIA HAS PASSED, BUT THE GOVERNMENT IS STILL TALKING ABOUT KEEPING TABS ON ANY ESPECIALLY *POWERFUL* MUTANTS.

LIKE *ME.*

MAYBE *I* SHOULD REGISTER, BEFORE MY SECRET COMES OUT ON ITS OWN... BEFORE SOMEONE COMES AFTER *ME.*

SHE'S THE ONE WE WANT. SNAG HER AND DITCH HER FRIEND.

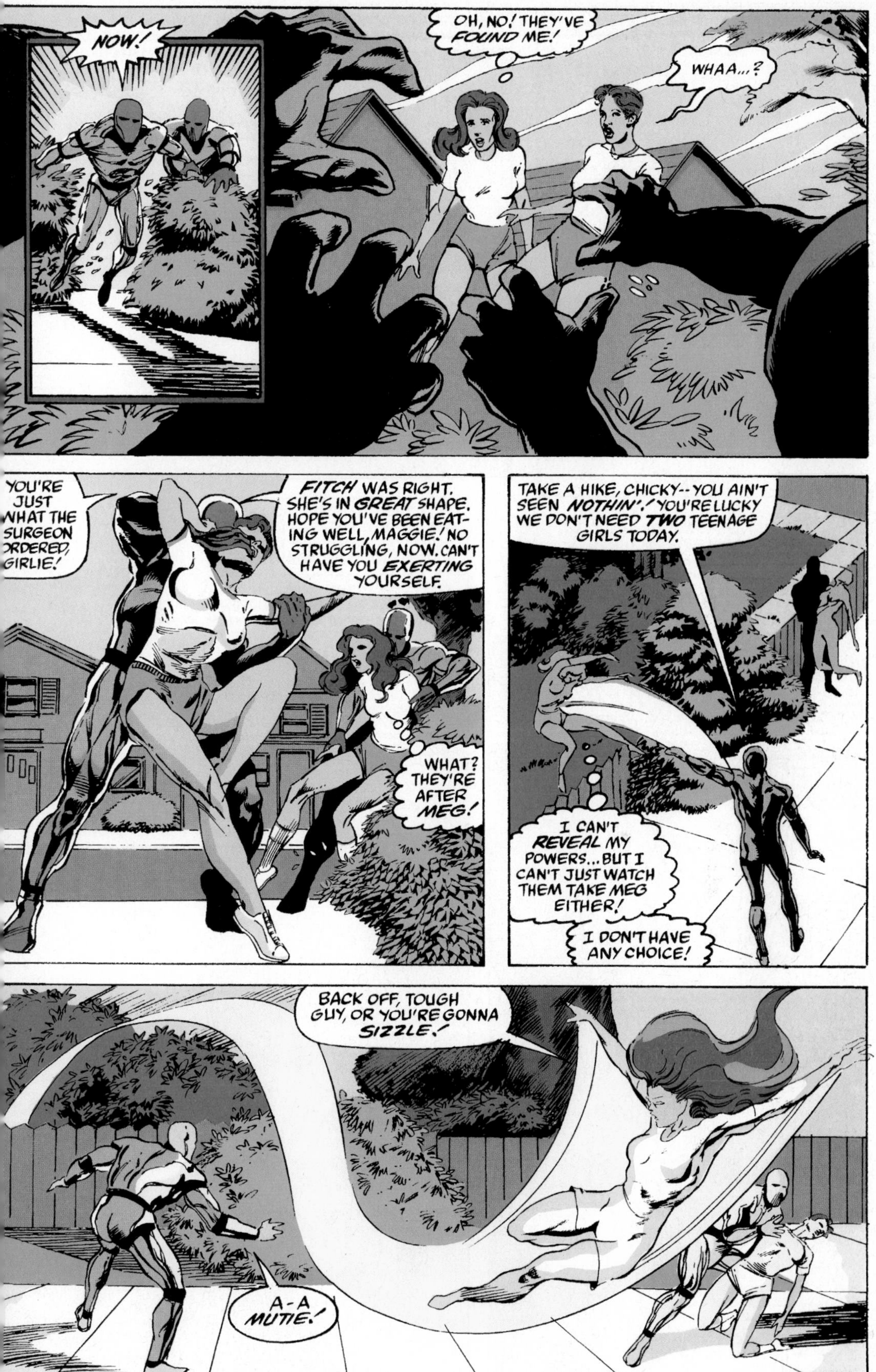
NOW!
OH, NO! THEY'VE FOUND ME!
WHAA...?
YOU'RE JUST WHAT THE SURGEON ORDERED, GIRLIE!
FITCH WAS RIGHT. SHE'S IN GREAT SHAPE. HOPE YOU'VE BEEN EATING WELL, MAGGIE! NO STRUGGLING, NOW. CAN'T HAVE YOU EXERTING YOURSELF.
WHAT? THEY'RE AFTER MEG!
TAKE A HIKE, CHICKY-- YOU AIN'T SEEN NOTHIN'! YOU'RE LUCKY WE DON'T NEED TWO TEENAGE GIRLS TODAY.
I CAN'T REVEAL MY POWERS... BUT I CAN'T JUST WATCH THEM TAKE MEG EITHER!
I DON'T HAVE ANY CHOICE!
BACK OFF, TOUGH GUY, OR YOU'RE GONNA SIZZLE!
A-A MUTIE!

YOU'RE OUT OF YOUR *LEAGUE*, BABY-DOLL! THESE ARE THE *BIG BOYS'* GAMES.

OH, STOP. YOU'RE SCARING ME.

LEAVE NOW. YOU'VE DONE ENOUGH DAMAGE.

YOU *MAY* HAVE DESTROYED MY LIFE-- YOU *DEFINITELY* MADE ME BREAK A VERY IMPORTANT PROMISE...

DOHNPH!

...AND YOUR FRIEND'S *NOT* GOING TO BE ABLE TO HELP YOU FOR A WHILE.

ZWARP

I HAVE *POWERS* AND I KNOW HOW TO *USE* THEM. GET OUT OF HERE *NOW*, AND I WON'T DESTROY YOU.

WE'LL SEE WHO DESTROYS *WHO*, PRINCESS.

BDDRRP BDDRRP BDDRRP

I GOT *UZIS* IN MY FISTS, AND I KNOW HOW TO USE *THEM*, TOO.

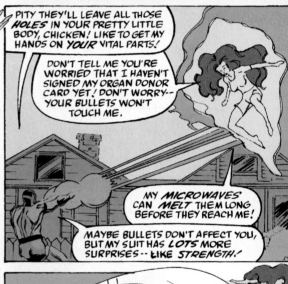

PITY THEY'LL LEAVE ALL THOSE *HOLES* IN YOUR PRETTY LITTLE BODY, CHICKEN! LIKE TO GET MY HANDS ON *YOUR* VITAL PARTS!

DON'T TELL ME YOU'RE WORRIED THAT I HAVEN'T SIGNED MY ORGAN DONOR CARD YET! DON'T WORRY-- YOUR BULLETS WON'T TOUCH ME.

MY *MICROWAVES* CAN *MELT* THEM LONG BEFORE THEY REACH ME!

MAYBE BULLETS DON'T AFFECT YOU, BUT MY SUIT HAS *LOTS* MORE SURPRISES-- LIKE *STRENGTH!*

YOU WANNA PLAY *HARDBALL*, CHICKEN? LET'S GO!

I'M MORE OF A SOCCER PLAYER MYSELF.

BUT THAT'S OKAY... I STILL KNOW HOW TO CATCH USING MY HANDS--

WRENCH

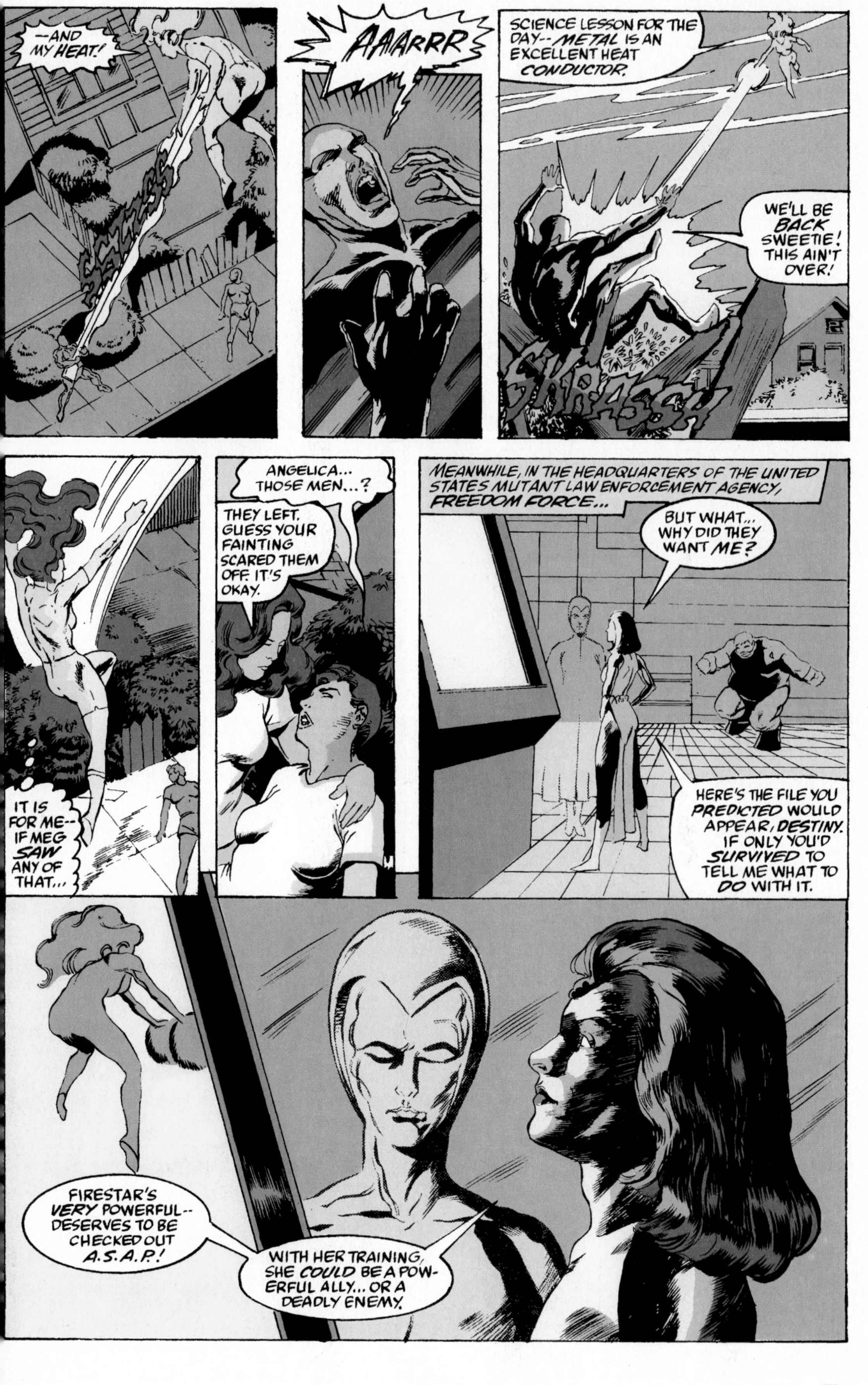

--AND MY HEAT!
AAAARRR
SCIENCE LESSON FOR THE DAY--METAL IS AN EXCELLENT HEAT CONDUCTOR.
WE'LL BE BACK SWEETIE! THIS AIN'T OVER!
SHRASSH
IT IS FOR ME--IF MEG SAW ANY OF THAT...
ANGELICA... THOSE MEN...?
THEY LEFT. GUESS YOUR FAINTING SCARED THEM OFF. IT'S OKAY.
MEANWHILE, IN THE HEADQUARTERS OF THE UNITED STATES MUTANT LAW ENFORCEMENT AGENCY, FREEDOM FORCE...
BUT WHAT... WHY DID THEY WANT ME?
HERE'S THE FILE YOU PREDICTED WOULD APPEAR, DESTINY. IF ONLY YOU'D SURVIVED TO TELL ME WHAT TO DO WITH IT.
FIRESTAR'S VERY POWERFUL--DESERVES TO BE CHECKED OUT A.S.A.P.!
WITH HER TRAINING, SHE COULD BE A POW-ERFUL ALLY... OR A DEADLY ENEMY.

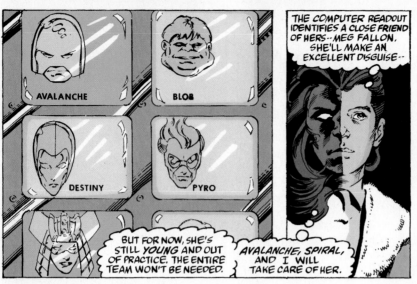

AVALANCHE

BLOB

DESTINY

PYRO

THE COMPUTER READOUT IDENTIFIES A CLOSE FRIEND OF HERS--MEG FALLON. SHE'LL MAKE AN EXCELLENT DISGUISE--

--TO ENSURE THAT FIRE-STAR USES HER POWER FOR THE GREATER GOOD OF *FREEDOM FORCE*... OR NOT AT ALL!

BUT FOR NOW, SHE'S STILL *YOUNG* AND OUT OF PRACTICE. THE ENTIRE TEAM WON'T BE NEEDED.

AVALANCHE, SPIRAL, AND I WILL TAKE CARE OF HER.

--*EVER*, YOU SAID! HOW COULD YOU?

YOU *KNOW* IT'S DANGEROUS TO USE YOUR POWERS IN PUBLIC! YOU *PROMISED*!

BUT, DAD... THEY WERE AFTER *MEG*...

WHAT IF SOMEBODY *SAW* YOU? YOU KNOW WHAT HAPPENED LAST TIME WITH THAT AWFUL EMMA FROST CHARACTER!

PROMISE ME *AGAIN*, ANGELICA. PROMISE ME YOU'LL NEVER USE THOSE POWERS AGAIN. *NEVER*.

I... I... I CAN'T.

170

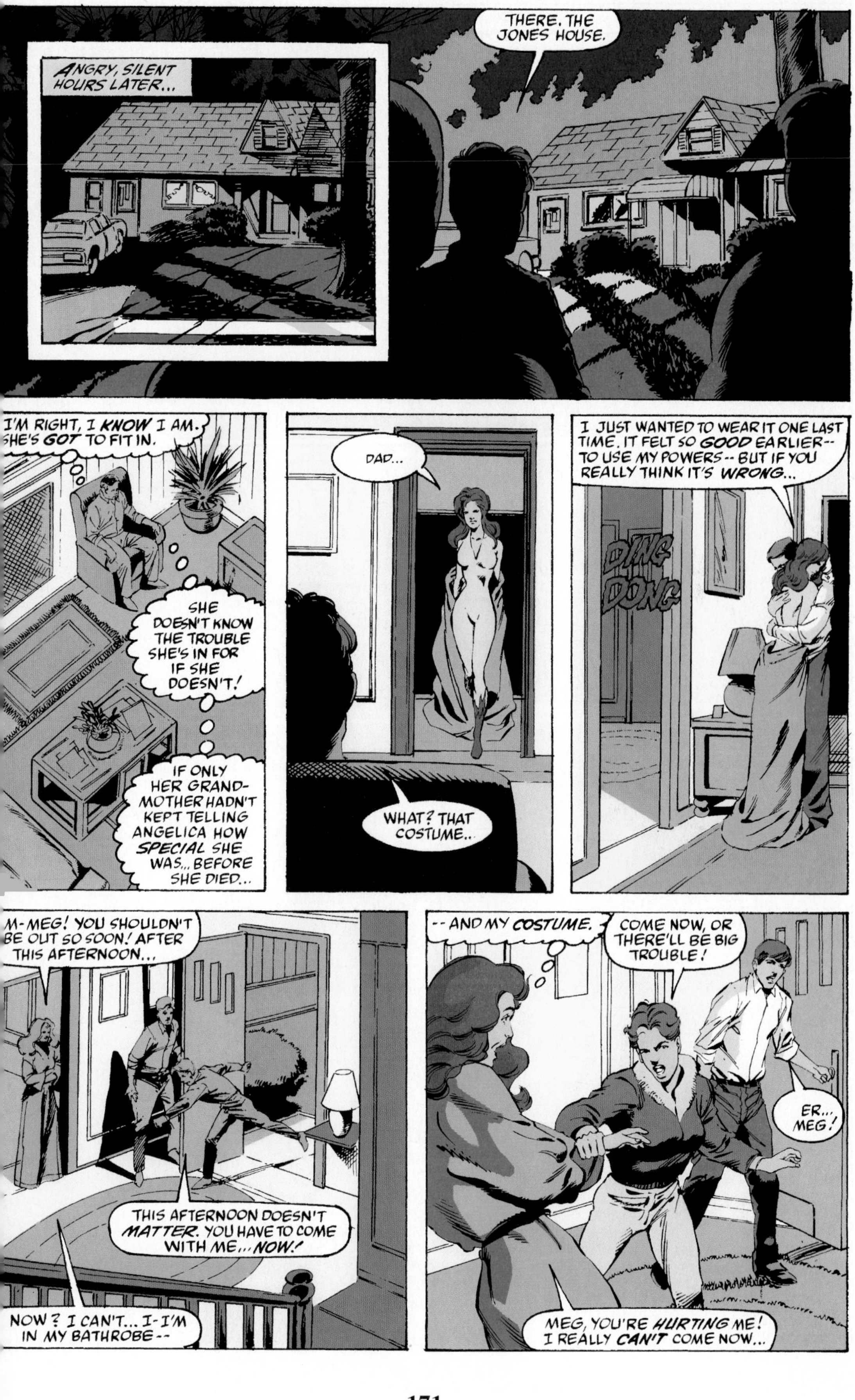
ANGRY, SILENT HOURS LATER...
THERE. THE JONES HOUSE.
I'M RIGHT, I KNOW I AM. SHE'S GOT TO FIT IN.
SHE DOESN'T KNOW THE TROUBLE SHE'S IN FOR IF SHE DOESN'T!
IF ONLY HER GRAND-MOTHER HADN'T KEPT TELLING ANGELICA HOW SPECIAL SHE WAS... BEFORE SHE DIED...
DAD...
WHAT? THAT COSTUME..
I JUST WANTED TO WEAR IT ONE LAST TIME. IT FELT SO GOOD EARLIER-- TO USE MY POWERS -- BUT IF YOU REALLY THINK IT'S WRONG...
DING DONG
M-MEG! YOU SHOULDN'T BE OUT SO SOON! AFTER THIS AFTERNOON...
THIS AFTERNOON DOESN'T MATTER. YOU HAVE TO COME WITH ME... NOW!
NOW? I CAN'T... I-I'M IN MY BATHROBE --
-- AND MY COSTUME.
COME NOW, OR THERE'LL BE BIG TROUBLE!
ER... MEG!
MEG, YOU'RE HURTING ME! I REALLY CAN'T COME NOW...

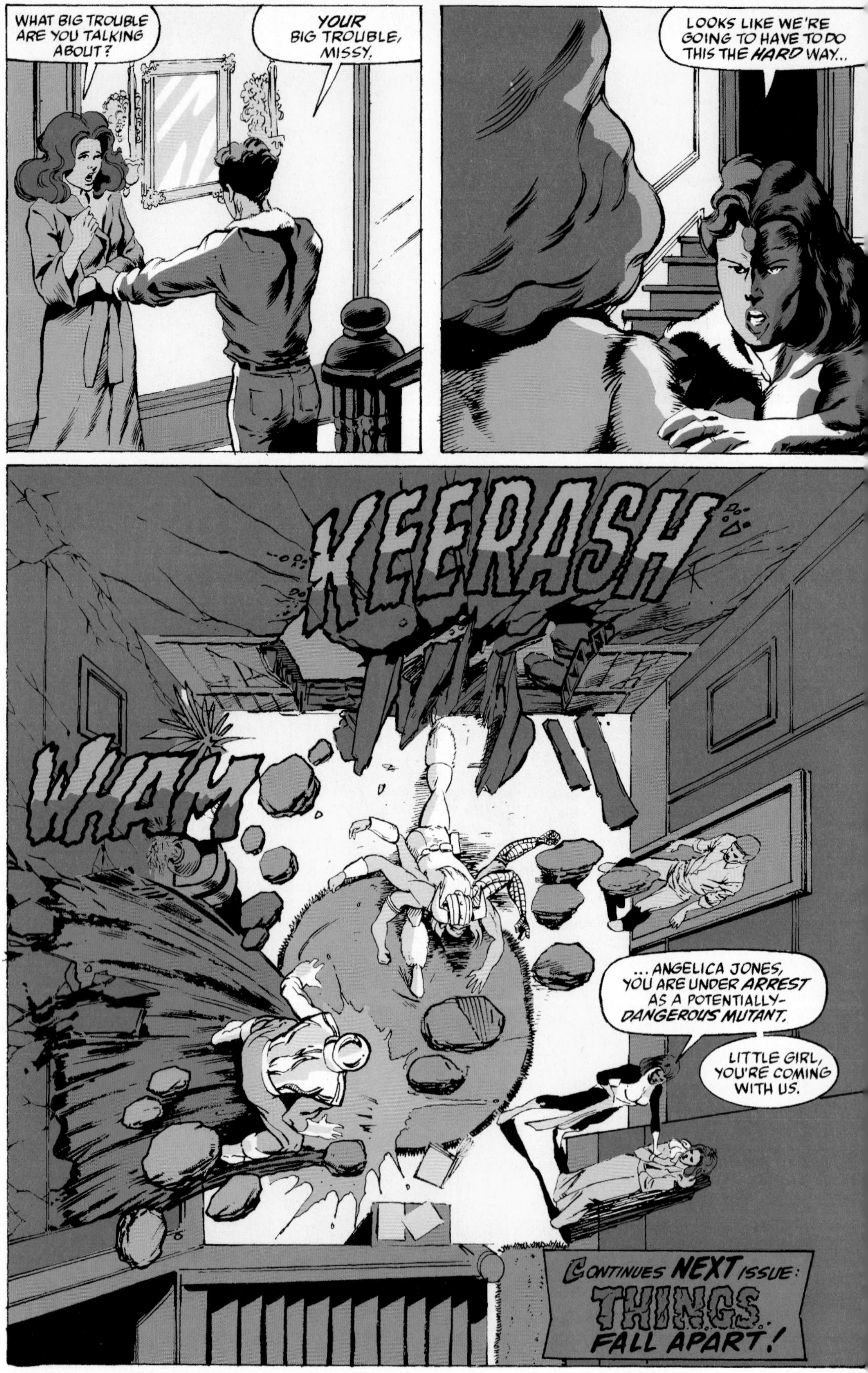
WHAT BIG TROUBLE ARE YOU TALKING ABOUT?
YOUR BIG TROUBLE, MISSY.
LOOKS LIKE WE'RE GOING TO HAVE TO DO THIS THE HARD WAY...
KEERASH
WHAM
...ANGELICA JONES, YOU ARE UNDER ARREST AS A POTENTIALLY-DANGEROUS MUTANT.
LITTLE GIRL, YOU'RE COMING WITH US.
CONTINUES NEXT ISSUE:
THINGS FALL APART!

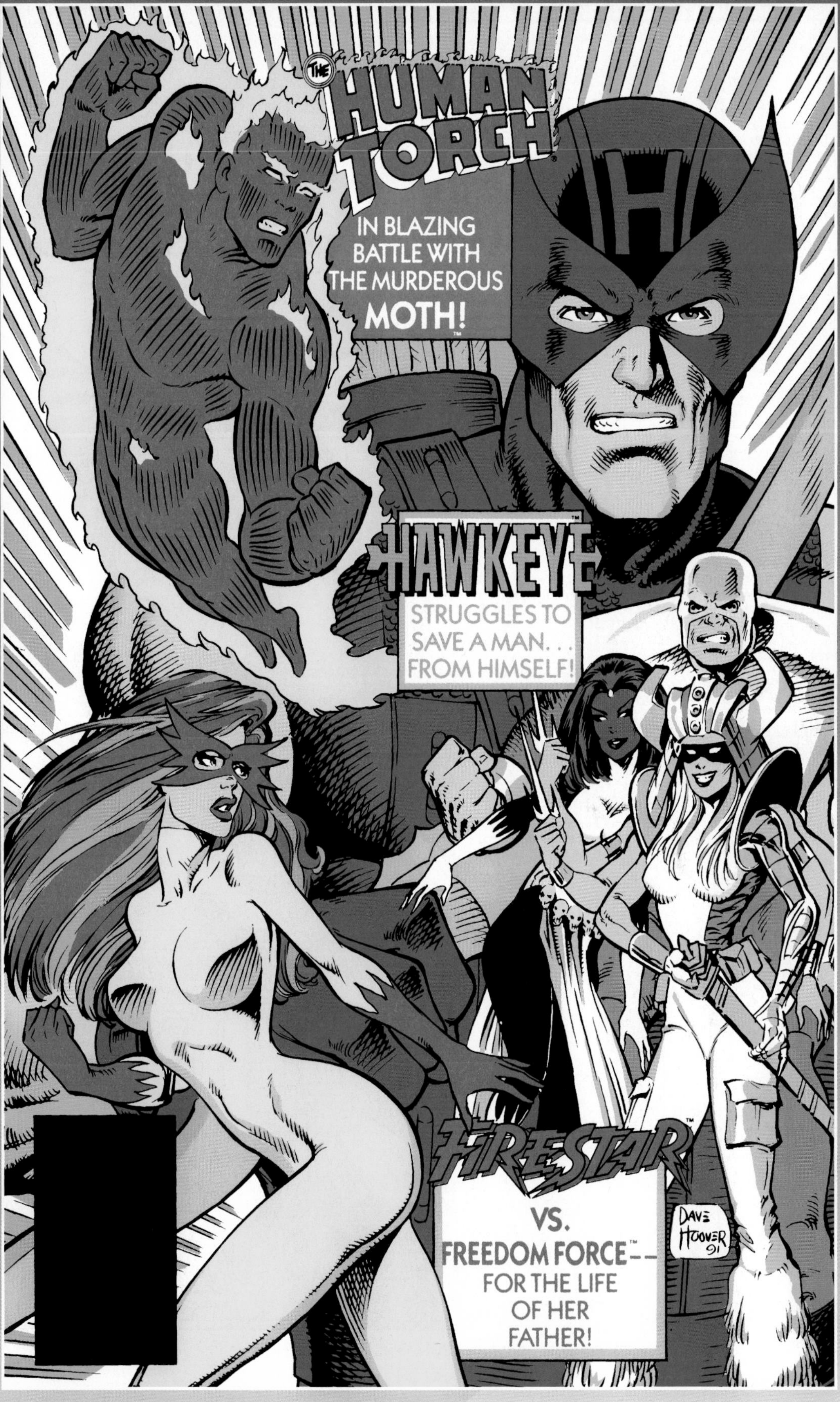
THE HUMAN TORCH
IN BLAZING BATTLE WITH THE MURDEROUS MOTH!
HAWKEYE
STRUGGLES TO SAVE A MAN. . . FROM HIMSELF!
FIRESTAR
VS. FREEDOM FORCE-- FOR THE LIFE OF HER FATHER!
DAVE HOOVER 91

Writers: Marie Javins & Marcus McLaurin • Penciler: Dwayne Turner • Inker: Jose Marzan Jr. • Colorist: Marcus McLaurin
Letterer: Rick Parker • Assistant Editor: Mark Powers • Editor: Terry Kavanagh

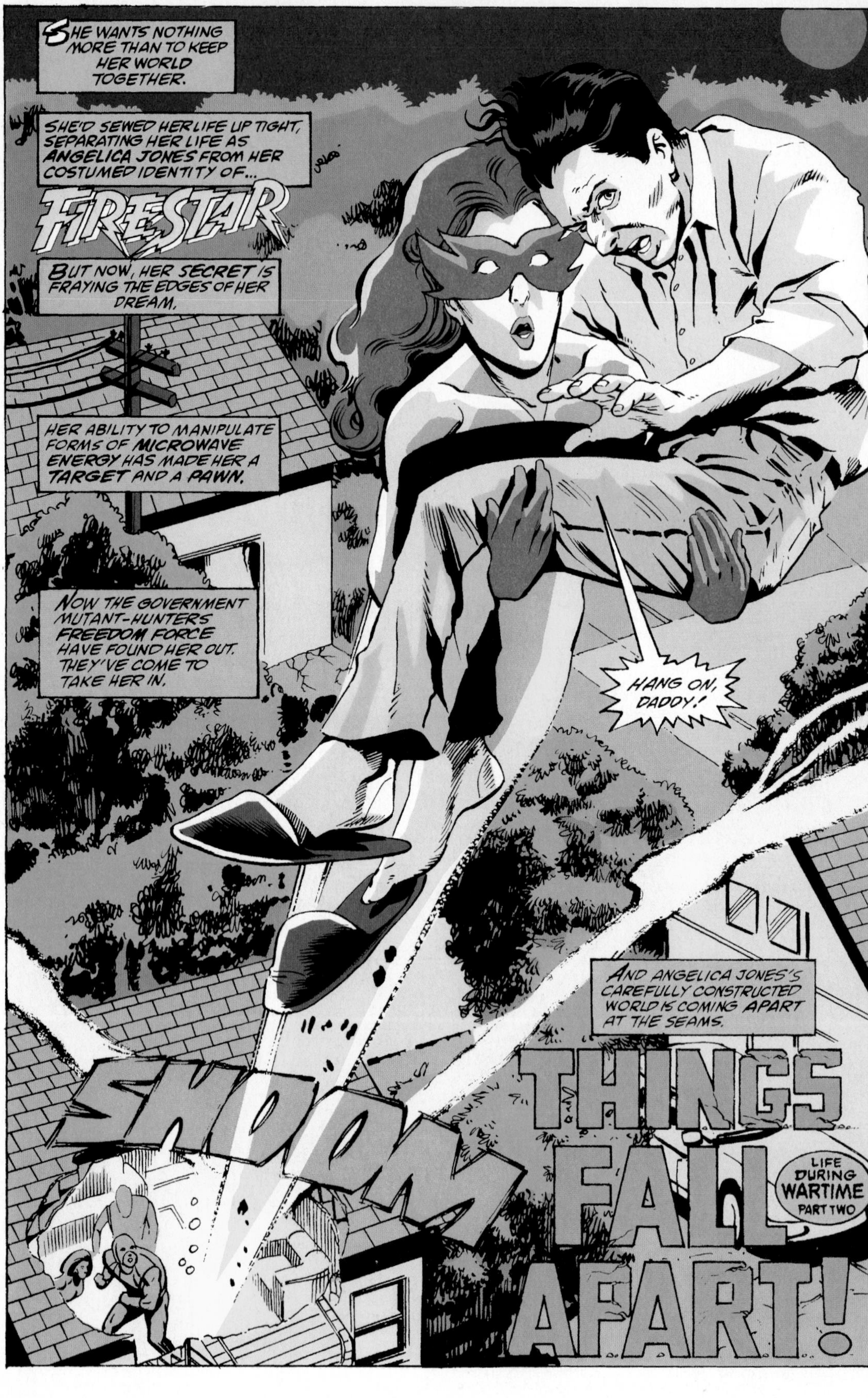

SHE WANTS NOTHING MORE THAN TO KEEP HER WORLD TOGETHER.
SHE'D SEWED HER LIFE UP TIGHT, SEPARATING HER LIFE AS ANGELICA JONES FROM HER COSTUMED IDENTITY OF...
FIRESTAR
BUT NOW, HER SECRET IS FRAYING THE EDGES OF HER DREAM.
HER ABILITY TO MANIPULATE FORMS OF MICROWAVE ENERGY HAS MADE HER A TARGET AND A PAWN.
NOW THE GOVERNMENT MUTANT-HUNTERS FREEDOM FORCE HAVE FOUND HER OUT. THEY'VE COME TO TAKE HER IN.
HANG ON, DADDY!
AND ANGELICA JONES'S CAREFULLY CONSTRUCTED WORLD IS COMING APART AT THE SEAMS.
SHOOM
THINGS FALL APART!
LIFE DURING WARTIME PART TWO

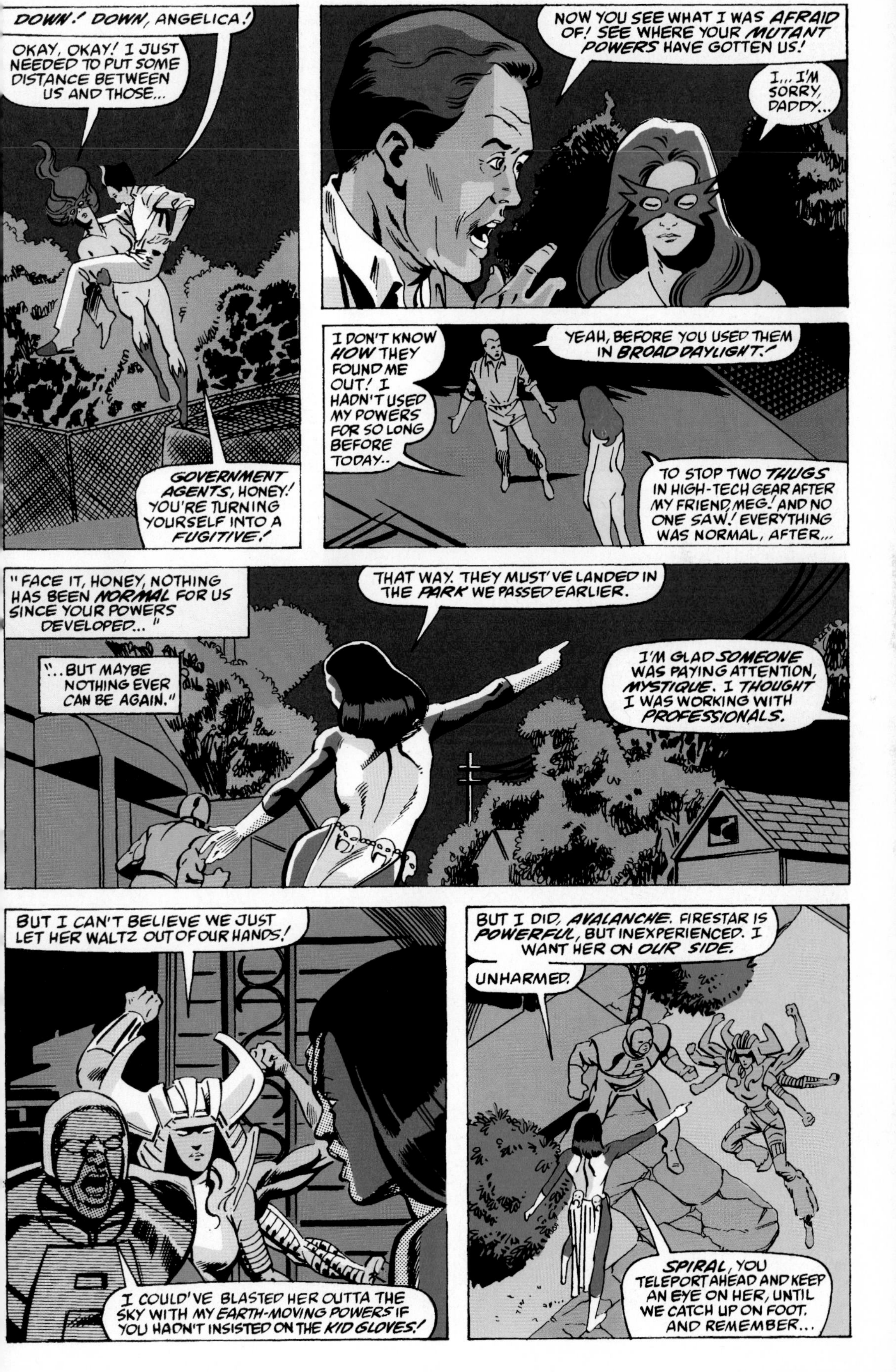

DOWN! DOWN, ANGELICA!
OKAY, OKAY! I JUST NEEDED TO PUT SOME DISTANCE BETWEEN US AND THOSE...
GOVERNMENT AGENTS, HONEY! YOU'RE TURNING YOURSELF INTO A FUGITIVE!
NOW YOU SEE WHAT I WAS AFRAID OF! SEE WHERE YOUR MUTANT POWERS HAVE GOTTEN US!
I... I'M SORRY, DADDY...
I DON'T KNOW HOW THEY FOUND ME OUT! I HADN'T USED MY POWERS FOR SO LONG BEFORE TODAY..
YEAH, BEFORE YOU USED THEM IN BROAD DAYLIGHT!
TO STOP TWO THUGS IN HIGH-TECH GEAR AFTER MY FRIEND, MEG! AND NO ONE SAW! EVERYTHING WAS NORMAL, AFTER...
"FACE IT, HONEY, NOTHING HAS BEEN NORMAL FOR US SINCE YOUR POWERS DEVELOPED..."
"...BUT MAYBE NOTHING EVER CAN BE AGAIN."
THAT WAY. THEY MUST'VE LANDED IN THE PARK WE PASSED EARLIER.
I'M GLAD SOMEONE WAS PAYING ATTENTION, MYSTIQUE. I THOUGHT I WAS WORKING WITH PROFESSIONALS.
BUT I CAN'T BELIEVE WE JUST LET HER WALTZ OUT OF OUR HANDS!
I COULD'VE BLASTED HER OUTTA THE SKY WITH MY EARTH-MOVING POWERS IF YOU HADN'T INSISTED ON THE KID GLOVES!
BUT I DID, AVALANCHE. FIRESTAR IS POWERFUL, BUT INEXPERIENCED. I WANT HER ON OUR SIDE.
UNHARMED.
SPIRAL, YOU TELEPORT AHEAD AND KEEP AN EYE ON HER, UNTIL WE CATCH UP ON FOOT. AND REMEMBER...

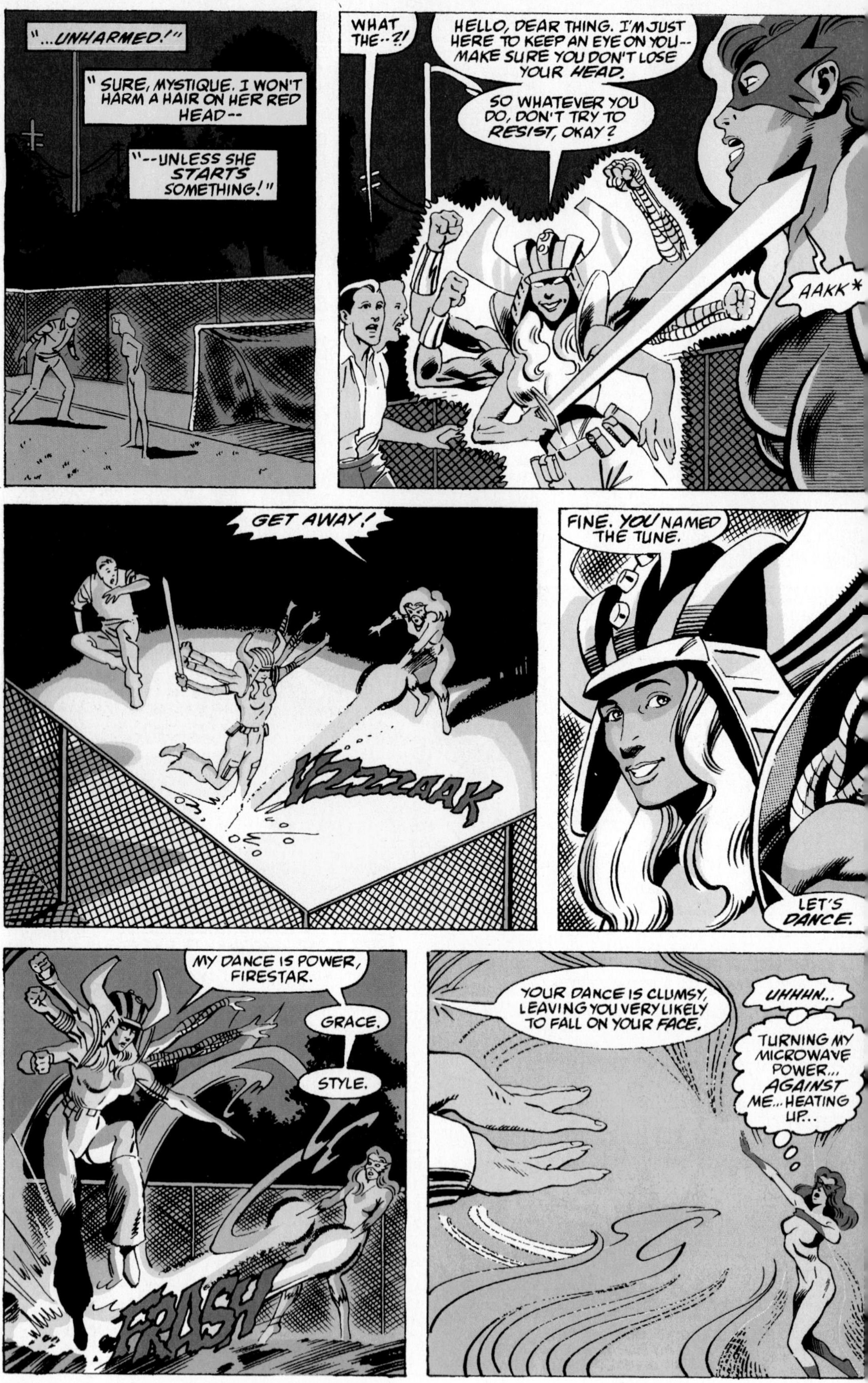

"...UNHARMED!"
" SURE, MYSTIQUE. I WON'T HARM A HAIR ON HER RED HEAD--
"--UNLESS SHE STARTS SOMETHING!"
WHAT THE--?!
HELLO, DEAR THING. I'M JUST HERE TO KEEP AN EYE ON YOU-- MAKE SURE YOU DON'T LOSE YOUR HEAD.
SO WHATEVER YOU DO, DON'T TRY TO RESIST, OKAY?
AAKK*
GET AWAY!
VZZZZAAK
FINE. YOU NAMED THE TUNE.
LET'S DANCE.
MY DANCE IS POWER, FIRESTAR.
GRACE.
STYLE.
FRASH
YOUR DANCE IS CLUMSY, LEAVING YOU VERY LIKELY TO FALL ON YOUR FACE.
UHHHN...
TURNING MY MICROWAVE POWER... AGAINST ME...HEATING UP..

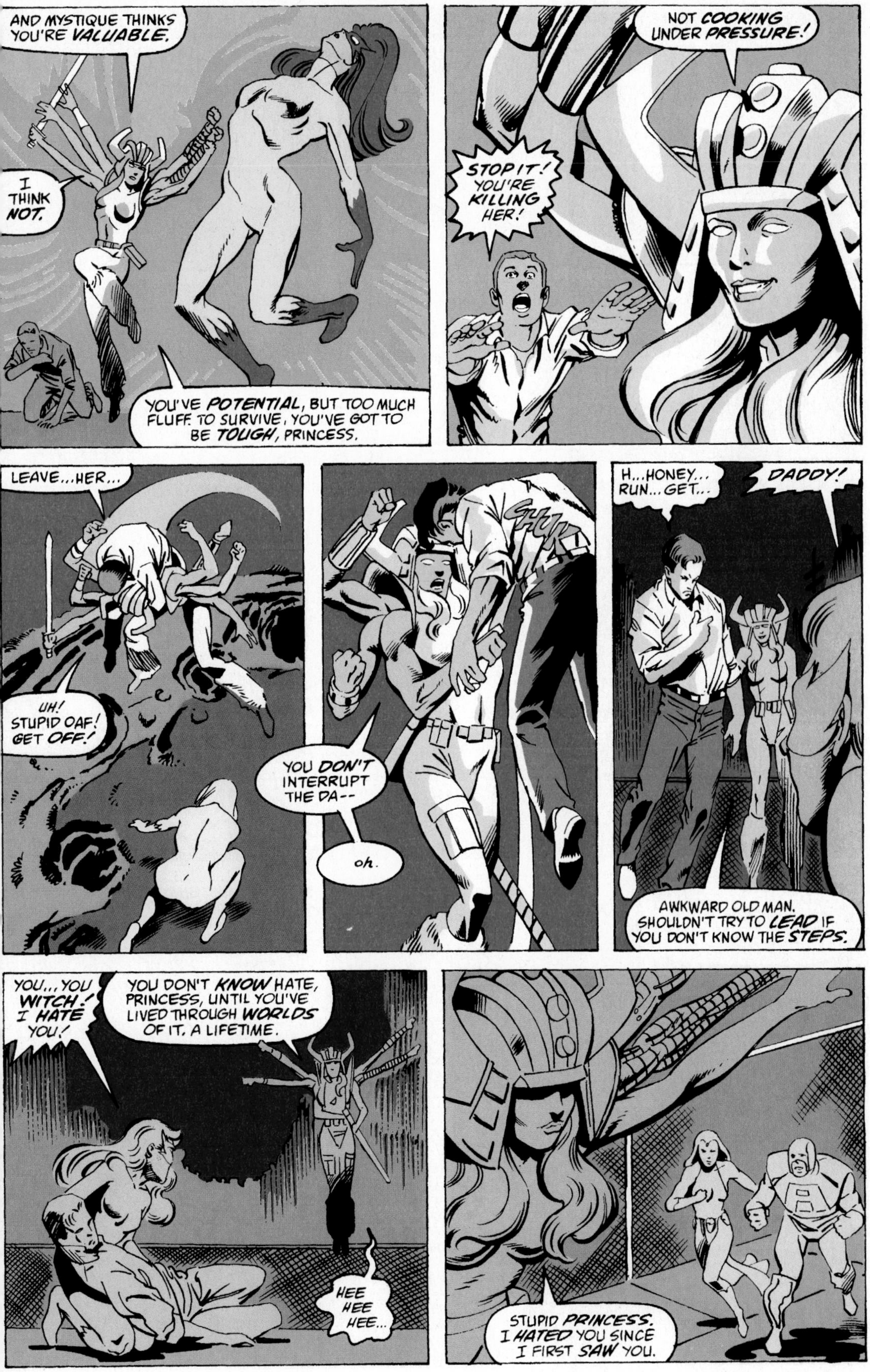
AND MYSTIQUE THINKS YOU'RE VALUABLE.
I THINK NOT.
YOU'VE POTENTIAL, BUT TOO MUCH FLUFF TO SURVIVE. YOU'VE GOT TO BE TOUGH, PRINCESS.
NOT COOKING UNDER PRESSURE!
STOP IT! YOU'RE KILLING HER!
LEAVE...HER...
UH! STUPID OAF! GET OFF!
YOU DON'T INTERRUPT THE DA--
oh.
H...HONEY... RUN... GET...
DADDY!
AWKWARD OLD MAN. SHOULDN'T TRY TO LEAD IF YOU DON'T KNOW THE STEPS.
YOU...YOU WITCH! I HATE YOU!
YOU DON'T KNOW HATE, PRINCESS, UNTIL YOU'VE LIVED THROUGH WORLDS OF IT. A LIFETIME.
HEE HEE HEE...
STUPID PRINCESS. I HATED YOU SINCE I FIRST SAW YOU.

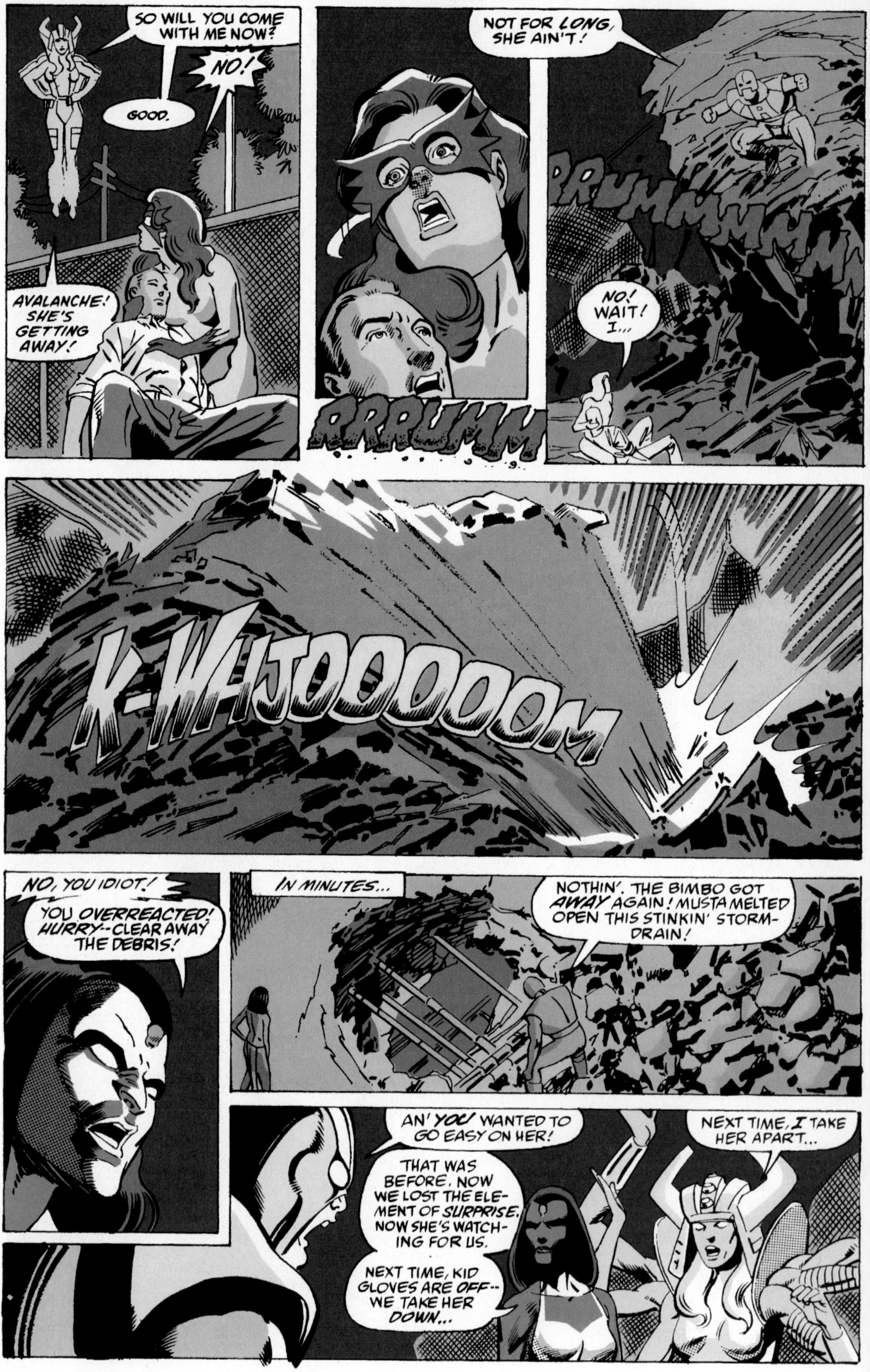
SO WILL YOU COME WITH ME NOW?
NO!
GOOD.
AVALANCHE! SHE'S GETTING AWAY!
NOT FOR LONG, SHE AIN'T!
RRRUMM
RRUMMMMMM
NO! WAIT! I...
K-WHOOOOOOM
NO, YOU IDIOT!
YOU OVERREACTED! HURRY--CLEAR AWAY THE DEBRIS!
IN MINUTES...
NOTHIN'. THE BIMBO GOT AWAY AGAIN! MUSTA MELTED OPEN THIS STINKIN' STORM-DRAIN!
AN' YOU WANTED TO GO EASY ON HER!
THAT WAS BEFORE. NOW WE LOST THE ELEMENT OF SURPRISE. NOW SHE'S WATCHING FOR US.
NEXT TIME, KID GLOVES ARE OFF-- WE TAKE HER DOWN...
NEXT TIME, I TAKE HER APART...

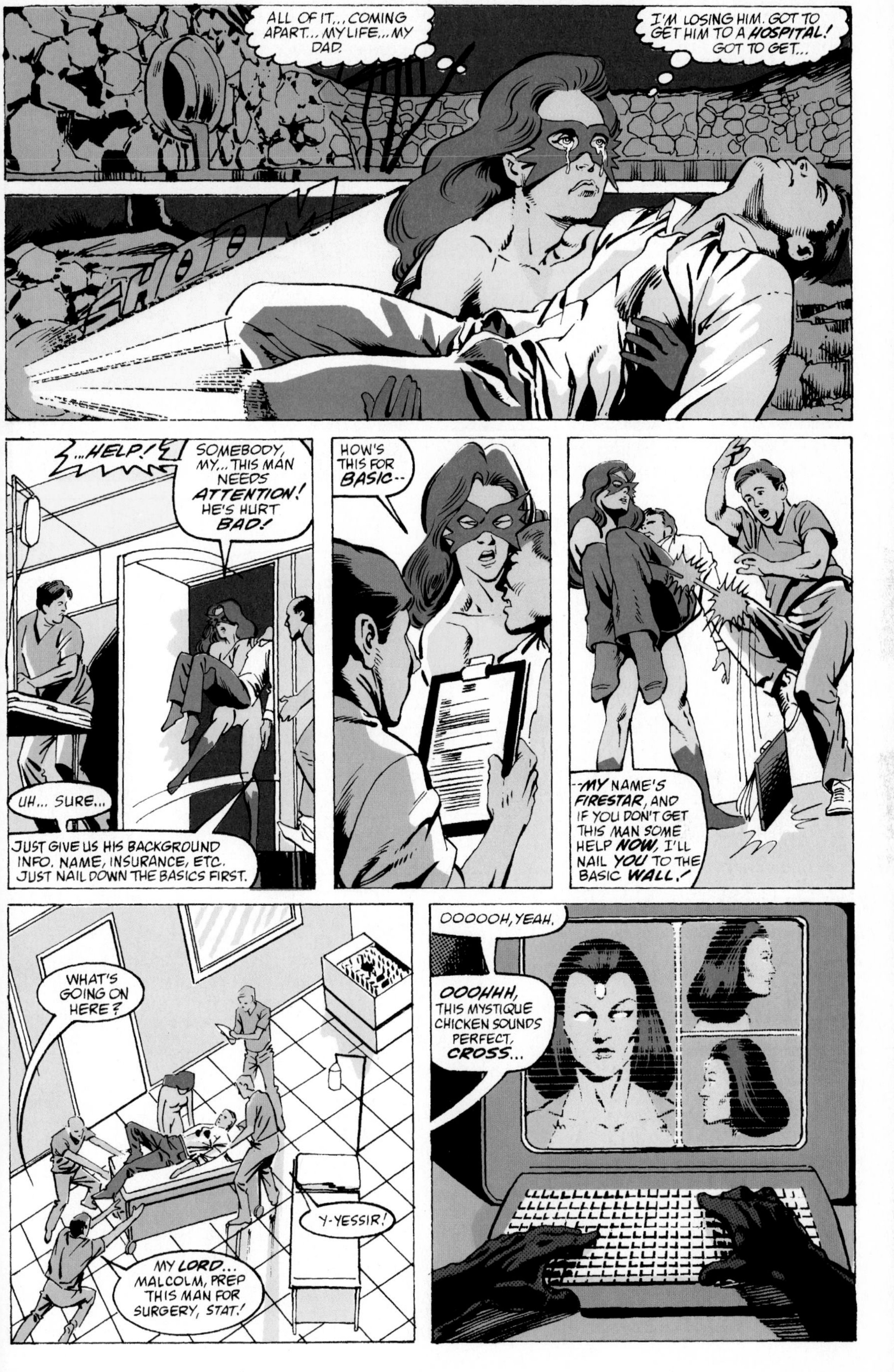
ALL OF IT... COMING APART... MY LIFE... MY DAD.
I'M LOSING HIM. GOT TO GET HIM TO A HOSPITAL! GOT TO GET...
SHOOOM
...HELP!
SOMEBODY, MY... THIS MAN NEEDS ATTENTION! HE'S HURT BAD!
UH... SURE...
JUST GIVE US HIS BACKGROUND INFO. NAME, INSURANCE, ETC. JUST NAIL DOWN THE BASICS FIRST.
HOW'S THIS FOR BASIC--
--MY NAME'S FIRESTAR, AND IF YOU DON'T GET THIS MAN SOME HELP NOW, I'LL NAIL YOU TO THE BASIC WALL.!
WHAT'S GOING ON HERE?
MY LORD... MALCOLM, PREP THIS MAN FOR SURGERY, STAT!
Y-YESSIR!
OOOOOH, YEAH.
OOOHHH, THIS MYSTIQUE CHICKEN SOUNDS PERFECT, CROSS...

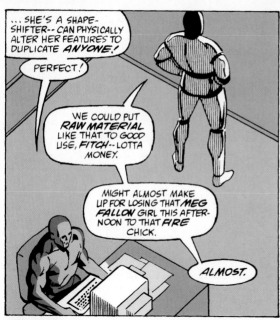

...SHE'S A SHAPE-SHIFTER-- CAN PHYSICALLY ALTER HER FEATURES TO DUPLICATE *ANYONE!*

PERFECT!

WE COULD PUT *RAW MATERIAL* LIKE THAT TO GOOD USE, *FITCH*-- LOTTA MONEY.

MIGHT ALMOST MAKE UP FOR LOSING THAT *MEG FALLON* GIRL THIS AFTERNOON TO THAT *FIRE* CHICK.

ALMOST.

BIGGEST PROB IS THAT MYSTIQUE'S A *GOVERNMENT AGENT.* GOT A WHOLE *MUTANT FORCE* BEHIND HER.

WE'LL NEED SOME WAY TO *SNAG* HER THAT CAN'T BE TRACED BACK TO US IF SOMETHING GOES WRONG.

"WE *NEED* A HEAVYWEIGHT *PATSY.*"

MISS...?

FIRESTAR, DOC. IS...IS THAT *MAN* GOING TO BE OKAY?

MAYBE. HE'S STABLE, BUT HE'S SUFFERED DAMAGE TO HIS LUNG AND KIDNEYS. HE'LL NEED A *TRANSPLANT,* AND SOON.

BUT I'LL BE HONEST, THE PROCESS ISN'T CHEAP, OR GUARANTEED.

WE'VE STARTED LOOKING, BUT THE SEARCH COULD TAKE HOURS... OR MONTHS.

AND I DON'T THINK HE'S GOT *THAT LONG.*

I'LL DO *ANYTHING* TO MAKE SURE HE GETS THE *BEST.*

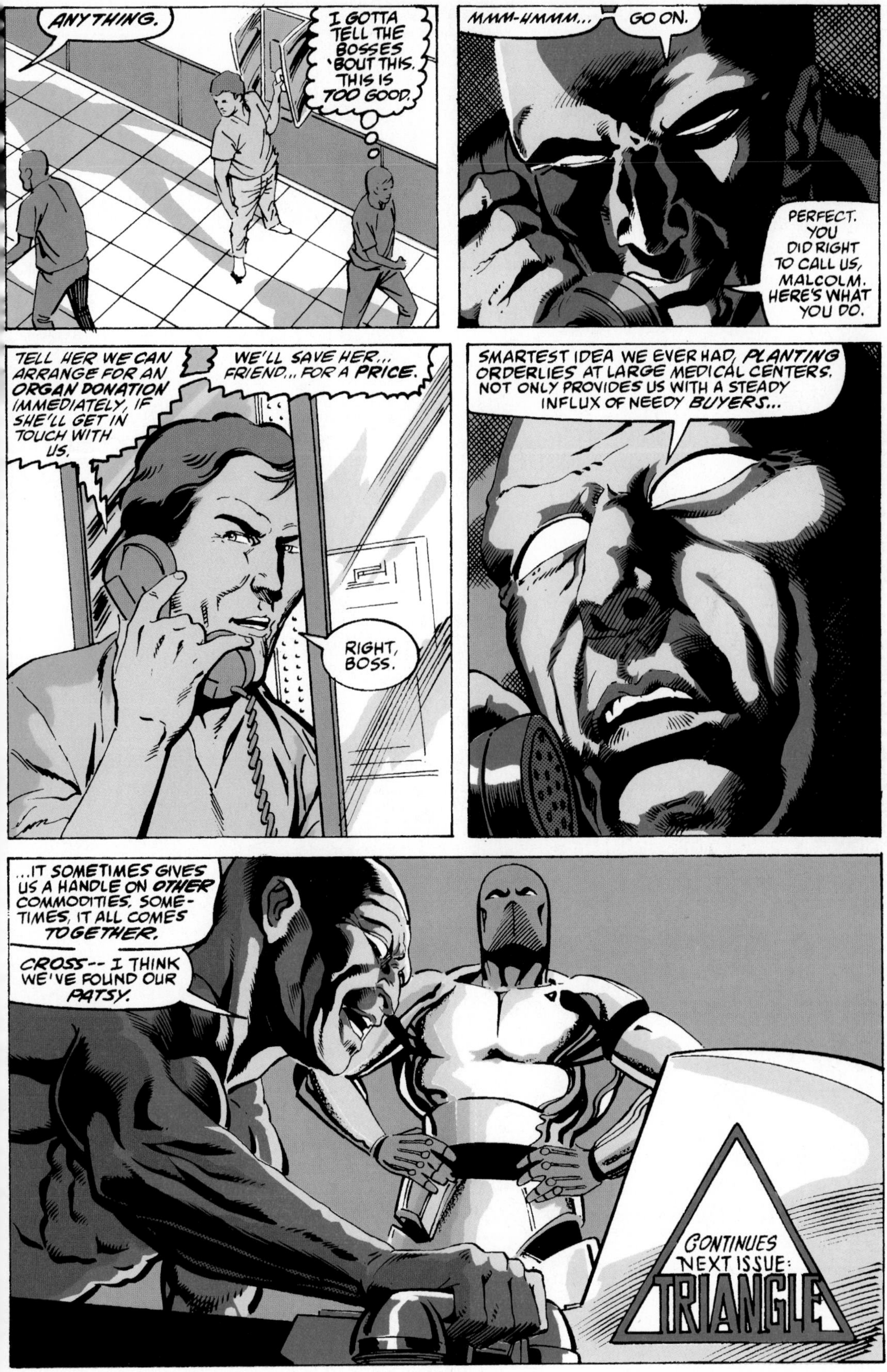
ANYTHING.
I GOTTA TELL THE BOSSES 'BOUT THIS. THIS IS TOO GOOD.
MMM-HMMM...
GO ON.
PERFECT. YOU DID RIGHT TO CALL US, MALCOLM. HERE'S WHAT YOU DO.
TELL HER WE CAN ARRANGE FOR AN ORGAN DONATION IMMEDIATELY, IF SHE'LL GET IN TOUCH WITH US.
WE'LL SAVE HER... FRIEND... FOR A PRICE.
RIGHT, BOSS.
SMARTEST IDEA WE EVER HAD, PLANTING ORDERLIES AT LARGE MEDICAL CENTERS. NOT ONLY PROVIDES US WITH A STEADY INFLUX OF NEEDY BUYERS...
...IT SOMETIMES GIVES US A HANDLE ON OTHER COMMODITIES. SOMETIMES, IT ALL COMES TOGETHER.
CROSS-- I THINK WE'VE FOUND OUR PATSY.
CONTINUES NEXT ISSUE:
TRIANGLE

Marvel Comics Presents #84

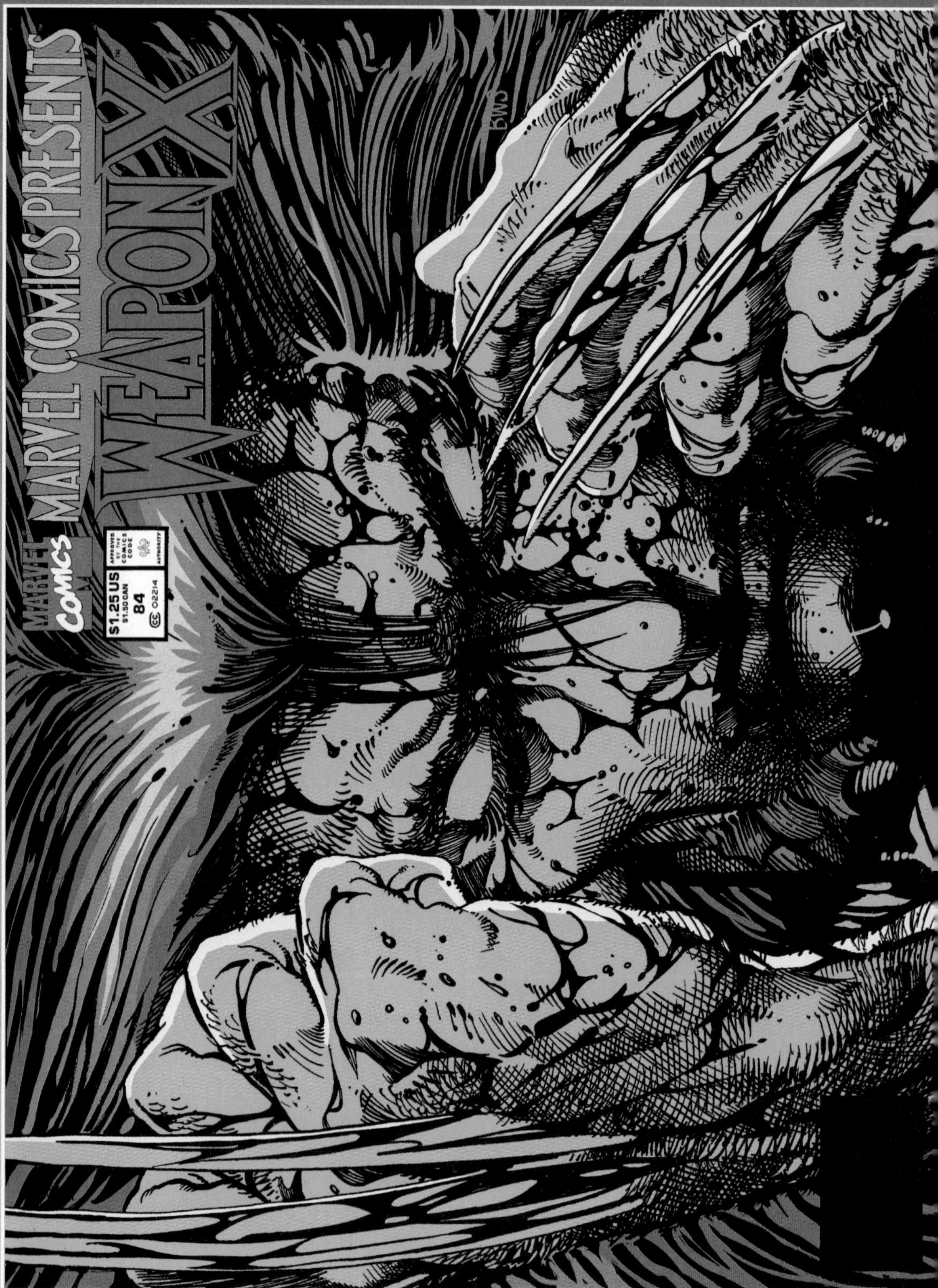
MARVEL COMICS
MARVEL COMICS PRESENTS
WEAPON X
$1.25 US
$1.50 CAN
84
APPROVED BY THE COMICS CODE AUTHORITY
BWS

Writers: Marcus McLaurin & Marie Javins • Penciler: Dwayne Turner • Inker: Jose Marzan Jr. • Colorist: Marcus McLaurin
Letterer: Rick Parker • Assistant Editor: Mark Powers • Editor: Terry Kavanagh

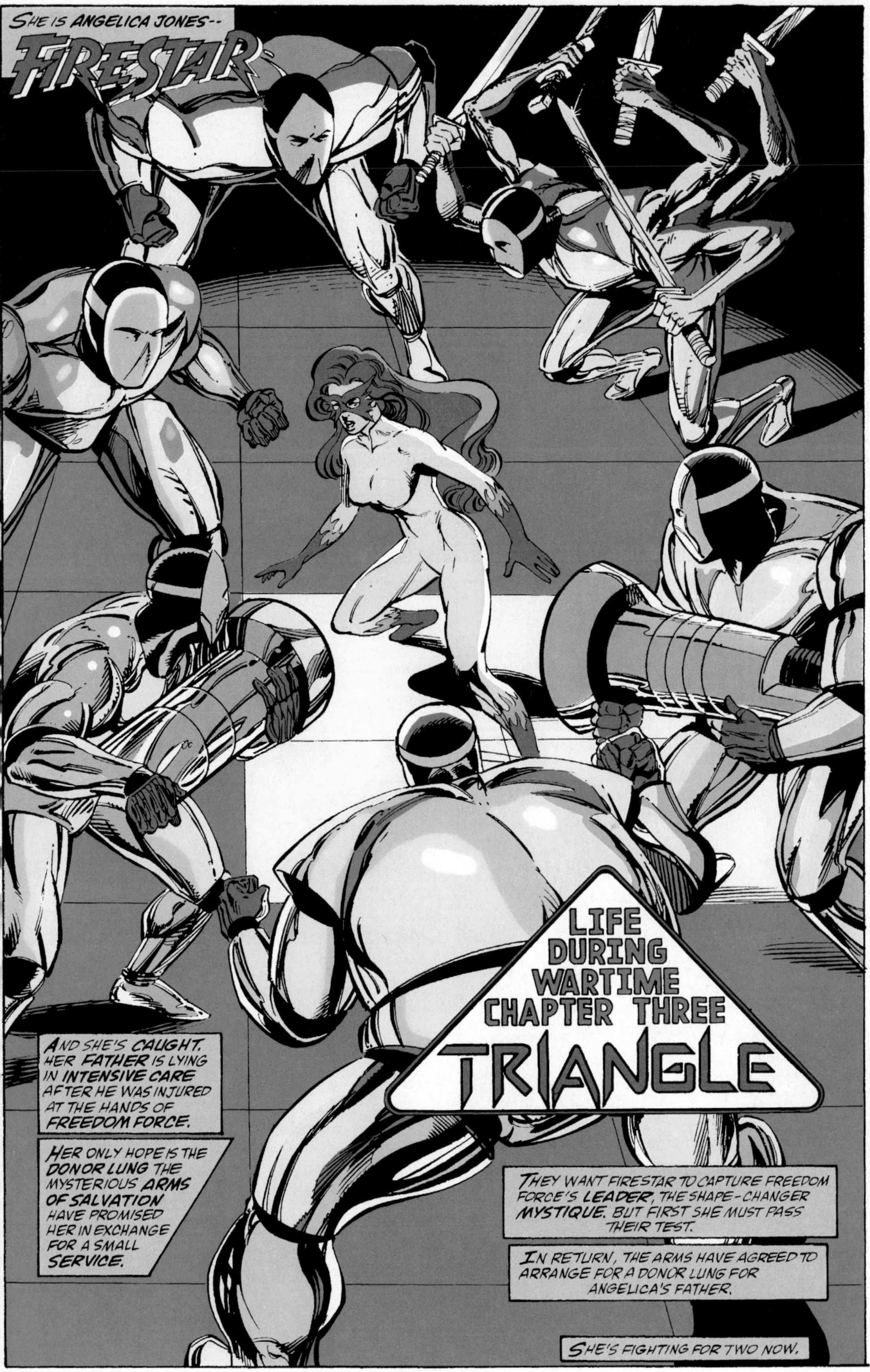
SHE IS ANGELICA JONES--
FIRESTAR
LIFE DURING WARTIME CHAPTER THREE
TRIANGLE
AND SHE'S CAUGHT. HER FATHER IS LYING IN INTENSIVE CARE AFTER HE WAS INJURED AT THE HANDS OF FREEDOM FORCE.
HER ONLY HOPE IS THE DONOR LUNG THE MYSTERIOUS ARMS OF SALVATION HAVE PROMISED HER IN EXCHANGE FOR A SMALL SERVICE.
THEY WANT FIRESTAR TO CAPTURE FREEDOM FORCE'S LEADER, THE SHAPE-CHANGER MYSTIQUE. BUT FIRST SHE MUST PASS THEIR TEST.
IN RETURN, THE ARMS HAVE AGREED TO ARRANGE FOR A DONOR LUNG FOR ANGELICA'S FATHER.
SHE'S FIGHTING FOR TWO NOW.

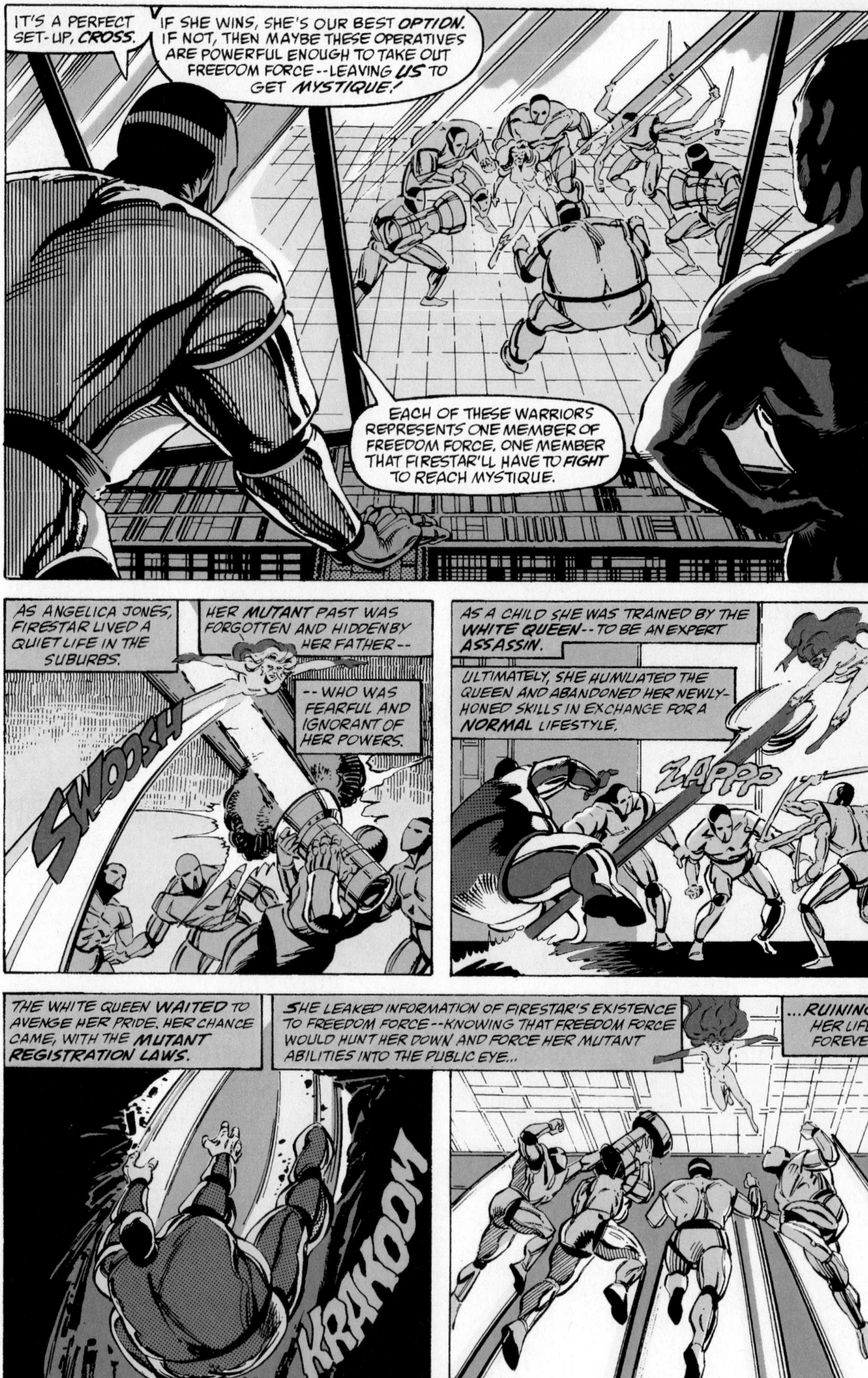
IT'S A PERFECT SET-UP, CROSS.
IF SHE WINS, SHE'S OUR BEST OPTION. IF NOT, THEN MAYBE THESE OPERATIVES ARE POWERFUL ENOUGH TO TAKE OUT FREEDOM FORCE--LEAVING US TO GET MYSTIQUE!
EACH OF THESE WARRIORS REPRESENTS ONE MEMBER OF FREEDOM FORCE, ONE MEMBER THAT FIRESTAR'LL HAVE TO FIGHT TO REACH MYSTIQUE.
AS ANGELICA JONES, FIRESTAR LIVED A QUIET LIFE IN THE SUBURBS.
HER MUTANT PAST WAS FORGOTTEN AND HIDDEN BY HER FATHER--
--WHO WAS FEARFUL AND IGNORANT OF HER POWERS.
SWOOSH
AS A CHILD SHE WAS TRAINED BY THE WHITE QUEEN--TO BE AN EXPERT ASSASSIN.
ULTIMATELY, SHE HUMILIATED THE QUEEN AND ABANDONED HER NEWLY-HONED SKILLS IN EXCHANGE FOR A NORMAL LIFESTYLE.
ZAPPP
THE WHITE QUEEN WAITED TO AVENGE HER PRIDE. HER CHANCE CAME, WITH THE MUTANT REGISTRATION LAWS.
KRAKOOM
SHE LEAKED INFORMATION OF FIRESTAR'S EXISTENCE TO FREEDOM FORCE--KNOWING THAT FREEDOM FORCE WOULD HUNT HER DOWN AND FORCE HER MUTANT ABILITIES INTO THE PUBLIC EYE...
...RUINING HER LIFE FOREVER.

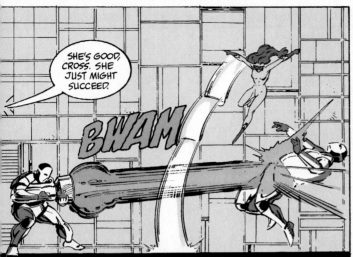

SHE'S GOOD, CROSS. SHE JUST MIGHT SUCCEED.

BWAM

REMEMBER-- WE'RE TELLING FIRESTAR WE NEED MYSTIQUE FOR HER UNIQUE PHYSIOLOGY, FOR D.N.A. RESEARCH-- WE'LL *RELEASE* HER WHEN WE'RE DONE.

HWUMP

FIRESTAR'S *HATE* FOR THE WOMAN WHO INJURED HER FATHER WILL KEEP HER FROM ASKING *TOO* MANY QUESTIONS.

MAKE NO MENTION OF OUR *REAL* PURPOSE-- KEEP THE CONVERSATION ON THE *SURFACE*.

FIRESTAR ISN'T SOMEONE I'D LIKE *AGAINST* US. SHE MIGHT REALIZE THAT SHE'S OUR *NEXT* LIKELY VICTIM.

FWOOOSH

BUT MYSTIQUE WILL BE TREATED NO DIFFERENT THAN OUR *OTHER* DONORS, RIGHT, *FITCH*?

S.O.P., CROSS. STANDARD *OPERATING* PROCEDURE.

FWMM

185

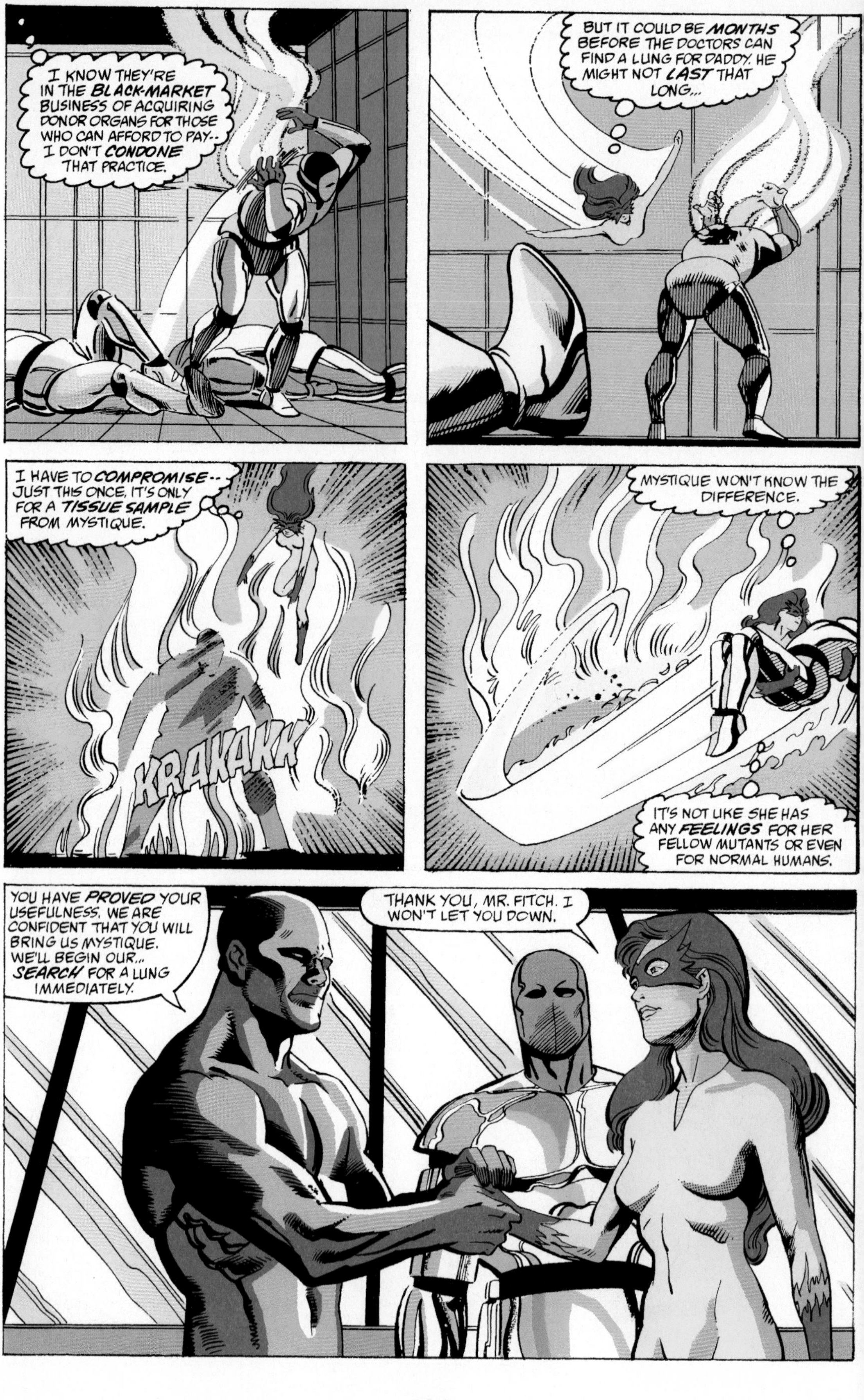
I KNOW THEY'RE IN THE BLACK-MARKET BUSINESS OF ACQUIRING DONOR ORGANS FOR THOSE WHO CAN AFFORD TO PAY-- I DON'T CONDONE THAT PRACTICE.
BUT IT COULD BE MONTHS BEFORE THE DOCTORS CAN FIND A LUNG FOR DADDY. HE MIGHT NOT LAST THAT LONG...
I HAVE TO COMPROMISE-- JUST THIS ONCE. IT'S ONLY FOR A TISSUE SAMPLE FROM MYSTIQUE.
KRAKAKK
MYSTIQUE WON'T KNOW THE DIFFERENCE.
IT'S NOT LIKE SHE HAS ANY FEELINGS FOR HER FELLOW MUTANTS OR EVEN FOR NORMAL HUMANS.
YOU HAVE PROVED YOUR USEFULNESS. WE ARE CONFIDENT THAT YOU WILL BRING US MYSTIQUE. WE'LL BEGIN OUR... SEARCH FOR A LUNG IMMEDIATELY.
THANK YOU, MR. FITCH. I WON'T LET YOU DOWN.

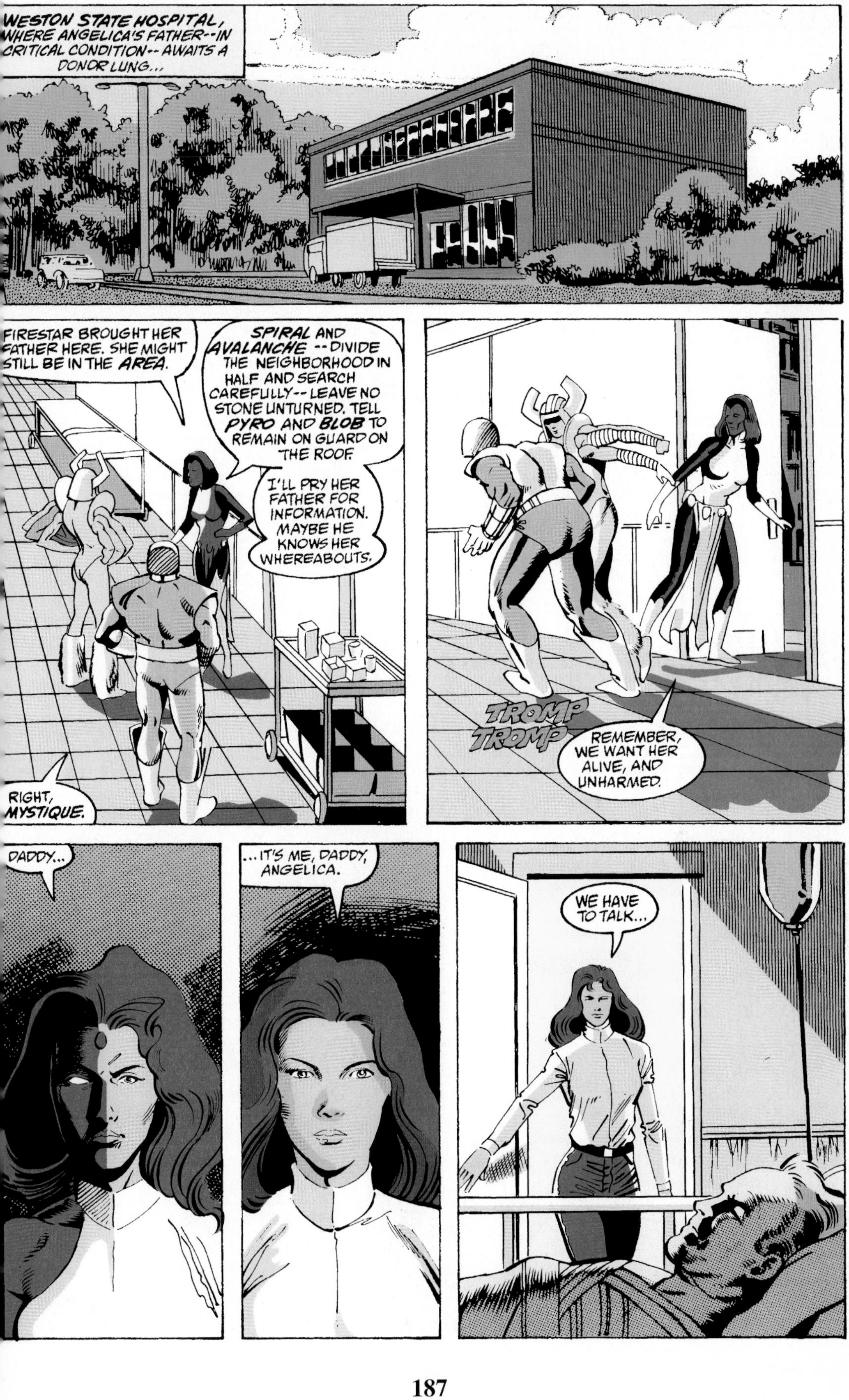
WESTON STATE HOSPITAL, WHERE ANGELICA'S FATHER--IN CRITICAL CONDITION--AWAITS A DONOR LUNG...
FIRESTAR BROUGHT HER FATHER HERE. SHE MIGHT STILL BE IN THE AREA.
SPIRAL AND AVALANCHE--DIVIDE THE NEIGHBORHOOD IN HALF AND SEARCH CAREFULLY--LEAVE NO STONE UNTURNED. TELL PYRO AND BLOB TO REMAIN ON GUARD ON THE ROOF.
I'LL PRY HER FATHER FOR INFORMATION. MAYBE HE KNOWS HER WHEREABOUTS.
RIGHT, MYSTIQUE.
TROMP TROMP
REMEMBER, WE WANT HER ALIVE, AND UNHARMED.
DADDY...
...IT'S ME, DADDY, ANGELICA.
WE HAVE TO TALK...

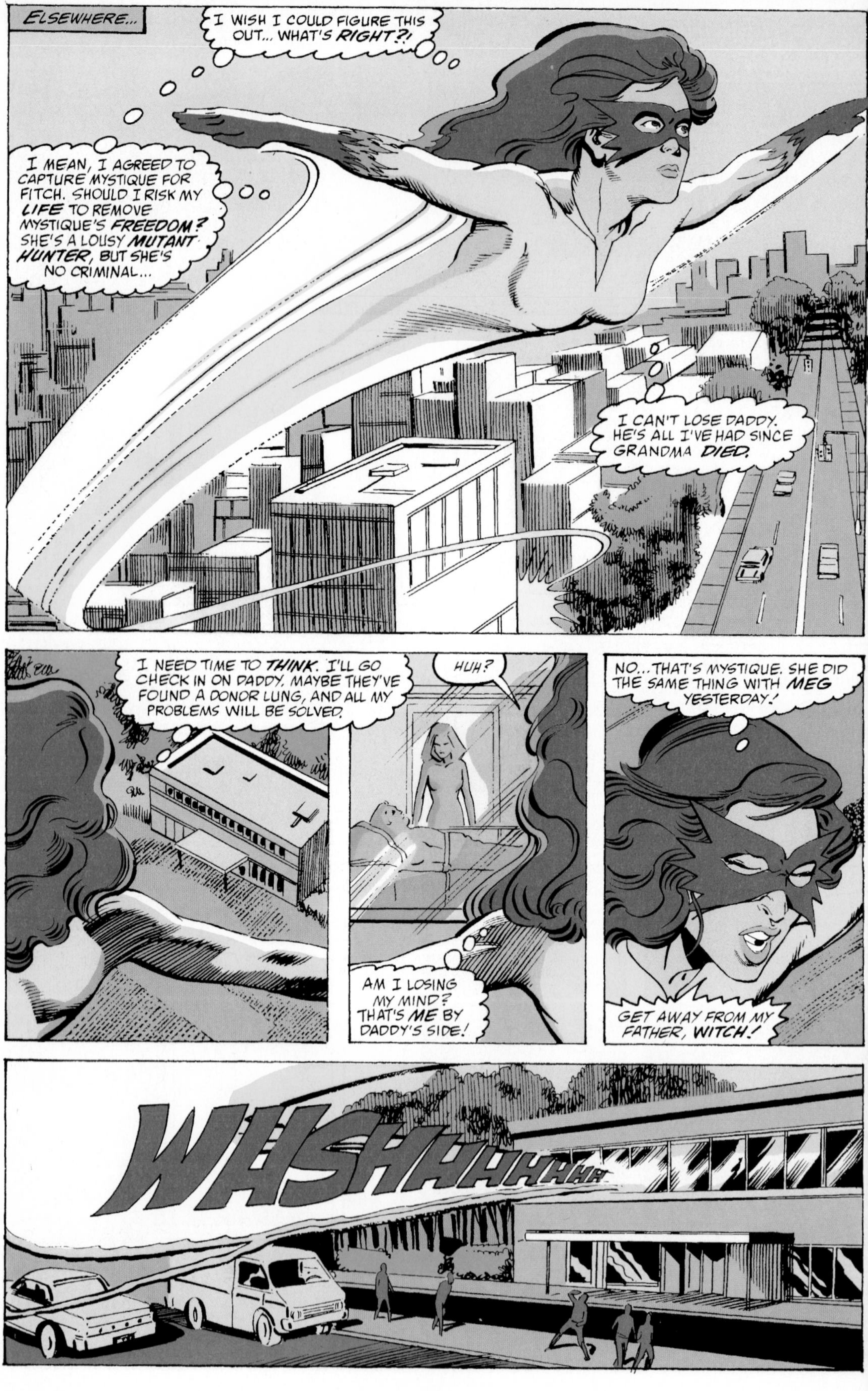

ELSEWHERE...
I WISH I COULD FIGURE THIS OUT... WHAT'S RIGHT?!
I MEAN, I AGREED TO CAPTURE MYSTIQUE FOR FITCH. SHOULD I RISK MY LIFE TO REMOVE MYSTIQUE'S FREEDOM? SHE'S A LOUSY MUTANT HUNTER, BUT SHE'S NO CRIMINAL...
I CAN'T LOSE DADDY. HE'S ALL I'VE HAD SINCE GRANDMA DIED.
I NEED TIME TO THINK. I'LL GO CHECK IN ON DADDY. MAYBE THEY'VE FOUND A DONOR LUNG, AND ALL MY PROBLEMS WILL BE SOLVED.
HUH?
AM I LOSING MY MIND? THAT'S ME BY DADDY'S SIDE!
NO... THAT'S MYSTIQUE. SHE DID THE SAME THING WITH MEG YESTERDAY!
GET AWAY FROM MY FATHER, WITCH!
WHSHHHHHH

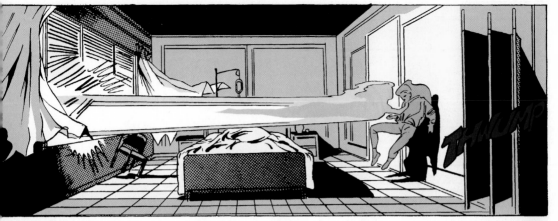

LOOKS LIKE I'VE GOT COMPA-- *OUCH!*

TWISTED MY ANKLE, *STUPID!* SHOULD'VE BEEN MORE CAREFUL!

THIS ISN'T SOME *SECOND-RATE* MUTIE I'M DEALING WITH -- SHE'S GOT ASSASSINATION TRAINING STRAIGHT FROM THE DANGER ROOM OF THE WHITE QUEEN.

HAVEN'T YOU DONE *ENOUGH*, MYSTIQUE? MUST YOU *CONTINUE* TO HARASS MY FATHER? IT'S YOUR FAULT HE'S EVEN HERE -- YOU ATTACKED OUR HOME! WHY CAN'T YOU LEAVE US *ALONE?*

THEY MAY HAVE BENCHED THE MUTANT REGISTRATION ACT, BUT THE N.S.C. STILL DEMANDS THAT *ALL* DANGEROUS MUTANTS BE *REGISTERED!*

WHY *IS* THAT, MYSTIQUE? DON'T YOU EVER QUESTION AUTHORITY?

I CAN'T *AFFORD* TO, LITTLE GIRL...

WELL, YOU'RE GOING TO *PAY* FOR YOUR LACK OF CURIOSITY RIGHT HERE, RIGHT NOW--

184

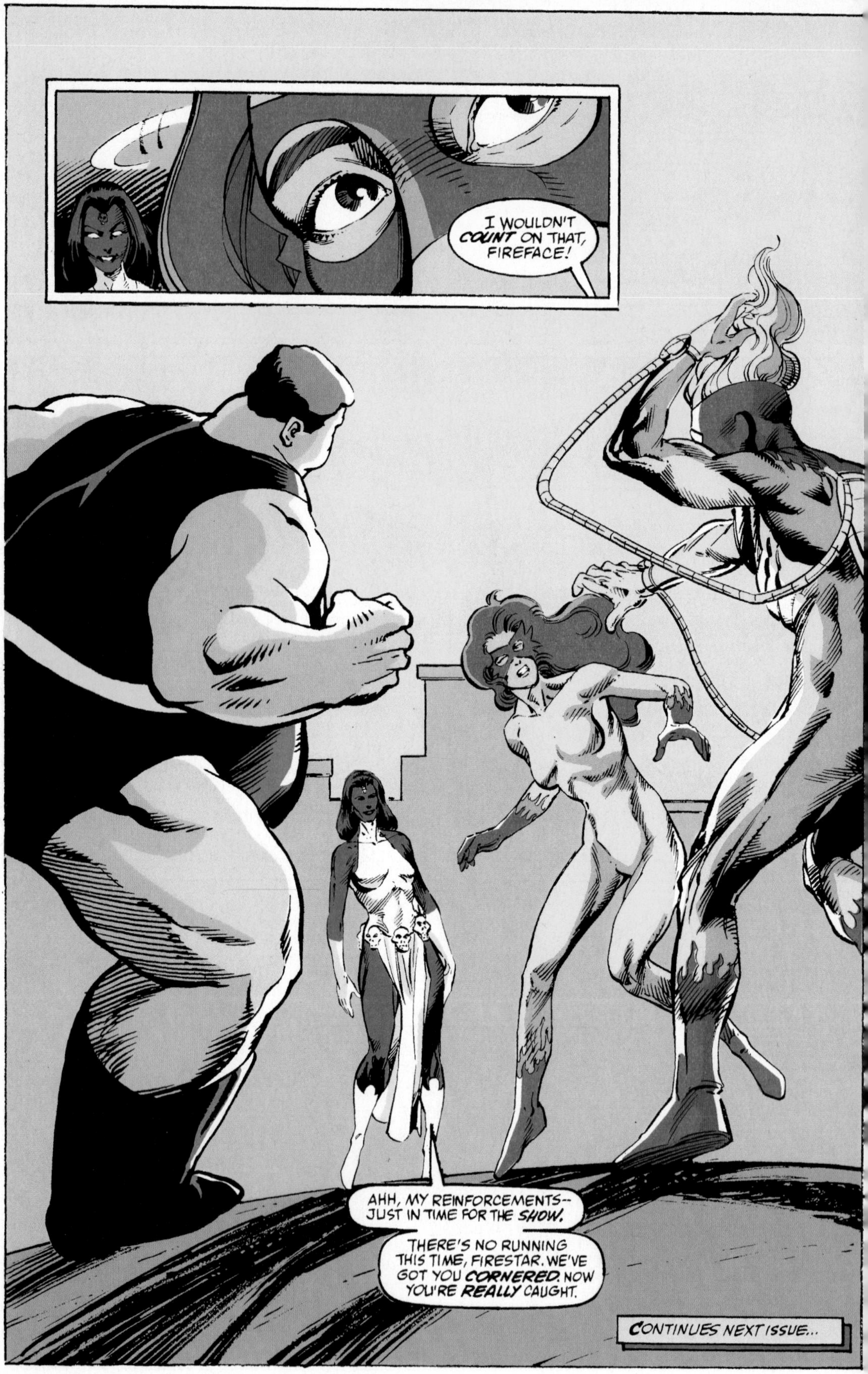
I WOULDN'T COUNT ON THAT, FIREFACE!
AHH, MY REINFORCEMENTS-- JUST IN TIME FOR THE SHOW.
THERE'S NO RUNNING THIS TIME, FIRESTAR. WE'VE GOT YOU CORNERED. NOW YOU'RE REALLY CAUGHT.
CONTINUES NEXT ISSUE...

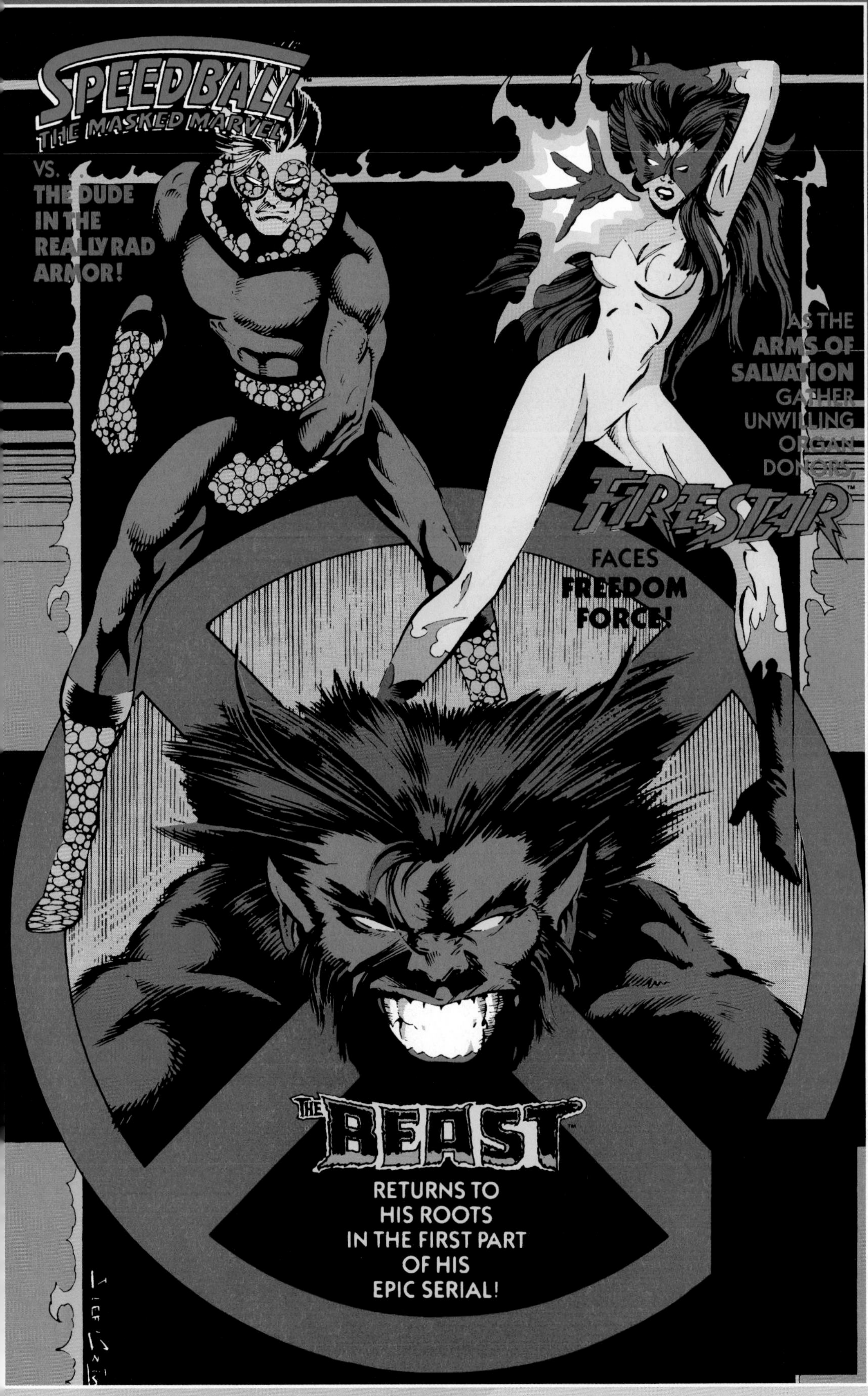
SPEEDBALL
THE MASKED MARVEL
VS. . . THE DUDE IN THE REALLY RAD ARMOR!
AS THE ARMS OF SALVATION GATHER UNWILLING ORGAN DONORS,
FIRESTAR
FACES FREEDOM FORCE!
THE BEAST
RETURNS TO HIS ROOTS IN THE FIRST PART OF HIS EPIC SERIAL!

Writers: Marcus McLaurin & Marie Javins • Penciler: Dwayne Turner • Inkers: Chris Ivy & Jose Marzan Jr.
Colorist: Marcus McLaurin • Letterer: Rick Parker • Assistant Editor: Mark Powers • Editor: Terry Kavanagh

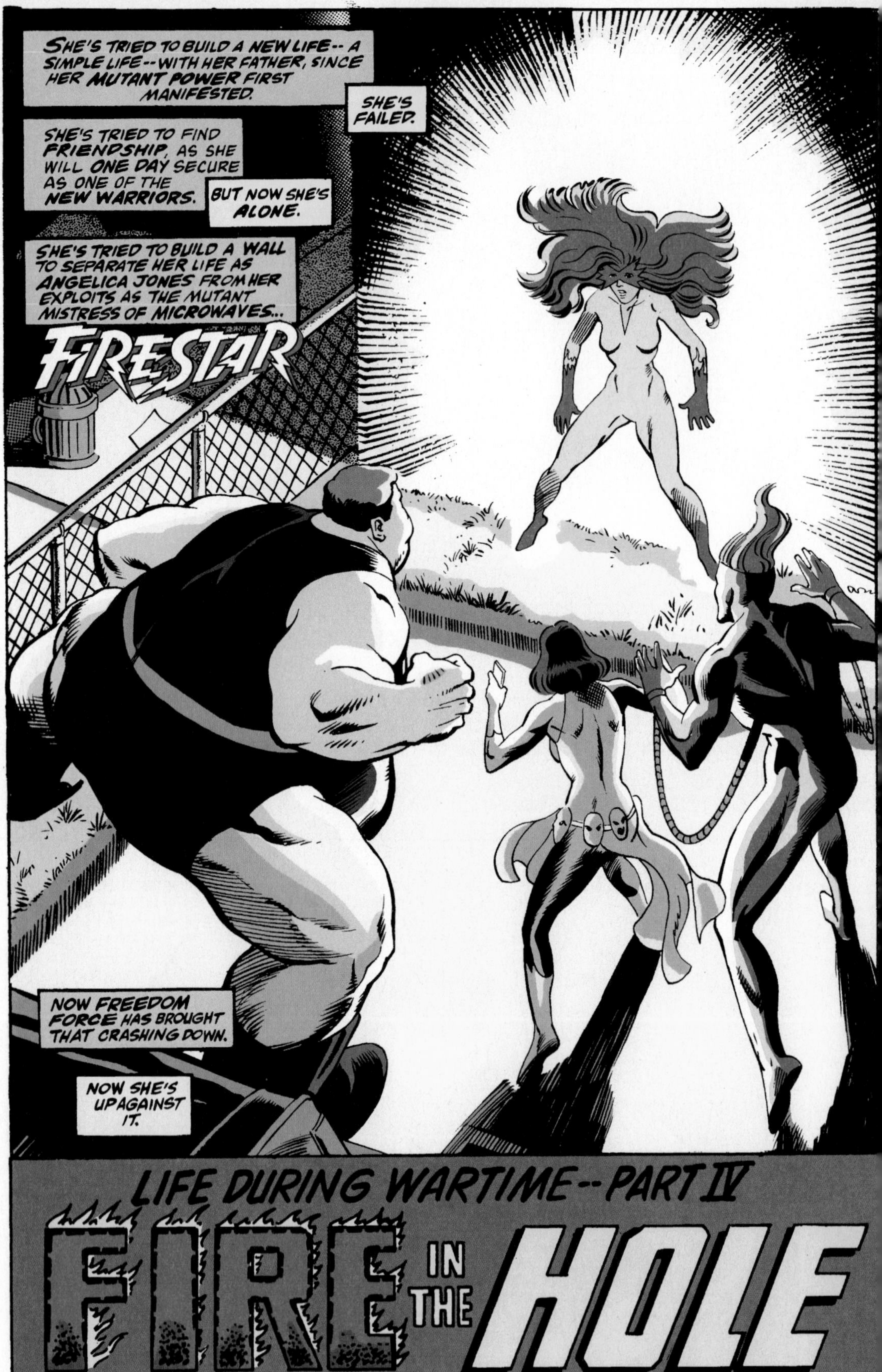
SHE'S TRIED TO BUILD A NEW LIFE-- A SIMPLE LIFE--WITH HER FATHER, SINCE HER MUTANT POWER FIRST MANIFESTED.
SHE'S FAILED.
SHE'S TRIED TO FIND FRIENDSHIP, AS SHE WILL ONE DAY SECURE AS ONE OF THE NEW WARRIORS.
BUT NOW SHE'S ALONE.
SHE'S TRIED TO BUILD A WALL TO SEPARATE HER LIFE AS ANGELICA JONES FROM HER EXPLOITS AS THE MUTANT MISTRESS OF MICROWAVES...
FIRESTAR
NOW FREEDOM FORCE HAS BROUGHT THAT CRASHING DOWN.
NOW SHE'S UP AGAINST IT.
LIFE DURING WARTIME-- PART IV
FIRE IN THE HOLE

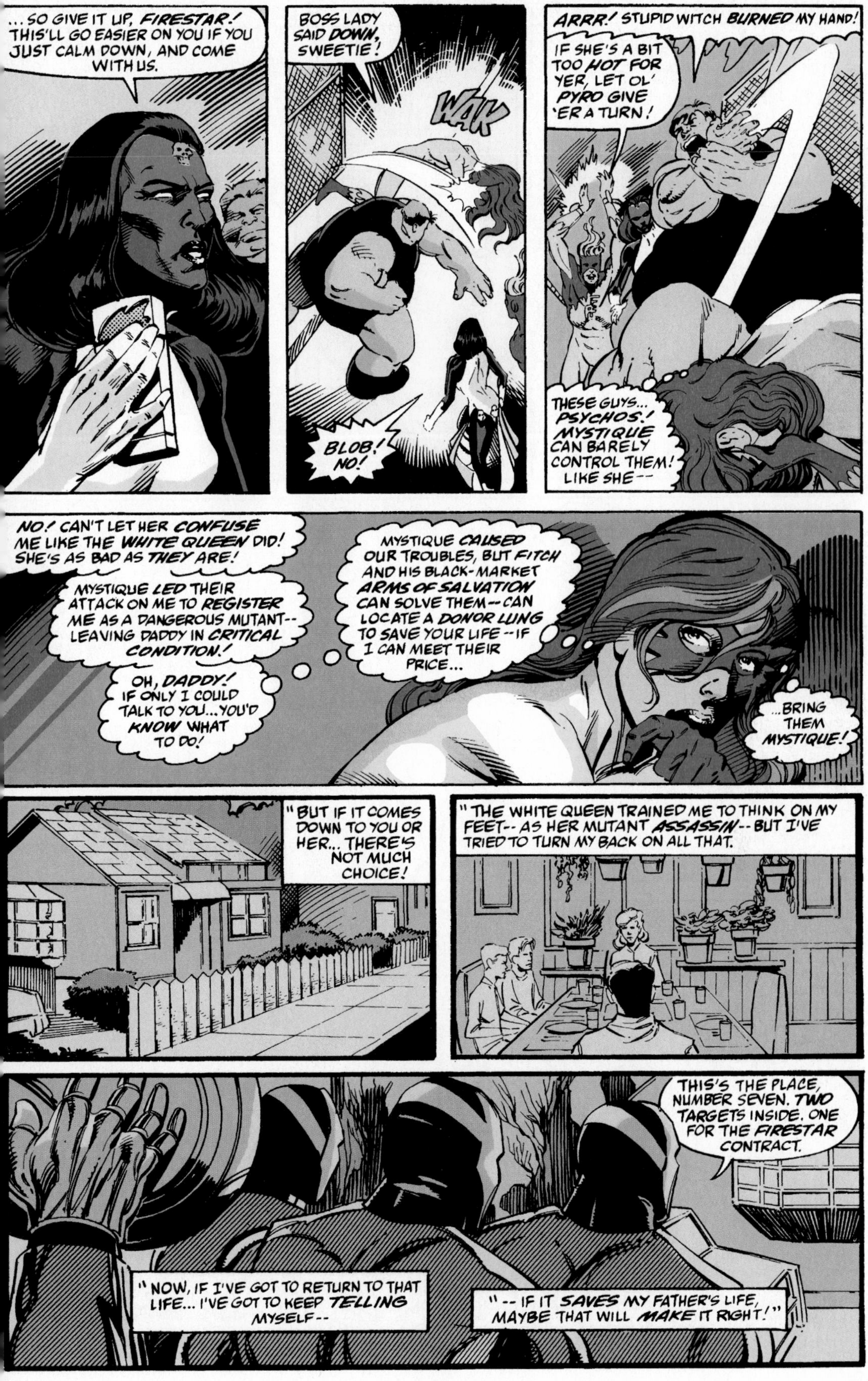

...SO GIVE IT UP, FIRESTAR! THIS'LL GO EASIER ON YOU IF YOU JUST CALM DOWN, AND COME WITH US.
BOSS LADY SAID DOWN, SWEETIE!
WAK
BLOB! NO!
ARRR! STUPID WITCH BURNED MY HAND!
IF SHE'S A BIT TOO HOT FOR YER, LET OL' PYRO GIVE 'ER A TURN!
THESE GUYS... PSYCHOS! MYSTIQUE CAN BARELY CONTROL THEM! LIKE SHE--
NO! CAN'T LET HER CONFUSE ME LIKE THE WHITE QUEEN DID! SHE'S AS BAD AS THEY ARE!
MYSTIQUE LED THEIR ATTACK ON ME TO REGISTER ME AS A DANGEROUS MUTANT-- LEAVING DADDY IN CRITICAL CONDITION!
OH, DADDY! IF ONLY I COULD TALK TO YOU...YOU'D KNOW WHAT TO DO!
MYSTIQUE CAUSED OUR TROUBLES, BUT FITCH AND HIS BLACK-MARKET ARMS OF SALVATION CAN SOLVE THEM--CAN LOCATE A DONOR LUNG TO SAVE YOUR LIFE--IF I CAN MEET THEIR PRICE...
...BRING THEM MYSTIQUE!
"BUT IF IT COMES DOWN TO YOU OR HER... THERE'S NOT MUCH CHOICE!
"THE WHITE QUEEN TRAINED ME TO THINK ON MY FEET-- AS HER MUTANT ASSASSIN-- BUT I'VE TRIED TO TURN MY BACK ON ALL THAT.
THIS'S THE PLACE, NUMBER SEVEN. TWO TARGETS INSIDE. ONE FOR THE FIRESTAR CONTRACT.
"NOW, IF I'VE GOT TO RETURN TO THAT LIFE... I'VE GOT TO KEEP TELLING MYSELF--
"--IF IT SAVES MY FATHER'S LIFE, MAYBE THAT WILL MAKE IT RIGHT!"

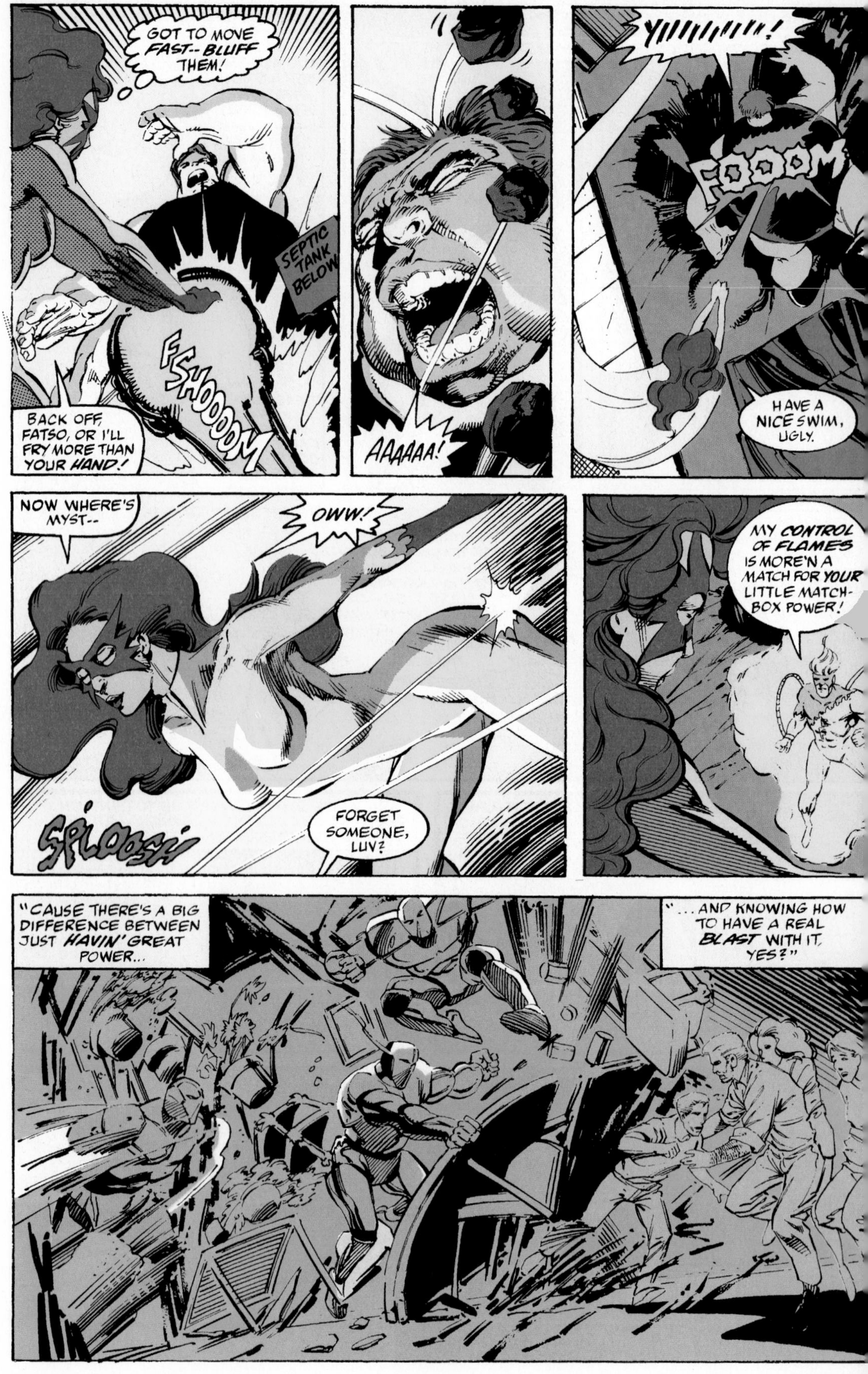

GOT TO MOVE FAST-- BLUFF THEM!
SEPTIC TANK BELOW
FSHOOOOM
BACK OFF, FATSO, OR I'LL FRY MORE THAN YOUR HAND!
AAAAAA!
YIIIIIIII!
FOOOM
HAVE A NICE SWIM, UGLY.
NOW WHERE'S MYST--
OWW!
SPLOOSH
FORGET SOMEONE, LUV?
MY CONTROL OF FLAMES IS MORE'N A MATCH FOR YOUR LITTLE MATCH-BOX POWER!
"CAUSE THERE'S A BIG DIFFERENCE BETWEEN JUST HAVIN' GREAT POWER...
"...AND KNOWING HOW TO HAVE A REAL BLAST WITH IT, YES?"

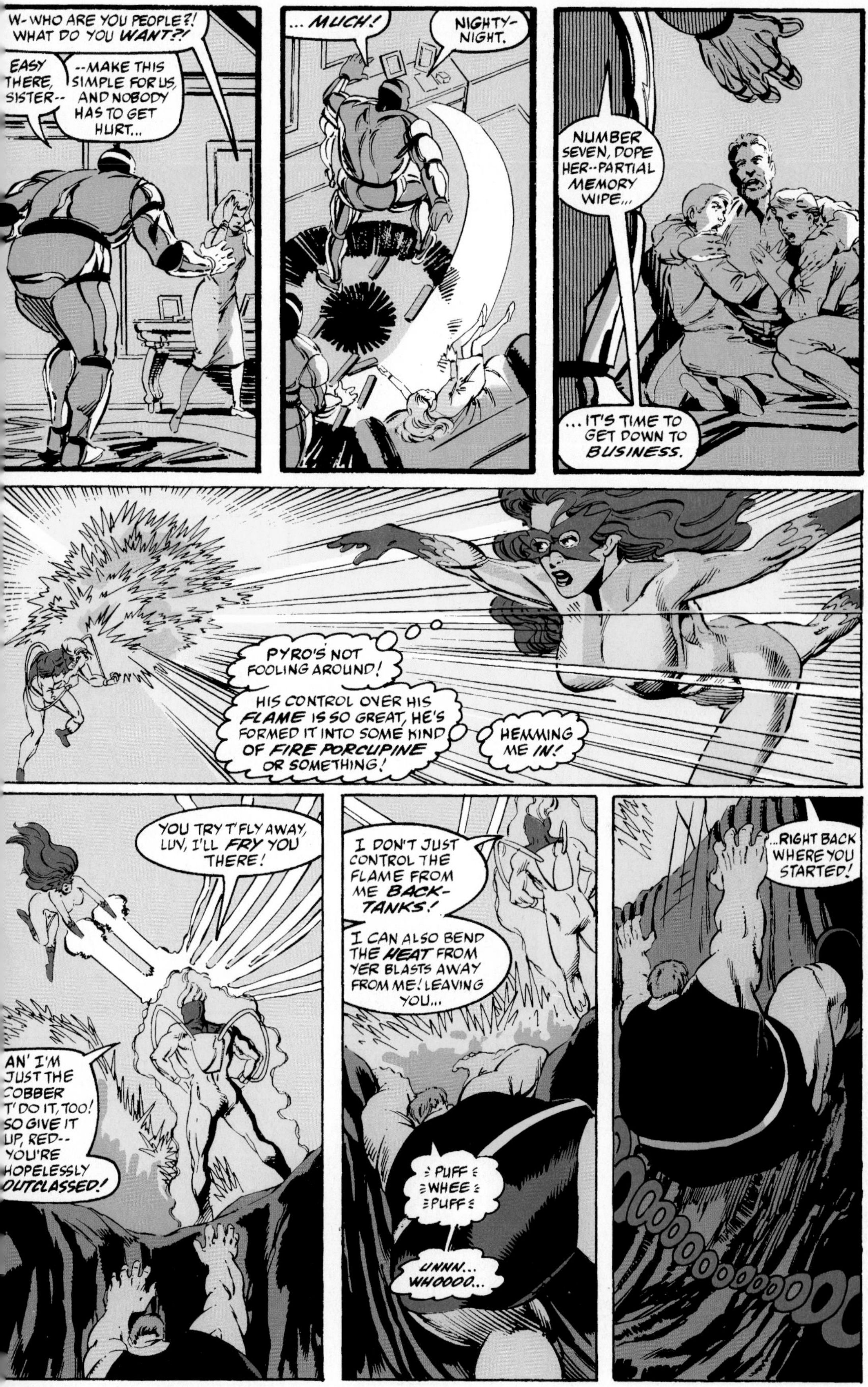
W-WHO ARE YOU PEOPLE?! WHAT DO YOU WANT?!
EASY THERE, SISTER--
--MAKE THIS SIMPLE FOR US, AND NOBODY HAS TO GET HURT...
...MUCH!
NIGHTY-NIGHT.
NUMBER SEVEN, DOPE HER--PARTIAL MEMORY WIPE...
...IT'S TIME TO GET DOWN TO BUSINESS.
PYRO'S NOT FOOLING AROUND!
HIS CONTROL OVER HIS FLAME IS SO GREAT, HE'S FORMED IT INTO SOME KIND OF FIRE PORCUPINE OR SOMETHING!
HEMMING ME IN!
YOU TRY T'FLY AWAY, LUV, I'LL FRY YOU THERE!
AN' I'M JUST THE COBBER T'DO IT, TOO! SO GIVE IT UP, RED-- YOU'RE HOPELESSLY OUTCLASSED!
I DON'T JUST CONTROL THE FLAME FROM ME BACK-TANKS!
I CAN ALSO BEND THE HEAT FROM YER BLASTS AWAY FROM ME! LEAVING YOU...
PUFF WHEE PUFF
UNNN... WHOOOO...
...RIGHT BACK WHERE YOU STARTED!

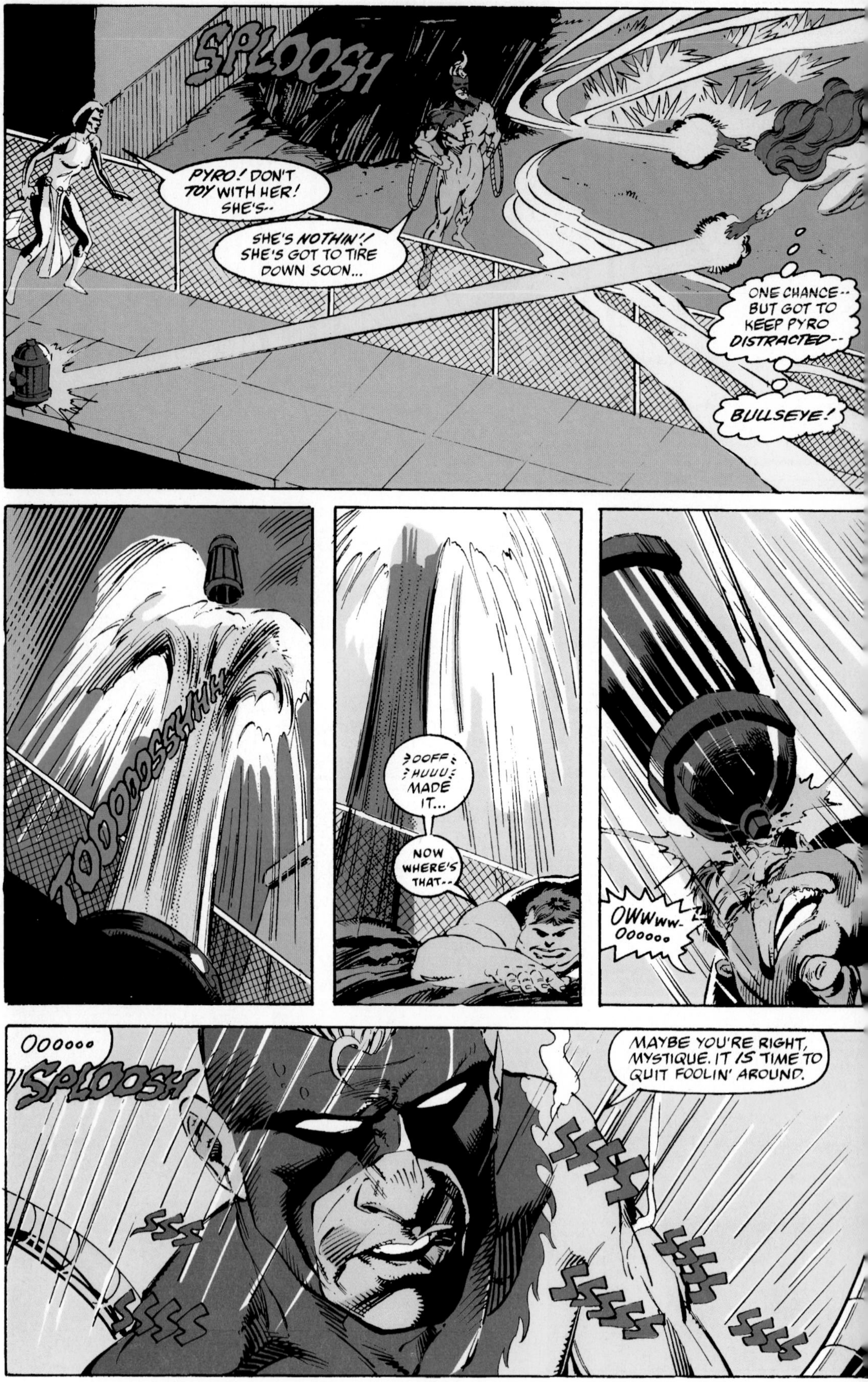
SPLOOSH
PYRO! DON'T TOY WITH HER! SHE'S--
SHE'S NOTHIN'! SHE'S GOT TO TIRE DOWN SOON...
ONE CHANCE-- BUT GOT TO KEEP PYRO DISTRACTED--
BULLSEYE!
OOFF HUUU MADE IT...
NOW WHERE'S THAT--
OWWww-Oooooo
Oooooo
SPLOOSH
MAYBE YOU'RE RIGHT, MYSTIQUE. IT IS TIME TO QUIT FOOLIN' AROUND.

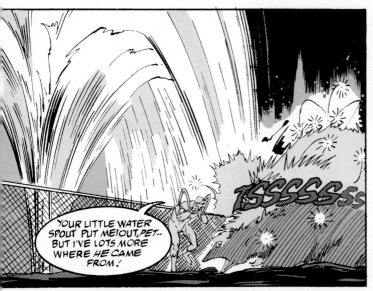

YOUR LITTLE WATER SPOUT PUT ME OUT, PET-- BUT I'VE LOTS MORE WHERE *HE* CAME FROM!

WHILE...

LEAVE HER ALONE!

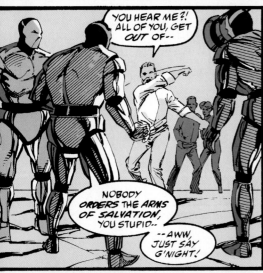

YOU HEAR ME?! ALL OF YOU, GET *OUT OF--*

NOBODY *ORDERS* THE *ARMS OF SALVATION,* YOU STUPID--

--AWW, JUST SAY G'NIGHT!

CAREFUL! HE'S ONE OF THE *TARGETS,* NUMBER FIVE! WE NEED HIS LUNG. THE *FACE,* YOU CAN HAVE FUN WITH.

BUT DON'T BRUISE THE *BODY.*

M... MY LUNG? BUT... THAT'LL...

...KILL YOU, YOU LITTLE *WITCH!*

YOUR LITTLE WATER SHOW WON'T STOP ME FROM *FRYING* YOU!

KWHAM

YEAH, BUT A LITTLE MICROWAVE ENERGY TO THE INTERIOR OF YOUR *TANKS* MIGHT!

NO! PYRO, YOU'LL--

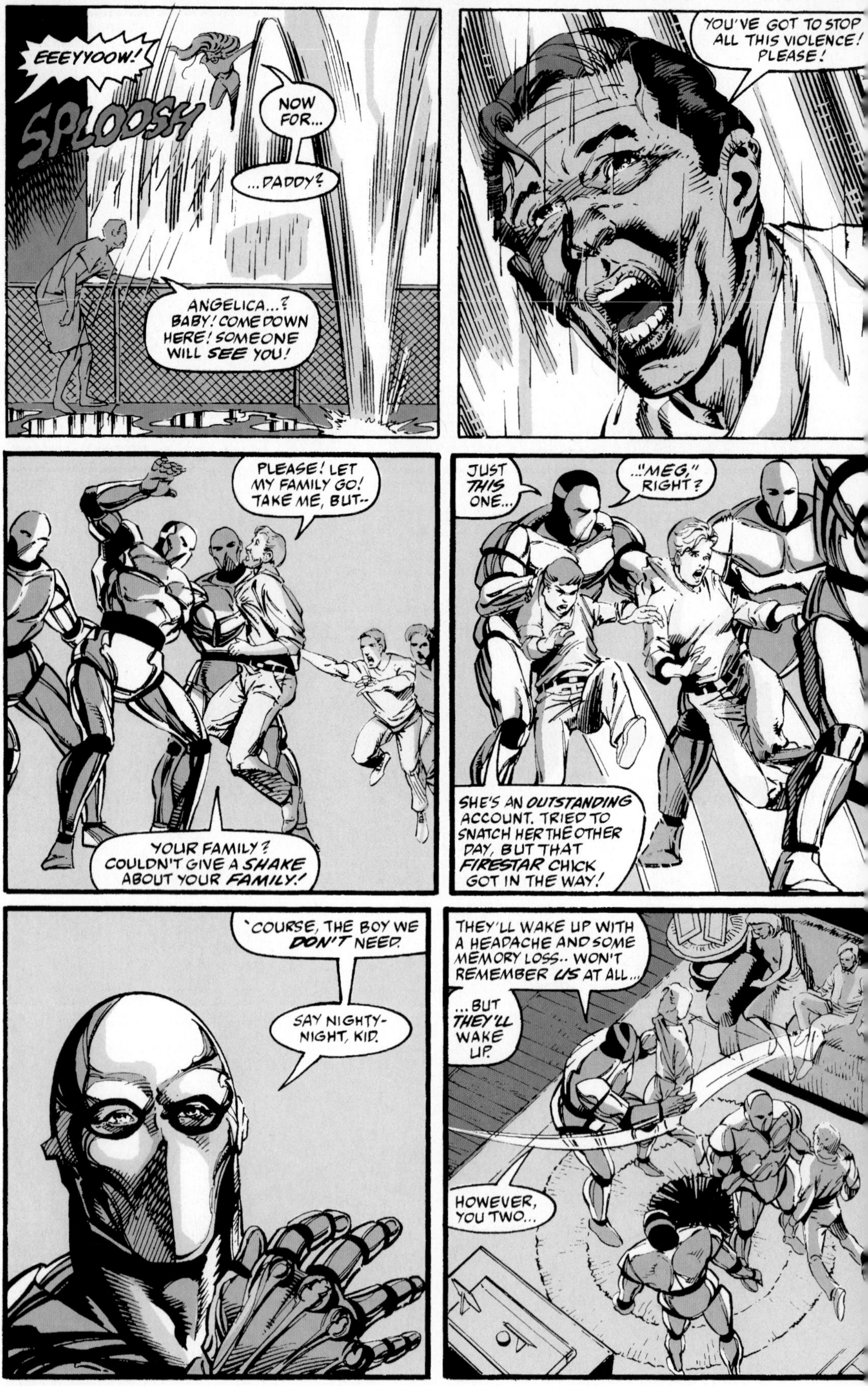
EEEYYOOW!
SPLOOSH
NOW FOR...
...DADDY?
ANGELICA...? BABY! COME DOWN HERE! SOMEONE WILL SEE YOU!
YOU'VE GOT TO STOP ALL THIS VIOLENCE! PLEASE!
PLEASE! LET MY FAMILY GO! TAKE ME, BUT--
YOUR FAMILY? COULDN'T GIVE A SHAKE ABOUT YOUR FAMILY!
JUST THIS ONE...
..."MEG," RIGHT?
SHE'S AN OUTSTANDING ACCOUNT. TRIED TO SNATCH HER THE OTHER DAY, BUT THAT FIRESTAR CHICK GOT IN THE WAY!
'COURSE, THE BOY WE DON'T NEED.
SAY NIGHTY-NIGHT, KID.
THEY'LL WAKE UP WITH A HEADACHE AND SOME MEMORY LOSS.. WON'T REMEMBER US AT ALL...
...BUT THEY'LL WAKE UP.
HOWEVER, YOU TWO...

ENOUGH, ANGELICA... ...FREEDOM FORCE IS ON YOUR SIDE. THEY WANT YOU TO REGISTER--MAYBE BECOME ONE OF THEM.

DADDY?

IT'S A CHANCE, BABY. A CHANCE AT FREEDOM, AND A REAL NEW LIFE.

A CHANCE TO BE ALL THE WHITE QUEEN KNEW YOU COULD BE!

NO!

THE WHITE QUEEN PRETENDED TO CARE ABOUT ME--

--THEN BETRAYED ME WHEN I REFUSED TO BE HER PET MUTIE SHARK!

WHOK

MY FATHER KNEW THAT...

...MYSTIQUE!

YOU OUGHT TO GET YOUR FACTS STRAIGHT BEFORE YOU GET INTO SOMETHING, MYSTIQUE--

ZZZAAKOOK

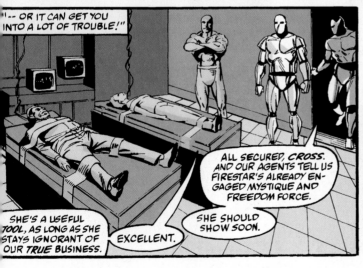

"-- OR IT CAN GET YOU INTO A LOT OF TROUBLE!"

ALL SECURED, CROSS. AND OUR AGENTS TELL US FIRESTAR'S ALREADY ENGAGED MYSTIQUE AND FREEDOM FORCE.

SHE'S A USEFUL TOOL, AS LONG AS SHE STAYS IGNORANT OF OUR TRUE BUSINESS.

EXCELLENT.

SHE SHOULD SHOW SOON.

AND IF SHE GETS TOO CURIOUS?

LONG BEFORE THAT HAPPENS, FITCH, SHE'LL BE A FOND, BLOODY MEMORY!

CONTINUES NEXT ISSUE › TRUE COLORS!

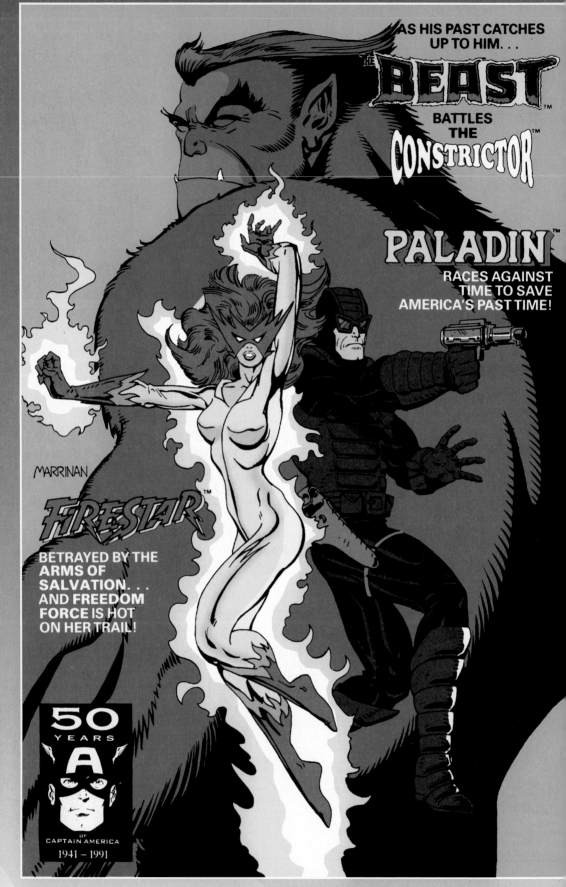

AS HIS PAST CATCHES
UP TO HIM. . .

THE
BEAST™
BATTLES
THE
CONSTRICTOR™

PALADIN™
RACES AGAINST
TIME TO SAVE
AMERICA'S PAST TIME!

MARRINAN

FIRESTAR™

BETRAYED BY THE
ARMS OF
SALVATION. . .
AND **FREEDOM
FORCE** IS HOT
ON HER TRAIL!

**50
YEARS**

A

OF
CAPTAIN AMERICA
1941 - 1991

Writers: Marie Javins & Marcus McLaurin • Penciler: Dwayne Turner • Inker: Chris Ivy • Colorist: Marcus McLaurin
Letterer: Dave Sharpe • Assistant Editor: Mark Powers • Editor: Terry Kavanagh

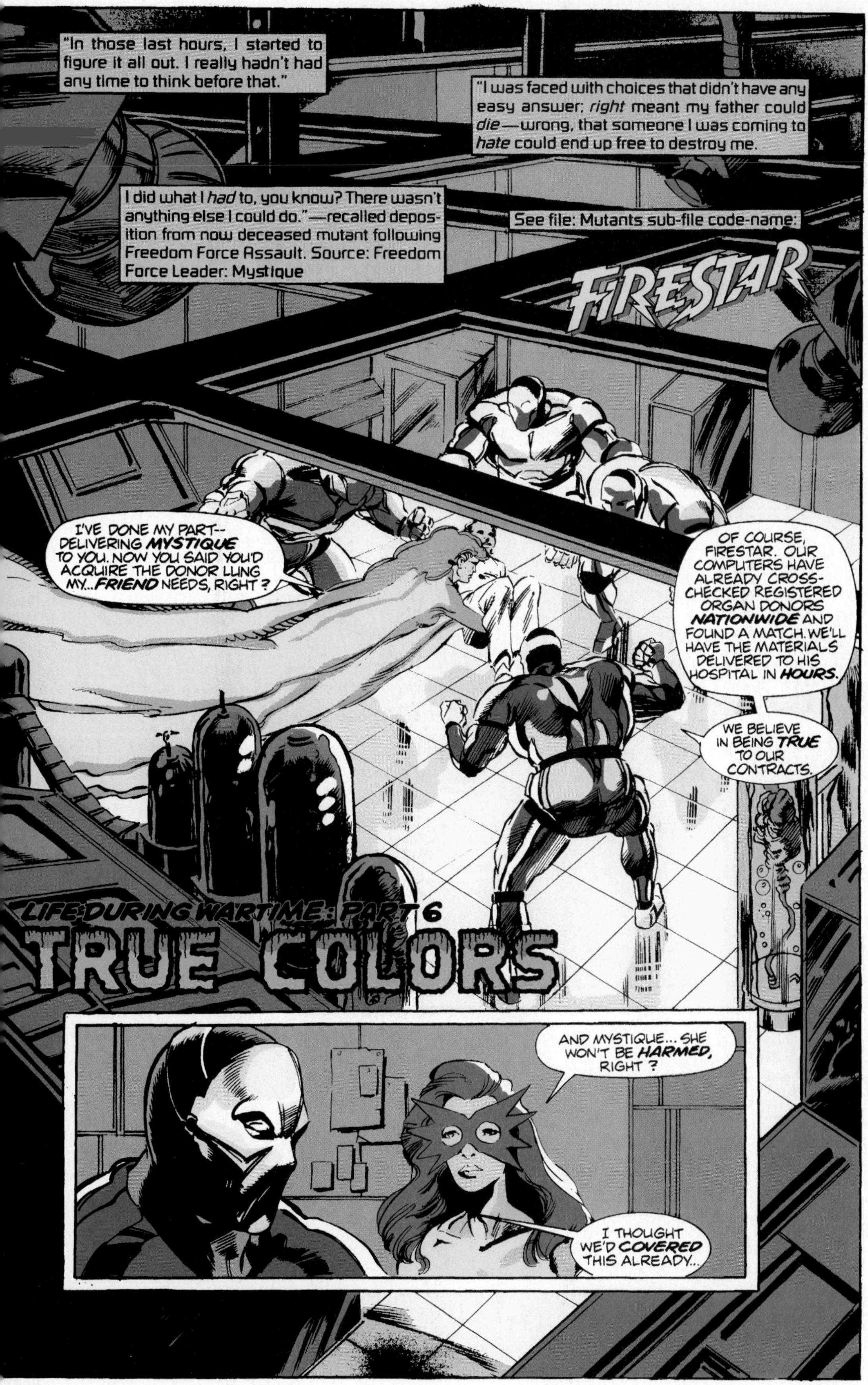
"In those last hours, I started to figure it all out. I really hadn't had any time to think before that."
"I was faced with choices that didn't have any easy answer; right meant my father could die—wrong, that someone I was coming to hate could end up free to destroy me.
I did what I had to, you know? There wasn't anything else I could do."—recalled deposition from now deceased mutant following Freedom Force Assault. Source: Freedom Force Leader: Mystique
See file: Mutants sub-file code-name:
FIRESTAR
I'VE DONE MY PART-- DELIVERING MYSTIQUE TO YOU. NOW YOU SAID YOU'D ACQUIRE THE DONOR LUNG MY...FRIEND NEEDS, RIGHT?
OF COURSE, FIRESTAR. OUR COMPUTERS HAVE ALREADY CROSS-CHECKED REGISTERED ORGAN DONORS NATIONWIDE AND FOUND A MATCH. WE'LL HAVE THE MATERIALS DELIVERED TO HIS HOSPITAL IN HOURS.
WE BELIEVE IN BEING TRUE TO OUR CONTRACTS.
LIFE DURING WARTIME: PART 6
TRUE COLORS
AND MYSTIQUE... SHE WON'T BE HARMED, RIGHT?
I THOUGHT WE'D COVERED THIS ALREADY...

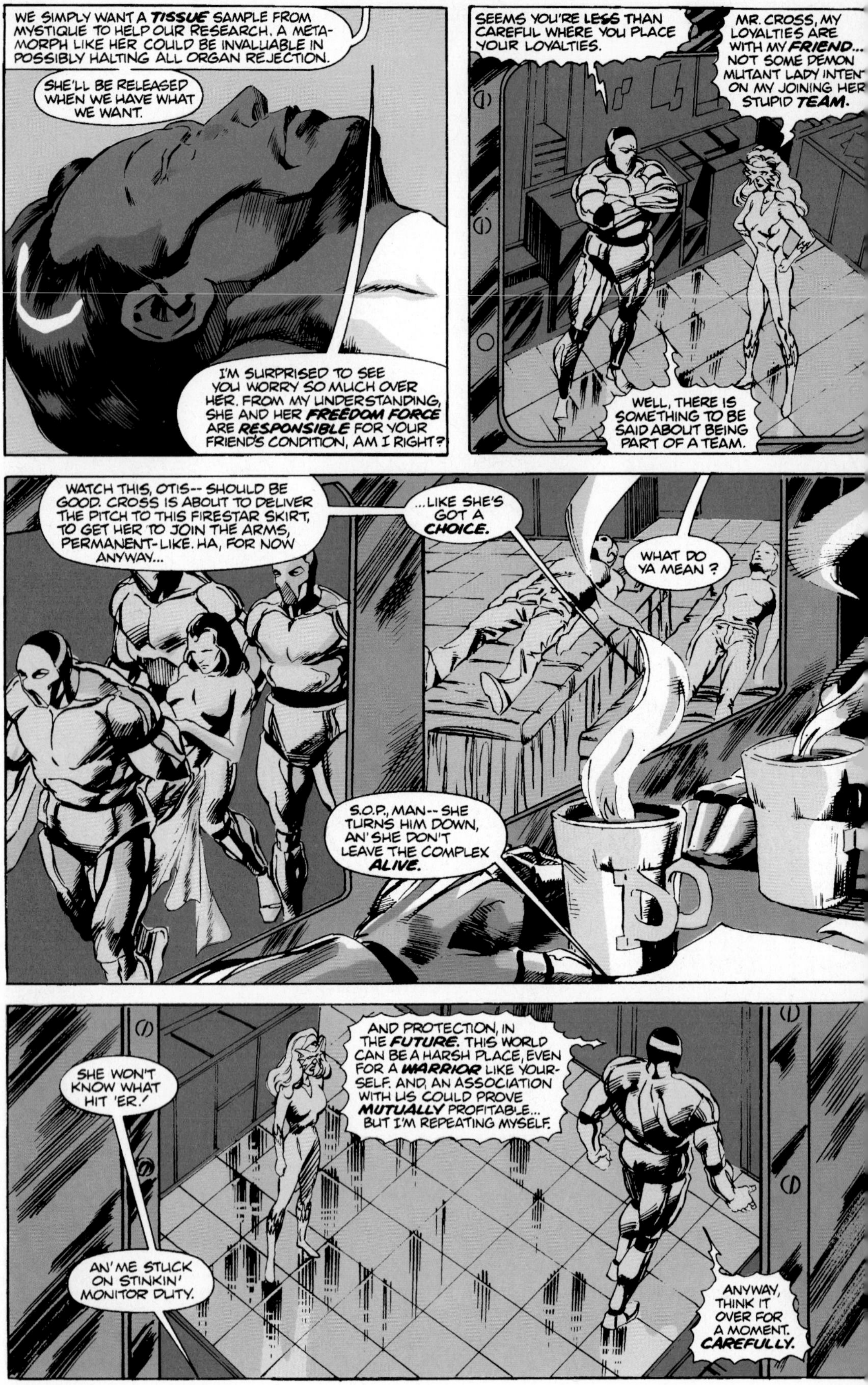
WE SIMPLY WANT A TISSUE SAMPLE FROM MYSTIQUE TO HELP OUR RESEARCH. A METAMORPH LIKE HER COULD BE INVALUABLE IN POSSIBLY HALTING ALL ORGAN REJECTION.
SHE'LL BE RELEASED WHEN WE HAVE WHAT WE WANT.
I'M SURPRISED TO SEE YOU WORRY SO MUCH OVER HER. FROM MY UNDERSTANDING, SHE AND HER FREEDOM FORCE ARE RESPONSIBLE FOR YOUR FRIEND'S CONDITION, AM I RIGHT?
SEEMS YOU'RE LESS THAN CAREFUL WHERE YOU PLACE YOUR LOYALTIES.
MR. CROSS, MY LOYALTIES ARE WITH MY FRIEND... NOT SOME DEMON MUTANT LADY INTEN ON MY JOINING HER STUPID TEAM.
WELL, THERE IS SOMETHING TO BE SAID ABOUT BEING PART OF A TEAM.
WATCH THIS, OTIS-- SHOULD BE GOOD. CROSS IS ABOUT TO DELIVER THE PITCH TO THIS FIRESTAR SKIRT, TO GET HER TO JOIN THE ARMS, PERMANENT-LIKE. HA, FOR NOW ANYWAY...
...LIKE SHE'S GOT A CHOICE.
WHAT DO YA MEAN ?
S.O.P., MAN-- SHE TURNS HIM DOWN, AN' SHE DON'T LEAVE THE COMPLEX ALIVE.
SHE WON'T KNOW WHAT HIT 'ER.'
AN' ME STUCK ON STINKIN' MONITOR DUTY.
AND PROTECTION, IN THE FUTURE. THIS WORLD CAN BE A HARSH PLACE, EVEN FOR A WARRIOR LIKE YOURSELF. AND, AN ASSOCIATION WITH US COULD PROVE MUTUALLY PROFITABLE... BUT I'M REPEATING MYSELF.
ANYWAY, THINK IT OVER FOR A MOMENT. CAREFULLY.

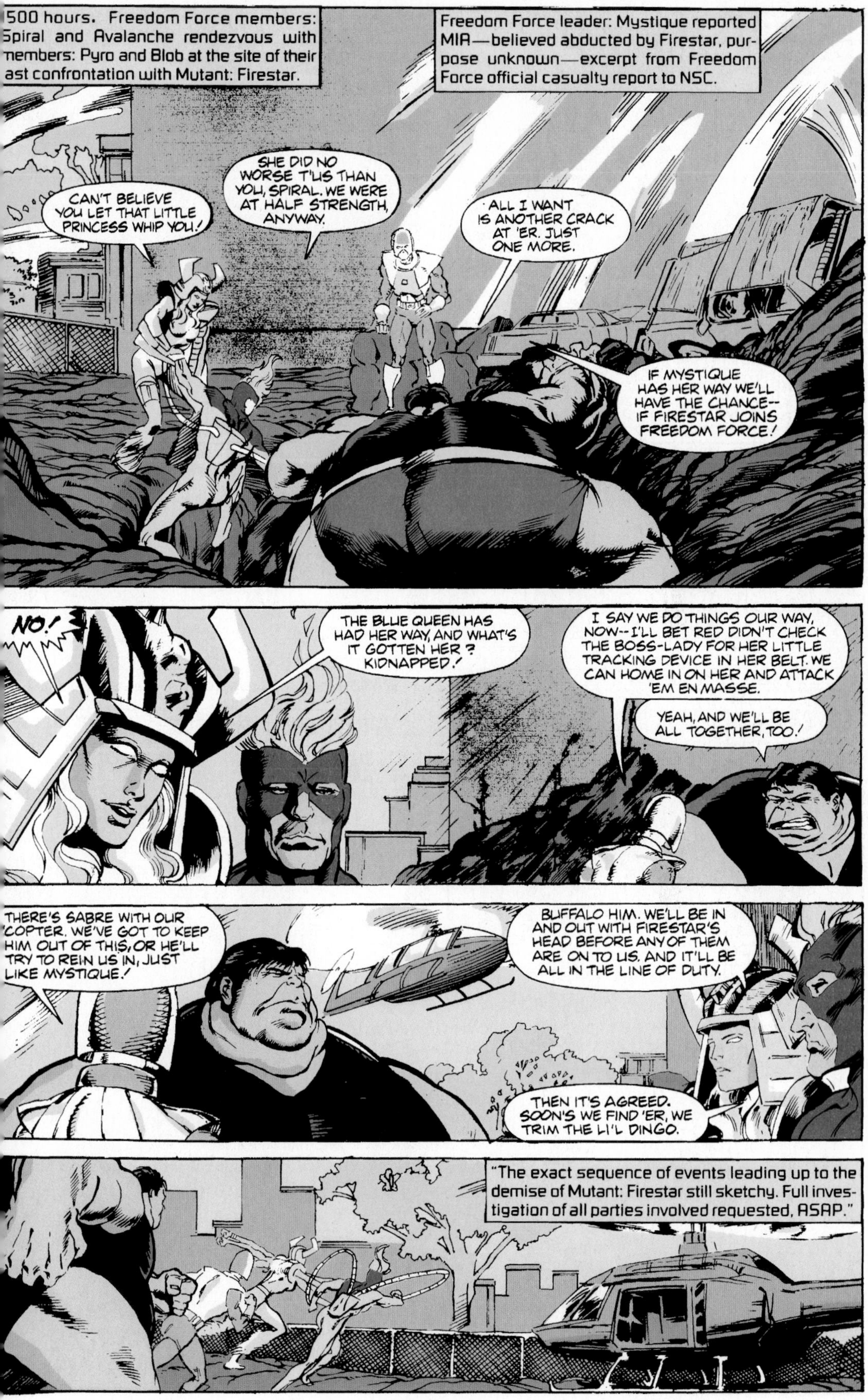
1500 hours. Freedom Force members: Spiral and Avalanche rendezvous with members: Pyro and Blob at the site of their last confrontation with Mutant: Firestar.
Freedom Force leader: Mystique reported MIA—believed abducted by Firestar, purpose unknown—excerpt from Freedom Force official casualty report to NSC.
CAN'T BELIEVE YOU LET THAT LITTLE PRINCESS WHIP YOU!
SHE DID NO WORSE T'US THAN YOU, SPIRAL. WE WERE AT HALF STRENGTH, ANYWAY.
ALL I WANT IS ANOTHER CRACK AT 'ER. JUST ONE MORE.
IF MYSTIQUE HAS HER WAY WE'LL HAVE THE CHANCE-- IF FIRESTAR JOINS FREEDOM FORCE!
NO!
THE BLUE QUEEN HAS HAD HER WAY, AND WHAT'S IT GOTTEN HER? KIDNAPPED!
I SAY WE DO THINGS OUR WAY, NOW--I'LL BET RED DIDN'T CHECK THE BOSS-LADY FOR HER LITTLE TRACKING DEVICE IN HER BELT. WE CAN HOME IN ON HER AND ATTACK 'EM EN MASSE.
YEAH, AND WE'LL BE ALL TOGETHER, TOO!
THERE'S SABRE WITH OUR 'COPTER. WE'VE GOT TO KEEP HIM OUT OF THIS, OR HE'LL TRY TO REIN US IN, JUST LIKE MYSTIQUE!
BUFFALO HIM. WE'LL BE IN AND OUT WITH FIRESTAR'S HEAD BEFORE ANY OF THEM ARE ON TO US, AND IT'LL BE ALL IN THE LINE OF DUTY.
THEN IT'S AGREED. SOON'S WE FIND 'ER, WE TRIM THE LI'L DINGO.
"The exact sequence of events leading up to the demise of Mutant: Firestar still sketchy. Full investigation of all parties involved requested, ASAP."

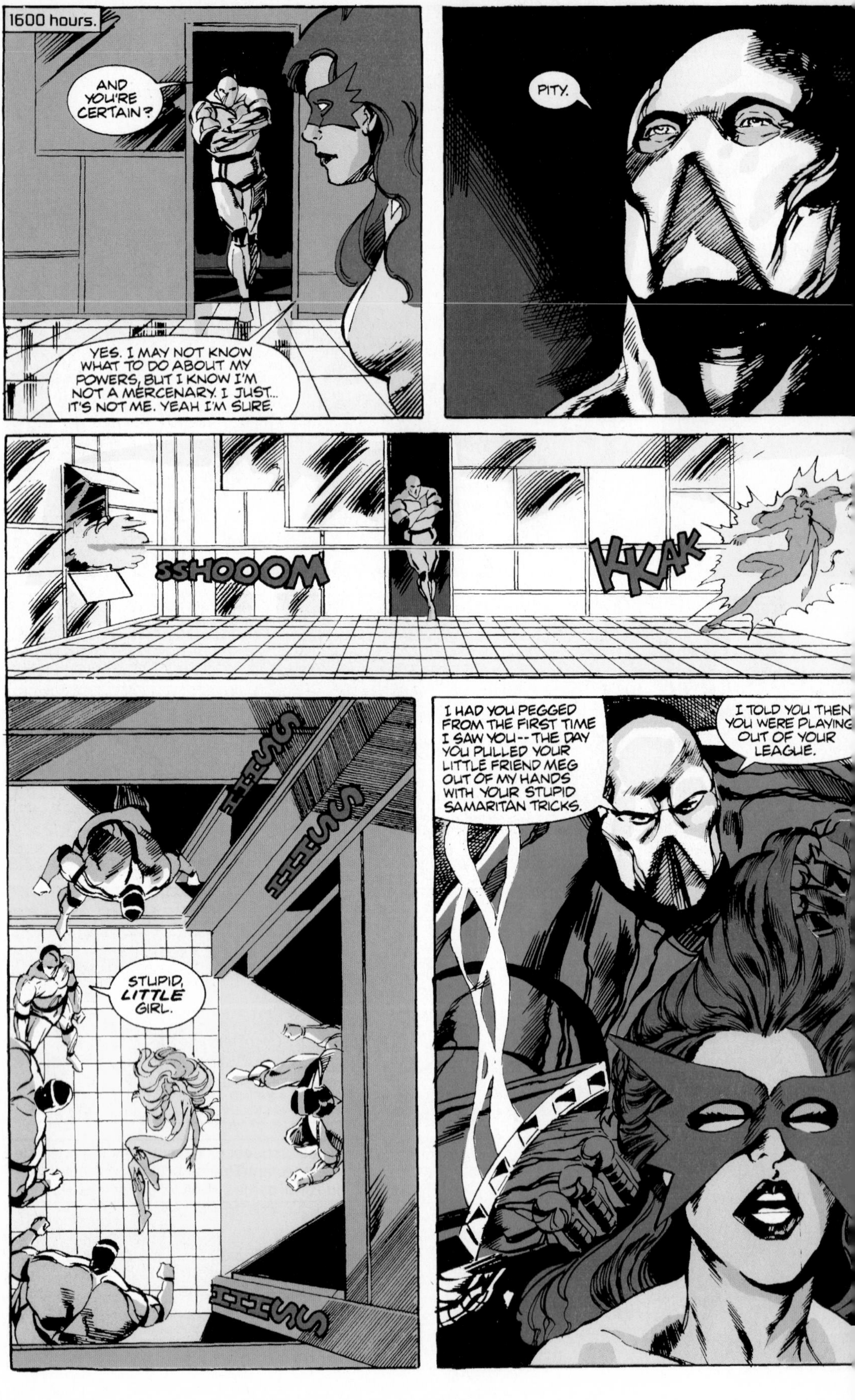
1600 hours.
AND YOU'RE CERTAIN?
YES. I MAY NOT KNOW WHAT TO DO ABOUT MY POWERS, BUT I KNOW I'M NOT A MERCENARY. I JUST... IT'S NOT ME. YEAH I'M SURE.
PITY.
SSHOOOM
VKKAK
STUPID, LITTLE GIRL.
I HAD YOU PEGGED FROM THE FIRST TIME I SAW YOU--THE DAY YOU PULLED YOUR LITTLE FRIEND MEG OUT OF MY HANDS WITH YOUR STUPID SAMARITAN TRICKS.
I TOLD YOU THEN YOU WERE PLAYING OUT OF YOUR LEAGUE.

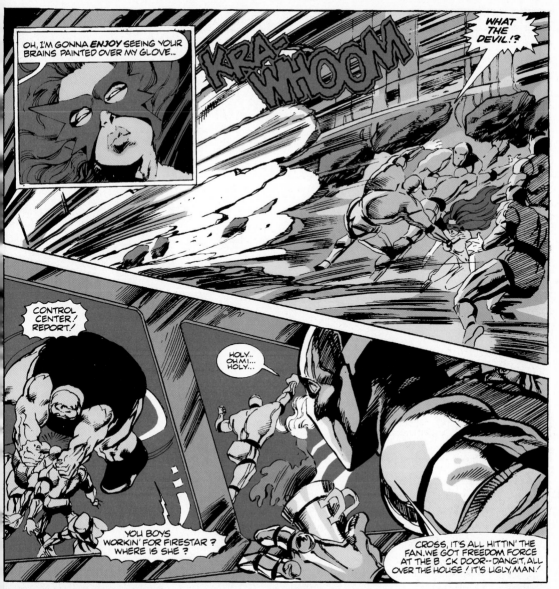

OH, I'M GONNA *ENJOY* SEEING YOUR BRAINS PAINTED OVER MY GLOVE...

KRA-WHOOM

WHAT THE DEVIL!?

CONTROL CENTER! REPORT!

HOLY... OH MI... HOLY...

YOU BOYS WORKIN' FOR FIRESTAR? WHERE IS SHE?

CROSS, IT'S ALL HITTIN' THE FAN. WE GOT FREEDOM FORCE AT THE B CK DOOR--DANGIT, ALL OVER THE HOUSE! IT'S UGLY, MAN!

CHOOM

KA'CHOOM

YOU STUPID...! YOU LED FREEDOM FORCE RIGHT TO US!

I'M NOT SURE I'M HAPPY ABOUT IT, EITHER--EVEN THOUGH THEY MAY HAVE SAVED MY LIFE!

EZZK

205

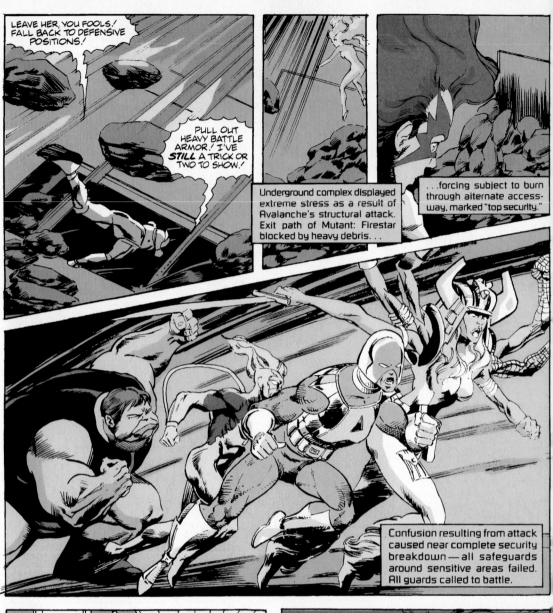

LEAVE HER, YOU FOOLS.! FALL BACK TO DEFENSIVE POSITIONS!

PULL OUT HEAVY BATTLE ARMOR.! I'VE **STILL** A TRICK OR TWO TO SHOW.!

Underground complex displayed extreme stress as a result of Avalanche's structural attack. Exit path of Mutant: Firestar blocked by heavy debris...

...forcing subject to burn through alternate access-way, marked "top security."

Confusion resulting from attack caused near complete security breakdown — all safeguards around sensitive areas failed. All guards called to battle.

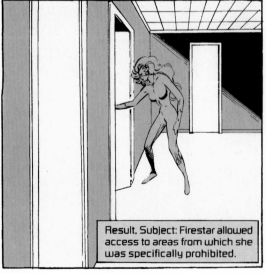

Result, Subject: Firestar allowed access to areas from which she was specifically prohibited.

She saw what she was never meant to see.

206

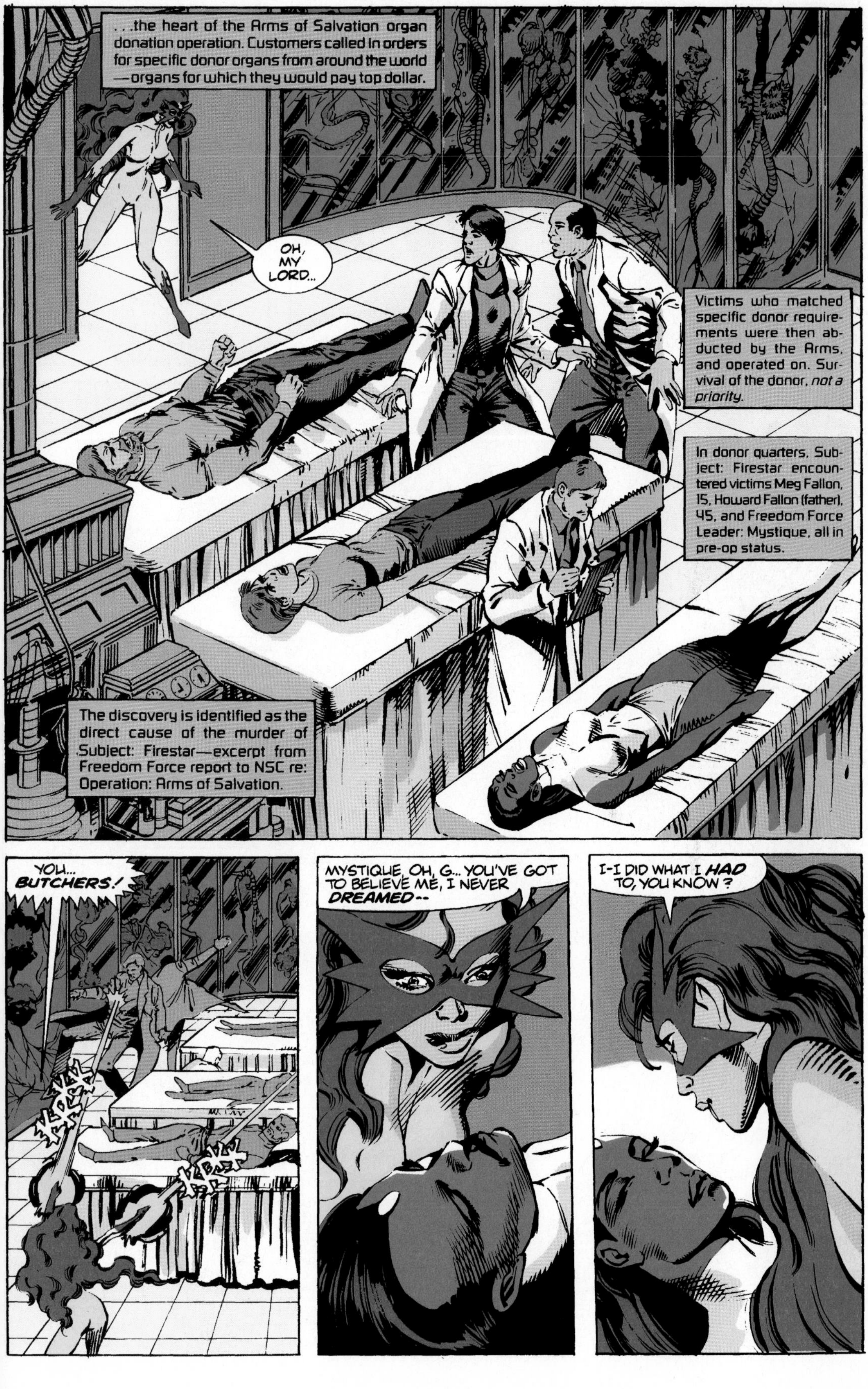
. . .the heart of the Arms of Salvation organ donation operation. Customers called in orders for specific donor organs from around the world —organs for which they would pay top dollar.
OH, MY LORD...
Victims who matched specific donor requirements were then abducted by the Arms, and operated on. Survival of the donor, *not a priority*.
In donor quarters, Subject: Firestar encountered victims Meg Fallon, 15, Howard Fallon (father), 45, and Freedom Force Leader: Mystique, all in pre-op status.
The discovery is identified as the direct cause of the murder of Subject: Firestar—excerpt from Freedom Force report to NSC re: Operation: Arms of Salvation.
YOU... **BUTCHERS!**
MYSTIQUE, OH, G... YOU'VE GOT TO BELIEVE ME, I NEVER **DREAMED**--
I-I DID WHAT I **HAD** TO, YOU KNOW?

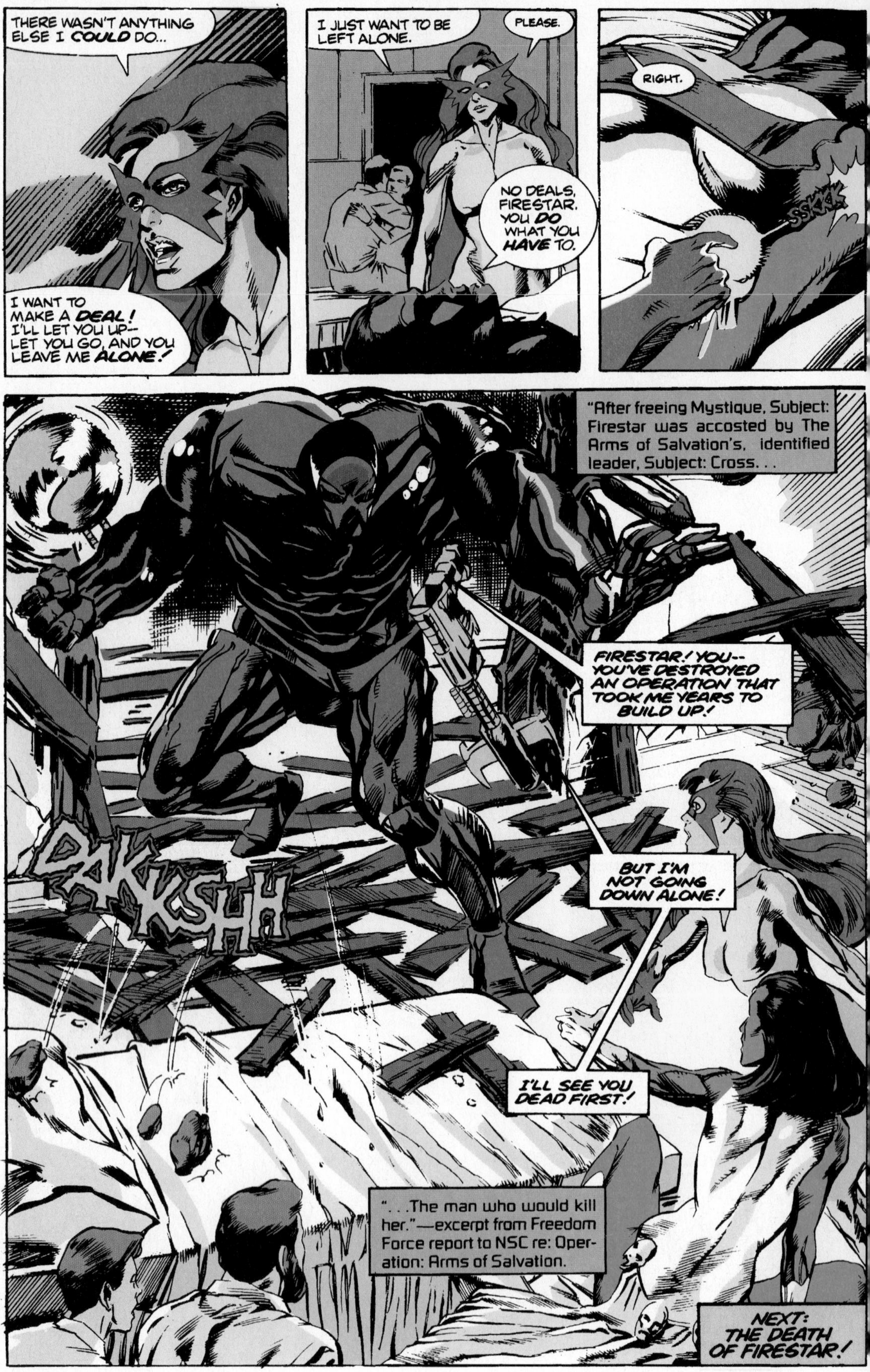
THERE WASN'T ANYTHING ELSE I COULD DO...
I WANT TO MAKE A DEAL! I'LL LET YOU UP-- LET YOU GO, AND YOU LEAVE ME ALONE!
I JUST WANT TO BE LEFT ALONE.
PLEASE.
NO DEALS, FIRESTAR. YOU DO WHAT YOU HAVE TO.
RIGHT.
"After freeing Mystique, Subject: Firestar was accosted by The Arms of Salvation's, identified leader, Subject: Cross. . .
FIRESTAR! YOU-- YOU'VE DESTROYED AN OPERATION THAT TOOK ME YEARS TO BUILD UP!
DAKSH
BUT I'M NOT GOING DOWN ALONE!
I'LL SEE YOU DEAD FIRST!
". . .The man who would kill her."—excerpt from Freedom Force report to NSC re: Operation: Arms of Salvation.
NEXT: THE DEATH OF FIRESTAR!

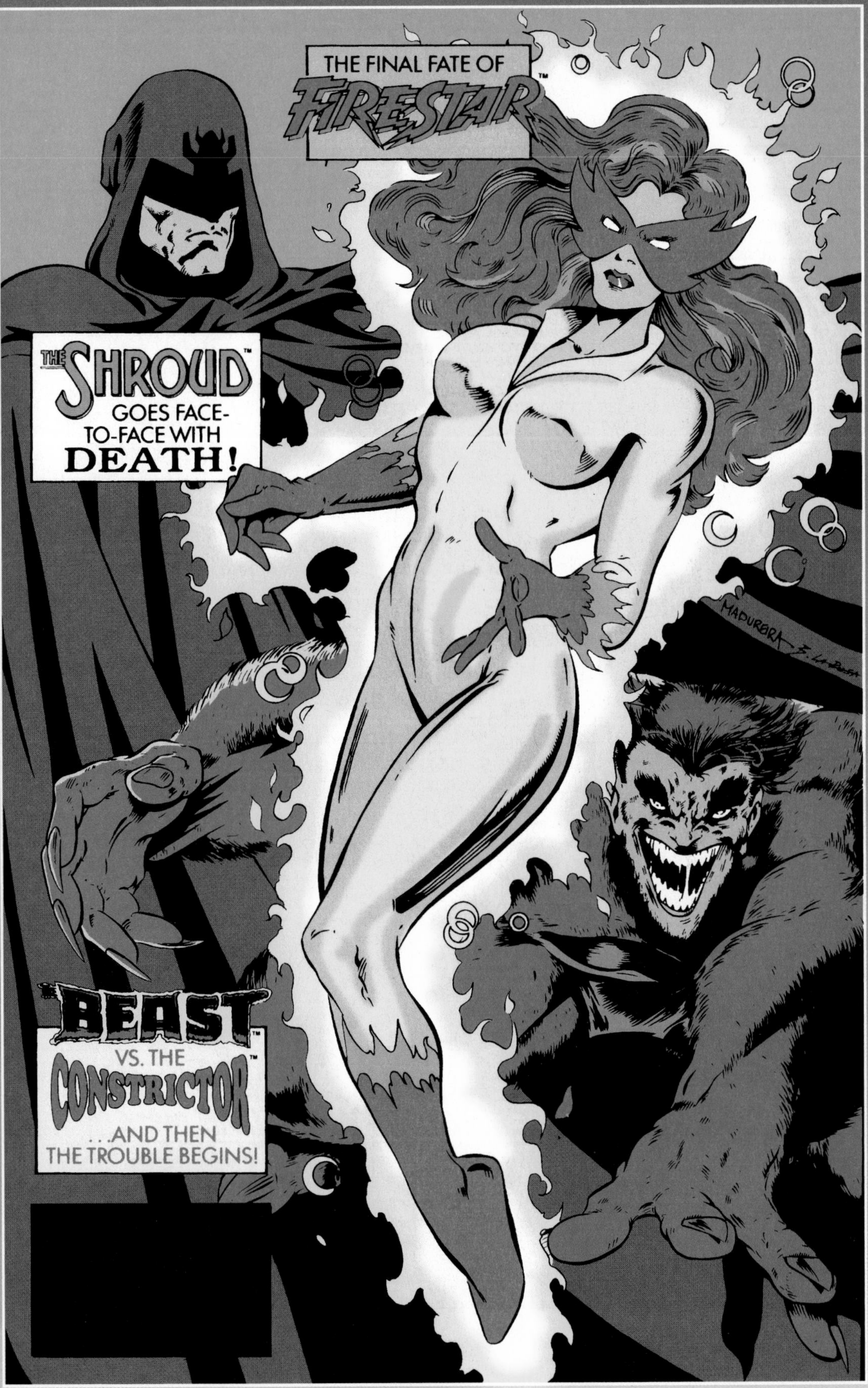
THE FINAL FATE OF
FIRESTAR™
THE SHROUD™
GOES FACE-
TO-FACE WITH
DEATH!
THE BEAST™
VS. THE
CONSTRICTOR™
. . .AND THEN
THE TROUBLE BEGINS!

Writers: Marcus McLaurin & Marie Javins • Penciler: Dwayne Turner • Inker: Chris Ivy • Colorist: Marcus McLaurin
Letterers: Diana Albers & Dave Sharpe • Assistant Editor: Mark Powers • Editor: Terry Kavanagh

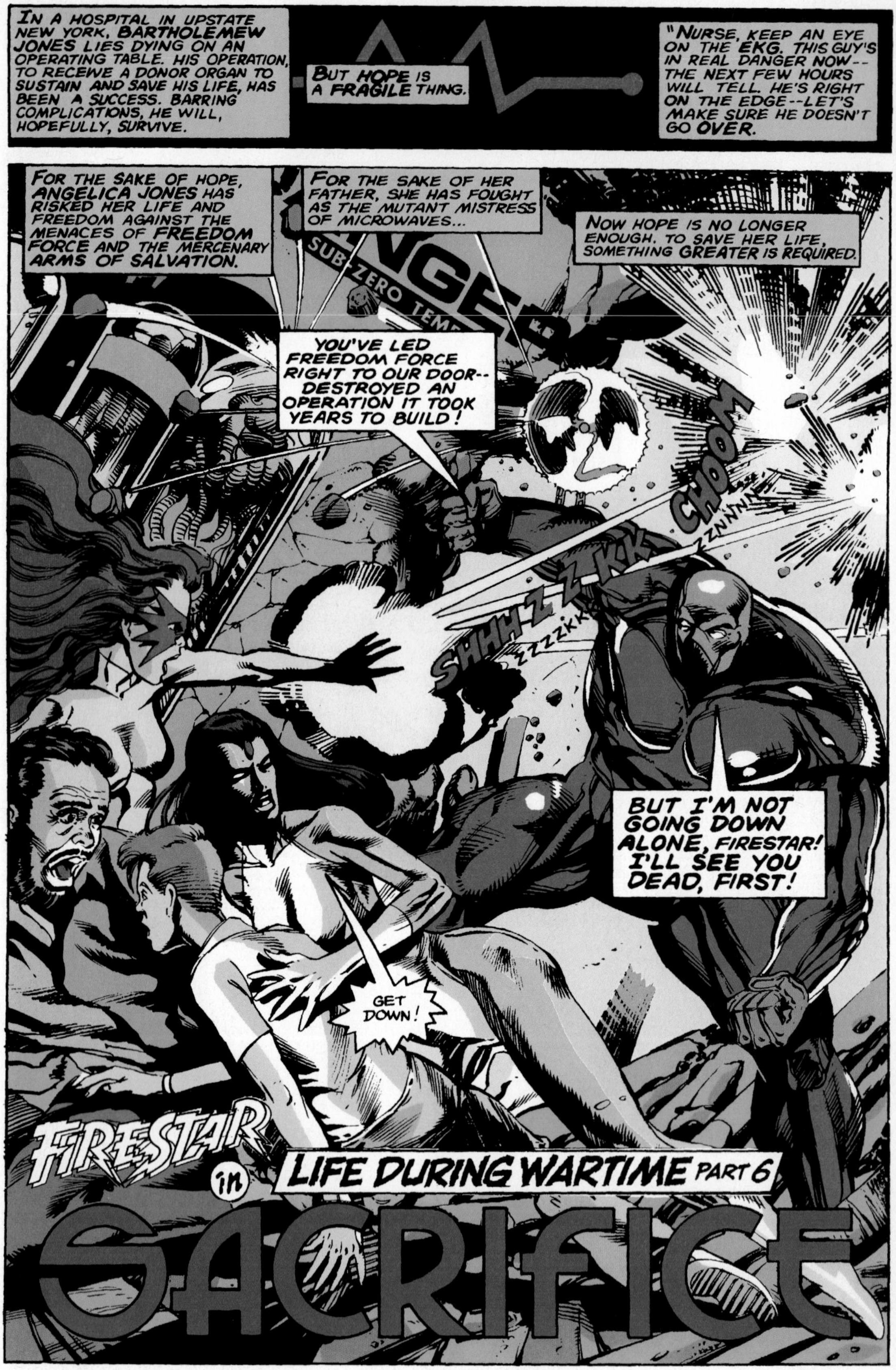

IN A HOSPITAL IN UPSTATE NEW YORK, BARTHOLEMEW JONES LIES DYING ON AN OPERATING TABLE. HIS OPERATION, TO RECEIVE A DONOR ORGAN TO SUSTAIN AND SAVE HIS LIFE, HAS BEEN A SUCCESS. BARRING COMPLICATIONS, HE WILL, HOPEFULLY, SURVIVE.
BUT HOPE IS A FRAGILE THING.
"NURSE, KEEP AN EYE ON THE EKG. THIS GUY'S IN REAL DANGER NOW-- THE NEXT FEW HOURS WILL TELL. HE'S RIGHT ON THE EDGE--LET'S MAKE SURE HE DOESN'T GO OVER.
FOR THE SAKE OF HOPE, ANGELICA JONES HAS RISKED HER LIFE AND FREEDOM AGAINST THE MENACES OF FREEDOM FORCE AND THE MERCENARY ARMS OF SALVATION.
FOR THE SAKE OF HER FATHER, SHE HAS FOUGHT AS THE MUTANT MISTRESS OF MICROWAVES...
NOW HOPE IS NO LONGER ENOUGH. TO SAVE HER LIFE, SOMETHING GREATER IS REQUIRED.
SUB-ZERO TEMP
YOU'VE LED FREEDOM FORCE RIGHT TO OUR DOOR-- DESTROYED AN OPERATION IT TOOK YEARS TO BUILD!
CHOOM
SHHHZZZKKK
ZZZZKK
ZNNNN
BUT I'M NOT GOING DOWN ALONE, FIRESTAR! I'LL SEE YOU DEAD, FIRST!
GET DOWN!
FIRESTAR in
LIFE DURING WARTIME PART 6
SACRIFICE

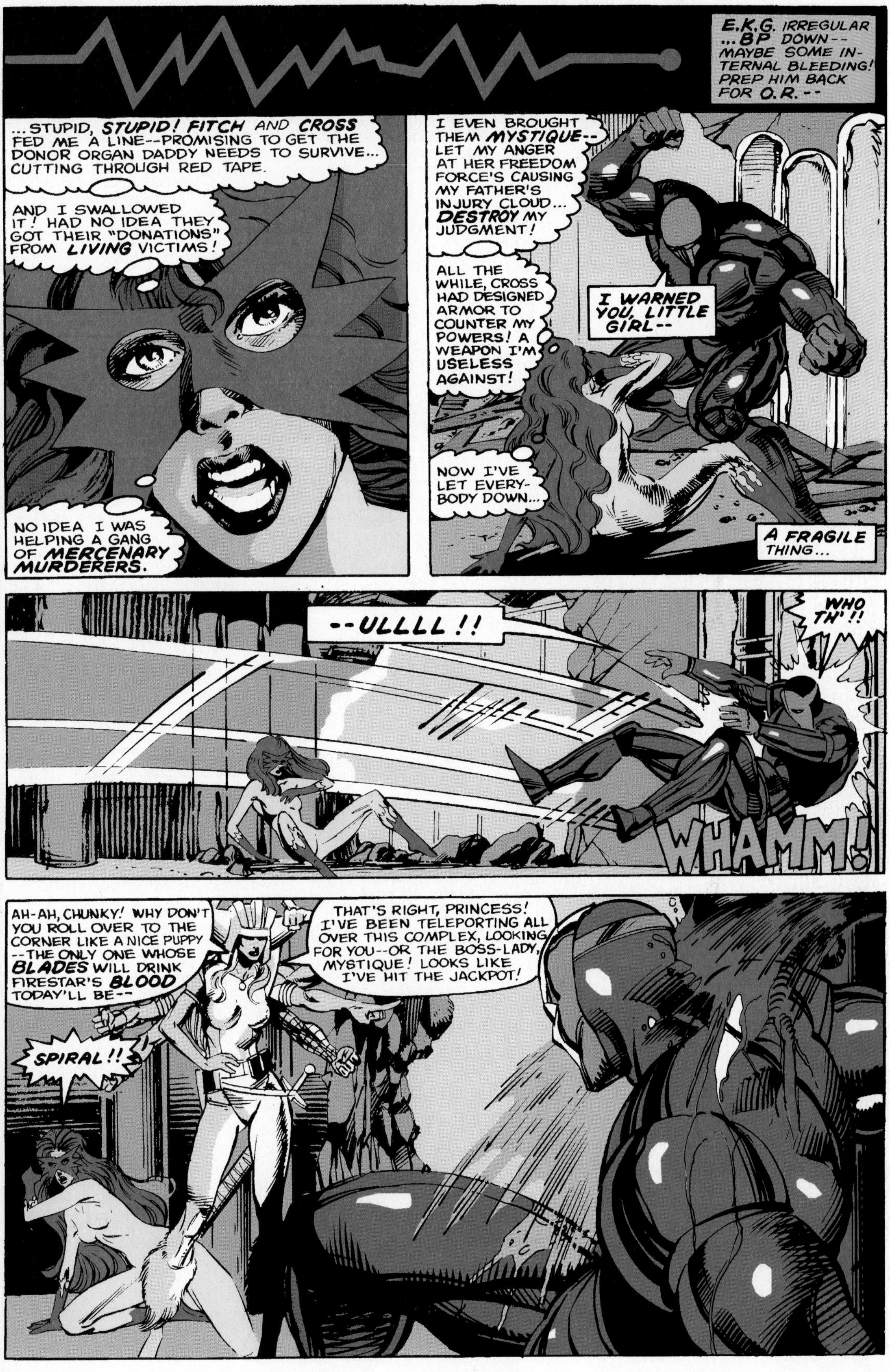
E.K.G. IRREGULAR ...BP DOWN-- MAYBE SOME INTERNAL BLEEDING! PREP HIM BACK FOR O.R.--
...STUPID, STUPID! FITCH AND CROSS FED ME A LINE--PROMISING TO GET THE DONOR ORGAN DADDY NEEDS TO SURVIVE... CUTTING THROUGH RED TAPE.
AND I SWALLOWED IT! HAD NO IDEA THEY GOT THEIR "DONATIONS" FROM LIVING VICTIMS!
NO IDEA I WAS HELPING A GANG OF MERCENARY MURDERERS.
I EVEN BROUGHT THEM MYSTIQUE--LET MY ANGER AT HER FREEDOM FORCE'S CAUSING MY FATHER'S INJURY CLOUD... DESTROY MY JUDGMENT!
ALL THE WHILE, CROSS HAD DESIGNED ARMOR TO COUNTER MY POWERS! A WEAPON I'M USELESS AGAINST!
I WARNED YOU, LITTLE GIRL--
NOW I'VE LET EVERYBODY DOWN...
A FRAGILE THING...
--ULLLL!!
WHO TH'!!
WHAMM!
AH-AH, CHUNKY! WHY DON'T YOU ROLL OVER TO THE CORNER LIKE A NICE PUPPY --THE ONLY ONE WHOSE BLADES WILL DRINK FIRESTAR'S BLOOD TODAY'LL BE--
THAT'S RIGHT, PRINCESS! I'VE BEEN TELEPORTING ALL OVER THIS COMPLEX, LOOKING FOR YOU--OR THE BOSS-LADY, MYSTIQUE! LOOKS LIKE I'VE HIT THE JACKPOT!
SPIRAL!!

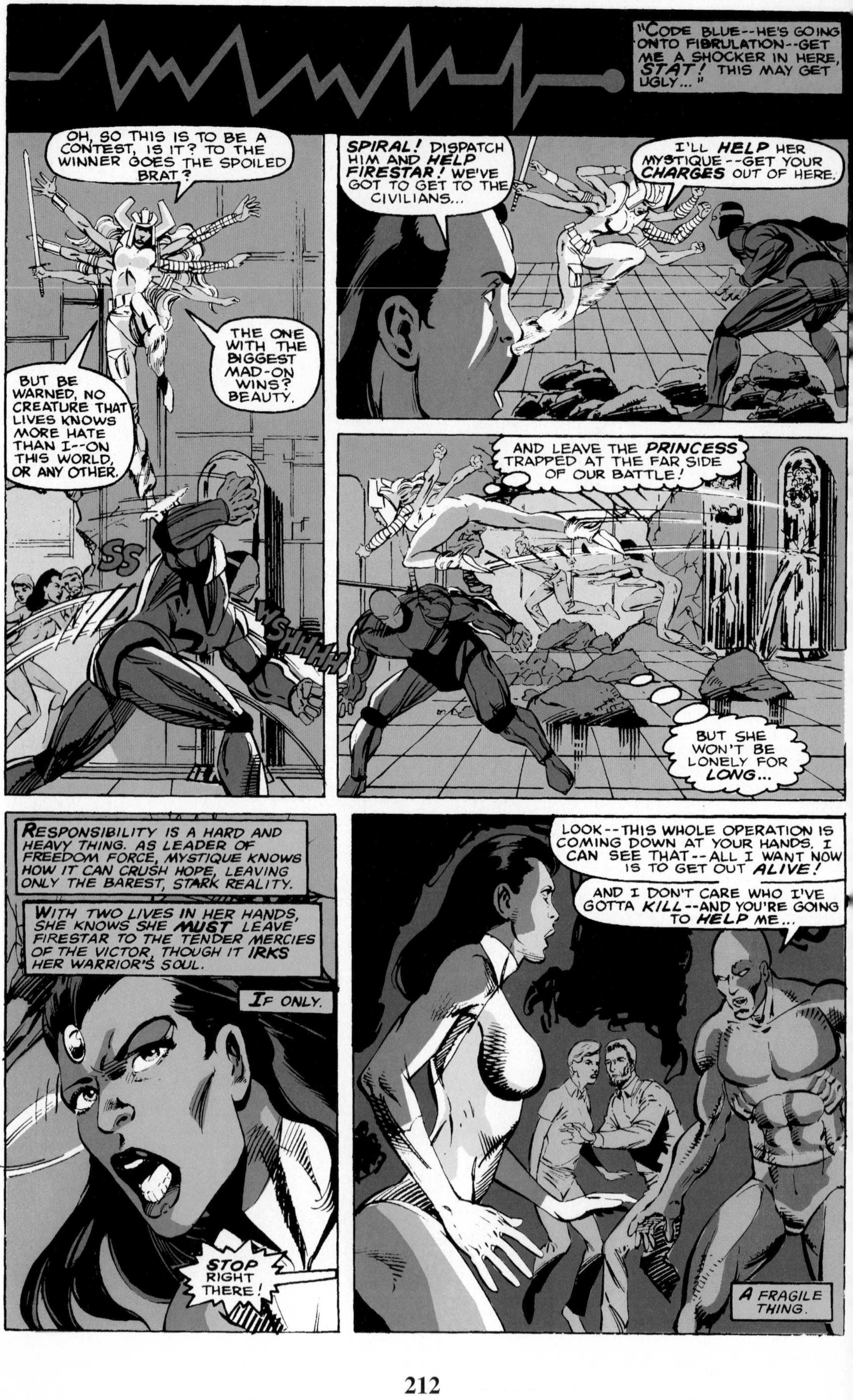
"CODE BLUE--HE'S GOING ONTO FIBRULATION--GET ME A SHOCKER IN HERE, STAT! THIS MAY GET UGLY..."
OH, SO THIS IS TO BE A CONTEST, IS IT? TO THE WINNER GOES THE SPOILED BRAT?
BUT BE WARNED, NO CREATURE THAT LIVES KNOWS MORE HATE THAN I--ON THIS WORLD, OR ANY OTHER.
THE ONE WITH THE BIGGEST MAD-ON WINS? BEAUTY.
SS
WSHHHH
SPIRAL! DISPATCH HIM AND HELP FIRESTAR! WE'VE GOT TO GET TO THE CIVILIANS...
I'LL HELP HER MYSTIQUE--GET YOUR CHARGES OUT OF HERE.
AND LEAVE THE PRINCESS TRAPPED AT THE FAR SIDE OF OUR BATTLE!
BUT SHE WON'T BE LONELY FOR LONG...
RESPONSIBILITY IS A HARD AND HEAVY THING. AS LEADER OF FREEDOM FORCE, MYSTIQUE KNOWS HOW IT CAN CRUSH HOPE, LEAVING ONLY THE BAREST, STARK REALITY.
WITH TWO LIVES IN HER HANDS, SHE KNOWS SHE MUST LEAVE FIRESTAR TO THE TENDER MERCIES OF THE VICTOR, THOUGH IT IRKS HER WARRIOR'S SOUL.
IF ONLY.
STOP RIGHT THERE!
LOOK--THIS WHOLE OPERATION IS COMING DOWN AT YOUR HANDS. I CAN SEE THAT--ALL I WANT NOW IS TO GET OUT ALIVE!
AND I DON'T CARE WHO I'VE GOTTA KILL--AND YOU'RE GOING TO HELP ME...
A FRAGILE THING.

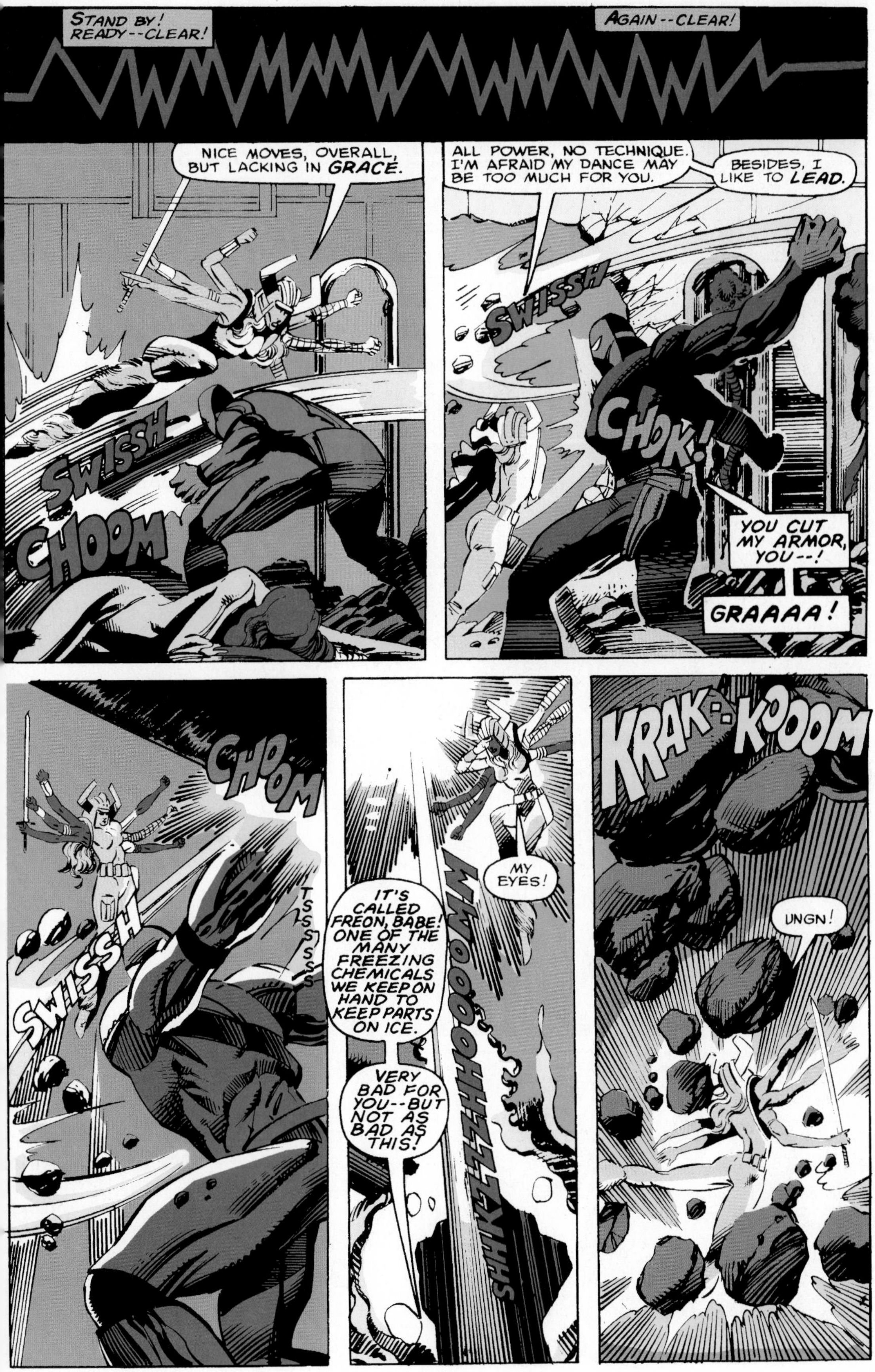
STAND BY! READY--CLEAR!
AGAIN--CLEAR!
NICE MOVES, OVERALL, BUT LACKING IN GRACE.
SWISSH
CHOOM
ALL POWER, NO TECHNIQUE. I'M AFRAID MY DANCE MAY BE TOO MUCH FOR YOU.
BESIDES, I LIKE TO LEAD.
SWISSH
CHOK!
YOU CUT MY ARMOR, YOU--!
GRAAAA!
CHOOM
SWISSH
TSSSSSS
MY EYES!
IT'S CALLED FREON, BABE! ONE OF THE MANY FREEZING CHEMICALS WE KEEP ON HAND TO KEEP PARTS ON ICE.
VERY BAD FOR YOU--BUT NOT AS BAD AS THIS!
SHHKZZHHOOOOOWM
KRAK-KOOOM
UNGN!

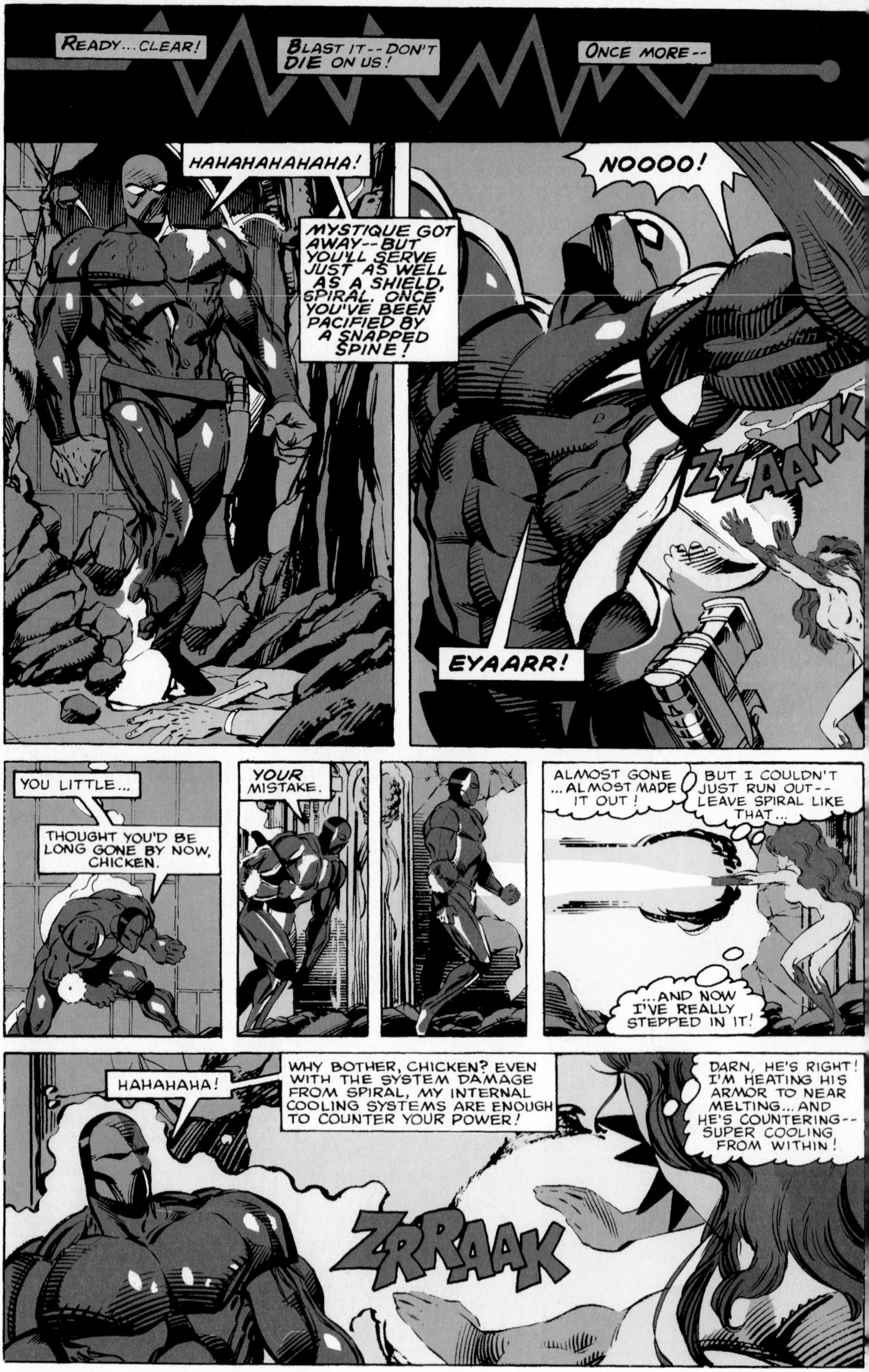

READY... CLEAR!
BLAST IT--DON'T DIE ON US!
ONCE MORE--
HAHAHAHAHAHA!
MYSTIQUE GOT AWAY--BUT YOU'LL SERVE JUST AS WELL AS A SHIELD, SPIRAL. ONCE YOU'VE BEEN PACIFIED BY A SNAPPED SPINE!
NOOOO!
ZZAAKK
EYAARR!
YOU LITTLE...
THOUGHT YOU'D BE LONG GONE BY NOW, CHICKEN.
YOUR MISTAKE.
ALMOST GONE ...ALMOST MADE IT OUT!
BUT I COULDN'T JUST RUN OUT--LEAVE SPIRAL LIKE THAT...
...AND NOW I'VE REALLY STEPPED IN IT!
HAHAHAHA!
WHY BOTHER, CHICKEN? EVEN WITH THE SYSTEM DAMAGE FROM SPIRAL, MY INTERNAL COOLING SYSTEMS ARE ENOUGH TO COUNTER YOUR POWER!
DARN, HE'S RIGHT! I'M HEATING HIS ARMOR TO NEAR MELTING... AND HE'S COUNTERING--SUPER COOLING FROM WITHIN!
ZRRAAK

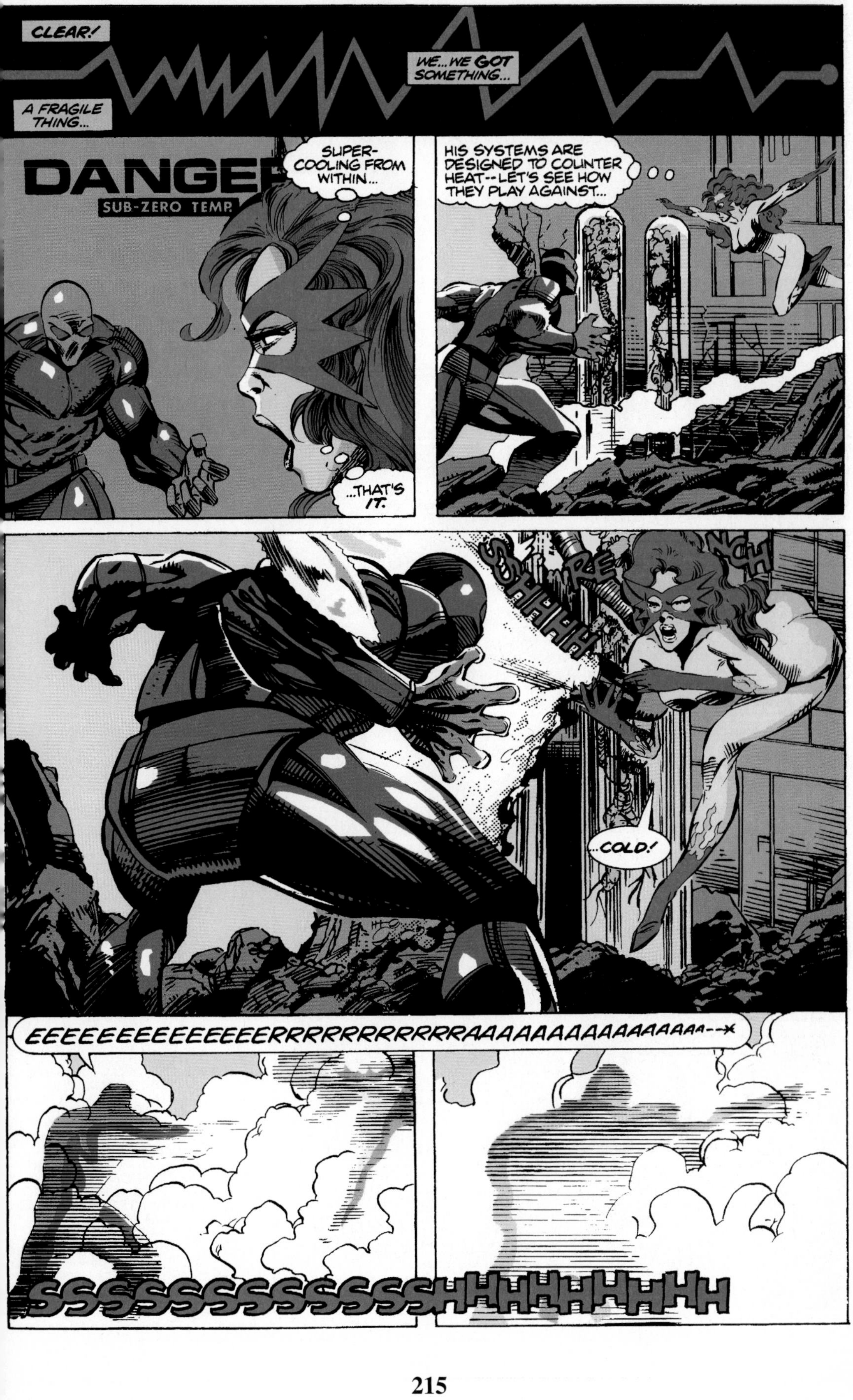
CLEAR!
A FRAGILE THING...
WE... WE GOT SOMETHING...
DANGER
SUB-ZERO TEMP.
SUPER-COOLING FROM WITHIN...
...THAT'S IT.
HIS SYSTEMS ARE DESIGNED TO COUNTER HEAT--LET'S SEE HOW THEY PLAY AGAINST...
SSHHHHH
...COLD!
EEEEEEEEEEEEEEERRRRRRRRRRRAAAAAAAAAAAAAA--
SSSSSSSSSSSSSSSHHHHHHHHHHH

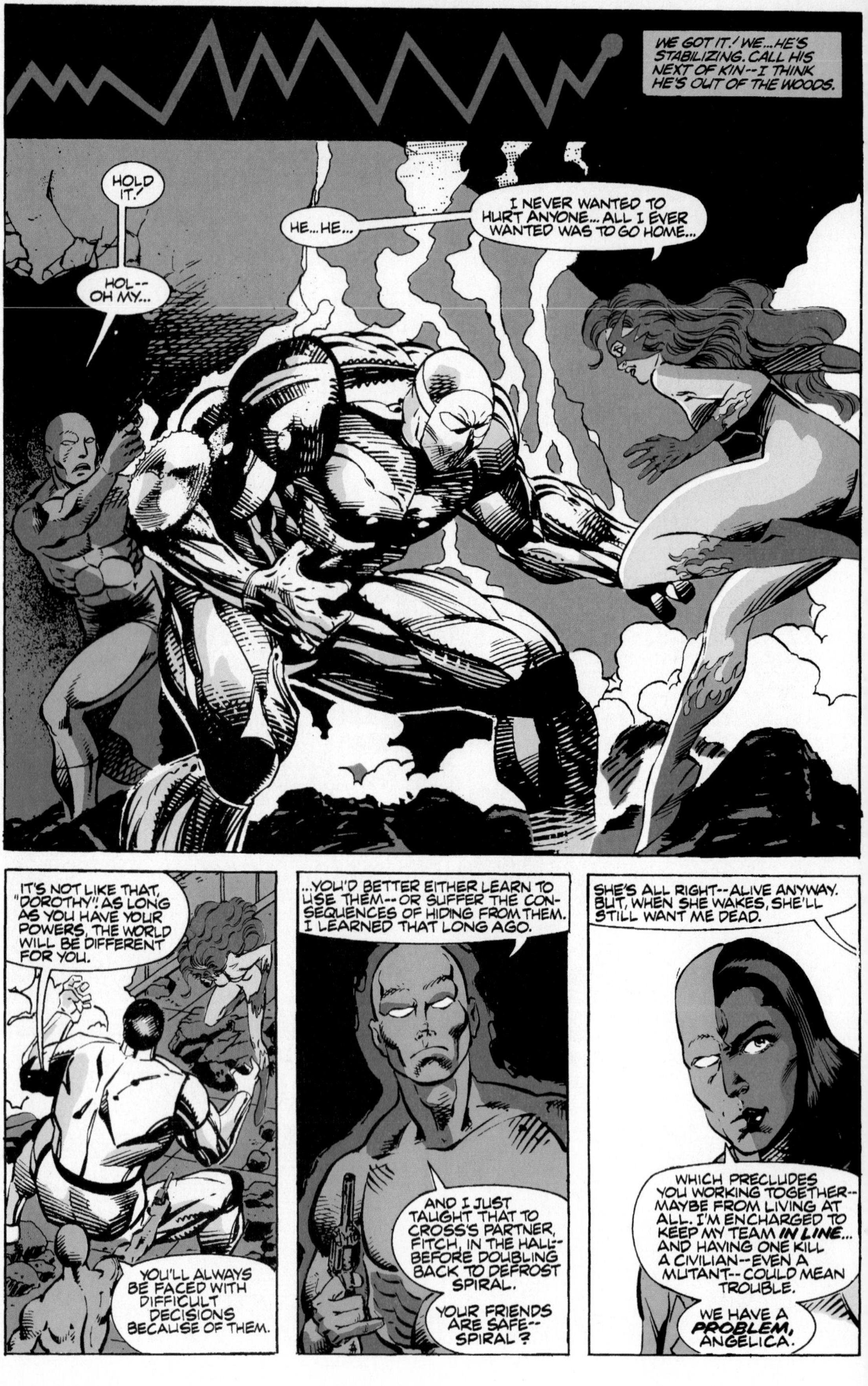
WE GOT IT! WE...HE'S STABILIZING. CALL HIS NEXT OF KIN--I THINK HE'S OUT OF THE WOODS.
HOLD IT!
HOL-- OH MY...
HE...HE...
I NEVER WANTED TO HURT ANYONE... ALL I EVER WANTED WAS TO GO HOME...
IT'S NOT LIKE THAT, "DOROTHY"! AS LONG AS YOU HAVE YOUR POWERS, THE WORLD WILL BE DIFFERENT FOR YOU.
YOU'LL ALWAYS BE FACED WITH DIFFICULT DECISIONS BECAUSE OF THEM.
...YOU'D BETTER EITHER LEARN TO USE THEM--OR SUFFER THE CONSEQUENCES OF HIDING FROM THEM. I LEARNED THAT LONG AGO.
AND I JUST TAUGHT THAT TO CROSS'S PARTNER, FITCH, IN THE HALL--BEFORE DOUBLING BACK TO DEFROST SPIRAL.
YOUR FRIENDS ARE SAFE--SPIRAL?
SHE'S ALL RIGHT--ALIVE ANYWAY. BUT, WHEN SHE WAKES, SHE'LL STILL WANT ME DEAD.
WHICH PRECLUDES YOU WORKING TOGETHER--MAYBE FROM LIVING AT ALL. I'M ENCHARGED TO KEEP MY TEAM IN LINE... AND HAVING ONE KILL A CIVILIAN--EVEN A MUTANT--COULD MEAN TROUBLE.
WE HAVE A PROBLEM, ANGELICA.

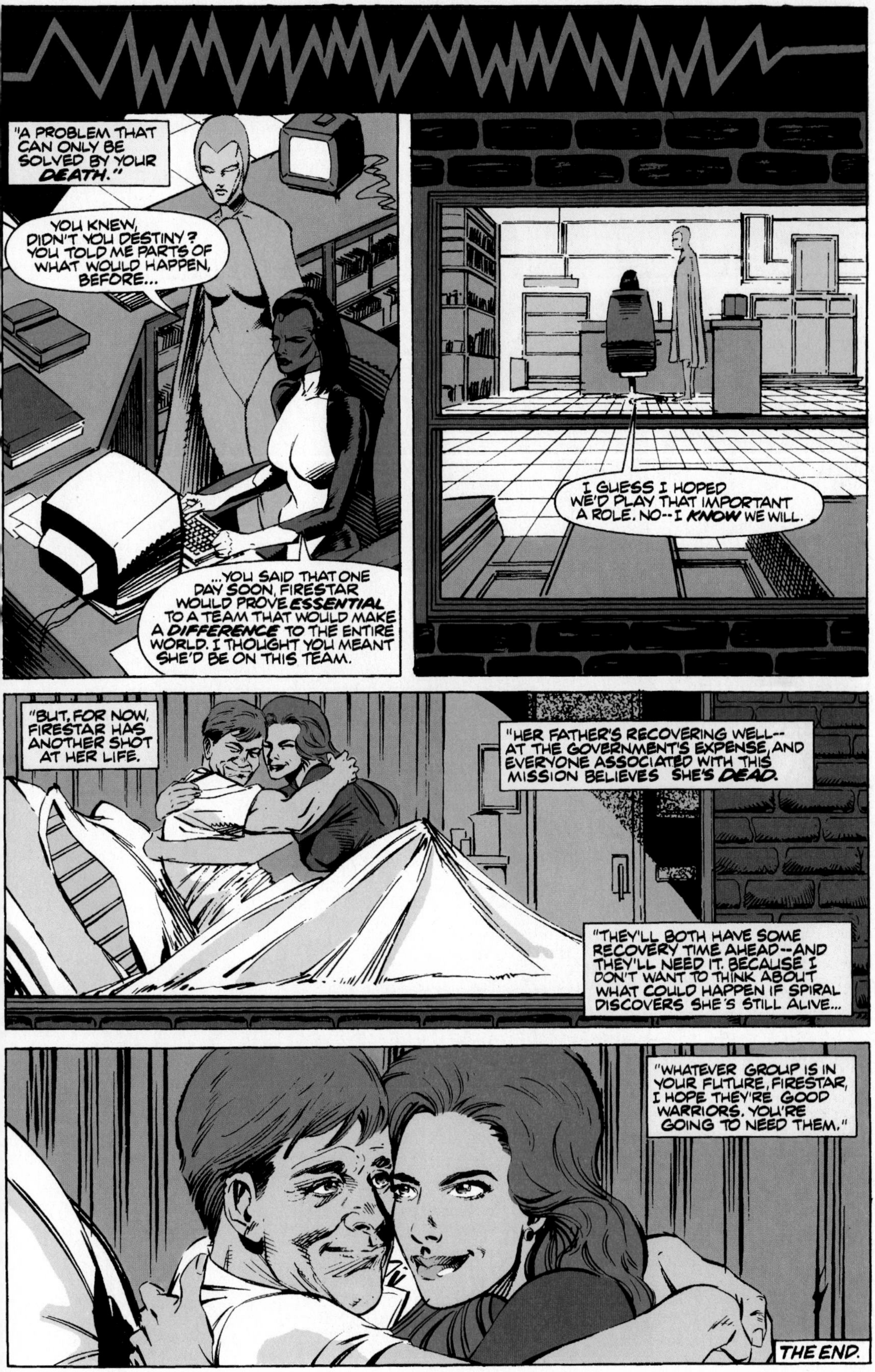
"A PROBLEM THAT CAN ONLY BE SOLVED BY YOUR DEATH."
YOU KNEW, DIDN'T YOU DESTINY? YOU TOLD ME PARTS OF WHAT WOULD HAPPEN, BEFORE...
...YOU SAID THAT ONE DAY SOON, FIRESTAR WOULD PROVE ESSENTIAL TO A TEAM THAT WOULD MAKE A DIFFERENCE TO THE ENTIRE WORLD. I THOUGHT YOU MEANT SHE'D BE ON THIS TEAM.
I GUESS I HOPED WE'D PLAY THAT IMPORTANT A ROLE. NO--I KNOW WE WILL.
"BUT, FOR NOW, FIRESTAR HAS ANOTHER SHOT AT HER LIFE.
"HER FATHER'S RECOVERING WELL--AT THE GOVERNMENT'S EXPENSE, AND EVERYONE ASSOCIATED WITH THIS MISSION BELIEVES SHE'S DEAD.
"THEY'LL BOTH HAVE SOME RECOVERY TIME AHEAD--AND THEY'LL NEED IT. BECAUSE I DON'T WANT TO THINK ABOUT WHAT COULD HAPPEN IF SPIRAL DISCOVERS SHE'S STILL ALIVE...
"WHATEVER GROUP IS IN YOUR FUTURE, FIRESTAR, I HOPE THEY'RE GOOD WARRIORS. YOU'RE GOING TO NEED THEM."
THE END.

To celebrate the 25th anniversary of the *Amazing Friends* cartoon, Marvel published a one-shot that brought the three TV stars together in the mainstream Marvel Universe — and included several tongue-in-cheek references to the cartoon.

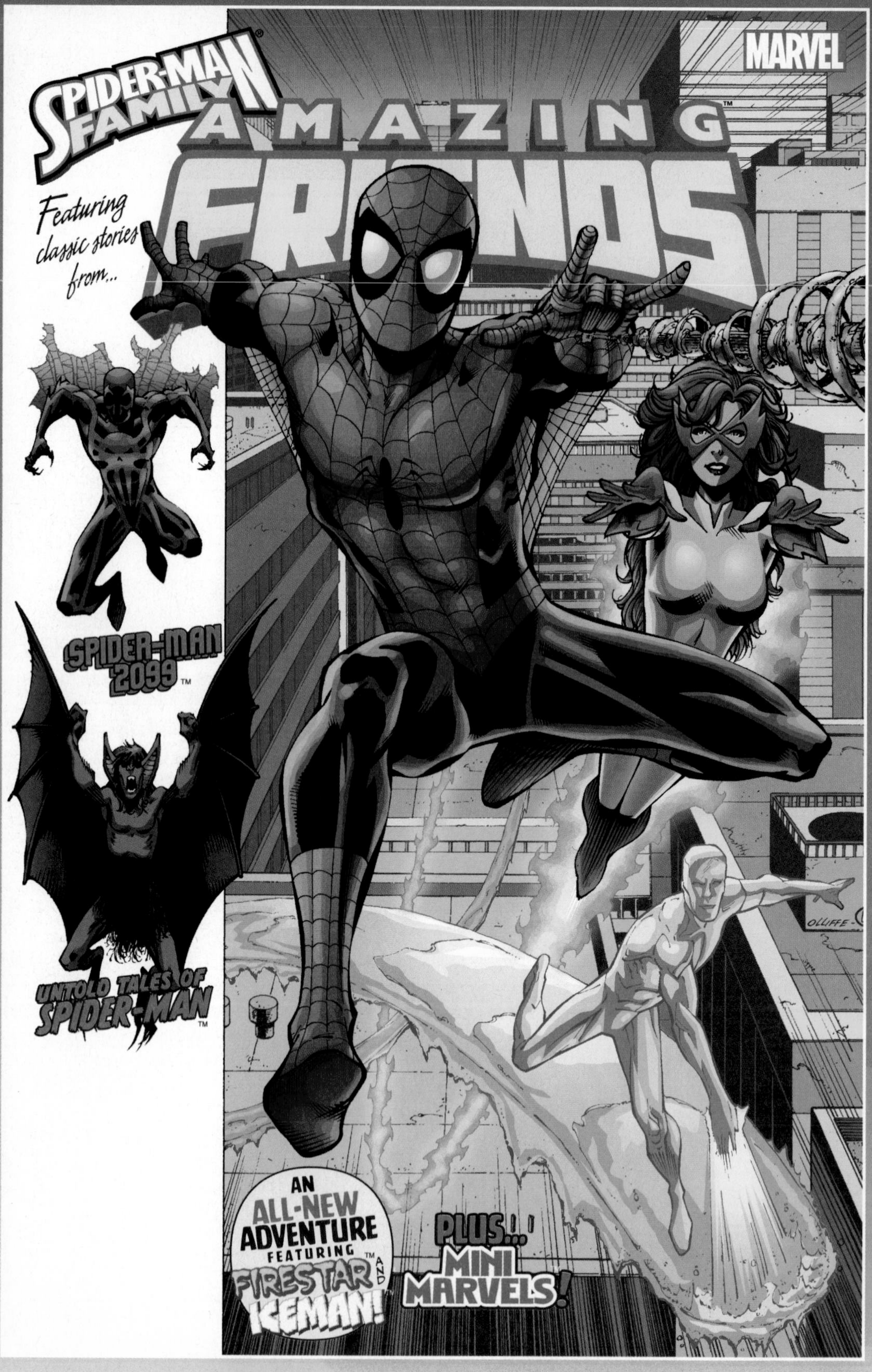

MARVEL
SPIDER-MAN FAMILY
AMAZING FRIENDS
Featuring classic stories from...
SPIDER-MAN 2099
UNTOLD TALES OF SPIDER-MAN
OLLIFFE
AN ALL-NEW ADVENTURE FEATURING FIRESTAR AND ICEMAN!
PLUS...! MINI MARVELS!

Writer: Sean McKeever • Pencilers: Patrick Olliffe, Casey Jones, Kano & Nick Dragotta • Inkers: Livesay, Vince Russell, Kano, Alvaro Lopez & Nick Dragotta
Colorist: Lee Loughridge • Letterer: Artmonkeys' Melanie Olsen • Consulting Editor: Mark Paniccia • Editor: Nathan Cosby

[This story takes place prior to *Web of Spider-Man #75*, which also featured a team-up between Spider-Man, Firestar and Iceman.]

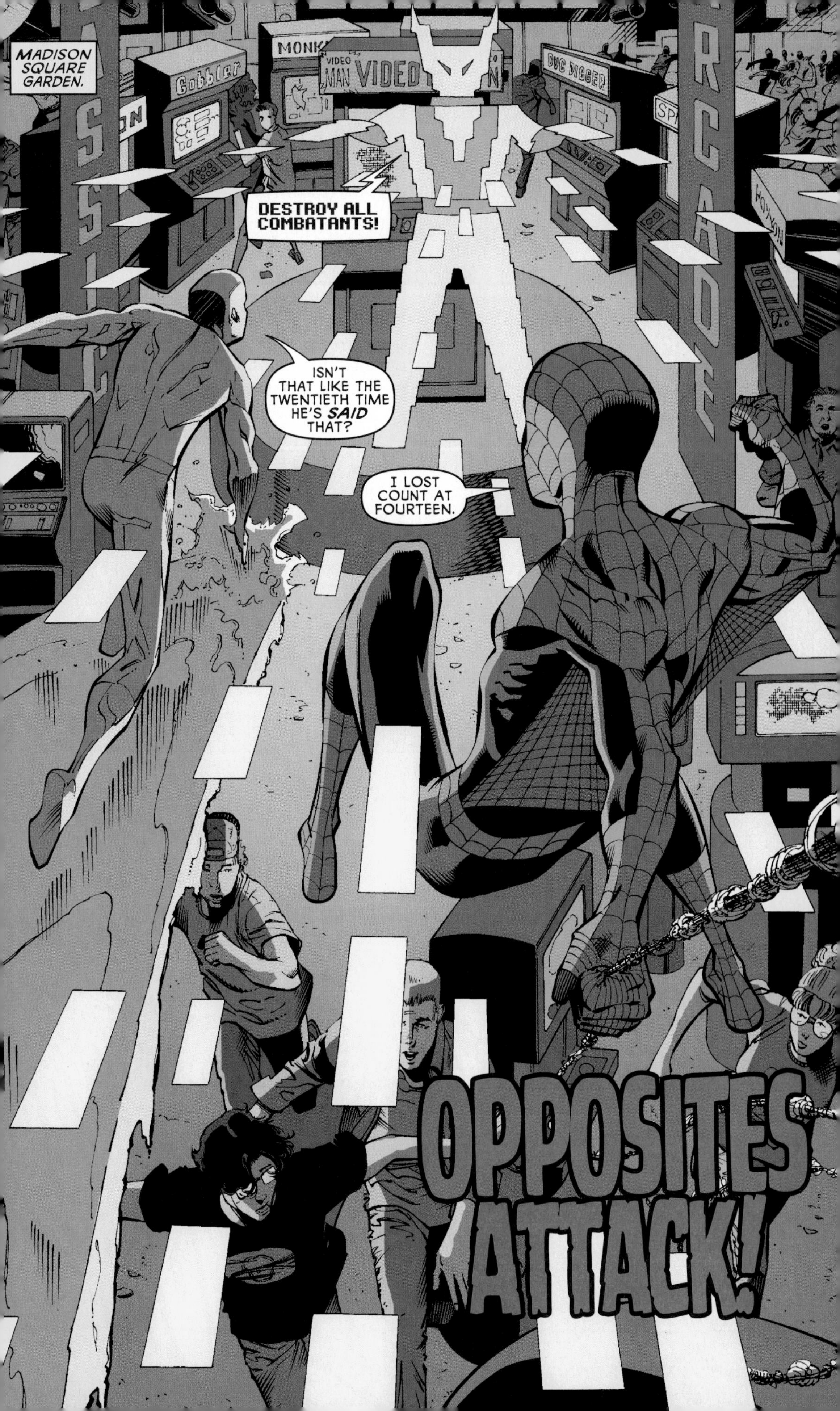
MADISON SQUARE GARDEN.
DESTROY ALL COMBATANTS!
ISN'T THAT LIKE THE TWENTIETH TIME HE'S *SAID* THAT?
I LOST COUNT AT FOURTEEN.
OPPOSITES ATTACK!

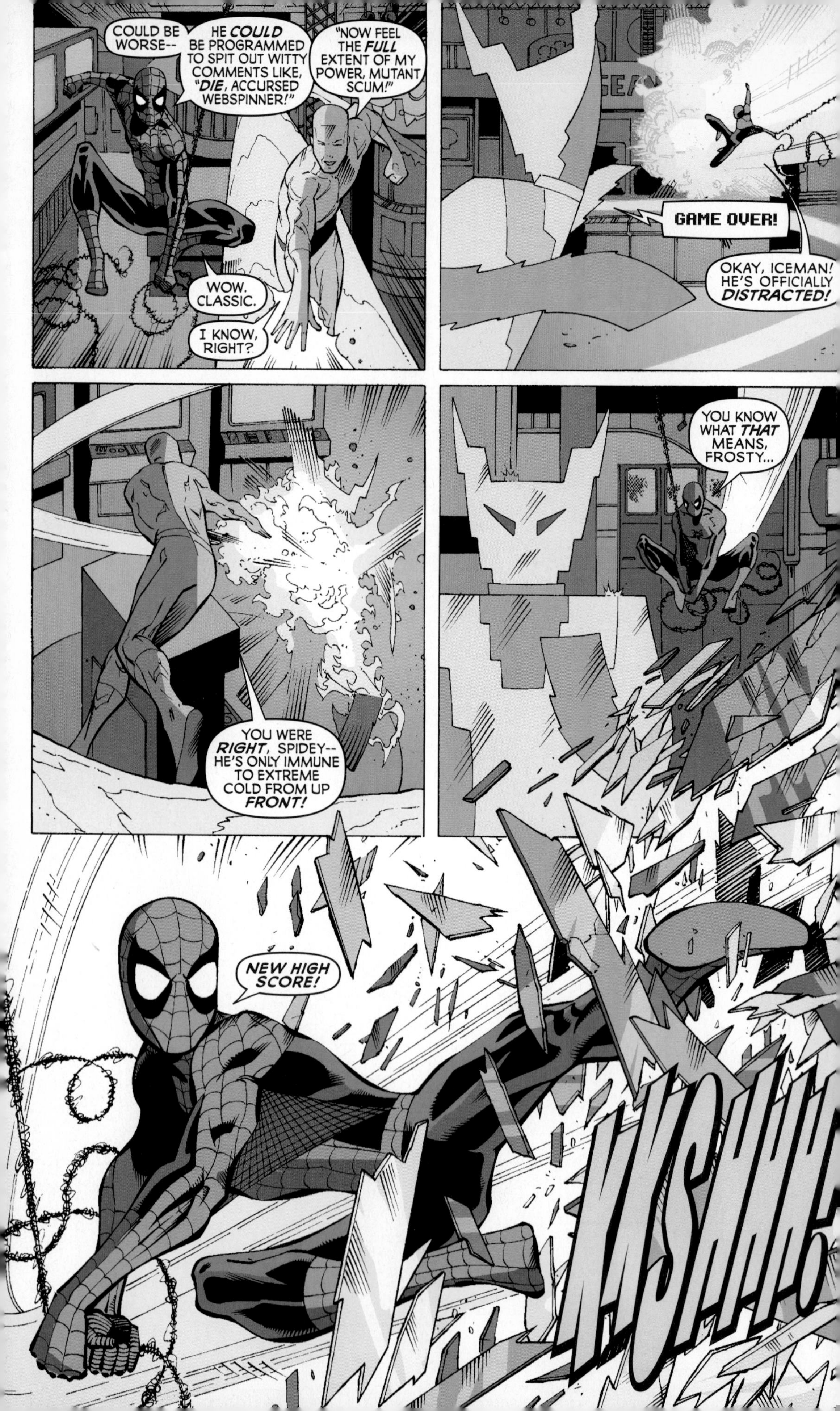

COULD BE WORSE--
HE COULD BE PROGRAMMED TO SPIT OUT WITTY COMMENTS LIKE, "DIE, ACCURSED WEBSPINNER!"
"NOW FEEL THE FULL EXTENT OF MY POWER, MUTANT SCUM!"
WOW. CLASSIC.
I KNOW, RIGHT?
GAME OVER!
OKAY, ICEMAN! HE'S OFFICIALLY DISTRACTED!
YOU WERE RIGHT, SPIDEY--HE'S ONLY IMMUNE TO EXTREME COLD FROM UP FRONT!
YOU KNOW WHAT THAT MEANS, FROSTY...
NEW HIGH SCORE!

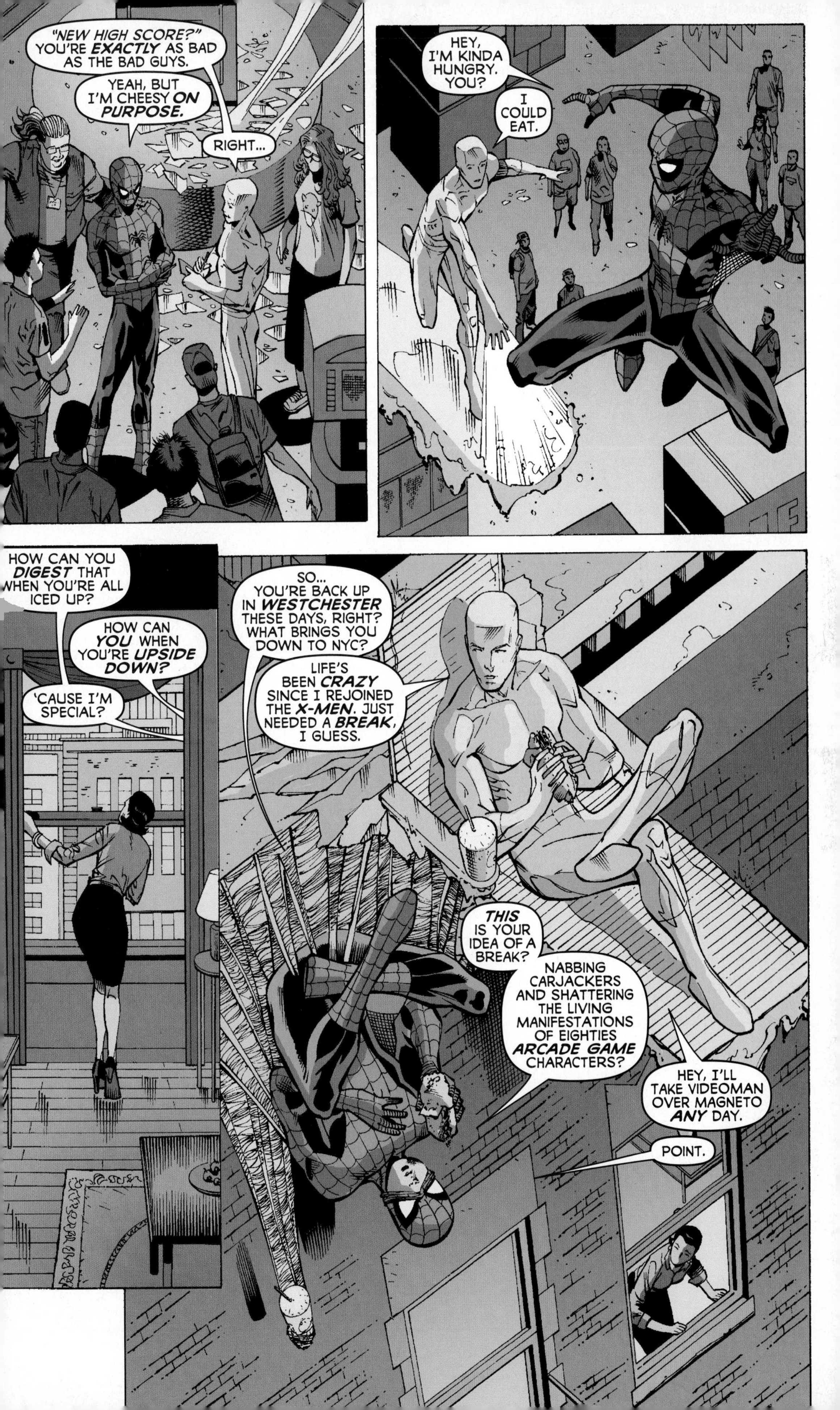
"NEW HIGH SCORE?" YOU'RE EXACTLY AS BAD AS THE BAD GUYS.
YEAH, BUT I'M CHEESY ON PURPOSE.
RIGHT...
HEY, I'M KINDA HUNGRY. YOU?
I COULD EAT.
HOW CAN YOU DIGEST THAT WHEN YOU'RE ALL ICED UP?
HOW CAN YOU WHEN YOU'RE UPSIDE DOWN?
'CAUSE I'M SPECIAL?
SO... YOU'RE BACK UP IN WESTCHESTER THESE DAYS, RIGHT? WHAT BRINGS YOU DOWN TO NYC?
LIFE'S BEEN CRAZY SINCE I REJOINED THE X-MEN. JUST NEEDED A BREAK, I GUESS.
THIS IS YOUR IDEA OF A BREAK?
NABBING CARJACKERS AND SHATTERING THE LIVING MANIFESTATIONS OF EIGHTIES ARCADE GAME CHARACTERS?
HEY, I'LL TAKE VIDEOMAN OVER MAGNETO ANY DAY.
POINT.

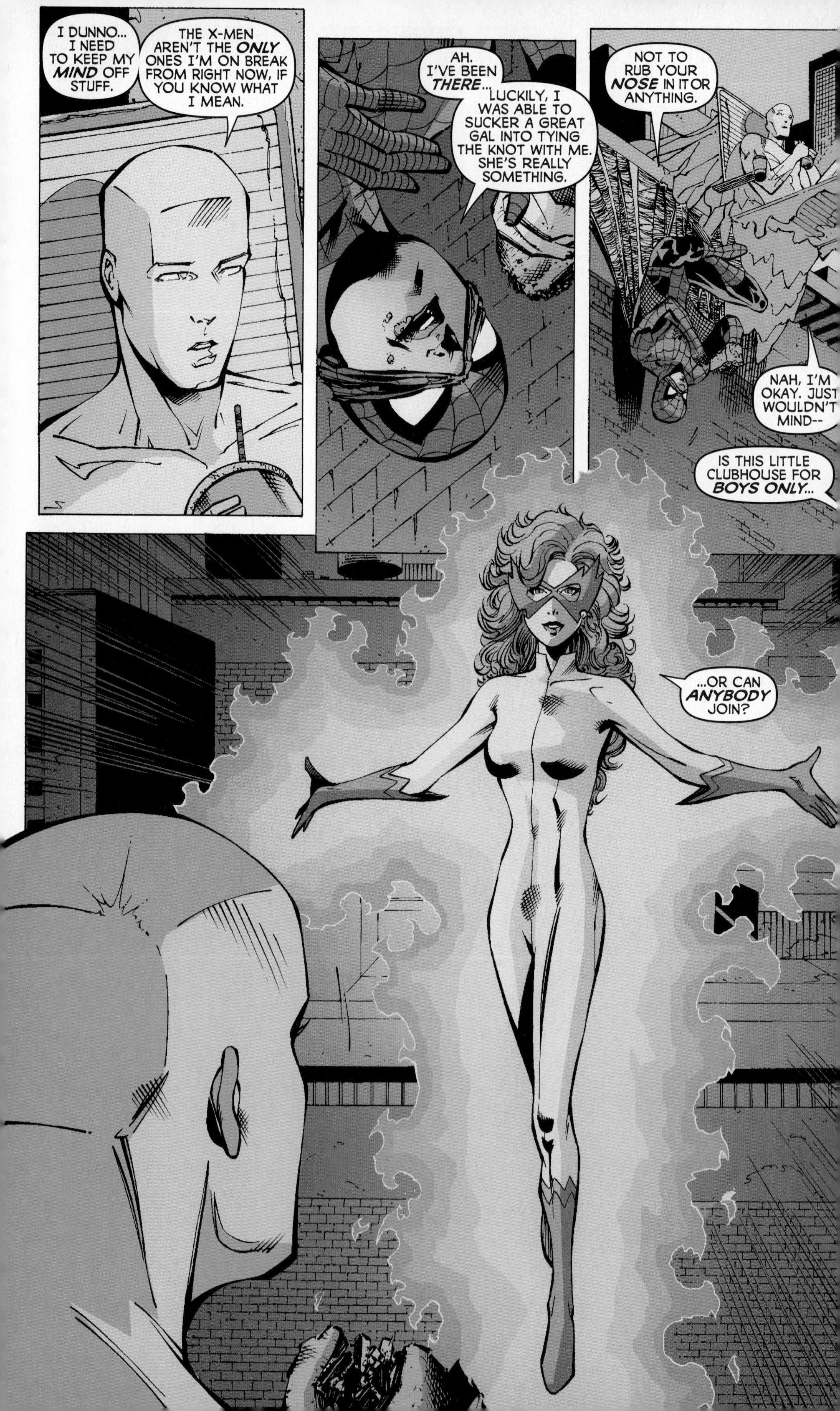
I DUNNO... I NEED TO KEEP MY *MIND* OFF STUFF.
THE X-MEN AREN'T THE *ONLY* ONES I'M ON BREAK FROM RIGHT NOW, IF YOU KNOW WHAT I MEAN.
AH. I'VE BEEN *THERE*...
LUCKILY, I WAS ABLE TO SUCKER A GREAT GAL INTO TYING THE KNOT WITH ME. SHE'S REALLY SOMETHING.
NOT TO RUB YOUR *NOSE* IN IT OR ANYTHING.
NAH, I'M OKAY. JUST WOULDN'T MIND--
IS THIS LITTLE CLUBHOUSE FOR *BOYS ONLY*...
...OR CAN *ANYBODY* JOIN?

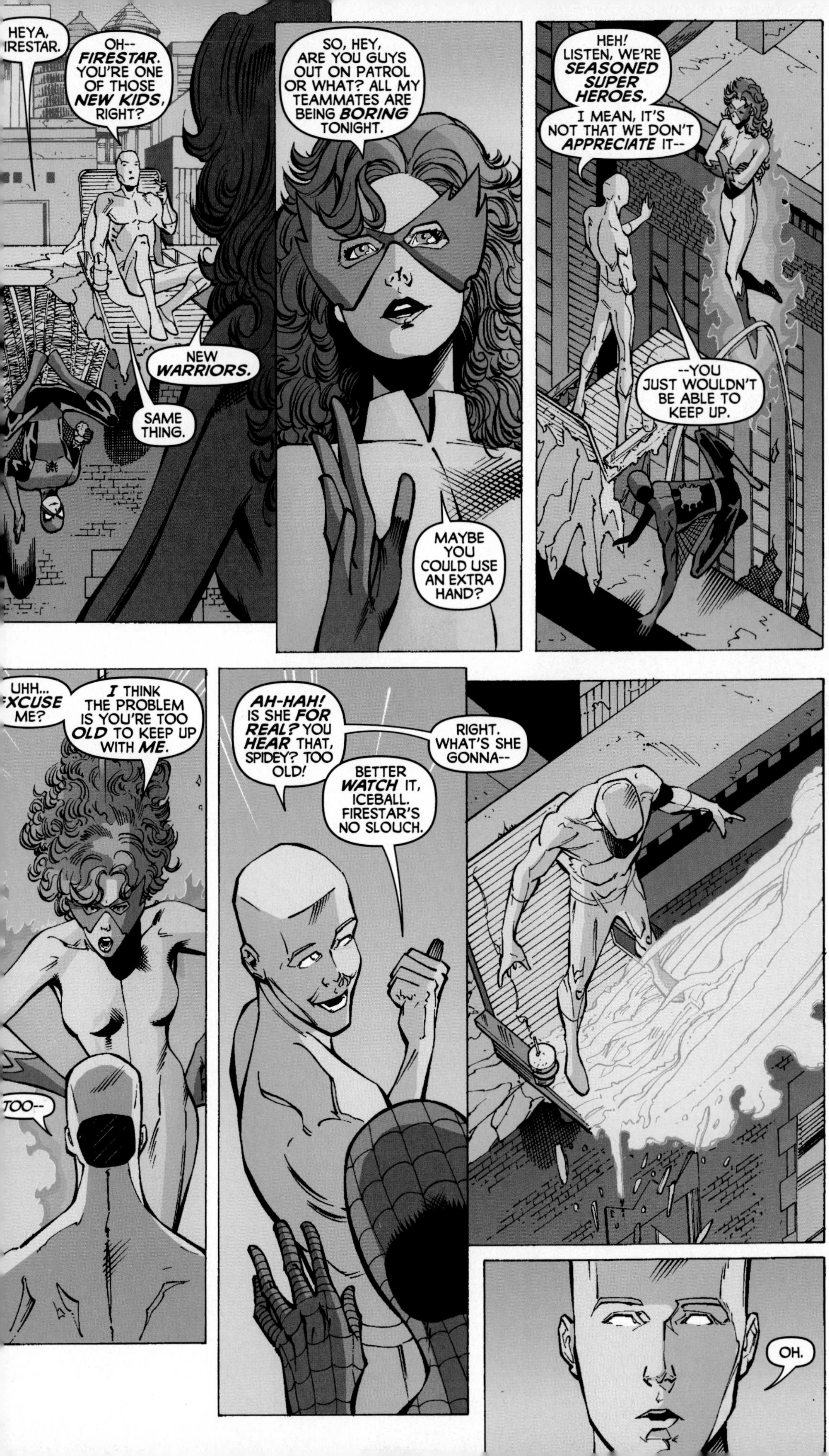
HEYA, IRESTAR.
OH-- FIRESTAR. YOU'RE ONE OF THOSE NEW KIDS, RIGHT?
NEW WARRIORS.
SAME THING.
SO, HEY, ARE YOU GUYS OUT ON PATROL OR WHAT? ALL MY TEAMMATES ARE BEING BORING TONIGHT.
MAYBE YOU COULD USE AN EXTRA HAND?
HEH! LISTEN, WE'RE SEASONED SUPER HEROES.
I MEAN, IT'S NOT THAT WE DON'T APPRECIATE IT--
--YOU JUST WOULDN'T BE ABLE TO KEEP UP.
UHH... EXCUSE ME?
I THINK THE PROBLEM IS YOU'RE TOO OLD TO KEEP UP WITH ME.
TOO--
AH-HAH! IS SHE FOR REAL? YOU HEAR THAT, SPIDEY? TOO OLD!
BETTER WATCH IT, ICEBALL. FIRESTAR'S NO SLOUCH.
RIGHT. WHAT'S SHE GONNA--
OH.

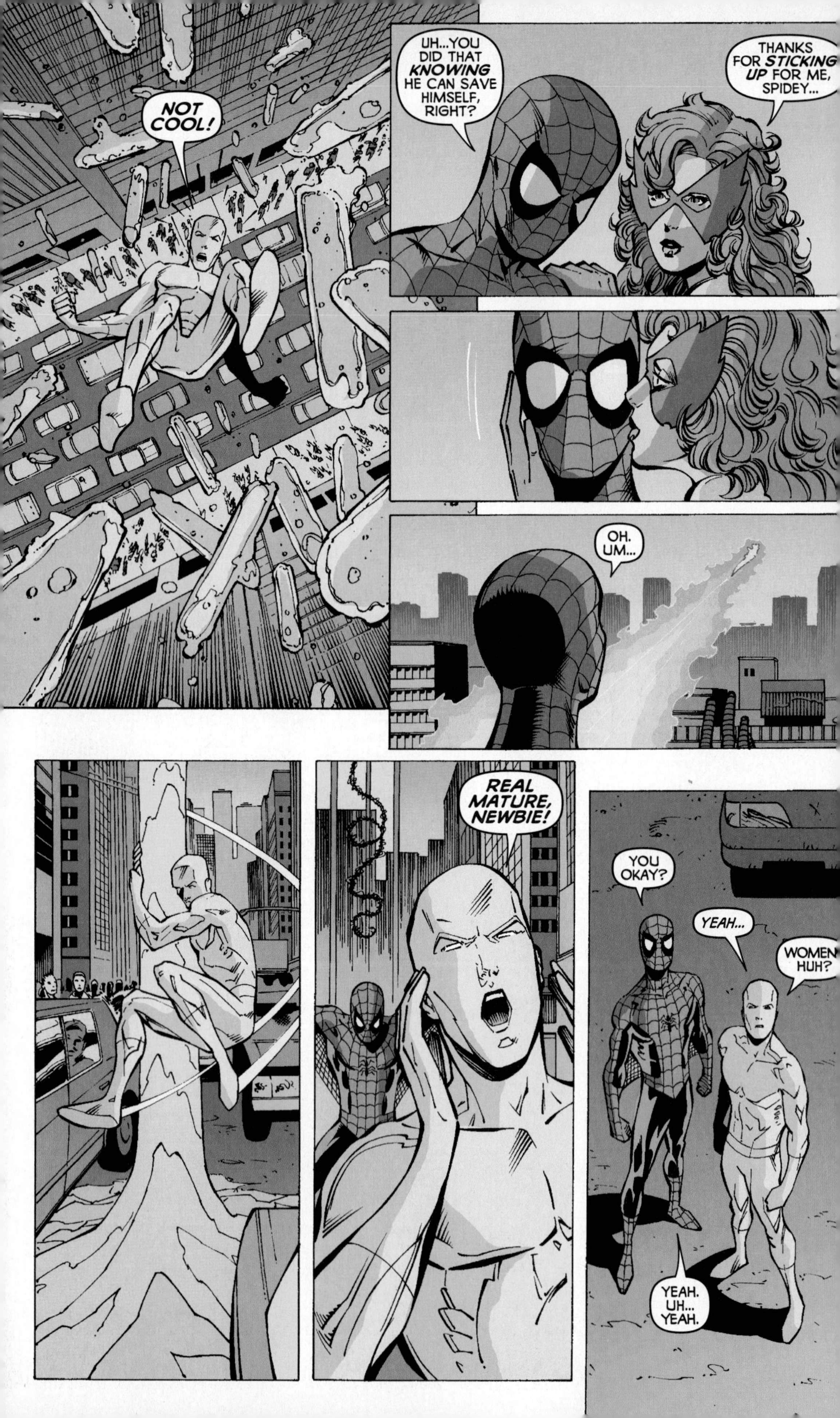
NOT COOL!
UH...YOU DID THAT KNOWING HE CAN SAVE HIMSELF, RIGHT?
THANKS FOR STICKING UP FOR ME, SPIDEY...
OH. UM...
REAL MATURE, NEWBIE!
YOU OKAY?
YEAH...
WOMEN HUH?
YEAH. UH... YEAH.

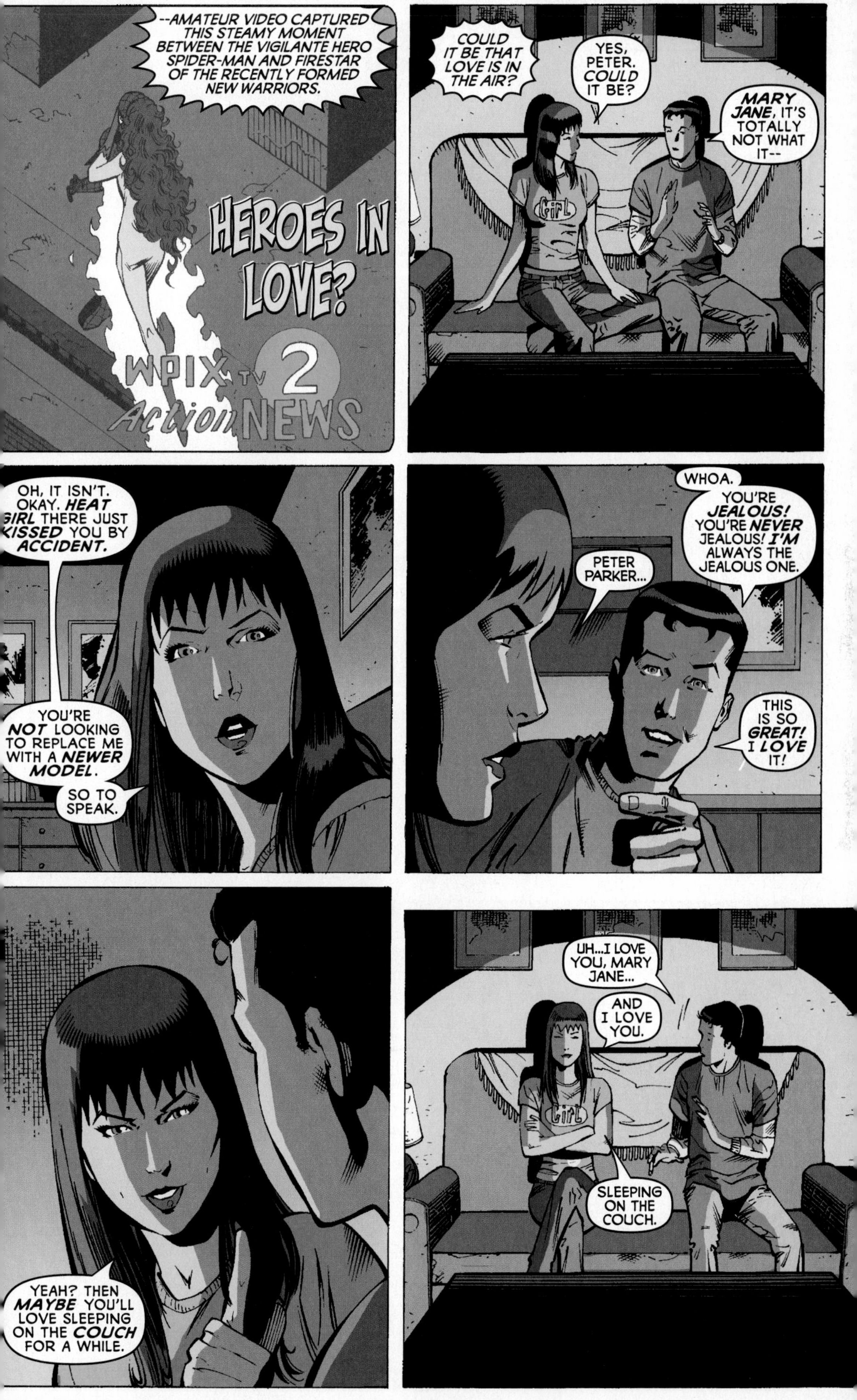
--AMATEUR VIDEO CAPTURED THIS STEAMY MOMENT BETWEEN THE VIGILANTE HERO SPIDER-MAN AND FIRESTAR OF THE RECENTLY FORMED NEW WARRIORS.
HEROES IN LOVE?
WPIX TV 2 Action NEWS
COULD IT BE THAT LOVE IS IN THE AIR?
YES, PETER. COULD IT BE?
MARY JANE, IT'S TOTALLY NOT WHAT IT--
OH, IT ISN'T. OKAY. HEAT GIRL THERE JUST KISSED YOU BY ACCIDENT.
YOU'RE NOT LOOKING TO REPLACE ME WITH A NEWER MODEL.
SO TO SPEAK.
PETER PARKER...
WHOA.
YOU'RE JEALOUS! YOU'RE NEVER JEALOUS! I'M ALWAYS THE JEALOUS ONE.
THIS IS SO GREAT! I LOVE IT!
YEAH? THEN MAYBE YOU'LL LOVE SLEEPING ON THE COUCH FOR A WHILE.
UH...I LOVE YOU, MARY JANE...
AND I LOVE YOU.
SLEEPING ON THE COUCH.

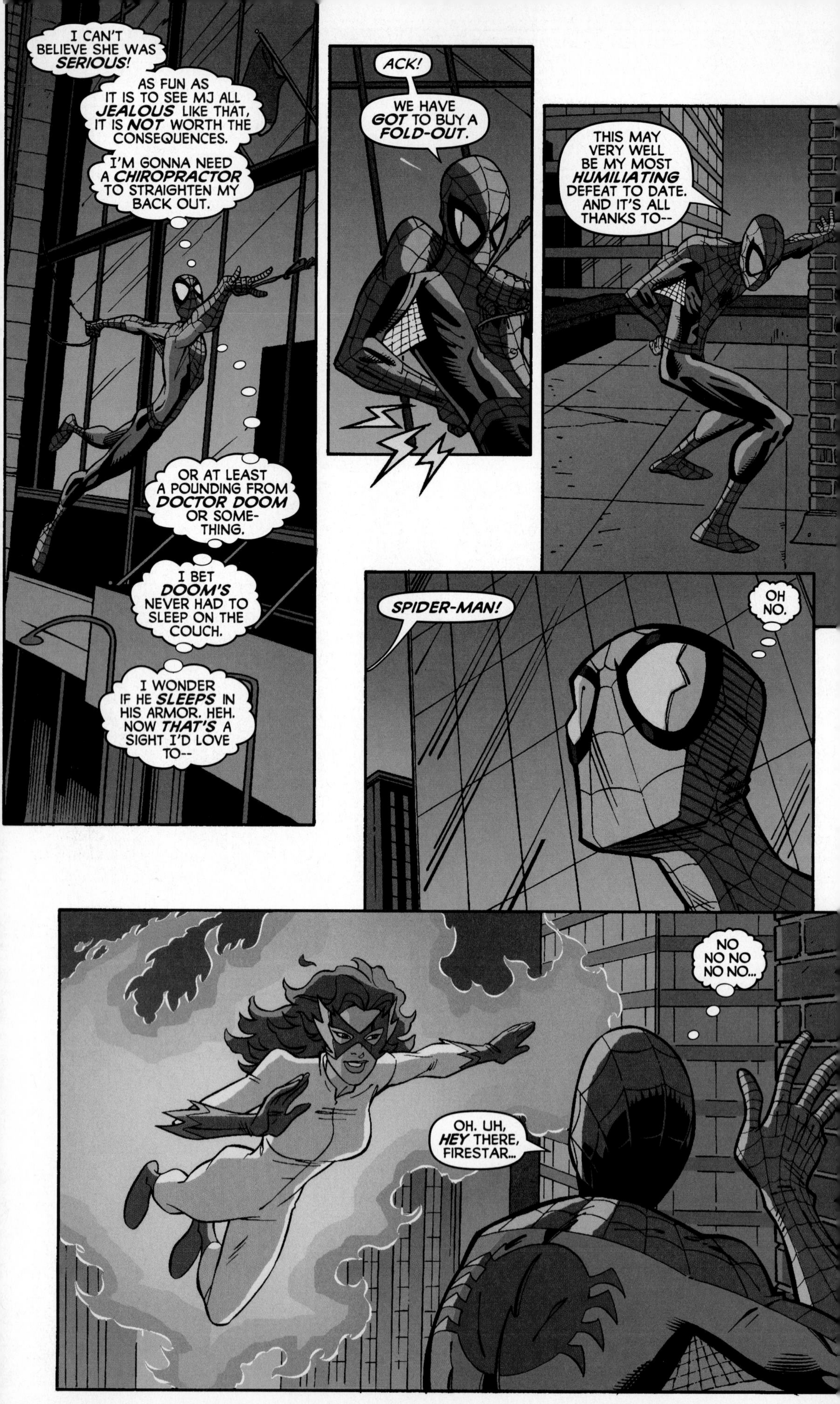
I CAN'T BELIEVE SHE WAS *SERIOUS!*
AS FUN AS IT IS TO SEE MJ ALL *JEALOUS* LIKE THAT, IT IS *NOT* WORTH THE CONSEQUENCES.
I'M GONNA NEED A *CHIROPRACTOR* TO STRAIGHTEN MY BACK OUT.
OR AT LEAST A POUNDING FROM *DOCTOR DOOM* OR SOME-THING.
I BET *DOOM'S* NEVER HAD TO SLEEP ON THE COUCH.
I WONDER IF HE *SLEEPS* IN HIS ARMOR. HEH. NOW *THAT'S* A SIGHT I'D LOVE TO--
ACK!
WE HAVE *GOT* TO BUY A *FOLD-OUT*.
THIS MAY VERY WELL BE MY MOST *HUMILIATING* DEFEAT TO DATE. AND IT'S ALL THANKS TO--
SPIDER-MAN!
OH NO.
NO NO NO NO NO...
OH. UH, *HEY* THERE, FIRESTAR...

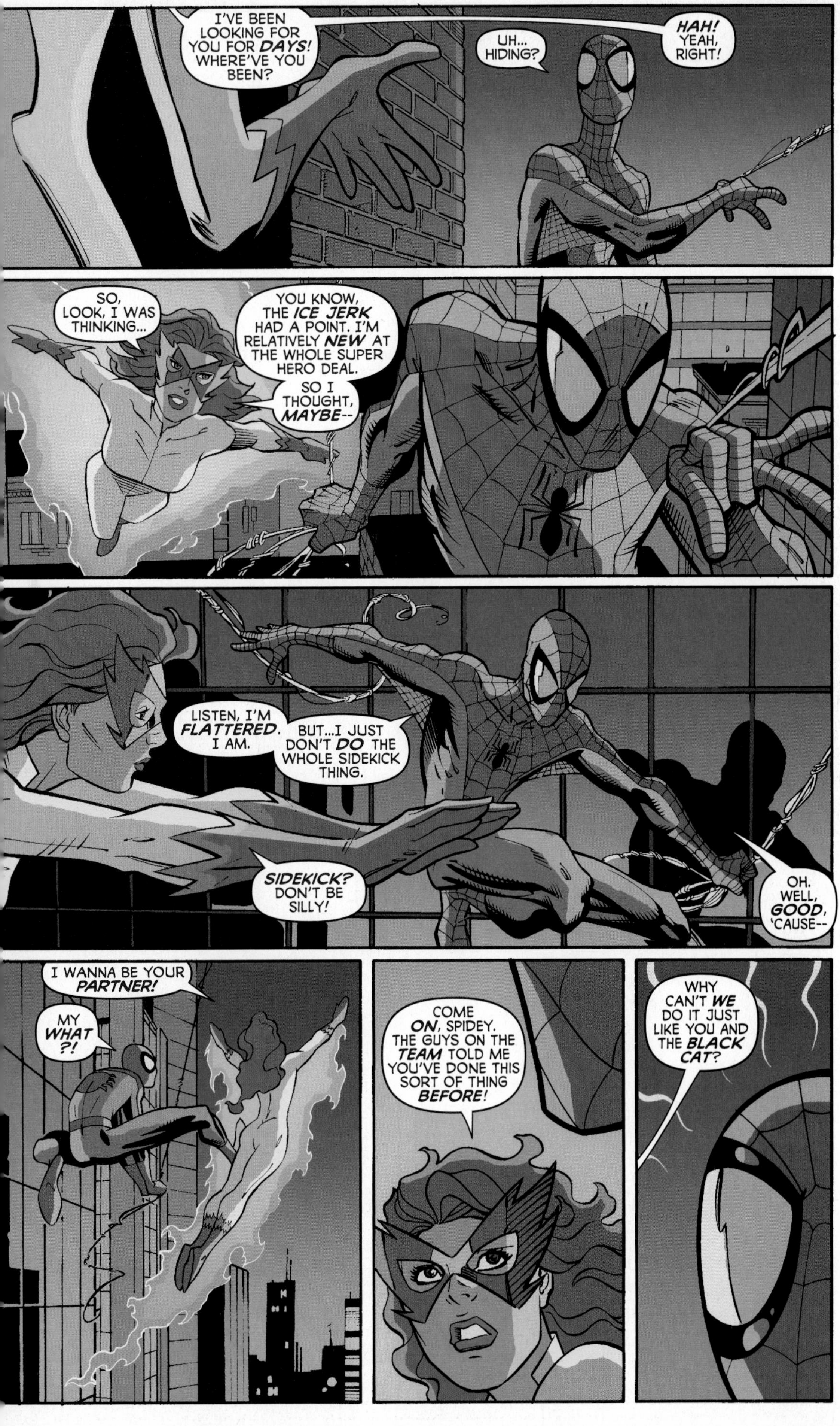
I'VE BEEN LOOKING FOR YOU FOR DAYS! WHERE'VE YOU BEEN?
UH... HIDING?
HAH! YEAH, RIGHT!
SO, LOOK, I WAS THINKING...
YOU KNOW, THE ICE JERK HAD A POINT. I'M RELATIVELY NEW AT THE WHOLE SUPER HERO DEAL.
SO I THOUGHT, MAYBE--
LISTEN, I'M FLATTERED. I AM.
BUT...I JUST DON'T DO THE WHOLE SIDEKICK THING.
SIDEKICK? DON'T BE SILLY!
OH. WELL, GOOD, 'CAUSE--
I WANNA BE YOUR PARTNER!
MY WHAT?!
COME ON, SPIDEY. THE GUYS ON THE TEAM TOLD ME YOU'VE DONE THIS SORT OF THING BEFORE!
WHY CAN'T WE DO IT JUST LIKE YOU AND THE BLACK CAT?

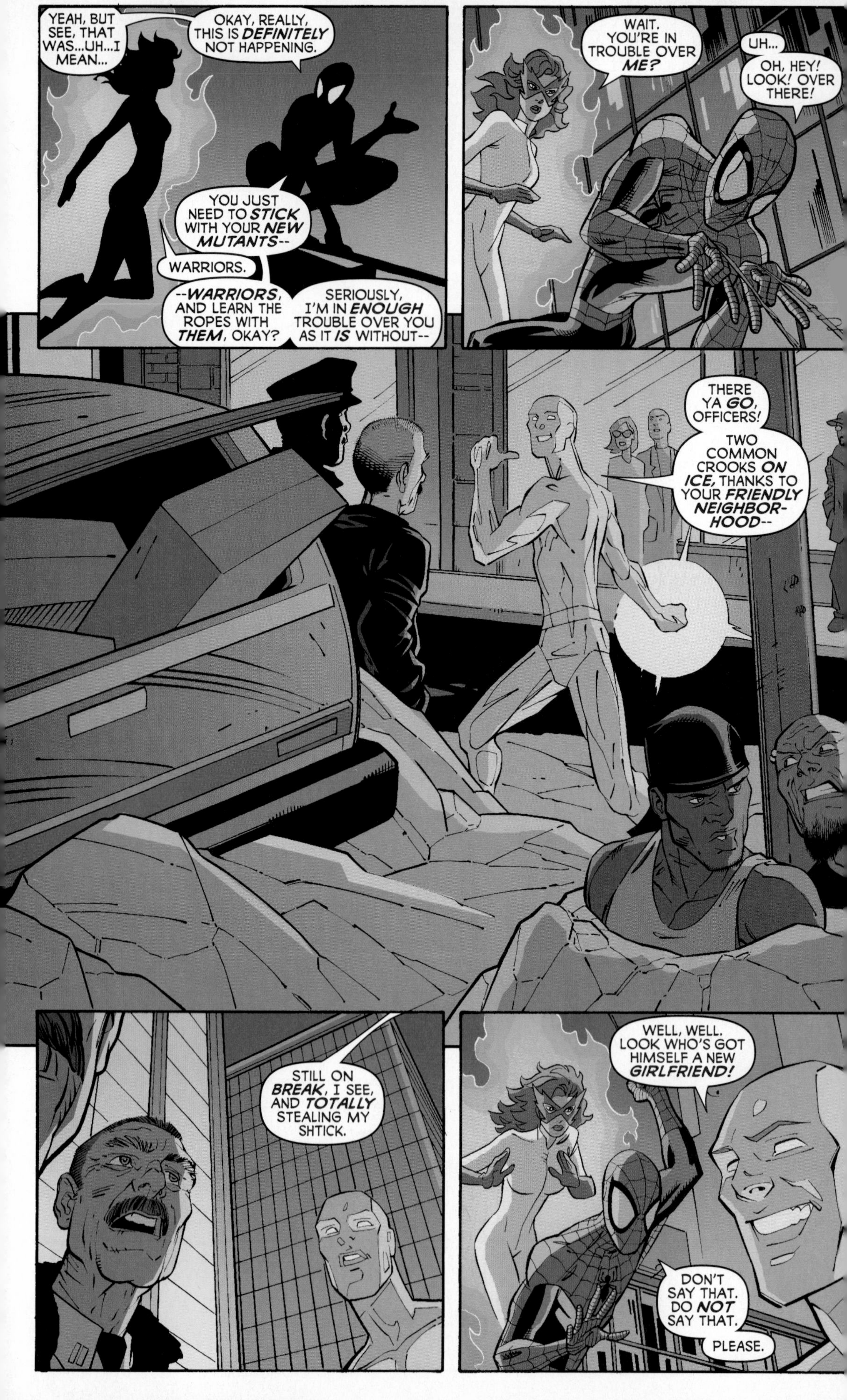
YEAH, BUT SEE, THAT WAS...UH...I MEAN...
OKAY, REALLY, THIS IS DEFINITELY NOT HAPPENING.
YOU JUST NEED TO STICK WITH YOUR NEW MUTANTS--
WARRIORS.
--WARRIORS, AND LEARN THE ROPES WITH THEM, OKAY?
SERIOUSLY, I'M IN ENOUGH TROUBLE OVER YOU AS IT IS WITHOUT--
WAIT. YOU'RE IN TROUBLE OVER ME?
UH...
OH, HEY! LOOK! OVER THERE!
THERE YA GO, OFFICERS!
TWO COMMON CROOKS ON ICE, THANKS TO YOUR FRIENDLY NEIGHBOR-HOOD--
STILL ON BREAK, I SEE, AND TOTALLY STEALING MY SHTICK.
WELL, WELL. LOOK WHO'S GOT HIMSELF A NEW GIRLFRIEND!
DON'T SAY THAT. DO NOT SAY THAT.
PLEASE.

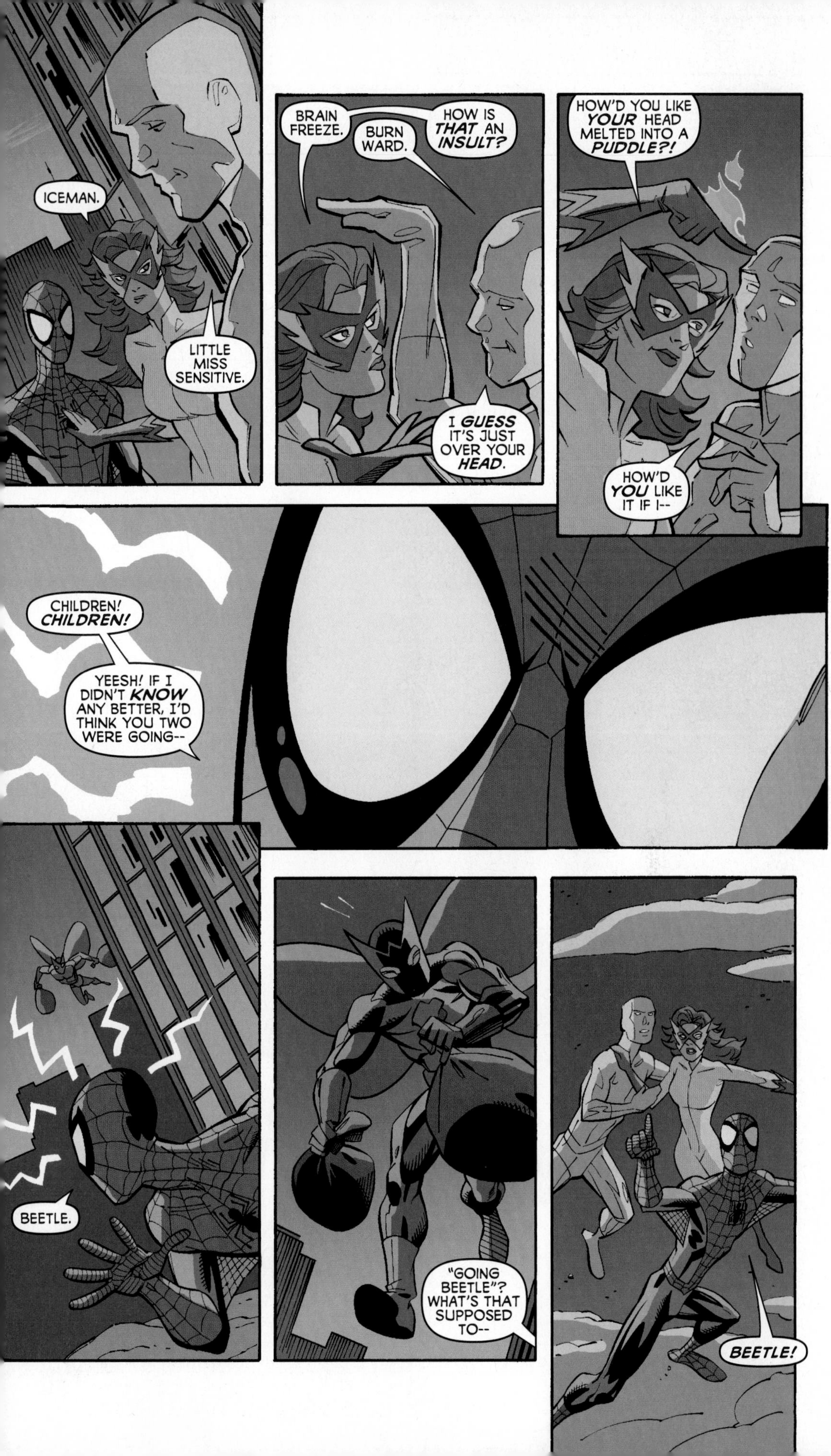
ICEMAN.
LITTLE MISS SENSITIVE.
BRAIN FREEZE.
BURN WARD.
HOW IS *THAT* AN *INSULT?*
I *GUESS* IT'S JUST OVER YOUR *HEAD*.
HOW'D YOU LIKE *YOUR* HEAD MELTED INTO A *PUDDLE?!*
HOW'D *YOU* LIKE IT IF I--
CHILDREN! *CHILDREN!*
YEESH! IF I DIDN'T *KNOW* ANY BETTER, I'D THINK YOU TWO WERE GOING--
BEETLE.
"GOING BEETLE"? WHAT'S THAT SUPPOSED TO--
BEETLE!

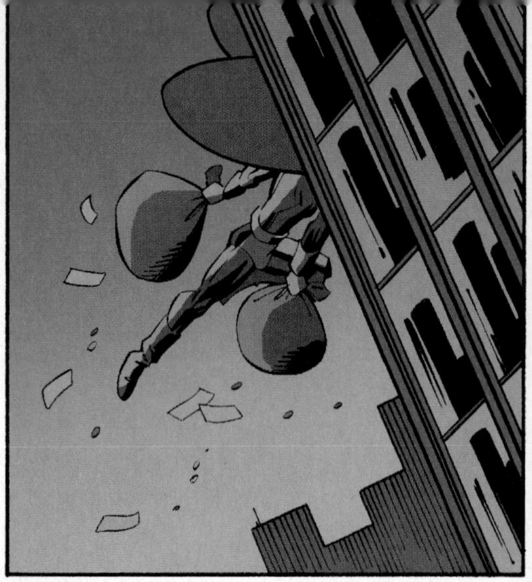

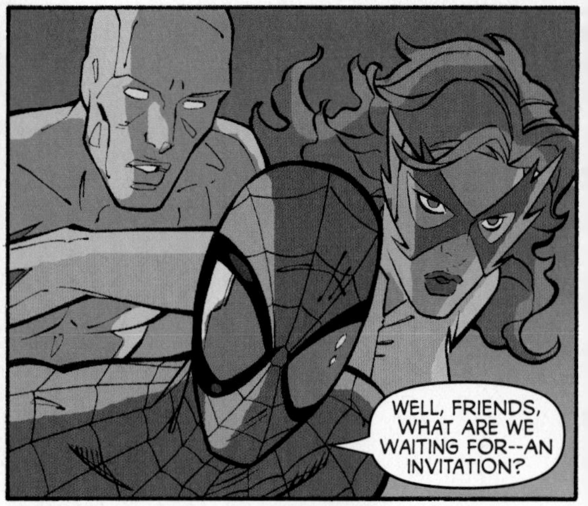
WELL, FRIENDS, WHAT ARE WE WAITING FOR--AN INVITATION?

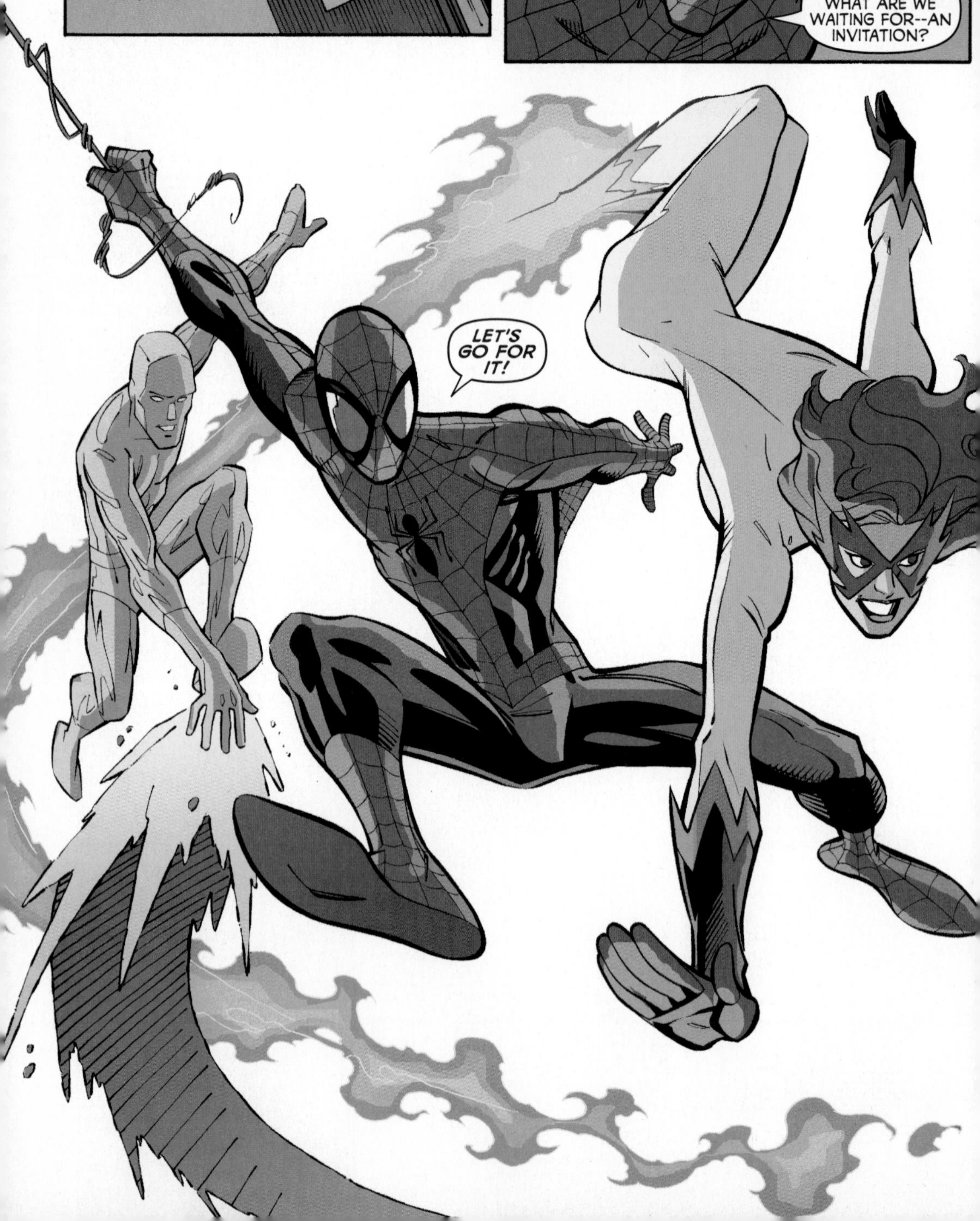
LET'S GO FOR IT!

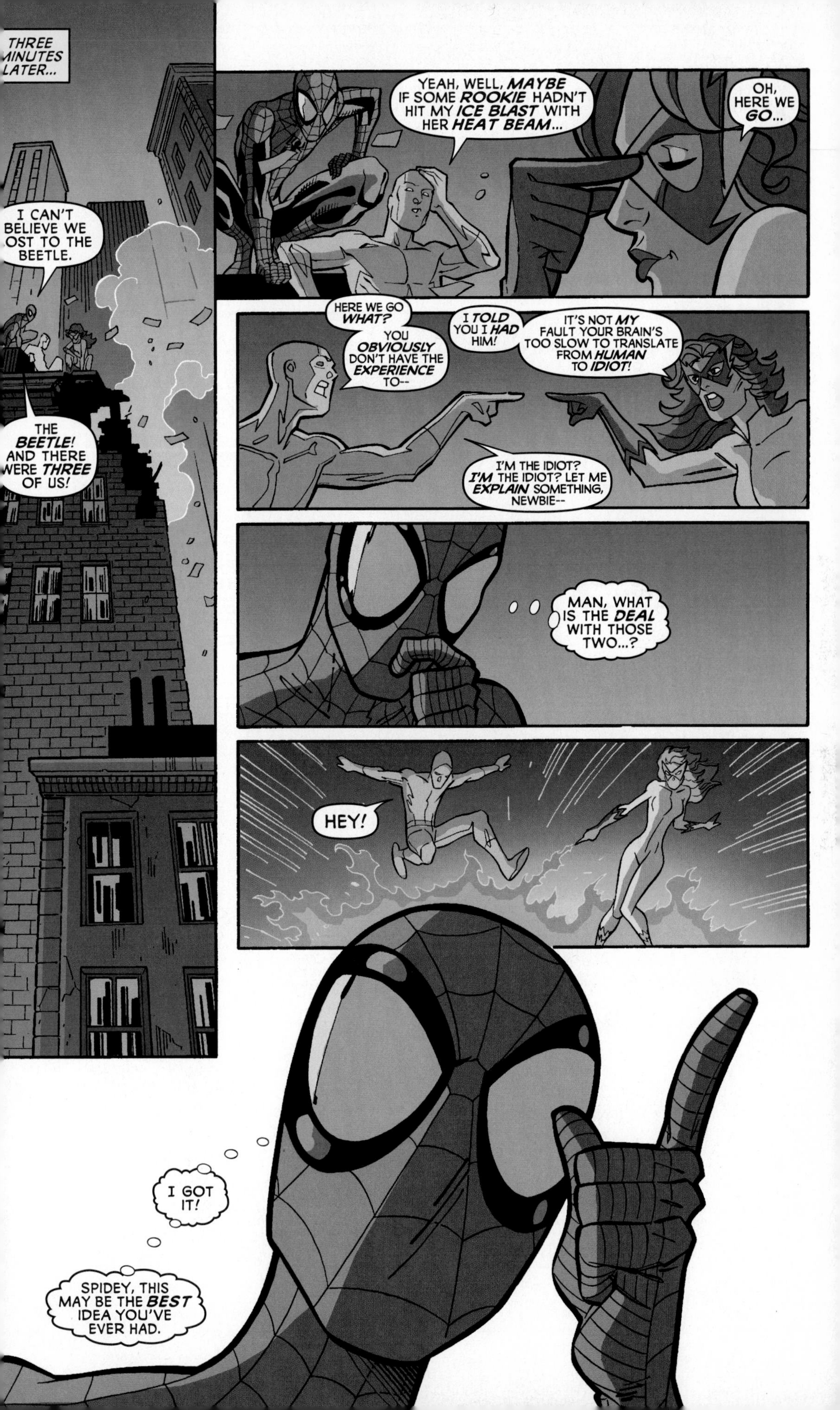

THREE MINUTES LATER...
I CAN'T BELIEVE WE LOST TO THE BEETLE.
THE BEETLE! AND THERE WERE THREE OF US!
YEAH, WELL, MAYBE IF SOME ROOKIE HADN'T HIT MY ICE BLAST WITH HER HEAT BEAM...
OH, HERE WE GO...
HERE WE GO WHAT?
YOU OBVIOUSLY DON'T HAVE THE EXPERIENCE TO--
I TOLD YOU I HAD HIM!
IT'S NOT MY FAULT YOUR BRAIN'S TOO SLOW TO TRANSLATE FROM HUMAN TO IDIOT!
I'M THE IDIOT? I'M THE IDIOT? LET ME EXPLAIN SOMETHING, NEWBIE--
MAN, WHAT IS THE DEAL WITH THOSE TWO...?
HEY!
I GOT IT!
SPIDEY, THIS MAY BE THE BEST IDEA YOU'VE EVER HAD.

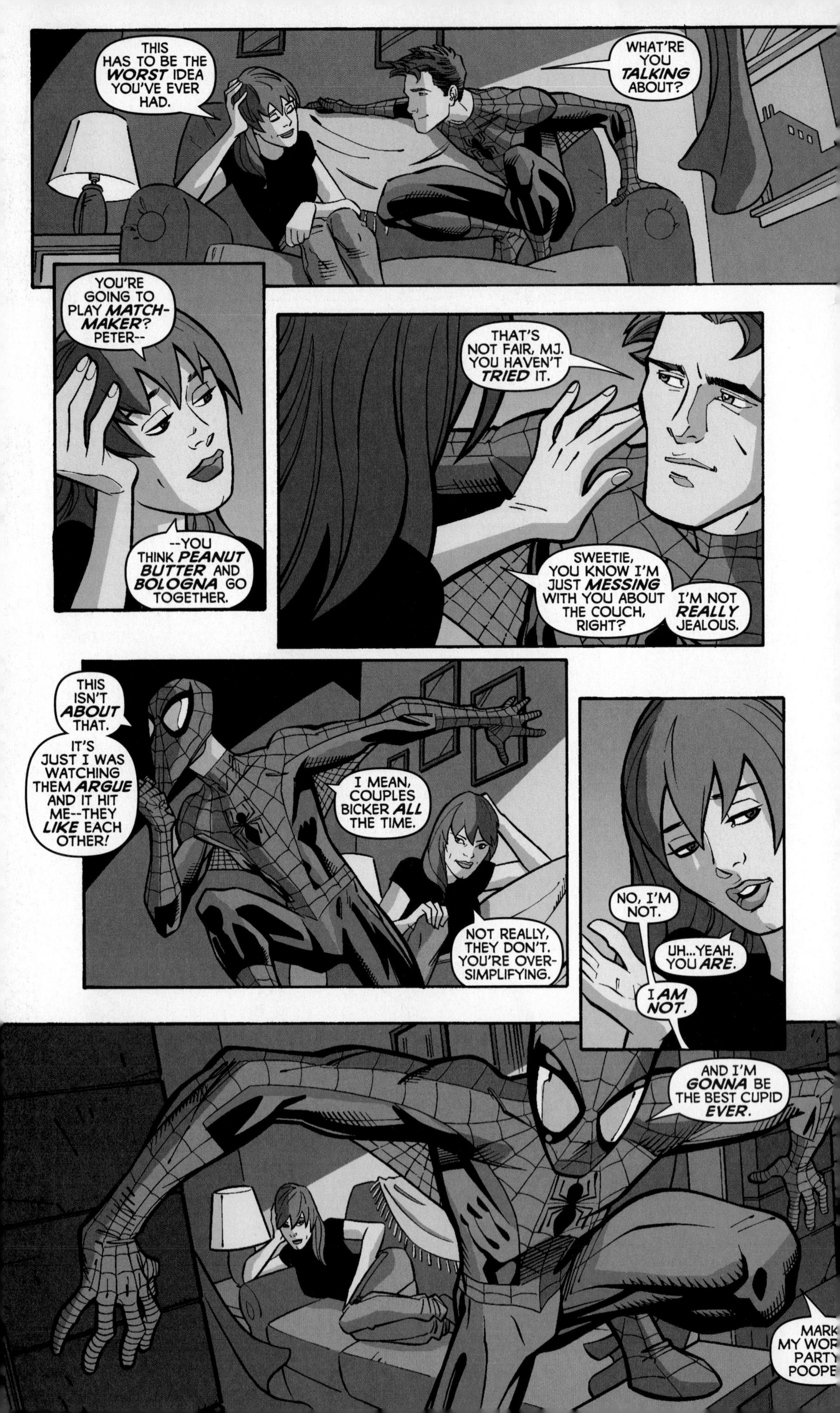
THIS HAS TO BE THE WORST IDEA YOU'VE EVER HAD.
WHAT'RE YOU TALKING ABOUT?
YOU'RE GOING TO PLAY MATCH-MAKER? PETER--
--YOU THINK PEANUT BUTTER AND BOLOGNA GO TOGETHER.
THAT'S NOT FAIR, MJ. YOU HAVEN'T TRIED IT.
SWEETIE, YOU KNOW I'M JUST MESSING WITH YOU ABOUT THE COUCH, RIGHT?
I'M NOT REALLY JEALOUS.
THIS ISN'T ABOUT THAT.
IT'S JUST I WAS WATCHING THEM ARGUE AND IT HIT ME--THEY LIKE EACH OTHER!
I MEAN, COUPLES BICKER ALL THE TIME.
NOT REALLY, THEY DON'T. YOU'RE OVER-SIMPLIFYING.
NO, I'M NOT.
UH...YEAH. YOU ARE.
I AM NOT.
AND I'M GONNA BE THE BEST CUPID EVER.

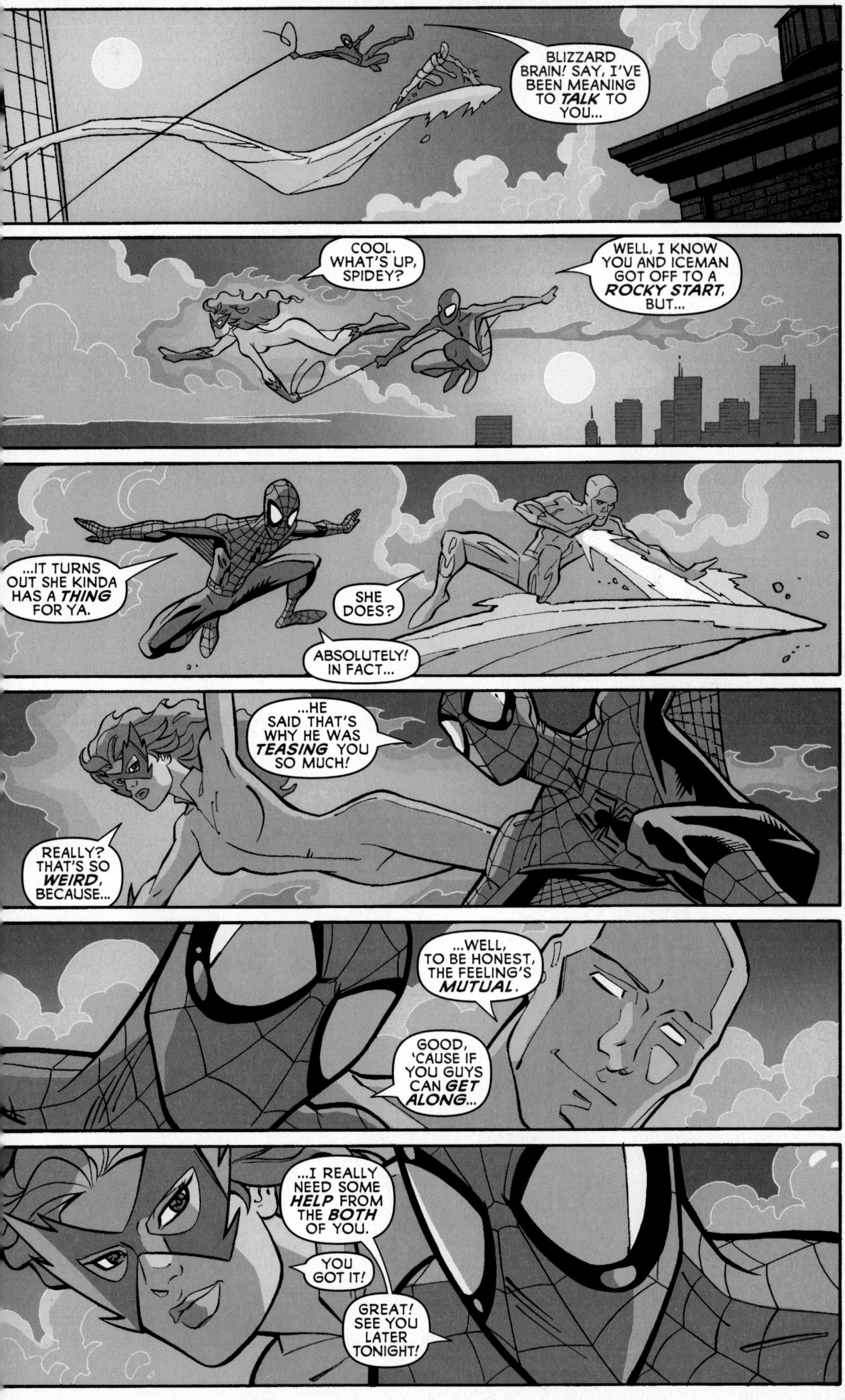
BLIZZARD BRAIN! SAY, I'VE BEEN MEANING TO *TALK* TO YOU...
COOL. WHAT'S UP, SPIDEY?
WELL, I KNOW YOU AND ICEMAN GOT OFF TO A *ROCKY START*, BUT...
...IT TURNS OUT SHE KINDA HAS A *THING* FOR YA.
SHE DOES?
ABSOLUTELY! IN FACT...
...HE SAID THAT'S WHY HE WAS *TEASING* YOU SO MUCH!
REALLY? THAT'S SO *WEIRD*, BECAUSE...
...WELL, TO BE HONEST, THE FEELING'S *MUTUAL*.
GOOD, 'CAUSE IF YOU GUYS CAN *GET ALONG*...
...I REALLY NEED SOME *HELP* FROM THE *BOTH* OF YOU.
YOU GOT IT!
GREAT! SEE YOU LATER TONIGHT!

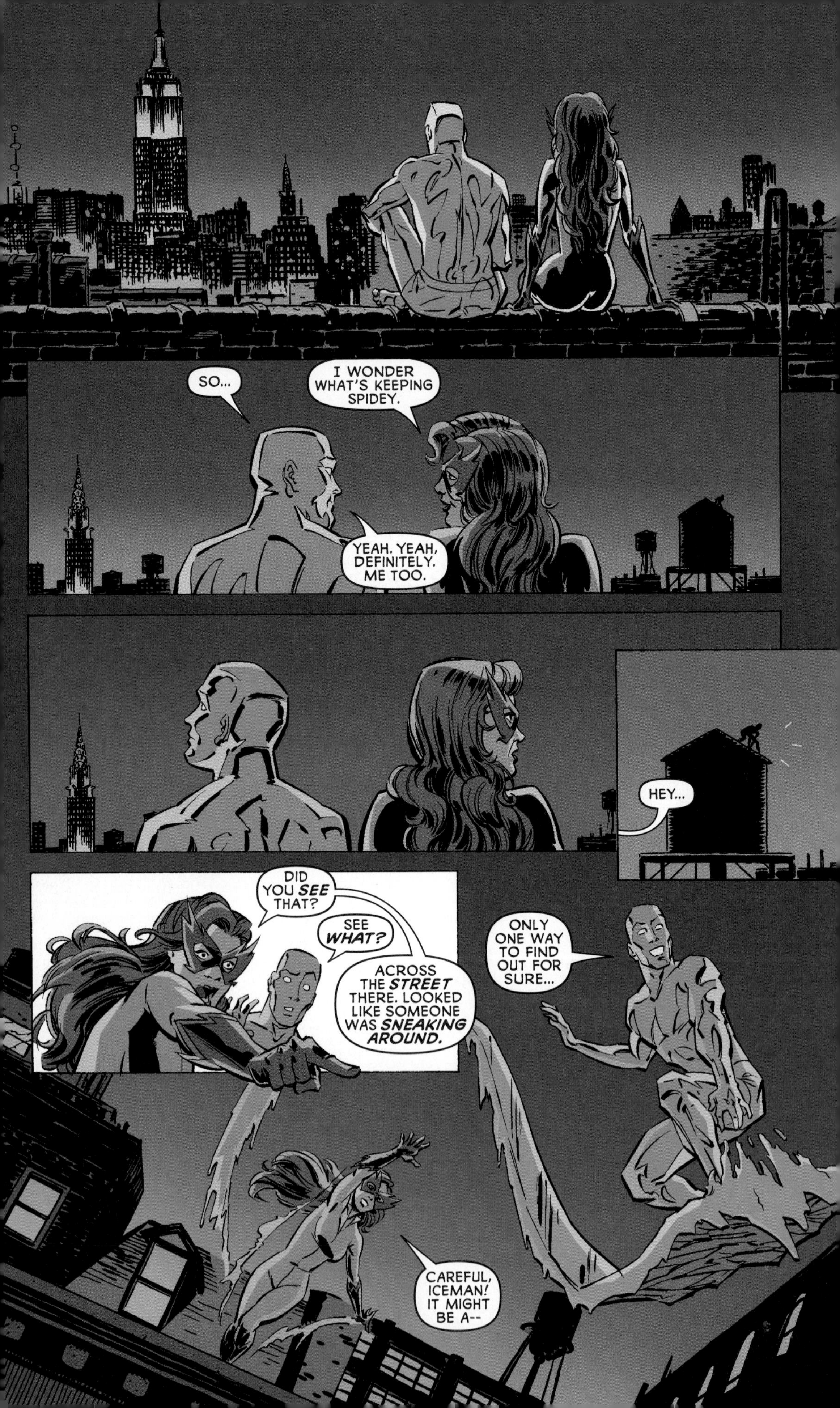
SO...
I WONDER WHAT'S KEEPING SPIDEY.
YEAH. YEAH, DEFINITELY. ME TOO.
HEY...
DID YOU SEE THAT?
SEE WHAT?
ACROSS THE STREET THERE. LOOKED LIKE SOMEONE WAS SNEAKING AROUND.
ONLY ONE WAY TO FIND OUT FOR SURE...
CAREFUL, ICEMAN! IT MIGHT BE A--

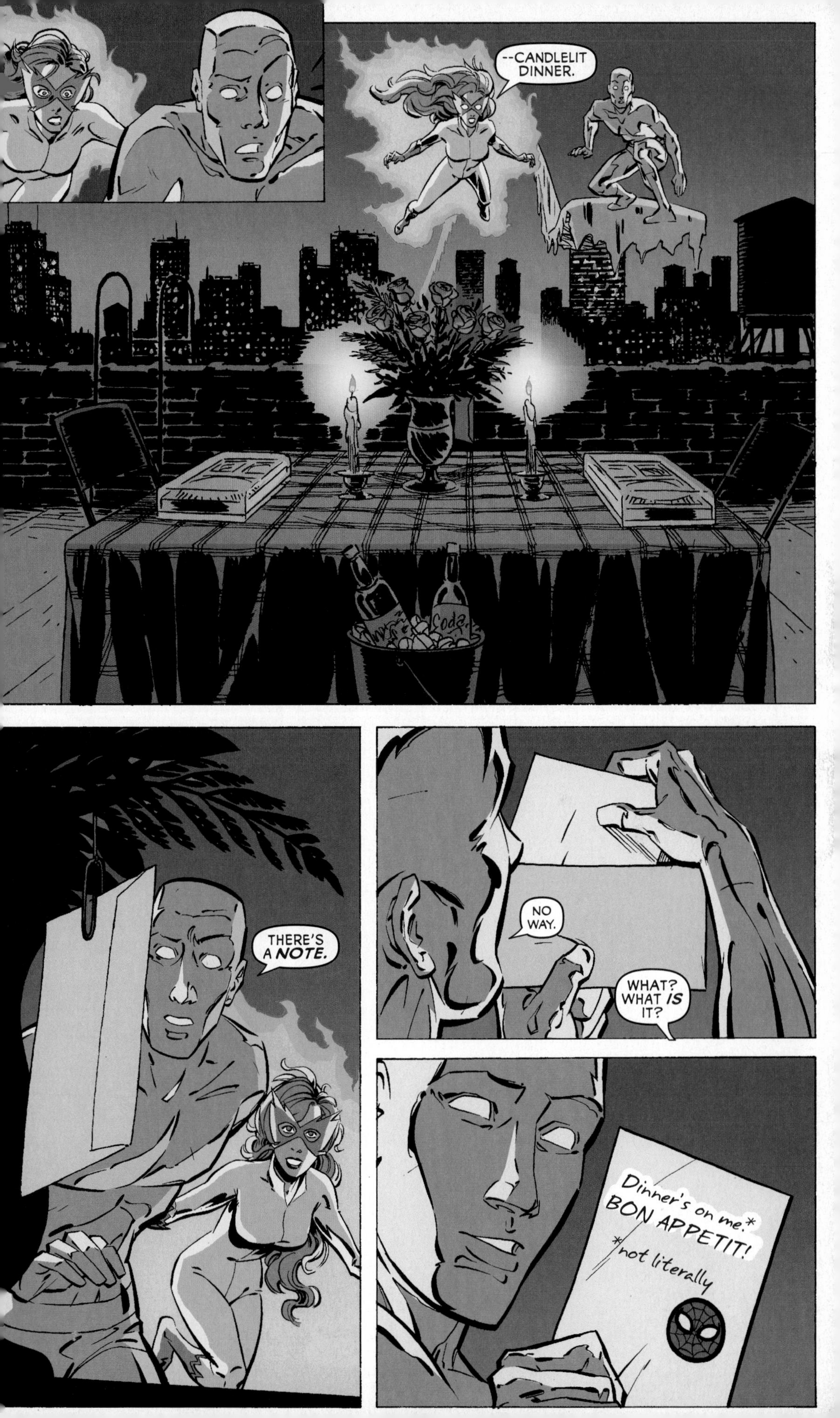
--CANDLELIT DINNER.
CODA
THERE'S A NOTE.
NO WAY.
WHAT? WHAT IS IT?
Dinner's on me.*
BON APPETIT!
*not literally

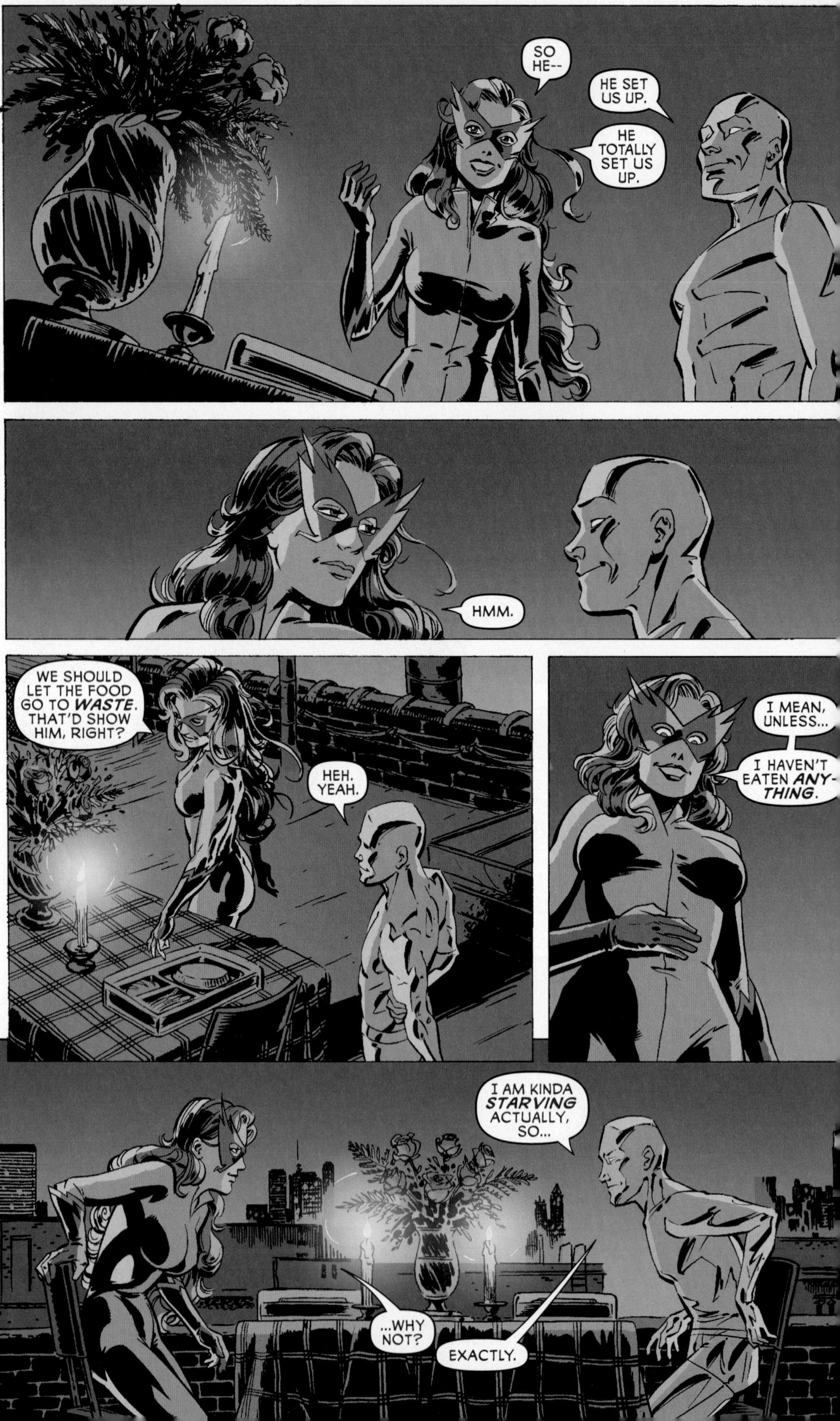
SO HE--
HE SET US UP.
HE TOTALLY SET US UP.
HMM.
WE SHOULD LET THE FOOD GO TO *WASTE*. THAT'D SHOW HIM, RIGHT?
HEH. YEAH.
I MEAN, UNLESS...
I HAVEN'T EATEN *ANYTHING*.
I AM KINDA *STARVING* ACTUALLY, SO...
...WHY NOT?
EXACTLY.

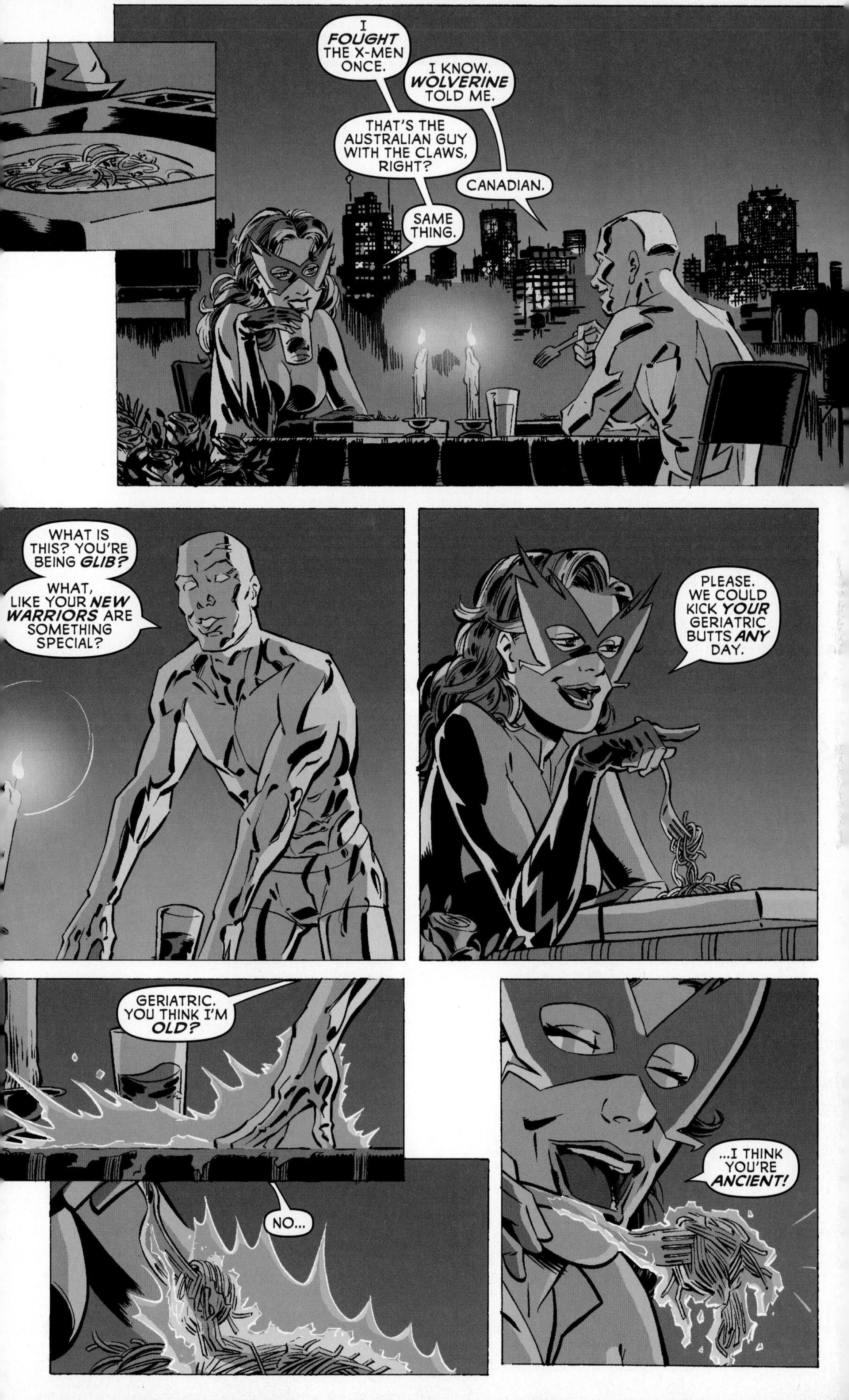

I FOUGHT THE X-MEN ONCE.
I KNOW. WOLVERINE TOLD ME.
THAT'S THE AUSTRALIAN GUY WITH THE CLAWS, RIGHT?
CANADIAN.
SAME THING.
WHAT IS THIS? YOU'RE BEING GLIB?
WHAT, LIKE YOUR NEW WARRIORS ARE SOMETHING SPECIAL?
PLEASE. WE COULD KICK YOUR GERIATRIC BUTTS ANY DAY.
GERIATRIC. YOU THINK I'M OLD?
NO...
...I THINK YOU'RE ANCIENT!

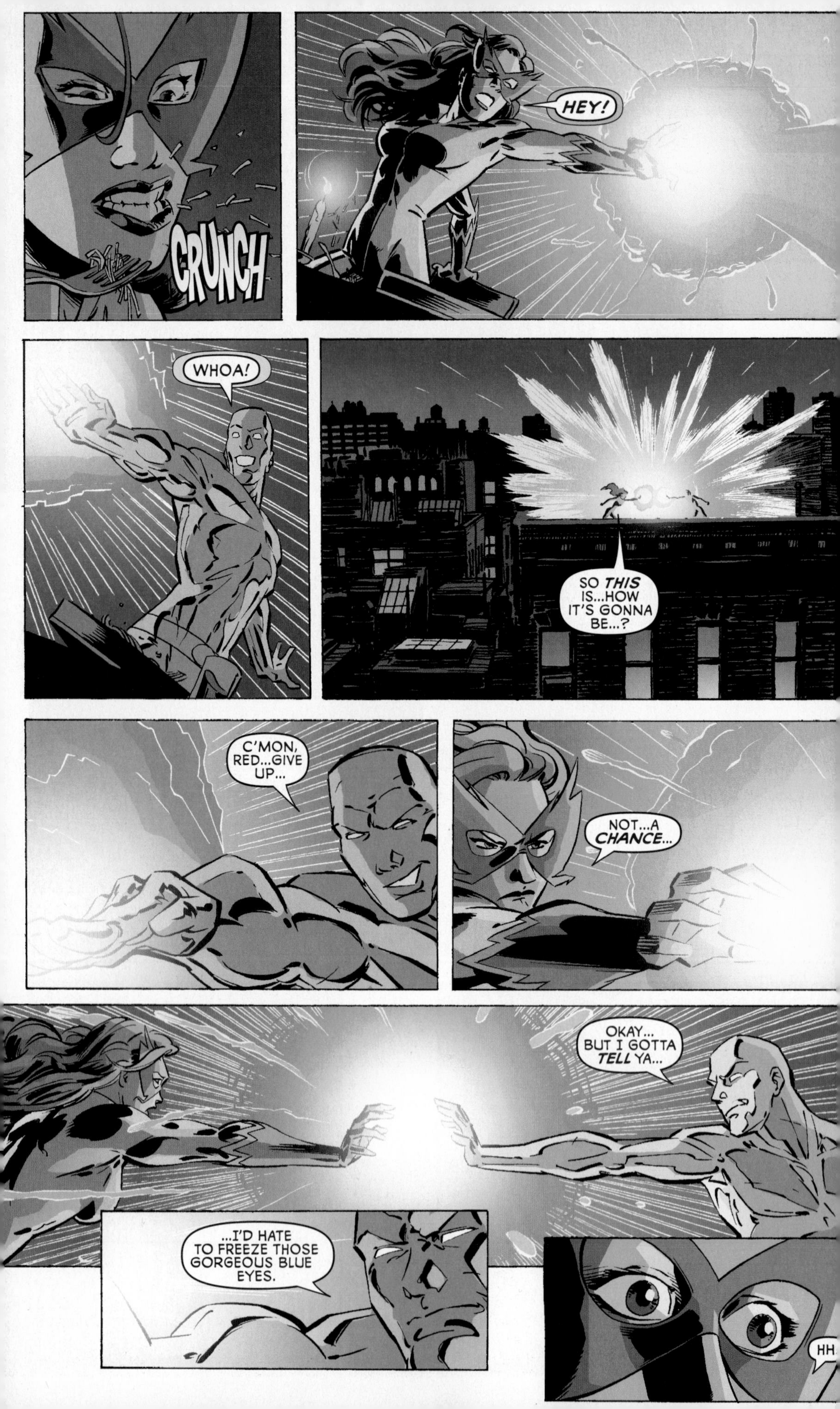
CRUNCH
HEY!
WHOA!
SO THIS IS...HOW IT'S GONNA BE...?
C'MON, RED...GIVE UP...
NOT...A CHANCE...
OKAY... BUT I GOTTA TELL YA...
...I'D HATE TO FREEZE THOSE GORGEOUS BLUE EYES.
HH

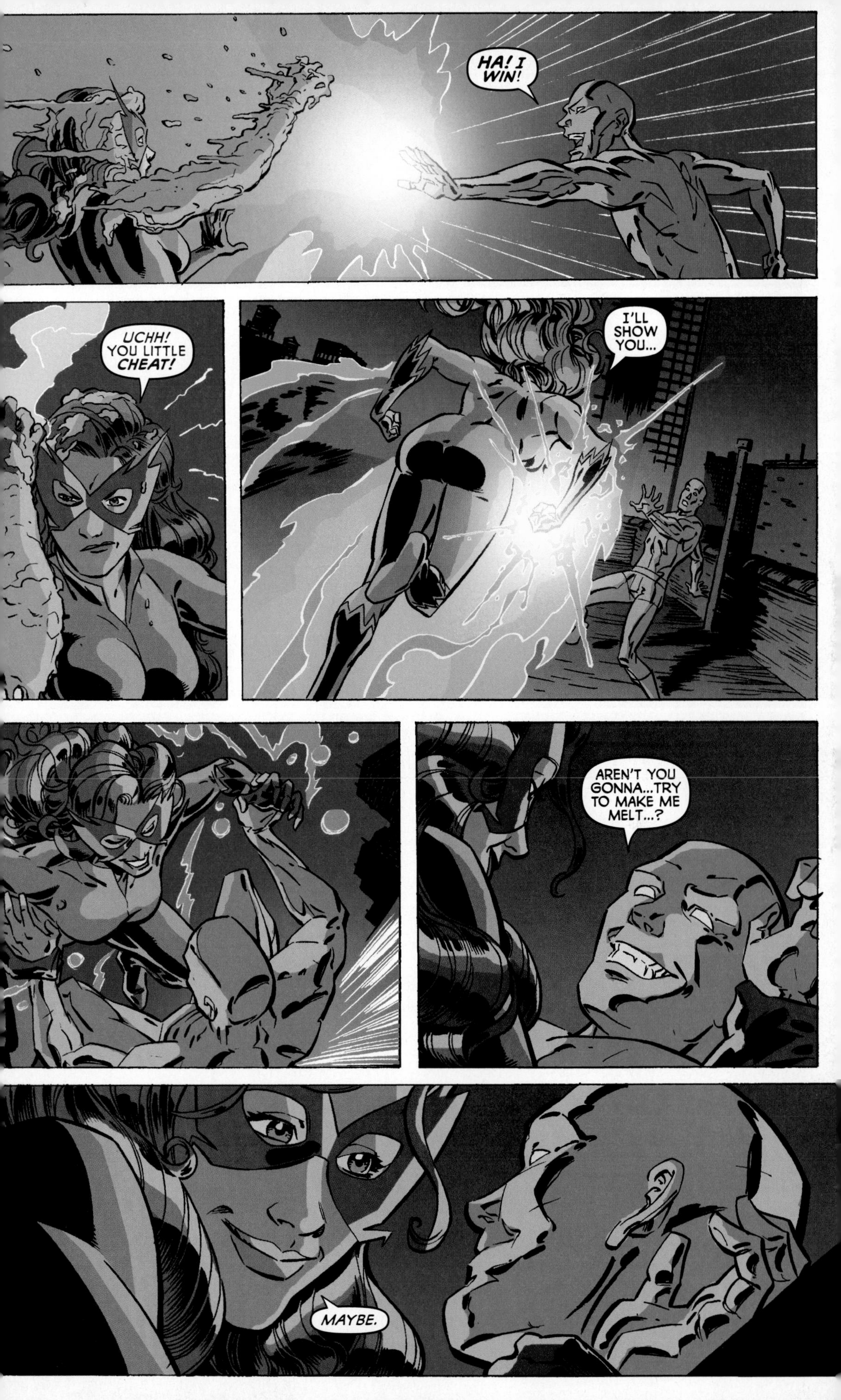
HA! I WIN!
UCHH! YOU LITTLE CHEAT!
I'LL SHOW YOU...
AREN'T YOU GONNA...TRY TO MAKE ME MELT...?
MAYBE.

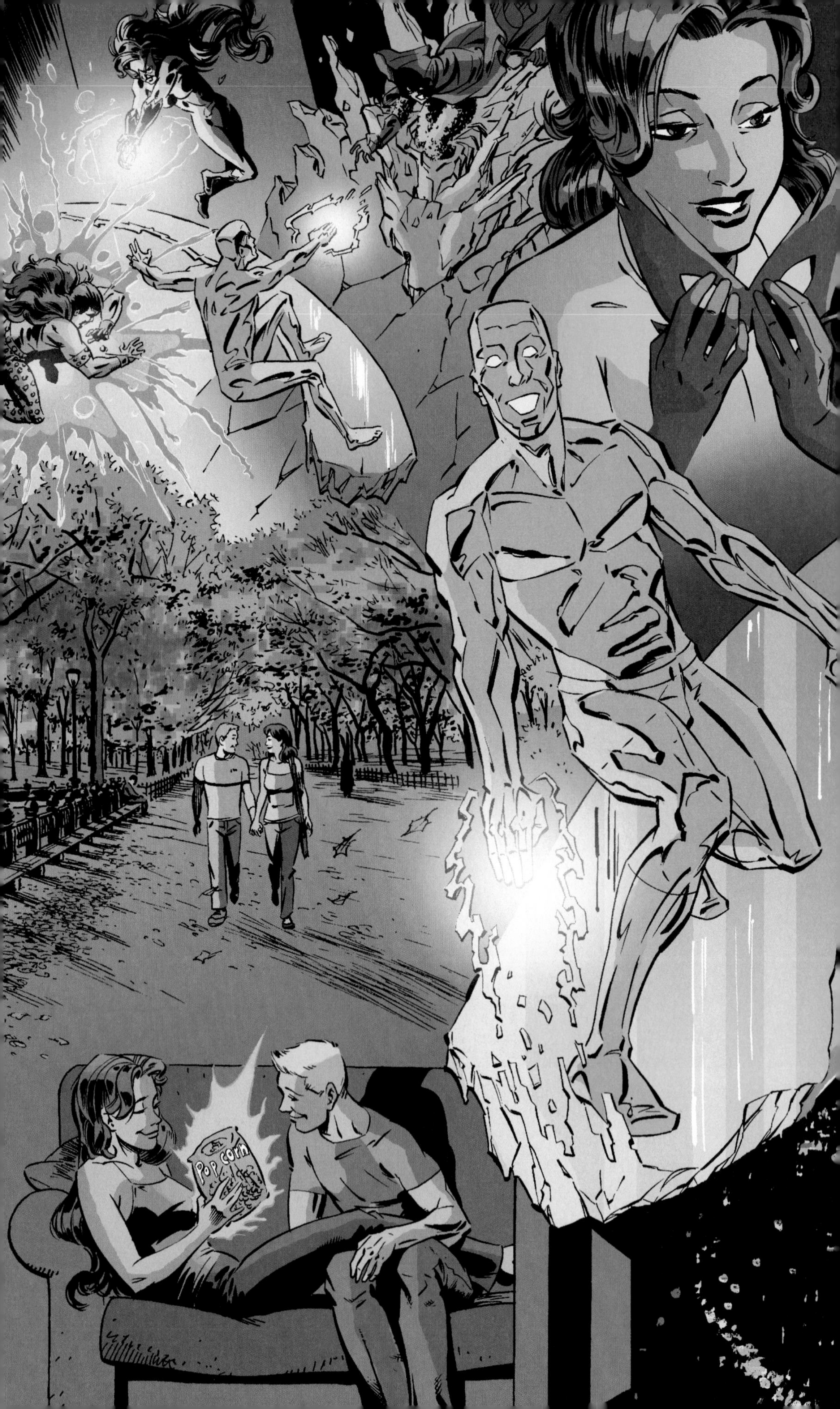
Pop corn

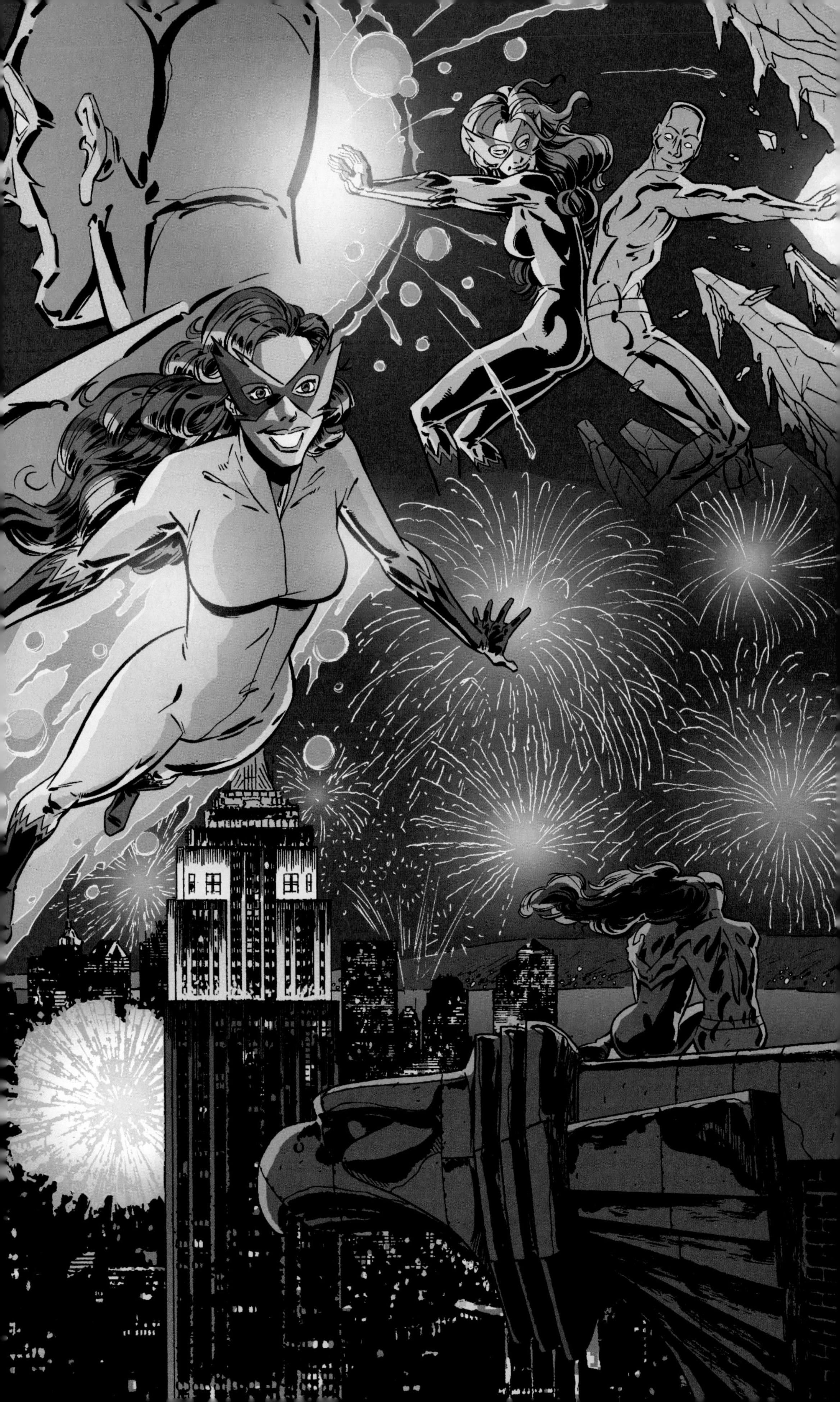

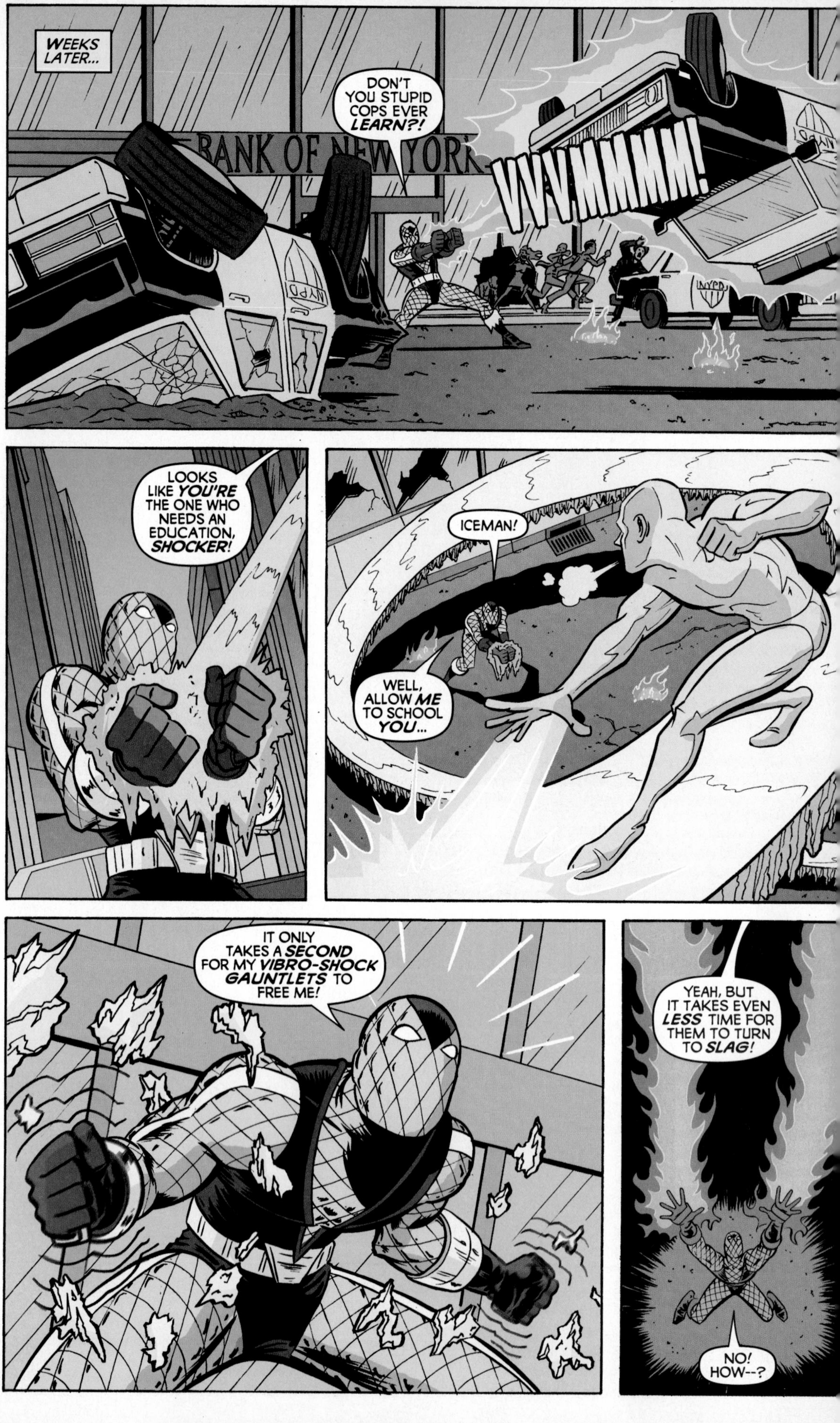
WEEKS LATER...
DON'T YOU STUPID COPS EVER LEARN?!
BANK OF NEW YORK
VVVMMMM!
NYPD
LOOKS LIKE YOU'RE THE ONE WHO NEEDS AN EDUCATION, SHOCKER!
ICEMAN!
WELL, ALLOW ME TO SCHOOL YOU...
IT ONLY TAKES A SECOND FOR MY VIBRO-SHOCK GAUNTLETS TO FREE ME!
YEAH, BUT IT TAKES EVEN LESS TIME FOR THEM TO TURN TO SLAG!
NO! HOW--?

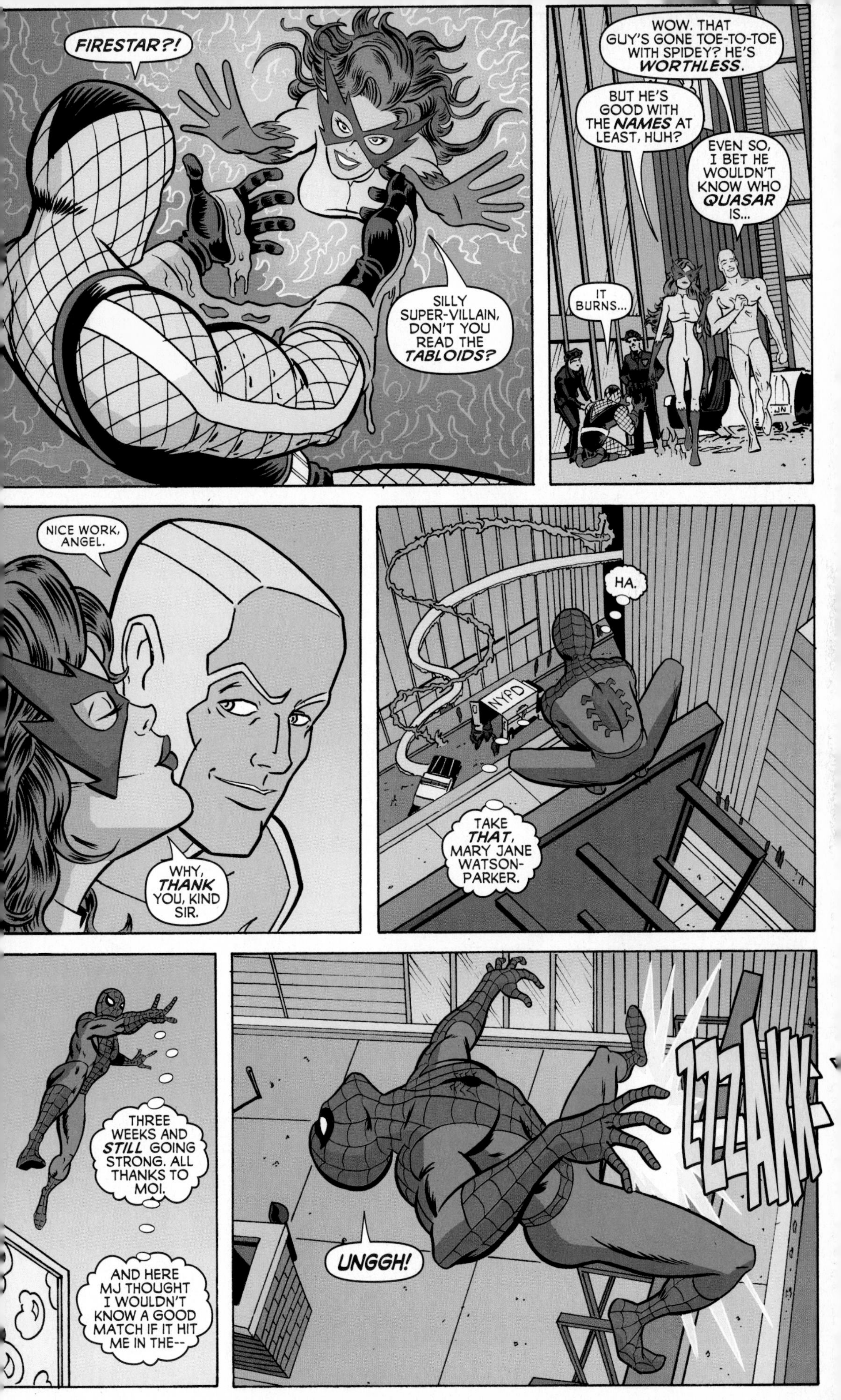
FIRESTAR?!
SILLY SUPER-VILLAIN, DON'T YOU READ THE TABLOIDS?
WOW. THAT GUY'S GONE TOE-TO-TOE WITH SPIDEY? HE'S WORTHLESS.
BUT HE'S GOOD WITH THE NAMES AT LEAST, HUH?
EVEN SO, I BET HE WOULDN'T KNOW WHO QUASAR IS...
IT BURNS...
NICE WORK, ANGEL.
WHY, THANK YOU, KIND SIR.
HA.
TAKE THAT, MARY JANE WATSON-PARKER.
THREE WEEKS AND STILL GOING STRONG. ALL THANKS TO MOI.
AND HERE MJ THOUGHT I WOULDN'T KNOW A GOOD MATCH IF IT HIT ME IN THE--
UNGGH!
ZZZAKK

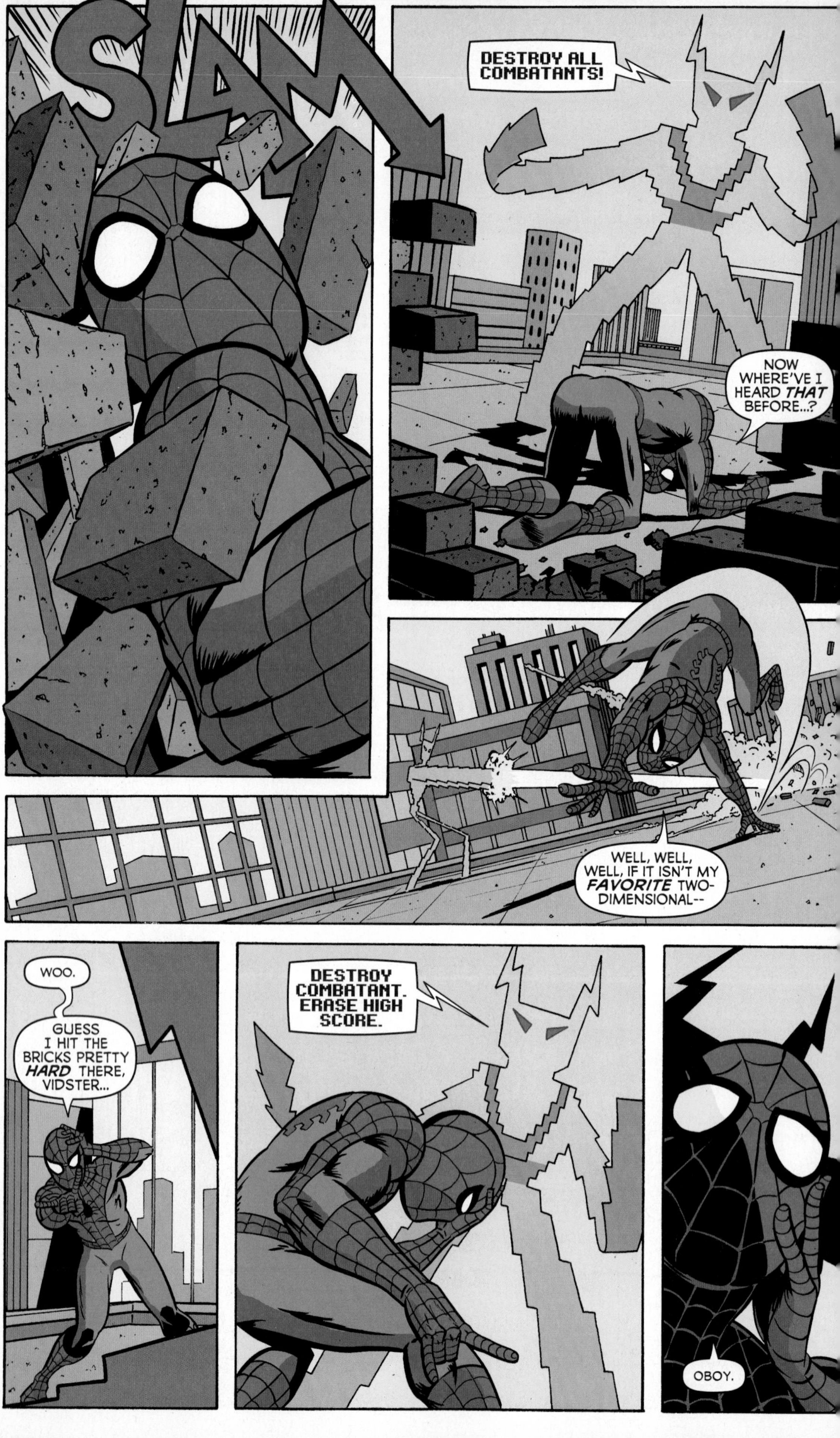
SLAM
DESTROY ALL COMBATANTS!
NOW WHERE'VE I HEARD *THAT* BEFORE...?
WELL, WELL, WELL, IF IT ISN'T MY *FAVORITE* TWO-DIMENSIONAL--
WOO.
GUESS I HIT THE BRICKS PRETTY *HARD* THERE, VIDSTER...
DESTROY COMBATANT. ERASE HIGH SCORE.
OBOY.

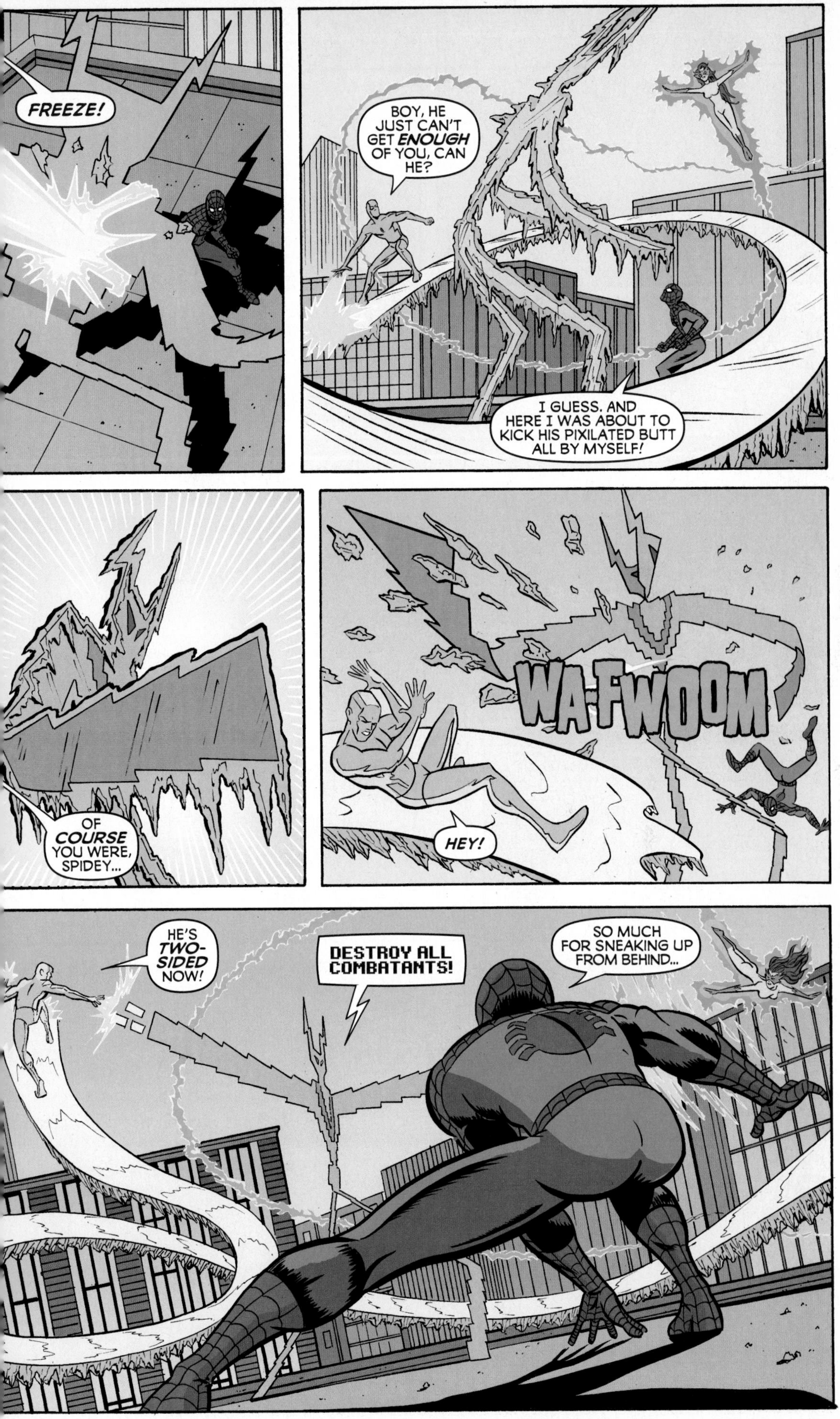
FREEZE!
BOY, HE JUST CAN'T GET ENOUGH OF YOU, CAN HE?
I GUESS. AND HERE I WAS ABOUT TO KICK HIS PIXILATED BUTT ALL BY MYSELF!
OF COURSE YOU WERE, SPIDEY...
WA-FWOOM
HEY!
HE'S TWO-SIDED NOW!
DESTROY ALL COMBATANTS!
SO MUCH FOR SNEAKING UP FROM BEHIND...

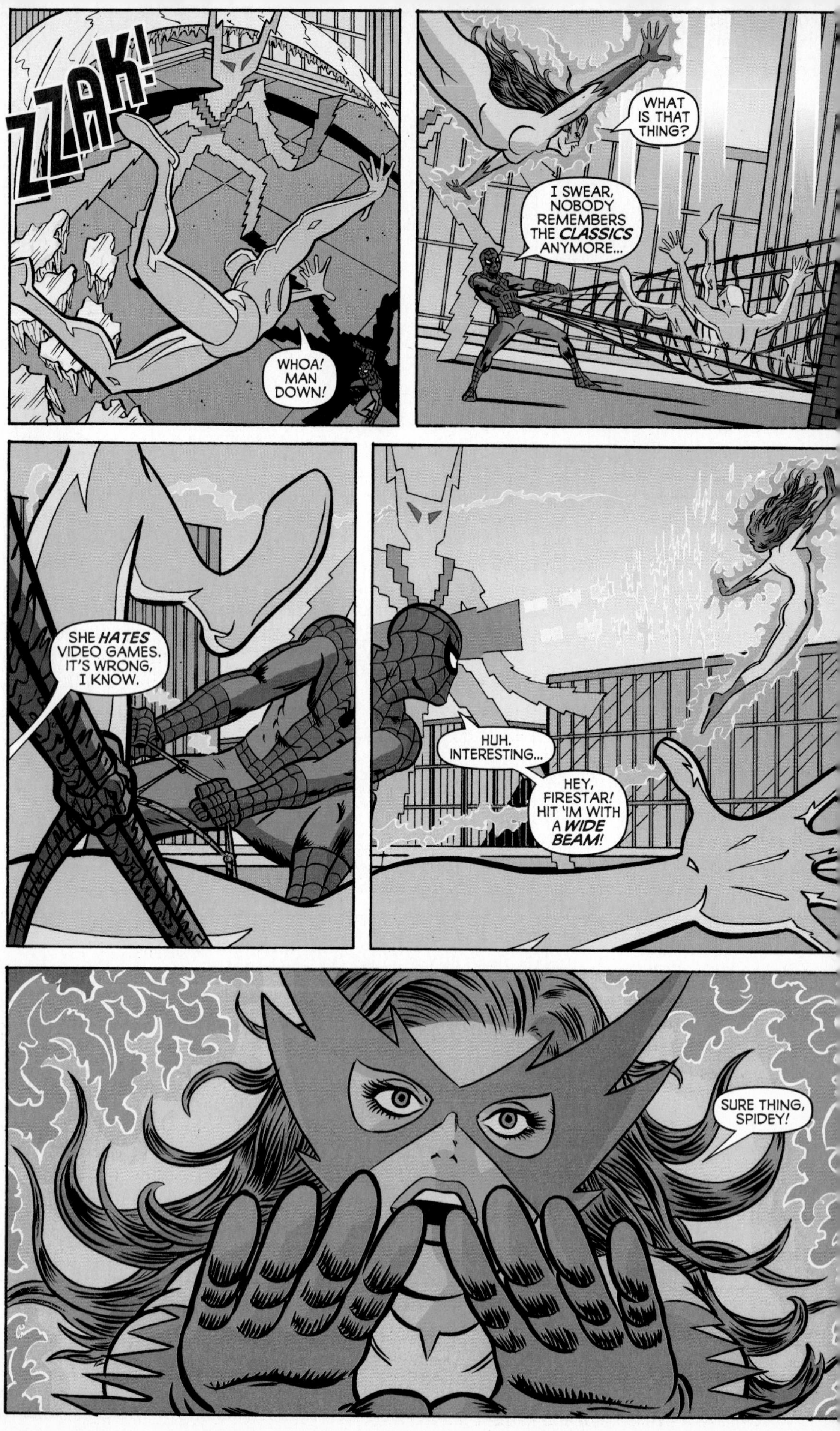
ZZAK!
WHOA! MAN DOWN!
WHAT IS THAT THING?
I SWEAR, NOBODY REMEMBERS THE CLASSICS ANYMORE...
SHE HATES VIDEO GAMES. IT'S WRONG, I KNOW.
HUH. INTERESTING...
HEY, FIRESTAR! HIT 'IM WITH A WIDE BEAM!
SURE THING, SPIDEY!

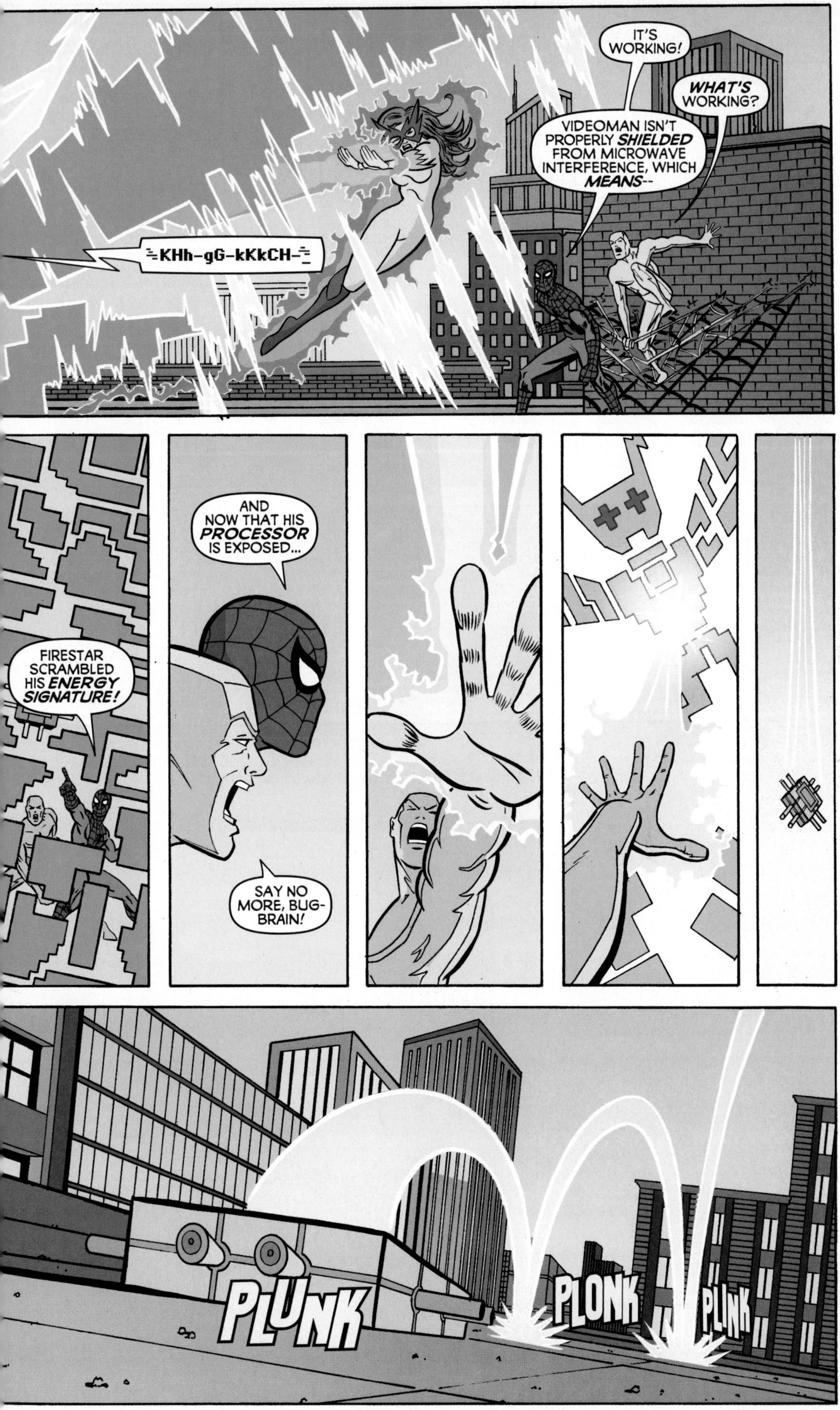

IT'S WORKING!
WHAT'S WORKING?
VIDEOMAN ISN'T PROPERLY SHIELDED FROM MICROWAVE INTERFERENCE, WHICH MEANS--
KHh-gG-kKkCH-
FIRESTAR SCRAMBLED HIS ENERGY SIGNATURE!
AND NOW THAT HIS PROCESSOR IS EXPOSED...
SAY NO MORE, BUG-BRAIN!
PLUNK
PLONK
PLINK

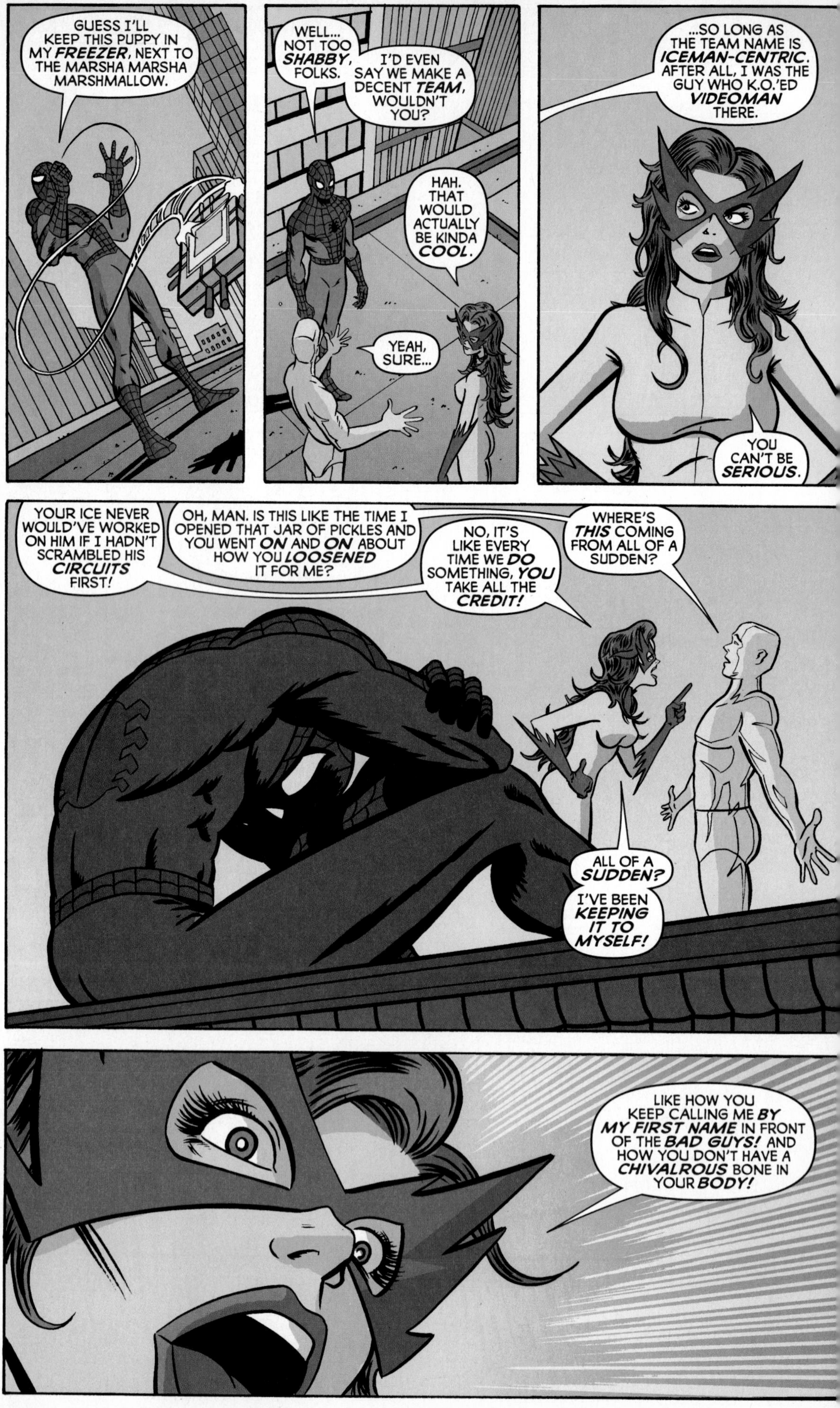
GUESS I'LL KEEP THIS PUPPY IN MY FREEZER, NEXT TO THE MARSHA MARSHA MARSHMALLOW.
WELL... NOT TOO SHABBY, FOLKS.
I'D EVEN SAY WE MAKE A DECENT TEAM, WOULDN'T YOU?
HAH. THAT WOULD ACTUALLY BE KINDA COOL.
YEAH, SURE...
...SO LONG AS THE TEAM NAME IS ICEMAN-CENTRIC. AFTER ALL, I WAS THE GUY WHO K.O.'ED VIDEOMAN THERE.
YOU CAN'T BE SERIOUS.
YOUR ICE NEVER WOULD'VE WORKED ON HIM IF I HADN'T SCRAMBLED HIS CIRCUITS FIRST!
OH, MAN. IS THIS LIKE THE TIME I OPENED THAT JAR OF PICKLES AND YOU WENT ON AND ON ABOUT HOW YOU LOOSENED IT FOR ME?
NO, IT'S LIKE EVERY TIME WE DO SOMETHING, YOU TAKE ALL THE CREDIT!
WHERE'S THIS COMING FROM ALL OF A SUDDEN?
ALL OF A SUDDEN?
I'VE BEEN KEEPING IT TO MYSELF!
LIKE HOW YOU KEEP CALLING ME BY MY FIRST NAME IN FRONT OF THE BAD GUYS! AND HOW YOU DON'T HAVE A CHIVALROUS BONE IN YOUR BODY!

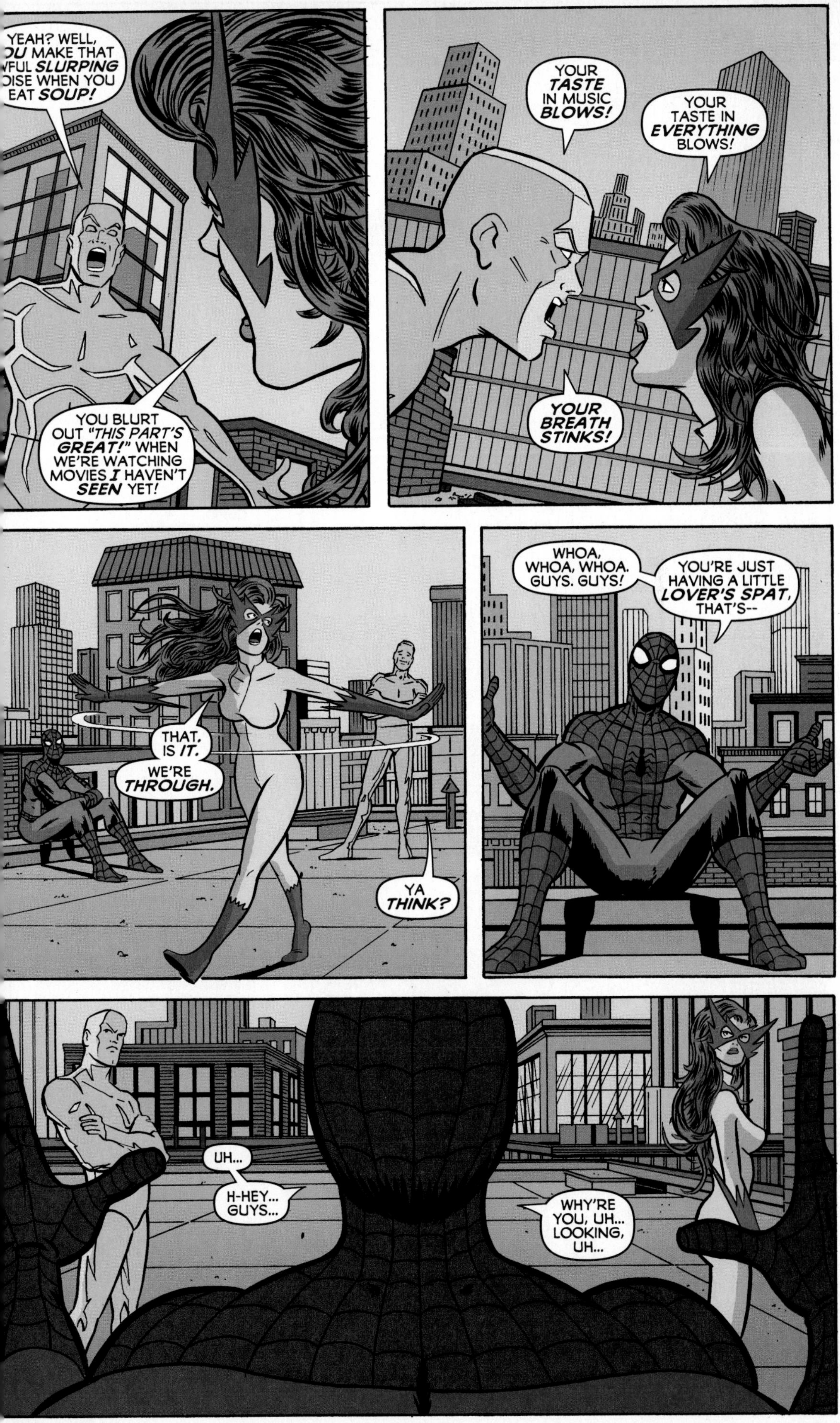

YEAH? WELL, OU MAKE THAT WFUL SLURPING OISE WHEN YOU EAT SOUP!
YOU BLURT OUT "THIS PART'S GREAT!" WHEN WE'RE WATCHING MOVIES I HAVEN'T SEEN YET!
YOUR TASTE IN MUSIC BLOWS!
YOUR TASTE IN EVERYTHING BLOWS!
YOUR BREATH STINKS!
THAT. IS IT. WE'RE THROUGH.
YA THINK?
WHOA, WHOA, WHOA. GUYS. GUYS!
YOU'RE JUST HAVING A LITTLE LOVER'S SPAT, THAT'S--
UH...
H-HEY... GUYS...
WHY'RE YOU, UH... LOOKING, UH...

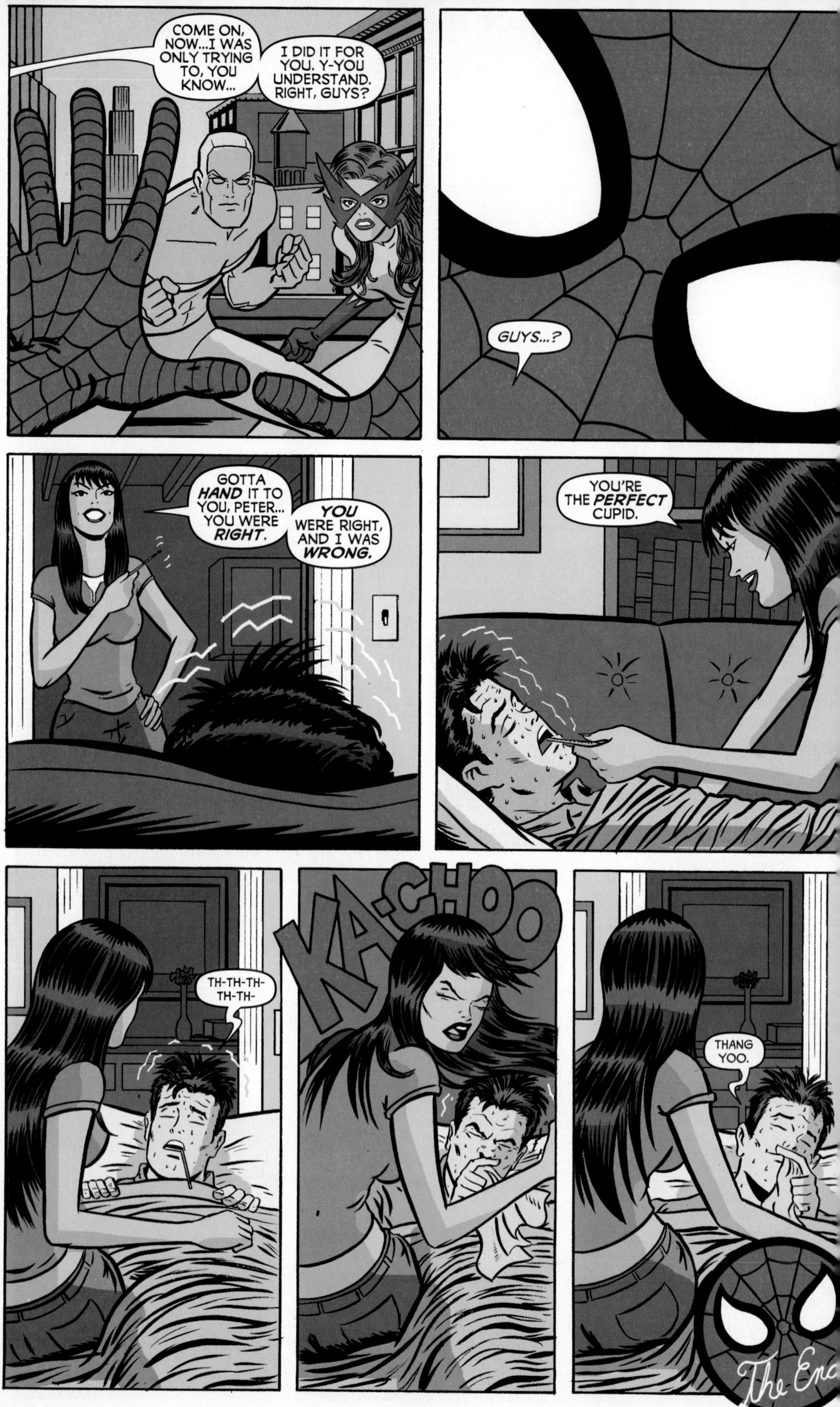
COME ON, NOW...I WAS ONLY TRYING TO, YOU KNOW...
I DID IT FOR YOU. Y-YOU UNDERSTAND. RIGHT, GUYS?
GUYS...?
GOTTA HAND IT TO YOU, PETER... YOU WERE RIGHT.
YOU WERE RIGHT, AND I WAS WRONG.
YOU'RE THE PERFECT CUPID.
TH-TH-TH-TH-TH-
KA-CHOO
THANG YOO.
The End

THE MINI MARVELS IN SPIDEY AND HIS AMAZING ~~FRIENDS~~ CO-WORKERS

ritten by **SEAN McKEEVER** (seanmckeever.com) • illustrated by **CHRIS GIARRUSSO** (chrisgcomics.com)
nsulted by **MARK PANICCIA** • edited by **NATHAN COSBY** • chiefed by **JOE QUESADA** • published by **DAN BUCKLEY**

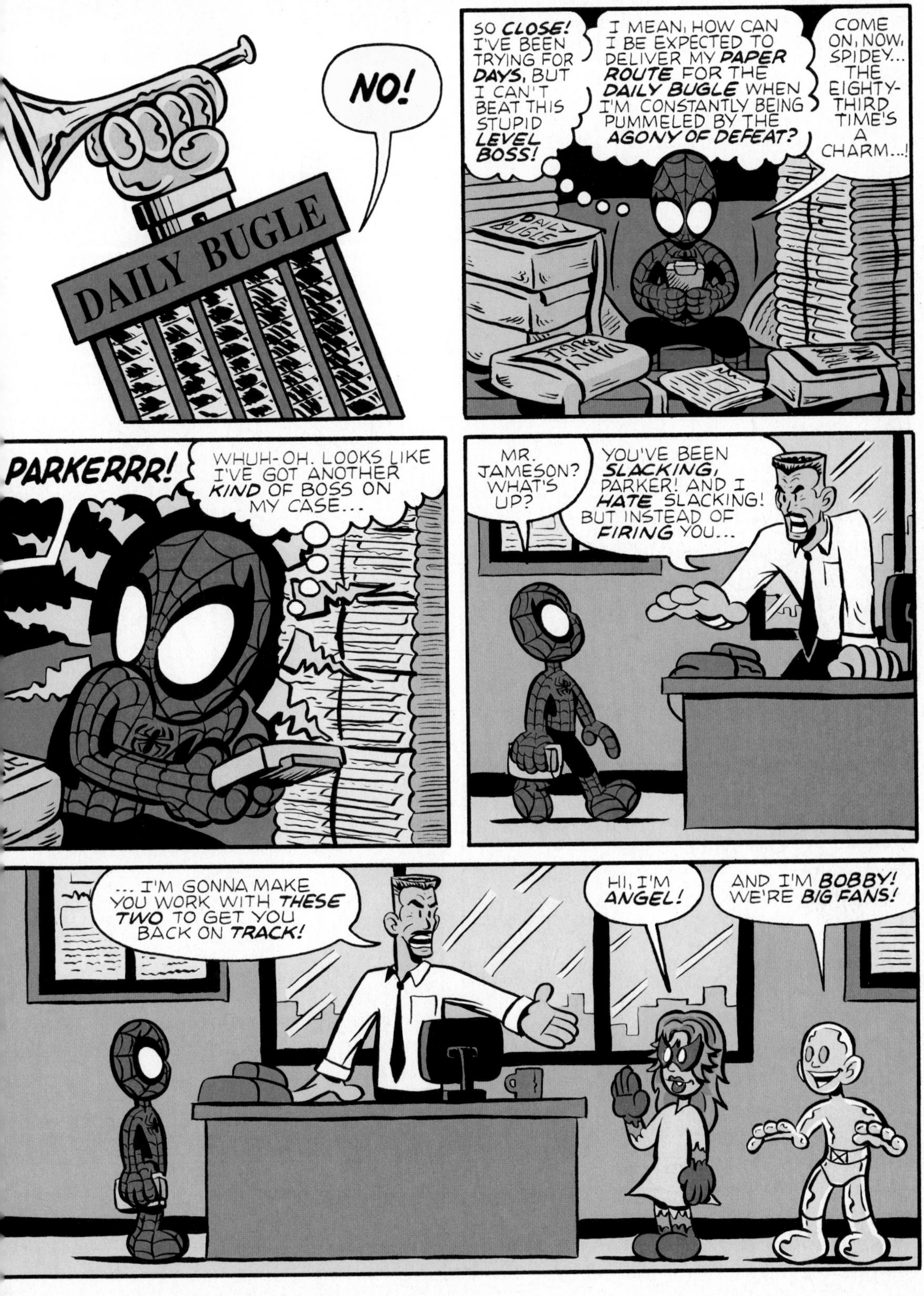
NO!
DAILY BUGLE
SO CLOSE! I'VE BEEN TRYING FOR DAYS, BUT I CAN'T BEAT THIS STUPID LEVEL BOSS!
I MEAN, HOW CAN I BE EXPECTED TO DELIVER MY PAPER ROUTE FOR THE DAILY BUGLE WHEN I'M CONSTANTLY BEING PUMMELED BY THE AGONY OF DEFEAT?
COME ON, NOW, SPIDEY... THE EIGHTY-THIRD TIME'S A CHARM...!
PARKERRR!
WHUH-OH. LOOKS LIKE I'VE GOT ANOTHER KIND OF BOSS ON MY CASE...
MR. JAMESON? WHAT'S UP?
YOU'VE BEEN SLACKING, PARKER! AND I HATE SLACKING! BUT INSTEAD OF FIRING YOU...
... I'M GONNA MAKE YOU WORK WITH THESE TWO TO GET YOU BACK ON TRACK!
HI, I'M ANGEL!
AND I'M BOBBY! WE'RE BIG FANS!

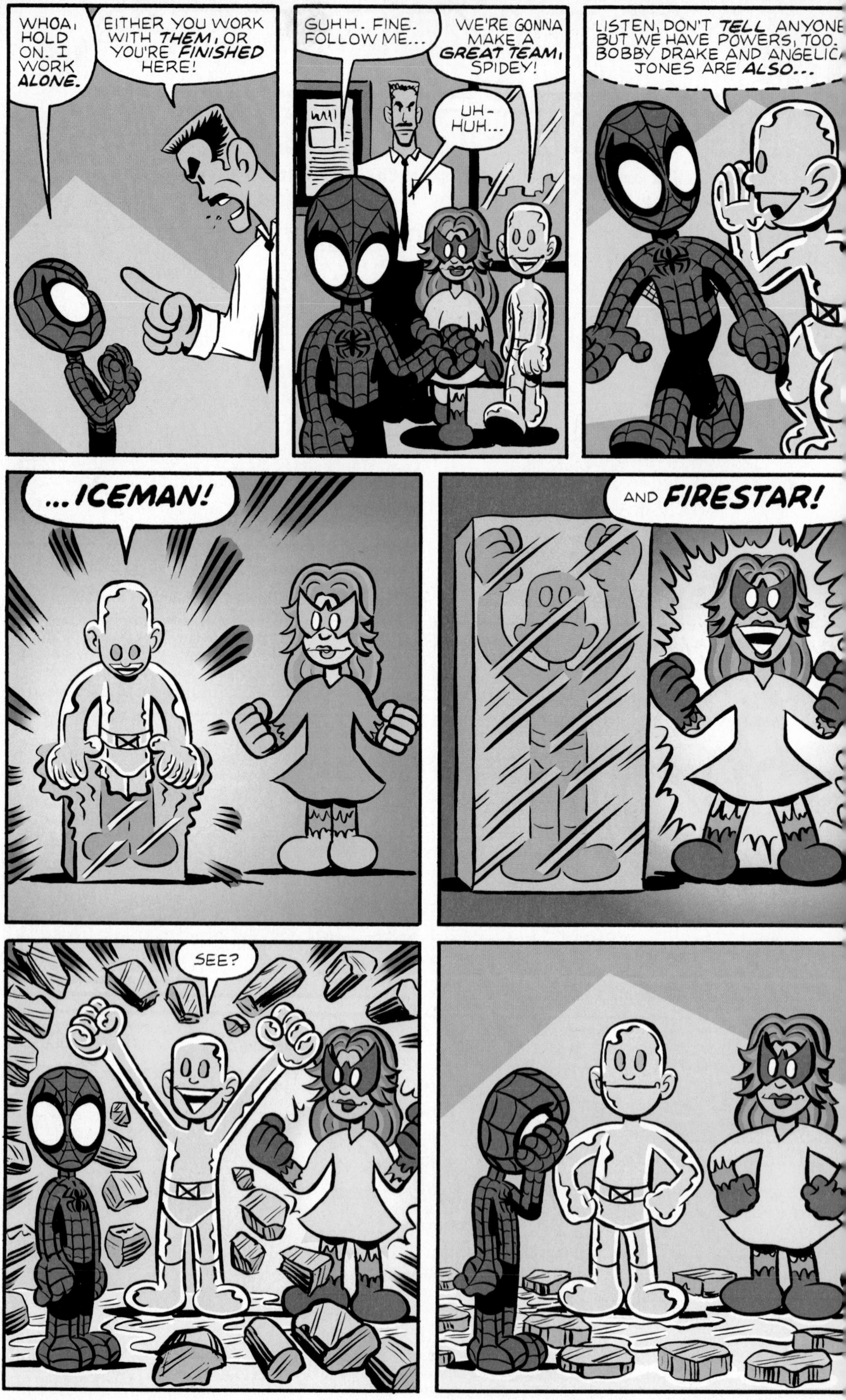
WHOA, HOLD ON. I WORK ALONE.
EITHER YOU WORK WITH THEM, OR YOU'RE FINISHED HERE!
GUHH. FINE. FOLLOW ME...
WE'RE GONNA MAKE A GREAT TEAM, SPIDEY!
UH-HUH...
LISTEN, DON'T TELL ANYONE BUT WE HAVE POWERS, TOO. BOBBY DRAKE AND ANGELICA JONES ARE ALSO...
...ICEMAN!
AND FIRESTAR!
SEE?

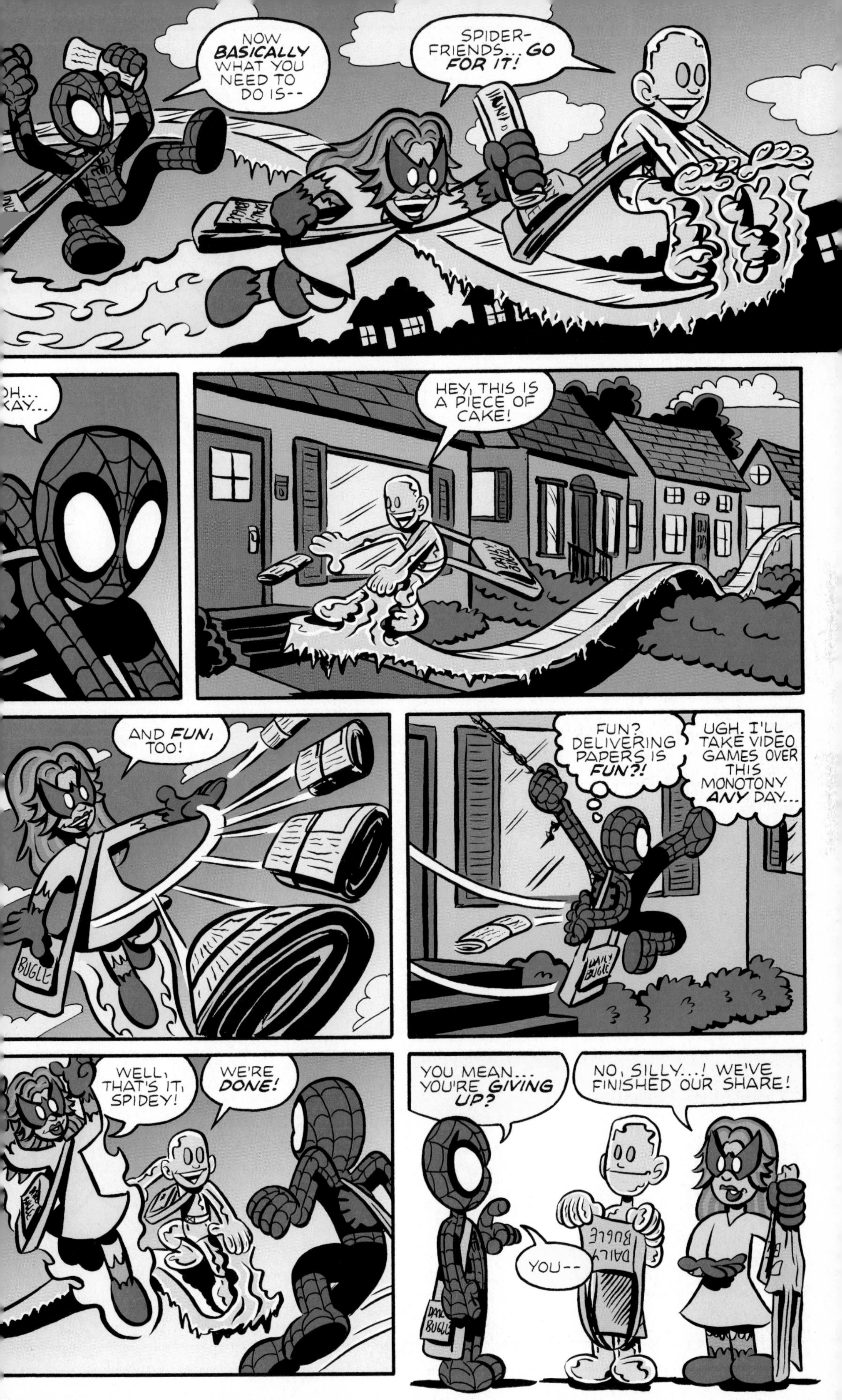
NOW BASICALLY WHAT YOU NEED TO DO IS--
SPIDER-FRIENDS... GO FOR IT!
OH... KAY...
HEY, THIS IS A PIECE OF CAKE!
AND FUN, TOO!
FUN? DELIVERING PAPERS IS FUN?!
UGH. I'LL TAKE VIDEO GAMES OVER THIS MONOTONY ANY DAY...
WELL, THAT'S IT, SPIDEY!
WE'RE DONE!
YOU MEAN... YOU'RE GIVING UP?
NO, SILLY...! WE'VE FINISHED OUR SHARE!
YOU--
DAILY BUGLE

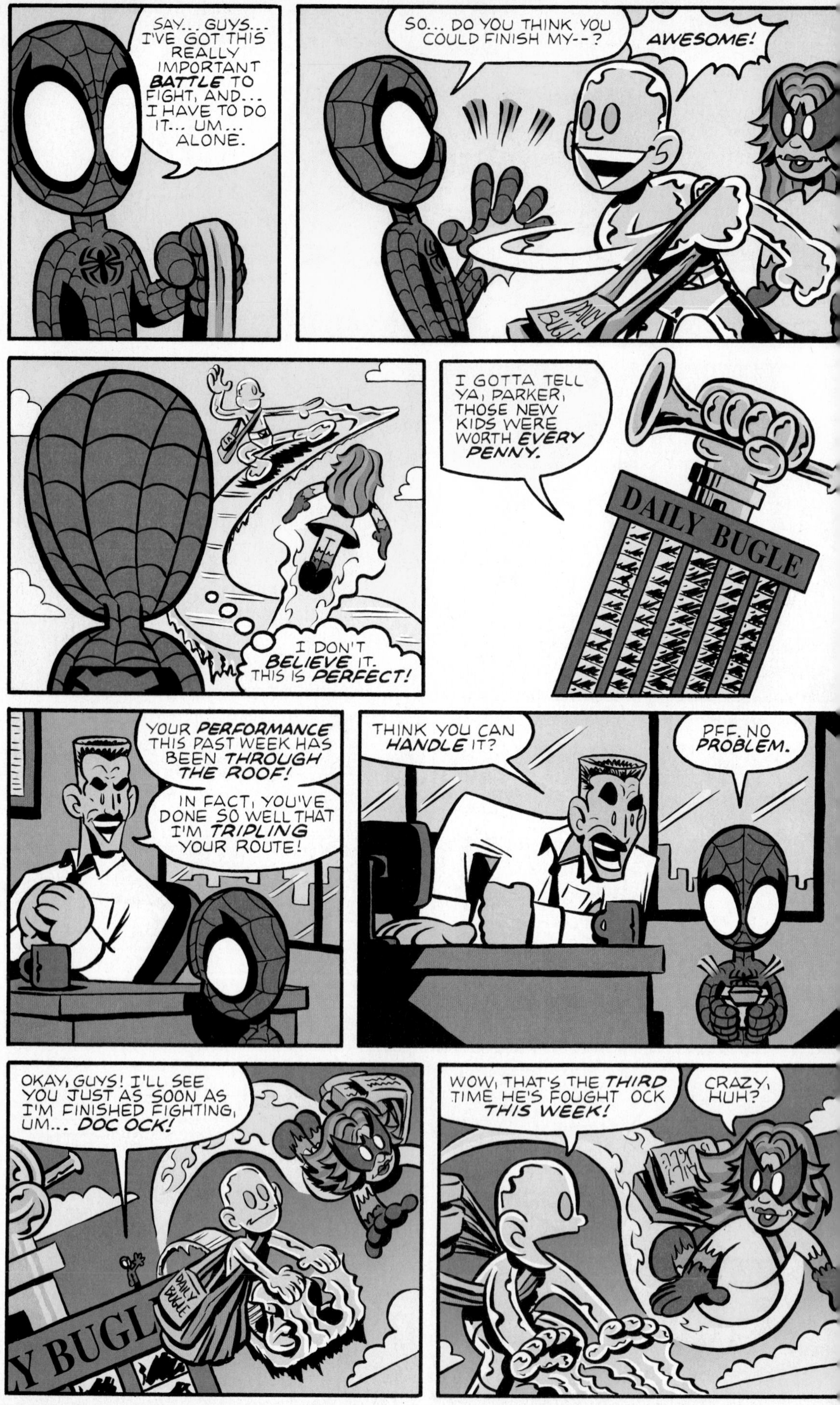
SAY... GUYS... I'VE GOT THIS REALLY IMPORTANT BATTLE TO FIGHT, AND... I HAVE TO DO IT... UM... ALONE.
SO... DO YOU THINK YOU COULD FINISH MY--?
AWESOME!
DAILY BUGLE
I DON'T BELIEVE IT. THIS IS PERFECT!
I GOTTA TELL YA, PARKER, THOSE NEW KIDS WERE WORTH EVERY PENNY.
DAILY BUGLE
YOUR PERFORMANCE THIS PAST WEEK HAS BEEN THROUGH THE ROOF!
IN FACT, YOU'VE DONE SO WELL THAT I'M TRIPLING YOUR ROUTE!
THINK YOU CAN HANDLE IT?
PFF. NO PROBLEM.
OKAY, GUYS! I'LL SEE YOU JUST AS SOON AS I'M FINISHED FIGHTING, UM... DOC OCK!
DAILY BUGLE
Y BUGL
WOW, THAT'S THE THIRD TIME HE'S FOUGHT OCK THIS WEEK!
CRAZY, HUH?

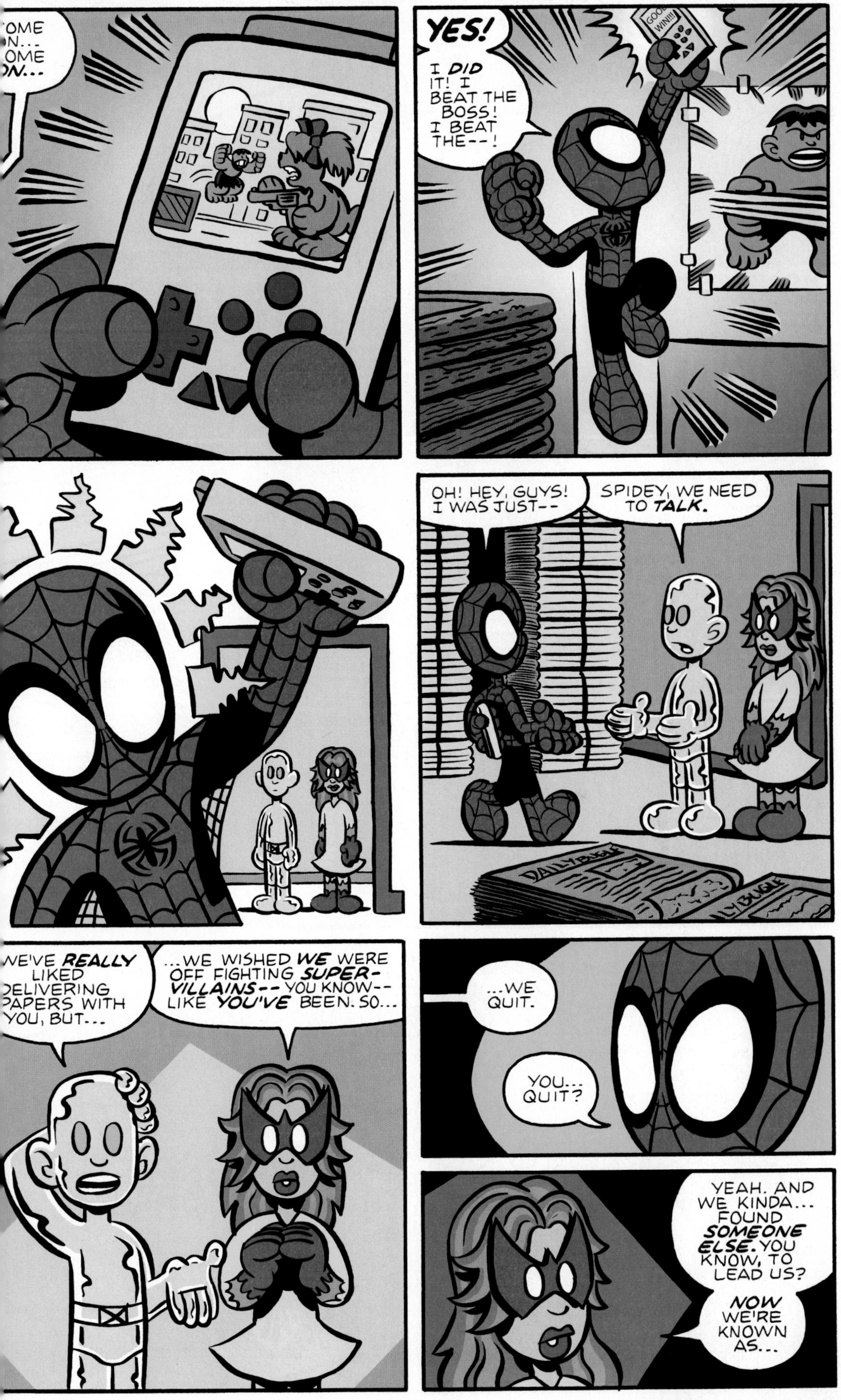

OME
N...
OME
N...
YES!
I DID IT! I BEAT THE BOSS! I BEAT THE--!
OH! HEY, GUYS! I WAS JUST--
SPIDEY, WE NEED TO TALK.
DAILY BUGLE
WE'VE REALLY LIKED DELIVERING PAPERS WITH YOU, BUT...
...WE WISHED WE WERE OFF FIGHTING SUPER-VILLAINS-- YOU KNOW-- LIKE YOU'VE BEEN. SO...
...WE QUIT.
YOU... QUIT?
YEAH. AND WE KINDA... FOUND SOMEONE ELSE. YOU KNOW, TO LEAD US?
NOW WE'RE KNOWN AS...

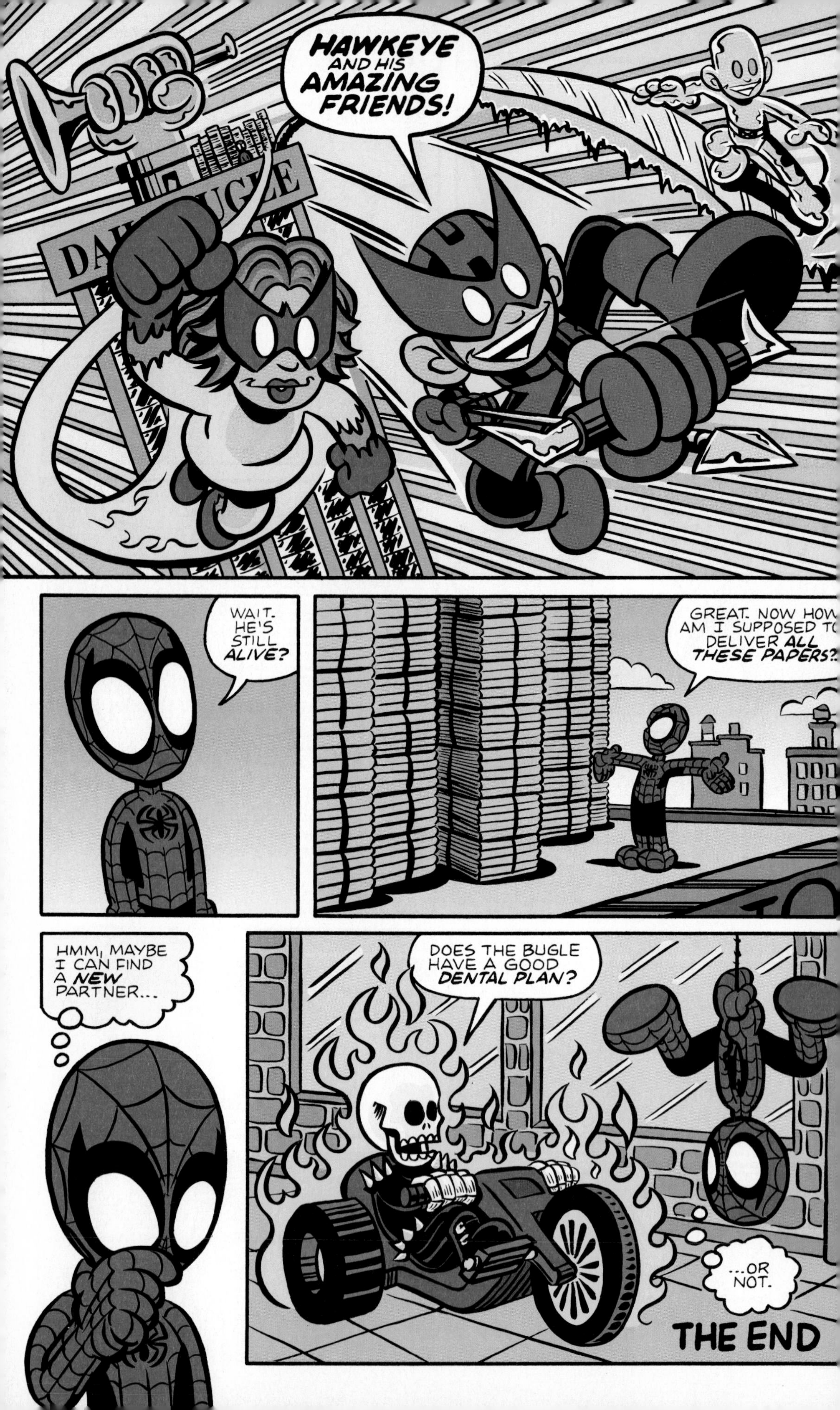
HAWKEYE AND HIS AMAZING FRIENDS!
DAILY BUGLE
WAIT. HE'S STILL ALIVE?
GREAT. NOW HOW AM I SUPPOSED TO DELIVER ALL THESE PAPERS?!
HMM, MAYBE I CAN FIND A NEW PARTNER...
DOES THE BUGLE HAVE A GOOD DENTAL PLAN?
...OR NOT.
THE END

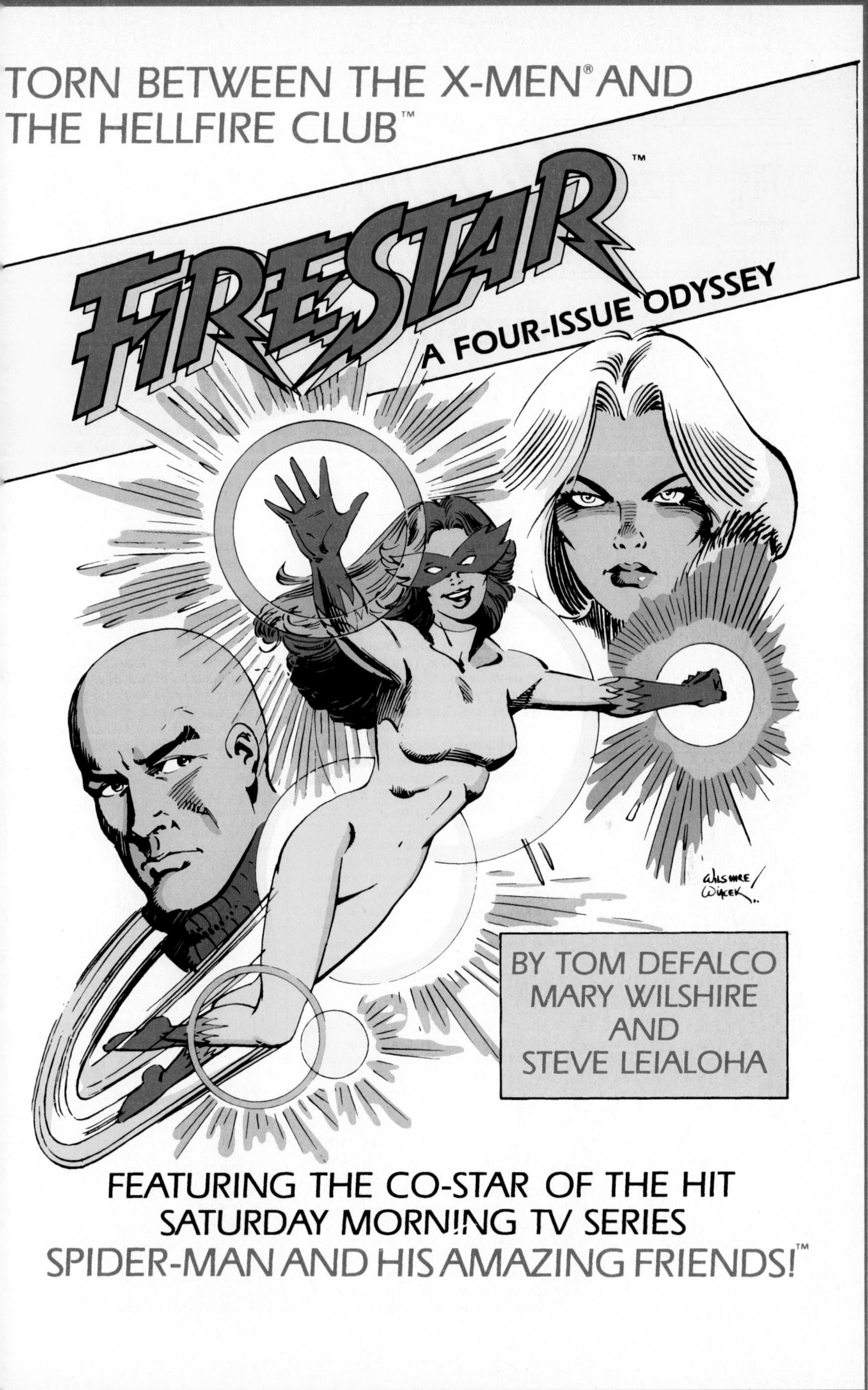
TORN BETWEEN THE X-MEN® AND
THE HELLFIRE CLUB™
FIRESTAR™
A FOUR-ISSUE ODYSSEY
WILSHIRE/ WIACEK
BY TOM DEFALCO
MARY WILSHIRE
AND
STEVE LEIALOHA
FEATURING THE CO-STAR OF THE HIT
SATURDAY MORNING TV SERIES
SPIDER-MAN AND HIS AMAZING FRIENDS!™

1986 house ad by **Mary Wilshire** & **Bob Wiacek**

THE *MUTANT* REPORT

VOLUME 1   "The Next Step in News Evolution!"   NUMBER 6

Firestar: New Mutant on the Horizon

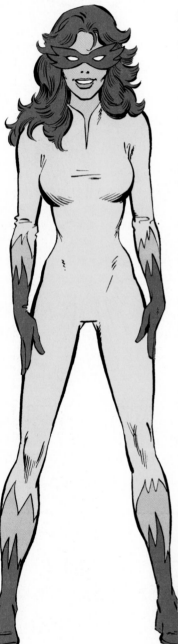

She's been a staple on Saturday morning television for a number of years now, but so far she has appeared in only one regular Marvel comic. That's about to change. Get ready to meet the latest addition to Marvel's mutant line-up in a four issue Limited Series, FIRESTAR.

Written by Tom DeFalco and illustrated by Mary Wilshire and Steve Leialoha, FIRESTAR will reintroduce us to the character who made one brief appearance in the X-MEN. We'll learn a lot about this mysterious young girl, her powers, and why she became a member of the Hellfire Club-controlled Hellions!

"The Limited Series deals with a young girl who, to her own horror, discovers that she's got a deep, mysterious, and powerful ability to do things that can hurt and even kill people," explained Tom, "and that frightens her to no end."

When we first meet young Firestar, she lives with her father and grandmother. "As her powers begin to emerge, she learns that she is capable of great destruction," said Tom. "The more she learns about this uncontrollable power, the more terrified she becomes. This reflects the theme of the Limited Series, a theme that deals with the secrets we find deep within us as we just try to survive."

But then comes the fatal switch in the FIRESTAR story. Usually at this point in the story, when the young and frightened hero discovers her new-found powers, the X-Men or Professor Xavier would appear and take the new mutant under wing to train and help her cope. But not this time.

"On many occasions we've seen good people discover that they were mutants, that they had special powers, as Firestar discovers," explained Tom. "Usually the X-Men manage to show up and train them to use their powers for good. In this case, the bad guys win."

Enter Emma Frost, the White Queen from the dreaded Hellfire Club. Frost has gathered her own group of young mutants in an evil and destructive parody of Xavier's work. She calls them the Hellions and trains them at her Massachusetts Academy for her own purposes.

"We have a basically good person being trained by a basically evil person for her own ends," said Tom. "This is where we, and Firestar, discover a frightening aspect and application of her powers."

Firestar's powers work on microwaves, and she can use that energy in a number of very lethal ways. "She could become the perfect as-

ACTUALLY, I PLAN TO LET HUMANS DO MOST OF THE FIGHTING FOR US AND THEN, AT THE APPROPRIATE MOMENT, TIP THE BALANCE IRREVOCABLY IN OUR FAVOR, BY UNLEASHING...

...FIRESTAR!

HI, MANUEL! HIYA, JENNIFER!

sassin for the Hellfire Club. Picture Firestar walking past her intended target. She could use her powers to burn out the person's insides in the same manner as a microwave oven works. Just cook him from the inside out, watch him fall over dead, and walk away. No one would have any idea what happened until she were long gone."

Firestar's powers reflect the theme of the Limited Series, that being "the terror from within." "I think it's something a lot of us can identify with," said Tom. "Many times we all feel we have a terrible thing or secret deep within us and we're afraid of it being unleashed. This young girl has this in a very practical respect. And unfortunately, she's all alone with this problem."

This is a lot different from the Firestar we've come to know on the Saturday morning "Spider-Man and his Amazing Friends" television program. In terms of depth of character, there are substantial differences between the TV version of Firestar and the comic book's. "TV, because of its restrictions regarding Saturday morning animation, lacks true depth of character. The programs are more interested in what someone is doing, rather than who someone is and why they are that way," explained Tom.

"We're more interested in the person than in the person jumping around. Action defines character, as far as we're concerned and you'll see that in the Limited Series," he said.

"Traditionally we have taken characters with a lot of depth and conflict and, to a certain extent, watered them down in order to have them portrayed on TV and in animation. With FIRESTAR, we are taking a character that was created for Saturday morning animation and we're adding depth and personality to the character," said Tom.

With the Limited Series, Firestar becomes a bonafide member of the Marvel Universe. Other creators around the Marvel offices have found her fascinating and Tom explained that there has been talk of giving her her own book. "That will depend largely on sales and reader reaction," he said. "Chris Claremont, on the basis of the plots for the Limited Series, liked the character so much that he wanted her to make an appearance in the X-MEN. All this just goes to show that we can do the reverse, we can add the depth of character that's necessary in order to make the transition from television to comics."

The artwork on FIRESTAR is nothing short of spectacular! This adds another dimension to the theme and brings it out more strongly. "Mary has a tremendous amount of sensitivity when dealing with people and people situations. She shows this in the way she portrays the very frightened young girl that Firestar really is. The terror that comes across in the art is incredible. She's just done a spectacular job on it," said Tom.

The four issues will be full of other mutant characters as well. The Hellfire Club, the Hellions, the X-Men, and the New Mutants will all appear and in some way influence the life of young Firestar.

Readers should also look for Tom's sense of humor which is re-flected in certain aspects of his stories. He likes to have fun with his work and hopes the reader will find these touches and have fun, too.

"Every year I do a Limited Series," said Tom. "I've done RED SONJA and MACHINE MAN in the past and people seemed to like them and they were well received. This year my contribution is FIRESTAR, and hopefully it will get the same reactions as well."

Will Firestar learn to deal with her powers? Will she become an assassin for the Hellfire Club? Will the bad guys really win out in the end? Don't miss the FIRESTAR Limited Series. The answers may just surprise you.

—*Bill Slavicsek*

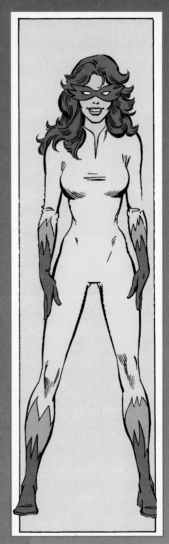

Official Handbook of the Marvel Universe: Deluxe Edition (1985) profile art by
Mary Wilshire, Josef Rubinstein & **Andy Yanchus**

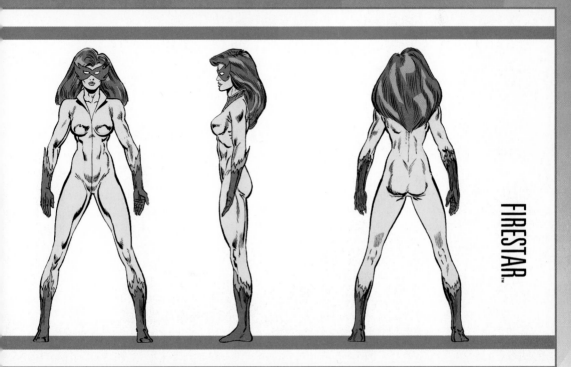

FIRESTAR™

Official Handbook of the Marvel Universe: Master Edition (1991) profile art by **Keith Pollard**, **Josef Rubinstein** & **Andy Yanchus**

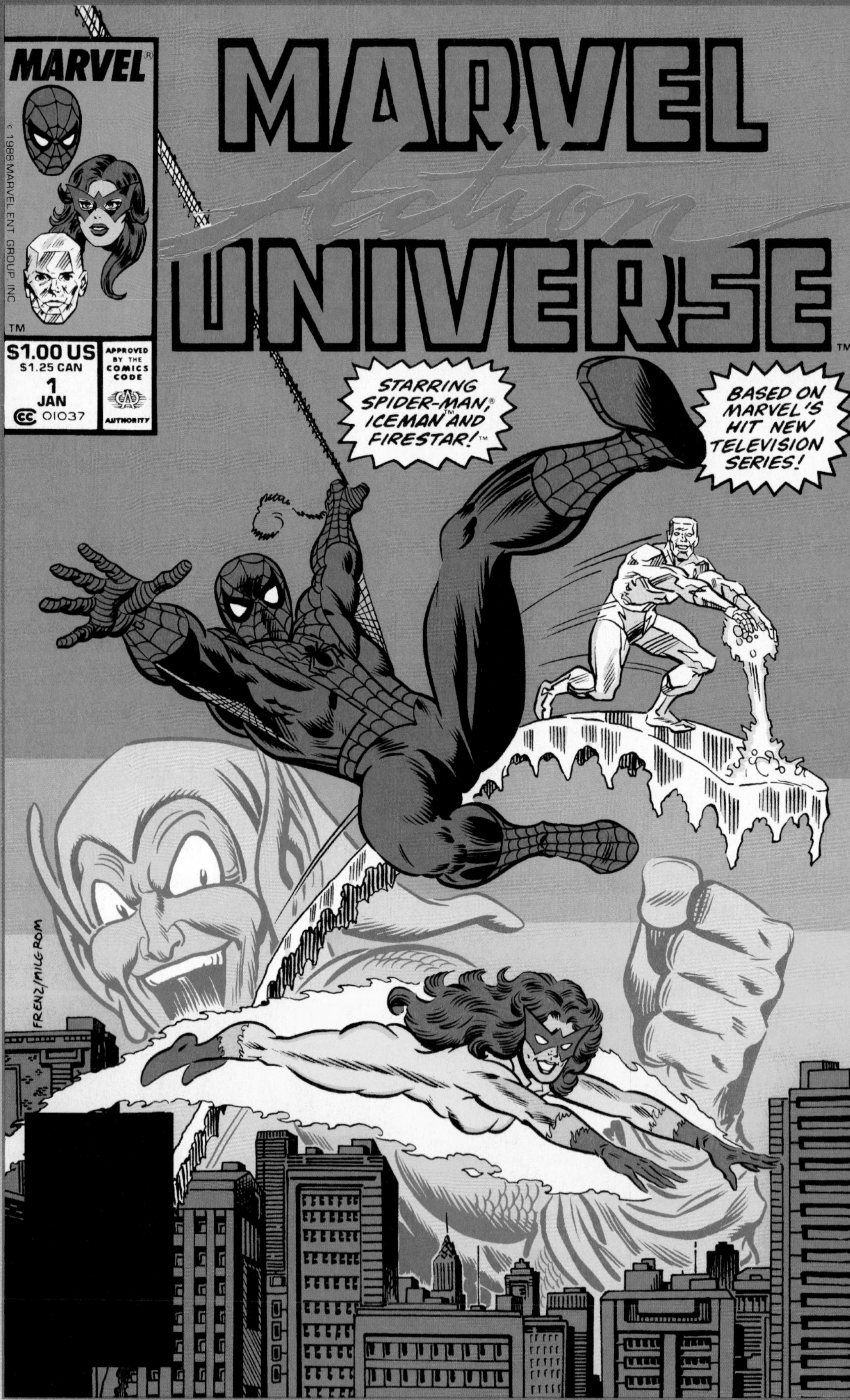
MARVEL
© 1988 MARVEL ENT. GROUP, INC.
TM
$1.00 US
$1.25 CAN
1
JAN
01037
APPROVED BY THE COMICS CODE AUTHORITY
MARVEL Action UNIVERSE
STARRING SPIDER-MAN, ICEMAN AND FIRESTAR!
BASED ON MARVEL'S HIT NEW TELEVISION SERIES!
FRENZ/MILGROM

Marvel Action Universe #1 reprinted *Spider-Man and His Amazing Friends #1*. Cover art by **Ron Frenz** & **Al Milgrom**.

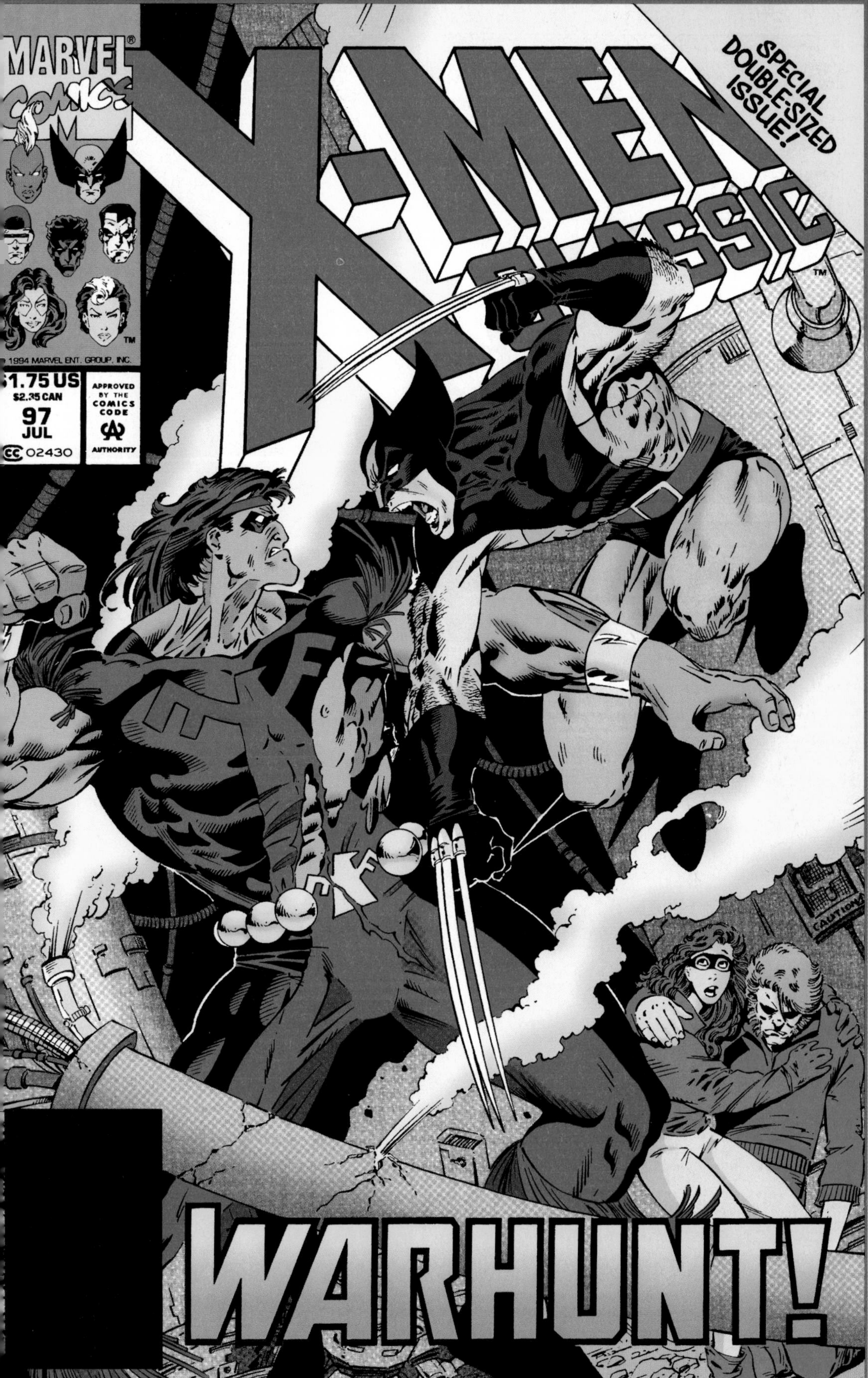
MARVEL COMICS
X-MEN CLASSIC
SPECIAL DOUBLE-SIZED ISSUE!
© 1994 MARVEL ENT. GROUP, INC.
$1.75 US
$2.35 CAN
97
JUL
02430
APPROVED BY THE COMICS CODE AUTHORITY
CAUTION
WARHUNT!

X-Men Classic #97 reprinted *Uncanny X-Men* #193. Cover art by **Matthew Ryan**.

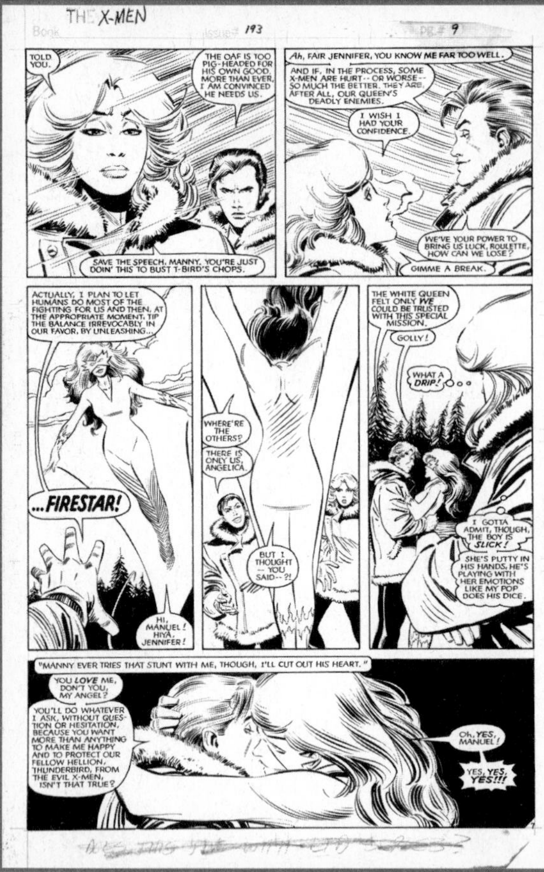

THE X-MEN
Book
Issue# 193
PG # 9
TOLD YOU.
THE OAF IS TOO PIG-HEADED FOR HIS OWN GOOD. MORE THAN EVER, I AM CONVINCED HE NEEDS US.
SAVE THE SPEECH, MANNY. YOU'RE JUST DOIN' THIS TO BUST T-BIRD'S CHOPS.
Ah, FAIR JENNIFER, YOU KNOW ME FAR TOO WELL.
AND IF, IN THE PROCESS, SOME X-MEN ARE HURT-- OR WORSE-- SO MUCH THE BETTER. THEY ARE, AFTER ALL, OUR QUEEN'S DEADLY ENEMIES.
I WISH I HAD YOUR CONFIDENCE.
WE'VE YOUR POWER TO BRING US LUCK, ROULETTE, HOW CAN WE LOSE?
GIMME A BREAK.
ACTUALLY, I PLAN TO LET HUMANS DO MOST OF THE FIGHTING FOR US AND THEN, AT THE APPROPRIATE MOMENT, TIP THE BALANCE IRREVOCABLY IN OUR FAVOR, BY UNLEASHING...
...FIRESTAR!
HI, MANUEL! HIYA, JENNIFER!
WHERE'RE THE OTHERS?
THERE IS ONLY US, ANGELICA.
BUT I THOUGHT -- YOU SAID-- ?!
THE WHITE QUEEN FELT ONLY WE COULD BE TRUSTED WITH THIS SPECIAL MISSION.
GOLLY!
WHAT A DRIP!
I GOTTA ADMIT, THOUGH, THE BOY IS SLICK!
SHE'S PUTTY IN HIS HANDS. HE'S PLAYING WITH HER EMOTIONS LIKE MY POP DOES HIS DICE.
"MANNY EVER TRIES THAT STUNT WITH ME, THOUGH, I'LL CUT OUT HIS HEART."
YOU LOVE ME, DON'T YOU, MY ANGEL?
YOU'LL DO WHATEVER I ASK, WITHOUT QUESTION OR HESITATION, BECAUSE YOU WANT MORE THAN ANYTHING TO MAKE ME HAPPY AND TO PROTECT OUR FELLOW HELLION, THUNDERBIRD, FROM THE EVIL X-MEN, ISN'T THAT TRUE?
Oh, YES, MANUEL!
YES, YES, YES!!!
7

Uncanny X-Men #193, page 7, art by **John Romita Jr.** & **Dan Green**

Courtesy of HeritageAuctions.com

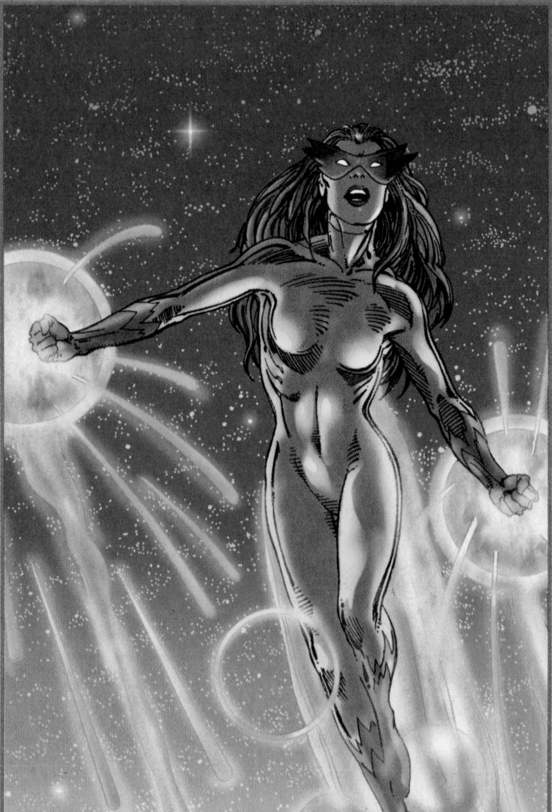

X-Men: Firestar Digest cover art by **Barry Windsor-Smith** & **Tom Smith**

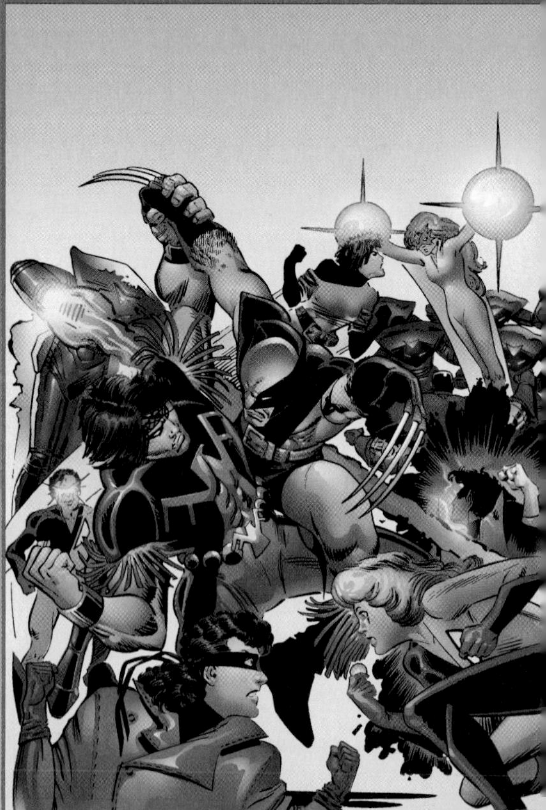

JRJRDG84

Essential X-Men Vol. 5 TPB cover art by **John Romita Jr.**, **Dan Green** & **Avalon's Matt Milla**